the

ALSACE
EMIGRATION BOOK

Volume I

compiled by
Cornelia Schrader-Muggenthaler

CLOSSON PRESS
Printers and Publishers
Apollo   1989

International Standard Book Number 1-55856-035-1

Special thanks to Mrs. Helene Goerger Vogt who shared her 40 years experience and found many of the emigrants listed. I learned a lot while working with her.

In preparing this manuscript I wish to express my appreciation also to Mrs. Hanne Kaisik and Miss Mirjam Dornauer for their eager assistance.

Finally, I express appreciation to the Genealogical Library of the Church of Jesus Christ of Latter-Day Saints in Munich for letting me use their microfilms, reader-printer and library rooms.

FOREWORD

From 1984 to 1987 I worked for the Weimer Genealogical Society, Albuquerque, New Mexico. My assignment was to sort out all emigrated Weimer (Wimmer) families in Alsace and trace their genealogies. During that time I traced several hundred families back to the time before church books began or their Swiss origin in 1600.

While working on this project I had the idea to compile and later publish all emigrants found from and through Alsace to the United States with their place or origin.

Sources include pass lists, ship lists, church books, private genealogies, people searched for through newspapers and in this edition, microfilms.

I sorted out the Alsace emigration index which was microfilmed by the Genealogical Society of the Latter Day Saints. My reason for wanting to computerize and published this already collected and alphabetized card file system was to gather all possible emigrants in published form making it more easily accessible.

It is my sincere hope that this book will be of great help for anyone tracing their roots.

A second book is in progress with the idea to list emigrants who migrated without permission and emigrants found in private and less accessible sources.

THE ALSACE
HISTORY, GEOGRAPHY AND GENERAL INFORMATION

The area of Alsace has been a very troubled one in history. This beautiful region was always in the interest of the surrounding countries.

The first settlements in Alsace were Celtic.

In 58 B.C. it was conquered by Caesar and then belonged to the Provincia Germania Superior.

During the Migration 'of' Nations period it became Alemanic. With the victory of Chlodwig against the Alemannes, the Franconians conquerred and christianized the Alsace area in 496.

With the Empire Division in the contract of Mersen in 870 it became part of the East Franconian Empire. Through this contract Ludwig II receives after the death of Lothar II the east half of Lothringen.

Since 925 Alsace belonged to the Dukedom Swabia.

After the region of the House of Staufer, it was separated into the countries Lower and Upper Alsace. The Free Cities beside Strassbourg and Muelhausen, built the Ten 'City' Alliance in 1354 (Zehnstadtebund).

With the "Westfalian Peace" the properties of the House of Habsburg were given to France.

Louis the 14th extended his power control also to the Free Cities (Reichsstadte). Strassbourg has been occupied, but its connections to Germany still existed.

During the French Revolution the Alsace became part of France.

After the French Revolution the first invasions came to Alsace. The situation in the Upper Alsace was especially horrible. The first large emigration period started in 1815 due to this and years and starvation (1816-1817).

Many young men migrated in the 1840s because they did not want to become soldiers. About 125,000 Alsacians and Lorraines migrated at this time to America, but also to Algeria.

When Bismarck and his troops beat Emperor Napoleon II in 1817, the Alsace was taken over by Germany. It became the German Reichsland Alsace'Lorraine, including Bas'Rhin (Lower Alsace) and Haut'Rhin (Upper Alsace). The western part of Haut Rhin fought against the accession by Germany. This part was born in 1871 and named the Territory of Belfort.

In this time period many optants migrated because they did not want to be German. They migrated to America and Algeria and have been replaced with German citizens.

In 1819 it became French again and still remains to this day beside a short break in the years of the German Occupation (1940-1944).

INTRODUCTION

This book contains mainly emigrants from Upper and Lower Alsace, but also includes families who migrated through Alsace from Germany, Switzerland and other countries.

During this time period many people were not able to read and write and therefore were unable to fill out their passport or emigration application. The passport officers had to write down the information by phonic spellings.

Due to this fact there are many misspellings which made it difficult to find the villages and their locations. We did our very best to make the list as complete as possible on the following pages. If you cannot find the village you are looking for in the index, look up the closest spelling.

Remember also that the area of Alsace was bilingual (French and German) and the same village often had two spellings such as:

Zinsweiler = Zinswiller, Mulhouse = Mulhausen
Steinbourg = Steinburg, Burckenwald = Birckenwald
Soultz = Sultz, Liepre = Liepvre
and so on

If you cannot find the village in the index, it can belong either to Germany, France or Switzerland.

Many men migrated with their families. In some cases it lists who migrated with who and how many family members. Single men or women are listed also. It is not shown if they migrated alone or with family.

Many children are listed who migrated without parents. They possibly have been in the companyof a neighbor, friend or relative.

The emigration date is not always the date of emigration but may also, in many cases, be the date of application for passport.

The birth year is not always correct. It is counted back from the age given on the passport.

In several cases, only the year of emigration is given. For example, in this case, we wrote 01/01/1848.

Weimer family datas (Weimer, Wimmer and similar spellings) of emigrated families are available through the Weimer Genealogical Society, Dr. Robert Weimer, P.O. Box, Albuquerque, N.M. 87192.

EXPLANATION OF THE SOURCES :

No.2

956 persons are listed in this book with source No.2 The information from this source has been taken from records about emigration from the Kanton Weissenburg, Lower Alsace, Signatur Nr.414 D 276 / 2154, Landesarchiv Strassburg. This records have not been sorted out before.

Film

More than 10000 persons are listed in this book with sourcefilm. The information from this source has been taken from the Alsace Emigration index, a cardfile archive put on microfilm by the Mormon archives in Salt Lake City. It does include immigrants to USA, Russia , Germany and many other countries. We only sorted out the emigrants to USA for this book.
If the emigrationyear is 1817 and filmsouce, it can be that some of the listed people migrated to Russia not America, they applied for a passport for both.
If the emigrationyear is 1828 and filmsource, it can be that these persons migrated between 1828 and 1838. They applied for a passport, but the correct year of emigration is not listed.The most common profession on the filmlist are :Farmer,farmworker, winegrowers , daylaborers, laborers and craftsmen like, butcher, baker, shoemaker carpenter and weaver.

bull

98 persons are listed in this book with source bull. The information from this source has been taken from the Bulletin des Cercle genealoqique du Bas' Rhin '
Nr. 1987/4
Nr. 1779/1

suess

94 persons are listed in this book with source Suess. This is a genealogy of anabaptised and protestant families.The Priest Suess wrote it from churchbooks and it contains more then 50 books.

pass.ship

254 pass, 294 ship are listed from the book L.P. Lutten , " Castroville 'Texas " Published 1986 Strassbourg. Bueb and Reumaux

No.1..priv

105 persons are listed with No.1 and 312 persons with abbrevation Priv. These are from private researches and genealogies.

ABBREVATIONS

w = wife of
h = husband of
f = father of
si = sister of
s = son of
d = daughter of
br = brother of
m = mother of

w ch or ch or only c = with ..children
example = ch 5 = with 5 children

CA = California
CL = Calveston
PA = Pennsylvania
NY = New York
NO = New Orleans
LO = Louisville
LV = "   "
BA = Bavaria
W = Wßüßrtemberg
CH = Chicago
HR = Haut Rhin
MI = Miami
SCO = Scotland

BR = Bas Rhin
IL = Illinois
Al = Algeria
TX = Texas
OH = Ohio
Ph = Philadelphia
BO = Boston
B = Baden
SW = Swiss
IA = Iowa
BE = Belgium
CN or CD = Canada
CI = Cincinatti

carp = carpenter
tayl = taylor
mill = miller
dayl = daylaborer
bake = baker
brla = bricklayer
serv = servant
farm = farmer
Join = joiner
butc = Butcher
fact = factoryworker
serr or lock = blacksmith
tonm = tonmaker
file = spinner
host = host
tena = tenant
draw = drawer
mier = milliner
teac = teacher
prin = printer
vine = vine grower
merc = merchant
shep = shephard
gard = gardener
arch = architect
hoow = houseowner
fobu = fountain builder
salk = saloonkeeper

farr = farrier
bama = bagmaker
coop = cooper
hadr = hairdresser
exmi = exmilitary
shma = shoemaker
chau = driver
layb = layborer
tiss or weav = weaver
cult = farmer or farmworker
char = trainworker
gwon = groundowner
cler = clerk
tann = tanner
sold = soldier
dyer = dyer
poet = poet
woca = wood carver
prie = priest
carm = carmaker
driv = driver
sadd = saddler
work = worker
file = spinner
ston = stone mason
comb = combmaker
mech = mechanics

ARCHIVE DEPARTEMENT DU BAS-RHIN
THE VILLAGES BELONGING TO THE LOWER ALSACE AND THEREFORE
TO THE ARCHIVES IN STRASSBOURG.

Adamswiller, Altdorf, Altenstadt, Altweiler, Andlau bas Rhin,
Aschbach, Asswiller, Auenheim,

Baerendorf, Balbronn, Baldenheim, Batzendorf, Behlenheim, Beinheim, Berg,
Bernardswiller, Berneville pas de cs.,Bernolsheim, Berstheim, Bettwiller, Bindernheim,
Brickenwald =Burckenwald, Bischheim, Birlenbach, Bischholtz, Bischofsheim,Bischwiller,
Bissert, Biswiller, Boersch, Boofsheim,Bosselshausen, Bruchez, Bourg, Bouxwiller,
Brettenau,Bremmelbach, Brumath, Buhl, Burbach, Bust, Butten,

Chatenois, Cleebourg, Climbach, Cosswiller, Croetwiller,

Dalhunden,Dambach, Dauendorf, Dehlingen, Dettwiller, Diebolsheim, Diedendorf,
Diemeringen, Dossenheim, Drachenbronn,Drulingen, Drusenheim, Duntzenheim,
Durrenbach, Durstel,Duettlenheim,

Eberbach, Ebermuenster, Eckolsheim, Euhwersheim, Eckwersheim, Engenthal, Engwiller,
Enscholtzmatt, Erckartswiller, Ergersheim, Ernolsheim, Erstein, Eschbach, Eschbourg,
Ettendorf,

Fegersheim, Fessenheim, Forstfeld, Forstheim, Fort Louis, Fouchy, Friesenheim,
Froeschwiller, Frohmuhl, Furdenheim, Furchhausen,

Geipolsheim, Geiswiller, Gerstheim, Goersdorf, Goerlingen,Gottenhouse, Grassendorf,
Grendelbruch, Gries, Griesheim,Gumbrechtshoffen, Gundershoffen, Gungwiller, Gunstett,

Haegen, Haguenau bas Rhin, Hambach, Harskirchen, Hatten, Hattmatt, Hegeney,
Hengwiller, Herbitzheim, Hermerswiller, Hirschland, Hochstett, Hoerdt, Hoffen, Hohwiller,
Holtzheim,Hohatzenheim,Hohengoeft, Hunspach, Huttendorf,

Illkirch Imbsheim, Ingenheim, Ingwiller, Isssenhausen,Ingolsheim,

Katenhouse, Kauffenheim, Keffenbach, Keskastel,Kienheim, Killstatt, Kintzheim, Kirchheim
, Kirrberg, Kirrwiller, Klentzheim, Kuttolsheim, Krautwiller, Krautergersheim Kuhlendorf,
Kurtzenhouse,

La Petit Pierre, Langensoultzbach, Lauterbourg, Lembach,Leutenheim, Lichtenberg,
Lingolsheim, Lipsheim, Lochwiller, Lohr, Lorentzen, Lupstein,

Mackwiller, Marckolsheim, Marlenheim, Marmoutier, Marsbronn, Mattstall, Metzenheim,
Melsheim, Memmelshofen, Menchhoffen, Merckwiller, Mertzwiller, Mietersheim,
Mietesheim, Minversheim, Mitschdorf, Molkirch, Molsheim, Mommenheim, Morsbronn,
Morschwiller, Mothern, Muehlhausen, Mulhausen, Munchhausen, Mutzen,

Neewiller, Nehwiller, Neuhaeusel, Niederbetschdorf, Niederbronn, Niederhausbergen,
Niedermodern, Niedernai, Niederroedern, Niederschaffolsheim, Niederseebach,
Niedersoultzbach, Niedersteinbach,

Obenheim, Oberbetschdorf, Oberbronn, Oberdorf, Oberhausbergen, Oberhofen, Oberhoffen, Oberlauterbach, Obermodern, Obernai, Oberroedern, Oberseebach, Obersoultzbach, Obersteinbach, Oermingen, Offenheim, Offwiller, Offendorf, Ohlungen, Ohnenheim, Ostwald, Ottersthal, Offwiller,

Petersbach, Pfaffenhoffen, Pfalzweyer, Plobsheim, Preuschdorf, Printzheim, Puberg,

Ratzwiller, Rauwiller, Reichshoffen, Reimerswiller, Reinhardsmuenster, Repertswiller, Retschwiller, Rexingen, Rhinau, Riedheim, Riedseltz, Rimsdorf, Ringeldorf, Rittershofen, Roeschwog, Romanswiller, Roppenheim, Rosteig, Rothbach, Rott, Rumersheim,

Salenthal, Salmbach, Sarre Union, Sarrewerden, Scheibenhard, Scherlenheim, Schillersdorf, Schiltigheim, Schirrheim, Schirrhofen, Schleithal, Schoenau, Schoenbourg, Schweighouse, Schwidratzheim, Schwobsheim, Selestat, Seltz, Sessenheim, Siegen, Siewiller, Siltzheim, Singrist, Soufflenheim, Soultz le Bains, Soultz sous Forets, Sparsbach, Stattmatten, Steinbourg, Steinseltz, Still, Strasbourg, Struth, Stundwiller, Surbourg,

Thal Marmoutier, Thal, Tieffenbach, Trimbach

Ueberach, Uhlwiller, Uhrwiller, Uttwiller,

Vendenheim Voellardingen, Volksberg,

Waldowisheim, Wangen, Wangenbourg, Wasselone, Waltenheim, Wantzenau, Weinbourg, Weislingen, Weitbruch, Wetterswiller, Westhoffen, Weyer, Wickersheim, Willgottheim, Wilmisheim, Wimmenau, Windstein, Wingen, Wintzenbach, Witternheim, Wittisheim, Woellenheim, Woerth, Wolschheim,

Zinswiller, Zittersheim, Zoebersdorf,

ARCHIVE DEPARTEMENTALES DU HAUT RHIN
VILLAGES THAT BELONG TO THE UPPER ALSACE AND THEREFORE
THE ARCHIVES IN COLMAR.

Algolsheim, Altkirch, Altwiller = Altweier?, Ammerschwihr, Ammerzwiller, Andolzheim, Appenweier= Appenwihr, Artzenheim, Aspach le Haut, Aspach le Bas, Attenschwiller

Baldersheim, Balgau, Ballersdorf, Balschwiller, Bannwihr, Banviller, Bartenheim, Battenheim, Beblenheim, Bellemagny, Bendorf, Bennwihr, Berentzwiller, Bergeheim, Bergholtz, Bergholtzzell, Berrwiller, Bettendorf, Bettlach, Biederthal, Biesheim, Biltzheim, Bisel, Bitschwiller Les Thann, Blodelsheim, Blotzheim, Bollwiller, Bonhomme= le Bonhomme, Bourbach le Bas, Bourgfelden, BreitenbachBas Rhin, Bruebach le Bas, Brun'statt, Buchsweiler, Buethwiller, Buhl, Burnhaupt le Bas, Burnhaupt le Haut, Buschwiller

Carspach, Cernay, Chavanne Sur-Létang, Colmar, Courtavon

Dannemarie, Dessenheim, Diedenheim, Dirlingsdorf, Durlinsdorf, Durmenach Haut Rhin, Durrenentzen Haut Rhin

Eguisheim, Elbach, Emlingen, Enisheim, Enschingen, Eschbach, Eschentzwiller, Eteimbes

Falkwiller, Feldbach, Feldkirch, Fellering, Felleringen, Ferette, Fessenheim, Fislis, Folgenbourg, Fortschwihr, Franken, Freland, Friesen, Froeningen, Fulleren

Galfingue, Geishausen, Geispitzen, Gildwiller, Goldbach, Gommersdorf, Grentzingen, Griesbach, Grussenheim, Guebenheim, Gueberschwihr, Guebwiller, Guemar, Guewenheim, Gundolsheim

Habsheim, Hagenheim, Hagenthal le Bas, Hattstatt, Hausgauen,
Hecken, Hegenheim, Heimersdorf, Helfrantzkirch, Herrlisheim, Hettenschlag, Hesingue, Hindlingen, Hirsingen, Hirtzbach, Hirtzfelden, Hochstadt, Holtzwihr, Hombourg, Horbourg, Houssen, Hunawihr Hundsbach, Huningue, Husseren Wesserling, Husseren les Chateaux

Illhaeusern, Illfurth, Illzach, Ingersheim, Issenheim, Jebsheim, Jungholtz

Kappelen Haut Rhin, Kayserberg, Kientzheim, Kiffis, Kirchberg, Koestlach, Kruth, Kunheim, Kembs

Lallemand Rombach or Rambach, Lapoutroie, Largitzen, Lautenbach, Lautenbach Zell, Leimbach, Leymen, Liebenswiller, Liepvre orLiepre, Liebsdorf, Linthal, Logelsheim or Logelnheim, Lucelle, Lutter, Lutterbach, Lutran

Magny, Malmerspach, Manspach, Massevaux, Mertzen, Merxheim, Meyenheim, Michelbach, Michelbach le Bas, Mittelwihr, Mittlach, Mitzach, Moernau, Mollau, Montreux Jeune, Moos, Moosach, Moosch, Morschwiller, Mortzwiller, Muhlbach sur Munster, Mulhausen, Mulhouse, Munchausen or Muenckhausen, Muntzenheim, Murbach

Nambsheim, Neu Breisach, Neuf Brisach, Niederbruck, Niederentzen, Niederhagenthal, Niederhergheim, Niederlarg, Niedermorschwiller, Niedersteinbrunn, Niffer

Oberbruck, Oberdorf, Oberenesisheim, Oberentzen, Oberhergheim, Oberhagenthal, Obermerschwiller, Obermichelbach, Oberrodern, Obersteinbrunn, Oderem, Oltingue, Orbey, Orschwier, Ostheim

Pfaffenheim, Pfastatt, Pfefferhausen= Pfetterhausen, Pulversheim

Raedersheim, Raedersdorff, Ramersmatt,Ranspach, Reguisheim, Reiningue, Retzwiller, Ribeauville, Richwiller, Riedisheim, Riespach, Rimbach, Rimbachzell, Riquewihr, Rixheim, Roderen, Romagny, Rombach le France, Roppentzwiller, Rouffach, Ruelisheim, Rumersheim

Sainte Marie aux mines, Sainte Croix aux Mines, Sausheim, Schweighausen, Schweighouse, Schwoben, Sentheim, Seppois le Bas, Seppois Le haut, Sewen, Sickert, Sierentz, Sigolsheim, Sondernach, Sondersdorf, Soppe Le Bas, Sondersdorf, Soultz, Soultzbach les Bains, Staffelfelden, Steffen, Steinbach, Steinbrunn le bas, Steinbrunn le haut, Steinsoultz, Sternenberg, Storckensohn, Stosswihr, Sundhoffen

Tagolsheim, Thann, Thannenkirch, Traubach le Bas, Traubach leHaut, Turckheim

Uberkumen, Uffheim, Ungersheim, Urbes, Urschenheim

Valdieu, Vieux-Thann, Voegtlinshoffen, Vogelsheim

Walbach , Walheim, Waltenheim, Wattwiller, Weckolsheim, Wegscheid, Wintzenheim, Wittenheim, Wittersdorf, Wittelsheim, Wolfersdorf, Wolfgantzen

Zell, Zellenberg, Zillisheim, Zimmerbach, Zimmersheim

GERMAN VILLAGES AND TOWNS, MAINLY, WÜRTTEMBERG, BADEN AND PALATINATE.

SOME OF THE BELOW LISTED VILLAGES WERE NOT FOUND IN ANY REGISTER,BUT WERE LISTED ON THE OLD RECORDS AS BEING GERMANY. THIS MIGHT PERHAPS BE MISSPELLINGS.

Albirsbach, Adelsheim, Altendorf, Altensteig, Altschweyer, Alzey,Andel,Annweiler

Baar Baden, Badersdorf, Baiersbronn, Balingen, Bartenstein, Beisingen, Berghaupten, Betten, Billingen, Bimbach or Burbach, Birckersdorf, Bittesbronn, Bittersheim, Blaufelden, Botzingen, Bremen, Bretten, Broggingen, Bruchheim, Bruehl, Bubenheim, Buchenwald, Buehl, Buehlertal, Busenbach, Buttenheim, Buren

Cappel, Celbronn,Codtnau

Dalle, Danningen, Deggingen, Dehlingen, Dennach, Detzeln, Dobel, Dollendorf, Donaueschingen. Dornach, Dueren, Dueringen, Duerrenbach, Durach, , Durmersheim, Dusslingen, Duerckheim

Eckendorf, Edlingen, Egenhausen ,Ehrenstetten, Eisingern, Emmendingen, Endersbach, Endingen ,Ensheim, Ensisheim, Erbach, Erlach ,Eschenberg, Ettenheim Ettlingen, Etzingen, Essingen

Frankfurt, Freistett,Freudenstadt, Friedenheim, Friedenstadt, Friesenheim

Gasbricher., Geiningen, Geisingen, Gengenbach, Gernsbach, Gesbrichen, Graben, Grafenhausen, Griesheim, Grosswallstadt, Grossweiher, Grunholtz, Gundelfingen, Gutach

Haagen, Haigerloch, Hainfeld, Haslach, Hatten, Heitersheim, Hemmendorf, Hengenlau, Hillstett, Hilpertsau, Hirlingen, Horb, Horgen, Hornberg, Hostetten, Homhourg, Hugsweiler, Huppach, Hutten, Huttenheim

Ichenhausen, Ichenheim, Iffetsheim, Immendingen, Jebenhausen

Kandel, Kandstadt ,Kappel-Rodeck, Karlsruhe, Kehl, Kerhofen, Kentzingen, Kiechlingsbergen, Kilpertsau, Kippenheimweiler, Kirchenhofen, Klaenthof, Korb, Kratzingen, Kuentzel, Kuppenheim, Kusel

Lahn, Lahr, Lakingen, Landau, Landshausen, Langenenzlingen, Laubenheim, Laucherthal, Lauderthal, Lauffenburg, Lautenbach, Leiderheim, Lemberg, Ligsdorf, Lohr, Loerrach Lenzkirchen, Leutkirch, Ludingen

Marlen, Marxheim, Meisenthal, Membrechtshofen, Merchenthal, Merdingen, Mieringen, Moehringen, Muenster, Munich, Munningen, Musbach

Nechardensheigen, Nerdingen, Neuenbrueck, Neuhoff Prussia, Neusatz, Neustadt, Neufreistett, Niederheim, Niederbergheim, Niederlauterbach, Niederhausen, Niederrad, Norstadt, Nortingen, Nunenheyer, Nussbach

Oberhergheim, Oberlangenwaldau, Oberndorf, Obernheim, Oder, Oehrignen, Oelbronn, Oensbach, Offfenburg, Olpe, Oos, Oppenau, Ottenbourg, Ottingen

Petersthal, Pforzheim, Phillipsburg, Pirmasens, Printzbach

Rambach, Rastadt, Rattenweiler, Reichenbach, Remingen, Remlisdorf, Renchen, Reningen, Riebeningue, Riegel, Roedersdorf, Roedersheim, Romersweyer, Rothenburg, Ruppe = Ruppen?, Rust

Schaffhausen, Schallersdorf, Scheibenhardt, Schelingen, Schertzheim, Schliedorf, Schlierstadt, Schwaldorf, Schwann, Schwartzenberg, Schwenningen, Sellbach, Simonswald, Sinsheim, Soultz, Speck, Speihingen, Stadelhofen, Stauffenberg, Stein, Steinbach, Sternberg, Straussdorf, Stupferich, Sulzbach, Szein

Teubingen, Trulben

Unterachern, Untermelingen, Unzhurst, Ulm

Voclerschbach, Voerden

Waiblingen, Weden,Weiden, Weil, Weiler, Weisach, Weissenborn, Weissenburg, Weitingen, Wessach, Wettelsheim, Wildberg, Winkel, Wittendorf, Wolfershoffen, Wurmlingen, Wurzach

Zehringen, Zell, Zeppenhorn, Zierolshofen, Zinsheim

B O U N D A R I E S   T O D A Y

GERMANY

Palatinate
today
Rhine-Palatinate

•Karlsruhe

Strassbourg

Stuttgart

BADEN-WÜRTTEMBERG

A L S A C E

Colmar•

Muehlhsn •

•Freiburg

Lake
Constanz

FRANCE

Zuerich•

S W I T Z E R L A N D

Lastname	Firstname	Birth Year	Birthplace	Emigration	De	Prof	Source
AAD	VALENTIN	1827	MOLLAU	12/19/1848	NY		NO.2
ABBA WW 1 CH	AUGUSTIN		ENGENTHAL	03/06/1838	A		NO.2
ABRAHAM	CATHERINE	1805	NIEDERENTZEN	06/27/1857	NO		NO.2
ABRAHAM	JOSEPH	1837	NIEDERENTZEN	06/27/1857	NO		NO.2
ABRAHAM	RAPHAEL		REICHSHOFFEN	01/01/1869	A		NO.2
ABRY	ANTOINE	1823	JONCHERY	02/17/1849	NY		NO.2
ABRY	FRANCOIS	1845	GRANDVILLAR	06/19/1866	NY		NO.2
ABRY	JEAN GEORGES	1813	RIGUEWIHR	05/01/1846	NO		NO.2
ABRY	LOUIS	1825	JONCHERY	02/19/1865	NY		NO.2
ABRY	PIERRE	1841	MEMONCOURT	09/27/1865	NY		NO.2
ABT	LAURENT	1816	RIEDISHEIM	01/01/1844	TX	VIGN	PASS
ABT	MICHEL		STADTMATTEN	01/01/1828	A		FILM
ACKERMANN	BERNARD	1807	CERNAY	08/14/1852	NY		FILM
ACKERMANN	BERNARD	1851	MULHOUSE	03/31/1857	NY		FILM
ACKERMANN	CHARLES	1832	COLMAR	08/05/1856	NY		FILM
ACKERMANN	DOMINIQUE	1817	GUEBWILLER	10/01/1848	NY		FILM
ACKERMANN	FERDINAND	1813	LINTHAL	10/21/1852	NO		FILM
ACKERMANN	FRANCOIS		VOLKSBERG	01/01/1828	A		FILM
ACKERMANN	FRANCOIS XAVIER	1822	SUAREE	02/27/1851	NY		FILM
ACKERMANN	FRED		BACKNANG(W)	07/30/1849	A		FILM
ACKERMANN	GEORGE		IMBSHEIM	01/01/1828	A		FILM
ACKERMANN	IGNACE	1802	JUNGHOLTZ	10/14/1850	NY		FILM
ACKERMANN	LOUIS BERNARD	1830	CERNAY	02/25/1853	A		FILM
ACKERMANN	VIKTORIA		BERRWILLER	01/01/1854	TX		SHIP
ACREMANN	MARIE THERESE	1821	FAREROIS	05/10/1850	NO		FILM
ADAM	ANDRE		PLOBSHEIM	01/01/1828	A		FILM
ADAM	CHARLES	1826	BONHOMME	02/14/1853	NY		FILM
ADAM	GEORGES		HIRSCHLAND	01/01/1828	A		FILM
ADAM	JOSEPH	1801	KLIENTZHEIM	05/19/1849	NY		FILM
ADAM MN TENN	MARIE ANNE	1806	SIGOLSHEIM	09/23/1850	A		FILM
ADELSHEIMER	FANNY	1851	NIEDERROEDERN	01/01/1867	NY		NO.2
ADOLFF	PIERRE		DOSSENHEIM	01/01/1828	A		FILM
ADRIAN	JOSEPH	1820	ST. MARTIN	11/09/1854	NY		FILM
ADRIEN MN SPOERY	JOSEPHINE	1827	RIBEAUVILLE	09/27/1855	NY		FILM
AEBY W URBAN JOSEPH	REINE WH AND D	1787		11/10/1854	A		FILM
AEDERMANN WW CH 2	JU JAQUES		ADAMSWILLER	03/17/1817	A		FILM
AEICHERT	ELISABETH		NEUHEUSEL	01/01/1828	A		FILM
AFFHOLDEN	PIERRE	1818	BURNHAUPT LE BAS	05/13/1839	NY		FILM
AHL	NICOLAS		EYWILLER	01/01/1828	A		FILM
AHL WW CH 1	MARTIN		HIRSHLAND	03/20/1817	A		FILM
AHR	CATHERINE	1820	OBERENTZEN	09/01/1851	TX		PASS
AHR	CATHERINE	1820	OBERENTZEN	09/10/1851	TX		FILM
AHR	ETIENNE	1821	OBERENTZEN	09/01/1846	TX	MARF	PASS
AHR	ETIENNE	1821	OBERENTZEN	09/14/1846	TX		FILM
AHR	LAURENT	1828	OBERENTZEN	09/01/1848	TX	MARF	PASS
AHR	LAURENT	1828	OBERENTZEN	11/04/1848	TX		FILM
ALBENISIUS	LORENZ	1840	SCHAFFHAUSEN	01/01/1865	NY	FARM	NO.2
ALBERT	GEORG	1845	HERMERSWEILER	01/01/1866	NY		MO.2
ALBERT	JEAN BAPTISTE	1819	LIEPRE	08/14/1838	NO		FILM
ALBERT	JEAN PIERRE	1819	LIEPRE	07/06/1848	NO		FILM

Lastname	Firstname	Birth Year	Birthplace	Emigration	De	Prof	Source
ALBERT	MARIE JEANNE	1815	LIEPRE	03/29/1841	NO		FILM
ALBERT	MARTIN	1819	HERMERSWEILER	01/01/1866	NY	FARM	NO.2
ALBERT W CH	MAGDALENA	1828	HERMERSWEILER	01/01/1866	NY		NO.2
ALBITZ	GEORGES	1824	URSCHENHEIM	05/04/1847	NY		FILM
ALBRECHT	PLAZENS	1798	DETZELN B	10/25/1843	TX		NO.2
ALBRECHT	PLAZEUS	1798	DETZELN (B)	10/25/1843	TX		FILM
ALBRECHT D DERN	MARIE D MARGUER	1854	MULHOUSE	10/08/1856	NY		FILM
ALBRECHT W DERN CH 1	MARGUERITE	1829	MULHOUSE	10/08/1856	NY		FILM
ALBRECHT W W 5 CH	FRANCOIS	1823	THANN	12/08/1845	NY		NO.2
ALBRECHT WW AND CH 3	FRANCOIS	1813	THANN	12/08/1845	NY		FILM
ALIMANN	JEAN	1826	RICHWILLER	01/03/1852	NY		NO.2
ALLEMAND	JAQUES	1812	VALDOIS	02/21/1857	NY		FILM
ALLEMAND	JOSEPH FILS	1836	COLMAR	08/09/1854	NY		FILM
ALLEMAND CH 4	ANNE MARIE	1790	ELOIE	03/11/1854	A		FILM
ALLEMAND WW	FRANCOIS	1807	COLMAR	03/31/1852	PH		FILM
ALLEMANN WW	JEAN	1816	RAEDERSDORFF	02/20/1852	NY		FILM
ALLENBRAND	EMILE	1837	MULHOUSE	09/29/1855	NY		FILM
ALLENBRAND	GEORGES	1829	MULHOUSE	07/03/1852	NY		FILM
ALLGEIER	XAVIER		MULLENBACH	08/31/1898	A		FILM
ALLIMANG	CHRETIEN		KIRRBERG	01/01/1828	A		FILM
ALLIMANG	HENRY		KIRRBERG	01/01/1828	A		FILM
ALLIMANG	JAQUES		KIRRBERG	01/01/1828	A		FILM
ALLIMANG	MARGERITE		KIRRBERG	03/12/1838	A		FILM
ALLIMANG F OF 9	JAQUES		KIRRBERG	03/12/1818	A		FILM
ALLIMANN	JOSEPH	1827	RICHWILLER	04/07/1857	A		FILM
ALLIMANN MN HIRTH	MARGUERITE	1827	RICHWILLER	07/01/1857	A		FILM
ALMONT WW AND CH 2	MARTINE		ZITTERSHEIM	03/11/1817	A		FILM
ALT	JAQUES		OTTERSTHAL	01/01/1828	A		FILM
ALT	MARX		OTTERSTHAL	01/01/1828	A		FILM
ALTHEIMER	JOSEPH MARTIN	1815	THANN	06/15/1847	SL		FILM
ALTHOFER WW AND CH 1	DAMIEN	1818	ARTZENHEIM	06/23/1846	PH		FILM
ALTINGER	ROSINE	1834	FALTZSTETTEN(W)	07/15/1854	NY		FILM
ALTMANN	JEAN	1826	RICHWILLER	01/03/1852	NY		FILM
ALZHAUSER WW AND CH3	ANDRE		MARCKOLSHEIM	06/27/1833	A		FILM
AMAN	JAQUES	1830	NIEDERHAGENTHAL	08/11/1849	NY		FILM
AMAND	JOSEPH		SCHIRRHEIN	01/01/1828	A		FILM
AMAND	MICHEL		SCHIRRHEIN	01/01/1828	A		FILM
AMANN	CHARLES	1835	ST MARIE AUX MINES	02/04/1847	BO		FILM
AMANN	JEAN FILS	1826	ST MARIE AUX MINES	03/22/1847	NY		FILM
AMANN	JOSEPH		STANDWEILER	06/18/1836	A		FILM
AMANN	MICHEL		SCHIRRHEIN	01/01/1828	A		FILM
AMANN WW AND CH	SERAPHIN	1810	AUGENTHAL LE SAS	10/17/1846	A		FILM
AMANN WW AND CH 1	FRANCOIS		SAVENNE	03/31/1817	A		FILM
AMBACHER	FREDERIC	1814	MULHAUSEN	08/07/1838	A		FILM
AMBACHER	MADELAINE	1822	WINTHERTHUR	03/06/1848	NY		NO.2
AMBARD	FRANCOIS XAVIER	1819	AUXELLES-HAUT	02/08/1853	NO		
AMBIEHL	JOSEPH		SOULTZ	10/26/1850	NY		FILM
AMBROISE	JEAN		DAUENDORF	01/01/1828	A		FILM
AMBS	JOSEPH		HUTTENDORF	01/01/1828	NY		FILM
AMBS	XAVIER		HOCHFELDEN	01/01/1828	A		FILM

Lastname	Firstname	Birth Year	Birthplace	Emigration	De	Prof	Source
AMBS WW AND CH	JEAN	1820	BOTZINGEN (B)	02/09/1852	NY		FILM
AMMEL	J. GEORGES		PLOBSHEIM	01/01/1828	A		FILM
AMMEL	JEAN		PLOBSHEIM	01/01/1828	A		FILM
AMMEL WW	MICHEL		PLOBSHEIM	01/01/1828	A		FILM
AMREIN	GREGORIE JOSEPH	1835	ROUFFACH	04/21/1856	NY		FILM
AMSTATZ	EUGENE	1827	ETAPES(DOUBS)	05/27/1846	NO		FILM
AMSTATZ	MARIE	1830	GRANDVILLARS	09/13/1852	NO		NO.2
AMSTUTZ	FRANCHISE	1829	GRANDVILLERS	03/22/1855	NY		FILM
AMSTUTZ	FRANCOISE	1829	GRANDVILLERS	03/22/1855	NY		FILM
AMSTUTZ	JOSEPH	1814	LEYMEN	10/29/1834	NY		FILM
AMSTUTZ	JOSEPH	1819	LEYMEN	07/04/1844	NY		FILM
AMSTUTZ	PIERRE	1816	LEYMEN	03/15/1838	NY		FILM
ANCEL	FRANCOIS	1800	LIEPRE	03/21/1839	NO		NO.2
ANCEL	JEAN CLAUDE	1820	ST. CROIX AUX MINES	06/23/1843	NO		FILM
ANCHLIN	LAURENT PAUL	1822	KIENTZHEIM	09/08/1847	NY		FILM
ANDING	SEBASTIAN		SCHIRRHEIN	01/01/1828	A		FILM
ANDRE	JEAN JOSEPH	8122	LIEPRE	08/17/1847	NY		FILM
ANDRE	MICHEL	1808	LIEPRE	04/08/1839	A		FILM
ANDRE WW AND CH 3	PIERRE	1800	ST CROIX AUX MINES	05/08/1847	SL		FILM
ANDREAS	CATHERINE		NUNENHEYER	10/06/1849	A		FILM
ANDREAS	JAQUES		NUNENHEYER(B)	10/06/1849	A		FILM
ANDREAS	JOSEPH		NUNENHEYER	10/06/1849	A		FILM
ANDRES	BENEDICT	1815	GAECHLIWIL,SWISS	12/15/1846	TX		FILM
ANDRES	JACOB	1837	CLEEBURG	01/01/1866	NY	TAYL	PRIV
ANDRES	JAQUES	1816	CLEEBOURG	01/01/1855	NY	TAYL	PRIV
ANDRES	JEAN		MALSHEIM	03/29/1840	A		FILM
ANDRES	JOSEPH		REINHARDSMUNSTER	01/01/1828	A		FILM
ANDRES	MICHEL		SINGRIST	01/01/1828	A		FILM
ANDRES	NIKOLAUS	1783	GACHLIEVIL	11/15/1846	TX		FILM
ANDRES	NIKOLAUS	1827	GACHLIEVIL	11/15/1846	TX		FILM
ANDRES	THERESE		REINHARDSMUNSTER	01/01/1828	A		FILM
ANDRES D NIKOLAUS	ELISABETH	1846	GACHLIEVIL	11/15/1846	TX		FILM
ANDRES F OF 2	BLAISE		SINGRIST	01/01/1828	A		NO.2
ANDRES W NIKOLAUS	ELISABETH	1805	GACHLIEVIL	11/15/1846	TX		FILM
ANDRES WW AND CH 1	NIKOLAUS	1811	GACHLIEVIL	11/15/1846	TX		FILM
ANDRES WW CH 6	MEINRAD	1791	ZIMMERSHEIM	12/01/1844	TX	CULT	SHIP
ANDRETZ F OF 2	MICHEL		DETTWILLER	01/01/1828	A		NO.2
ANGEL	ALEXANDRE	1825	ST. CROIX AUX MINES	10/09/1846	NY		FILM
ANGEL	FRANCOISE	1800	LIEPRE	03/21/1839	NO		FILM
ANIEL	ALEXANDRE	1825	ST. CROIX AUX MINES	10/09/1846	NY		FILM
ANNA WW AND CH 2	THIEBAUD		CARMINGEN	03/23/1817	A		FILM
ANSCHER	BERTHA	1850	OBERLAUTERBACH	01/01/1868	NY		NO.2
ANSCHER	BERTHE	1850	OBERLAUTERBACH	01/01/1868	NY		PRIV
ANSCHER	CHARLOTTE	1849	NIEDERROEDERN	01/01/1868	NO		NO.2
ANSCHER	SAMUEL	1812	OBERLAUTERBACH	01/01/1868	NY	MERC	PRIV
ANSCHUTZ WW AND CH	PIERRE		ZINSWILLER	03/16/1818	A		FILM
ANSEL	MARTIN	1827	ESCHBACH	04/14/1855	NY		FILM
ANSEL	SERAPHIN	1814	THANNENKIRCH	11/16/1853	NY		FILM
ANSELM	ADAM	1803	ZINSWEILLER	02/16/1817	A		FILM
ANSELM	ANTOINE	1791	GUEBWILLER	02/12/1849	NY		FILM

Lastname	Firstname	Birth Year	Birthplace	Emigration	De	Prof	Source
ANSELM	AUGUSTE	1828	GUEBWILLER	08/02/1852	A		FILM
ANSELM	CH		STUTTGART(W)	02/05/1864	A		FILM
ANSELM D JAQUES	BARBE	1806	ZINSWEILLER	02/16/1817	A		FILM
ANSELM D JAQUES	CHRISTINE	1813	ZINSWEILLER	02/16/1817	A		FILM
ANSELM D JAQUES	MADELEINE	1811	ZINSWEILLER	02/16/1817	A		FILM
ANSELM D JAQUES	MARIE ANNE	1800	ZINSWEILLER	02/16/1817	A		FILM
ANSELM D JAQUES	THERESE	1815	ZINSWEILLER	02/16/1817	A		FILM
ANSELM S JAQUES	ADAM	1803	ZINSWEILLER	02/16/1817	A		FILM
ANSELM S JAQUES	FRANCOIS	1807	ZINSWEILLER	02/16/1817	A		FILM
ANSELM S JAQUES	FRANCOIS	1808	ZINSWEILLER	02/16/1817	A		FILM
ANSELM S JAQUES	FRANCOIS JAQUES	1796	ZINSWEILLER	02/16/1817	A		FILM
ANSELM S JAQUES	FRANCOIS JOSEPH	1798	ZINSWEILLER	02/16/1817	A		FILM
ANSELM S JAQUES	GEORGE	1799	ZINSWEILLER	02/16/1817	A		FILM
ANSELM WW	AUGUSTE	1828	GUEBWILLER	08/02/1852	A		FILM
ANSELM WW AND CH	JAQUES	1763	ZINSWEILLER	02/16/1817	A		FILM
ANSMINGER F OF 5	CONRAD		DIEMERINGEN	03/03/1838	A		FILM
ANSTATT	GEORGE		INGVILLER	01/01/1828	A		FILM
ANSTEIN	JEAN GEORGE	1833	COLMAR	10/22/1854	A		FILM
ANSTETT	JEAN		BRUMATH	01/01/1828	A		FILM
ANTHOIN	JEAN BAPTISTE	1823	ST. CROIX AUX MINES	10/19/1853	SL		FILM
ANTHOINE	ALEXANDRE	1824	LIEPRE	03/31/1855	NY		FILM
ANTHON	BARBARA	1843	ALTENSTADT	01/01/1866	NY		NO.2
ANTHON	MARIA	1844	ALTENSTADT	01/01/1869	NY		NO.2
ANTOINE	ELISABETH		INGENHEIM	01/01/1828	A		FILM
ANTOINE	THIEBAUD	1828	CHEVREMONT	05/11/1847	NY		FILM
APFELL	FRIDERICKE	1852	WEISSENBURG	01/01/1865	NY		NO.2
APFELL	HEINRICH	1847	WEISSENBURG	01/01/1865	NY		NO.2
APFELL	LINA	1851	WEISSENBURG	01/01/1865	NY		NO.2
APFELL	MARGARETHA	1846	WEISSENBURG	01/01/1865	NY		NO.2
APFELL W 4CH	MARGARETHA	1823	WEISSENBURG	01/01/1865	NY		NO.2
APRIL	ROSINA	1842	LEMBACH	01/01/1866	NY		NO.2
ARBOGAST	EDUARD		OBERSTEINBACH	01/01/1854	NY		NO.2
ARBOGAST F OF 4	JEAN		INGENHEIM	01/01/1828	A		FILM
ARBOGAST F OF 7	IGNACE		ROESCHWOOG	01/01/1828	A		FILM
ARGAST	FRANCOIS	1839	HERICOURT	10/01/1866	NY		FILM
ARLEN	GEORGE		HOERDT	01/01/1828	A		FILM
ARMBRUST	JOHANN		RIEDSELTZ	01/01/1868	A		NO.2
ARMBRUST	PHILLIP	1839	SCHLEITHAL	01/01/1866	NY		NO.2
ARNETH F OF 9	FRANCOIS ANTOIN		ROESCHWOOG	01/01/1828	A		FILM
ARNOLD	AGATHE	1818	FELLERINGEN	11/22/1843	TX		FILM
ARNOLD	AGATHE	1835	KRUTH	08/01/1860	TX	TISS	PASS
ARNOLD	ALEXANDRE	1827	KRUTH	08/01/1855	TX	CULT	PASS
ARNOLD	ALEXANDRE	1827	RANSPACH	08/06/1855	TX		FILM
ARNOLD	BARBARA		GERMANY	04/12/1849	NY		FILM
ARNOLD	CECILE D ANTOIN	1851	KRUTH	10/01/1859	TX		PASS
ARNOLD	CHRISTIEN		MUTTERSHOLTZ	01/01/1828	A		FILM
ARNOLD	CLAIRE D ANTOIN	1859	KRUTH	10/01/1859	TX		PASS
ARNOLD	ETIENNE	1826	ROUGEMONT	09/19/1857	A		FILM
ARNOLD	GEORG	1803	MOLLKIRCH	10/25/1843	TX		FILM
ARNOLD	GEORGE		BALDENHEIM	03/06/1838	A		FILM

Lastname	Firstname	Birth Year	Birthplace	Emigration	De	Prof	Source
ARNOLD	GEORGE		FROHMUHL	01/01/1828	A		FILM
ARNOLD	GEORGE		ROMANSWILLER	01/01/1828	A		FILM
ARNOLD	HENRI		ROPPENHEIM	01/01/1828	A		NO.2
ARNOLD	IRENEE D ANTOIN	1857	KRUTH	10/01/1859	TX		PASS
ARNOLD	JACQUES	1827	KRUTH	08/01/1855	TX	CULT	PASS
ARNOLD	JAQUES		OFFWILLER	03/11/1817	A		FILM
ARNOLD	JAQUES	1827	KRUTH	08/06/1855	TX		FILM
ARNOLD	JAQUES	1830	KRUTH	10/05/1854	NY		FILM
ARNOLD	JEAN	1832	KRUTH	01/01/1853	TX		SHIP
ARNOLD	JEAN	1832	KRUTH	08/01/1855	TX	CARP	PASS
ARNOLD	JEAN	1832	KRUTH	08/21/1855	TX		FILM
ARNOLD	LAURENT	1822	KRUTH	08/01/1860	TX		PASS
ARNOLD	MARIE ANNE	1826	KRUTH	09/14/1854	NY		FILM
ARNOLD	ODILE D ANTOINE	1853	KRUTH	10/01/1859	TX		PASS
ARNOLD	PAUL	1836	KRUTH	08/01/1860	TX		PASS
ARNOLD	PIERRE	1820	GOLDBACH	08/28/1853	NY		FILM
ARNOLD CH 2	ANTOINE	1827	KRUTH	01/01/1867	TX	CARP	PASS
ARNOLD CH 4	ANTOINE	1823	KRUTH	10/01/1859	TX	JOUR	PASS
ARNOLD D MICHAEL	CAROLINE		ROPPENHEIM	01/01/1843	A		NO.1
ARNOLD H SALOME	MICHAEL		ROPPENHEIM	03/15/1846	A		NO.1
ARNOLD S GEORGE	LORENZ	1835	MOLLKIRCH	10/25/1843	TX		FILM
ARNOLD S GEORGE	MICHAEL	1841	MOLLKIRCH	10/25/1843	TX		FILM
ARNOLD S GEORGE	XAVER	1837	MOLLKIRCH	10/25/1843	TX		FILM
ARNOLD S GEORGES	LAURENT	1855	MOLLKIRCH	10/01/1843	TX		SHIP
ARNOLD S GEORGES	MICHEL	1841	MOLLKIRCH	10/01/1843	TX		SHIP
ARNOLD S GEORGES	XAVIER	1857	MOLLKIRCH	10/01/1843	TX		SHIP
ARNOLD S JACQUES	HENRI		ROPPENHEIM	01/01/1828	A		FILM
ARNOLD W GEORGE	MAGDALENA	1810	MOLLKIRCH	10/25/1843	TX		FILM
ARNOLD W MICHAEL	SALOME		ROPPENHEIM	01/15/1846	A		NO.1
ARNOLD WW AND CH 3	GEORGES	1803	MOLLKIRCH	10/01/1843	TX	CULT	SHIP
ARNOLD WW AND CH 4	JOSEPH		TIEFFENBACH	03/11/1817	A		FILM
ARNOLDT H EVE 5CH	PHILLIP GEORGES	1800	ROPPENHEIM	01/01/1831	A		NO.1
ARNOLDT MN CLAUSS	EVE ELSIABETH	1800	ROPPENHEIM	01/01/1831	A		NO.1
ARNOULD	QUIRIN	1828	LIEPRE	08/21/1847	NY		FILM
ARON	MAX		RENINGEN	04/18/1849	NY		FILM
ART MN HARRER	THERESE	1828	MUNTZENHEIM	01/19/1853	A		FILM
ARTH	CASPAR	1843	EBERBACH	01/01/1867	NY	SHMA	NO.2
ARTH	CATHERINA	1837	EBERBACH	01/01/1867	NY		NO.2
ARTH	JOHANN	1841	EBERBACH	01/01/1865	NY	FARM	NO.2
ASCHBACHER	CATHERINE		NIEDERLAUTERBACH	01/01/1850	NO		PRIV
ASCHBACHER	CATHERINE	1843	NIEDERLAUTERBACH	01/01/1861	NO		PRIV
ASCHBACHER	JEAN		NIEDERLAUTERBACH	01/01/1850	NO		PRIV
ASCHBACHER	JEAN	1840	NIEDERLAUTERBACH	01/01/1861	A	DAYL	PRIV
ASSENMACHER	HEINRICH	1826	EUPEN(BELGIEN)	11/15/1846	TX		FILM
ASSINOUR	JOHANN BAPT.	1808	DURBACH	04/09/1844	TX		NO.2
AST	JEAN	1824	NIFFER	05/02/1852	NO		FILM
AST	JOSEPHINE	1833	PFASTATT	03/18/1857	A		NO.2
AST	NICOLAS		SILTZHEIM	01/01/1828	A		FILM
ATTENBACH WW AND CH5	ETIENNE	1800	SONDERSDORF	04/09/1847	NY		FILM
ATTINGER	FRANCOIS	1833	MOOS	09/28/1853	NY		FILM

Lastname	Firstname	Birth Year	Birthplace	Emigration	De	Prof	Source
ATTINGER	FRANCOISE ANTOI	1833	MOOS	09/20/1853	NY	DAYL	FILM
ATZEL	ANNE MARIE		STATTMATTEN	01/01/1828	A		FILM
ATZEL	TOBIE		STATTMATTEN	01/01/1828	A		FILM
AUBRY	HENRIETTE	1795		09/17/1845	TX		FILM
AUCH F OF 10	ADAM		DOSSENHEIM	01/01/1828	A		FILM
AUDRAN	GUILLAUME ALEX	1783	DANNEMARIE	04/20/1846	NY		FILM
AUER F OF 4	GEORGE		WEISLINGEN	01/01/1828	A		FILM
AUFSCHNEIDER	THERESE		BALBRONN	01/01/1828	A		FILM
AUGSBURGER	AMRIE	1815	STRASSBOURG	05/16/1849	A		NO.2
AUGSBURGER WW CH 7	CHRETIEN		STRASBOURG	05/12/1817	A		FILM
AUGUSTI	CATHERINE	1817	BAUXWILLER	05/14/1841	NY		FILM
AUGUSTIN WW CH 6	IGNACE	1797	CERNAY	08/10/1847	SL		FILM
AUSCHER	CHARLOTTE		NIEDEROEDERN	01/01/1866	NO		PRIV
AUTZMANN WW	JEAN BAPTISTE	1805	LIEPRE	10/15/1838	NO		FILM

Lastname	Firstname	Birth Year	Birthplace	Emigration	De	Prof	Source
BABON		1819	HAUT-RHIN	12/01/1844	TX	CULT	PRIV
BABON	MARIE MADELEINE	1809	HAUT-RHIN	12/01/1844	TX		SHIP
BABON	VIKTORIA	1840	HAUT-RHIN	12/01/1844	TX		SHIP
BABON CH1	MARIE	1814	HAUT-RHIN	12/01/1844	TX		SHIP
BABON S MADELEINE	HIPPOLYTE	1836	HAUT-RHIN	12/01/1844	TX		SHIP
BABSER	JEAN	1819	RETZWILLER	01/30/1847	NO		FILM
BACH	FRANZ	1837	BITCHE LOTHRINGEN	01/01/1866	NY		NO.2
BACH	JAQUES		KASKASTEL	01/01/1828	A		FILM
BACH	JEAN-ADAM		KASKASTEL	01/01/1828	A		FILM
BACH	MARIA	1850	BITCHE LOTHRING	01/01/1866	NY		NO.2
BACH	PIERRE LE JEUN		SIEWILLER	01/01/1828	A		FILM
BACH	REGINA	1842	BITCHE LOTHRING	01/01/1866	NY		NO.2
BACH	ROSALI	1844	BITCHE LOTHRING	01/01/1866	NY		NO.2
BACHARACH	FRANCOISE	1829	HARTMANNSWILLER	10/19/1854	A		FILM
BACHER WW AND CH 2	JEAN LOUIS	1826	COLMAR	06/24/1854	NY		FILM
BACHMANN	JAQUES		MACKWILLER	03/03/1817	A		PRIV
BACHMANN	LOUIS		HAAGEN	01/01/1828	A		FILM
BACHMANN	MADELEINE	1827	BOUXWILLER	05/25/1850	A		FILM
BACHMANN	NICOLAS		RANWILLER	01/01/1828	A		FILM
BACHMANN	SEBASTIEN	1793	BLITZHEIM	09/01/1846	TX	JOUR	PASS
BACHMANN	SEBASTIEN	1793	ROUFFACH	09/17/1846	TX		FILM
BACHMANN WW AND CH 5	JAQUES		MACKWILLER	03/03/1817	A		FILM
BACHMAY	JOCKS	1830	SENTHEIM	12/07/1855	NY		FILM
BACKEL WW AND CH 7	JEAN	1790	GUEMAR	08/25/1847	NY		FILM
BADAIRE	VIRGINIS	1845	ROUGEGOUTTE	05/20/1865	NY		FILM
BADER	ANNE MARIE	1814	UFFHOLTZ	12/31/1856	TX		FILM
BADER	JOSEPH	1837	UFFHOLTZ	12/01/1860	TX	BUTC	PASS
BADER AND CH	JOSEPH	1800	WITTELSHEIM	11/22/1843	TX		FILM
BADER D JOSEPH	MARIA ANNA	1825	WITTELSHEIM	11/22/1843	TX		FILM
BADER D JOSEPH I	ANNE-MARIE	1825	WITTELSHEIM	11/01/1843	TX		SHIP
BADER H ANNE-MARIE	JOSEPH I	1800	WITTELSHEIM	11/01/1843	TX	CULT	SHIP
BADER MN SCHOTT	ANNE MARIE		WITTELSHEIM	01/01/1845	TX		SHIP
BADER S JOSEPH I	JOSEPH II	1833	WITTELSHEIM	11/01/1843	TX		SHIP
BADER WH AND CH 3	MARIE ANNE	1803	HOMMERT	10/01/1850	NY		FILM
BADIQUEZ	JOSEPH	1815	PETIT CROIX	05/01/1857	NY		FILM
BAECHELE	ALEXANDRE	1830	CERNAY	05/16/1849	NY		FILM
BAECHER	VALENTIN	1816	HEGENHEIM	09/27/1847	NY		FILM
BAECHLE	ANDRE	1824	CERNAY	03/06/1848	NY		FILM
BAECHLI	JEAN JAQUES	1826	MULHOUSE	12/24/1852	NY		FILM
BAEHR	ADAM		KASKASTEL	01/01/1828	A		FILM
BAEHR	MICHEL		GERSTHEIM	03/03/1838	A		FILM
BAEHR WW AND CH 7	JOSEPH		ETTENDORF	01/01/1828	A		FILM
BAER	ADOLF	1848	KUTZENHAUSEN	01/01/1865	NY	FARM	NO.2
BAER	JEAN		BAERENTHAL(TIROL)	09/30/1849	A		FILM
BAER	JEAN BAPTISTE	1827	OHER ASPACH	06/28/1865	NY		FILM
BAER	MARIE ANNE	1818	OHER ASPACH	06/28/1865	NY		FILM
BAER AND CH 2	CATHERINE ELISA		NEHWILLER	06/23/1819	A		FILM
BAERINGEN	EMANUEL		OELBRONN(B)	04/11/1849	A		FILM
BAESSLER	GASPARD	1825	BITSCHWILLER	08/30/1853	NY		FILM
BAET	JOSEPH		WEISLINGEN	01/01/1828	A		FILM

Lastname	Firstname	Birth Year	Birthplace	Emigration	De	Prof	Source
BAGNEN	HANNI	1825	MULHOUSE	08/30/1854	NY		FILM
BAHL	CHARLES	1828	MULHOUSE	11/08/1853	NY		FILM
BAHL	LUDWIG	1864	SELTZ	01/01/1865	NY		NO.2
BAHL MN OGER	MAGDALENA		SELTZ	01/01/1865	NY		NO.2
BAHL W W 1 CH	JOSEF	1838	SELTZ	01/01/1865	NY	FARM	NO.2
BAILAT WW AND CH	GEORGES	1815	MULHOUSE	10/02/1848	NY		FILM
BAILLEUX	CHARLES	1824	HAUT-RHIN	12/01/1844	TX	CULT	SHIP
BAILLEUX W FRANCOIS	JULIE	1802	HAUT-RHIN	12/01/1844	TX		SHIP
BAILLEUX WW	FRANCOIS	1800	HAUT-RHIN	12/01/1844	TX	CULT	SHIP
BAILLY	WW AND CH2	1805	ST. GERMAIN	07/02/1837	NY		FILM
BAIMER WW AND CH2	DOMENIQUE	1811	GUEBWILLER	01/21/1854	A		FILM
BAIMER WW AND CH 2	DOMENIQUE	1811	GUEBWILLER	01/21/1854	A		FILM
BAJO	JEAN PIERRE	1838	ST. CROIX AUX MINES	12/05/1856	CA		FILM
BALDENSCHWEILER	BLASIUS	1809	LAUFFENBURG	11/22/1843	TX		FILM
BALDENSCHWEILER	MARIA ANNA	1813	LAUFFENBURG	11/22/1843	TX		FILM
BALDENSPERGER	GEORGE		BALDENHEIM	03/06/1838	A		FILM
BALDENSPERGER	PHILIPPE		BALDENHEIM	01/01/1828	A		FILM
BALDESCHWILLER	B.			12/01/1843	TX		SHIP
BALDINGER	FRANCOIS JOSEPH	1822	THANNENKIRCH	04/10/1855	SL		FILM
BALDINGER	WENDELIN	1820	THANNEKIRCH	08/20/1854	CH		FILM
BALDINGER W HERZOG	ELISABETH CH 4	1810	THANNENKIRCH	10/31/1846	NO		FILM
BALDNER	ANDRE		SCHWEIGHAUSEN	01/01/1828	A		FILM
BALDT WW AND CH6	JEAN		SCHWABWILLER	03/22/1817	A		FILM
BALIS	MAGDALENA	1801	LEMBACH	01/01/1866	NY		NO.2
BALL	JOSEPH		GERMANY	04/17/1849	A		FILM
BALL	LUDWIG.	1845	NIEDERBETSCHDORF	01/01/1866	OH	MILL	NO.2
BALLAY	ADELE	1822	MULHOUSE	03/16/1857	NY		FILM
BALLAY	ADOLPHE	1851	FRAHIER	07/30/1866	NO		FILM
BALLAY	DOROTHEE	1850	FRAHIER	07/30/1866	NO		FILM
BALLAY	FRANCOIS	1826	ERRARAT	03/09/1852	SL		FILM
BALLAY	FRANCOIS CONSTA	1835	BITSCHWILLER	04/07/1852	NY		FILM
BALLAY	WW AND CH2	1793	RONCHAMP	02/01/1857	NY		FILM
BALLAY D JEAN BAPTIS		1822	RONCHAMP	02/01/1857	NY		FILM
BALLAY D JEAN BAPTIS		1830	RONCHAMP	02/01/1857	NY		FILM
BALLAY W JEAN BAPTIS		1797	RONCHAMP	02/01/1857	NY		FILM
BALLIET	JAQUES PIERRE		RONWILLER	01/01/1828	A		FILM
BALLWEBER	ADELINE	1865	WEISSENBURG	01/01/1868	NY		NO.2
BALLWEBER	BARBARA	1867	WEISSENBURG	01/01/1868	NY		NO.2
BALLWEBER	JOHANN	1847	ALTENSTADT	01/01/1869	NO		NO.2
BALLWEBER	JOHANN	1847	ASCHPACH	01/01/1869	NO	FARM	NO.2
BALLWEBER	KARL	1860	ALTENSTADT	01/01/1869	NY		NO.2
BALLWEBER	SOPHIE	1864	WEISSENBURG	01/01/1868	NY		NO.2
BALLWEBER MN SAUVING	ROSINE		WEISSENBURG	01/01/1868	NY		NO.2
BALLWEBER W W 3 CH	JACOB	1818	WEISSENBURG	01/01/1868	NY	FARM	NO.2
BALLY W VERDUN FRANC	M.A. LOUISE	1833	VETRIGNE	09/22/1857	NY		FILM
BALME WW AND CH 4	WENDELIN	1813	BOURG	04/16/1851	NY		FILM
BALMER	PIERRE		MALSHEIM	01/01/1828	A		FILM
BALTENRECK	MARIE CATHERINE	1812	COLMAR	05/16/1845	A		FILM
BALTENWECK	LEON JEAN	1813	COLMAR	03/22/1857	NY		FILM
BALTHASAR W IMBERMOT	MARIE LOUISE	1838	KAYSERSBERG	11/06/1856	NO		FILM

Lastname	Firstname	Birth Year	Birthplace	Emigration	De	Prof	Source
BALTZER	HENRI		INGVILLER	01/01/1828	A		FILM
BALZLI	JAQUES		HATTMATT	01/01/1828	A		FILM
BAMDSAI	CATHERINE	1819	LANGRANGE	08/27/1850	NY		FILM
BANCKART	FERDINAND	1817	HARTMANNSWILLER	03/01/1848	TX	CULT	PASS
BANDSEPT	JEAN NICOLAS	1809	FRELAND	02/28/1849	A		FILM
BANET	FRANCOIS	1830	BAVILLIERS	03/05/1852	SL		FILM
BANGARD	FRANCOIS	1829	LIEPRE	10/13/1852	NO		FILM
BANGARD	JEAN FRANCOIS	1824	LIEPRE	10/22/1842	NO		FILM
BANQUEREL WW	LOUIS	1789	FONTAINE MEULOT	04/05/1855	NY		FILM
BANSEPT	TIMOTHEI	1830	ROMBACH	06/24/1851	NO		FILM
BAPET	ELOYSE	1849	VOLGENSBURG	04/11/1866	NY		FILM
BAPET H MARIE ANNE	JEAN	1821	VOLGENSBURG	04/11/1866	NY		FILM
BAPET S JEAN	EMILE	1855	VOLGENSBURG	04/11/1866	NY		FILM
BAPET S JEAN	EMILE	1859	VOLGENSBURG	04/11/1866	NY		FILM
BAPET W JEAN	MARIE ANNE	1822	VOLGENSBURG	04/11/1866	NY		FILM
BAPST			LAUTERBOURG	01/01/1850	NO		PRIV
BARBARAS WW AND CH 2	JAQUES	1798	OSTHEIM	03/17/1845	NY		FILM
BARBARAS WW AND CH 3	GEORGES	1805	OSTHEIM	04/12/1847	NY		FILM
BARBARAS WW AND CH 4	JEAN	1809	OSTHEIM	03/19/1853	NY		FILM
BARBEN	ELISE		GERMANY	04/17/1849	A		FILM
BARBERET	JEAN GEORGE	1824	GROSMAGNY	01/30/1851	NY		FILM
BARBERET WW AND CH 6	JEAN BAPTISTE	1807	GROSMAGNY	02/20/1852	A		FILM
BARBIER	ANNE MARIE		MORSCHWILLER	01/01/1828	A		FILM
BARBIER	JAQUES	1810	GROSNE	03/09/1847	NY	CULT	FILM
BARBIER	JEAN PIERRE	1813	GROSNE	09/12/1850	NY	DAYL	FILM
BARBIER	MARIE BARBE	1802	LIEPRE	09/09/1847	NO		FILM
BARBIER	SEBASTIEN	1802	LIEPRE	08/18/1838	NO	PLAT	FILM
BARBIER	THERESE		MORSCHWILLER	01/01/1828	A		FILM
BARCK BACHLER	FRANCOIS ANTOIN	1808	HATTEN	09/16/1842	A		FILM
BARCKBUCHLIER	FRANCOISE	1808	HATTEN	09/16/1842	NY	FACT	FILM
BARCKHARD	CAROLINE		OELBRONN(B)	04/11/1849			FILM
BARCKHARD	CHRISTIAN		OELBRONN(B)	04/11/1849	A		FILM
BARDOL	MICHEL		SCHWEIGHAUSEN	01/01/1828	A		FILM
BARDOT	CHARLES	1824	SERMAMAGNY	09/16/1845	NY	CULT	FILM
BARDOT	JEAN CLAUDE		LA CHAPELLE	09/03/1844	NY	CULT	FILM
BARDOT	LOUIS	1825	SERMAMAGNY	03/04/1857	SL		FILM
BARDOT	PIERRE FRANCOIS	1823	LA CHAPELLE	09/03/1844	NY	CULT	FILM
BAREN	JEAN PIERRE	1810	BRETAGNE	02/09/1844	NY	CULT	FILM
BARGUNDEN	SOPHIE MARIE	1814	STORCKENSOHN	03/10/1842	NO		FILM
BARGY	NICOLAS	1811	HERLISHEIM	10/21/1846	TX	SALK	FILM
BARHUS	JEAN THEOPHILE	1822	RIQUEWIHR	08/21/1854	A	JOIN	FILM
BARIDO	CARTHERINE		WINGEN	01/01/1828	A		FILM
BARLEMENT	MICHEL		ERNOLSHEIM	01/01/1828	A	TAYL	FILM
BARLEN	SEBASTIEN	1810	BENNWIHR	04/11/1846	CH	WINE	FILM
BARNARD W 2CH	MARIE	1812	COEURE SWISS	02/28/1848	NY		FILM
BARRE	PIERRE GEORGE	1825	GREMAGNY	10/30/1856	NY		FILM
BARRER	IGNACE	1820	CUEWENHEIM	02/16/1846	NY		FILM
BARRUS	CHRISTINE	1835	THANN	04/11/1857	NY	TAYL	FILM
BARTENBACH	JEAN GEORGES	1830	KIENHEIM	08/14/1852	A		FILM
BARTH	ADAM	1813	MUELHAUSEN	11/22/1843	TX	CULT	FILM

Lastname	Firstname	Birth Year	Birthplace	Emigration	De	Prof	Source
BARTH	BARBE		WANGENBOURG	01/01/1828	A		FILM
BARTH	BERTHOLD	1818	BISCHOFSHEIM(B)	10/25/1845	TX		FILM
BARTH	CHARLES		KARLSRUHE(B)	07/31/1849	A		FILM
BARTH	DOROTHEE		FROHMUHL	01/01/1828	A		FILM
BARTH	JAQUES		KASKASTEL	01/01/1828	A	CULT	FILM
BARTH	JEAN		REITWEILER	01/01/1828	A	BRLA	FILM
BARTH	JEAN-MICHEL	1814	STRASBOURG	11/01/1843	TX		SHIP
BARTH	JOHANN MICHEL	1814	STRASBOURG ELSASS	11/22/1843	TX	CULT	FILM
BARTH	JOSEPH		FROHMUHL	01/01/1828	TX	DAYL	FILM
BARTH CH 2	MARIE		BADEN	06/27/1833	A		FILM
BARTHEL	GEORGE	1804	SCHLEITHAL	02/25/1852	NO	GARD	FILM
BARTHEL	JAQUES		INGENHEIM	01/01/1828	A	CULT	FILM
BARTHEL	JEAN		INGENHEIM	01/01/1828	A	CULT	FILM
BARTHEL	MARIE		INGENHEIM	01/01/1828	A		FILM
BARTHEL	VALENTIN		INGENHEIM	01/01/1828	A	CULT	FILM
BARTHELEMY	THERESA			04/17/1849	A		FILM
BARTHOLOME	ARNAUD		WINGEN	01/01/1828	A	TISS	FILM
BARTZ	BARBE	1824	LEMBERG	09/16/1846	TX	FACT	FILM
BARTZ	BARBE	1824	MULHOUSE	09/01/1846	TX	FACT	PASS
BARTZ H MADELEINE	MAURICE	1827	THANN	10/01/1843	TX	CULT	SHIP
BARTZ H SALOME	ADAM	1813	MULHOUSE	11/01/1843	TX	CULT	SHIP
BARTZ W ADAM	SALOME	1813	MULHOUSE	11/01/1843	TX		SHIP
BARTZ W MAURICE	MADELEINE	1797	THANN	10/01/1843	TX		SHIP
BARUCH	LANY	1833	DURMENACH	10/25/1852	A	MERC	FILM
BASCH	GEORGE		ROESCHWOOG	01/01/1828	A	CARP	FILM
BASCHY	JEAN	1822	RIXHEIM	09/19/1857	A		FILM
BAST	MATHIAS	1818	ROUFFACH	07/30/1840	A		FILM
BASTIAN	MARIE CATHARINE		INGENHEIM	01/01/1828	A		FILM
BASTIAN	PHILLIP	1844	WEILER	01/01/1866	NY	FARM	NO.2
BASTIEN	JOSEPH		THANNENKIRCH	01/01/1828	SL		FILM
BASTIEN	JOSEPH	1833	THANNENKIRCH	03/27/1855	SL		FILM
BATHELEMY	JOSEPH	1833	BLODELSHEIM	05/19/1842	NY	FARR	FILM
BATOT	JEAN	1865	MITTELWIHR	06/27/1846	TX		FILM
BATOT	JEAN BAPTISTE	1821	LAPUTROIS	03/08/1854	NY		FILM
BATOT CH 4	JEAN	1806	MITTELWIHR	06/01/1846	TX	DAYL	PASS
BATOT MN TORETAN	THERESE			06/01/1846			PASS
BATT	JOSEPH		MOESCHVILLER	01/01/1828	A	CULT	FILM
BATT	JOSEPH	1841	HEGENEY	01/01/1866	NY	FARM	NO.2
BATTICK	JOSEPH	1821	HERGISWYL	07/01/1851	NY	VACK	FILM
BATTINGER	XAVIER	1819	LARGITZEN	03/05/1852	NY	DAYL	FILM
BAU	BERNARD		FLOBSHEIM	01/01/1828	A	DAYL	FILM
BAUBEG	GERMAIN	1810	OFFEMONT	01/30/1840	SL	CULT	FILM
BAUD	ANTOINE		HEIMBACH(B)	04/19/1849	A		FILM
BAUDROIT	CHARLES	1831	ABEVILELRS	02/10/1864	NY	CULT	FILM
BAUDROIT	LOUIS	1859	ABEVILLERS	02/10/1864	NY		FILM
BAUDROIT	LOUISE	1862	ABEVILLERS	02/10/1864	NY		FILM
BAUDROIT	MARIANNE	1832	ABEVILLERS	02/10/1864	NY	CULT	FILM
BAUDROY	FREDERIC	1801	CLAY	03/28/1863	NY	CULT	FILM
BAUER			OEHRINGEN(W)	08/17/1849	A		FILM
BAUER		1787	MEMPRECHTSHOFEN(B)	09/17/1845	TX		FILM

Lastname	Firstname	Birth Year	Birthplace	Emigration	De	Prof	Source
BAUER	CATHERINA	1754	ERSCHWILL	04/09/1844	TX		FILM
BAUER	EMERANCIA		BEISINGEN (W)	06/01/1849	A		FILM
BAUER	GEORGES		HERBITZHEIM	01/01/1828	A	DAYL	FILM
BAUER	JAKOB	1807	MEMPRECHTSHOFEN(B)	09/17/1845	TX		FILM
BAUER	JAQUES	1822	SUNDHOFFEN	06/29/1853	A	EBEN	FILM
BAUER	JEAN		SCHWALDORF(W)	05/03/1849	NY		FILM
BAUER	JEAN		UHRWILLER	03/11/1817	A	BRLA	FILM
BAUER	JEAN	1829	RIQUEWIHR	11/26/1853	NY	VINE	FILM
BAUER	JEAN GEORGES		BINDENHEIM	02/28/1838	A	DAYL	FILM
BAUER	JEAN GEORGES	1831	SUNDHOFFEN	01/22/1852	SL		FILM
BAUER	JOH		BRETTEN(B)	06/21/1849	A		FILM
BAUER	JOHANN		UHRWILLER	01/01/1817	A		NO.2
BAUER	JOSEPH		LAUF(B)	05/22/1849	A		FILM
BAUER	KATHARINA	1824	ERSHWIL(SW)	05/29/1844	TX		FILM
BAUER	LEONART		STRUTH	05/20/1817	A	BRLA	FILM
BAUER	MADELEINE	1823	ADELSHEIM	02/04/1856	SL		FILM
BAUER	MARGARETHA	1843	CROETTWILLER	01/01/1868	NY		NO.2
BAUER	NICOLAS		HERBITZHEIM	01/01/1828	A	DAYL	FILM
BAUER	NICOLAS	1828	SUNDHOFFEN	01/22/1852	SL	BLAC	FILM
BAUER	VICTORIA		REICHENBACH(B)	08/27/1849	A		FILM
BAUER CH1	MADELEINE		WESSACH(W)	06/01/1849	SL		FILM
BAUER W MUELLER MART	MAGDALENA	1811	ERSCHWIL	05/29/1844	TX		FILM
BAUERLE	ALOISE		BUEHLENTAL(B)	04/19/1849	NY		FILM
BAUM	CASPAR		WURMLINGEN (W)	07/23/1849	A		FILM
BAUM:BAUER	ABRAHAM		GUNDERSHOFEN	01/01/1869	NY		NO.2
BAUMANN	ANDRE	1807	HUNDSBACH	03/25/1852	A	CHAR	FILM
BAUMANN	CASPAR		NIEDERLAUTERBACH	01/01/1861	NO		PRIV
BAUMANN	GASPARD	1807	NIEDERLAUTERBACH	01/01/1861	NO	DAYL	PRIV
BAUMANN	GEORGES	1834	JEBSHEIM	11/09/1854	A	SERV	FILM
BAUMANN	JACQUES	1827	JEBSHEIM	01/30/1857	NY	CULT	FILM
BAUMANN	JEAN	1832	ATTENSCHWILLER	05/26/1866	NY	JOIN	FILM
BAUMANN	JEAN JAQUES	1822	JEBSHEIM	08/12/1854	NY	TISS	FILM
BAUMANN	JOHANN		MOTHERN	01/01/1868	NY		NO.2
BAUMANN	JOHANN GEORG	1849	MUNCHHOUSE	01/01/1868	NY		NO.2
BAUMANN	JOSEPH		NIEDERLAUTERBACH	01/01/1850	NO		PRIV
BAUMANN	JOSEPH		NIEDERLAUTERBACH	01/01/1861	NO		PRIV
BAUMANN	MATHAEUS		CAPPEL(B)	05/24/1849	A		FILM
BAUMANN	MATHEUS		CAPPEL(B)	01/01/1828	A		FILM
BAUMANN	MICHEL	1824	MOTHERN	01/01/1867	NY	FARM	NO.2
BAUMANN MN WALDI	CATHERINE	1813	NIEDERLAUTERBACH	01/01/1865	NO		NO.2
BAUME	JACQUES	1825	OFFEMONT	05/19/1847	NY		FILM
BAUME	JAQUES	1825	OFFEMONT	05/10/1847	A		FILM
BAUME	JAQUES	1825	OFTEMONT	05/10/1847	A		FILM
BAUMER	ALEXANDRE	1836	GUEBWILLER	10/09/1857	A		FILM
BAUMER	APPOLONIA	1842	MUNCHHOUSE	01/01/1867	NY		NO.2
BAUMER	JOSEF		MOTHERN	01/01/1868	NY		NO.2
BAUMGARTEN	AMAND		SARENNE	01/01/1828	A		FILM
BAUMGARTEN	AMAND		SAVERNE	01/01/1828	A		FILM
BAUMGARTEN	JOSEPH		OFFENDORF	01/01/1828	A		FILM
BAUMGARTNER	MARIE ANNE	1832	NIEDERBRUCK	05/02/1854	A		FILM

Lastname	Firstname	Birth Year	Birthplace	Emigration	De	Prof	Source
BAUMGARTNER	MARIE ANNE	1832	NIEDERBRUCK	05/02/1854	NY		FILM
BAUMGARTNER	NICOLAS		SCHELINGEN(B)	04/11/1849	A		FILM
BAUMGARTNER	RENAUD	1800	MASEVAUX	10/31/1844	A		FILM
BAUMGARTNER	RENAUD	1800	MASEVAUX	10/31/1844	NO		FILM
BAUMGARTNER WW	RENAUD	1801	SENTHEIM	12/01/1844	TX	SHMA	SHIP
BAUMGARTNER WW	ALOYCE	1796	NEU-GERSCHWIL	08/10/1846	NO		FILM
BAUMGARTNER WW	ALOYCE	1796	NEUGERSCHWIL	05/10/1846	A		FILM
BAUMLER WW AND D	JEAN	1794	BUHL	05/17/1838	NY		FILM
BAUMLER WW AND WD	JEAN	1794	BUHL	05/17/1838	A		FILM
BAUMSTARCK	ELISABETH		LEUTENHEIM	01/01/1828	A		FILM
BAUMSTARCK	ELSIABETH		LEUTENHEIM	01/01/1828	A		FILM
BAUMSTAUCH	ELISABETH		LEUTENHEIM	01/01/1828	A		FILM
BAUNOURT	MARIE ANNE	1820	ENSHEIM	08/27/1850	NY		FILM
BAUNOURT	MARIE ANNE	1820	ENSISHEIM	08/27/1850	A		FILM
BAUR	AUGUSTE	1823	COLMAR	02/29/1856	A		FILM
BAUR	AUGUSTE	1823	COLMAR	02/29/1856	NY		FILM
BAUR	LEOPOLD LOUIS	1819	COLMAR	01/08/1853	A		FILM
BAUR	MATHIAS		STRASBOURG	06/04/1817	A		FILM
BAUR CH 5	MICHEL	1826	MASEVAUX	09/01/1847	TX	CHAR	PASS
BAUR MN KOCHE	MARIE ANNE	1789	BERNWILLER	07/17/1856	A		FILM
BAUR MN KOEHE	MARIE ANNE	1789	BERNWILLER	07/17/1856	NY		FILM
BAUR W BINCHE JOSEPH	MARIE	1800	CHERMICHELBACH	04/21/1857	NY		FILM
BAUR W JOSEPH	MARIE	1800	CHERMICHELBACH	04/21/1857	A		FILM
BAURAIS	FRANCOIS			01/23/1854	A		FILM
BAURAIS	JEAN-CLAUDE	1823	GRANDVILLERS	04/10/1850	A		FILM
BAURARD WW	JEAN CLAUDE	1823	GRANDVILLARS	09/10/1850	NY		FILM
BAURARD WW	JEAN CLAUDE	1823	GRANDVILLERS	09/10/1850	NY		FILM
BAUT WW AND CH	MATHIAS		STRASBOURG	06/04/1817	A		FILM
BAYA	GEORG	1853	WEISSENBURG	01/01/1868	NY		NO.2
BAYER	ANTOINE		MOTHERN	01/01/1850	OO		PRIV
BAYER	JEAN		MOTHERN	01/01/1850	NO		PRIV
BAYER	MICHEL		NEEWILLER	01/01/1850	NO		PRIV
BAYER-LANG	MARIE		MOTHERN	01/01/1850	NO		PRIV
BEAU	MARIE	1796	SERMAMAGNY	09/28/1854	SL		FILM
BEAU MN GUICHO	MARIE	1796	SERMAMAGNY	09/28/1854	A		FILM
BEAUD	ANTOINE		HEIMBACH	04/19/1844	A		FILM
BEAUD	ANTOINE		HEIMBACH	04/19/1844	NY		FILM
BEAUJEUX	FRANCOIS	1823	RONCHAMP	02/03/1866	A		FILM
BEAUJEUX	FRANCOIS	1823	RONCHAMP	02/03/1866	NY		FILM
BEAUJEUX	JEAN BAPTISTE	1818	BARILLIERS	07/24/1852	A		FILM
BEAUJEUX	THERESE	1821	RONCHAMP	02/03/1866	NY		FILM
BEAUJEUX	VICTOR	1848	RONCHAMP	02/03/1866	NY		FILM
BEAUJEUX S FRANCOIS	VICTOR	1848	RONCHAMP	02/03/1866	A		FILM
BEAUJEUX W FRANCOIS	THERESE	1821	RONCHAMP	02/03/1866	A		FILM
BEAUJEUX WW AND CH 3	JEAN BAPTISTE	1818	BARILLIERS	07/24/1852	NY		FILM
BEAUMENT	LOUIS	1823	MORILLARS	02/13/1849	NY		FILM
BEAUMENT	LOUIS	1823	MORRILARS	02/13/1849	A		FILM
BEAUSEIGNEUR	MARTIN	1832	THIANCOURT	01/20/1852	A		FILM
BEAUSEIGNEUR	MARTIN	1832	THIANCOURT	01/20/1852	NY		FILM
BEAUSEIGNEUR WW A C3	AUGUSTE	1821	THIANCOURT	04/02/1855	A		FILM

```
                                Birth                                      13
Lastname            Firstname   Year  Birthplace        Emigration De Prof Source
----------------------------------------------------------------------------------
BEAUSEIGNEUR WW CH2 AUGUSTE     1821  THIANCOURT        04/02/1855 NY      FILM
BECHEL              GEORGE            SCHIRRHEIM        01/01/1828 A       FILM
BECHEL              JEAN              SCHIRRHEIN        01/01/1828 A       FILM
BECHEL              MARTIN            SCHIRRHEIN        01/01/1828 A       FILM
BECHLE              FERDINAND   1826  CERNAY            09/27/1847 A       FILM

BECHLE              FERDINAND   1826  CERNAY            09/27/1847 NY      FILM
BECHTHOLD           SCH               ALTSCHWEIER ?     09/30/1849 A       FILM
BECHTHOLD           SEBASTIEN         EISINGEN          08/21/1849 A       FILM
BECHTOLD            J                 ALTSCHWERER ?     09/30/1849 A       FILM
BECHTOLD            SEBASTIEN         EISINGEN          08/21/1849 A       FILM

BECK                ADAM              SCHOENBOURG       01/01/1828 A       FILM
BECK                ANDRES            WILWISHEIM        01/01/1828 A       FILM
BECK                AUGUSTA           PFORZHEIM         05/09/1849 A       FILM
BECK                CHRETIEN          LOHR              01/01/1828 A       FILM
BECK                CHRISTINE         WEINBOURG         01/01/1828 A       FILM

BECK                EDMOND            PFORZHEIM         05/09/1849 NY      FILM
BECK                ERNA              PFORZHEIM         05/09/1849 A       FILM
BECK                FRANCOIS JOSEPH 1801 SENTHEIM       09/11/1846 A       FILM
BECK                FREDERIC          SCHILTIGHEIM      03/03/1817 A       FILM
BECK                GEORG       1853  WEISSENBURG       01/01/1869 NY      NO.2

BECK                GEORGES     1822  SENTHEIM          09/01/1851 TX CULT PASS
BECK                GEORGES     1822  SENTHEIM          09/30/1851 A       FILM
BECK                GEORGES     1822  SENTHEIM          09/30/1851 TX      FILM
BECK                HEIMRICH    1852  WEISSENBURG       01/01/1869 NY      NO.2
BECK                JAQUES            WEINBOURG         01/01/1828 A       FILM

BECK                JOSEPH            SENTHEIM          01/01/1854 TX      SHIP
BECK                LAURENT           WILMISHEIM        01/01/1828 A       FILM
BECK                MADELAINE   1829  HIRSINGEN         09/03/1857 A       FILM
BECK                MARGUERITE        WEINBOURG         01/01/1828 A       FILM
BECK                MICHEL      1808  CARSPACH          05/02/1846 A       FILM

BECK                NIKOLAUS    1816  BLISWANGEN        11/22/1843 TX      FILM
BECK                OBERT             PFORZHEIM         05/09/1849 NY      FILM
BECK                PHILIPPE          ERNOLSHEIM        01/01/1828 A       FILM
BECK                WILHELM     1847  WEISSENBURG       01/01/1869 NY KNSH NO.2
BECK                WILHELMINE  1825  WEISSENBURG       01/01/1869 NY      NO.2

BECK   WW AND CH 5  FRANCOIS ANTOIN 1798 SENTHEIM      08/23/1847 A       FILM
BECK MN OLFF CH 4   SARA        1811  REGUISHEIM        07/25/1853 A       FILM
BECK WW AND CH 2    HENRI             SCHEONBOURG       01/01/1828 A       FILM
BECK WW AND CH 2    HENRI             SCHOENBOURG       01/01/1828 A       FILM
BECK WW AND CH 5    FRANCOIS ANTOIN 1798 SENTHEIM      08/23/1847 OH      FILM

BECK WW AND CH 5    JEAN BAPTISTE     VIEUX FERRETTE    12/27/1839 NY      FILM
BECK WW AND CH 5    JEAN BAPTISTE     VIEUX-FERRETTE    12/27/1839 A       FILM
BECKER              ANNE MARIE        BUSENBACH         09/30/1849 A       FILM
BECKER              AUGUSTE     1818  OBERLANGENWALDAU SIL 04/08/1843 A? SHMA FILM
BECKER              FRANCOIS          KIRRBERG          01/01/1828 A       FILM

BECKER              FRANCOIS JOSEPH 1821 BENNWIHR       07/31/1850 A       FILM
BECKER              GEORG       1839  BIRLENBACH        01/01/1866 NY BAKE NO.2
BECKER              GEORGE            HOARDT            01/01/1828 A       FILM
BECKER              GEORGES     1819  SOULTZ-SOUS-FORETS 03/08/1850 A      FILM
BECKER              GEROGES           KIRRBERG          01/01/1828 A       FILM
```

Lastname	Firstname	Birth Year	Birthplace	Emigration	De	Prof	Source
BECKER	JEAN	1797	KUSEL(BA)	05/28/1851	A		FILM
BECKER	KARL	1841	LEMBACH	01/01/1869	NY		NO.2
BECKER	LAURENT		ROSSCHWOOG	01/01/1828	A		FILM
BECKER	MARIE ANNA		KAIDENBURG	01/01/1869	NY		NO.2
BECKER W W 5 CH	AURLETT		HARSKIRCHEN	03/03/1817	A		FILM
BECKER MN GUCKERT C4	MADELEINE	1806	HEITERSHEIM	04/14/1848	A		FILM
BECKERICH	JOSEPH	1836	MEISENTHAL	05/13/1857	A		FILM
BECKERT MN STEPHAN	PHILIPPINE	1813	BERGHAUPTEN(B)	07/15/1856	A		FILM
BECKORRICH WW	ANDRE	1830	MEISENTHAL	10/02/1854	A		FILM
BEEG WW CH 2	JEAN JAQUES			06/27/1833	A		FILM
BEETZNER	GEORGES	1835	ST.CROIX AUX MINES	12/10/1856	A		FILM
BEGEY H MARIE	ALBERT		VESOUL (F)	10/06/1866	A		FILM
BEGEY W ALBERT	MARIE	1839	VESOUL (F)	10/06/1866	A		FILM
BEGINA WW AND CH 2	JEAN	1809	TRAUBACH-LE-HAUT	05/09/1851	A		FILM
BEH CH 3	LANCALIN		JACH	07/28/1854	A		FILM
BEHE WW AND CH 2	GEORGES		BRUNSTATT	11/01/1844	TX		SHIP
BEHL	MARGUERITE	1827	BRECHAUMONT	03/12/1847	A		FILM
BEHR	THIEBAUD		HARSKIRCHEN	01/01/1828	A		FILM
BEHRA	ALEXANDRE	1817	RIMBACH	04/08/1852	A		FILM
BEHRA	ANDRE	1810	RODEREN	03/17/1854	A		FILM
BEIGEL	MATHIAS		WISSEMBOURG	11/19/1855	A		FILM
BEIL	BENEDICT		GEISINGEN	05/12/1849	A		FILM
BEISER WW	ADOLPH	1803	RIBEAUVILLE	06/21/1852	A		FILM
BELAET	JOSEPH	1823	VELESCOT	12/19/1843	A		FILM
BELECHIN WW CH 4	URBAIN		GRAND DUCHY OF BADEN	06/27/1833	A		FILM
BELET	MARTIN	1812	DELLE	04/25/1851	A		FILM
BELET WW	FRANCOIS	1817	ROUGEMONT	03/07/1840	A		FILM
BELFILS WW	JAQUES FREDERIC	1805	AUDINCOURT	04/09/1850	A		FILM
BELL	ADOLPHE		APPENWEIER	08/11/1849	A		FILM
BELLE	VENDOLIN	1816	ATTKIRCH	03/13/1848	A		FILM
BELOT	ALEXIN	1847	CHAUX TERR BELFORT	03/18/1856	NY		FILM
BELOT	ALEXIN	1849	CHAUX	03/18/1856	A		FILM
BELOT	AMBROISE	1832	URCEREY	01/25/1855	A		FILM
BELOT	AMBROISE	1832	URGEREY TERR BELFORT	01/25/1855	NY		FILM
BELOT	CHRISTOPH	1830	URCEREY	08/06/1852	A		FILM
BELOT	FELIX	1830	SERMAMAGNY	11/11/1851	A		FILM
BELOT	FELIX	1830	SERMAMAGNY TERR BELF	11/11/1851	SL	FARM	FILM
BELOT	FRANCOIS XAVER	1802	SERMAMAGNY TERR BELF	08/19/1819	NY	FARM	FILM
BELOT	FRANCOIS XAVER	1836	SERMAMAGNY TERR BELF	04/21/1854	NO	FARM	FILM
BELOT	FRANCOIS XAVIER	1796	SCHYNDEL	03/30/1853	NY	FARM	FILM
BELOT	FRANCOIS XAVIER	1802	SERMAMAGNY	08/19/1839	A		FILM
BELOT	FRANCOIS XAVIER	1836	SERMAMAGNY	04/21/1854	A		FILM
BELOT	LEOPLD	1834	SERMAMAGNY	01/16/1853	A		FILM
BELOT	LEOPOLD	1834	SERMAMAGNY TERR.BELF	01/10/1853	NO		FILM
BELOT	LOUIS	1832	SERMAMAGNY	11/11/1851	A		FILM
BELOT	LOUIS	1832	SERMAMAGNY TERR BELF	11/11/1851	SL	FARM	FILM
BELOT W W	CHRISTOPHE	1830	URCEREY TERR.BELFORT	08/06/1852	NY		FILM
BELOT W W CH	VINCENT	1823	SERMAMAGNY	04/09/1853	NY		FILM
BELOT WW CH 1	VINCENT	1823	SERMAMAGNY	04/09/1853	A		FILM
BELOT WW CH 7	FRANCOIS XAVIER	1796	SCHYNDEL	03/30/1853	A		FILM

Lastname	Firstname	Birth Year	Birthplace	Emigration	De	Prof	Source
BELTZ	GEORGES	1825	LANDCHER	02/10/1853	A		FILM
BELTZ	GEORGES	1825	LANDIER	02/10/1853	NY		FILM
BELTZ	HENRY	1829	MULHOUSE	06/10/1850	A		FILM
BELTZ	VINCENT	1821	SOULTZ	11/17/1848	NY	SHMA	FILM
BELTZ WW CH 3	VINCENT	1821	SOULTZ	11/17/1848	A		FILM
BENDEICH	FRANCOIS	1812	NECKURRALEN	09/23/1851	A		FILM
BENDEL	FRANCOIS THOMAS		FORT LOUIS	01/01/1828	A		FILM
BENDEL FAMILY OF 2	FRANCOIS THOMAS		BETELLIER	01/01/1828	A		FILM
BENDELE	JAKOB	1829	NIEDERENTZEN	11/15/1846	A		FILM
BENDELE	JOSEPH	1825	NIEDERENTZEN	04/01/1852	TX	DAYL	SHIP
BENDELE	MARTIN	1778	HERRLISHEIM	03/25/1847	NY	WINE	FILM
BENDELE	MARTIN	1783	HERRLISHEIM	03/25/1847	A		FILM
BENDELE CH 3	JEAN-JAQUES I	1801	NIEDERENTZEN	09/01/1846	TX	CULT	PASS
BENDELE D JEAN-JAQUE	JAQUES II	1829	NIEDERENTZEN	11/01/1846	TX		PASS
BENDELE D JEAN-JAQUE	MARIE-AGATHE	1828	NIEDERENTZEN	09/01/1846	TX		PASS
BENDELE MN BRAUCH	MARIE			/ /			
BENDELE MN BURGER	CATHERINE			09/01/1846			PASS
BENDELE S JEAN-JAQUE	ANDRE	1834	NIEDERENTZEN	09/01/1846	TX		PASS
BENDELE W W 3 CH	SEBASTIEN	1809	EGUISHEIM	03/16/1852	NO	WINE	FILM
BENDELE WW CH 3	JAQUES	1801	ST CROIX EN PLAINE	09/07/1846	A		FILM
BENDELE WW CH 3	SEBASTIEN	1809	EGUISHEIM	03/16/1852	A		FILM
BENDELE'W W 3 CH	JAQUES	1801	ST.CROUX EN PLAINE	09/07/1846	TX	FARM	FILM
BENDER			REICHENBACH	04/27/1849	A		FILM
BENDER	DANIEL		LANGENSOULTZBACH	01/01/1861	A		SUESS
BENDER	JOSEPH		HAYERLOCH	08/24/1849	A		FILM
BENDER	JOSEPH		HAYERLOCH B	08/24/1849	A		FILM
BENDER	LOUIS		HARSKIRCHEN	01/01/1828	A		FILM
BENGEL	FERDINAND		GERSTHEIM	03/03/1838	A		FILM
BENGEL	FERDINAND		GERSTHEIM	03/05/1838	A	CHRR	FILM
BENGUEREL	ZELIME HENRY	1813	LA CHAUX DE FONDS	02/09/1848	A		FILM
BENGUEREL	ZELIME HENRY	1822	LA CHAUX DE FONDS	11/06/1844	A		FILM
BENGUEREL	ZELIN HENRY	1813	LA CHAUX DE FONDS SW	02/09/1848	NO		FILM
BENGUEREL	ZELIN HENRY	1841	LA CHAUX DE FONDS SW	11/06/1844	NO	JOIN	FILM
BENITZ	AUGUSTE		BAERENTHAL TIROL	09/30/1849	A		FILM
BENNER	JEAN HENRY	1824	MULHOUSE	04/10/1849	A		FILM
BENNER	JEAN HENRY	1824	MULHOUSE	04/10/1849	NY	ARCH	FILM
BENNINGER CH 1	GEORGE		DRUSENHEIM	03/24/1838	A		FILM
BENNINGER 1 CH	GEORGE		DRUSENHEIM BISCHWILL	03/24/1838	A	WEAV	FILM
BENNINGER W W 1 CH	FRANOIS JOSEPH		DRUSENHEIM BISCHWILL	03/24/1838	A	WEAV	FILM
BENNINGER WW CH 1	FRANCOIS JOSEPH		DUSENHEIM	03/24/1838	A		FILM
BENO BERNARD			BURCKENWALD =BIRCKEN	04/11/1853	A		FILM
BENOIT	JEAN JOSEPH	1821	LEPURE	02/21/1848	NO	WEAV	FILM
BENOIT	JEAN JOSEPH	1822	LIEPRE	02/21/1849	A		FILM
BENOIT	JOSEPH	1814	ST MARIE AUX MINES	06/06/1840	A		FILM
BENOIT	JOSEPH	1824	ST MARIE AUX MINES	06/06/1840	NO	LAYB	FILM
BENOIT D THERES	THERES		ST. MARIE AUX MINES	10/15/1857	A		FILM
BENOIT M HENRY	THERESE	1823	ST MARIE AUX MINES	10/15/1857	A		FILM
BENOIT M THERESE	THERESE		ST MARIE AUX MINES	10/15/1857	A		FILM
BENOIT S THERES	HENRY		ST. MARIE AUX MINES	10/15/1857	A		FILM
BENOIT S THERESE	HENRY		ST MARIE AUX MINES	10/15/1857	A		FILM

Lastname	Firstname	Birth Year	Birthplace	Emigration	De	Prof	Source
BENOIT W 2 CH	THERES		ST. MARIE AUX MINES	10/15/1857	A		FILM
BENTZ	ANTOINE		HAGENAU	01/01/1828	A		FILM
BENTZ	ANTOINE		HAGUENAU	01/01/1828	A		FILM
BENTZ	ANTOINE	1823	GUEBWILLER	03/08/1848	A		FILM
BENTZ	ANTON		RIEGEL	06/04/1849	A		FILM
BENTZ	ANTON		RIEGEL B	06/04/1849	A		FILM
BENTZ	GREGOIRE	1826	HECKEN	02/19/1850	A		FILM
BENZ	MICHEL		ERBACH B	07/29/1849	A		FILM
BENZ	MICHEL		ERLACH	07/29/1849	A		FILM
BENZINGER	CHRIST W.		MAINTS BAS-RHIN	01/01/1845	A		FILM
BEON W W 1 CHILD	JEAN PIERRE	1806	ALEXANDRIE PIEMONT	03/29/1847	NY		FILM
BEON WW CH 1	JEAN PIERRE	1806	ALEXANDRE	03/29/1847	A		FILM
BERARD	XAVIER	1848	SERMAMAGNY	10/07/1865	A		FILM
BERARD	XAVIER	1848	SERMANGNY TERR BELFO	10/07/1865	NY		FILM
BERBET	CATHERINE	1837	GRENTZINGEN	08/16/1865	A		FILM
BERBY WW	ANDRE	1810	DELLE	06/11/1844	A		FILM
BERDELLE	XAVIER		HAGENAU	01/01/1828	A		FILM
BERDELLE	XAVIER		HAGUENAU	01/01/1828	A		FILM
BERDOZ W W	FRANCOIS	1822	BANVILLERS?	09/18/1850	CH	BAKE	FILM
BERDOZ WW	FRANCOIS	1822	BANVILLARS	09/19/1850	A		FILM
BERENTER	LOUISE	1830	COLMAR	05/04/1852	A		FILM
BERG	FRANCOIS		BADEN	09/21/1849	A		FILM
BERG	MATHIAS	1812	BüHL	02/05/1848	A		FILM
BERG	MATHIAS	1814	BUEHL	02/05/1848	NY		FILM
BERGANS	JOSEPH		DOSSENHEIM	01/01/1828	A		FILM
BERGANS FAMILY OF 6	JOSEPH		DOSSENHEIM	01/01/1828	A	DAYL	FARM
BERGANTZ	MADELAINE		SCHAFFHAUSEN	01/01/1828	A		FILM
BERGANTZ	PIERRE		STEINBOURG	01/01/1828	A		FILM
BERGANTZ FAMILY OF 5	PIERRE		STEINBOURG	01/01/1828	A	SHMA	FILM
BERGDOLE W W 1 CH	PIERRE		OTTWILLER	03/07/1817	A	WEAV	FILM
BERGDOLE W W 3 CH	CHRISTIAN		OTTWILLER	03/03/1817	A	WEAV	FILM
BERGDOLL	JOSEPH	1800	ROPPEVILLER	02/27/1846	A		FILM
BERGDOLL	JOSEPH	1800	ROPPEVILLER MOSELLE	02/27/1846	NO	CHAU	FILM
BERGDOLL	NICOLAS	1829	ROPPEVILLER	07/29/1857	A		FILM
BERGER	FRANCOIS		NEUWILLER	01/01/1828	A		FILM
BERGER	FRANCOIS ANTOIN	1817	BISEL	04/29/1847	A		FILM
BERGER	FRANCOIS ANTONI	1817	BISEL	04/29/1847	NY		FILM
BERGER	JEAN	1802	OSENS	06/28/1850	A		FILM
BERGER	JEAN	1802	OSENS HAUTES PYRENEE	01/28/1850	NY		FILM
BERGER	JOSEPH	1837	BELFORT	01/12/1866	A		FILM
BERGER FAMILY OF 8	FRANCOIS		NEUWILLER	01/01/1828	A		FILM
BERGER FAMILY OF 3	JAQUES		KIRCHBERG	03/12/1838	A		FILM
BERGHOLD	JAQUES		GENDERTHEIM	01/01/1828	A		FILM
BERGMANN	HEINRICH		NIEDERKUNTZENHAUSEN	01/01/1870	A	FARR	SUESS
BERGMANN	MICHEL		WEITERSWILLER	01/01/1828	A		FILM
BERGMEIER	FERDINAND		SARENNE	01/01/1828	A		FILM
BERGTOLD	GEORGE		BRUMATH	01/01/1828	A		FILM
BERGTOLD	JAQUES JUN		BRUMATH	01/01/1828	A		FILM
BERGTOLD	JAQUES SEN		BRUMATH	01/01/1828	A		FILM
BERGUENTZLE WW CH 2	SEBASTIEN	1828	AMMERSCHWIR	01/05/1855	A		FILM

Lastname	Firstname	Birth Year	Birthplace	Emigration	De	Prof	Source
BERLING	JEAN PIERRE		NIEDERBRONN	03/21/1817	A		FILM
BERLING	JOHANN PETER		NIEDERBRONN	01/01/1817	A		NO.2
BERLING	VALENTIN		LEUTENHEIM	01/01/1828	A		FILM
BERLIOZ	VICTORINE	1836	ST CROIX AUX MINES	10/27/1857	A		FILM
BERMEN	JAQUES JOSEPH	1816	MORVILLARS	10/26/1852	A		FILM
BERMER	LOUISE	1808	MUNSTER	04/06/1840	A		FILM
BERMONT	EMILE	1843	MORVILLARD	05/23/1865	A		FILM
BERMOTOT	MARIE BARBE	1820	CERNAY	01/08/1844	A		FILM
BERNA	FRANCOIS ANTOIN	1821	MOOSCH	05/09/1849	A		FILM
BERNA WW CH 1	EUGENE	1823	MUNSTER	04/26/1854	A		FILM
BERNA WW CH 5	PHILIPPE ANTOIN	1816	MARSEILLE	08/04/1854	A		FILM
BERNAHRD	JOSEPH	1832	MASSEVAUX	09/09/1852	TX	LAYB	FILM
BERNARD	FRANCOIS XAVIER	1822	MASSEVAUX	09/16/1847	A		FILM
BERNARD	GERTRUDE	1813	FAVEROIS	08/12/1857	A		FILM
BERNARD	JEAN PIERRE	1820	FAVEROIS	07/17/1840	A		FILM
BERNARD	JOSEPH	1826	FAVEROIS	02/25/1852	A		FILM
BERNARD	LOUISE	1847	EGUENIGUE	06/09/1864	A		FILM
BERNARD	MADELEINE	1824	KAYSERSBERG	03/20/1847	A		FILM
BERNARD	MARIE	1818	FAVEROIS	08/12/1857	A		FILM
BERNAUER	CHARLES		SCHA(O)N(E)AU	04/23/1844	A		FILM
BERNER	CAROLINE		OFFENBOURG	08/11/1844	A		FILM
BERNERT F OF 5	JOSEPH		ST.JEAN DE CHOUX	01/01/1828	A		FILM
BERNERT F OF 7	MICHEL		ST JEAN DE CHOUX	01/01/1828	A		FILM
BERNHARD	JACOB		DAMBACH	01/01/1817	A		NO.2
BERNHARD	JACQUES		DAMBACH	03/11/1817	A		NO.2
BERNHARD	JEAN BAPTISTE		HAGENAU	01/01/1828	A		FILM
BERNHARD	JEAN BAPTISTE		HAGUENAU	01/01/1828	A		FILM
BERNHARD	JOSEPH	1832	MASEVAUX	09/01/1853	TX	FACT	PASS
BERNHARD	JOSEPH	1832	MASSEVAUX	09/09/1852	A		FILM
BERNHARD	JOSEPH	1832	MASSEVAUX	09/13/1853	A		FILM
BERNHARD	NICOLAS		STRUTH	01/01/1828	A		FILM
BERNHARD W LIENHARD	CATHERINE	1802	CERNAY	07/30/1856	A		FILM
BERNHARD W W CH 6	CAROLINE		FREUDENSTADT	09/12/1844	A		FILM
BERNHARDT	MADELEINE		FREUDENSTADT	04/20/1849	A		FILM
BERNHEIM	JAQUES		STRUTH	01/01/1828	A		FILM
BERNICHER	MADELEINE	1831	KAFFENACH	08/11/1854	A		FILM
BERNOT	GEORGE	1837	MONTRELLIARD	11/26/1864	NY	FARM	FILM
BERNZWILLER WW CH 2	JEAN	1805	SOULTZ	03/05/1850	A		FILM
BERO F OF 7	ANTOINE		FORT LOUIS	01/01/1828	A		FILM
BERO WW CH 4	JOSEPH	1803	LA CROIX AUX MINES	05/07/1840	A		FILM
BERON	NICOLAS		WEISLINGEN	01/01/1828	A		FILM
BERON F OF 4	ADAM		WEISLINGEN	01/01/1828	A		FILM
BEROND	FRANCOIS	1821	MONTREUX VIEUX	07/15/1848	A		
BERREN	CHRISTINE		ESCHBOURG	01/01/1828	A		FILM
BERREN	JEAN		ESCHBOURG	01/01/1828	A		FILM
BERREN	JUAQUES		ESCHBOURG	01/01/1828	A		FILM
BERRING CH 1	THIEBAUD	1819	UFFHOLTZ	07/18/1854	A		FILM
BERRITTER	LOUISE	1830	COLMAR	05/04/1852	NY		FILM
BERRON	DANIEL		WAXX	01/01/1828	A		FILM
BERSCHANDY	JEAN JAQUES	1812	BEBLENHEIM	04/21/1854	A		FILM

Lastname	Firstname	Birth Year	Birthplace	Emigration	De	Prof	Source
BERSCHIG	MICHEL		OBERKIRCH	04/06/1849	A		FILM
BERTHE	REINE	1841	HERICOURT	08/30/1866	A		FILM
BERTHOLDY	FRIEDRICH	1826	WINTZENBACH	01/01/1869	NY	FARM	NO.2
BERTIN	JAQUES	1826	FAREROIS	03/31/1846	A		FILM
BERTSCH	AGATHE	1840	HOCHSTATT	07/04/1866	A		FILM
BERTSCH	CLEMENT	1832	HOCHSTATT	07/04/1866	A		FILM
BERTSCH	FLORIAN		GERMANY	04/01/1849	A		FILM
BERTSCH	THERESE	1843	HOCHSTATT	07/04/1866	A		FILM
BERTSCHY	CATHERINA	1848	WINTZENBACH	01/01/1869	NY		NO.2
BERTSCHY	FRIEDRICH	1863	WINTZENBACH	01/01/1869	NY		NO.2
BERTSCHY	GEORG	1865	WINTZENBACH	01/01/1869	NY		NO.2
BERTSCHY	HENRY		KIRRBERG	03/12/1838	A		FILM
BERTSCHY	JEAN	1818	MULHOUSE	01/31/1843	A		FILM
BERTSCHY	MAGDALENA	1862	WINTZENBACH	01/01/1869	NY		NO.2
BERTSCHY	PIERRE		KIRRBERG	01/01/1828	A		FILM
BERTSCHY MN ZIMMERMA	MAGDALENA	1829	WINTZENBACH	01/01/1869	NY		NO.2
BERTSCHY WW 3 CH	FRIEDRICH	1826	WINTZENBACH	01/01/1869	NY		NO.2
BESANCENEZ	JAQUES	1840	FRAHIER	09/29/1865	A		FILM
BESANCON	ANTOINE	1776	STRASBOURG	05/29/1847	A		FILM
BESANCON	CATHERINE	1840	FRAHIER	12/07/1865	A		FILM
BESANCON	ERINE	1825	BEAUCOURT	09/27/1865	A		FILM
BESANCON	FRANCOISE	1838	DENNEY	11/06/1863	A		FILM
BESANCON	FRITZ	1848	AUDINCOURT	02/19/1866	A		FILM
BESANCON	HORTENSE	1844	ROPPE	09/22/1866	A		FILM
BESANCON WW CH 3	FRANCOIS	1801	DENNEY	03/14/1846	A		FILM
BESTLER	JOHANN	1797	SAUSIER	11/15/1846	A		FILM
BESTLER	JOHANN	1797	SOUSIER	11/15/1846	TX		FILM
BETHARI	JOSEF		SIEGEN	01/01/1868	NY		NO.2
BETRINGER	GEORGES	1810	HAUT-RHIN	12/01/1844	TX	CULT	SHIP
BETSCH	JEAN	1832	PFETTENHAUSEN	06/01/1861	A		FILM
BETTERLY W W 3CH	JOSEPH	1822	URBAY	09/01/1854	TX		FILM
BETTRICH	MARGUERITE	1828	MITTELWIHR	11/09/1848	A		FILM
BETZER	JOHANN	1847	ALTENSTADT	01/01/1866	NY	FARM	NO.2
BETZINGER	CHRIST	1819	BORON	03/24/1848	A		FILM
BETZINGER	JEAN JAQUES	1811	TRAUBACH-LE-HAUT	11/14/1844	A		FILM
BEUCHAT	JEAN CLAUDE	1823	BORON	03/17/1857	A		FILM
BEUCLER	ANA	1859	BARR = BART DOUBE ?	03/01/1865	NY		FILM
BEUCLER	ARTHUR	1865	BARR= BART DOUBE?	03/03/1865	NY		FILM
BEUCLER	CATHARINE	1834	BARR ? BART DOUBE	03/03/1865	NY	FARM	FILM
BEUCLER	CHARLOTTE	1836	VALENTIGNY	02/19/1866	NY	FARM	FILM
BEUCLER	EUGENE	1826	AUDINCOURT	04/10/1864	NY	FARM	FILM
BEUCLER	FREDERICH	1843	BARR = BART DOUBE ?	03/03/1865	NY	FARM	FILM
BEUCLER	G. EMILIE	1846	AUDINCOURT	04/30/1864	NY	FARM	FILM
BEUCLER	JACQUES	1834	VALENTIGNEY	02/19/1866	NY	FARM	FILM
BEUCLER	LUCIE	1863	BARR DOUBE=BART DOUB	03/03/1865	NY		FILM
BEUCLER	MARGUERITE	1842	ABSVILLER	02/15/1864	NY	FARM	FILM
BEUCLER D JAQUES	ANE	1857	BARR	03/03/1865	A		FILM
BEUCLER D JAQUES	ALINE	1857	BARR	03/03/1865	A		FILM
BEUCLER W W 3 CH	JACQUES	1829	BARR DOUBE=BART DOUB	03/03/1865	NY	FARM	FILM
BEUDEL F OF 2	FRANCOIS THOMAS		FORT LOUIS	01/01/1828	A		FILM

Lastname	Firstname	Birth Year	Birthplace	Emigration	De	Prof	Source
BEUDIN	ROSINE	1781	WINDSTEIN BAS RHIN	02/20/1817	A		FILM
BEUDIN W PAUL DANIEL	ROSINE		WINDSTEIN	02/20/1817	A		FILM
BEUGLET	CELESTINE	1836	VALDIEU	08/09/1855	NO	DAYL	FILM
BEUGRATH	EMILIE	1839	THANN	03/22/1855	NY	LAYB	FILM
BEUMAYER	JULES	1821	FRIBOURG SWISS	03/20/1851	A		FILM
BEURELL H MADELEINE	JOSEPH I CH 10	1803	ALTDORF	05/01/1844	TX	CULT	SHIP
BEURRET	AUGUSTIN	1841	LARIVIERRE	02/28/1863	NY		FILM
BEUTELSCHOEN	MARGARETTA		KIRCHHEIM U TECK W	05/23/1849	A		FILM
BEUTELSTETTER F OF 4	JACQUES		NIEDERSOULTZBACH	01/01/1828	A	DAYL	FILM
BEUTER	GERTRUDE		HIRLINGEN BA	04/17/1849	NY		FILM
BEUTER	JEAN		HIRLINGEN BA	04/17/1849	NY		FILM
BEUTER	NIZIDAS		BIETENHAUSEN HOHENZO	04/17/1849	NY		FILM
BEY	GEORG		MATTSTALL	01/01/1817	NY		NO.2
BEY	JOSEPH		MOMMENHEIM	01/01/1828	A		FILM
BEYER	ALOYSIUS	1839	MOTHERN	01/01/1867	NY	WAMA	NO.2
BEYER	BALTHASAR		UHRWILLER	03/02/1817	A	TAYL	FILM
BEYER	CATHERINA	1849	SOULTZ-SOUS-FORET	01/01/1869	NY		NO.2
BEYER	DAVID	1866	MOTHERN	01/01/1868	NY		NO.2
BEYER	JOHANN	1847	MOTHERN	01/01/1866	NY		NO.2
BEYER	KARL	1865	MOTHERN	01/01/1868	NY		NO.2
BEYER	MAGDALENA	1849	MOTHERN	01/01/1867	NY		NO.2
BEYER	MAGDALENA	1868	MOTHERN	01/01/1868	NY		NO.2
BEYER	MICHEL	1845	MOTHERN	01/01/1866	NY		NO.2
BEYER	ROSINA	1844	OBERSEEBACH	01/01/1868	NY		NO.2
BEYER	WENDELIN		MOTHERN	01/01/1868	NY		NO.2
BEYER W W 6 CH	JACQUES		RAUWILLER	03/31/1817	A		FILM
BEYER F OF 2	JEAN		GOTTENHAUSEN	01/01/1822	A	DAYL	FILM
BEYER MN HANSCHEN	BARBARA		MOTHERN	01/01/1868	NY		NO.2
BEYER W W 3 CH	KARL	1838	MOTHERN	01/01/1868	NY	FARM	NO.2
BEYHURST	ALOIS	1839	SOULTZ-SOUOS-FORET	01/01/1869	NY		NO.2
BEYLER	BALTHAZAR		UHRWILLER	01/01/1817	A		NO.2
BEYLER F OF 9	GEORGE		DOSSENHEIM	01/01/1828	A		FILM
BEYWAND	SEBASTIEN	1826	BENNWIHR	12/31/1852	NY		FILM
BICHLER	FREDERIC		FREUDENSTADT W	09/12/1849	A		FILM
BICHLER	NICOLAS		STRUTH	01/01/1828	A	DAYL	FILM
BICHLER F OF 5	JACQUES		BOUXWILLER	01/01/1828	A		FILM
BICHLER W S	XAVIER	1841	GUEBWILLER	05/10/1863	A	FARM	FILM
BICKART	CELERIE	1827	WINTZENHEIM	05/02/1853	NY		FILM
BICKART	EVE	1826	WINTZENHEIM	05/02/1853	NY		FILM
BICKART	SAMUEL	1840	HORBOURG	07/22/1857	NO		FILM
BICKEL	JEAN	1820	SUNDHOFFEN	09/22/1857	CH	DAYL	FILM
BICKEL MN SCHILLER	HENRIETTE W D	1828	COLMAR	09/14/1855	NO		FILM
BICKELHAUB W W	JEAN SIEGFRIED		STRASSBOURG	06/11/1817	A		FILM
BICKERT	MOISE	1833	WINTZENHEIM	05/27/1853	NY		FILM
BIDEAUX	FRANCOIS	1787	VILLARE LE SEC	08/12/1837	A	DAYL	FILM
BIEBER	ADAM		ASSWILLER	01/01/1828	A	FARM	FILM
BIEBER	ADAM		LOHR	01/01/1828	A	DAYL	FILM
BIEBER	ADAM		LOHR	01/01/1828	A	SHMA	FILM
BIEBER	CHRISTINE		HIRSCHLAND	01/01/1828	A		FILM
BIEBER	CHRISTINE		LOHR	01/01/1828	A	DAYL	FILM

Lastname	Firstname	Birth Year	Birthplace	Emigration	De	Prof	Source
BIEBER	GEORGE		HAMBACH	03/20/1817	A	DAYL	FILM
BIEBER	HENRI		DURSTEL	03/29/1817	A	FARM	FILM
BIEBER	HENRY		SCHOENBOURG	01/01/1828	A	FARM	FILM
BIEBER	JAQUES		LOHR	01/01/1828	A		FILM
BIEBER	JAQUES		SCHOENBOURG	01/01/1828	A	DAYL	FILM
BIEBER	JAQUES		WEINBOURG	01/01/1828	A	TAYL	FILM
BIEBER	JEAN ADAM		PFALSWEYER	01/01/1828	A		FILM
BIEBER	NICOLAS		DIEDENDORF	01/01/1828	A	DAYL	FILM
BIEBER	PHILIPPE		LOHR	01/01/1828	A	DAYL	FILM
BIEBER	PIERRE		LOHR	01/01/1828	A	DAYL	FILM
BIEBLER	BARBE	1822	NEUF BRISACH	04/15/1857	A		FILM
BIECHER	SEBASTIEN	1823	KIENTZHEIM	03/13/1849	NY	BAKE	FILM
BIEDERMANN	ANDRE		OBERMODERN	01/01/1828	A		FILM
BIEDERMANN	JACQUES		OBERMODERN	01/01/1828	A		FILM
BIEHL WW AND CH 3	MICHAEL		HIRTZFWK	/ /			
BIEHL WW AND CH 3	MICHEL		HIRTZFELDEN	09/01/1843	TX		SHIP
BIEHLER	ANTOINE	1831	GUEBWILLER	06/24/1854	NY		FILM
BIEHLER	CHRETIEN		STRUTH	01/01/1828	A	SHMA	FILM
BIEHLER	DOMINIQUE	1826	GUEBWILLER	02/21/1849	NY	PAIN	FILM
BIEHLER	FREDERIC		FREUDENSTADT W	09/12/1849	A		FILM
BIEHLER	JEAN BAPTISTE	1814	GUEBWILLER	11/05/1846	NY	BAKE	FILM
BIEHLER	MADELAINE	1832	GUEBWILLER	08/04/1854	NY		FILM
BIEHLMANN	MICHEL	1813	HUNSWIHR	02/17/1847	NY		FILM
BIEHLMANN W W 1 CH	ANTOINE	1790	GUEWENHEIM	08/26/1847	OH		FILM
BIER	ANDRE		PETERSTHAL B	08/21/1849	A		FILM
BIER	JOSEPH		DAUENDORF	04/12/1845	A		FILM
BIERCKEL	FRANCOIS		HAGUENAU	03/01/1838	A		FILM
BIERLE	GEORG		INGWILLER	01/01/1828	A		FILM
BIESSIG	EMANUELLE JEAN		STRASSBOURG	03/20/1819	A		FILM
BIETH	PIERRE		WANTZENAU	01/01/1828	A	WAV	FILM
BIETIGER D JEAN	AGATHE	1841	FALKWILLER	12/01/1844	TX		SHIP
BIETIGER D JEAN	MARIANNE	1836	FALKWILLER	12/01/1844	TX		SHIP
BIETIGER H AGATHA M	JEAN CH 5	1808	FALKWILLER	12/01/1844	TX	DAYL	SHIP
BIETIGER S JEAN	JAQUES	1835	FALKWILLER	12/01/1844	TX		SHIP
BIETIGER S JEAN	JEAN-MICHEL	1833	FALKWILLER	12/01/1844	TX		SHIP
BIETIGER S JEAN	JOSEPH	1843	FALKWILLER	12/01/1844	TX		SHIP
BIETIGER W JAEN	AGATHA	1811	FALKWILLER	12/01/1844	TX		SHIP
BIGARD	LOUISE	1811	SEPPOIS LE BAS	10/28/1857	NY		FILM
BIGEARD	JEAN PIERRE	1823	MEROUX	03/11/1854	NY		FILM
BIGEARD W 3 D 1 S	CATHERINE	1798	MEROUX	03/04/1857	NY	DAYL	FILM
BIGINO 1CH	ELISABETH	1820	CERNAY	12/17/1845	A	COOK	FILM
BIHL	ANNE MARIE	1844	BRECHAUMONT	06/04/1846	NY		FILM
BIHL	JEAN	1794	BRECHAUMONT	04/21/1857	A	DAYL	FILM
BIHL	JEAN	1818	TRAUBACH LE HAUT	02/12/1845	NY	FARM	FILM
BIHL	JEAN	1819	FUELLEREN ?	04/25/1857	A		FILM
BIHL	JEAN	1829	BRECHAUMONT	04/23/1857	A		FILM
BIHL	KATHERINE	1818	HIRZFELDEN	11/15/1846	TX		FILM
BIHL	MARIE	1826	HIRZFELDEN	11/15/1846	TX		FILM
BIHL W W 2 CH	JOSEPH	1816	HIRTZFELDEN	09/24/1846	TX	CARP	FILM
BIHL CH 1	MICHEL	1816	HIRTZFELDEN	11/01/1846	TX	DAYL	SHIP

Lastname	Firstname	Birth Year	Birthplace	Emigration	De	Prof	Source
BIHL D JOSEPH	ROSE	1846	HIRTZFELDEN	11/01/1846	TX		SHIP
BIHL D MICHEL	MARIE	1844	HIRTZFELDEN	11/01/1846	TX		SHIP
BIHL H CATHERINE	JOSEPH	1816	HIRTZFELDEN	11/01/1846	TX	CARP	SHIP
BIHL MN STRASSER	THERESE	1800	HIRTZFELDEN	02/06/1850	TX	FARM	FILM
BIHL W JOSEPH	CATHERINE	1818	HIRTZFELDEN	11/01/1846	TX		SHIP
BIHL W W	MICHEL	1796	HIRZFELDEN	09/21/1846	TX		FILM
BIHL W W 5 CH	CASPARD	1807	BRECHAUMONT	09/02/1847	NY	LAYB	FILM
BIHLER W W	APPOLLINAIRE	1794	BOURBACH LE BAS	04/19/1847	NY	DAYL	FILM
BILDSTEIN	IGNACE		INGWILLER	01/01/1828	A		FILM
BILDSTEIN	LOUIS HENRI ALE	1818	GUEBWILLER	05/06/1842	A		FILM
BILDSTEIN	LOUIS HENRY	1818	GUEBWILLER	04/06/1840	NY		FILM
BILGER	ANTOINE	1831	ESTLACH	06/11/1866	NY	LAYB	FILM
BILGER	JOSEPH	1818	HIRTZBACH	01/10/1848	NY	CARP	FILM
BILGER	MICHEL		DORLISHEIM	01/01/1828	A	BAKE	FILM
BILGER	MICHEL	1813	RIESPACH	01/25/1840	NY	WEAV	FILM
BILGER	NIKOLAS	1829	STETTEN	07/04/1854	NY	DAYL	FILM
BILGER W W 3 CH	BERNARD		NEUHOFF? NEUHAUSEL ?	03/03/1817	A	DAYL	FILM
BILHARTZ	JOSEPH	1800	SOPPE LE BAS	10/08/1844	PH	BUTC	FILM
BILHARTZ D FRANCOIS	ANNE-MARIE	1831	SOPPE-LE-BAS	12/01/1844	TX		SHIP
BILHARTZ D FRANCOIS	MARIANNE	1830	SOPPE-LE-BAS	12/01/1844	TX		SHIP
BILHARTZ H MARIE ANN	FRANCOIS-JOSEPH	1808	FALKWILLER	12/01/1844	TX	DAYL	SHIP
BILHARTZ MN REITZER	MARIE-ANNE CH 6	1802	SOPPE-LE-BAS	12/01/1844	TX		SHIP
BILHARTZ S FRANCOIS	JEAN-BAPTISTE	1839	SOPPE-LE-BAS	12/01/1844	TX		SHIP
BILHARTZ S FRANCOIS	JOSEPH	1834	SOPPE-LE-BAS	12/01/1844	TX		SHIP
BILHARTZ S FRANCOIS	VINCENT	1841	SOPPE-LE-BAS	12/01/1844	TX		SHIP
BILHARTZ S FRANCOIS	XAVIER	1844	SOPPE-LE-BAS	12/01/1844	TX		SHIP
BILL	CARL	1841	ROPPENHEIM	04/28/1844	A		NO.1
BILL	CAROLINE	1835	ROPPENHEIM	04/28/1844	A		NO.1
BILL	GEORG	1838	ROPPENHEIM	04/28/1844	A		NO.1
BILL	GEORG MICHAEL	1811		04/28/1844	A		PRIV
BILL D GEORG MICHAEL	MAGDALENA	1843		04/28/1844	A		PRIV
BILL D GEORG MICHAEL	SALOME	1837		04/28/1844	A		PRIV
BILL D MICHEL	CAROLINE	1835		04/28/1844	A		PRIV
BILL H MAREY 5 CH	GEORG MICHAEL	1811	ROPPENHEIM	04/28/1844	A		NO.1
BILL MN MAREY	CAROLINE	1807		04/28/1844	A		PRIV
BILL MN MAREY	CAROLINE	1807	ROPPENHEIM	04/28/1844	A		NO.1
BILL S GEORG MICHAEL	CARL	1841		04/28/1844	A		PRIV
BILL S GEORG MICHAEL	GEORG MICHAEL	1838		04/28/1844	A		PRIV
BILLACH	CERF ?			11/03/1847	A		FILM
BILLAR	JACQUES		KIRRBERG	01/01/1828	A	DAYL	FILM
BILLAR	PAUL		KIRRBERG	01/01/1828	A		FILM
BILLAR F OF 6	CHRETIEN		KIRRBERG	01/01/1828	A	DAYL	FILM
BILLMANN	MARTIN	1840	ALTENSTADT	01/01/1867	NY	FARM	NO.2
BIMBEL W W 3 CH	MARTIN		LA PETITE PIERRE	03/03/1817	A		FILM
BINDEICH	ANNE MARIE	1811	BITSCHE	04/25/1856	NY		FILM
BINDER	JACQUES		SESSENHEIM	01/01/1828	A		FILM
BINDER	JEAN	1833	FELLERINGEN	09/08/1853	A	LAYB	FILM
BINDER	JOSEPH	1825	FELLERINGEN	08/27/1844	NY	LAYB	FILM
BINDER F OF 6	JACUQES		DETTWILLER	01/01/1828	A	WEAV	FILM
BINDNER 3 CH	MICHEL		KESKASTEL	01/01/1817	A		FILM

Lastname	Firstname	Birth Year	Birthplace	Emigration	De	Prof	Source
BINDSWEDLER	HENRI EDUARD	1831	THANN	03/29/1853	A	MECH	FILM
BINNERT W W 4 CH	ANTOIN		LIPSHEIM	03/27/1817	A		FILM
BIPPERT W W 2 CH	JACQUES	1799	MITTELWHIR	09/23/1846	TX	WINE	FILM
BIR	EMILIE	1841	LUTTER	07/17/1864	NY	DAYL	FILM
BIRCKEL	CHRETIEN FREDER	1827	BEBLENHEIM	05/27/1848	CH		FILM
BIRCKEL	MADELAINE	1831	RIBEAUVILLE	03/06/1855	NO		FILM
BIRCKEL W W	JEAN			04/06/1849	NY		FILM
BIRCKEL W W 1 CH	JEAN		KESKASTEL	01/01/1817	A	DAYL	FILM
BIRCKENSTOCK	CATHERINA		NIEDERLAUTERBACH	01/01/1865	NO		PRIV
BIRCKENSTOCK	CATHERINE		NIEDERLAUTERBACH	01/01/1850	NO		PRIV
BIRCKENSTOCK	JEAN		NIEDERLAUTERBACH	01/01/1850	NO		PRIV
BIRCKENSTOCK	JEAN	1847	NIEDERLAUTERBACH	01/01/1866	NO		PRIV
BIRE F OF 3	ANTOINE		STEINBOURG	01/01/1828	A		FILM
BIRENBECHER	JEAN GEORGE	1814	CARSPACH	02/24/1848	NY		FILM
BIRKLE	MARIE		ORSCHWEIER B	04/23/1849	A		FILM
BIRLE WW AND CH 9	JOSEPH		ALTDORF	01/01/1854	TX		SHIP
BIRLE MN HOTTINGER	MARIE ANNE		ALTDORF	01/01/1854	TX		SHIP
BIRR	LAURENT	1826	REGUISHEIM ? REGNISH	12/20/1851	NO		FILM
BIRRER	JEAN CORNEL	1814	WILLER	04/08/1847	NY	LAYB	FILM
BIRRER W W 2 CH	NICOLAS	1817	BOURBACH LE BAS	04/26/1845	NY	DAYL	FILM
BIRY	BENJAMIN	1822	OBERENTZEN	09/01/1850	TX		SHIP
BIRY	BENJAMIN	1822	OBERENTZEN	09/01/1850	TX	CULT	PASS
BIRY	JAQUES	1816	OBERENTZEN	09/01/1846	TX	SHMA	PASS
BIRY S BENJAMIN	THERESE	1837	OBERENTZEN	09/01/1850	TX		PASS
BIRY W S	BENJAMIN	1822	OBERENTZEN	09/21/1850	TX	FARM	FILM
BISANTZ	JOSEPH	1836	THANN	10/31/1854	NY		FILM
BISANTZ	MARIE AGATHE	1830	BURNHAUPT LE BAS	02/18/1857	NY		FILM
BISANTZ	PIERRE	1799	STEINSOULTZ	12/21/1839	NY		FILM
BISCH F OF 3	MARTIN		FORT LOUIS	01/01/1828	A	SHMA	FILM
BISCH W W 4 CH	VALENTIN		OBERNAI	05/26/1817	A		FILM
BISCHLER CH 2	JEAN-BAPTISTE	1804	HEITEREN	12/01/1851	TX	CULT	PASS
BISCHLER W W 2 SONS	JEAN BAPTISTE	1803	HEITEREH ?	12/26/1851	TX	LAYB	FILM
BISCHOFF	ANTON	1813	DISSLINGEN B	10/25/1843	TX		FILM
BISCHOFF	JEAN	1808	STERNENBERG	01/31/1851	NY	FARM	FILM
BISCHOFF	JOSEPH	1831	SOPPE LE BAS	10/30/1851	NY		FILM
BISCHOFF	PHIL.JACQUE	1833	GERSTHEIM	04/14/1852	NY	BAKE	FILM
BISCHOFF	THIEBAUD	1780	CERNAY	08/28/1839	NY	FARM	FILM
BISCHOFF H THERESE	JEAN		SENTHEIM	01/01/1854	TX		SHIP
BISCHOFF W JEAN	THERESE MN BECK		SENTHEIM	01/01/1854	TX		SHIP
BISCHOFF W W 2 CH	DOMINIQUE	1819	OBERHERGHEIM	11/20/1852	NO	DAYL	FILM
BISQUADOR	FREDERIC		HAMBACH MOSELLE	03/20/1817	A	CARP	FILM
BISSLER 2 CH	JEAN	1790	BOURBACH	12/01/1847	A	FARM	FILM
BISSLER W W	FERDINAND	1823	BOURBACH	12/01/1847	NY	DAYL	FILM
BITSCH	FRANCOIS JOSEPH	1791	BURNHAUPT LE RHIN	05/21/1839	NY	WEAV	FILM
BITSCH	JEAN	1814	BURNHAUPT LE RHIN	05/23/1838	NY	DAYL	FILM
BITSCH	JEAN BAPTISTE	1826	PFASTATT	09/16/1847	NY		FILM
BITSCH	JOSEPH		HOCHFELDEN	01/09/1838	A		FILM
BITSCH	NIKOLAS	1816	GUEVENATTEN HAUT RHI	03/17/1847	NY	WAEV	FILM
BITSCH W W 3 CH	JOSEPH	1802	TRAUBACH	06/08/1846	NY	DAYL	FILM
BITSCHEZ W W 6 CH	MICHEL		SOUFFLENHEIM	01/01/1828	A	CARP	FILM

Lastname	Firstname	Birth Year	Birthplace	Emigration	De	Prof	Source
BITTER	ETIENNE	1821	MASSEVAUX	03/25/1852	A		FILM
BITTERLIN W W 7CH	PIERRE PAUL	1799	WETTELSHEIM	09/17/1846	TX	FARM	FILM
BITTERLY CH 3	JOSEPH	1822	FELLERING	09/01/1854	TX	CULT	PASS
BITTERLY W W 3 CH	JOSEPH	1822	URBAY	09/01/1854	TX		FILM
BITTERMANN	MADELAINE		BERSTHEIM	01/01/1828	A		FILM
BITTGER W W 1 CH	MICHEL		SAVERNE	01/01/1817	A		FILM
BITTNER	BARBE	1835	JEBSHEIM	01/30/1857	NY	LAYB	FILM
BITZ	JEAN		NEUHAUESEL	01/01/1828	A	LAYB	FILM
BIZOT W CH	ANTOINE JOSEPH	1814	DELLE	02/22/1856	NY	FARM	FILM
BLAES	LOUIS		KESKASTEL	01/01/1828	A	DAYL	FILM
BLAES W W	PIERRE	1822	BIMBACH? BURBACH ?	02/18/1854	NY		FILM
BLAESS	MICHEL		INGENHEIM	01/01/1828	A	FARM	FILM
BLAESS	THIEBAUD		INGENHEIM	01/01/1828	A	TAYL	FILM
BLAISE	JEAN BAPTISTE	1801	ORBAY	04/09/1857	NY		FILM
BLANC	MARIE	1807	ELOIE TERR BELFORT	08/08/1838	NY	LAYB	FILM
BLANC W W 3 CH	LAURENT	1798	ELOY	01/04/1843	A		FILM
BLANC W W 4 CH	GEORGES	1793	ROUGEMONT	02/24/1840	PH		FILM
BLANC 3 CH A M INLAW	JACQUES	1810	LIESBERG SWISS	09/23/1847	NY	LAYB	FILM
BLANCK	CATHERINE	1807	KAYSERSBERG	08/10/1849	A		FILM
BLANCK	JOSEPH	1824	BANNWIHR	02/23/1857	NO		FILM
BLANCK	MATHILDE		NIEDERLAUTERBACH	01/01/1850	NO		PRIV
BLANCK W W 6 CH	GOERG		INGERSHEIM	/ /	NO	WINE	FILM
BLANCK MN OEHLINGER	CATHERINE	1820	BANNWIHR	02/23/1857	NO		FILM
BLANK	MARIE	1807	ELOIS TERR ·BELFORT	08/08/1838	NY	LAYB	FILM
BLANK	REINHARD		ETTENHEIM B	04/03/1849	NY		FILM
BLASIARD	FRANCOIS	1835	TRAUBACH LE BAS	09/02/1856	A		FILM
BLASIARD	JEAN	1824	TRAUBACH LE BAS	06/19/1845	CD	LAYB	FILM
BLASIARD	JOSEPH	1827	TRAUBACH LE BAS	05/03/1855	NY	DAYL	FILM
BLATT	FRANCISKA	1818	MOTHERN	01/01/1867	NY		NO.2
BLATT W W 3 CH	JEAN		BISSERT	03/06/1817	A	DAYL	FILM
BLAUCH	MATHILDE	1842	NIEDERLAUTERBACH	01/01/1861	NO		PRIV
BLEACH W W 5 CH	MORAND	1824	BIXHEIM	11/18/1851	TX	DAYL	FILM
BLEGER	CHARLES	1836	ST. HYPOLITE	01/20/1854	PH		FILM
BLEGER	GEORGES	1817	ST.HYPOLITE	10/27/1853	NY	FARM	FILM
BLEGER	JEAN BAPTISTE	1829	ST. HYPOLITE	07/27/1853	NY		FILM
BLEGER	THERES	1826	ST.HYPOLITE	03/15/1854	CH		FILM
BLEICH	CATHERINE		NEUENBRUECK W	09/09/1849	A		FILM
BLEICH	CHARLES FRANC.		NEUENBRUECK W	09/09/1849	A		FILM
BLEIGER	IGNACE	1843	NIEDERLAUTERBACH	01/01/1861	NO	HADR	PRIV
BLENCK CH 5	MORAND		RIXHEIM	11/01/1851	TX	DAYL	PASS
BLENDE W W	JEAN THIEBAUD	1817	BRECHAUMONT	02/19/1850	NY		FILM
BLESSIG	EMMANUEL JEAN		STRASSBOURG	03/20/1838	A		FILM
BLEU	FRANCOIS JOSEPH	1815	KAYSERSBERG	07/18/1853	NY	WINE	FILM
BLEU	GEORGES	1826	KAYSERSBERG	02/03/1854	NO	WINE	FILM
BLEU	JOSEPHINE	1824	KAYSERBERG	02/08/1854	NO		FILM
BLEUX	JEAN PIERRE	1818	BETHENVILLIERS	01/30/1851	NY	SHMA	FILM
BLEYER	FREDERIC	1820	MITTELWIHR	08/12/1846	NY		FILM
BLEYER	GEORGES	1817	ST.HYPOLITE	10/27/1853	NY	FARM	FILM
BLEYER	JEAN	1814	MITTELWIHR	04/29/1853	NY	BUTC	FILM
BLEYER	JEAN DAVID	1817	MITTELWIHR	08/12/1846	NY		FILM

Lastname	Firstname	Birth Year	Birthplace	Emigration	De	Prof	Source
BLEYER W W	SEBASTIEN	1783	DIEFMATTEN?	02/20/1845	NY	DAYL	FILM
BLEYER W W 5 CH	JEAN	1785	DIEFMATTEN	02/08/1845	NY	DAYL	FILM
BLIND	ELAINE	1820	KIFFIS	04/05/1854	NY	DAYL	FILM
BLIND	GREGOIRE	1821	KIFFIS	01/17/1842	NY	TAYL	FILM
BLIND	JEAN JACQUES	1796	STRASBOURG	08/17/1838			FILM
BLIND	JOSEPH ANTOINE	1833	PFATTERHAUSEN	04/01/1853	NY	FARM	FILM
BLIND M ORTSCHEID JE	MARIE		VIEUX FERRETTE	07/11/1857	NY		FILM
BLIND W S AND D	MARIE	1801	SONDERSDORFF	07/11/1857	NY		FILM
BLIS MN URSPRUNG	MARIE ANNE	1793	HEITEREN	08/28/1855	NY		FILM
BLISS	J.B.		GRASSENHEIM	04/16/1846	NY		FILM
BLOCH	ALPHONSE	1840	DURMENACH HAUT RHIN	10/26/1864	NY		FILM
BLOCH	ARON	1834	HORBOURG	01/26/1857	NY		FILM
BLOCH	BABETTE	1850	DRACHENBRINN	01/01/1868	NY		NO.2
BLOCH	CATHERINE	1822	VAUTHIERMONT T.BELF	06/19/1854	NY		FILM
BLOCH	CHARLES	1828	FOUSSEMAGNE	09/21/1849	NO		FILM
BLOCH	FROMMEL		SCHWEIGHAUSEN	01/01/1828	A		FILM
BLOCH	JACQUES		SAVERNE	01/01/1828	A		FILM
BLOCH	JEAN NICOLAS		DIEDENDORF	01/01/1828	A	TAYL	FILM
BLOCH	JEANETTE		GUEBWILLER	09/12/1856	NY		FILM
BLOCH	LEOPOLD	1831	GUEBWILLER	09/12/1856	NY		FILM
BLOCH	LOUIS	1827	SOULTZ	11/03/1854	NY	BAKE	FILM
BLOCH	REINE	1831	GUEBWILLER	09/16/1856	NY		FILM
BLOCH	SALOMON	1826	GUEBWILLER	07/10/1852	NY		FILM
BLOCH	SARA	1834	GUEBWILLER	09/12/1856	NY		FILM
BLOCH	SARA	1843	DRACHENBRONN	01/01/1863	NY		NO.2
BLOCH	THEODORE	1836	CERNAY	04/24/1857	NY		FILM
BLOCH	W	1840	PHAFFANS TERR. BELF	11/03/1862	NY	FARM	FILM
BLOCH	WOLFF	1825	INGWILLER	01/01/1866	NY	MERC	NO.2
BLOCHE	JACQUES	1837	DUETTLENHEIM	10/29/1857	A		FILM
BLOCHMANN	SOPHIE		INGENHEIM	01/01/1828	A		FILM
BLOHZER	GENOFEVA	1828	ODEREN HAUT RHIN	11/22/1843	TX		FILM
BLOHZER	LEO	1826	ODEREN HAUT RHIN	11/22/1843	TX		FILM
BLOHZER	MAGDALENA		ODEREN HAUT RHIN	11/22/1843	TX		FILM
BLOHZER	NICOLAS	1834	ODEREN HAUT RHIN	11/22/1843	TX		FILM
BLOHZER	PETER	1807	ODEREN HAUT RHIN	11/22/1843	TX	FARM	FILM
BLOHZER	SIPLUS	1841	ODEREN HAUT RHIN	11/22/1843	TX		FILM
BLOHZER	THERESE	1805	ODEREN HAUT RHIN	11/22/1843	TX		FILM
BLOHZER	THERESE	1835	ODEREN HAUT RHIN	11/22/1843	TX		FILM
BLOHZER	URBAN	1831	ODEREN HAUT RHIN	11/22/1843	TX		FILM
BLONDE	FRANCOIS JOSEPH	1809	BRECHAUMONT	03/13/1844	NY	FARM	FILM
BLONDE	JOSEPH	1828	BRECHAUMONT	03/12/1847	NY	FARM	FILM
BLONDE	JOSEPH	1829	GUEVENATTEN	02/23/1846	CN	FARM	FILM
BLONDE	NICOLAS	1805	BRECHAUMONT	03/12/1847	NY	FARM	FILM
BLONDE	NICOLAS	1819	BRECHAUMONT	03/21/1844	NY	FARM	FILM
BLONDE W W 2 D	JOSEPH	1806	TRAUBACH 5E HAUT	11/25/1854	NY	FARM	FILM
BLONDE W W 3 CH	JOSEPH	1785	TRAUBACH LE HAUT	12/09/1847	NY	LAYB	FILM
BLONZER W W 8CH	PETER	1807	ODEREN	11/22/1843	TX		FILM
BLUCKER	MARIE ANN		HOCHFELDEN	01/01/1828	A		FILM
BLUM	CHRETIEN	1802	ALGOLSHEIM	02/17/1853	NY		FILM
BLUM	ELISABETH		OBERNAI	01/01/1850	NO		PRIV

Lastname	Firstname	Birth Year	Birthplace	Emigration	De	Prof	Source
BLUM	FANNY	1842	NIEDERROEDERN	01/01/1865	NY		NO.2
BLUM	JACQUES	1818	MUTTERHOLTZ	05/01/1849	NY		FILM
BLUM	JACQUES	1825	BERGHEIM	03/17/1849	NO		FILM
BLUM	JOSEF		REICHSHOFFEN	/ /	LA		BULL
BLUM	JOSEPH	1815	STEINBACH	12/31/1851	NO	DAYL	FILM
BLUM	MELANIE		REICHSHOFFEN	/ /	LA		BULL
BLUM	PIERRE		WEIL	05/03/1849	NY		FILM
BLUM W 3CH	MADELAINE	1806	BRETAGNE	10/08/1847	NY		FILM
BLUMSTEIN	HENRY	1832	STE CROIX AUX MINES	05/31/1854	NY		FILM
BLUMSTEIN	JOSEPH	1839	STE CROIX AUX MINES	03/20/1857	NY		FILM
BLUMSTEIN	MARIE	1831	ST CROIX AUX MINES	03/20/1857	NY		FILM
BLUMSTEIN	MARIE	1856	STE CROIX AUX MINES	03/20/1857	NY		FILM
BLUMSTEIN	SEBASTIEN	1843	STE CROIX AUX MINES	03/20/1857	NY		FILM
BLUMSTEIN D OF MARIE	MARIE	1857	STE CROIX AUX MINES	03/20/1857	NY		FILM
BLUMSTEIN MN BRUNETT	MARIE ANNE W D		STE CROIX AUX MINES	03/20/1857	NY		FILM
BLUN	FRANCOIS JOSEPH	1826	KIFFIS	01/17/1848	NY		FILM
BLUNTZER D PETER	GENEVIEVE	1828	ODEREN	11/01/1843	TX		SHIP
BLUNTZER D PETER	MARIE MADELEINE	1843	ODEREN	11/01/1843	TX		SHIP
BLUNTZER D PETER	SIXTE	1841	ODEREN	11/01/1843	TX		SHIP
BLUNTZER D PETER	THERESE	1836	ODEREN	11/01/1843	TX		SHIP
BLUNTZER D PETER	VENERANDE	1838	ODEREN	11/01/1843	TX		SHIP
BLUNTZER H THERESE	PETER CH 8	1805	ODEREN	11/01/1843	TX	TISS	SHIP
BLUNTZER S PETER	LEON	1826	ODEREN	11/01/1843	TX		SHIP
BLUNTZER S PETER	NICOLAS	1834	ODEREN	11/01/1843	TX		SHIP
BLUNTZER S PETER	URBAIN	1831	ODEREN	11/01/1843	TX		SHIP
BLUNTZER S PETER	URBAIN	1831	ODERENM	/ /			SHIP
BLUNTZER W PETER	THERESE		ODEREN	11/01/1843	TX		SHIP
BLUSS W W 5 CH	JEAN	1798	NIEDERWILLER	08/05/1845	A	FARM	FILM
BLUST	LOUIS		SCHIRRHEIM	01/01/1828	A	FARM	FILM
BLUST	NICOLAS		SCHIRRHEIN	01/01/1828	A	FARM	FILM
BOBAY	THIEBAUD	1830	ST.GERMAIN	04/04/1851	NY		FILM
BOBAY W W 4 CH	JEAN PIERRE	1799	ST GERMAIN	07/30/1842	NY	DAYL	FILM
BOBBARD	CHRETIEN	1833	GALFINGUE	10/30/1852	NY		FILM
BOBBARD W W 4 CH	JOSEPH	1790	HUNSWIHR	06/17/1840	NY		FILM
BOBBELE	GUILEUME	1822	COLMAR	05/11/1852	NY	FARM	FILM
BOBENRIETH	JAKOB	1812	FELLERINGEN	04/09/1844	TX		FILM
BOBENRIETH	JEAN	1812	FELLERING	04/01/1844	TX	PRIN	SHIP
BOBENRIETH	JEAN	1812	FELLERINGEN	04/01/1844	TX	PRIN	SHIP
BOBENRIETH	JEAN	1818	FELLERINGEN	11/05/1844	NY	PRIN	FILM
BOBENRIETH	JOSEPH	1816	HUSSEREN WESSERLING	01/07/1845	NO		FILM
BOBENRIETH	RENE	1825	FELLERINGEN	08/27/1844	NY		FILM
BOBENRIETH W 6 CH	ANNE MARIE	1800	RANSPACH	07/16/1846	NY	LAYB	FILM
BOBENRIETH W W 2 CH	GEORGES ANTOINE	1806	ODEREN	06/02/1845	NY	SHMA	FILM
BOBEY	THIEDBAUD	1830	ST GERMAIN	04/04/1851	NY	EXMI	FILM
BOCHHOLZ	LORENZ	1816	BIRKERSDORF	05/29/1844	TX		FILM
BOCHLER	ALPHONSE	1835	MULHOUSE	10/06/1855	NY		FILM
BOCK	JEAN		ALTECKENDORF	01/01/1828	A	WEAV	FILM
BOCK	WILHELM	1829	WEISSENBURG	01/01/1865	NY		NO.2
BODAIRE	VIRGINIA	1845	RONGAGOUTTE	05/20/1865	NY		FILM
BOEBION F OF 5	PIERRE		PFALZWEYER	01/01/1828	A		FILM

Lastname	Firstname	Birth Year	Birthplace	Emigration	De	Prof	Source
BOECHEL	MARTIN		SCHIRRHEIM	07/24/1837	A		FILM
BOECKER	SARA		DUSSLINGEN W	06/18/1849	A		FILM
BOEGER F OF 7	CHRETIEN		ROESCHWOOG	01/01/1828	A		FILM
BOEGLIN	JEAN	1819	BUSCHWILLER	10/04/1845	A	TAYL	FILM
BOEGLIN	XAVIER	1808	MANSPACH ?	02/21/1839	NY	DAYL	FILM
BOEGLIN W W 3 CH	JEAN	1796	BUSCHWILLER	08/07/1850	NY	DAYL	FILM
BOEGLIN W W 6CH	IGNACE	1802	CARSPACH	10/25/1853	A	FARM	FILM
BOEHLER	ALPHONSE	1835	MULHOUSE	10/06/1855	A		FILM
BOEHNE	MARIE ANNE		RENCHEN B	10/27/1849	A		FILM
BOELL	MICHEL	1851	WEISSENBURG	01/01/1865	NY		NO.2
BOEPPELE	ANTOINE		MULLENBACH	08/23/1849	A		FILM
BOERLEN W W 2 CH	ANTOINE	1823	BURRHAUPT LE HAUT	01/01/1823	NY		FILM
BOERLEN W W 3 CH	APOLLO	1808	BURNHAUPT LE BAS	05/07/1839	NY		FILM
BOESCH	AUGUSTE	1813	SOULTZMATT	11/22/1852	NO	BAKE	FILM
BOESCH	EDUARD	1816	SOULTZ	07/05/1853	NY		FILM
BOESCH	JEAN CASPAR	1785	NESLAU SWISS	01/17/1840	A		FILM
BOESCHLIN	CATHERINE	1826	JEBSHEIM	03/21/1857	NY		FILM
BOESCHLIN	GEORGES	1855	JEBSHEIM	03/21/1857	NY		FILM
BOESCHLIN	JEAN	1823	JEBSHEIM	03/21/1857	NY	LAYB	FILM
BOESCHLIN	JEAN	1847	JEBSHEIM	03/21/1857	NY		FILM
BOESCHLIN H CATHERIN	JEAN		JEBSGEIM	03/21/1857	NY		FILM
BOESCHLIN W W 1 D	JACQUES	1804	JEBSHEIM	09/30/1857	NY	LAYB	FILM
BOESCHLIN W W 2CH	MARTIN	1815	JEBSHEIM	08/14/1855	NY		FILM
BOETSCH	ANDRE	1795	VIEUX- FERRETTE	05/02/1845	NY	DAYL	FILM
BOETSCH	JOSEPH	1791	VIEUX FERRETTE	05/26/1845	NY		FILM
BOETTIGER	CHRISTIAN		WITTENDORF W	05/12/1849	A		FILM
BOETTIGER	CHRISTOPH		WITTENDORF OR DORNHE	05/12/1849	A		FILM
BOGELEN	JEAN	1814	GILDWILLER	08/30/1848	A	WEAV	FILM
BOGEN	GANGOLF	1817	BENNWIHR	02/17/1847	NY		FILM
BOGNER	MARIA ANNA		KAIDENBURG	01/01/1869	NY		NO.2
BOH	JACQUES	1809	OTTENBACH	02/22/1851	NO		FILM
BOHIN	EMILIE	1833	BEAUCOURT	04/26/1854	NY		FILM
BOHL	ANTOINE	1793	HAUT-RHIN	12/01/1844	TX	CULT	SHIP
BOHL	JEAN	1813	MASSEVAUX	04/03/1847	NY		FILM
BOHL	JEAN	1830	MORTWILLER	09/01/1853	NY	FARM	BOHL
BOHL	LOUIS		HERRLISHEIM	/ /	NY		FILM
BOHL D JOSEPH	CAROLINE	1837	BOURBACH	12/01/1844	TX		SHIP
BOHL D JOSEPH	FRANCOIS	1834	BOURBACH	12/01/1844	TX		SHIP
BOHL S JOSEPH	APPOLONTAR	1830	BOURBACH	12/01/1844	TX		SHIP
BOHL S JOSEPH	EDOUARD	1842	BOURBACH	12/01/1844	TX		SHIP
BOHL S JOSEPH	JOSEPH	1840	BOURBACH	12/01/1844	TX		SHIP
BOHL S JOSEPH	PHILIPPE	1844	BOURBACH	12/01/1844	TX		SHIP
BOHL W W	ANTOINE	1820	SOPPE LE HAUT	02/12/1851	NY		FILM
BOHL WW AND CH 6	JOSEPH	1796	BOURBACH	12/01/1844	TX	CULT	SHIP
BOHM MN LOSINGER 3CH	BARBE	1800	COLMAR	09/20/1854	NY		FILM
BOHN F OF 7	PHILIPPE		BETTWILLER	08/14/1855	NY		FILM
BOHNENKAMP	ARNOLD	1800	WESTFALEN	09/17/1845	TX		FILM
BOHNENKAMP	MARIE	1795	WESTFALEN	09/17/1845	TX		FILM
BOHREO W W 1D	MICHEL	1819	PFASTATT	03/20/1854	SL		FILM
BOHRER	JEAN BAPTISTE	1804	WILLER	03/04/1839	NY		FILM

Lastname	Firstname	Birth Year	Birthplace	Emigration	De	Prof	Source
BOIG	ANDRE	1820	BERNARDSWILLER	02/12/1846	NO		FILM
BOIGEOT	GENEREUSE	1822	JOUCHERAY TERR LE BF	03/13/1848	NY		FILM
BOIGY W W 4 CH	JOSEPH	1812	NEUWILLER	10/04/1845	A	CHRR	FILM
BOILLON	PIERRE FREDERIE	1823	VALENTIGNEY	02/28/1863	NY		FILM
BOIRIER	VICTOR	1829	BESSONCOURT	03/31/1865	NY		FILM
BOISCHIEN ?	VICTOR	1821	ETROITS FONTAINE	04/21/1854	NY		FILM
BOLE	FRANCOIS	1815	LIEUPRE	08/14/1838	NO	WEAV	FILM
BOLEE	MARIE	1835	SAINTE CROIX AUX MIN	10/19/1854	SL		FILM
BOLEF	MARIE	1835	ST CROIX AUX MINES	10/19/1854	SL		FILM
BOLET	JULIEN	1830	GIROMAGNY	09/14/1854	NY	OFFI	FILM
BOLF	FRANCOIS	1815	LIEPVRE	08/14/1838	NO		FILM
BOLLACH	MICHEL	1846	RIEDSELTZ	01/01/1867	NY	MERC	NO.2
BOLLACK	HEINRICH	1842	WEISSENBURG	01/01/1868	NO	MAMA	NO.2
BOLLACK	HENRIETTE	1846	WEISSENBURG	01/01/1869	NY		NO.2
BOLLACK	JOSEPF	1847	WEISSENBURG	01/01/1865	NY		NO.2
BOLLAK	HENRI		WISSEMBOURG	01/01/1869	NO		PRIV
BOLLE W W CH	JOSEPH	1818	LIEPVRE	09/02/1847	NO	FARM	FILM
BOLLENBACH	JEAN PIERRE	1805	OSTHEIM	12/22/1853	NY	FARM	FILM
BOLLENBACH	MICHEL	1832	OSTHEIM	09/02/1853	NY	BAKE	FILM
BOLLINGER	GEORGES	1833	BEBLENHEIM	06/16/1854	NY		FILM
BOLLINGER	JACQUES	1829	BEHLENHEIM	05/06/1851	NY	FARM	FILM
BOLLINGER	JULIE	1840	VOLSCHWILLER	05/17/1866	NY		FILM
BOLOT	M. JOSEPHINE	1826	CERNAY	08/09/1853	NO		FILM
BOLT	OSWALD	1847	KIFFIS	05/21/1866	NY	DAYL	FILM
BOMBERG	HENRY	1814	MULHOUSE	07/06/1848	NY		FILM
BOMINGER	SIMON	1815	ZIMMERSHEIM	03/13/1852	NO		FILM
BONAT	HENRI,LEON	1832	VAUTHIERMONT	10/01/1860	TX	DAYL	PASS
BONAT	NICOLAS	1818	ROPPE	03/21/1846	NY	FARM	FILM
BONBEZ	JACQUES	1821	AUXELLES BAS	01/18/1853	NO		FILM
BONNERONT W W 1 CH	JACQUES	1808	WEINBOURG BAS RHIN	04/06/1840	NY	FARM	FILM
BONNET W W A SISTER	FRANCOIS	1828	BESSONCOURT	08/13/1847	NY		FILM
BONNINGER	SIMON	1815	ZIMMERSHEIM	03/13/1852	NO	MISS	FILM
BONOTAL	CATHERINE	1843	CHENEBIER	03/17/1865	NY	FARM	FILM
BONOTAL	EUGENE	1839	CHENEBIER	03/10/1865	NY	FARM	FILM
BONTEMPS	JEAN BAPTISTE	1829	MASSEVAUX	10/13/1857	A		FILM
BONY	AUGUSTE	1830	BOURAGNE	04/20/1849	NY		FILM
BOOS	JACQUES		MENCHHOFFEN?	01/01/1828	A		FILM
BOOS	XAVIER		STATTMATTEN	01/01/1828	A	FARM	FILM
BORGUEREL	LUCIE	1831	ST.URSANNE SWISS	09/21/1850	NY		FILM
BORMANN	JAUQES	1821	ST. MARIE AUX MINES	05/30/1842	NO		FILM
BORN	CATHERINE		ECKARTSWILLER	01/01/1828	A		FILM
BORNEQUE	THIEBAUT	1825	PHAFFANS	11/09/1862	NY	FARM	FILM
BORNMANN	JEAN FREDERIC	1816	ST MARIE AUX MINES	04/24/1840	NO		FILM
BORNMANN	JEAN JACQUEZ	1821	ST MARIE AUX MINES	05/30/1842	NO		FILM
BORNMANN	NICOLAUS		UHRWILLER	05/13/1736	A		FILM
BORST	AGATHE		LAUF B	05/22/1849	A		FILM
BORTET	MARIE ANN	1831	LA POUTROIE	05/05/1852	A		FILM
BORTMANN W W 2 CH	JEAN	1802	ESCHHOLTZMATT SWISS	04/18/1840	NY		FILM
BOSCHEURICHTER	IGNACE		MATZENHEIM	02/28/1838	A	TAYL	FILM
BOSSARD	CHRETIEN	1833	GALFINGUE	10/30/1852	NY		FILM

Lastname	Firstname	Birth Year	Birthplace	Emigration	De	Prof	Source
BOSSARD W W 4CH	JSOEPH	1790	HUNAWIHR	06/17/1840	NY		FILM
BOSSART W SI	CATHERINE	1826	ILLFURTH	04/10/1855	NY	LAYB	FILM
BOSSART W W 2 CH	ANDRE	1816	BERGHEIM	09/14/1854	NY	WINE	FILM
BOSSELE	LOUIS		WASSELONNE	01/01/1828	A		FILM
BOSSEMEYER	XAVER	1843	KALTENHOUSE	01/01/1868	NY	FARM	NO.2
BOSSENMEYER	X		KALTENHOUSE	01/01/1850	NO		PRIV
BOSSERT W W CH BR	MATHIEU	1808	GUEBWILLER	04/12/1839	NY	FARM	FILM
BOSSHARDT	FRANCOIS ANTOIE	1826	GRUSSENHEIM	10/31/1853	NY	FARM	FILM
BOSSHART	JACQUES	1819	BAUMR SWISS	07/23/1851	NY		FILM
BOSSLER	FRANCOIS	1821	BOURBACH LE BAS	07/09/1838	A	LAYB	FILM
BOSSLER	IGNACE	1825	BOURBACH LE BAS	07/09/1838	A		FILM
BOSSLER	JOSEPH	1824	STAFFELFELDEN	05/05/0186	NY		FILM
BOSSLER W W 9 CH	ANTOINE	1783	BOURBACH LE BAS	10/22/1845	NY	DAYL	FILM
BOSTETTER D MARTIN	ANNA MARIA	1828		01/01/1851	A		PRIV
BOSTETTER D MARTIN	ANNA MARIEA	1828	ROPPENHEIM	01/01/1851	A		NO.1
BOSTETTER F OF 5	MARTIN		FORSTFELD BISCHWILLR	03/03/1838	A		FILM
BOSTETTER H GEYER4CH	MARTIN	1806	ROPPENHEIM	08/13/1852	A		NO.1
BOSTETTER H MARIE A	MARTIN	1806		08/13/1852	A		PRIV
BOSTETTER MN GEYER	MARIE ANNE	1803		08/13/1852	A		PRIV
BOSTETTER MN GEYER	MARIE ANNE	1803	ROPPENHEIM	08/13/1852	A		NO.1
BOTT	LOUIS	1818	RIBEAUVILLE	11/26/1840	NY		FILM
BOTZAUER	LOUISE	1848	MUNCHHOUSE	01/01/1868	NY		NO.2
BOTZMEYER	PHILLIP	1835	GUNSTETT	01/01/1867	NY	DAYL	NO.2
BOTZY	JEAN	1808	VIEUX FERRETTE	12/27/1845	NY		FILM
BOUBEZ	JACQUES FRANCOI	1821	AUXELLES BAS	01/18/1753	NO		FILM
BOUCHE		1825	VERSAILLES	09/17/1845	TX		FILM
BOUCHER	FRANCOIS		ROPPENHEIM	03/06/1838	A		FILM
BOUCHER	GEORGES		ROPPENHEIM	03/06/1838	A	FARM	FILM
BOUCHER	HENRI		ROPPENHEIM	03/06/1838	A		FILM
BOUCHER	SEBASTIEN		ROPPENHEIM	03/06/1838	A	BUTC	FILM
BOUCHEZ		1825	VERSAILLES	09/17/1845	TX		FILM
BOUCHEZ	ALEXIS	1781	SALBERT TERR BELFORT	02/18/1849	NO		FILM
BOUCHEZ	JACQUEZ ETIENNE	1808	SALBERT TERR BELFORT	04/23/1847	NO		FILM
BOUCHEZ W W	FRANCOIS	1812	SALBER TERR BELFORT	02/18/1847	NO	FARM	FILM
BOUDIN	FELICE	1830	SWITZERLAND	09/30/1866	NY		FILM
BOUDIN	JOSEPH	1833	SWITZERLAND	09/30/1866	NY		FILM
BOUER	KATHERINE	1824	ERSCHWIL SWISS	05/29/1844	TX		FILM
BOUILLARD	ALEXANDRE	1831	MAROUX	04/11/1857	NY	FARM	FILM
BOUILLARD	JEAN PIERRE	1828	DAUJOUTIN	10/11/1847	NY		FILM
BOULANGER	PIERRE	1824	ARGIESANSE T.BELFORT	10/25/1852	NY		FILM
BOULANGER MN RHEINET	MADELAINE	1804	HUNAWIHR	12/09/1854	NY		FILM
BOULARD	JOSEPHINE	1808	LEEGERWOOD MAUSE SCO	04/08/1843	TX		FILM
BOUQUARDEZ	CELESTIN	1840	PHAFFANS	09/02/1865		FARM	FILM
BOUQUET	ANTOINE	1807	CHATENOIS	08/09/1853	NY	FARM	FILM
BOUQUET	CATHERINE	1836	LA RIVIERE	10/31/1866	NY		FILM
BOUQUET	CATHERINE	1862	LA RIEVIERE	10/31/1866	NY		FILM
BOUQUET	LOUIS	1833	LA RIEVIERE	10/31/1866	NY		FILM
BOUQUET	MARIE	1864	LA RIEVIERE	10/31/1866	NY		FILM
BOUQUET W W CH	LOUIS	1833	LARIEVIERE	10/31/1866	NY	FARM	FILM
BOUQUOT W W CH ,F	RENI	1805	MERZHEIM	12/22/1852	NY	LAYB	FILM

Lastname	Firstname	Birth Year	Birthplace	Emigration	De	Prof	Source
BOUR	JEAN	1811	SPICHEREN MOSELLE	08/02/1854	NO	TAYL	FILM
BOURCART	JACQUEZ	1807	MULHOSE	09/19/1857	NO		FILM
BOURELLIN 2CH	REINE	1825	MEYENHEIM	08/28/1855	NY		FILM
BOUREZ	JACQUES	1821	CERNAY	01/18/1853	NO		FILM
BOURG	CELESTIN		PHAFFANS	04/09/1863	NY		FILM
BOURG	CELESTIN	1846	PHAFFANS	04/09/1863	NY	FARM	FILM
BOURGARD	MARGERITE	1767	ZINSWEILER	02/16/1817	A		FILM
BOURGENOT W W 2CH	XAVIER JOSEPH	1816	GIROMAGNY	08/16/1850	NY		FILM
BOURGEOIS	JOSEPH SIMON	1797	ROMANC SUR ISERE	10/25/1843	TX	FARM	FILM
BOURGEOIS	M	1837	HIRSINGUE	03/14/1864	NY	FARM	FILM
BOURGEOIS	MARIE ANNE	1822	DAUJOUTIN	02/17/1848	NO	FARM	FILM
BOURGEOIS W W 5CH	XAVIER	1811	HAUTTE OR HACELLE ?	05/17/1850	A		FILM
BOURGER W W 5 CH	JEAN		UHRWILLER	03/11/1817	A	WEAV	FILM
BOURGES	JOHANN		TRIEMBACH	01/01/1817	A		NO.2
BOURGMEYER	GUSTAV	1809	HIRSINGUE	02/22/1851	NY	CARP	FILM
BOURGONNIER	JOSEPH FRANCOIS	1821	BREST	01/17/1852	NY	SOLD	FILM
BOURGUARD	PIERRE JOSEPH	1824	ROPPE TERR DE BELFOT	09/03/1846	A	BAKE	FILM
BOURGUENOT	XAVIER JOSPH	1816	GIROMAGNY	08/16/1850	NY		FILM
BOURGUNIOT	JULIE	1818	GIROMAGNY	07/21/1845	A		FILM
BOURIER	VIKTOR	1839	BESSONCOURT	03/31/1865	NY		FILM
BOURLARD	JOSEPHINE	1808	LEEGERWOOD MENGE SCO	11/22/1843	TX		FILM
BOURLET	MAGDALENA	1847	ALTENSTADT	01/01/1868	NY		NO.2
BOURQUARDEZ	ALPHONSE		LA RIEVIERE	08/08/1861	NY		FILM
BOURQUARDEZ	AUGUSTIN	1855	LA RIVIERE	08/08/1861	NY		FILM
BOURQUARDEZ	FRANCOIS	1818	SOPPE LE BAS	05/12/1840	NY		FILM
BOURQUARDEZ	JOSEPH	1829	LA RIVIERE	08/08/1861	NY	FARM	FILM
BOURQUARDEZ	JOSEPHINE	1833	LA RIVIERE	08/08/1861	NY	FARM	FILM
BOURQUARDEZ	LOUIS	1831	BRECHAUMONT	06/15/1857	NY	BAKE	FILM
BOURQUARDEZ	VIRGINIA	1859	LA RIVIERE	08/08/1861	NY		FILM
BOURQUIN	AUGUSTINE	1863	CHAMPAGNEY	02/27/1866			FILM
BOURQUIN	GEORGE	1833	FRAISSE HAUT SONNE	02/27/1866	NY		FILM
BOURQUIN	JULES	1864	CHAMPAGNEY	02/27/1866	NY		FILM
BOURQUIN	MARIE	1866	CHAMPAGNEY	02/27/1866	NY		FILM
BOURQUIN	MARIE EUGENE	1839	CHAMPAGNEY	02/27/1866	NY		FILM
BOURQUIN	PIERRE	1842	VELENTIGNEY	05/06/1865	NY	FARM	FILM
BOURQUIN CH 2	FRANCOIS	1819	MULHOUSE	09/01/1846	TX	SERR	PASS
BOURQUIN W W 2 CH	FRANCOIS		GROSNE	09/16/1846	TX		FILM
BOURRON	FRANCOIS	1813	PFATTERSHAUSEN	09/22/1853	NY	DAYL	FILM
BOURY	CELESTIN	1846	PHAFFANS	04/09/1863	NY		FILM
BOUSSING W W 2 CH	JEAN		HIRSCHLAND	03/20/1817	A		
BOUTEILLER	CATHERINE	1833	MEZIRE	04/18/1857	NY		FILM
BOUTEILLER	EUGENE	1845	ETOBON	02/05/1866	NY		FILM
BOUVIER	JOSEPHINE	1828	BITSCHWILLER	03/12/1852	A		FILM
BOUVIER	LOUIS	1846	MONTBELIARD	04/25/1865	NY	FARM	FILM
BOUVIER	MARIE	1847	MONTBELIARD	05/29/1865	NY	FARM	FILM
BOUVIER	MICHEL		BOUXWILLER	01/01/1828	A		FILM
BOWMANN			NIEDERLAUTERBACH	01/01/1850	N0		PRIV
BOX	FRANCOIS	1813	THANN	05/15/1849	NY		FILM
BOYOT	ADELE	1860	VALENTIGNEY DOUBE	03/17/1865	NY		FILM
BOYOT	CATHERINE	1819	VALENTIGNEY	03/17/1865	NY	FARM	FILM

Lastname	Firstname	Birth Year	Birthplace	Emigration	De	Prof	Source
BOYOT	CATHERINE	1859	VALENTIGNEY	03/17/1865	NY		FILM
BOYOT	ELISE	1854	VALENTIGNEY DOUBE	03/17/1865	NY		FILM
BOYOT	EUGENE	1846	VALENTIGNEY	03/17/1865	NY	FARM	FILM
BOYOT	GEORGES	1823	VALENTIGNEY	03/17/1865	NY		FILM
BOYOT	GEORGES	1848	VALENTIGNEY DOUBE	03/17/1865	NY	FARM	FILM
BOYOT	LOUISE	1850	VALENTIGNEY DOUBE	03/17/1865	NY	FARM	FILM
BRACHMANN	SEBASTIEN	1791	ROUFFACH	09/17/1846	TX	LAYB	FILM
BRAECKLE W W 3 CH	MICHEL		NEUHOFF	03/03/1817	A	CARP	FILM
BRAENDLE	CATHERINE		APPENWEIER	08/11/1849	A		FILM
BRAENDLE	FRANCOISE		APPENWEIER	08/11/1849	A		FILM
BRAM	JACQUEZ	1826	DURRENENTZEN	05/15/1847	CH		FILM
BRAND	BONIFACE	1815	BURNHAUPT LE HAUT	12/23/1845	NY		FILM
BRAND	CATHERINE	1791	BURNHAUPT LE HAUT	09/28/1843	A		PRIV
BRAND	MARIE URSULA	1834	HEIMERSDORFF	01/01/1857	NY		FILM
BRAND MN BEISSINGER	ROSINE W 6 CH	1810	MULHOUSE	10/24/1850	NY		FILM
BRAND W W 5 CH	BONIFACE	1794	BURNHAUPT LE HAUT	04/08/1840	NY	SHMA	FILM
BRANDENBERGER	JACQUES	1831	BLOTZHEIM	09/11/1855	NY	LAYB	FILM
BRANDENBERGER	JEAN GEORGES	1802	BEBLENHEIM	12/13/1853	NO	FARM	FILM
BRANDER	JOSEPH	1818	GUEMAR	03/06/1855	NY	SHMA	FILM
BRANDNER	ALEXANDRE SEBAT	1826	COLMAR	02/22/1848	NY		FILM
BRANDSTETTER	FRANCE		ZIEROLSHOFEN B	07/31/1849	A		FILM
BRANDSTETTER	JACQUES	1821	FERRETTE	03/03/1846	NO		FILM
BRAUER	ADOLPHE	1841	RIBEAUVILLE	08/11/1853	NY		FILM
BRAUN	BALTHAZAR	1858	MOTHERN	01/01/1867	NY		NO.2
BRAUN	BENEDIKT	1861	MOTHERN	01/01/1867	NY		NO.2
BRAUN	CASPAR	1849	LAUTERBURG	01/01/1865	NY		NO.2
BRAUN	DANIEL	1860	LAUTERBURG	01/01/1866	NY		NO.2
BRAUN	ELISABETH	1825	MOTHERN	01/01/1867	NY		NO.2
BRAUN	FRANZ	1851	LAUTERBURG	01/01/1866	NY		NO.2
BRAUN	JACOB	1840	ALTENSTADT	01/01/1869	NY	FARM	NO.2
BRAUN	JAQUES	1804	SOULTZ	01/27/1853	NY		FILM
BRAUN	JEAN BAPTISTE	1805	WATTWILLER	09/25/1850	NY	LAYB	FILM
BRAUN	JOHANN	1859	MOTHERN	01/01/1867	NY		NO.2
BRAUN	JOSEF	1856	MOTHERN	01/01/1867	NY		NO.2
BRAUN	JOSEPH		DURBACH B	09/05/1849	A		FILM
BRAUN	LOUIS FREDERIC		DURSTEL	03/18/1838	A	TAYL	FILM
BRAUN	MARIA	1857	LAUTERBURG	01/01/1866	NY		NO.2
BRAUN	MARIE		ALTKIRCH	09/07/1854	NY		FILM
BRAUN	MARTIN LOUIS	1821	KAYSERSBERG	09/25/1848	NO	TAYL	FILM
BRAUN	MARTIN LOUIS	1803	CONSTETT W	09/05/1849	NO		FILM
BRAUN	MATHIEU	1809	MULHAUSEN	12/08/1840	A		FILM
BRAUN	MATHIEU	1810	MULHAUSEN	04/03/1843	NY		FILM
BRAUN	MOSES	1841	WEISSENBURG	01/01/1867	A		NO.2
BRAUN	SEBASTIEN	1837	BREMMELBACH	01/01/1867	NY	CARP	NO.2
BRAUN F OF3	JACQUES		WEITERSWILLER	01/01/1828	A	DAYL	FILM
BRAUN W W 2 CH	NICOLAS	1822	NEUWILLER	03/14/1849	NY		FILM
BRAUN D LOUIS	JOSEPHINE	1834	HAUT-RHIN	12/01/1844	TX		SHIP
BRAUN D LOUIS	LOUISE	1830	HAUT-RHIN	12/01/1844	TX		SHIP
BRAUN H SALOME CH 3	LOUIS	1805	HAUT-RHIN	12/01/1844	TX	SHMA	SHIP
BRAUN S LOUIS	LOUIS	1844	HAUT-RHIN	12/01/1844	TX		SHIP

```
-----------------------------------------------------------------------------------------
BRAUN W LOUIS         SALOME        1805 HAUT-RHIN            12/01/1844 TX        SHIP
BRAUN W W 2 CH        XAVIER        1814 LAUTENBACH-ZELL      01/24/1848 NY FARM FILM
BRAUN W W 4 CH        MICHEL        1824 MOTHERN              01/01/1867 NY        NO.2
BRAUNSCHWIG           SAMUEL        1834 DURMENACH            08/29/1854 NY        FILM
BRECHBIEHL W W 1D     NICOLAS       1802 BREITENBACH BAS RHIN 03/17/1855 NY FARM FILM
-----------------------------------------------------------------------------------------
BRECHBUHLER W W 3 CH  JEAN          1797 OSTHEIM              03/26/1845 NY DAYL FILM
BRECHENMACHER         JACQUES            IMBSHEIM             01/01/1828 A        FILM
BRECHENMACHER         PHILLIPE           INGWILLER            01/01/1828 A   WEAV FILM
BRECHIER              FRANCOIS      1803 GRANDVILLARS         02/05/1851 CH FARM FILM
BRECHON               PIERRE        1831 DENNEY TERR BELFORT  01/16/1856 NY FARM FILM
-----------------------------------------------------------------------------------------
BREIDT                GEORG HEINRICH 1866 WEISSENBURG         01/01/1866 NY BAKE NO.2
BREINING F OF 11      MICHEL             WILWISHEIM           01/01/1828 A   FARM FILM
BREINING F OF 8       JOSEPH             WILWISHEIM           01/01/1828    FARM FILM
BREITEL               MELCHIOR      1826 ST.HYPOLITE          08/10/1852 PH DAYL FILM
BREITENBUCHER         CHRETIEN           VENDENHEIM           01/01/1828 A        FILM
-----------------------------------------------------------------------------------------
BRENCKLE              JOSEF         1844 LAUTERBURG           01/01/1865 NY DAYL NO.2
BRENCKLE              MARGERITE     1848 NIEDERLAUTERBACH     01/01/1866 NO        PRIV
BRENCKLE              MARGUERITE         NIEDERLAUTERBACH     01/01/1850 NO        PRIV
BRENDEL               JEAN GEORGES  1814 ECKBOLSHEIM BAS RHIN 03/24/1848 NY        FILM
BRENDEL               LOUIS         1819 RIBEAUVILLE          08/30/1849 NY MERC FILM
-----------------------------------------------------------------------------------------
BRENDER               AGNES              CODTNAU? B           03/24/1848 SL        FILM
BRENDGARD             AUGUSTIN      1824 HIRTZFELDEN          02/16/1850 TX        FILM
BRENDLE               CRESZENE           EHRENSTETTEN B       12/26/1849 A        FILM
BRENDLE               SEBASTIEN          EHRENSTETTEN B       12/26/1849 A        FILM
BRENGARD              AUGUSTIN      1824 HIRTZFELDEN          02/01/1850 TX CHAR PASS
-----------------------------------------------------------------------------------------
BRENIER               FRANCOIS JOSEPH 1815 ZINSWEILER        02/16/1817 A        FILM
BRENIER               MARTIN        1817 ZINSWEILER           02/16/1817 A        FILM
BRENIER MN POSTE      MARGARITE          ZINSWEILER           02/16/1817 A        FILM
BRENIER W W 2 CH      MARTIN        1766 ZINSWEILER           02/16/1817 A        FILM
BRENNER W CH          VALENTIN           ROESCHWOOG           11/25/1854 NO        FILM
-----------------------------------------------------------------------------------------
BRENNOT               GEORGES       1837 MONTBELLIARD         11/26/1864 NY        FILM
BRESCH W W CH         JEAN          1826 STOSSWIHR            06/01/1854 A        FILM
BRETTEY               CHARLES       1850 AUDINCOURT           03/03/1866 NY        FILM
BREUNIG W W 4 CH      HENRI              GRIESBACH            01/01/1817 NY        NO.2
BRICKA                MARIE CATHERINE 1769 WOERTH SUR SAUER   07/23/1828 A        FILM
-----------------------------------------------------------------------------------------
BRIDEN W W 5 CH       ANDRE         1807 OBERENTZEN           09/14/1846 TX        FILM
BRIEDEN CH 5          ANDRE I       1807 OBERENTZEN           09/01/1846 TX CULT PASS
BRIEDEN MN ZURCHER    ELISABETH          OBERENTZEN           09/01/1846 TX        PASS
BRIEDEN S ANDRE I     ANDRE II      1838 OBERENTZEN           09/01/1846 TX        PASS
BRIEDEN S ANDRE I     JAQUES        1840 OBERENTZEN           09/01/1846 TX        PASS
-----------------------------------------------------------------------------------------
BRIEDEN S ANDRE I     JEAN-BAPTISTE 1846 OBERENTZEN           09/01/1846 TX        PASS
BRIEDEN S ANDRE I     JOSEPH        1842 OBERENTZEN           09/01/1846 TX        PASS
BRIEDEN S ANDRE I     LEOPOLD       1845 OBERENTZEN           09/01/1846 TX        PASS
BRIENTZ ?             MATHIAS       1828 RAEDERSHEIM          03/02/1854 A        FILM
BRIGALDIN             MARIE              NIEDERLAUTERBACH     01/01/1850 NO        PRIV
-----------------------------------------------------------------------------------------
BRIGUELEUR            FRANCOIS XAVIER 1824 CHAUX TERR. BELFORT 02/05/1847 NO FARM FILM
BRILL    F OF 3       JEAN               NEUWILLER            01/01/1828 A        FILM
BRILL ?               GEORGE             UHRWILLER            04/09/1819 A        FILM
BRILLMANN             MATHIAS            LAUCHERTHAL          05/12/1849 A        FILM
BRINCKHOFF            ANNA          1777 WESTFALEN            09/17/1845 TX        FILM
```

Lastname	Firstname	Birth Year	Birthplace	Emigration	De	Prof	Source
BRINCKHOFF	BERNHARD	1836	WESTFALEN	09/17/1845	NY		FILM
BRINCKHOFF	GERHARD	1839	WESTFALEN	09/17/1845	TX		FILM
BRINCKHOFF	GERTRAUD	1816	WESTFALEN	09/17/1845	TX		FILM
BRINCKHOFF	HEINRICH	1776	WESTFALEN	09/17/1845	TX		FILM
BRINCKHOFF	THEODOR	1845	WESTFALEN	09/17/1845	TX		FILM
BRINCKHOFF W W 3 CH	HEINRICH	1806	WESTFALEN	09/17/1845	TX		FILM
BRINGARD	ANNA	1829	ROUGEROUTTE	05/20/1865	NY		FILM
BRINGARD	EMILIE	1859	ROUGEGOUTTE	05/20/1865	NY		FILM
BRINGARD	GEORGES	1848	ROUGEGOUTTE	05/20/1865	NY		FILM
BRINGARD	JEAN PIERRE	1827	ROUGEGOUTTE	12/30/1851		FARM	FILM
BRINGARD	JULIENNE	1837	ROUGEGOUTTE	05/20/1865	NY		FILM
BRINGARD	LEONIE	1855	ROUGEGOUTTE	05/20/1865	NY		FILM
BRINGARD	MARIE	1862	ROUGEGOUTTE	05/20/1865	NY		FILM
BRINGARD	OCTAVE	1861	ROUGEGOUTTE	05/20/1865	NY		FILM
BRINGARD	PIERRE JOSEPH	1828	GROSMAGNY	02/19/1852	LV		FILM
BRINGARD	VIKTOR	1834	ROUGEGOUTTE	05/20/1865	NY		FILM
BRINGARD MN MERMIER	FRANCOISE	1795	ANJOUTEY	07/09/1850	LV		FILM
BRINIG	THIEBAUT	1828	GUEWENHEIM	01/17/1852	NY	TAYL	FILM
BRIQUELER	LOUIS	1834	CHAUX TERR. BELFORT	12/04/1855	NO	FARM	FILM
BRIQUELEUR	JACQUES FRANCOS	1828	CHAUX TERR. BELFOR	03/18/1856	NY		FILM
BRISACH	GEORG HEINRICH		NIEDERROEDERN	01/01/1817	A		NO.2
BRISACH	GEORGE HENRY		NIEDERBRONN	02/26/1817	A		FILM
BRISACH W W	GEORG HENRI		NIEDERBRONN	01/01/1817	A	DAYL	FILM
BRISEWALD	VERONIQUE		SWISS	/ /	NY		FILM
BRISINGER	FERDINAND	1824	BENDORF	01/18/1851	NY	TAYL	FILM
BRISVALTER	ANDRE	1828	ROUGEMONT	11/21/1848	CD		FILM
BRIVOH W W 4 CH	MATHIAS ·		DURSTAL? DURETAL?	03/06/1817	A		FILM
BRIWA	ARMAND		STRUTH	01/01/1828	A		FILM
BROBECKER W W	XAVIER	1817	RIBEAUVILLE	03/05/1852	NY	WINE	FILM
BROCHIER W W 6 CH	FRANCOIS	1803	GRANDVILLARS	02/05/1851	CH	FARM	FILM
BROCKHULSEN	GERRET	1825	ZWOLLE NETHERLANDS	04/09/1844	TX		FILM
BROD	ANTON	1824	HIRSCHWIESEN	10/25/1843	TX		FILM
BROD	JOHANN	1822	HIRSCHWIESEN	10/25/1843	TX		FILM
BROD	JOHANN	1793	HIRSCHWIESEN PRUSSIA	10/25/1843	TX		FILM
BRODAG H BARBE	JOSEPH	1809	BLODELSHEIM	12/01/1844	TX	CULT	SHIP
BRODAG MN WEIXLER	URSULA			/ /			
BRODAG W JOSEPH	BARBE	1818	BLODELSHEIM	12/01/1844	TX		SHIP
BRODHAG W W	JOSEPH	1810	BLODELSHEIM	10/11/1844	NO		FILM
BROESCHLIN W W 2 CH	MARTIN	1815	JEBSHEIM	08/14/1855	NY	FARM	FILM
BROGLE	CONRAD	1800	UNTERMELINGEN B	11/30/1854	NY		FILM
BROGLE W W A SI	CONRAD	1820	MULHOUSE	10/31/1853	NY		FILM
BROGLY	MARIE ANNA	1828	ST AMARIN	06/13/1854	A	WEAV	FILM
BROGNARD	GEORGE FREDERIC	1843	AUDINCOURT	04/28/1865	NY		FILM
BROHMANN	JOSEPH		RUNTZENHEIM	01/01/1828	A	LAYB	FILM
BROIHIER W W 6 CH	FRANCOIS	1803	GRANDVILLERS	02/05/1851	CH	FARM	FILM
BROMARD	CONSTANT	1848	AUDINCOURT FRANCE	02/23/1866	NY		FILM
BROMDEL W W 2 CH	JEAN	1813	RIBEAUVILLE	09/13/1853	NY		FILM
BROMLER	MARIE	1815	MUNINGEN	07/05/1854	NY	FARM	FILM
BRONNE	FREDERIC	1818	MULHAUSEN	03/10/1847	NY		FILM
BRONNER	JEAN		DETTWILLER	01/01/1828	A		FILM

Lastname	Firstname	Birth Year	Birthplace	Emigration	De	Prof	Source
BRONNER	JEAN	1828	ILLSACH ?	07/27/1854	NY		FILM
BROSIDE		1830	PLEIN SWISS	12/30/1864	NY		FILM
BROSMANN	MATHIAS		STATTMATTEN	01/01/1828	A		FILM
BROSSE 2 CH	BARBE	1806	RODEREN	09/01/1854	A		FILM
BROSSI	CHARLES		KESKASTEL	03/31/1817	A		FILM
BROUNER	GEORGE		INGENHEIM	01/01/1828	A	DAYL	FILM
BROUNER	JACQUES		INGENHEIM	01/01/1828	A		FILM
BROUNER	MARGUERITE		INGENHEIM	01/01/1828	A		FILM
BROUNER	THIEBAUD		INGENHEIM	01/01/1828	A	DAYL	FILM
BROYEZ	FRANCOIS	1822	RECOUVRANCE TERR. BL	02/15/1847	NY	FARM	FILM
BRUA	HENRI		WOLFSKIRCHEN	01/01/1828	A		FILM
BRUA	JACQUES		WOLFSKIRCHEN	01/01/1828	A		FILM
BRUA	JEAN		HIRSCHLAND	01/01/1828	A		FILM
BRUCHMANN 1 CH	MARIE CATHERINE		FREUDENSTADT W	09/02/1849	A		FILM
BRUCK	SEBASTIEN	1817	NIEDERENTZEN	09/01/1846	TX	DAYL	PASS
BRUCK	SEBASTIEN	1827	NIEDERENTZEN	09/07/1846	TX	DAYL	FILM
BRUCKBUECHLER	GABRIEL	1833	NIEDERLAUTERBACH	01/01/1867	NO	HADR	PRIV
BRUCKER	CHRISTINE		ECKENDORF W	07/21/1849	A		FILM
BRUCKER	GOTTLIEB		ECKENDORF W	07/21/1849	A		FILM
BRUCKER	JEAN	1818	GEISPITZEN	08/21/1854	A	HADR	FILM
BRUCKER	LOUIS PHILLIPE	1838	BERGHEIM ELSASS	10/25/1844	TX		FILM
BRUCKER	MARIE ANNE		HOCHFELDEN	01/01/1828	A		FILM
BRUCKER	THERESE	1807	BERGHEIM ELSASS	10/25/1843	TX		FILM
BRUCKER W W 1 CH	ANTON	1804	BERGHEIM ELSASS	10/25/1843	TX		FILM
BRUCKER W W 5 CH	JOSEPH	1809	RIQUEWIHR	03/07/1855	NO	FARM	FILM
BRUCKS	ELISABETH	1838	WESTFALEN	09/17/1845	TX		FILM
BRUCKS	GERTRAUD	1800	WESTFALEN	09/17/1845	TX		FILM
BRUCKS	GERTRUD	1834	WESTFALEN	09/17/1845	TX		FILM
BRUCKS	HEINRICH	1838	WESTFALEN	09/17/1845	TX		FILM
BRUCKS	JOHANN BERNHARD	1796	WESTFALEN	09/17/1845	TX		FILM
BRUCKS	JOHANN BERNHARD	1837	WESTFALEN	09/17/1845	TX		FILM
BRUECHEL	JOSEPH	1798	BASSECOURT SWISS	04/09/1844	TX		FILM
BRUECHEL	MARGARETHE	1808	BASSECOURT SWISS	04/09/1844	TX		FILM
BRUEDER	BENJAMIN	1821	ST AMARIN	09/27/1856	NY		FILM
BRUEDER	JOSEPH	1826	ST AMARIN	08/01/1844	NY		FILM
BRUEDERLE	JOSEPH		HASLACH B	05/12/1849	A		FILM
BRUEGGEMANN	ANNA	1842	WESTFALEN	09/17/1845	TX		FILM
BRUEGGEMANN	HERMANN	1838	WESTFALEN	09/17/1845	TX		FILM
BRUEGGEMANN	JOHANN THEODOR	1840	WESTFALEN	09/17/1845	TX		FILM
BRUEGGEMANN	WALBURGA	1844	WESTFALEN	09/17/1845	TX		FILM
BRUEGGEMANN W W 5CH	BERNHARD	1807	WESTFALEN	09/17/1845	TX		FILM
BRUEHL	CHRETIEN		BACKNANG W	07/30/1849	A		FILM
BRUEZ	PACIFIQUE		SCHYNDEL	03/30/1853	NY	FARM	FILM
BRUEZ MN BELOT	MARGARETE	1817	SERMAMAGNY TERR BELF	02/29/1856	NO		FILM
BRUEZ MN BELOT	MARGUERITE	1817	SERMAMAGNY	02/29/1856	A		FILM
BRUEZ W W 3 CH	PACIFIQUE	1813	SERMAMAGNY	02/29/1856	NO	CARP	FILM
BRUHON	GUSTAVE	1861	DENNEY	10/27/1863	NY		FILM
BRUHON	JULES	1862	DENNEY	10/27/1863	NY		FILM
BRUHON	MARGERITE	1822	DENNEY	10/27/1863	NY	FARM	FILM
BRUHON	MARIE	1863	DENNEY	10/27/1863	NY		FILM

Lastname	Firstname	Birth Year	Birthplace	Emigration	De	Prof	Source
BRUHON	PIERRE	1846	DENNEY	10/27/1863	NY		FILM
BRUHON W W 4 CH	JOSEPH	1826	DENNEY	10/27/1863	NY		FILM
BRUM	CHRETIEN		LA PETITE PIERRE	01/01/1828	A	SHMA	FILM
BRUM	GUSTAVE		LA PETITE PIERRE	01/01/1828	A		FILM
BRUM	JACQUES	1826	DURRENENTZEN	05/15/1847	CH		FILM
BRUM	PIERRE		LA PETITE PIERRE	01/01/1828	A		FILM
BRUME	LOUIS	1821	ILLZACH	06/23/1847	NY	LAYB	FILM
BRUMER W 4 CH	MAX BARBE	1792	TEUBINGEN W	07/13/1848	LV		FILM
BRUMM	CHRETIEN	1784	ROSTEIG BAS RHIN	03/16/1849	NO	DAYL	FILM
BRUMM	JEAN ADAM		ROSTEIG	01/01/1828	A		FILM
BRUMMER	JACQUES		KEHL B	09/27/1849	A		FILM
BRUN	ANTOINE	1812	ESCHOLTZMATT SWISS	04/09/1851	NY	FARM	FILM
BRUN	AUGUSTIN	1848	CHENEBIER	03/28/1863	NY		FILM
BRUN	FLORIN		CHENEBIER	03/28/1863	NY		FILM
BRUN	MARIE	1860	CHENEBIER	03/28/1863	NY		FILM
BRUN	MIRAND	1791	HAGENBACH	10/13/1847	A		FILM
BRUN	PIERRE	1840	ROPPENTWILLER	08/16/1865	NY		FILM
BRUN	THERESE	1826	STEINSOULTZ	04/03/1849	NY		FILM
BRUN W W 4 CH AND NH	BERNARD	1798	FERRETTE	12/23/1838	NY		FILM
BRUNBY	LAURENT	1817	DIEDENHEIM	11/04/1841	PH		FILM
BRUNDNER	SEBASTIEN	1826	COLMAR	02/29/1848	NY		FILM
BRUNER F OF 9	MICHEL		HOUXWILLER	01/01/1828	A		FILM
BRUNETTE	JOSEPH	1829	ST CROIX AUX MINES	03/20/1857	NY		FILM
BRUNETTE	SEBASTIEN	1831	ST CROIX AUX MINES	03/20/1857	NY		FILM
BRUNETTE	SEBASTIEN	1843	ST.CROIX AUX MINES	03/20/1857	NY		FILM
BRUNETTE W 2 S	MARGUERITE	1803	ST CROIX AUX MINES	03/20/1857	NY		FILM
BRUNGARD	JOSEPH	1803	BALSCHWILLER	02/22/1854	NY	FARM	FILM
BRUNNER	ANNE MARIE	1822	HEGENHEIM	04/03/1849	NY		FILM
BRUNNER	ANTOINE	1833	RIMBACH	03/05/1853	NY	FARM	FILM
BRUNNER	CALVERTON	1834		11/25/1854	NO		FILM
BRUNNER	CATHERINE	1832	WERENTZHAUSEN	06/11/1857	PH	DAYL	FILM
BRUNNER W CH	VALENTIN		ROESCHWOOG	11/25/1854	NO		FILM
BRUNNER W D	JEAN	1792	EMMENDINGEN B	10/24/1851	NY		FILM
BRUNNER W W	BERNHARD	1823	FESSENHEIM	10/24/1851	NY		FILM
BRUNNER W W 2 CH	MERAUD	1808	FERRETTE	07/10/1850	NY		FILM
BRUNNER W W 3 CH	FRANCOIS JOSEPH	1822	FESSENEHM	03/27/1847	NY		FILM
BRUNSCHWICK	CECILE	1818	BELFORT	07/12/1844	NO		FILM
BRUNSER	JEAN		NIEDERLAUTERBACH	01/01/1865	NO		PRIV
BRUNTZ	LAURENT	1817	DIDENHEIM HAUT RHIN	11/04/1841	PH		FILM
BRUNTZ	MATHIEU	1828	RAEDERSHEIM	03/07/1854	NY		FILM
BRUNTZ	MATHIEU	1838	RAEDERSHEIM	09/30/1857	NY		FILM
BRUSSI W W 2 CH	CHARLES		KESKASTEL	01/01/1817	A	DAYL	FILM
BRUST W W 3 CH	FRANCOIS JOSEPH		NIEDERBRONN	03/17/1817	A	CARP	FILM
BRUTSCHY	ANDRE	1827	SOPPE LE BAS	03/07/1854	NY		FILM
BUCH W W 1CH	FRANCOIS ANTOIN		HERMERSWILLER	/ /	A		FILM
BUCHEIT			SCHWEIGHAUSEN	04/12/1845	A		FILM
BUCHELE W W 7 CH	JEAN ULRICH	1816	MALTERS SWISS	03/11/1854	NY		FILM
BUCHER	JEAN THIEBAUT	1821	SCHWEIGHAUSEN	04/26/1847	NY		FILM
BUCHER	PHILLIPE		BALDENHEIM	03/06/1838	A	SHMA	FILM
BUCHER F OF 5	ANTOINE		SCHIRRHEIM	01/01/1828	A	CARP	FILM

Lastname	Firstname	Birth Year	Birthplace	Emigration	De	Prof	Source
BUCHERT	JOSEPH		GUNDERSHOFFEN	01/01/1869	NY		NO.2
BUCHERT W W	JOSEPH		GUNDERSHOFFEN	03/11/1817	A	DAYL	FILM
BUCHES F OF 5	ANTOINE		SCHIRRHEIM	03/05/1838	A	CARP	FILM
BUCHLE W W	LOUIS		STRASSBOURG	03/27/1817	A		FILM
BUCHLER	JEAN		BURCKENWALD	01/01/1828	A		FILM
BUCHLER	JOSEPH		BURCKENWALD	01/01/1828	A		FILM
BUCHLER	LORENZ		GESBRICHEN W	05/08/1849	A		FILM
BUCHLER	LOUIS		BURCKENWALD	01/01/1828	A		FILM
BUCHLER W M	JEAN	1830	HUNSWIHR	11/25/1854	NY		FILM
BUCHLER W W 1 D	JEAN	1808	COLMAR	07/27/1854	NY	WEAV	FILM
BUCHMANN	MICHEL		ALTWILLER	01/01/1828	A	FAMR	FILM
BUCHMUELLER	CHARLES		DURMERSHEIM B	06/21/1849	A		FILM
BUCHS	GEORGE		ESCHBOURG	01/01/1828	A	SHMA	FILM
BUCHTERSTUHL	EMILE	1855	ANJOUTEY	08/11/1866	NY		FILM
BUCHWALDER	JOSEPH	1838	ALTKIRCH	10/02/1866	NY	FARM	FILM
BUCK W W 1 CH	FRANCOIS ANTOIE		HERMERSWILLER	03/29/1817	A	LAYB	FILM
BUCKEL	MICHEL	1825	FORTSCHWIR	08/24/1854	NO		FILM
BUCKEL W W 7 CH	JEAN	1790	CULMAR ? = COLMAR	08/25/1847	NY		FILM
BUCKENMEYER	CARL		STETTEN	04/17/1849	NY		FILM
BUCKENMEYER	MADELEINE		NEEWILLER	01/01/1850	NO		PRIV
BUCKENMEYER	MARTIEN		NEEWILLER	01/01/1850	NO		PRIV
BUCKENMEYER	MARTIN		NEEWILLER	01/01/1850	NO		PRIV
BUCKENMEYER	MARTIN	1808	NEHWILLER	01/01/1866	NO		NO.2
BUCKENMEYER	MARTIN	1864	NEHWILLER	01/01/1866	NO		NO.2
BUCKENMEYER MN WEIBL	MAGDALENA	1842	NEHWILLER	01/01/1866	NO		NO.2
BUCKENMEYER W W 1CH	MARTIN	1840	NEHWILLER	01/01/1866	NO	FARM	NO.2
BUDA	CHARLES		DIEMERINGEN	03/03/1838	A		FILM
BUECHEL	ANTOINE		ROESCHWOOG	01/01/1828	A	LAYB	FILM
BUECHER	JEAN	1835	GUEBWILLER	09/13/1853	NY		FILM
BUECHER	JOSEPH	1808	WINDENTOHLEN?	10/08/1838	NO		FILM
BUECHI F OF 6	PIERRE		PETERSBACH	01/01/1828	A	WEAV	FILM
BUECHI W W 3CH	ANDRE		SCHOENBURG	01/01/1828	A		FILM
BUECHI W W 5 CH	PIERRE		SCHOENBOURG	01/01/1828	A		FILM
BUECHMANN	JOSEPH	1824	ALTKIRCH	03/16/1849		FARR	FILM
BUEHL	MICHEL		ORSCHWEIER B	04/23/1849	A		FILM
BUEHLER W M	MICHEL	1810	HUGSWEIER B	11/22/1843	TX		FILM
BUERLEN	PIERRE PAUL	1818	BENNWIHR	12/11/1856	NY	WINE	FILM
BUERRER	JOSEPH	1818	THANN	09/24/1845	NY		FILM
BUERRER	LOUIS JOSEPH	1840	BITSCHWILLER	05/14/1855	NY		FILM
BUESCH	MARIE		HEIMBACH B	04/19/1849	NY		FILM
BUESS	ANTOINE	1827	ENSISHEIM	12/06/1854	NY		FILM
BUESS	JOSEPH	1828	ENSISHEIM	12/26/1854	NY		FILM
BUGGLE W W 7 CH	JOSEPH		IMMENDINGEN	04/21/1849	NY		FILM
BUGNION	ELISABETHA	1842	CHENEBIER	03/28/1863	NY	FARM	FILM
BUGNOT	LOUISE	1841	ETOBON	08/23/1866	NY	FARM	FILM
BUGVON		1837	ETOBON	03/18/1866	NY		FILM
BUHL	CHARLES	1828	MULHOUSE	11/02/1853	NY		FILM
BUHL	JEAN FREDERIC	1826	MULHOUSE	07/24/1849	NY		FILM
BUHL	MATHIAS	1784	BREITENBACH	11/11/1851	SL		FILM
BUHL	MATHIAS	1786	BREITENBACH	03/16/1846	A		FILM

Lastname	Firstname	Birth Year	Birthplace	Emigration	De	Prof	Source
BUHL CH 6	JOSEPH	1806	MEYENHEIM	02/01/1852	TX	BRLA	PASS
BUHLER	FREDERIC		FREUDENSTADT W	09/12/1842	A		FILM
BUHLER	GASPARD	1808	ST AMARIN	06/13/1850	A		FILM
BUHLER	JOSEPH	1824	VIEUX THANN	05/07/1852	NY		FILM
BUHLER	PAUL		RAUWILLER	03/07/1838	A		FILM
BUHLER	QUILLE		LAHN B	09/30/1849	A		FILM
BUHLMANN	CAROLINE		OFFENBOURG	08/11/1849	A		FILM
BULACHER	FRANZISKA	1798	RIXHEIM	10/25/1843	TX		FILM
BULACHER	FRANZISKA	1825	RIXHEIM	10/25/1843	TX		FILM
BULACHER	JOHANN	1822	RIXHEIM	10/25/1845	TX		FILM
BULACHER D JUSTIN	FRANCOISE	1825	RIXHEIM	10/01/1843	TX		SHIP
BULACHER H FRANCOISE	JUSTIN CH 2	1793	RIXHEIM	10/01/1843	TX	CULT	SHIP
BULACHER S JUSTIN	JEAN	1829	RIXHEIM	10/01/1843	TX		SHIP
BULACHER W JUSTIN	FRANCOISE	1798	RIXHEIM	10/01/1843	TX		SHIP
BULACHER W W 2 CH	JUSTINE	1793	RIXHEIM	10/25/1843	TX		FILM
BULGADIN	ANNE MARIE	1845	NIEDERLAUTERBACH	01/01/1866	NO		PRIV
BULL W W 6CH F INLAW	JOSEPH	1806	OBERSEEBACH BAS RHIN	02/13/1852	TX		FILM
BULLJUNG	ANDRE		OERMINGEN	03/23/1817	A		FILM
BULLMANN	JOSEF	1818	NIEDERLAUTERBACH	01/01/1866	NO		NO.2
BULLMANN	MARIE EVE	1818	NIEDERLAUTERBACH	01/01/1866	NO		PRIV
BUMB	SEBASTIEN	1811	FLEMLINGEN BA	04/15/1842	A		FILM
BUMER	MARIE MARGERITE	1818	MUNSTER	09/23/1844	A		FILM
BUNDSEPT	BENJAMIN	1820	FRELAND	03/06/1848	A	WEAV	FILM
BUNDSEPT	JEAN NICOLAS	1809	FRELAND	02/18/1849	A		FILM
BUNER F OF 9	MICHEL		BOUXVILLER	01/01/1828	A	DRIV	FILM
BUNZ	BABETTE		ECKENDORF W	06/21/1849	A		FILM
BUNZ	JEAN		ECKENDORF W	06/21/1849	A		FILM
BUNZ 2	JEAN		ECKENDORF	01/01/1828	A		FILM
BUOCH F OF 5	FRANCOIS JOSEPH		NIEDERNAI	03/03/1838	A		FILM
BUR W W 7 CH	PHILIPPE		OERMINGEN	03/23/1817	A		FILM
BURCH W W 3 CH	LAURENT	1814	ST MARIE AUX MINES	12/06/1854	NY		FILM
BURCHER	CATHERINE	1806	BLOTZHEIM	05/01/1861	A		FILM
BURCKARDT	CHRISTIAN		VIENBACHE B?	08/24/1849	A		FILM
BURCKBUCHLER	GABRIEL		NIEDERLAUTERBACH	01/01/1850	NO		PRIV
BURCKBUECHLER	FRAN ANTON		REICHSHOFFEN	01/01/1819	A		NO.2
BURCKBUEHLER	GABRIEL	1833	NIEDERLAUTERBACH	01/01/1867	NO	HADR	NO.2
BURCKEL	FRANCOIS		HAGUENAU	01/01/1828	A		FILM
BURCKHARD	JACQUES		NEHWILLERB	04/11/1849	A		FILM
BURCKHARDT	EDUARD		MOTHERN	01/01/1868	NY		NO.2
BURCKHARDT	JACOB	1839	STEINSELTZ	01/01/1866	NY		NO.2
BURCKHARDT	JOSEPH	1832	NIEDERLAUTERBACH	01/01/1866	NO		PRIV
BURCKHARDT	MARTIN	1847	STEINSELTZ	01/01/1868	NY		NO.2
BURCKLE	ANNE	1830	EGENHAUSEN	07/07/1854	NY		FILM
BURCKLE	CHRETIEN	1814	EGENHAUSEN	04/13/1849	NY		FILM
BURCKLE W CH	JOSEPH		ENDERSBACH B OR W	04/21/1849	A		FILM
BURELL D JOSEPH I	ANNE MARIE	1826	ALTDORF	05/01/1844	TX		SHIP
BURELL D JOSEPH I	CATHERINE	1841	ALTDORF	05/01/1844	TX		SHIP
BURELL D JOSEPH I	MADELEINE	1836	ALTDORF	05/01/1844	TX		SHIP
BURELL D JOSEPH I	THERESE	1844	ALTDORF	05/01/1844	TX		SHIP
BURELL MN HABY W JOS	MADELEINE	1805	ALTDORF	05/01/1844	TX		SHIP

Lastname	Firstname	Birth Year	Birthplace	Emigration	De	Prof	Source
BURELL S JOSEPH I	ALOISE	1838	ALTDORF	05/01/1844	TX		SHIP
BURELL S JOSEPH I	BENOIT	1840	ALTDORF	05/01/1844	TX		SHIP
BURELL S JOSEPH I	CYRIAC	1835	ALTDORF	05/01/1844	TX		SHIP
BURELL S JOSEPH I	ETIENNE	1832	ALTDORF	05/01/1844	TX		SHIP
BURELL S JOSEPH I	JEAN BAPTISTE	1830	ALTDORF	05/01/1844	TX		SHIP
BURELL S JOSEPH I	JOSEPH II	1827	ALTDORF	05/01/1844	TX		SHIP
BURG	ANTOINE		HAGUENAU	01/01/1828	A		FILM
BURG	GERTRUD		OHLUNGEN	01/01/1828	A		FILM
BURG	JAQUES	1829	CLEEBURG	01/01/1868	NY	FARM	PRIV
BURG	JEAN	1815	GILDWILLER	08/02/1840	NY		FILM
BURG	JOSEPH	1839	CLEEBURG	01/01/1868	NY		PRIV
BURG	MARIE ANNE		OHLUNGEN	01/01/1828	A		FILM
BURG F OF 3	PHILLIP		WEISLINGEN	01/01/1828	A	CARP	FILM
BURG F OF 4	PIERRE		WEISLINGEN	01/01/1828	A		FILM
BURG F OF 6	BARTOLOME		WEISLINGEN	01/01/1828	A		FILM
BURG F OF 6	GEORGE		SPARSBACH	01/01/1828	A		FILM
BURG W W	PHILIPPE		ECHBOURG	01/01/1828	A	SHMA	FILM
BURG W W 1 CH	MICHEL		ESCHBOURG	01/01/1828	A	TAYL	FILM
BURGARD 2 CH	ANASTASIA	1797	LUTTERBACH	03/11/1854	NY		FILM
BURGARD F OF 2	PIERRE		ERCKARTSWILLER	01/01/1828	A	FARM	FILM
BURGARD MN MUSSE 4CH	MADELAINE	1813	MUENSTER OR MUNSTER	04/02/1856	NY		FILM
BURGATT	EMILIE	1829	THANN	03/22/1855	NY	LAYB	FILM
BURGER	SERAPHIN	1837	MOOSCH	08/11/1853	A	CARP	FILM
BURGER	ANNE MARIE	1808	UFFHOLZ	12/31/1856	TX	LAYB	FILM
BURGER	CATHERINE		OBENHEIM	03/10/1838	A		FILM
BURGER	FRANCOIS ANTOI		UFFHOLTZ	01/05/1857	A		FILM
BURGER	FRANCOIS-ANTOIN	1844	UFFHOLTZ	01/01/1857	TX	DAYL	PASS
BURGER	JEAN	1826	RUSTENHART	07/25/1854	NO		FILM
BURGER	JEAN	1838	SOUFFLENHEIM	03/02/1838	A		FILM
BURGER	JOSEPH	1814	HAGUENAU	01/25/1848	NY		FILM
BURGER	LOUIS	1818	WITTELSHEIM	12/03/1846	PH	DAYL	FILM
BURGER	SOHPIE		GENGENBACH B	05/28/1849	A		FILM
BURGER W 2 S	ELISABETH	1824	CERNAY	08/23/1856	NO		FILM
BURGER CH 3	CHRISTOSOME	1812	MOOSCH	10/01/1853	TX	GOWN	PASS
BURGER CH 8	MADELEINE	1813	WITTELSHEIM	11/01/1854	TX		PASS
BURGER H MADELEINE	JOSEPH CH 7		WITTELSHEIM	01/01/1854	TX		SHIP
BURGER MN SCHOTT	MADELEINE		WITTELSHEIM	01/01/1854	TX		SHIP
BURGER MN SENN	MARIE-ANNE			01/01/1857	TX		PASS
BURGER W BADER ANTOI	ANNE-MARIE	1814	UFFHOLTZ	12/01/1856	TX	DAYL	PASS
BURGER W W 3 CH	CHRETIEN	1812	MOOSCH	10/22/1853	TX		FILM
BURGER W W 8 CH	IGNACE		SOUFFLENHEIM	01/01/1828	A		FILM
BURGERMEISTER	AUGUSTE	1822	WITTERSDORFF	04/14/1851	NO		FILM
BURGHARD	JACQUEZ		NEHWILLER	04/11/1818	A		FILM
BURGHARD	JEAN	1824	MUNTZENHEIM	03/07/1854	A	FARM	FILM
BURGHARD	MARTIN	1830	MUNTZENHEIM	01/20/1852	A	FARM	FILM
BURGHARD MN BAER 2CH	CATHERINA ELISH		NEHWILLER	06/23/1819	A		FILM
BURGHART W W 4 CH	JEAN	1801	MUNTZENHEIM	11/11/1854	CH	FARM	FILM
BURGHOLTZER	JEAN	1845	EBERSMUENSTER BAS RH	09/11/1856	NY		FILM
BURGHOLTZER	MARIE	1850	EBERSMUENSTER BAS RH	09/11/1856	NY		FILM
BURGHOLTZER	MARTIN	1854	EBERSMUENSTER BAS RH	09/11/1856	NY		FILM

Lastname	Firstname	Birth Year	Birthplace	Emigration	De	Prof	Source
BURGHOLTZER	PHILLIPINE	1855	EBERSMUENSTER BAS RH	09/11/1856	NY		FILM
BURGHOLTZER 4CH	CAROLINE	1822	EBERSMUENSTER BAS RH	09/11/1186	NY		FILM
BURGLIN	ANDRE	1818	MARXHEIM	03/29/1852	A	SHMA	FILM
BURGUNDER	MARIE	1842	ST.AMARIN	08/01/1860	TX		PASS
BURGUNDER	PIERRE	1810	STORCKENSOHN	08/20/1841	NO		FILM
BURGUNDER	PIERRE	1821	SONDERSDORF HAUT RHI	04/28/1842	NY	LAYB	FILM
BURGUNDER W W	SYLVESTRE	1824	MOLLAU	09/28/1854	A		FILM
BURGUNDER W W ,NEPHW	SERAPHIN	1815	RANSPACH	12/29/1847	NY		FILM
BURGY	FRANCOIS JOSEPH	1810	HERRLISHEIM	02/03/1848	SL	FARM	FILM
BURGY	JEAN	1830	HERRLISHEIM	10/08/1851	NO	DAYL	FILM
BURGY	MADELAINE	1824	LOGELHEIM	02/12/1853	SL		FILM
BURGY	NICOLAS	1811	OBERHERGHEIM	10/01/1846	TX		PASS
BURGY	SEBASTIEN	1821	LOGELHEIM	03/20/1850	SL		FILM
BURKARD	WENDELIN		BUEHLERTHAL B	04/19/1849	NY		FILM
BURKART	GEORGE		BLAUFELDEN W	06/21/1849	A		FILM
BURKHALTER	NICOLAS		DURSTEL	01/01/1828	A	DAYL	FILM
BURKHARD	CAROLINE		CELBRONN	04/11/1849	A		FILM
BURKHARD	CHRISTIAN		CELBRONN B	04/11/1849	A		FILM
BURLEN	JEAN BAPTISTE	1837	BENNWIHR	07/25/1853	NY	WINE	FILM
BURNER	JOSEPH	1825	BRUNSTATT HAUT RHIN	03/18/1847	NY		FILM
BURR	FREDERIC		BERG	03/01/1838	A		FILM
BURR	HENRI		GUNGWILLER	03/02/1838	A	DAYL	FILM
BURR	JEAN	1825	HIRTZBACH	01/03/1847	NY	BUTC	FILM
BURR	NICOLAS		BETTWILLER	02/28/1838	A		FILM
BURR	PHILIPPE		BETTWILLER	02/28/1838	A	FARM	FILM
BURRER	CATHERINE	1828	THANN	06/16/1846	NY		FILM
BURRER	CHARLES	1826	THANN	09/30/1845	NY		FILM
BURRER	MARIE ANN	1783	ROMMERSMATT ?	07/09/1846	NY		FILM
BURRER W W CH	IGNACE	1820	GUEBENHEIM	02/16/1846	NY		FILM
BURRI	MICHEL		SCHOENBOURG	01/01/1828	A	WEAV	FILM
BURRUS	CHRISTINE	1825	THANN	04/11/1857	NY		FILM
BURRUS	GEORGES		MARLENHEIM	01/01/1828	A		FILM
BURTECHERT W W CH	PIERRE FRANCOIS	1829	ROUFFACH	06/09/1847	NY		FILM
BURTSCH	SOPHIE	1825	BERNARDSWILLER	12/08/1854	NO		FILM
BURTSCHY	ELAINE	1824	BISEL	01/20/1852	NY	WEAV	FILM
BURTSCHY	JEAN	1815	BISEL	12/10/1839	NO	FARM	FILM
BURTZ	GEORGES	1813	ARTZENHEIM	01/22/1849	NY	FARM	FILM
BURTZ	MADELAINE	1797	THANN	10/25/1843	AX		FILM
BURTZ	MAGDALENA	1797	THANN	10/25/1843	TX		FILM
BURTZ	MORITZ	1808	THANN	10/25/1843	TX		FILM
BURTZ W W	MORITZ	1811	THANN	10/25/1843	TX		FILM
BURY	HENRI		BRUMATH	01/01/1828	A		FILM
BURY	JEAN	1815	GILDWILLER	08/02/1840	NY		FILM
BURY	JEAN	1820	KUENHEIM	07/11/1850	CH	WEAV	FILM
BURY	JEAN	1822	GILDWILLER	02/26/1845	CN		FILM
BURY W 4 CH	MADELAINE	1809	BURRHAUPT LE BAS	05/20/1857	NY	DAYL	FILM
BUSCH	ADELE	1844	SCHAFFHAUSEN	01/01/1865	NY		NO.2
BUSCH	CATHERINE	1829	BANNWIHR	02/23/1857	NO		FILM
BUSCH	CATHERINE	1829	MULHOUSE	02/25/1857	NO		FILM
BUSCH	JOHANN	1845	WINTZENBACH	01/01/1869	NY		NO.2

Lastname	Firstname	Birth Year	Birthplace	Emigration	De	Prof	39 Source
BUSCH	JUSTINE	1854	BANNWIHR	02/23/1857	NO		FILM
BUSCHER	LEOPOLD	1801	BITZUM AUSTRIA	08/26/1852	PH		FILM
BUSCHLER	CAROLINE		GASBRICHEN ? W	05/06/1849	A		FILM
BUSSINGER	XAVIER	1806	WITTNAU SWISS	01/14/1849	NY		FILM
BUSSLER	JOSEPH	1801	TRAUBACH LE HAUT	05/23/1846	A	FARM	FILM
BUTIGER W W 5CH	JEAN	1818	FALKWILLER HAUT-RHIN	08/28/1844	NO		FILM
BUTTERLIN CH 7	PIERRE PAUL	1805	ROUFFACH	09/01/1846	TX	TONM	PASS
BUZY W W 2 CH	HENRY		GOERSDORF	03/22/1817	A		FILM

40   Birth
Lastname   Firstname   Year Birthplace   Emigration De Prof Source
----
CACHEUX   CONSTANT   1836 BELFORT   02/17/1853 A   FILM
CACHOT CH 2   DOMINIQUE   1799 GRANGES   11/13/1845 NY   FILM
CAESAR   JEAN PHILIPPE   1820 MULHOUSE   01/26/1850 NY   FILM
CAESAR   MAXIMILIAN FERD 1815 STRASSBOURG   10/11/1850 NO   FILM
CALMELAT   MARGUERITE   1820 HAUT-RHIN   12/01/1844 TX   SHIP

CALMELAT WW AND CH 2   JAQUES   1802 SENTHEIM   12/01/1844 TX CULT SHIP
CALMELAT WW AND CH 9   JAQUES   BRETTEN   10/31/1844 PH   FILM
CANAL H ROSE   PIERRE FRANCOIS 1815 AUXELLES-BAS   07/14/1854 NY   FILM
CARDOT   JEAN BAPTISTE   EVETTE   10/06/1865 NY   FILM
CARDOT   JEAN BAPTISTE   1823 ERETTE   10/08/1865 NY   FILM

CAREL   JOSEPH   PLOBSHEIM   01/01/1828 A   FILM
CARL   ANNE MARIE   WEITBRUCH   01/01/1828 A   FILM
CARL   MARGHUERITE   WEITBRUCH   01/01/1828 A   FILM
CASPAR   BAUW   WURMLINGEN   07/03/1849 A   FILM
CASPAR   JAQUES   WEITTERSWILLER   01/01/1828 A   FILM

CASSEL   ADAM   STRUTH   01/01/1828 A   FILM
CASSEL   ADAM   VOLKSBERG   01/01/1828 A   FILM
CASSEL   GEORGES   SIEWILLER   03/02/1838 A   FILM
CASTIAN   ANTOINE   NIEDERSCHAEFFOLSHEIM   01/01/1828 A   FILM
CATHEY   CATHERINE   1830 DENNEY   12/01/1865 NO   FILM

CATTE   PROSPER   1831 CUNELIERES   04/25/1854 NY   FILM
CATTE WW AND CH 4   PIERRE LOUIS   1804 CUNELIERES   04/16/1853 NY   FILM
CATTEY   FELIX   1823 FAVEROIS   08/06/1855 NO   FILM
CATTEY   FRANCOIS   1823 FAVEROIS   11/04/1857 NY   FILM
CATTEY   VERONIQUE   1814 FAVEROIS   08/17/1840 NY   FILM

CATTEY H MARIANNE   JEAN CLAUDE   1839 DENNEY   01/06/1866 NY   FILM
CATTEY S JEAN CLAUDE   PIERRE   1866 DENNEY   01/06/1866 NY   FILM
CATTEY W JEAN CLAUDE   MARIANNE   1841 DENNEY   01/06/1866 NY   FILM
CATTEZ   JOSEPH   1828 JONCHEREY   04/17/1855 NY   FILM
CATTY   LOUIS   1829 JONCHEREY   02/22/1866 NY   FILM

CAUSE   HENRI   1830 STRASBOURG   12/13/1853 A   FILM
CAYOT   PIERRE   1828 ROPPE   03/25/1846 NY   FILM
CAYOT CH 3   GEORGES   1808 ROPPE   02/08/1856 NY   FILM
CAYOT D GEORGES   MARGUERITE   1838 ROPPE   02/08/1856 NY   FILM
CAYOT S GEORGES   GEORGES   1840 ROPPE   02/08/1856 NY   FILM

CAYOT S GEORGES   PIERRE   1842 ROPPE   02/08/1856 NY   FILM
CAYOT WW   PIERRE FRANCOIS 1822 PHAFFANS   06/15/1853 NY   FILM
CAYOT WW AND CH 4   FRANCOIS   1799 RENNEY   09/05/1843 NY   FILM
CAYOT WW AND CH 4   GEORGES   PHAFFANS   / /   NY   FILM
CAYOT WW AND CH 5   FRANCOIS   1806 BESSONCOURT   10/05/1846 NY   FILM

CEASAR   MAXIMILIAN FERD 1815 STRASBOURG   10/11/1850 NO   FILM
CENLIVRES   CHARLES LOUIS   1828 LUTRAN   09/03/1850 NO   FILM
CENTLIVRE   CELESTIN   BELFORT   01/07/1853 NY   FILM
CENTLIVRE   CHARLES LEVY   1828 LUTRAN   07/26/1847 A   FILM
CENTLIVRE   MARIE   1814 LUTRAN   03/14/1842 NY   FILM

CENTLIVRE CH 3   CELESTIN   1804 BELFORT   01/07/1863 NY   FILM
CENTLIVRE D CELESTIN   CELESTIN   1850 BELFORT   01/07/1863 NY   FILM
CENTLIVRE D CELESTIN   CLEMENTIN   1854 BELFORT   01/07/1863 NY   FILM
CENTLIVRE S CELESTIN   CHARLES   1848 BELFORT   01/07/1863 NY   FILM
CENTLIVRES   MADELEINE   1825 LUTRAN   05/10/1852 NY   FILM
```
```

Lastname	Firstname	Birth Year	Birthplace	Emigration	De	Prof	Source
CERICH	JEAN	1825	HORBOURG	05/27/1852	NY		FILM
CHABERT	GREGOIRE	1818	SCHOENAU	08/09/1849	PH		FILM
CHABOUDE WW AND CH 2	JOSEPH	1820	BOUROGNE	04/07/1845	NY		FILM
CHANEY W MARCHAND JO	MARIE	1817	BRETAGNE	03/03/1846	NY		FILM
CHAPOUTOT	JULIE	1838	COURCHATON	02/15/1866	NY		FILM
CHAPPE WW AND CH 2	XAVIER	1800	DENNY	08/23/1845	NY		FILM
CHAPPUIS	AUGUSTE	1860	ESCHAVANNE	02/23/1863	NY		FILM
CHAPPUIS	JEANE	1825	ESCHAVANNE	02/23/1863	NY		FILM
CHAPPUIS	JULIE	1856	ESCHAVANNE	02/23/1863	NY		FILM
CHAPPUIS	SIMONE	1828	ESCAVANNE	02/23/1863	NY		FILM
CHAPPUIS WW AND CH	FERDINAND	1810	CHAPELLE	10/06/1846	A		FILM
CHAPPUIS WW AND CH 1	NICOLAS	1793	GUEBWILLER	05/01/1857	NY		FILM
CHAPUIS	FRANCOIS XAVIER	1827	CROIX	11/07/1854	NO		FILM
CHAPUIS	FREDERIC	1830	CROIX	01/25/1844	NY		FILM
CHAPUIS	MARGUERITE	1827	LEPUIX	04/13/1849	NY		FILM
CHAPUIS	PIERRE JULIEN	1807	CHAPELLE	10/10/1846	A		FILM
CHAPUIS	PIERRE JULIEN	1807	LA CHAPELLE SOUS CHA	02/13/1845	NY		FILM
CHAPUIS WW AND CH 2	JEAN BAPTISTE	1802	LA CHAPELLE SOUS CHA	02/21/1845	NY		FILM
CHAPUIS WW AND CH 2	THIEBAUD	1792	SERMAMAGNY	02/05/1847	NO		FILM
CHARDON	AUGUSTE	1839	CHALONVILLARS	02/13/1866	NY		FILM
CHARDON	XAVIER	1833	DANIJOUTIN	05/06/1851	NY		FILM
CHARPENTIER	FRANCOIS	1826	URCEREY	10/21/1851	NY		FILM
CHARPIAT	FRANCOIS JOSEPH	1825	FAVEROIS	06/03/1845	NO		FILM
CHARPIAT	MATHIAS	1819	FAVEROIS	08/17/1840	NY		FILM
CHARPIOT	ADELE	1834	BARD	05/04/1866	NY		FILM
CHARPIOT	SUSANNE	1835	AUDINCOURT	04/28/1865	NY		FILM
CHARTON	PIERRE	1834	DANJOUTIN	11/22/1853	NY		
CHARTON WW AND CH 3	PIERRE	1809	BLAMONT	04/06/1846	NY		FILM
CHASSIGNET	JEAN BAPTISTE	1825	BAVILLIERS	01/25/1855	A		FILM
CHASSIGNET	JOSEPH	1822	PUIX	03/09/1839	NY		FILM
CHATELOT	FRANCOIS	1818	ESSERT	03/04/1846	NY		FILM
CHATELOT CH 2	SOPHIE	1826	ESSERT	09/01/1854	A		FILM
CHATELOT WW CH 1	JOSEPH	1824	SALBERT	09/20/1852	NY		FILM
CHATILLON	LOUIS	1838	SERMAMAGNY	10/04/1865	NY		FILM
CHATILLON	MARIE JOSEPHINE	1809	SALBERT	02/18/1846	NY		FILM
CHAUVEZ	FRANCOIS	1838	VALDORS	02/21/1857	NY		FILM
CHAVANN	JEAN	1824	ASPACH	03/28/1855	NY		FILM
CHAVANN	THERESE	1822	MASSEVAUX	10/01/1847	NY		FILM
CHAVAUX WW AND CH 3	MAURICE	1807	ST. DIZIER	04/09/1847	NY		FILM
CHEMER	ANTON	1821	HAMBACH PRUSSIA	04/09/1844	TX		FILM
CHENAL	NICOLAS	1835	ROMBACH	10/03/1856	NY		FILM
CHERAY WW AND CH 3	FRANCOIS	1797	BAVILLIERS	08/02/1846	NO		FILM
CHERENOT	CELESTIN	1834	MONTREUX JEUNE	12/15/1853	NY		FILM
CHERENOT CH 2	JAQUES	1792	MONTREUX JEUNE	05/29/1847	NY		FILM
CHETELAT	AGNES	1824	GUEBWILLER	08/22/1849	NY		FILM
CHEULLOT	PIERRE	1839	LEVAL	07/28/1855	NY		FILM
CHEVALIER	FRANCOIS	1830	MEROUX	04/11/1857	NY		FILM
CHEVALIER	IGNACE	1819	COLMAR	02/09/1852	NY		FILM
CHEVALIER	VIRGINIE		BREBOTTE	04/09/1863	NY		FILM
CHEVALIER	VIRGINIE	1839	BREBOTTE	04/09/1863	NY		FILM

Lastname	Firstname	Birth Year	Birthplace	Emigration	De	Prof	Source
CHEVILLIOT	MARIE	1849	CHALONVILLARD	02/17/1864	NY		FILM
CHEVILLOT	FRANCOIS	1822	ST. GERMAIN	04/03/1841	NY		FILM
CHEVILLOT	JULIE	1833	ST. GERMAIN	11/20/1853	NY		FILM
CHEVILLOT	PIERRE	1839	LEVAL	07/28/1855	NY		FILM
CHEVILLOT	PIERRE	1852	CHALONVILLARD	03/05/1865	NY		FILM
CHEVIRON	EUGENE	1826	BARLEDUC	10/19/1847	NY		FILM
CHIFFRE	JOSEPHINE	1845	CHENEBIE	03/13/1865	NY		FILM
CHIQUI F OF 5	JEAN		DAUENDORF	01/01/1828	A	DAYL	FILM
CHOFEY	JULES	1857	BEAUCOURT	02/22/1866	NY		FILM
CHOFFAT	PIERRE FRANCOIS	1813	FOUSSEMAGNE	03/02/1844	NY		
CHOFFAT	URSANNE	1785	WILDENSTEIN	09/05/1853	NY		FILM
CHOFFAT CH 3	CATHERINE	1807	BRETAGNE	09/05/1844	NY		FILM
CHOFFIN	ANDRE	1839	ROUGEMONT	02/28/1863	NY		FILM
CHOPAY	JOSEPH		SWISS	/ /	NY		FILM
CHOPAY	JULES	1840	SWISS	10/01/1863	NY		FILM
CHOPAY	LEONIC		SWISS	/ /	NY		FILM
CHOPAY	ROSALIE	1865	SWISS	/ /	NY		FILM
CHOPAY	VERONIQUE		SWISS	/ /	NY		FILM
CHOQUARD	ADELE	1833	DELLE	03/05/1853	NY		FILM
CHOULLAIRE	DESIRE	1818	HERSIGNE	03/14/1864	NY		FILM
CHRIST	JEAN	1811	FERETTE	05/22/1866	NY		FILM
CHRIST	JEAN PIERRE	1820	PLAINFAING	04/14/1856	NY		FILM
CHRIST	JOSEPH		LICHTENBERG	01/01/1828	A		FILM
CHRIST	LOUISE	1964	FERRETTE	05/22/1866	NY		FILM
CHRIST	MARC		FERRETTE	01/01/1828	NY		FILM
CHRIST	MARIE	1846	EBERBACH	01/01/1867	NY		NO.2
CHRIST	MICHEL		FERRETTE	01/01/1828	NY		FILM
CHRIST	MULLER	1818	ANDELNANS	02/17/1864	NY		FILM
CHRIST WW AND CH 4	LOUIS	1813	RIBEAUVILLE	09/22/1854	NO		FILM
CHRISTEN	FRANCOIS JOSEPH	1825	BALSCHWILLER	05/19/1847	NY		FILM
CHRISTEN	JEAN JAQUES	1823	BALSCHWILLER	04/13/1847	NY		FILM
CHRISTEN	JOSEPH	1824	ST. AMARIN	08/11/1854	NY		FILM
CHRISTEN	JOSEPH	1825	FELLERINGEN	01/06/1845	NY		FILM
CHRISTEN	MARIE ANNE	1820	ST. AMRIN	08/11/1854	CA		FILM
CHRISTEN	PIERRE	1826	BALSCHWILLER	06/10/1840	NY		FILM
CHRISTEN	THIEBAUT	1822	ST. AMARIN	08/11/1854	NY		FILM
CHRISTEN S CHARLES		1853	CERNAY	01/13/1857	NO		FILM
CHRISTEN S CHARLES		1856	CERNAY	01/13/1857	NO		FILM
CHRISTEN W CHARLES		1829	CERNAY	01/13/1857	NO		FILM
CHRISTEN WW AND CH 2	CHARLES	1830	CERNAY	01/13/1857	NO		FILM
CHRISTILES	JOSEPH	1769	BAS-RHIN	12/01/1844	TX	CULT	SHIP
CHRISTILES D PIERRE	BARBE	1833	BAS-RHIN	12/01/1844	TX		SHIP
CHRISTILES D PIERRE	CATHERINE	1828	BAS-RHIN	12/01/1844	TX		SHIP
CHRISTILES D PIERRE	SALOME	1835	BAS-RHIN	12/01/1844	TX		SHIP
CHRISTILES H MARIE	PIERRE GEORGES	1804	BAS-RHIN	12/01/1844	TX	CULT	SHIP
CHRISTILES MN FORST	MARIE SALOME	1802	BAS-RHIN	12/01/1844	TX		SHIP
CHRISTILES S PIERRE	GEORGES	1836	BAS-RHIN	12/01/1844	TX		SHIP
CHRISTILES S PIERRE	JOSEPH	1838	BAS-RHIN	12/01/1844	TX		SHIP
CHRISTILES S PIERRE	MICHEL	1840	BAS-RHIN	12/01/1844	TX		SHIP
CHRISTMANN	NICOLAS		VOLKSBERG	01/01/1828	A		FILM

Lastname	Firstname	Birth Year	Birthplace	Emigration	De	Prof	43 Source
CHRISTMANN WW CH 4	MICHEL		OBERHOFFEN	03/01/1838	A		FILM
CHRITEN	PAUL	1823	BALSCHWILLER	02/11/1852	NY		FILM
CIMBS WW AND CH	JEAN	1815	BOTZINGEN	02/09/1852	NY		FILM
CLAD	DIDIER	1837	MOLLAU	02/18/1854	PH		FILM
CLADEN	MORAND	1833	HOCHSTADT	10/01/1860	NY		FILM
CLADONG	AUGUSTIN		ENGENTHAL	01/01/1828	A		FILM
CLADY WW AND CH	PIERRE		BERSTHEIM	01/01/1828	A		FILM
CLAERR	JEAN	1814	FELLERINGEN	04/13/1844	NY		FILM
CLAERR H ANAIS CH 1	JEAN	1813	HAUT-RHIN	12/01/1844	TX		SHIP
CLAERR S JEAN	XAVIER	1843	HAUT-RHIN	12/01/1844	TX		SHIP
CLAERR W JEAN	ANAIS	1819	HAUT-RHIN	12/01/1844	TX		SHIP
CLAIROTEL	DOMINIQUE CONST	1813	NEUF BRISACH	05/07/1844	TX		FILM
CLAIROTET	DOMINIQUE CONST	1813	CERNAY	05/01/1844	TX	CLER	PASS
CLARC CH 4	ANNE	1803	FELLERINGEN	03/28/1854	NY		FILM
CLAREQUIN	JOSEPH	1823	VOURRENANS	06/13/1853	NY		FILM
CLAREYNIN	MATHIEU	1815	BELFORT	03/20/1863	NY		FILM
CLAUSS	ANTOINE		ROPPENHEIM	03/06/1838	A		FILM
CLAUSS	CHARLES	1834	COLMAR	09/13/1851	NO		FILM
CLAUSS	GEORGE		LEUTENHEIM	03/01/1838	A		FILM
CLAUSS	GEORGE MICHEL	1813	ZINSWEILLER	02/16/1817	A		FILM
CLAUSS	GEORGES		BOUXWILLER	01/01/1828	A		FILM
CLAUSS	NICOLAS		WEITBRUCH	01/01/1828	A		FILM
CLAUSS CH1	JAQUES	1803	HATTEN	01/22/1848	A		FILM
CLAUSS D JOSEPH	MAGDELAINE	1811	ZINSWEILER	02/16/1817	A		FILM
CLAUSS D JOSEPH	MARIE ANNE	1817	ZINSWEILER	02/16/1817	A		FILM
CLAUSS F GEORGE MICH	JOSEPH	1786	ZINSWEILER	02/16/1817	A		FILM
CLEISS	GEORGE		WEINBOURG	01/01/1828	A		FILM
CLEMANN	JEAN	1835	MULHOUSE	05/22/1857	NY		FILM
CLEMENT WW AND CH	JOSEPH		ESCHBOURG	01/01/1828	A		FILM
CLEMENTZ	ANTOINE	1816	KRUTH	06/24/1851	NY		FILM
CLEMENTZ	CARHERINE		ESCHBOURG	01/01/1828	A		FILM
CLEMENTZ	CATHERINE		ESCHBOURG	01/01/1828	A		FILM
CLEMENTZ	JEAN		ESCHBOURG	01/01/1828	A		FILM
CLEMENTZ	MADELEINE		ESCHBOURG	01/01/1828	A		FILM
CLEMENTZ	VINCENT		OTTERSTHAL	01/01/1828	A		FILM
CLER	XAVIER	1829	BRECHAUMONT	03/12/1847	NY		FILM
CLER CH 3	MADELAINE	1812	HERICOURT	03/19/1845	NY		FILM
CLERC	CHARLES JEAN B	1842	HERICOURT	03/13/1865	NY		FILM
CLERC	CONRAD	1842	FRAHIER	09/29/1865	NY		FILM
CLERC	FRANCOIS AUGUST	1837	OFFEMONT	11/22/1856	NY		FILM
CLERC	LOUIS	1829	ROUGEGOUTTE	07/01/1852	NY		FILM
CLERC	ROSINE	1833	OFFEMONT	11/22/1856	NY		FILM
CLO WW AND CH 4	MATHIAS	1825	NIEDERMORSCHWIHR	07/25/1853	CI		FILM
CLODONG	ANTOINE		ENGENTHAL	01/01/1828	A		FILM
CLODONG	AUGUSTIN		ENGENTHAL	01/01/1828	A		FILM
CLOR	JEAN THEIBAUD			/ /			
CLOR	JEAN THEIBAUD	1814	BRECHAUMONT	03/13/1844	NY		FILM
CLOR WW	JEAN BAPTISTE	1824	BRECHAUMONT	02/05/1845	OH		FILM
CLOR WW AND CH 3	FRANCOIS JOSEPH	1812	MOOS	05/03/1851	NY		FILM
CLOU	ANNE MARIE	1821	BRECHAUMONT	04/09/1847	NY		FILM

Lastname	Firstname	Birth Year	Birthplace	Emigration	De	Prof	Source
COCHETAILLE D BLAISE	JULIE	1851	MORVILLARS	10/06/1865	NY		FILM
COCHETAILLE H AGATHE	BLAISE	1807	MORVILLARS	10/06/1865	NY		
COCHETAILLE S BLAISE	HUBERT	1849	MORVILLARS	10/06/1865	NY		FILM
COCHETAILLE S BLAISE	HUMBERT	1859	MORVILLARS	10/06/1865	NY		FILM
COCHETAILLE W BLAISE	AGATHE CH 3	1820	MORVILLARS	10/06/1865	NY		FILM
COIGON		1816	DAMRAT	08/31/1866	NO		FILM
COLETTE	ALOISE	1834	MULHOUSE	02/20/1864	NY		FILM
COLIN	JAQUES	1807	PUIX	03/04/1839	NY		FILM
COLIN	JEAN BAPTISTE	1822	PUIX	09/03/1852	NY		FILM
COLIN	JOSEPH	1814	PUIX	02/14/1844	NY		FILM
COLLAS	JEAN BAPTISTE	1830	ST.MARIE AUX MINES	03/14/1850	NO		FILM
COLLET	SEBASTIEN		NOMMENHEIM	01/01/1828	A		FILM
COLLEZ	FRANCOIS		CHENEBIER	03/28/1863	NY		FILM
COLLEZ	FRANCOIS	1839	CHERREBIER	03/28/1863	NY		FILM
COLLIGNON	CATHERINE	1831	LIEPRE	10/02/1854	NO		FILM
COLLIGNON	JEAN GEORGE	1821	LIEPRE	02/21/1848	NO		FILM
COLLIGNON	JOSEPH	1814	LIEPRE	09/02/1847	NO		FILM
COLLIGNON	MARIE ROSE	1819	LIEPRE	03/21/1841	NO		FILM
COLLIN	CATHERINE	1805	ROMBACH	01/13/1857	NO		FILM
COLLIN	HENRY	1827	LIEPRE	09/02/1847	NO		FILM
COLLIN	JEAN BAPTISTE	1819	LIEPRE	03/30/1839	NO		FILM
COLLIN	JEAN FRANCOIS	1803	ROMBACH	04/22/1839	A		FILM
COLLIN	JEAN FREDERIC	1835	LIEPRE	10/02/1854	NO		FILM
COLLIN CH 5	JUSTINE	1808	LUCELLE	03/30/1854	NY		FILM
COMMENT	MARCEL	1837	MONTBELIARD	01/30/1863	NY		FILM
COMMENT	SEBASTIEN	1823	SWISS	03/13/1863	NY		FILM
COMMERG WW AND CH 4	JEAN LE JEUN	1798	OSTHEIM	04/23/1844	NY		FILM
COMMERY	JEAN	1826	OSTHEIM	05/23/1845	NY		FILM
CONCLAST	JOSEPHINE	1824	KAYSERSBERG	02/03/1854	NO		FILM
CONDRE WW AND CH 4	NICOLAS	1802	BRETTEN	11/06/1844	PH		FILM
CONNETTI	ALFRED	1847	HERICOURT	08/30/1866	A		FILM
CONRAD	EUGENE	1822	BERGHEIM	03/25/1852	NO		FILM
CONRAD	HENRY	1806	ZINSWEILLER	02/16/1817	A		FILM
CONRAD	JAQUES CHRISTOP	1821	BELFORT	08/10/1839	NO		FILM
CONRAD	JOSEPH		LA CHAPELLE	01/01/1855	TX	PROF	SHIP
CONRAD	MADELEINE	1808	ZINSWEILLER	02/16/1817	A		FILM
CONRAD	PIERRE	1783	ZINSWEILLER	02/16/1817	A		FILM
CONRAD	PIERRE	1804	ZINSWEILLER	02/16/1817	A		FILM
CONRAD	ZACHARIE	1819	FELLERINGEN	08/14/1844	NO		FILM
CONRAD D PIERRE	CATHERINE	1814	ZINSWEILLER	02/16/1817	A		FILM
CONRAD D PIERRE	DOROTHEE	1812	ZINSWEILLER	02/16/1817	A		FILM
CONRAD WW AND CH 4	CHARLES		HARSKIRCHEN	01/01/1828	A		FILM
CONSTANS	MARGUERITE		GUNGWILLER	03/02/1838	NY		FILM
CONTE WW AND CH 3	JEAN FRANCOIS	1824	BOTANS	09/28/1854	NY		FILM
COPIN	FRANCOIS	1833	GROSMAGNY	09/22/1853	NY		FILM
CORBAT	FRANCOIS XAVIER	1839	SWISS	10/30/1866	NY		FILM
CORBIS	MEINRAD ALPHONS	1826	BELFORT	07/18/1853	NY		FILM
CORDIER	ADELE	1829	MONTBELIARD	09/30/1864	NY		FILM
CORDIER	JEAN		BOERSCH	01/01/1854	TX		SHIP
CORDIER	JEAN BAPTISTE	1804	BRETTEN	10/15/1844	PH		FILM

Lastname	Firstname	Birth Year	Birthplace	Emigration	De	Prof	Source
CORDIER	MARIE	1848	VALDOIE	03/27/1865	NY		FILM
CORDIER	REMIS	1810	BRETTEN	10/25/1843	TX		FILM
CORDIER H MAGARET CH	JEAN FRANCOIS	1804	BRETTEN	12/01/1844	TX	CULT	SHIP
CORDIER S JEAN-FRANC	CELESTIN	1841	BRETTEN	12/01/1844	TX		SHIP
CORDIER S JEAN-FRANC	FRANCOIS	1844	BRETTEN	12/01/1844	TX		SHIP
CORDIER S JEAN-FRANC	JOSEPH	1843	BRETTEN	12/01/1844	TX		SHIP
CORDIER S JEAN-FRANC	NICOLAS	1839	BRETTEN	12/01/1844	TX		SHIP
CORDIER W JEAN FRANC	MARGARET	1825	BRETTEN	12/01/1844	TX		SHIP
CORDONNIER	JEAN	1798	LA CHAPELLE	12/01/1844	TX	CULT	SHIP
CORDONNIER	NICOLAS	1804	BRETTEN	09/21/1844	PH		FILM
CORDONNIER	NICOLAS	1811	HAUT-RHIN	12/01/1844	TX	CULT	SHIP
CORE	J.CLAUDE	1841	ROMAGNY FRANCE	10/05/1866	NY	FARM	FILM
CORTOLENDY W W 2 CH	NICOLAS	1817	GRIESBACH	07/22/1852	NY	POTM	FILM
COTTEL	DAVID	1829	SAINTE MARIE AUX MIS	11/10/1854	NY	FARM	FILM
COTTEL W W 5 CH	FRANCOIS JOSEPH	1802	BOUROGNE	03/26/1844	NY	FARM	FILM
COTTET	GEORGE	1836	MORVILLERS	08/28/1866	NY	FARM	FILM
COTTET	LEONIE	1855	MORVILLERS	08/28/1866	NY		FILM
COTTET	MARIE ANNE	1777	FROIDEFONTAIN	02/03/1852	CH		FILM
COTTET	ROSE	1823	GRANVILLARN	07/15/1854	NY		FILM
COTTET	VICTIORE	1841	MORVILLARS	08/28/1866	NY		FILM
COTTET W CANAL PIERR	ROSE	1819	AUXELLES BAS	07/14/1854	NY		FILM
COTTEY	JEAN PIERRE	1818	TANCHEREY?	04/20/1848	NY		FILM
COULERENT	JAQUES	1823	BERNEVILLE PAS DE CS	04/20/1848	NY		FILM
COULERENT W W A D	JAQUES	1857	BERNEVILLE PAS DE CS	03/17/1857	NY	LAYB	FILM
COURAND	JOSEPH	1821	LA CHAPELLE SOUS ROU	04/03/1855	A	FARM	FILM
COURANT	LAURENT EDUARD	1801	POISSE SERRE ET OISE	10/05/1839	NY		FILM
COUREAUX	JEAN LOUIS	1818	THANNENKIRCHEN	10/06/1852	CH	FARM	FILM
COURNIER	JOSEPH	1819	LEPUIZ	08/11/1853	NY	FARM	FILM
COURS	EUGENE	1833	ARCEY	10/10/1865	NY		FILM
COURTET	FRANCOIS	1826	ANDETHANS? TERR BELF	11/10/1846	NY	FARM	FILM
COURTOD	NICOLAS	1825	OFFEMONT	07/08/1851	NY		FILM
COURTOIS	FRANCOIS	1800	ST FERREOL SAVOIS	06/26/1856	A		PRIV
COURTOT	FLORENTINE	1832	BOTANS TERR BELFORT	04/28/1855	NY	FARM	FILM
COURTOT	JAQUES	1805	OFFEMONT	03/27/1843	NY	FARM	FILM
COURTOT	JEAN PIERRE	1806	CHATENOIS	02/13/1840	NY	FARM	FILM
COURTOT	JOSEPH	1826	SEVENANS TERR BELFOT	11/10/1846	NY	CARP	FILM
COURTOT	LEONIE	1845	OFFEMONT	10/18/1866	NY		FILM
COUTURIER	CATHERINE	1827	MONTREUX JEUNE	05/02/1854	NY		FILM
COUVERT	HENRY	1843	REAUCOURT	09/30/1864	NY	FARM	FILM
COUVET	FRANCOIS	1828	FERRETTE	01/27/1847	NY		FILM
COYOT	JEAN CLAUDE	1818	BESSONCOURT	02/25/1848	NY	FARM	FILM
COYOT	JOSEPHINE	1830	BESSONCOURT	03/03/1848	NY	FARM	FILM
CRAVE	JEAN BAPTISTE	1828	ST GERMAIN	02/12/1847	NY	FARM	FILM
CRAVE	JEAN BAPTISTE	1832	ST GERMAIN	01/21/1851	NY	FARM	FILM
CRAVE	MADELEINE	1843	EGUENIGE	06/03/1864	NY	FARM	FILM
CRAVE	PIERRE	1846	EGUENIGUE	06/03/1864	NY	FARM	FILM
CRAVE W W 2 CH	PIERRE CLAUDE	1813	ST GERMAIN	06/24/1854	NY		FILM
CRAX	LOUIS		SCHILTIGHEIM	03/03/1817	A		FILM
CRENNES	MADELAINE		PARIS	06/18/1850	NY		FILM
CRESD	VINCENT	1819	SOPPE LE BAS	08/18/1848	A		FILM

Lastname	Firstname	Birth Year	Birthplace	Emigration	De	Prof	Source
CREUEL W W 3 CH	CHARLES		ADAMSWILLER	03/17/1817	A		FILM
CREVOISERAT	JOSEPH	1824	DELLE	02/07/1839	NY		FILM
CRIQUE	MICHEL		ETTENDORF	10/30/1854	A		FILM
CRIQUI	ANDREAS	1866	DUERRENBACH	01/01/1866	NY		NO.2
CRIQUI	ANTOINE		ETTENDORF	01/01/1828	A	SHMA	FILM
CRIQUI	CATHERINA	1860	DUERRENBACH	01/01/1866	NY		NO.2
CRIQUI	JAUES		ETTENDORF	01/01/1828	A	DAYL	FILM
CRIQUI	JOSEPH	1859	DUERRENBACH	01/01/1866	NY		NO.2
CRIQUI	KARL	1861	DUERRENBACH	01/01/1866	NY		NO.2
CRIQUI MN ZEHRINGER	CATHERINE		DUERRENBACH	01/01/1866	NY		NO.2
CRIQUI W W 4 CH	JOSEPH	1832	DUERRENBACH	01/01/1866	NY	BLSM	NO.2
CRITZ	ANNA EVE	1823	GUEVENATTEN	03/21/1845	A		FILM
CRITZ W W 7 CH	JOSEPH	1795	GUEVENATTEN	11/17/1847	A		FILM
CROENI	JEAN	1838	STRA⊥BOURG	07/06/1865	NY		FILM
CROMINAUD	FRANCOIS JOSEPH	1820	BERRWILLER	09/18/1854	NY		FILM
CROSSE W FAM	MARIE	1766	PEROUSE TERR. BELFOR	10/14/1852	NO		FILM
CUENAT	CASPARD		MARCKOLSHEIM	01/01/1828	A	DAYL	FILM
CUENAT	FRANCOIS	1842	ROUGEGOUTTE ?	05/01/1865	NY		FILM
CUENIN	CELESTIN	1828	BESSONCOURT	03/03/1848	NY		FILM
CUENIN	FERDINAND	1812	VENOLINCOURT	09/30/1864	NY		FILM
CUENOT W W 4 CH	ANTOINE	1794	OFFEMONT	01/30/1840	A		FILM
CUINEL	AUGUSTE	1828	DANJOUTIN	06/02/1847	NY		FILM
CUISINIER	MARIE JEAN	1806	VELESCOIT ?	04/17/1840	NY		FILM
CUISINIER W W 3 CH	ANTOINE	1801	VELLESCOT	01/25/1847	NY		FILM
CULLI	JEAN		RATZWILLER	01/01/1828	A	TAYL	FILM
CUNAL	MARIE ANNE	1831	GIROMAGNY	06/08/1852	A		FILM
CUNOT	PIERE FRANCOIS	1811	TERR. BELFORT	07/12/1864	NY		FILM
CUPPLES	CAMILLE	1793	WOOLER ENGLAND	09/17/1845	TX		FILM
CUPPLES	CHARLES	1825	WOOLER ENGLAND	09/17/1845	TX		FILM
CUPPLES	GEORGE	1816	LEEGERWOOD MANGO SCO	11/22/1843	TX	DMED	FILM
CUPPLES	JANE	1822	WOOLER ENGLAND	09/17/1845	TX		FILM
CUPPLES S OF GEORGE	ROBERT	1838	LEEGERWOOD MENGE SCO	11/22/1843	TX		FILM
CUPPLES W OF GEORGE	CHRISTINE	1816	LEEGERWOOD MENGE SCO	11/22/1843	TX		FILM
CUSANDIER OR CUSAUDR	DANIEL		FORT LOUIS	01/01/1828	A	LAYB	FILM
CUSAUDIER	JOSEPH		FORT LOUIS	01/01/1828	A		FILM
CUSAUDIER	MARGUERITE		FORT LOUIS	01/01/1828	A		FILM
CUTTEY	NICOLAS	1821	BAVEROIS	05/23/1840	NY	FARM	FILM
CUYOT	PIERRE	1828	ROPPE TERR. BELFORT	04/25/1846	NY	FARM	FILM
CUYOT W W 4 CH	GEORGES	1808	PHAFFANS TERR. BELFT	03/19/1846	NY	FARM	FILM

Lastname	Firstname	Birth Year	Birthplace	Emigration	De	Prof	Source
DABST	CATHERINA	1849	LAUTERBURG	01/01/1867	NY		NO.2
DABST	JOSEPHINE	1853	LAUTERBURG	01/01/1867	NY		NO.2
DABST	KARL FRANZ	1851	LAUTERBURG	01/01/1867	NY		NO.2
DABST	LUDWIG	1846	LAUTERBURG	01/01/1867	NY		NO.2
DABST	MAGDALENA	1857	LAUTERBURG	01/01/1867	NY		NO.2
DABST MN MICHEL	ELISABETH	1820	LAUTERBURG	01/01/1867	NY		NO.2
DABST W W 5 CH	FRANZ	1816	LAUTERBURG	01/01/1867	NY	BRLA	NO.2
DACH	JEAN		ENGENTHAL	03/05/1840	A		FILM
DACH	THERESE		WAGENBOURG	01/01/1828	A		FILM
DAEGELEN W F 5CH	XAVIER	1806	GUEWENHEIM	06/03/1846	A		
DAETER F OF 8			PFAFFENHOFEN	01/01/1828	A		FILM
DAGARD H MARIANNE	JAQUES CH 3	1804	HAUT-RHIN	12/01/1844	TX		SHIP
DAGARD S JAQUES	GEORGES	1830	HAUT-RHIN	12/01/1844	TX		SHIP
DAGARD S JAQUES	HENRI	1837	HAUT-RHIN	12/01/1844	TX		SHIP
DAGARD S JAQUES	JAQUES	1840	HAUT-RHIN	12/01/1844	TX		SHIP
DAGRD W JAQUES	MARIANNE	1811	HAUT-RHIN	12/01/1844	TX		SHIP
DAHLMANN	ABRAHAM	1851	SURBOURG	01/01/1869	NO		NO.2
DAHLMANN	ABRAHAM	1863	SURBOURG	01/01/1869	NO		NO.2
DAHLMANN	ADELE	1864	WEISSENBURG	01/01/1866	NY		NO.2
DAHLMANN	EMMA	1861	WEISSENBURG	01/01/1866	NY		NO.2
DAHLMANN	JULIUS	1858	WEISSENBURG	01/01/1866	NY		NO.2
DAHLMANN	LUCIA	1860	WEISSENBURG	01/01/1866	NY		NO.2
DAHLMANN W 4 CH	HORTENSE	1842	WEISSENBURG	01/01/1866	NY		NO.2
DAHMEN	CLARA	1800	HAMBACH(P)	04/09/1844	TX		FILM
DALIA W 3 CH	MADELEINE	1824	RIBEAUVILLE	09/25/1855	NO		FILM
DALLER	FRANCOIS JOSEPH	1832	GUNDOLSHEIM	11/13/1852	SL		FILM
DALSHEIMER	EDEL		TIEFFENBACH	01/01/1828	A		FILM
DALSHEIMER	GOTTFRIED		TIEFFENBACH	01/01/1828	A		FILM
DALSHEIMER	NATHAN		STRUTH	01/01/1828	A		FILM
DALSHEIMER	NAUSE		TIEFENBACH	01/01/1828	A		FILM
DAMBACH	JOSEPH		SCHLIERSTADT(B)	05/12/1849	A		FILM
DAMBACHER	NICOLAS		PFALZWEYER	01/01/1828	A		FILM
DAMBACHER F OF 3	JAQUES		PFALZWEYER	01/01/1828	A		FILM
DAMBACHER F OF 3	JEAN		PFALZWEYER	01/01/1828	A		FILM
DAMM	JACOB		WEIDEN W	05/23/1849	A		FILM
DAMMERONG	ETIENNE		DETTWILLER	01/01/1828	A		FILM
DAMOLTE	FRANCOIS GEORGE	1827	ARGIESANS	07/20/1847	NY		FILM
DANCOURT CH 2	SIGISMOND	1804	CROIX	04/01/1845	TX	GWON	PASS
DANGEL	BLAISE	1831	MOOS	09/26/1853	NY		FILM
DANGLER	JACOB	1850	OBERBETSCHDORF	01/01/1850	NY		NO.2
DANHEISER	MICHEL	1819	SAVERNE(BAS SIENE)	05/18/1846	NO		FILM
DANICHERT	XAVIER		MATZENHEIM	02/28/1838	A		FILM
DANIEL	MARIE ROSALIE	1824	AUDINCOURT	03/03/1845	NY		FILM
DANIEL	MARIE VICTOIRE	1830	MONDEURE	08/02/1849	NY		FILM
DANKER	CHARLES		HAMBACH	03/08/1838	A		FILM
DANKER	JEAN BAPTISTE	1818	HELFRANTZKIRCH	06/04/1857	NY		PRIV
DANKER	MATHIAS		HAMBACH	03/08/1838	A		FILM
DANKER	NICOLAS		HAMBACH	03/08/1836	A	TAYL	FILM
DANKER	PHILLIPE		HAMBACH	03/08/1836	A		FILM
DANKER	PIERRE		HAMBACH	03/08/1836	A		FILM

Lastname	Firstname	Birth Year	Birthplace	Emigration	De	Prof	Source
DANKER	VALENTIN		LAUTERBOURG	09/19/1855	NY		FILM
DANNE	CHARLES	1833	ST.MARIE AUX MINES	10/20/1854	NO		FILM
DANNECKER	ANDREAS			06/08/1837	A		FILM
DANNEMüLLER	BENOIT		SCHIRRHEIN	01/01/1828	A		FILM
DANNEMüLLER	GEORGE		SCHIRRHEIN	01/01/1828	A		FILM
DANNEMüLLER	JEAN		SCHIRRHEIN	01/01/1828	A		FILM
DANNER	GEORGE		NIEDERBRONN	06/30/1837	A		FILM
DANNER	JACOB		WEIDEN(W)	05/23/1849	A		FILM
DANNER	VALERIE	1826	MONTBELIARD(DOUBS)	10/20/1846	SL		FILM
DANNER W W 2CH	JOSEPH	1790	KAYSERSBERG	03/21/1854	NO		FILM
DANNHAEUSER	LEOPOLD	1840	WEISSENBURG	01/01/1865	NY		NO.2
DANOL	ELISE	1848	AUDINCOURT	04/30/1864	NY		FILM
DANSLIN		1791	STROUSSDORF(BA)	05/30/1839	NY		FILM
DANTZER W W 8CH	PIERRE MORAND	1807	ALTKIRCH	04/08/1848	NY		FILM
DANZAS	JENNY	1808	PARIS	05/26/1838	SL		FILM
DANZAS	JENNY	1808	PARIS	06/14/1841	SL		FILM
DANZAS	LUIS	1788	COLMAR	11/02/1847	SL		FILM
DASSBACH	JEAN		HATTMATT	01/01/1828	A		FILM
DATT	JEAN FREDERIC	1809	MUNSTER	07/27/1854	PH		FILM
DATTLER	FRANCOIS JOSEPH	1828	PFETTERHAUSEN	03/02/1847	NY		FILM
DAUCOURT	SIGISMOND	1804	CROIX (TERR OF BELFO	04/17/1845	TX		FILM
DAUER	JEAN BAPTISTE	1818	HELFRANTZKIRCH	06/04/1857	NY		FILM
DAUER	NICOLAS		HAMBACH	03/08/1838	A	DAYL	FILM
DAUER	VALENTIN		LAUTERBOURG	09/19/1855	NY		FILM
DAUKER	CH		HAMBACH	03/08/1838	A		FILM
DAUL	ANDRE		SOUFFLENHEIM	01/01/1828	A		FILM
DAUL	FRANCOIS ANTOIN	1815	ROESCHWOOG	08/21/1847	A		FILM
DAUL	IGNACE		SOUFFLENHEIM	01/01/1828	A		FILM
DAUL	IGNACE LE GRAND		SOUFFLENHEIM	01/01/1828	A		FILM
DAUL	JOSEPH		ROESCHWOOG	01/01/1828	A		FILM
DAUL	MARGUERITE	1786	ZINSWEILLER	02/16/1817	A		FILM
DAUL	XAVIER		SOUFFLENHEIM	01/01/1828	A		FILM
DAUM	JEAN BAPTISTE	1841	VOCLERSCHBACH(B)	12/18/1869	A		FILM
DAUMI	MICHAEL		GRIESBACH	03/31/1817	A		FILM
DAUMOURT	SIGISMOND	1804	CROIX	04/17/1845	TX		FILM
DAUNEN	GEORG		SOULTZ (W)	04/03/1898	NY		FILM
DAUSCHLER	MICHEL	1826	HAUT-RHIN	12/01/1844	TX	STON	SHIP
DAUSMANN	DAVID		DRACHENBRONN	03/28/1817	A		FILM
DAUW	JEAN		SCHWALDORF(W)	05/03/1849	NY		FILM
DAUW	MARTIN		SCHWALDORF(W)	05/03/1849	NY		FILM
DAVID	BENOIT	1806	BOURG AT BRANCHE	03/23/1840	NO		FILM
DAVID	CONRAD	1826	LIEPRE	05/12/1846	NO		FILM
DAVID	FREDERIC	1804	BRINKHEIM(B)	08/31/1848	NY		FILM
DAVID	THERESE		HECKING HOHENZOLLERN	03/16/1849	A		FILM
DEAR	JEAN PIERRE	1825	GRANDVILLARS	01/07/1847	NY		FILM
DEBAER	MAGDALENA	1861	OBERBETSCHDORF	01/01/1869	NY		NO.2
DEBAER W CH	MAGDALENA	1839	OBERBETSCHDORF	01/01/1869	NY		NO.2
DEBAIN	VICTOIRE	1836	MESIRE	03/17/1857	A		FILM
DEBENATH	SEBASTIEN	1814	LINTHAL	09/10/1857	NO		FILM
DEBS	JEAN DANIEL	1821	COLMAR	11/06/1848	NY		FILM

Lastname	Firstname	Birth Year	Birthplace	Emigration	De	Prof	Source
DECAT	CELESTIN	1840	VELSCOT	08/21/1861	NY		FILM
DECHER	JEAN		ETZINGEN	05/30/1849	NY		FILM
DECK	BENEDICT	1865	MOTHERN	01/01/1867	NY		NO.2
DECK	BENEDIKT		MOTHERN	01/01/1868	NY		NO.2
DECK	CATHERINA	1865	MOTHERN	01/01/1867	NY		NO.2
DECK	EDUARD	1866	MOTHERN	01/01/1867	NY		NO.2
DECK	FRANCOIS PIERRE	1815	GUEBWILLER	10/14/1850	NY		FILM
DECK	JOHANN	1854	MOTHERN	01/01/1867	NY		NO.2
DECK	JULIE VICTOIRE	1814	GUEBWILLER	09/18/1850	NY		FILM
DECK	LORENZ	1850	MOTHERN	01/01/1867	NY		NO.2
DECK	MAGDALENA	1858	MOTHERN	01/01/1867	NY		NO.2
DECK	MARTIN		LANDSHAUSEN	04/07/1849	NY		FILM
DECK	VALENTIN	1848	NEHWILLER	01/01/1866	NO		NO.2
DECK W 7 CH	JOHANN	1813	MOTHERN	01/01/1867	NY	FARM	NO.2
DECKER	CHRETIEN		DURSTEL	01/01/1828	A		FILM
DECKER	CRETIEN		PFALZWEYER	01/01/1828	A		FILM
DECKER	FRANCOIS		DURSTEL	03/18/1838	A		FILM
DECKER	LEOPOLD		PFALZWEYER	03/29/1817	A		FILM
DECKERT	BENOIT	1795	BLODELSHEIM	11/03/1846	TX		FILM
DECKERT	MICHEL	1807	BLODELSHEIM	08/06/1849	TX	CULT	PASS
DECKERT	MICHEL	1807	BLODELSHEIM	08/06/1849	TX		FILM
DECKERT CH 5	BENOIT	1795	BLODELSHEIM	11/01/1846	TX	MARF	PASS
DECKERT S BENOIT	BAPTISTE	1828	BLODELSHEIM	11/01/1846	TX		PASS
DECKERT S BENOIT	BENOIT	1824	BLODELSHEIM	11/01/1846	TX		PASS
DECKERT S BENOIT	FRANCOIS	1831	BLODELSHEIM	11/01/1846	TX		PASS
DECKERT S BENOIT	IGNACE	1835	BLODELSHEIM	11/01/1846	TX		PASS
DECKERT S BENOIT	ZACHARIE	1830	BLODELSHEIM	11/01/1846	TX		PASS
DECKERT W BENOIT	MARIANNE	1797		11/01/1846	TX		PASS
DECOMBE	ADELE	1835	VAL ST DIZIER	09/29/1865	NY		FILM
DECOMBE	ADELE	1863	VAL ST DIZIER	09/29/1865	NY		FILM
DECOR	ETIENNE	1830	VAL ST DIZIER	10/14/1865	NY		
DECOUE	J		PARIS	11/10/1863	NY		FILM
DECOUE	JULES		PARIS	09/04/1856	NY		FILM
DECOUVY	FRANCOIS JOSEPH	1820	ST CROIX EN PLEINE	04/28/1842	NO		FILM
DEES	FREDERIC		WOERTH SUR SAUER	07/13/1828	A		FILM
DEESS	JEAN PHILIPPE		WOERTH SUR SAUER	07/13/1828	A		FILM
DEFOURNEAUX	ANTOINE	1820	GRANDVILLARS	08/06/1851	NO		FILM
DEFOURNEAUX	JOSEPH	1835	LEBETAIN(BEL)	11/23/1854	NY		FILM
DEGENHARD	JOSEPH	1813	MASEVAUX	02/16/1846	NY		FILM
DEIBER	JEAN BAPTISTE	1820	DELLE(BEL)	08/14/1847	A		FILM
DEICKELBOHRER	NAZAIRE		BRUMATH	01/01/1828	A		FILM
DEIKER	FRANCOIS		GRIESBACH	01/01/1820	A		FILM
DEINEUSY	PIERRE OSINE	1828	PUIX	09/03/1852	NY		FILM
DEISS	FREDERIC	1824	BOUXWILLER	08/05/1841	NO		FILM
DEISS	GEORGE		OBERSOULTZBACH	01/01/1820	A		FILM
DEJOUX	FREDERIC LUCIEN	1811	ST MARIE AUX MINES	11/10/1854	NY		FILM
DELACROIX	JEAN	1819	LEYMEN	02/09/1847	NY		FILM
DELAET	CELESTIN	1840	BLODELSHEIM	01/01/1861	TX	CULT	PASS
DELAET	FERDINANT	1833	VELSCOT(BEL)	03/23/1855	NY		FILM
DELAET	JEAN PIERRE	1809	GROSNE(BEL)	02/17/1847	NY		FILM

Lastname	Firstname	Birth Year	Birthplace	Emigration	De	Prof	Source
DELAET	JOSEPH	1827	VELSCOT	03/02/1847	NY		FILM
DELAIT	FRANCOISE	1824	TURCKHEIM	02/08/1844	NY		FILM
DELAIT	HENRI	1793	VELLESCOT	09/04/1844	NY		FILM
DELARUE	CHRISTOPHE	1803	WERENTZ HOUSE	10/19/1844	VI		FILM
DELARUE	JEAN FRANCOIS	1801	LAUFFEN SWISS	08/07/1848	A		FILM
DELARUE	MICHEL	1812	ESCH (SWISS)	03/10/1841	A		FILM
DELARUE	SEBASTIEN	1805	WINKEL	08/23/1838	A		FILM
DELCOMBE	ADELE	1835	VAL ST. DIZIER	01/29/1865	NY		FILM
DELCOMBE	ADELE	1863	VAL ST DIZIER	09/29/1865	NY		FILM
DELLANG	IGNACE	1794	WOLFERSDORF	04/19/1847	NY		FILM
DELLENBACH	LEONARD	1835	ST MARIE AUX MINES	10/02/1854	NY		FILM
DELMISCH	JEAN ADAM	1817	PFETTERHAUSEN	03/02/1847	NY		FILM
DELOIE	CONSTANT	1849	FRAHIER	02/10/1866	NY		FILM
DELOYE	JOSEPH ALEXANDE	1832	FRAHIER	07/08/1847	NO		FILM
DELUNSCH	JEAN ADAM	1817	PFEFFERHAUSEN	03/02/1847	NY		FILM
DEMENSY	JEAN BAPTISTE	1833	ROUGEGOUTTE	10/30/1852	NY		FILM
DEMENUS	ADOLPHE	1834	CHAUX	09/27/1854	NY		FILM
DEMEUSY	FRANCOIS XAVIER	1836	VESCEMENT	09/05/1854	NY		FILM
DEMEUSY	GEORGE JEAN BAP	1824	ROUGEGOUTTE	10/30/1852	NY		FILM
DEMEUSY	MATHIAS	1815	PUIX	03/04/1839	NY		FILM
DEMONG	JEAN PIERRE	1805	ETEIMBES	03/14/1855	NY		FILM
DEMONGE	PIERRE	1813	ANGEOT	10/12/1844	A		FILM
DEMOUGE	JEAN PIERRE	1799	ETEIMBES	03/14/1855	NY		FILM
DEMOUGE	JEAN PIERRE	1805	ETEIMBES	03/14/1855	NY		FILM
DEMOUGEOT	LOUISE	1841	DUNG	05/04/1866	NY		FILM
DENIER	NICOLAS	1811	REPPE	09/05/1850	NY		FILM
DENIER CH 1	JAQUES	1807	HAUT-RHIN	12/01/1844	TX	CULT	SHIP
DENIER D JAQUES	CECILE	1843	HAUT-RHIN	12/01/1844	TX		SHIP
DENNER	MARIE ANTOINETT	1822	FRIESEN	08/07/1848	NY		FILM
DENNER W W D 2 S	IGNACE JEAN BAP	1792	GUEBWILLER	02/13/1852	A		FILM
DENNI F OF 4	HENRY		BOUXWILLER	01/01/1828	A		FILM
DENNI F OF 7	GEORGES		IMBSHEIM	01/01/1828	A		FILM
DENNINGER	MICHEL		HATTMATT	01/01/1828	A		FILM
DENNSTEIN WW AND CH6	JAQUES	1802	BLEICHEISEN	10/20/1854	NO		FILM
DENNY	VAL		TRIMBACH	01/01/1850	NO		PRIV
DENNY	VALENTIN	1849	TRIEMBACH	01/01/1867	NO	FARM	NO.2
DENNY H BA. ARNOLD	PETER		BUEHL	01/01/1843	A		SUESS
DENNY MN ARNOLD	BARBARA		BUEHL	01/01/1843	A		SUESS
DENTZ WW AND CH 1	FRIDOLIN		BINZGEN	01/01/1828	A		FILM
DENTZ W W 3CH	ADAM		BINZGEN	05/23/1833	A		FILM
DENTZ WW CH 1	FRIDOLIN		BINZGEN(B)	01/01/1828	A		FILM
DENVELINO	JAQUES		NEHWILLER	01/26/1817	A		FILM
DENVELINO	JAQUES		NEHWILLER	02/26/1817	A		FILM
DENZE WW	JOSEPH	1830	LUTTERBACH	05/25/1855	NY		FILM
DERAT	CELESTIN	1840	VELESCOT(TERR OF BEL	08/21/1861	NY		FILM
DERIE	LOUIS		WEISLINGEN	01/01/1828	A		FILM
DERIE	LOUIS		WESILINGEN	01/01/1828	A		FILM
DERN	CAROLINE	1822	EBERMUNSTER	09/11/1856	NY		FILM
DERN AND CH 1	MARGUERITE	1829	MULHOUSE	10/08/1856	NY		FILM
DERN CH 1	MARGUERITE	1829	MULHOUSE	10/08/1856	NY		FILM

Lastname	Firstname	Birth Year	Birthplace	Emigration	De	Prof	Source
DEROILLES	JULES	1842	PERCUSE	02/17/1864	NY		FILM
DEROILLES	JULES	1844	PERCUSE	02/17/1864	NY		FILM
DESALM	ANTON	1821	SENTHEIM	11/22/1843	TX		FILM
DESALM D ANTOINE	CATHERINE	1831	STRASBOURG	11/01/1843	TX		SHIP
DESALM D ANTOINE	MADELEINE	1829	STRASBOURG	11/01/1843	TX		SHIP
DESALM H MADELEINE	ANTOINE CH 4	1794	STRASBOURG	11/01/1843	TX	CULT	SHIP
DESALM MN ROTH W ANT	MADELEINE	1800	STRASBOURG	11/01/1843	TX		SHIP
DESALM S ANTOINE	ANTOINE II	1821	STRASBOURG	11/01/1843	TX		SHIP
DESALM S ANTOINE	JOSEPH	1834	STRASBOURG	11/01/1843	TX		SHIP
DESCH	MARIE ANNE	1818	RAEDERSHEIM	12/21/1852	NO		FILM
DESCH	MARIE ANNE	1818	RAEDERSHEIM	12/21/1852	NO		FILM
DESCHAMP W W 3CH	JOSEPH	1815	EBERSHEIM	02/17/1855	A		FILM
DESCHER	CHRETIEN		NEUWILLER	01/01/1828	A		FILM
DESDAMES	JEAN BAPTISTE	1824	ROPPE	01/24/1856	NY		FILM
DESDAMES	NICOLAS	1819	ROPPE	05/19/1846	NY		FILM
DESDAMES	SEBASTIEN	1817	ROPPE	08/03/1846	A		FILM
DESIEBER	PHILIPP	1846	WEISSENBURG	01/01/1867	NY	BAKE	NO.2
DESPOIRER	JEAN BAPTISTE	1795	EVETTE	09/27/1847	NY		FILM
DESPRETZ	XAVIER	1807	BRETANGE	09/08/1844	NY		FILM
DESPREZ		1831	BETRANGE	05/02/1854	NY		FILM
DESPREZ	ANDRE C	1824	CROSNE	12/05/1844	NY		FILM
DESPREZ	CELESTIN J.P.	1831	BETRANGE	05/02/1854	NY		FILM
DETE	JOSEPH	1806	LIEPRE	10/15/1838	NO		FILM
DETOURNEAUX	ANTOINE	1820	GRANDVILLARS	08/06/1851	NO		FILM
DETTLIN	PIERRE FREDERIC		WESTHOFFEN	01/01/1828	A		FILM
DEUBLER	THERESA		ROTHENBURG	05/09/1849	NY		FILM
DEUCHLER	CAROLINE	1843	NIEDERROEDERN	01/01/1868	NY		NO.2
DEUR	ETIENNE	1829	ST. DIZIER	11/07/1854	NO		FILM
DEUR	FRANCOIS	1829	ST. DIZIER	04/09/1847	NY		FILM
DEUR	GEORGES	1808	GRANDVILLERS	08/09/1855	NY		FILM
DEUR	JEAN PIERRE	1815	GRANDVILLER	01/07/1847	NY		FILM
DEUR	JEAN PIERRE	1825	GRANDVILLER	01/07/1847	NY		FILM
DEUR	JOSEPH	1830	GRANDVILLERS	08/13/1849	NY		FILM
DEUTSCH	J. GEORGE		PLOBSHEIM	01/01/1828	A		FILM
DEUTZ	ADAM		BINZGEN	05/23/1833	A		FILM
DEUTZ WW AND CH 1	FRIDOLIN		BINZGEN	05/23/1833	A		FILM
DEUTZ WW CH 3	ADAM		BINZGEN	05/25/1833	A		FILM
DEUTZER	JAQUES	1798	CLEEBOURG	01/22/1852	NY		FILM
DEVAILLE	JULES	1842	PEROUSE	02/17/1864	NY		FILM
DEYBACH	DOMINIQUE	1821	GUNDOLSHEIM	03/17/1853	NO		FILM
DEYLE	PRAX	1816	ETUEFFONT-HAUT	10/25/1839	NY		FILM
DICHT	JAQUES		BARR	02/27/1838	A		FILM
DICK	ANDRE FRANSKIND		ESCHBOURG	05/23/1817	A		FILM
DICK	CHRETIEN		DOSSENHEIM	01/01/1828	A		FILM
DICK	ETIENNE		MARCKENHEIM	05/01/1838	A		FILM
DICK	HENRI		DEHLINGEN	01/01/1828	A		FILM
DICK WW AND CH 1	ANDRE		ESCHBOURG	05/23/1817	A		FILM
DICKELBOHIER	SALOME	1836	BEBLENHEIM	07/28/1854	NY		FILM
DICKELICHIER	SALOME	1836	BEBLENHEIM	07/28/1854	NY		FILM
DICKMAN	MICHEL		WASSELONE	01/01/1828	A		FILM

Lastname	Firstname	Birth Year	Birthplace	Emigration	De	Prof	Source
DIDIER	JEAN CLAUDE		BONHOMME	04/21/1847	NY		FILM
DIDIER	JEAN CLAUDE	1815	ST. GERMAIN	05/13/1843	NY		FILM
DIDIER	NICOLAS	1807	ETUEFFORT-HAUT	11/26/1851	FL		FILM
DIDIER WW	ALEXIS	1823	PETIT MAGNY	10/06/1853	NY		FILM
DIDIER WW AND CH 1	JEAN BAPTISTE	1814	COURTEGENY SWISS	07/15/1844	PH		FILM
DIDIER WW CH 4	THEIBAUD	1803	EMEFFONT-HAUTE	05/07/1840	NY		FILM
DIDIER WW CH 5	FRANCOIS	1800	MEZIRE	04/01/1845	NY		FILM
DIDIERJEAN	VIRGINE	1821	ST CROIX AUX MINES	05/18/1856	NY		FILM
DIDIERLAURENT C 4	CONRAD	1832	FELLERING	06/01/1860	TX	FACT	PASS
DIDIERLAURENT D CONR	ALOISE	1857	FELLERING	09/01/1860	TX		PASS
DIDIERLAURENT S CONR	CHARLES	1860	FELLERING	01/01/1860	TX		PASS
DIDIERLAURENT S CONR	JEAN-BAPTISTE	1858	FELLERING	09/01/1860	TX		PASS
DIDIERLAURENT S CONR	JOSEPH	1857	FELLERING	09/01/1860	TX		PASS
DIDIERLAURENTMNBRUTS	WALBURG	1829		09/01/1860	TX		PASS
DIDION	JEAN BAPTISTE	1818	GUEMAR	05/21/1841	A		FILM
DIDION	JEAN BAPTISTE	1818	GUEMAR	03/26/1841	PH		FILM
DIEBOLD			KEHL	05/31/1849	A		FILM
DIEBOLD	ANNA		INGENHEIM	02/18/1828	A		FILM
DIEBOLD	CATHERINE		FROHMUHL	01/01/1828	A		
DIEBOLD	DAVID		HATTMATT	01/01/1828	A		FILM
DIEBOLD	ELISE		FROHMUHL	01/01/1828	A		FILM
DIEBOLD	MARIE		KORK	08/16/1842	A		FILM
DIEBOLD	MARIE		KORK	08/16/1842	NY		FILM
DIEBOLT	ANTOINE		DAUENDORF	01/01/1828	A		FILM
DIEBOLT	ANTOINE		SCHAFFHAUSEN	01/01/1828	A		FILM
DIEBOLT	IGNACE		DAUENDORF	01/01/1828	A		FILM
DIEBOLT	JAQUES		DAUERDORF	01/01/1828	A		FILM
DIEDERMANN	JEAN	1811	HAUT-RHIN	12/01/1844	TX	CULT	SHIP
DIEFF CH 4	XAVIER	1787	SOPPE-LE-HAUT	11/01/1844	TX	DAYL	PASS
DIEFFENE	JEANE G.		NIEDERBRONN	05/21/1817	A		FILM
DIEHL	JAQUES		BAAR	02/27/1838	A		FILM
DIEHL	JOHANNES		MANNHEIM	05/10/1816	A		FILM
DIEHL	LOUISE		BARR	02/27/1838	A		FILM
DIELENSCHNEIDER	L.		SINGRIST	01/01/1828	A		FILM
DIELLER	J.			01/01/1843	TX		SHIP
DIEMANN	FRANCOIS A.	1809	TRAUBACH-LE-HAUT	02/16/1854	A		FILM
DIEMER	CATHERINE		NIEDERMODERN	01/01/1828	A		FILM
DIEMER	JAQUES		NIEDERMODERN	01/01/1828	A		FILM
DIEMER	MADELAINE		NIEDERMODERN	01/01/1828	A		FILM
DIEMER	MARGRET		NIEDERMODERN	01/01/1828	A		FILM
DIEMERT	ANTOINE		DETTWILLER	01/01/1828	A		FILM
DIEMERT	ELISABETH		MORSHWILLER	01/01/1828	A		FILM
DIEMERT	PIERRE		ERCKARTSWILLER	01/01/1828	A		FILM
DIEMUNCH	JEAN NICOLAS	1796	MASEVAUX	05/29/1838			
DIEMUND	ROSALIE	1827	MASSEVAUX	05/31/1857	NY		FILM
DIEMUNSCH WW	BOURCARD	1803	KRUTH	01/09/1855	NY		FILM
DIENER	ANNE MARIE	1831	JEBESHEIM	08/14/1855	NY		FILM
DIENER	MICHEL		FROHMUHL	01/01/1817	A		FILM
DIENERT	ELISABETH		MORSHWILLER	01/01/1828	A		FILM
DIERKS	JOHANN K.	1814	MUEHLHAUSEN	10/25/1843	TX		FILM

Lastname	Firstname	Birth Year	Birthplace	Emigration	De	Prof	Source
DIERKS H CAROLINE	JEAN CHARLES	1814	MULHOUSE	10/01/1843	TX		CULT
DIERKS W JEAN CHARLE	CAROLINE	1819	MULHOUSE	10/01/1843	TX		SHIP
DIERR	CHARLES		EMMENDINGEN	05/24/1849	A		FILM
DIESSER	PROSE	1827	ALTKIRCH	05/22/1855	NY		FILM
DIESSER	ROSE	1827	ALTKIRCH	05/22/1855	NY		FILM
DIESTELRATH	GUILLAUME		NIDERLUZINGUE	/ /	A		FILM
DIETEMAIN	HENRI	1810	TRAUBACH-LE-HAUT	11/14/1844	NO		FILM
DIETEMAN	JOSEPH	1810	TRAUBACH-LE-HAUT	06/02/1846	NY		FILM
DIETEMANN	ANTOINE	1827	TRAUBACH-LE-HAUT	07/19/1857	NY		FILM
DIETEMANN	APPOLINAIRE	1831	TRAUBACH-LE-HAUT	02/18/1854	NY		FILM
DIETEMANN	JEAN	1832	TRAUBACH-LE-HAUT	05/22/1855	A		FILM
DIETEMANN	JOSEPH	1830	TRAUBACH-LE-HAUT	02/18/1854	NY		FILM
DIETEMANN D JEAN	JOSEPHINE		OBERTRAUBACH	12/01/1844	TX		SHIP
DIETEMANN H JUSTINE	JEAN CH 1		OBERTRAUBACH	12/01/1844	TX		SHIP
DIETEMANN MN MURE	JUSTINE		OBERTRAUBACH	12/01/1844	TX		SHIP
DIETERLE	JEAN	1824	COLMAR	09/01/1845	TX	MERC	SHIP
DIETERLE	JEAN	1824	INGERSHEIM	09/05/1845	NY		FILM
DIETERS	BERNARD H.	1806	WESTFALEN	09/17/1845	TX		FILM
DIETLER	FRANCOIS JOSEPH	1817	HAUT-RHIN	11/01/1843	TX	CULT	SHIP
DIETLER	FRANCOIS JOSEPH	1819	VALHEIM	11/22/1843	TX		FILM
DIETMANN	FRANCOIS	1809	TRAUBACH-LE-HAUT	02/16/1854	A		FILM
DIETRICH	ADOLPHE	1825	TURCKHEIM	07/07/1847	NY		FILM
DIETRICH	BERNARD	1823	TRUCKHEIM	09/05/1844	NY		FILM
DIETRICH	CHRETIEN		DURSTEL	05/18/1838	A		FILM
DIETRICH	CLEMENT		BERNARDSWILLER	05/12/1838	A		FILM
DIETRICH	ETIENNE	1835	MOOSACH	08/11/1853	A		FILM
DIETRICH	GILLER	1814	RUMERSHEIM	01/03/1848	NY		FILM
DIETRICH	JAQUES	1816	HERRLISHEIM	08/30/1849	NO		FILM
DIETRICH	JEAN THIBAUD	1831	MOOSCH	03/03/1852	NO	FOBU	FILM
DIETRICH	JOSEPH	1820	THANN	10/01/1843	TX	CULT	SHIP
DIETRICH	JOSEPH	1820	THANN HAUT RHIN	10/25/1843	TX		FILM
DIETRICH	JOSEPH ALOYSE	1838	MOOSCH	06/19/1854	NY		FILM
DIETRICH	MARIE ANNE		BERNARDSWILLER	01/01/1828	A	WEAV	FILM
DIETRICH	MARTIN	1798	MULHOUSE	12/29/1854	NY	FERR	FILM
DIETRICH	RICHARD	1833	MOOSCH	08/11/1853	PA	CARP	FILM
DIETRICH	SEBASTIEN	1816	RUMERSHEIM	04/14/1841	A	MECH	FILM
DIETRICH	THIEBAUD	1783	SOPPE LE HAUT	05/11/1838	NY		FILM
DIETRICH 3CH	JEAN JOSEPH	1805	RUMERSHEIM	01/03/1848	NY	LAYB	FILM
DIETRICH CH 1	THIEBAUD	1806	THANN	09/01/1845	TX	FILE	PAS
DIETRICH MN WILLIG	MARIE ANNE	1801	NIEDERHERGHEIM	09/16/1850	NO		FILM
DIETRICH W H	MARIE LOUISE		WILLER HAUT RHIN	07/27/1853	NY		FILM
DIETRICH W W 2CH	SEBASTIAN	1803	TRAUBACH LE HAUT	06/01/1852	IA	SHMA	FILM
DIETRICH W W 6CH	THIEBAUD	1806	THANN	09/04/1845	TX		FILM
DIETRICH W W 8CH	SIMON	1802	FAVEROIS	03/15/1847	NO	SHMA	FILM
DIETSCH	JOSEPH	1823	BIESHEIM	05/14/1850	SL		FILM
DIETSCHIN	ANNE	1841	HELFRANTSKIRCH	05/01/1857	NY		FILM
DIETSCHIN	THERESE	1839	HELFRANTSKIRCH	05/01/1857	NY		FILM
DIETSCHIN W 3 D	NICOLAS	1799	HELFRANTSKIRCH	05/01/1857	NY		FILM
DIETZ	GEOFREI EDUARD	1814	COLMAR	07/20/1854	NY		FILM
DIETZ	VALENTIN		ALT BISCHHEIM	09/30/1849	A		FILM

Lastname	Firstname	Birth Year	Birthplace	Emigration	De	Prof	Source
DIETZ W W 2 CH	JEAN	1817	TIEFFENBACH	01/01/1817	A		FILM
DIFFENE	JEAN GEORGE		NIEDERBRONN	01/01/1828	A		FILM
DIFFENE	JOHANN GEORG		NIEDERBRONN	01/01/1817	A		NO.2
DIHLET W W 3 CH	ANTOINE	1810	ALTKIRCH	06/03/1840	NY		FILM
DILGER W W 3 CH	MARTIN		RECHTENBACH	02/28/1852	NO		FILM
DILLEMAM S ANDRE	LOUIS	1841	HAUT-RHIN	12/01/1844	TX		SHIP
DILLEMAN H LOUISE CH	ANDRE	1812	HAUT-RHIN	12/01/1844	TX		SHIP
DILLEMAN W ANDRE	LOUISE	1812	HAUT-RHIN	12/01/1844	TX		SHIP
DILLER	LOUIS LEON	1823	SIGOLSHEIM	11/16/1844	NY		FILM
DILLINGER W D	BARBE	1800	KIENTZHEIM	08/29/1852	NO		FILM
DILLMANN	GEORG		LEMBACH	01/01/1867	NY		NO.2
DIM F OF 3	FRANCOIS		STRUTH	01/01/1828	A		FILM
DIMANCHE	ALEXANDRE	1841	CHALONVILLARD	03/05/1865	NY		FILM
DIMANCHE	EMILIE	1839	CHALONVILLARD	03/05/1865	NY		FILM
DIMANCHE	MARIE	1864	CHALONVILLARD	03/05/1865	NY		FILM
DIMSER	GASPARD	1835	ASPACH-LE-BAS	07/14/1855	NY		FILM
DINET MN TROY	CATHERINE		MORVILLARS	10/11/1855	NY		FILM
DING	FRANCOIS ANTOIE	1827	LEYMEN	03/03/1853	NY		FILM
DINGENS	CHRISTIAN		TIEFFENBACH	01/01/1828	A		FILM
DINGENS	GEORGES		TIEFFENBACH	01/01/1828	A		FILM
DINGENS	JEAN		TIEFFENBACH	01/01/1828	A		FILM
DINKEL	GEORGE		WEISLINGEN	01/01/1828	A		FILM
DINKEL	JACQUES		FROHMUHL	01/01/1828	A		FILM
DINKEL	LEOPOLD	1828	WURMERSHEIM	02/10/1851	NY		FILM
DINTINGER	GEORGE		WEISLINGEN	01/01/1828	A		FILM
DINTINGER	MARGUERITE		STRUTH	01/01/1828	A		FILM
DINTINGER	PHILLIPP		WEISLINGEN	01/01/1828	A		FILM
DINTINGER F OF 4	MICHEL		WEISLINGEN	01/01/1828	A		FILM
DINTINGER F OF 5	JEAN		WEISLINGEN	01/01/1828	A		FILM
DINTINGER F OF 6	HENRY		THAL CANTON DRULINGN	01/01/1828	A		FILM
DINTINGER W W	ADAM		HAMBACH	01/01/1817	A		FILM
DINTINGER W W 7 CH	CASPAR		STRUHT	01/01/1817	A		FILM
DINTINGER W W CH	MICHEL		STRUTH	01/01/1817	A		FILM
DIRIE	NICOLAS		FROHMUHL	01/01/1828	A		FILM
DIRIY	FRANC. ANTOIN	1828	LEYMEN	03/03/1852	A		FILM
DIRNINGER W W 6CH	IGNACE	1805	GUEBERSSCHWIHR	02/22/1848	A		FILM
DIRR W W 3 CH	SEBASTIEN	1803	REGUISHEIM	06/02/1849	NO		FILM
DIRRIG	LOUIS ALOYSE	1825	LEYMEN	02/27/1844	NY		FILM
DIRRIG	THIBAUD	1828	ALTRINGUE	01/24/1853	NY		FILM
DIRZ W W 3 CH	SEBASTIEN	1803	REGUISHEIM	06/20/1849	NO		FILM
DISCHER	CATHERINA	1828	MUENSTER	11/22/1856	SL		FILM
DISCHER	CHRETIEN		NEUWILLER	01/01/1828	A		FILM
DISCHER	JOSEPH	1817	FELLERINGEN	04/08/1844	TX	FARM	FILM
DISCHER F OF 3	MICHEL		NEUWILLER	01/01/1828	A		FILM
DISCHER WW 2CH	MICHEL		NEUWILLER	03/17/1817	A		FILM
DISCHLER	JOSEPH	1816	FELLERING	12/01/1843	TX	FARM	SHIP
DISS	LOUIS	1832	MAMOUTIER	09/16/1853	A		FILM
DISS F OF 4	PIERRE		HOCHFELDEN	01/01/1828	A		FILM
DISSEL	JEAN MICHEL		IMMENDINGEN	04/21/1849	NY		FILM
DISSEN	MADELAINE	1783	ALTKIRCH	04/12/1851	A		FILM

Lastname	Firstname	Birth Year	Birthplace	Emigration	De	Prof	Source
DISSER	ANTOINE		GOTTENHAUSEN	01/01/1828	A		FILM
DISSER	ANTOINE	1829	ALTKIRCH	01/24/1854	NY		FILM
DISSER	CHARLES	1819	HIRTZBACH	01/12/1848	NY		FILM
DISSER F OF 6	MICHEL		GOTTENHAUSEN	01/01/1828	A		FILM
DISSERT W W 4CH	JEAN GEORGES		RINGELDORF	01/01/1828	A		FILM
DITNER	PAUL	1808	BURNHAUPT-LE-BAS	05/23/1838	A	SHMA	FILM
DITNER	THIEBAUT	1809	AMMERZWILLER	01/10/1840	NY		FILM
DITNER W 8 CH	JOSEF	1801	BURNHAUPT-LE BAS	05/13/1840	NY		FILM
DITTOR W W	JEAN	1821	HUPACH	12/01/1847	A		FILM
DITZ	JOSEPH		DETTWILLER	01/01/1837	A		FILM
DIVIAS	HENRY	1826	CERNAY	02/29/1848	NY		FILM
DMENSY	MATHIAS	1815	PUIX	03/04/1839	NY		FILM
DOBEL	FRANCOIS		RIBEAUVILLE	08/14/1849	PH		FILM
DOBEL	JACQUES	1817	BERGHEIM	04/05/1849	PH		FILM
DOCHTER	GEORGE		SOSSENHEIM	01/01/1828	A		FILM
DODANE	CONSTANT	1850	CERNEUX SWISS	08/11/1865	NY		FILM
DODANE	EMILIE	1848	CERNEUX SWISS	08/11/1865	NY		FILM
DODANE	JEAN PIERRE	1810	CERNEUX SWISS	08/11/1865	NY		FILM
DODANE	PHILOMENE	1845	CERNEUX SWISS	08/11/1865	NY		FILM
DOEBELE	CAROLINE	1837	LUTTER	05/17/1866	NY		FILM
DOEBELE	MARIE URSULA	1836	LUTTER	05/17/1866	NY		FILM
DOEGELEN	XAVIER	1806	GUEWENHEIM	06/03/1846	NY		FILM
DOERNER	FRED		SINSHEIM B	10/11/1849	A		FILM
DOERNERT F OF 9	GEORGE		SCHWEIGHAUSEN	01/01/1828	A	FARM	FILM
DOESS	PHILLIP		PETERSBACH	01/01/1828	A	WEAV	FILM
DOHLINGER WW	GEORGES	1802	DEUX PONTS	09/07/1844	NY		FILM
DOLL	AMBROISE	1838	LUTTER	07/17/1864	NY		FILM
DOLL	CHARLES	1844	NIEDERLAUTERBACH	01/01/1867	NY		PRIV
DOLL	EUGEN	1866	HAGUENAU	01/01/1869	NY		NO.2
DOLL W S EUGEN	MARIE	1844	HAGUENAU	01/01/1869	MY		NO.2
DOLLFUS	JACQUES	1820	MULHOUSE	01/26/1849	NY		FILM
DOLLFUS	JEAN FRANCOIS	1820	MULHOUSE	08/08/1845	NY		FILM
DOLT	FRANZISQUE		STEINBACH B	04/21/1849	A		FILM
DOMECK W W 3 CH	LOUIS	1804	LANDAU BA	08/13/1855	NO	SHMA	FILM
DOMIDIAN F OF 3	ROSINE		STRASSBURG	01/01/1837	A		FILM
DOMIG WW	JEAN		STRASSBURG	05/28/1817	A	CARP	FILM
DOMINIQUE	JOSEPHINE	1816	FRAHIER	03/17/1865	NY	FARM	FILM
DOMINIQUE	PHILLIPPE	1799	ROMBACH	10/23/1838	NO		FILM
DONAU	ELISE	1848	AUDINCOURT	04/30/1864	NY		FILM
DONCHE	GAY	1834	SWISS	03/22/1863	NY		FILM
DONIAT	M.ANNE	1813	MEZIRE	07/29/1857	NY		FILM
DONIAT	PIERRE	1821	MEZIRE	08/08/1842	NY		FILM
DONIGT W FRANCOIS	MARIE ANNE	1813	MEZIRE	07/29/1857	NY		FILM
DONNENWERTH W 2 CH	GEORGE		UHRWILLER	03/11/1817	A		FILM
DONNENWERTH W W 2CH	JACQUES		MULHAUSEN BOUXWILLER	01/01/1828	A		FILM
DONNER	ANTOINE	1812	BERGHEIM	12/15/1852	A		FILM
DONNEWIRTH			TRIEMBACH	01/01/1817	A		NO.2
DONZE	PIERRE FRANC.	1810	BEAUCOURT	04/04/1844	NY		FILM
DONZE WW 2CH	DENIS	1821	MONTREUX CHATEAU	03/12/1847	A		FILM
DOPLER	CATHERINE THERE	1813	HAGENTHAL-LE-BAS	06/24/1842	A		FILM

56

Lastname	Firstname	Birth Year	Birthplace	Emigration	De	Prof	Source
DOPPELLER	MARIE CATHERINE		ZINSWEILER	02/16/1817	A		FILM
DOPPELLER	MARIE MAGDALEN		ZINSWEILER	02/20/1817	A		FILM
DOPPLER	ANDRE		STRUTH	01/01/1828	A		FILM
DOPPLER	CATHERINE		BIEDERTHAL	07/15/1850	NY		FILM
DOPPLER	FRANCOIS		TIEFFENBACH	01/01/1828	A		FILM
DOPPLER	GUSTAVE		STRUTH	01/01/1828	A		FILM
DOPPLER	JOSEPH	1837	HAGENTHAL	01/31/1859	NY		FILM
DOPPLER W W 2 CH	JEAN	1799	NIEDERHAGENTHAL	09/08/1846	NY		FILM
DORFER	ELISABETH		SCHIRRHOFEN	07/27/1853	A		FILM
DORIOT	CAMILLE	1851	ETUPES	09/15/1866	NY		FILM
DORIOT	SUSANNE	1813	ETUPES	09/15/1866	NY		FILM
DORMEYER	ADAM		VOLKSBERG	01/01/1828	A		FILM
DORMEYER	ANDRE		DIEMERINGEN	01/01/1817	A		FILM
DORMEYER	JACQUES		DIEMERINGEN	01/01/1817	A		FILM
DORMOG	ADELE	1846	MONTBELIARD	09/11/1866	NY		FILM
DORMOIS	PIERRE	1818	MULHOUSE	08/21/1847	A		FILM
DORMOIS	PIETTE	1823	HERICOURT	03/03/1846	NY		FILM
DORN S KARL	KARL		FROESCHWILLER	01/01/1876	A		SUESS
DORNBERGER	BERNARD		THAL	01/01/1828	A		FILM
DORSCH	JOHANN	1845	NIEDERSTEINBACH	01/01/1869	NY	FARM	NO.2
DORSY	CATHERINE	1820	BEAUCOURT	02/20/1866	NY		FILM
DORSY	SEBASTIEN	1818	BEAUCOURT	02/20/1866	NY		FILM
DORVEAUX	JEAN BAPTISTE	1842	BELFORT	04/17/1863	NY		FILM
DORY	FRANCOIS	1845	BEAUCOURT	02/18/1865	A		FILM
DOSSENBACH W W CH	JEAN BAPTISTE	1819	GUEBERSCHWIHR	04/22/1852	PH		FILM
DOTZAUAER	FRANZISKA	1804	SELTZ	01/01/1868	NY		NO.2
DOTZAUER	ANTON	1804	SELTZ	01/01/1868	NY	CARP	NO.2
DOTZAUER	LUDWIG	1854	SELTZ	01/01/1864	NY		NO.2
DOTZLER W W 1 CH	JACQUES	1812	COLMAR	02/21/1849	NY		FILM
DRACH	LOUIS		HERBITZHEIM	01/01/1828	A		FILM
DREGEL W D	GEORGE	1806	THANNENKIRCH	11/03/1852	NY		FILM
DREHER	FREDERIC	1787	ANNWEILER	03/11/1841	NO		FILM
DREHER	MATHIEU		PETERSTHAL	04/25/1849	NY		FILM
DREHER F OF 5	EMANUEL		INGWILLER	01/01/1828	A		FILM
DRESS	JEAN PHILLIPPE		WOERTH SUR SAMARA	07/13/1828	A		FILM
DRESSEL	PHILIPPE		BUEHLERTHAL B	04/19/1849	A		FILM
DRETSCH	CATHERINE	1845	MULHOUSE	04/19/1866	NY		FILM
DREY	ANTOINE	1823	DUERRENENTZEN	04/02/1841	NY		FILM
DREY	GEORGES	1827	DUERRENENTZEN	01/08/1846	A		FILM
DREY W W 6 CH	ANTOINE	1797	DUERRENTENTZEN	03/14/1845	CH		FILM
DREYEL W D	GEORGE	1806	THANNENKIRCHEN	11/03/1852	NY		FILM
DREYER	ANNA MARIA	1826	RANSPACH	11/22/1843	TX		FILM
DREYER	ANNE	1815	THANN	08/05/1848	A		FILM
DREYER	HEINRICH	1832	RANSPACH	11/22/1843	TX		FILM
DREYER	JEAN	1717	LEYMEN	02/27/1844	NY		FILM
DREYER	JEAN	1816	ASPACH	06/30/1847	NY		FILM
DREYER	JEAN	1827	BERGHOLZZELL	02/13/1854	NY		FILM
DREYER	KAROLINE	1830	RANSPACH	11/22/1843	TX		FILM
DREYER	KATHARINA	1822	RANSPACH	11/22/1843	TX		FILM
DREYER	KATHERINA	1797	RANSPACH	11/22/1843	TX		FILM

Lastname	Firstname	Birth Year	Birthplace	Emigration	De	Prof	Source
DREYER	MARIA ANNA	1828	RANSPACH	11/22/1843	TX		FILM
DREYER	MARTIN	1796	RANSPACH	11/22/1843	TX		FILM
DREYER	THERES	1819	RANSPACH	11/22/1843	TX		FILM
DREYER	URBAN	1810	RANSPACH	12/13/1856	TX		FILM
DREYER CH 2	BENOIT	1813	KRUTH	10/01/1855	TX	CULT	PASS
DREYER D MARTIN	ANNE-MARIE	1825	RANSPACH	11/01/1843	TX		SHIP
DREYER D MARTIN	CAROLINE	1829	RANSPACH	11/01/1843	TX		SHIP
DREYER D MARTIN	CATHERINE	1821	RANSPACH	11/01/1843	TX		SHIP
DREYER D MARTIN	MARIE-ANNE	1827	RANSPACH	11/01/1843	TX		SHIP
DREYER D MARTIN	THERESE	1818	RANSPACH	11/01/1843	TX		SHIP
DREYER H CATHERINE	MARTIN CH 6	1795	RANSPACH	01/01/1843	TX	CULT	SHIP
DREYER S MARTIN	HENRI	1832	RANSPACH	11/01/1843	TX		SHIP
DREYER W 3CH	JACQUES	1817	WECKOLSHEIM	07/04/1845	A		FILM
DREYER W MARTIN	CATHERINE		RANSPACH	11/01/1843	TX		SHIP
DREYER W W	BENOIT		GEISHAUSEN	11/07/1855	TX		FILM
DREYER W W 2 CH	ANTOINE			01/01/1817	A		FILM
DREYER WW AND CH 3	BENOIT	1813	KRUTH	10/01/1855	TX	CULT	SHIP
DREYFOUS	DANIEL	1795	PARIS	03/07/1838	NO		FILM
DREYFOUS	JULES	1817	BELFORT	08/02/1837	NO		FILM
DREYFUS	ARTHUR	1836		01/20/1853	A		FILM
DREYFUS	BENOIT	1801	ALTKIRCH	06/08/1854	NY		FILM
DREYFUS	FELIX	1824	SIERENTZ	08/01/1857	NY		FILM
DREYFUS	PAUL	1823	ALTKIRCH	08/13/1849	NY		FILM
DREYFUS W W 4 CH	LEHMANN	1807	RIXHEIM	07/16/1847	NY		FILM
DREYFUSS	BENJAMIN	1848	WEISSENBURG	01/01/1867	NY		NO.2
DREYFUSS	BENJAMIN	1853	SOULTZMATT	06/02/1852	NY		FILM
DREYFUSS	ELIAS	1823	CERNAY	01/01/1848	NO	MERC	PRIV
DREYFUSS	JACQUES	1805	RIBEAUVILLE	12/20/1850	NY		FILM
DREYFUSS	MOSES	1852	WEISSENBURG	01/01/1869	NO		NO.2
DREYFUSS	MOYSE		WISSEMBOURG	01/01/1869	NO		PRIV
DREYFUSS	SIMON	1849	WEISSENBURG	01/01/1865	NO		NO.2
DRIBER W W A BR	FREDERIC		MOLSHEIM	01/01/1817	A		FILM
DRISSEL F OF 6	CHRETIEN		WEISLINGEN	01/01/1828	A		FILM
DRIXEL	FLORENT		WANGENBOURG	01/01/1828	A		FILM
DROG	MARIE AGNES	1815	CHAUX	02/17/1844	NY		FILM
DROXLER	ANTOINE	1815	RIESPACH	01/27/1846	NY		FILM
DROZ	CLAUS JACQUES	1821	CHAUX	05/20/1854	NO		FILM
DROZ	GEORGES	1824	CHAUX	05/12/1846	NO		FILM
DROZ	JEAN CLAUDE	1821	CHAUX	02/10/1840	NY		FILM
DROZ	MARIE AGNES	1815	CHAUX	02/17/1844	NY		FILM
DROZ	MARIE THERES	1831	CHAUX	11/12/1850	NO		FILM
DROZ W S	MAXIMINE	1800	ILLHAEUSERN	08/17/1847	A		FILM
DROZ W W 1 CH	FRANCOISE	1815	CHAUX	02/27/1846	NO		FILM
DROZ W W 1 S	JEAN PIERRE	1783	CHAUX	08/21/1847	A		FILM
DROZ W W 2 CH	JOSEPH	1807	CHAUX	10/09/1852	NO		FILM
DRUMMER	GEORGE		ESCHBOURG	01/01/1828	A		FILM
DRUSSEL	JACQUES		HATTMATT	01/01/1828	A		FILM
DRUSSEL	MARGERITE		HATTMATT	01/01/1828	A		FILM
DRUSSEL F OF 5	MICHEL		HATTMATT	01/01/1828	A		FILM
DSDAMES	NICOLAS	1819	ROPPE	05/19/1846	NY		FILM

Lastname	Firstname	Birth Year	Birthplace	Emigration	De	Prof	Source
DUBER	BARBE		HAMBACH	03/08/1838	A		FILM
DUBER	CATHERINE		HAMBACH	03/08/1838	A		FILM
DUBER	CHRETIEN		HAMBACH	03/08/1838	A		FILM
DUBER	FREDERIC		HAMBACH	03/08/1838	A		FILM
DUBER	PHILIPPE		HAMBACH	03/08/1828	A		FILM
DUBER	PIERE		HAMBACH	03/08/1838	A		FILM
DUBERT	ANNE MARIE		HAEGEN	01/01/1828	A		FILM
DUBLER	JEAN BAPTISTE	1824	GUEBWILLER	10/14/1850	LV		FILM
DUBLER W 1CH	MARIE ANNE	1826	GUEBWILLER	11/29/1848	LV		FILM
DUBOIS	HENRY	1828	THANN	10/25/1843	TX		FILM
DUBOIS	JACOB	1835	NIEDERBRONN	01/01/1865	NY		NO.2
DUBOIS	KARL	1838	THANN	10/25/1843	TX		FILM
DUBORONSKI W W 4D	ETIENNE	1792	JOUCHERY	/ /	NY		FILM
DUBOSQUE W 1 CH	PROSPER		STRASSBOURG	05/12/1817	A		FILM
DUBS	CHARLES	1826	ST.MARIE AUX MINES	06/15/1847	NY		FILM
DUBS	CHARLES	1828	THANN	10/01/1843	TX		SHIP
DUBS	HENRY	1827	ST.MARIE AUX MINES	08/18/1848	NY		FILM
DUBS W W 7CH	BLAISE	1824	SCHWOBEN	11/24/1851	NY		FILM
DUCHANOIS	HENRY	1843	BELFORT	04/13/1866	NY		FILM
DUCHENE	JOSEPH	1798	ST.ABORD	10/02/1854	NY		FILM
DUCHMANN	ETTIENE		NIEDERMODERN	01/01/1828	A		FILM
DUCHMANN	MATHIEU		NIEDERMODERN	01/01/1828	A		FILM
DUCHMANN	THIEBAUT		NIEDERMODERN	01/01/1828	A		FILM
DUCLOS	MATHIAS		KALTENHAUSEN	01/01/1828	A		FILM
DUCLOUX	JACQUES	1829	FEVEROIS	08/06/1855	NO		FILM
DUCLOUX	PIERRE NICOLAS	1826	FAVEROIS	03/28/1846	NO		FILM
DUCOTEY	MARIE	1844		03/13/1865	NY		FILM
DUCROS W W 4CH	FRANCOIS		JUGWILLER	03/23/1817	A		FILM
DUENSER	GASPARD	1835	ASPACH LEBAS	07/14/1855	NY		FILM
DUERR	CHARLES		EMMENDINGEN B	05/24/1845	A		FILM
DUERR	FRANCOIS JOSEPH		LICHTENBERG	01/01/1828	A		FILM
DUERR	MARIE		WEYL	05/03/1849	NY		FILM
DUERR	SIMON	1818	SCHLIERBACH	09/19/1848	NY		FILM
DUERR W W	JOSEPH		REIPERTSWILLER	01/01/1817	A		FILM
DUERRFOIS	JOSEPH		LICHTENBERG	01/01/1828	A		FILM
DUFFNER	JOSEPH	1825	MOLSHEIM	10/12/1854	NY		FILM
DUIRE	ANTOINE	1828	LIEPVRE	12/04/1848	NO		FILM
DUKRO W W1CH	THOMAS		LICHTENBERG	01/01/1817	A		FILM
DUMEL	JOSEF	1832	LEIMBACK	08/20/1853	PH		FILM
DUMET W W	JOSEPH	1820	OLPE PR	08/20/1841	NY		FILM
DUMEY	AUGUSTE	1838	HEZIRE	09/15/1866	NY		FILM
DUMEY	FRANCOIS	1860	HEZIRE	09/15/1866	NY		FILM
DUMON	GEORGES	1833	VETRIGNE	09/22/1866	NY		FILM
DUMONT W W 1CH	PIERRE	1810	MANSPACH	03/18/1850	SL		FILM
DUMOULIN	MATHIAS		ROESCHWOOG	01/01/1828	A		FILM
DUMOULIN	WILLIBALD	1828	THANNENKIRCH	10/06/1852	CH		FILM
DUPALA	AUGUSTIN	1827	LIEPVRE	02/21/1849	NO		FILM
DUPE	JULIE	1829	MONTECHEROUIL	02/07/1865	NY		FILM
DUPERI	ELISABETH		GOTTENHAUSEN	01/01/1828	A		FILM
DUPLAIN	AUGUSTE LOUISE	1823	SEDAN	12/31/1851	CH		FILM

Lastname	Firstname	Birth Year	Birthplace	Emigration	De	Prof	Source
DUPLAIN	JOSEPH	1825	NANCY	08/05/1848	NY		FILM
DUPLAIN	JOSEPH W W 6CH	1800	GRANDVILLARS	12/31/1851	CH		FILM
DUPLAIN	JULES	1849	BELFORT	03/12/1866	NY		FILM
DUPLAIN	PIERRE	1813	BELFORT	03/12/1866	NY		FILM
DUPLAIN	PIERRE JOSEPH	1813	GRANDVILLARS	05/18/1840	NY		FILM
DUPLAIN W 4CH SI	MARIE ANNE	1806	GRANDVILLARS	02/16/1852	NY		FILM
DUPONT	CONSTATNT	1857	SAUNOT H.SAONE	01/10/1862	NY		FILM
DUPONT	HENRI FERDINAND	1836	ARGIESANS TERR BELF	05/15/1856	NY		FILM
DUPONT	JACQUES	1812	EGUENIGUE TERR BELF	02/07/1851	NY		FILM
DUPONT	JEAN CLAUDE			/ /			
DUPONT	JOSEPH	1862	SAUNOT	10/01/1862	NY		FILM
DUPONT	ROSALIE	1854	SAUNOT	10/01/1862	NY		FILM
DUPONT	SERAPHIN	1848	SAUNOT	10/01/1862	NY		FILM
DUPONT	THERESE	1851	SAUNOT	10/01/1862	NY		FILM
DUPONT W 2CH	JEAN CLAUDE	1779	ROUGEMONT	02/24/1840	PH		FILM
DUPONT W W 1CH	LEONIE	1859	SAUNOT H.-SAONE	10/01/1862	NY		FILM
DUPRE	FRANCOIS	1821	RUPPE	03/04/1847	NY		FILM
DUPRE W W 2CH	JEAN PIERRE	1818	ROPPE	07/04/1846	NY		FILM
DUPREZ	FRANCOIS	1825	LEBETAIN	03/30/1847	NY		FILM
DUPREZ	JULIE	1833	LEBETAIN	08/26/1854	NY		FILM
DUPREZ	PIERRE	1823	LEBETAIN	03/30/1847	NY		FILM
DURACHER W W 3CH	BARNABE	1808	ST MARIE AUX MINES	02/03/1847	NO		FILM
DURAND W W 6CH	JOSEPH		STRASSBOURG	05/27/1817	A		FILM
DURBAN	ANDRE	1826	DURRENTZEN	04/18/1848	CH		FILM
DURBAN	BARBE	1809	DURRENENTZEN	10/11/1837	NY		FILM
DURBAN	MARIE SALOME	1814	COLMAR	07/03/1849	CH		FILM
DURBAN	URSULA	1824	DURRENENTZEN	05/06/1848	CH		FILM
DURCK	ERNEST	1833	INGERSHEIM	11/15/1851	NY		FILM
DURELL	BARBE	1800	KIENTZHEIM	08/29/1852	NO		FILM
DURENBERGER	JEAN		ESCHBOURG	03/03/1817	A		FILM
DURENBERGER W W 5 CH	GEORGE		ESCHBOURG	03/17/1817	A		FILM
DURENWAECHTER	JEAN GEORGE	1818	OBERMAGSTATT	05/31/1854	NY		FILM
DURET	PIERRE LOUIS	1827	BEAUCOURT	02/29/1848	NY		FILM
DURGET W F	JOSEPH	1824	BITSCHWILLER	04/20/1852	NY		FILM
DURIN	LOUIS	1829	AUXELLES BAS	07/11/1853	NO		FILM
DURING	JEAN		OBERNDORF W	06/21/1849	A		FILM
DURLEAT W W 4CH	XAVIER	1801	BRECHAUMONT	02/05/1845	NY		FILM
DURLIAT	SEBASTIEN	1810	BRECHAUMONT	03/02/1847	NY		FILM
DURLIAT W W 1 S	LAURENT	1822	BRECHAUMONT	04/23/1853	A		FILM
DURLIAT W W 4CH	JACQUES	1815	BRECHAUMONT	02/20/1845	NY		FILM
DURMEYER	JEAN		WOLFSKIRCHEN	01/01/1828	A		FILM
DURR	ANDRE		ALEXANDERSREUTH W	05/18/1849	A		FILM
DURRMEYER	NICOLAS		ESCHBOURG	01/01/1828	A		FILM
DURRMEYER F OF 3	GEORGES		ESCHBOURG	01/01/1828	A		FILM
DURRMEYER F OF 4	DANIEL		REIPERTSWILLER	01/01/1828	A		FILM
DURRMEYER F OF 4	PHILIPPE		REIERTSWILLER	01/01/1828	A		FILM
DURRMEYER F OF 6	FREDERIC		REIPERTSWILLER	01/01/1828	A		FILM
DURRMEYER W D	NICOLAS		ESCHBOURG	01/01/1828	A		FILM
DURRWARTH	JACOB		BRETTEN B	06/21/1849	A		FILM
DURST	DAVID	1833	OSTHEIM	01/15/1857	NY		FILM

Lastname	Firstname	Birth Year	Birthplace	Emigration	De	Prof	Source
DUSCH F OF 5	GEORGE		MENCHHOFFEN	01/01/1828	A		FILM
DUSCH F OF 8	NICOLAS		BETTWILLER	01/01/1832	A		FILM
DUTEY	ELISABETH		KALTENHAUSEN	01/01/1828	A		FILM
DUVIC W W 1 S	JOSEPH	1794	LIEPVRE	11/06/1838	NO		FILM
DUVIE	ANTOINE	1828	LIEPVRE	12/04/1848	NO		FILM
DUVIE	CONRAD	1826	LIEPVRE	05/12/1846	NO		FILM
DUVIE	JEAN PHILLIPE	1822	LIEPVRE	11/06/1838	NO		FILM
DUVIE	MARIE ANNE		LIEPVRE	11/06/1838	NO		FILM
DUVIE	MARIE FRANCOISE	1828	LIEPVRE	05/12/1846	NO		FILM
DUWA W W 3CH	JEAN BAPTISTE	1820	MITTELWIHR	12/21/1852	NY		FILM
DYON	FRANCOIS ANTOIN	1822	BIESHEIM	01/09/1849	NY		FILM
DéCOUVY F OF ANNE MR	FRANCOIS JOSEPH		MUNCHHAUSEN BAS RHIN	/ /	A		FILM
DéCOUVY D OF FRA.JOS	MARIE ANNE		MUNCHHAUSEN	/ /	A		FILM

Lastname	Firstname	Birth Year	Birthplace	Emigration	De	Prof	Source
EARTH ? ERNST?	ANTON	1822	HORB W	01/01/1844	TX		FILM
EBEL	JOSEPH	1819	KILSTETT	12/31/1845	A		PRIV
EBEL W W	CHARLES		WANTZENAU	05/12/1817	A	LAYB	FILM
EBENSTEIN	ADOLPHE	1843	HAGENTHAL	07/10/1866	NY		FILM
EBERENZ	MARIE		GERMANY	04/17/1849	A		FILM
EBERHARD	JEAN GEORG	1830	MULHOUSE	03/12/1852	PH		FILM
EBERHARD	JONAS	1824	MULHOUSE	03/12/1849	NY		FILM
EBERHARD	MARGERITE		WEISLINGEN	01/01/1828	A		FILM
EBERHARD	NIKOLAUS		PETERSBACH	01/01/1828	A		FILM
EBERHARD W W 3CH	MARTIN		REMLISDORFF? W	/ /	NY		FILM
EBERHARD W W 8CH	JAQUES		TIEFFENBACH	03/11/1817	A	SHMA	FILM
EBERHARDT	JEAN GEORGE	1838	MULHOUSE	03/12/1844	PH		FILM
EBERHARDT	JONAS	1824	MULHOUSE	03/13/1844	NY		FILM
EBERHART	LOUIS	1821	KAYSERSBERG	07/25/1847	NO		FILM
EBERHART	MICHEL	1818	KAYSERSBERG	02/13/1849	NO	BUTC	FILM
EBERLE	EMILE		GERNSBACH B	09/28/1849	NY		FILM
EBERLE	MICHEL	1806	KLENTZHEIM	11/29/1851	NY		FILM
EBERLE	ROSINA	1850	NIEDERLAUTERBACH	01/01/1867	NO		PRIV
EBERLE	ROSINE		NIEDERLAUTERBACH	01/01/1850	NO		PRIV
EBERLE	SALOME		NIEDERHEIM B	04/25/1849	A		FILM
EBERLIN	ANDRE		NIEDERHEIM B	04/25/1849	A		FILM
EBERLIN	HENRI	1793	BALLERSDORFF	03/11/1848	NY		FILM
EBERLIN	MICHEL		INGENHEIM	01/01/1828	A	BAKE	FILM
EBERLIN W FAMILY	JEAN	1808	CARSPACH	03/09/1841	NY	DAYL	FILM
EBERLY	ANTOINE	1826	GUEWENHEIM	09/28/1854	NY	WEAV	FILM
EBERT	ANDREAS	1851	SELTZ	01/01/1869	NY	FARM	NO.2
EBERT FAMILY OF 8	GEOFROID		BRUMATH	01/01/1828	A	LAYB	FILM
EBING	CASPAR		WURMLINGEN W	07/25/1849	A		FILM
EBING	CASPARD		WURMLINGEN	07/03/1849	A		FILM
EBING	JEAN BAPTISTE	1830	DORNACH	10/15/1857	NY	SHMA	FILM
EBING	JOSEPH		WURMLINGEN	07/25/1849	A		FILM
EBING	JOSEPH		WURMLINGEN W	07/23/1849	A		FILM
EBIRCHER	ANTE (ANTOINE?)		FROHMUHL	01/01/1817	A		FILM
EBISCH	CHRETIEN		FROHMUHL	01/01/1828	A	DAYL	FILM
EBISCHER W W 5 CH	ANTE (ANTOINE)		FROHMUHL	01/01/1817	A		FILM
EBY	JEAN BAPTISTE	1829	ASPACH	02/23/1857	NY		FILM
ECHARDS OR ECKARDS	JULI		BOUXWILLER	01/01/1828	A		FILM
ECHENWALTHER	CAROLINE		ROMERSCHWEYER(?)B	06/03/1849	A		FILM
ECK W W 2 CH	AUGUSTIN		DIEBOLSHEIM	06/04/1817	A	WEAV	FILM
ECKART F OF 5	JOSEPH		DAUENDORF	01/01/1828	A	LAYB	FILM
ECKART W CH	GUILLAUME	1815	MULHOUSE	06/06/1849	A	COMB	FILM
ECKENFELD	LANDOLIN		FRIESENHEIM B	08/05/1849	A		FILM
ECKENWALTHER	CAROLINE		ROMERSWEYER B	06/01/1849	A		FILM
ECKER	ANNE MARIE	1828	KRUTH	09/14/1854	NY	WEAV	FILM
ECKER	CATHERINE		GERMANY	04/12/1849	A		FILM
ECKER	MATHIAS	1828	KRUTH	04/24/1855	NY	WEAV	FILM
ECKER	MICHEL		SIEWILLER	01/01/1828	A	WAIT	FILM
ECKERLIN W W 2 CH	ANTOINE	1813	THANN	03/29/1853	NY		FILM
ECKERT			SENTHEIM	12/01/1844	TX	COOK	SHIP
ECKERT	JOHANN	1844	NEHWILLER	01/01/1866	A		NO.2

Lastname	Firstname	Birth Year	Birthplace	Emigration	De	Prof	Source
ECKERT	MADELAINE	1838	CERNAY	09/07/1857	SF		FILM
ECKERT	MARTIN	1845	NEHWILLER	01/01/1866	A		NO.2
ECKHOFF	DAVID		ROMANSWILLER	01/01/1828	A		FILM
ECKI FAMILY OF 5	JEAN JAQUES		SCHWEIGHAUSEN	01/01/1828	A		FILM
ECKLE	FRANCOIS JOSEPH	1808	NIEDERMORSCHWIHR	10/30/1840	A		FILM
EDEL	JOSEPH	1830	INGERSHEIM	05/21/1852	NY	JOIN	FILM
EDELMANN	HENRY	1826	MULHOUSE	06/05/1848	PH	TINM	FILM
EDELMANN	MARTIN	1823	BERGHEIM	01/04/1854	NY	WINE	FILM
EDELMANN MN KNAB	JEANNE	1823	BERGHEIM	07/20/1854	NY	BAKE	FILM
EDER	CATHERINA	1834	LEMBACH	01/01/1866	NY		NO.2
EDER	GEORG	1841	MERTZWILLER	01/01/1866	NY		NO.2
EDER	GEORG HEINRICH	1844	HERMERSWEILER	01/01/1866	NY		NO.2
EDET	JOSEPH	1820	INGERSHEIM	05/21/1852	NY		FILM
EDIGHOFFEN	URSULA PHILLIPP	1805	COLMAR	09/16/1848	NO		FILM
EDINEUSY	PIERRE	1829	PUIX	09/03/1853	NY		FILM
EFFINGER	CONRAD	1845	WINTZENBACH	01/01/1869	NY		NO.2
EGELE	HYPOLITE	1834	ST.HYPOLITE	01/20/1854	PH		FILM
EGENSCHWILLER	XAVIER	1811	WINCKEL OR WINKEL	02/12/1838	NY		FILM
EGER	SABINE		BIETENHAUSEN HOHENZ	04/17/1849	NY		FILM
EGERZ	JOSEPH		HAIGERLOCH W	04/21/1849	A		FILM
EGGENSPIELER	JEAN	1837	ROPPENZWILLER	08/06/1865	NY	FARM	FILM
EGGENSPIELER D JEAN	EMILI	1861	ROPPENZWILLER	08/06/1865	NY		FILM
EGGENSPIELER S JEAN	ANDRE	1865	ROPPENTZWILLER	08/05/1865	NY		FILM
EGGENSPIELER S JEAN	XAVIER	1863	ROPPINGSWILLER	08/06/1865	NY		FILM
EGGLY	MARIE		LAUCHERTHAL SWISS	05/12/1849	A		FILM
EGLE W W 2 BR	JACQUES	1811	ECKBOLSHEIM	04/03/1847	NY		FILM
EGLIN	FELIX	1814	ARGIESANS	07/13/1847	NY		FILM
EGLIN	FRANCOIS XAVIER	1823	URCEREY	10/21/1851	NY		FILM
EGLIN	JEAN	1805	MULHAUSEN B	03/06/1838	NY		FILM
EGLINGER	FREDERIC DAGOBR	1825	HUSSEREN	08/22/1854	TX		FILM
EGLINGER	FREDERIC DAGOBT	1825	HUSSEREN	08/01/1854	TX	DAYL	PASS
EGLINGER	JOSEPH	1827	STEINBACH	07/11/1853	NO		FILM
EGLY	JACQUES	1816	SOPPE LE BAS	05/07/1840	NY		FILM
EGLY	JACQUES	1834	BLOTZHEIM	03/14/1853	NY		FILM
EGLY W 2 SI	JOSEPH	1832	BLETZHEIM	09/28/1854	NY		FILM
EGLY W W 4D	CHRETIEN	1806	MULHOUSE	03/14/1856	NY		FILM
EHLINGER	CHRISTINE	1814	STORCKENSOHN	08/25/1845	NO		FILM
EHLINGER	JACQUES	1823	MOOSCH	03/02/1847	NY		FILM
EHLINGER	MARC	1834	URBES	08/05/1854	PH		FILM
EHLINGER	NAPOLEON	1810	STORCKENSOHN	09/21/1844	NY		FILM
EHLINGER	NICOLAS	1831	ST AMARIN	05/04/1851	A		FILM
EHLINGER	SALOME	1824	WILLER	05/04/1846	NY		FILM
EHLINGER W 3CH	MARIE ANNE	1822	WILLER	05/04/1846	NY		FILM
EHLINGER W 5CH	MARIE ANNE	1801	BISCHWILLER	09/16/1843	A		FILM
EHLINGER W SI	CAROLINE	1827	STORCKENSOHN	03/05/1852	NY		FILM
EHNINGER	MARIE LOUISE	1828	ST MARIE AUX MINES	02/26/1850	NO		FILM
EHRENMANN	CHRETIENNE		ALEXANDERSREUTH W	05/18/1849	A		FILM
EHRENMANN	REGINE		ALEXANDERSREUT	05/18/1849	A		FILM
EHRET	ALBERT	1833	OBERBRUCK	04/13/1852	LV		FILM
EHRET	BERNARD	1822	RAMMERSMATT	08/06/1857	NY		FILM

Lastname	Firstname	Year	Birthplace	Emigration	De	Prof	Source
EHRET	CAMILLE	1825	OBERBRUCK	11/14/1849	NY		FILM
EHRET	CATHERINE	1824	RAMMERSMATT	09/13/1847	NY		FILM
EHRET	FRANCOIS	1801	MASSEVAUX	03/22/1849	NY		FILM
EHRET	FRANCOIS	1827	RAMMERSMATT	11/17/1849	NY		FILM
EHRET	FRANCOIS JOSEPH	1825	OBERBRUCK	04/21/1857	NY		FILM
EHRET	SIMON	1824	OBERBRUCK	04/21/1857	NY		FILM
EHRET	THERESE	1819	MOOSCH	03/16/1852	A		FILM
EHRET	VINCENT		WEGSCHEID	/ /	NY		FILM
EHRET W W	ANTOINE	1800	RAMMERSMATT	04/26/1847	NY		FILM
EHRET W F	ANTOINE	1802	RAMMERSMATT	04/17/1850	NO		FILM
EHRET W W	ANTOINE	1808	MASSEVAUX	04/13/1847	NY		FILM
EHRET W W 6CH	ANTOINE	1800	RAMMERSMATT	10/31/1845	NY		FILM
EHRETSMANN	JOSEPH	1841	SERMERSHEIM	07/17/1856	NY		FILM
EHRETSMANN	JOSEPH	1814	HUNAWIHR	01/13/1857	NY		FILM
EHRETSMANN W W	JEAN		HUNAWIHR	02/28/1853	NY		FILM
EHRHARD F OF 6	FREDERIC		DETTWILLER	01/01/1833	A		FILM
EHRHARDT	CATHERINE		OBERHOFF	03/01/1838	A		FILM
EHRHARDT	CONSTANTIN		RENCHEN B	10/05/1849	A		FILM
EHRHARDT	SIMON		RENCHEN	10/05/1849	A		FILM
EHRHART	BARBE	1829	THANN	09/08/1847	PH		FILM
EHRLIG	CAROLINE	1851	WEISSENBURG	01/01/1866	NY		NO.2
EIBEL	MICHEL		REICHSHOFFEN	01/01/1869	A		NO.2
EIBEL W W 2CH	MICHEL		REICHSHOFFEN	03/22/1817	A		FILM
EIBERLIN	FRANCOIS JOSEPH	1821	BLODELSHEIM	05/05/1849	NY		FILM
EICHENLAUB	CAROLINE		NEEWILLER	01/01/1850	NO		PRIV
EICHENLAUB	MARGARETHE	1831	ALTENSTADT	01/01/1869			NO.2
EICHER	ANNE MARIE	1824	ASPACH	03/16/1848	NY		FILM
EICHER	BARBE	1821	ALTKIRCH	04/17/1849	PH		FILM
EICHER	CHRETIEN	1820	BISCH OR BISEL	09/12/1844	NY		FILM
EICHER	DANIEL	1825	PULVERSHEIM	04/24/1845	OH		FILM
EICHER	JACQUES	1786	HEITEREN	04/15/1843	NY		FILM
EICHER	JACQUES	1822	ASPACH	03/22/1855	A		FILM
EICHER	JEAN	1800	BISEL	09/28/1840	NY		FILM
EICHER	JEAN	1828	ALTKIRCH	02/09/1852	NY		FILM
EICHER	MARTIN	1829	PULVERSHEIM	03/03/1848	C		FILM
EICHER	VERONIQUE	1825	ALTKIRCH	07/06/1857	PH		FILM
EICHER W W 1CH	JACQUES	1809	ROUGEMONT	04/14/1847	OH		FILM
EICHERT	JOSEPH		SINGRIST	01/01/1828	A		FILM
EICHHORN	SIMON	1816	BERRWILLER	03/13/1855	NY		FILM
EICHINGER W W 1D	JOSEPH	1815	TRAUBACH LE HAUT	02/12/1845	C		FILM
EICKHORM	SIMON	1816	BERRWILLER	03/13/1855	NY		FILM
EILD	MADELAINE		WANTZENAU	03/07/1838	A		FILM
EIM	DAVID		WANGENBOURG	01/01/1828	A		FILM
EIM	FRANCOISE		WANGENBOURG	01/01/1828	A		FILM
EIM	JACQUES		WANGENBOURG	01/01/1828	A		FILM
EIMEN	FANCOIS JOSEPH	1828	SOULTZ	07/05/1854	NY		FILM
EIMEN	MADELAINE	1828	NIEDERHERGHEIM	11/18/1851	SL		FILM
EIMEN	PIERRE			/ /			
EIMEN W W 2CH	PIERRE	1826	NIEDERHERGHEIM	07/04/1855	A		FILM
EINHART	EVA	1850	SELTZ	01/01/1869	NY		NO.2

Lastname	Firstname	Birth Year	Birthplace	Emigration	De	Prof	Source
EINHORN	BARBARA	1821	LEMBACH	01/01/1866	NY		NO.2
EINHORN	MICHEL	1821	LEMBACH	01/01/1866	NY		NO.2
EINHORN	MICHEL	1852	SCHOENBOURG	01/01/1866	NY		NO.2
EINNINGER	JOSEPH	1832	SELTZ	05/15/1849	NY		FILM
EISEL	GEORGE	1811	SECK IN NASSAU	10/25/1843	TX		FILM
EISELE	GEORGES	1829	ALTKIRCH	01/30/1849	A		FILM
EISEMANN	LAZARE	1840	CANTON DE NIEDERBRON	08/19/1863	NO		FILM
EISENLOB			ETTLINGEN B	04/27/1849	A		FILM
EISENMANN	EMMANUELL	1855	LEMBACH	01/01/1866	NY		NO.2
EISENMANN	JOHANETTA		LEMBACH	01/01/1866	NY		NO.2
EISENMANN	MAGDALENA	1863	LEMBACH	01/01/1866	NY		NO.2
EISENMANN W W 2CH	JOACHIM	1828	LEMBACH	01/01/1866	NY	DAYL	NO.2
EISENMENGER	MARTIN	1829	OBERSEEBACH	01/01/1868	NY		NO.2
EISENZIMMER W W 1CH	GEORGES	1832	NIEDERLAUTERBACH	01/04/1854	NY		FILM
EISSEMANN F OF 4	JACQUES		NEUHEUSEL	03/20/1838	A		FILM
EITEL F OF 2	JACQUES		ILLKIRCH	03/05/1838	A		FILM
EKIRCH	LOUIS VALENTIN	1832	ORSCHWIHR	05/31/1854	NY		FILM
ELBERT	LUDWIG	1847	ALTENSTADT	01/01/1865	NY	MECH	NO.2
ELCHINGER	GEORGE		NEUHEUSEL	03/20/1838	A		FILM
ELCHINGER	HENRY		AUENHEIM	03/14/1817	A		FILM
ELCHINGER	MADELAINE		RUNTZENHEIM	01/01/1828	A		FILM
ELGLISE	FRANCOIS		CHENEBIER	03/28/1863	NY		FILM
ELKAN	ABRAHAM	1850	ZILLISHEIM	04/25/1856	SF		FILM
ELKAN	MOISE	1845	ZILLISHEIM	04/25/1856	SF		FILM
ELLES W W 2CH	JACQUES		MOLSHEIM	03/03/1817	A		FILM
ELMENCH F OF 5	PIERRE`		DAUENDORF	02/28/1838	A		FILM
ELMERICH F OF 5	PIERRE		DAUENDORF	02/28/1838	A		FILM
ELMERICH W W 1CH	JACQUES		GUNDERSHOFFEN	03/11/1817	A		FILM
ELMLINGER	CONRAD		ESCHBACH B	10/11/1849	A		FILM
ELMLINGER	CONSTANTIN		ESCHBACH B	10/11/1849	A		FILM
ELMLINGER	FRANCOIS JOSEPH		ESCHBACH B	10/11/1849	A		FILM
ELMLINGER	ROSINE		ESCHBACH B	10/11/1840	A		FILM
ELMRICH W W 7CH	ANTOINE		UHLWILLER	03/14/1817	A		FILM
ELSASS	MICHEL		WIMMENAU	01/01/1828	A		FILM
ELSASS F OF 5	JACQUES		WIMMENAU	01/01/1828	A		FILM
ELSASS F OF 5	GEORGE		WIMMENAU	01/01/1828	A		FILM
ELSASS F OF 6	CHRETIEN 2ND		WIMMENAU	01/01/1828	A		FILM
ELSASS F OF 7	CHRETIEN 1ST		WIMMENAU	01/01/1828	A		FILM
ELSASSER F OF 4	JACQUES		BRUMATH	01/01/1828	A		FILM
ELSEN	ANTOINE	1838	HERRLISHEIM	09/22/1857	A		FILM
ELSER	GEORGES	1815	WILDENSOLEN	10/24/1854	NY		FILM
ELSER	IGNACE	1825	HERRLISHEIM	09/21/1850	A		FILM
EMANUEL	ELISE	1825	DURMENACH	07/05/1854	NY		FILM
EMERICH	JACOB		GUNDERSHOFFEN	01/01/1869	NY		NO.2
EMMENACHER	FRANZISKA	1811	SWISS	10/25/1843	TX		FILM
EMMENACHER W W 5CH	JOSEPH	1811	SWISS	10/25/1843	TX		FILM
EMMERT	JOSEPH	1834	MULHOUSE	02/28/1855	NY		FILM
END	JACOB		MARLEN B	09/30/1849	A		FILM
ENDELEN	VINCENT	1823	SOPPE LE BAS	09/28/1846	NY		FILM
ENDELIN	MARIE LOUISE	1859	OBERDORFF	11/12/1865	NY		PRIV

Lastname	Firstname	Birth Year	Birthplace	Emigration	De	Prof	Source
ENDELIN	ODILE	1855	DURLINSDORF	12/01/1860	NO		PRIV
ENDELIN	PHILOMENE	1851	DURLINSDORF	12/01/1860	NO		PRIV
ENDELIN	THERESE	1862	OBERDORF	11/12/1865	NY		PRIV
ENDELIN	THIEBAUT	1816	SAUSHEIM	03/16/1844	NY		PRIV
ENDELIN 8CH	PIERRE	1799	DURLINSDORF	12/01/1860	NO		PRIV
ENDERESS F OF 4	ADAM		PFALZWEYER	01/01/1828	A		FILM
ENDERLE	JEAN PIERRE		HAGUENAU	03/01/1838	A		FILM
ENDERLEN	PIERRE	1813	SOPPE LE BAS	04/19/1847	NY		FILM
ENDERLEN W 4CH	ANNE MARIE	1790	ELOISE	03/11/1854	DT		FILM
ENDERLEN W W 3CH	ANTOINE	1816	PFEFFERHAUSEN	02/08/1854	NY		FILM
ENDERLEN W W 3CH	JOSEPH	1787	STRUTH	11/16/1847	NY		FILM
ENDERLIN	EMILE	1865	OBERDORFF	11/12/1865	NY		FILM
ENDERLIN	FRANC. ANTOINE	1823	PFETTERHAUSEN	09/02/1853	A		FILM
ENDERLIN	FRANCOISE JOSEP	1832	GANSBRUNNEN SWISS	07/04/1852	NY		FILM
ENDERLIN	IGNACE	1843	DURLINSDORF	12/01/1860	NO		FILM
ENDERLIN	ISIDORE	1841	DURLINSDORF MULHOUS	01/20/1180	NO		FILM
ENDERLIN	JEAN GEORGES		KAMDRINGEN B (KUENDR	04/03/1849	NY		FILM
ENDERLIN	JOSEPH	1825	OBERDORFF SWISS	04/03/1852	NY		FILM
ENDERLIN	JOSEPH	1845	DURLINSDORF	12/01/1860	NO		FILM
ENDERLIN	JOSEPH	1860	OBERDORFF B-R	11/12/1865	NY		FILM
ENDERLIN	MADELAINE	1835	OBERDORFF	11/12/1865	NY		FILM
ENDERLIN	MARIE	1815	DURLINSDORF	12/01/1860	A		FILM
ENDERLIN H ELISABETH	HENRI	1802	COURTAVON	12/01/1844	TX	ENGI	SHIP
ENDERLIN W HENRI	ELISABETH	1804	COURTAVON	12/01/1844	TX		SHIP
ENDERLIN W W 1 CH	HENRI	1801	COURTAVON	04/11/1840	PH		FILM
ENDERLIN W W 2CH	DOMINIQUE	1829	PFEFFERHAUSEN	03/07/1854	NY		FILM
ENDERLIN W W 3CH	IGANCE	1836	OBERDORF	11/12/1865	NY		FILM
ENDERLIN W W CH	ANTOINE	1823	PFEFFERHAUSEN	09/21/1853	NY		FILM
ENDERLIN W W CH	ANTOINE	1824	PFEFFERHOUSE	09/13/1852	NY		FILM
ENDERS F OF 4			GERMANY	04/01/1849	NY		FILM
ENDRES F OF 5	ANTOINE		SIEWILLER	03/02/1838	A		FILM
ENG F OF 7	JEAN JACQUES		BRUMATH	01/01/1828	A		FILM
ENGASSER	JEAN MICHEL	1831	BLODELSHEIM	01/28/1852	NY		FILM
ENGEL	CHARLES	1830	GUEMAR	10/16/1852	NY		FILM
ENGEL	DANIEL	1841	BIRLENBACH	01/01/1869	NY		NO.2
ENGEL	DAVID		RAUWILLER OR RANWILR	03/07/1838	A		FILM
ENGEL	ELISABETH	1829	BATTENHEIM	04/26/1852	NY		FILM
ENGEL	GEORGE		MUSSIG	03/03/1838	A		FILM
ENGEL	JACOB		OFFWILLER	01/01/1817	A		NO.2
ENGEL	JEAN	1828	OFTHEIM	03/17/1854	NY		FILM
ENGEL	JEAN	1799	OSTHEIM	03/22/1850	CH		FILM
ENGEL	JEAN BAPTISTE	1833	BATTERHEIM	12/24/1852	NY		FILM
ENGEL	JEAN BAPTISTE	1832	GUEMAR	04/13/1853	NY		FILM
ENGEL	JOSEPH		MUSSI	03/03/1838	A		FILM
ENGEL	LAURENT	1823	GUEMAR	08/26/1857	MX		FILM
ENGEL	PHILIPPE		KESKASTEL	01/01/1828	A		FILM
ENGEL	PIERRE		PETERSBACH	01/01/1822	A		FILM
ENGEL	THEOBALD		OFFWILLER	01/01/1817	A	DAYL	NO.2
ENGEL W D	HEMERSY	1795	BATTENHEIM	08/21/1854	NY		FILM
ENGEL W W	HYMERE		BATTENHEIM	/ /	NO		FILM

Lastname	Firstname	Birth Year	Birthplace	Emigration	De	Prof	Source
ENGEL W W 2CH	JOSEPH	1820	CERNAY	01/16/1854	NY		FILM
ENGEL W W 4CH	THIEBAUT		OFFWILLER	03/03/1817	A		FILM
ENGEL W W 9CH	JACQUES		OFFWILLER	03/03/1817	A		FILM
ENGELHARDT	GEORG	1848	BREMMELBACH	01/01/1869	NY		NO.2
ENGELHARDT	JOHANN	1850	BREMMELBACH	01/01/1866	NY		NO.2
ENGELHARDT	JOSEF	1862	NIEDERLAUTERBACH	01/01/1866	NO		NO.2
ENGELHARDT	JOSEPH		NIEDERLAUTERBACH	01/01/1850	NO		PRIV
ENGELHARDT	JOSEPH	1819	NIEDERLAUTERBACH	01/01/1866			PRIV
ENGELHARDT	MARIE		NIEDERLAUTERBACH	01/01/1850	NO		PRIV
ENGELHARDT	MARIE	1845	NIEDERLAUTERBACH	01/01/1861	NO		PRIV
ENGELHARDT	PIERRE	1859	NIEDERLAUTERBACH	01/01/1866	NO		PRIV
ENGELHARDT F OF 3	JOSEPH		ROESCHWOOG	01/01/1828	A		FILM
ENGELHARDT MN HENTZ	MARIE	1824	NIEDERLAUTERBACH	01/01/1866	NO		PRIV
ENGELHARDT W W 2CH	FREDERIC	1802	ALTENSTATT	10/10/1845	NY		FILM
ENGELHARDT W W 2CH	JACQUES	1827	NIEDERLAUTERBACH	08/02/1854	A		FILM
ENGELMANN	FRANC LOUIS		PLOBSHEIM	03/19/1838	A		FILM
ENGELS	HENRY		RAUWILLER OR RANWILL	03/07/1838	A		FILM
ENGELSMANN	SIEGMUND		HASLACH B	08/21/1849	A		FILM
ENGER W W	ANTOINE		BERNOLSHEIM	03/03/1858	A		FILM
ENGLER	GEORGES	1829	MULHOUSE	08/30/1850	NY		FILM
ENSLIN	KARL	1818	KARLSRUHE B	10/25/1843	TX		FILM
ENSMINGER	CHRETIEN		HAMBACH	03/28/1828	A		FILM
ENSMINGER	JACQUES		TIEFFENBACH	01/01/1828	A		FILM
ENSMINGER	SAMUEL		TREFFENBACH	01/01/1828	A		FILM
ENSMINGER F OF 3	GUILLAUME		HAMBACH	03/08/1838	A		FILM
ENSMINGER F OF 4	PHILIPPE		DIEMERINGEN	01/03/1838	A		FILM
ENSMINGER F OF 8	JAKOB		RATZWILLER	01/01/1828	A		FILM
ENSMINGER W W CH	PHILIPPE		HAMBACH	05/26/1817	A		FILM
ENTZ	JOSEPH	1824	OBERHERGHEIM	01/12/1852	A		FILM
ENTZ	XAVIER	1827	OBERHERGHEIM	10/19/1854	NY		FILM
ENTZ W W 3CH	IGNACE	1798	ROUFFACH	09/30/1839	A		FILM
EPPLER	JEAN		DUERINGEN HESSEN	04/11/1849	A		FILM
ERB	CHARLES HENRI		BERGHAUSEN B	05/12/1849	NY		FILM
ERB	CHRETIEN		SELESTAT	03/03/1819	A		FILM
ERB	JEAN		SELSTAT	02/22/1819	A		FILM
ERB F OF 5	CHARLES		ALLENWILLER	01/01/1828	A		FILM
ERB F OF 9	NICLAS		ALTENWILLER	01/01/1828	A		FILM
ERCK W W 3CH	JEAN ANTOINE	1798	HERRLISHEIM	12/30/1847	SL		FILM
ERDMANN	CAROLINE	1829	GUEBWILLER	03/31/1857	NY		FILM
ERDMANN	CATHERINE	1797	GUNGWILLER	04/09/1842	PH		FILM
ERDMANN W W D	CHRETIEN	1796	REXINGEN BAS RHIN	10/24/1839	PH		FILM
ERGENSCHAEFTER	ALOYSE		BERGHEIM	/ /	A		FILM
ERHARD	JEAN	1830	BRUEBACH	03/28/1854	NY		FILM
ERHARD	JEAN ADAM		ASSWILLER	03/03/1817	A		FILM
ERHARD	JOSEPH	1819	UEBERSTRASS	07/08/1852	NY		FILM
ERHARD	JOSEPH		UEBERSTRASS	04/30/1846	NY		FILM
ERHARD	JOSEPH	1822	WILLER CANTON THANN	05/29/1846	NY		FILM
ERHARD	NICOLAS	1826	SOPPE LE BAS	10/30/1851	NY		FILM
ERHARD W W 5CH	ADAM		ASSWILLER	03/11/1817	A		FILM
ERHARDT	CATHERINE		OBERHOFFEN	03/01/1838	A		FILM

Lastname	Firstname	Birth Year	Birthplace	Emigration	De	Prof	Source
ERHARDT	JEAN		RENCHEN B	10/05/1849	A		FILM
ERHARDT W W 2CH	DANIEL		OBERHOFFEN	03/01/1838	A		FILM
ERHART	MORAND	1833	BRUEBACH	05/16/1854	NY		FILM
ERINHARD WW AND CH 3	LAURENT	1814	OSTHEIM	08/10/1854	NY		FILM
ERLENBACH	PIERRE		KESKASTEL	01/01/1828	A		FILM
ERNEWEIN	BRUNO		SOUFFLENHEIM	03/02/1838	A		FILM
ERNEWEIN	FREDERICE		BOUXWILLER	01/01/1828	A		FILM
ERNEWEIN W W 2CH	IGACE		SOUFFLENHEIM	03/02/1838	A		FILM
ERNIE	FREDERICE			/ /			
ERNIE W W 3CH	FREDERICE	1811	OBERSEEBACH	10/28/1839	NY		FILM
ERNST	ANNA	1844	MUNCHHOUSE	01/01/1865	NY		NO.2
ERNST	CHRISTE	1823	BORON TERR. BELFORT	10/05/1846	NY		FILM
ERNST	GREGOIRE		ZINSHEIM B	04/14/1849	NY		FILM
ERNST	IDA	1867	MUNCHHOUSE	01/01/1868	NY		NO.2
ERNST	JAKOB	1804	HORB W	10/23/1843	TX		FILM
ERNST	JAQUES	1804		10/01/1843	TX	CULT	SHIP
ERNST	JOSEPH	1808	BLODELSHEIM	10/01/1851	TX		PASS
ERNST	JOSEPH	1828	BLODELSHEIM	10/15/1851	TX		FILM
ERNST	JOSEPH	1836	BORON TERR BELFORT	12/15/1854	NY		FILM
ERNST	M.ANNA	1843	MUNCHHOUSE	01/01/1868	NY		NO.2
ERNST	MADELEINE		MUNCHHAUSEN	01/01/1850	NO		PRIV
ERNST	MAGDALENA	1845	MUNCHHOUSE	01/01/1867	NY		NO.2
ERNST	MAGDALENA	1865	MUNCHHOUSE	01/01/1868	NY		NO.2
ERNST	MARIE-ANNE	1838	MEYENHEIM	01/01/1856	TX		PASS
ERNST	MATHILDE	1862	MUNCHHOUSE	01/01/1868	NY		NO.2
ERNST	MATHILDE	1865	MUNCHHOUSE	01/01/1865	NY		NO.2
ERNST	MICHEL		IMBSHEIM	01/01/1828	A		FILM
ERNST	PIERRE	1828	BORON TERR BELFORT	07/05/1848	NY		FILM
ERNST CH 2	SERAPHIN	1814	BLODELSHEIM	11/01/1851	TX	BRLA	PASS
ERNST CH 6	FRANCOIS-ANTOIN	1816	BLODELSHEIM	10/01/1851	TX	BRLA	PASS
ERNST F OF 2	JACQUES		IMBSHEIM	04/14/1849	NY		FILM
ERNST W SI A 3CH	CATHERINE	1819	THANN	07/22/1847	NY		FILM
ERNST W W 1 CH	MARTIN	1836	MUNCHHOUSE	01/01/1865		FARM	NO.2
ERNST W W 3 CH	JOSEF	1808	MUNCHHOUSE	01/01/1868	NY		NO.2
ERNST W W 6CH	FRANCOIS ANTOI	1816	BLODELSHEIM	09/11/1851	TX		FILM
ERNWEIN	LOUIS		BURCKENWALD MARMOUTI	01/01/1828	A		FILM
ERNY	FREDRIC	1825	RIXHEIM	10/23/1849	NY		FILM
ERRICH	JEAN	1825	HORBOURG	05/27/1852	NY		FILM
ERTEL F OF 2	JACQUES		ILLKIRCH	05/03/1838	A		FILM
ERTZ	JEAN		BOUXWILLER	01/01/1828	A		FILM
ESCH	JACQUES		MONSWILLER	01/01/1828	A		FILM
ESCHBACH	JOSEPHINE	1828	INGERSHEIM	11/03/1854	NY		FILM
ESCHBACH W NIECE	MARGUERITE	1830	INGERSHEIM	01/10/1853	A		FILM
ESCHBACH W W 1CH	JEAN PIERRE	1823	INGERSHEIM	11/29/1851	NO		FILM
ESCHBACH W W 2CH	FRANCOIS JOSEPH		OBERNAI	05/26/1817	A		FILM
ESCHBACH W W 2CH	XAVIER	1814	INGERSHEIM	11/26/1851	NO		FILM
ESCHBACH W W 7CH	JOSEPH		HOHATZENHEIM	05/12/1817	A		FILM
ESCHEMANN W W 3CH	FRANCOIS	1817	EGUENIGUE	08/27/1846	NY		FILM
ESCHENBRENNER	BALTHASAR		WINGEN	01/01/1828	A		FILM
ESCHER 7 CH	JACQUES			/ /			

Lastname	Firstname	Birth Year	Birthplace	Emigration	De	Prof	Source
ESCHER F OF 5	MARTIN		BALDENHEIM	03/06/1838	A		FILM
ESCHER F OF 7	JACQUES		BALDENHEIM	03/06/1838	A		FILM
ESCHIENSCHANG W W 7C	ETINNE	1798	ROEDERSDORFF	03/18/1844	NY		FILM
ESCHLIMANN	PIERRE	1818	WILLER	02/16/1841	NY		FILM
ESCHRICH F OF 5	MICHEL		ALTECKENDORF	01/01/1828	A		FILM
ETSCHMANN	GUILLAUME		DURLACH	05/12/1849	NY		FILM
ETSCHMANN	LOUIS		DURLACH	05/12/1849	NY		FILM
ETTER	ADAM		SCHOENBOURG	01/01/1828	A		FILM
ETTER	ANNE MARIE		SCHOENBURG	01/01/1828	A		FILM
ETTER	JACQUES		PFALZWEYER	01/01/1828	A		FILM
ETTER	LAURENT TWIN		SCHOENBURG	01/01/1828	A		FILM
ETTER	LOUIS TWIN		SCHOENBURG	01/01/1828	A		FILM
ETTER	PIERRE		SCHOENBURG	01/01/1828	A		FILM
ETTER NIECE ETTER AM	ANNE MARIE		SCHOENBURG	01/01/1828	A		FILM
ETTERBRECHTOLD F OF6	ETIENNE		MARLENHEIM	01/01/1828	A		FILM
ETTLING F OF 4	GEORGE		OBERMODERN	01/01/1828	A		FILM
EUBEL	JOHANN		NEHWILLER	01/01/1817	A		NO.2
EUBEL W W 2CH	JEAN		NEHWILLER	03/11/1817	A		FILM
EURMILLER W W 2CH	PHILIPPE		ASSWILLER	03/03/1817	A		FILM
EURMINGER	JN PIERRE		MACKWILLER	03/18/1817	A		FILM
EURMINGER	PHILIPPE		MACKWILLER	03/18/1817	A		FILM
EUSMINGER W W 2CH	PHILIPPE		ASSWILLER	03/11/1817	A		FILM
EVA F OF 4	PHILIPPE		OERMINGEN	01/01/1828	A		FILM
EVA F OF 7	PHILIPPE		OERMINGEN	01/01/1828	A		FILM
EYERMANN	HEINRICH	1845	MERCKWILLER	01/01/1869	NY	FARM	NO.2
EYLIN	JACQUES	1830	BOURAGNE FRANCE	04/09/1866	NY		FILM
EYMANN	SEBASTIEN	1828	LIEPVRE	08/23/1850	NO		FILM
EYMEN	CATHERINE	1837	ILLZACH	07/01/1857	NY		FILM

Lastname	Firstname	Birth Year	Birthplace	Emigration	De	Prof	Source
FAAS	JUSTINE		SCHWARTZENBERG W	09/21/1849	A		FILM
FABER	SEBASTIEN		RIEGEL B	06/04/1849	A		FILM
FABER	VALENTIN	1832	MULHOUSE	10/21/1853	NY		FILM
FAERBER F OF 5	JACQUES		INGVILLER	01/01/1828	A		FILM
FAES W W 2 CH	NICOLAS		MACKWILLER	03/03/1817	A		FILM
FAESSEL	THERESE		WILWISHEIM	01/01/1828	A		FILM
FAESSEL	THERESE		WILWISHEIM	01/01/1828	A		FILM
FAESSLER	BENOIT		ICHENHEIM	04/23/1849	NY		FILM
FAHIS W S	MARIE ANN	1792	ANDELNANS	02/25/1848	NY		FILM
FAHR	JEAN		HAGUENAU	01/01/1828	A		FILM
FAHRMANN	MARKUS		MIERINGEN W	04/13/1849	NY		FILM
FAHRNE F OF 8	JEAN		SUNDHAUSEN	03/28/1837	A		FILM
FAHRNER	FRANCOIS JOSEF	1805	BALDENHEIM	11/08/1845	SL		FILM
FAHRNER	JEAN MICHEL	1810	BALDENHEIM	11/08/1845	SL		FILM
FAHRNER W W 2 CH	ANDRE	1817	BALDENHEIM	11/08/1845	SL		FILM
FAHRNER W W 4CH	FRANC.JOSEPH	1805	BALDENHEIM	12/19/1846	SL		FILM
FAIRET	FRANCOIS	1819	NOVILLARS	09/10/1850	NO		PRIV
FAIRET W F	LOUIS	1794	GRANDVILLARS	04/21/1854	NY		PRIV
FAITE W 5 CH	MARGERITE	1805	OFFEMONT	03/26/1847	NY		FILM
FAIVRE	FRANC.XAVIER	1824	OUXELLES BAS	06/05/1851	NY	FARM	FILM
FAIVRE	HENRY		NOMAIS DOUBS	11/20/1865	NY	FARM	FILM
FAIVRE	JEAN PIERRE	1820	RECHOTTE	04/04/1839	NY		FILM
FAIVRE	LOUIS	1797	RECHOTTE	03/31/1846	NY	FARM	FILM
FAIVRE	LOUIS JOSEPH	1822	VALDIEN	02/28/1849	NY	FARM	FILM
FAIVRE	MARIE ANNE	1821	VALDIEN	07/09/1847	NO		FILM
FAIVRE	SOPHIE MARIE	1820	VALDIEN	07/09/1847	NO		FILM
FAIVRE F OF 4	PIERRE		ASSWILLER	03/06/1838	A		FILM
FALK	CATHERINA	1820	MONTBELIARD	04/14/1866	NY		FILM
FALK	CHARLES	1846	MONTBELIARD	04/14/1866	NY		FILM
FALK	LOUISE	1848	MONTBELIARD	04/14/1866	NY		FILM
FALK	THIEBAUD	1838	SENTHEIM	12/07/1865	NY		FILM
FALLASTRE	MARIE ANNE		PEROUSE	10/14/1852	NO		FILM
FALLECKER	THIEBAUD	1821	LEIMBACH	04/06/1848	NY		FILM
FALLER	ALOYSE		ZEHRINGEN B	03/20/1828	A		FILM
FALLER	ENGELHARD		NEUKIRCH B	07/29/1849	A		FILM
FALLER	GREGOIRE	1813	GRUNHOLTZ B	08/11/1854	NY		FILM
FANDELEUR	MARIE FRANCOIS	1814	ETTNEFONT BAS	10/13/1852	A		FILM
FARNY	CHARLES	1813	ILLHAEUSERN	07/29/1853	NY		FILM
FARNY W W 4 CH	CHARLES	1809	ILLHAEUSERN	07/29/1853	NY		FILM
FARNY W W 6 CH	JACQUES	1806	ST.CROIX AUX MINES	/ /	NY		FILM
FARSCHOIR W W 5CH	SEBASTIEN	1805	BELLENBORN	10/24/1854	NY		FILM
FASCHEINER	JEAN CHRETIEN	1820	KAYSERSBERG	02/17/1849	NY		FILM
FATH	JOHANN	1839	BREMMELBACH	01/01/1866	NY		NO.2
FATZ	THIEBAUT		SENTHEIM	12/07/1865	NY		FILM
FAUCHE	ANNE MARGARETHE	1840		09/17/1845	TX		FILM
FAUCHE	ELISABETH	1801		09/17/1845	TX		FILM
FAUCHE	MARIE	1830		09/17/1845	TX		FILM
FAUCHE W W 2CH	FRANCOIR NICOLA	1798		09/17/1845	TX		FILM
FAUCKLER	ARBAJACH		HASLACH B	07/30/1849	A		FILM
FAUGLE	XAVIER	1839	GIROMAGNY	03/24/1865	NY		FILM

Lastname	Firstname	Birth Year	Birthplace	Emigration	De	Prof	Source
FAULLIMMEL	CATHERINE		KURTZENHAUSEN	01/01/1828	A		FILM
FAUST	BALTHASAR		TIEFFENBACH	01/01/1828	A		FILM
FAUST	JEAN BAPTISTE	1818	ROUFFACH	12/29/1842	A		FILM
FAUST	MICHEL	1838	ROUFFACH	02/22/1855	A		PRIV
FAUST	NICOLAS		TIEFFENBACH	01/01/1828	A		FILM
FAUST F OF 6	JEAN		LOCHWILLER	01/01/1828	A		FILM
FAUTH W W 4 CH	MICHEL		OELBRONN B	04/11/1849	A		FILM
FAUTSCH	FRANC. EUGEN	1830	ROUGEMONT	10/15/1844	NO		FILM
FAVET	ALEXANDRE	1826	HUGHVILLERS	02/17/1849	NY		PRIV
FAVRE	HENRI		ASSWILLER	01/01/1838	A		FILM
FAWET	ALEXANDRE	1826	HUGVILLERS	02/17/1849	NY		FILM
FAWET	FRANCOIS		MORVILLARS	02/17/1849	A		FILM
FAYARD	JEAN	1813	UNIEUX LOIRE	08/14/1189	NO		FILM
FEBER W W 2CH	MONRAD	1807	ST ULRICH	05/05/1847	NY		FILM
FECHTER	ZACHARIE		WAYERLOCH B	08/24/1849	A		FILM
FECKERT	MICHEL	1807	BLODELSHEIM	08/01/1849	TX	CULT	PASS
FECKLING F OF 9	JEAN		SCHILLERSDORF	01/01/1828	A		FILM
FEDERSPIEL	AUGUSTIN	1819	BISEL	11/27/1839	NY		FILM
FEGER	MARIE		WILWISHEIM	01/01/1828	A		FILM
FEGER	PAULINE	1824	ZELL B	08/23/1850	NY		FILM
FEHR	JACQUES		LICHTENBERG	01/01/1828	A		FILM
FEHR	PIERRE		LICHTENBERG	01/01/1828	A		
FEIGEL	GEORG MICHEL	1826	ROPPENHEIM	03/15/1846	A		NO.1
FEIGEL	PHILLIPE GEORGE		ROPPENHEIM	03/06/1838	A		FILM
FEIGEL S MICHEL	MADELAINE	1820	ROPPENHEIM	03/09/1848	A		NO.1
FEIL	JEAN BAPTISTE	1808	ALLEMAND ROMBACH	08/24/1838	NY		FILM
FEIST	ISAAC	1851	TRIEMBACH	01/01/1866	NY		NO.2
FEIST	JEAN GEORGES		GERMANY	04/03/1849	NY		FILM
FEIST	MARGARETHE	1846	KAIDENBURG	01/01/1869	NY		NO.2
FELDEN F OF 5	GEORGE		OBERMODERN	01/01/1828	A		FILM
FELDEN F OF 6	PHILIPPE		ZUTZENDORF	01/01/1828	A		FILM
FELDER	JOSEPH	1822	MULHOUSE	01/08/1848	NY		FILM
FELDER CH 6	FRANCOIS JOSEPH	1799	ST AMARIN	08/01/1844	TX	TOUR	PASS
FELDER CH 6	FRANCOIS JOSEPH	1799	ST. AMARIN	08/01/1844	TX		
FELDER W W 6CH	JEAN JOSEPH	1799	ST AMARIN	01/01/1828	NY		FILM
FELEY	FRANCOIS	1839	FRAHIER	10/15/1861	NY		FILM
FELLAT	LOUIS	1808	LIPEVRE	08/14/1838	NO		FILM
FELLMANN	JOSEPH	1824	HERRLISHEIM	03/27/1847	NY		FILM
FELLMANN W W CH	JOSEPH	1819	GUEBERSCHWIHR	04/18/1852	A		FILM
FELLRATH	LOUIS		ENGENTHAL	01/01/1828	A		FILM
FELTEN	MADELAINE		ROPPENHEIM	03/06/1838	A		FILM
FELTER	ANTOINE		LEUTENHEIM	03/01/1838	A		FILM
FELTER	JOSEPH		LEUTENHEIM	03/01/1838	A		FILM
FELTZ W F	LOUIS	1814	HUTTENHEIM	09/11/1851	TX		FILM
FENDENHEIM F OF 5	PHILIPPE		GERSTHEIM	03/03/1838	A		FILM
FENNER	CATHERINE		HATTMATT	01/01/1828	A		FILM
FENNER F OF 2	HENRY		HATTMATT	01/01/1828	A		FILM
FENNER F OF 7	JACQUES		ERNOLSHEIM	01/01/1828	A		FILM
FERARD	MARIE FRANCOISE	1828	FOUSSEMAGNE	03/08/1847	NY		FILM
FERBER	ALBERT	1835	MULHOUSE	06/12/1854	NY		FILM

Lastname	Firstname	Birth Year	Birthplace	Emigration	De	Prof	Source
FERBER W W 5CH	GEORGE		BOSSELSHAUSEN	01/01/1828	A		FILM
FERCHER	ANTOINE	1829	BIESHEIM	03/19/1851	NY		FILM
FERE	ZUERIN	1807	LIEPVRE	12/05/1848	NO		PRIV
FERE MN KNOLL	CECILE		LIEPVRE	11/05/1856	NO		PRIV
FERE W W S A D	LIEPVERE	1856	LIEPVRE	11/05/1856	NO		FILM
FERNBACH	ETIENNE		GRASSENDORFF	02/28/1838	A		FILM
FERNBACH F OF 6	JOSEPH		MORSCHWILLER	03/04/1838	A		FILM
FERNET	MARGUERITE	1845	ROUGEMONT	10/11/1866	NY		FILM
FERR W W 3CH	JEAN BAPTISTE	1803	MITTELWIHR	10/14/1846	TX		FILM
FERRIET W F	PHILIPPE	1795	BAUME LES DAMES	09/29/1851	NY		FILM
FERRIOT	PHILLIPPE FRANC	1832	DELLE	07/18/1849	NY		FILM
FERRY	MATHIAS		VESCEMENT	11/02/1865	NY		FILM
FESE	MADELAINE		WILWISHEIM	01/01/1828	A		FILM
FESSLER	FLORENT		LOCHWILLER	01/01/1828	A		FILM
FESSLER F OF 2	JOSEPH		LACHWILLER	01/01/1828	A		FILM
FESSMANN F OF 2	MICHEL		GEUDERTHEIM	03/01/1838	A		FILM
FEST	LOUIS	1819	HIRTZFELDEN	11/01/1850	TX	DAYL	PASS
FEST	SIMON	1827	HIRTZFELDEN	11/01/1846	TX	SERV	SHIP
FEST	SIMON	1827	HIRTZFELDEN	11/15/1846	TX		FILM
FEST	SIMON	1826	HIRTZFELDEN	11/15/1846	TX		FILM
FEST W F	LOUIS	1819	HIRTZFELDEN	11/28/1850	TX		FILM
FETE	LOUIS	1785	OFFEMONT	03/06/1841	NY		FILM
FETES	LOUIS	1821	OFFEMONT	02/01/1840	LV		FILM
FETTAT	LOUIS	1808	LIEPVRE	08/14/1838	NO		FILM
FETTEL W W	JEAN JOSEPH	1822	LIEPVRE	09/14/1854	NO		FILM
FETTER	ADELE	1845	BIRCKENWALD	05/09/1862	A		FILM
FETZER	JOSEPH	1819	HEGENHEIM	08/07/1850	NY		FILM
FEUDENHEIM				/ /			
FEUDENHEIM F OF 5	PHILIPPE		GERSTHEIM	03/03/1838	A		FILM
FEUDERICH	FIDELE		KUERTZEL B	09/30/1849	A		FILM
FEUERSTEIN	JOSEPH		THAL	01/01/1828	A		FILM
FEUERSTOSS	MARGUERITTE		KESKASTEL	01/01/1817	A		FILM
FEUERSTOSS	PHILLIPPE		KESKASTEL	01/01/1817	A		FILM
FEUVRE	FRANCOIS	1823	RECHOTTE	03/31/1846	NY		FILM
FEVE	JUSTINE	1836	LIEPVRE	08/01/1854	NO		FILM
FEY W 2CH MN MEY	MADELAINE	1800	HOHWILLER	10/06/1851	PA		FILM
FEYE W W 4CH	GEORGE		ST MAURICE	03/16/1838	A		FILM
FEYER	MADELAINE		WILWISHEIM	01/01/1828	A		FILM
FEYLER F OF 5	JOSEPH		DOSSENHEIM	01/01/1828	A		FILM
FEYLER W W 3CH	JEAN		DOSSENHEIM	03/31/1817	A		FILM
FIAT	CHARLES	1820	MASSEVAUX	04/02/1847	NY		FILM
FICHRER	FRIDOLIN	1823	SEPPOIS LE BAS	05/27/1852	PA		FILM
FICHT	BARBE		WOLSCHHEIM	01/01/1828	A		FILM
FICHT	PIERRE		FURCHHAUSEN	01/01/1828	A		FILM
FICHT F OF 2	PIERRE		HATTMATT	01/01/1828	A		FILM
FICHTER W 4CH	ANNE MARIE		SALESTAT	05/27/1817	A		FILM
FIDEL	PETER		GERMANY	04/12/1849	A		FILM
FIEGEL	ANTOINE F OF 2		BAERENDORF	03/01/1837	A		FILM
FIEGEL	ELISABETH		BAERENDORF	03/01/1837	A		FILM
FIEGEL	REMI		ESCHWILLER	03/01/1838	A		FILM

Lastname	Firstname	Birth Year	Birthplace	Emigration	De	Prof	Source
FIEGEL F OF 2	ANTOINE		BAERENDORF	03/01/1837	A		FILM
FIEGEL F OF 4	MICHEᵬ		TIEFFENBACH	01/01/1828	A		FILM
FIEGEL F OF 6	GEORGES		PFALZWEYER	01/01/1828	A		FILM
FIEHRER	FRIDOLIN	1823	SEPPOIS LE BAS	05/27/1852	A		FILM
FIELTZ	LOUIS	1814	STEINBACH	09/01/1851	TX	TEAC	PASS
FIESSINGEN W W	JOSEPH	1810	RIMBACH ZELL	01/22/1840	NY		FILM
FIETIER	FRANCOIS XAVIER	1828	VAULHIESMON	02/23/1857	NY		FILM
FIGEL W W 1CH	MICHEL		PETERSBACH	03/11/1817	A		FILM
FILLINGER	FRANCOIS ANTOIE	1824	OBERENTZEN	11/19/1855	TX		FILM
FILLINGER	FRANCOIS ANTOIM		OBERENTZEN	11/01/1855	TX	CHAR	PASS
FILLIPS W W 2CH	SEBASTIEN		SOUFFLENHEIM	03/02/1838	A		FILM
FILWEBER W 2D A GRCH	BARBE	1797	BERGHEIM	01/30/1856	NY		FILM
FINAINE W W	JEAN BAPTISTE	1824	ALLEMAND RIMBACH	08/12/1854	NO		FILM
FINAME	SEBASTIEN	1826	THANNENKIRCH	09/23/1852	MX		FILM
FINCK	ABRAHAM		BOSSELSHAUSEN	01/01/1828	A		FILM
FINCK W W	ANTOINE	1794	LANGENEGEZ AUSTRIA	12/15/1845	A		FILM
FINCKEBOHNER	FREDERIC	1814	BAHR	03/22/1841	NY		FILM
FINGER C 1	JOSEPH I	1816	OBERENTZEN	09/01/1846	TX	CULT	PASS
FINGER MN ZURCHER	ELISABETH			09/01/1846	TX		PASS
FINGER S JOSEPH I	JOSEPH II			09/01/1846	TX		PASS
FINGER W W 1 CH	JOSEPH	1816	OBERENTZEN	09/08/1846	A		FILM
FINOT W W	FRANCOIS XAVIER	1810	CERNAY	01/08/1850	NO		FILM
FIRET MN GERENT.3CH		1814	BEAUCOURT	02/07/1842	NY		FILM
FISCHER	ALBIN		GERMANY	05/04/1849	NY		FILM
FISCHER	B. A E. LADIES		GERMANY	03/31/1849	A		FILM
FISCHER	CAROLINE PHILIP		STRASSBOURG	06/04/1817	A		FILM
FISCHER	CATHERINE		KESKASTEL	01/01/1828	A		FILM
FISCHER	CHRETIEN		ZOLLINGEN	01/01/1828	A		FILM
FISCHER	DANIEL		ZOLLINGEN	01/01/1828	A		FILM
FISCHER	ETIENNE	1818	ZIMMERSHEIM	09/19/1849	NY		FILM
FISCHER	EUGENE	1844	WOLFGANTZEN	04/21/1857	NY		FILM
FISCHER	FREDERIC		PFAFFENHOFFEN W	03/01/1837	A		FILM
FISCHER	FRIDOLIN	1823	SEPPOIS LE BAS	05/27/1852	PA		FILM
FISCHER	GEORGE	1817	KUNHEIM	03/30/1846	NY		FILM
FISCHER	JACQUES		PFAFFENHOFFEN W	01/03/1837	A		FILM
FISCHER	JACQUES	1839	SIEGEN	01/26/1857	NY		FILM
FISCHER	JAKOB		GERMANY	04/01/1849	NY		FILM
FISCHER	JEAN JACQUES	1828	KUENHEIM	08/13/1854	CH		FILM
FISCHER	LOUIS		KESKASTEL	01/01/1828	A		FILM
FISCHER	MARIE ANNE	1848	ASCHPACH	01/01/1868	NY		NO.2
FISCHER	MARTIN	1861	ASCHPACH	01/01/1868	NY		NO.2
FISCHER	SEBASTIEN	1824	ODEREN	09/01/1860	TX	DAYL	PASS
FISCHER	THIEBAUD	1822	HINDLINGEN	02/20/1847	NY		FILM
FISCHER	THIEBAUT		SCHOPPERTEN	01/01/1828	A		FILM
FISCHER F OF 2	MICHEL		BOUXWILLER	01/01/1828	A		FILM
FISCHER F OF 5	FREDERIC		NEUWILLER	01/01/1828	A		FILM
FISCHER F OF 6	ANDRE		KESKASTEL	01/01/1828	A		FILM
FISCHER F OF 6	ANDRE		KESKASTEL	01/20/1828	A		FILM
FISCHER W 4CH	YVE RETSET		ERCKARTSWILLER	03/11/1817	A		FILM
FISCHER W SI 2CH	THIRRI	1819	ZILLISHEIM	12/11/1849	PA		FILM

Lastname	Firstname	Birth Year	Birthplace	Emigration	De	Prof	Source
FISCHER W W	PIERRE		LORENTZEN	01/01/1828	A		FILM
FISCHER W W 2CH	GEORGES	1792	KUNHEIM	05/08/1847	NY		FILM
FISCHER W W 2CH	JOSEPH	1810	JONCHERRY	03/06/1847	NY		FILM
FISCHER W W 7CH	GEORGE		KESKASTEL	01/01/1817	A		FILM
FISCHER W W7 CH	MICHEL		BAERENDORF	03/18/1817	A		FILM
FISCHESSER	THERESE	1826	BATTENHEIM	08/29/1854	NY		FILM
FLACH W W 5CH	CHARLES DAVID		HARSKIRCHEN	01/01/1828	A		FILM
FLANS W W M A 7CH	DAVID	1801	HUNAWIHR	04/12/1847	NY		FILM
FLECKSTEIN	NICOLAS		LOHR	01/01/1828	A		FILM
FLEIG	JOSEPH	1810	GRAFENHAUSEN B	01/06/1835	A		FILM
FLEIG W W 5 CH	ANTOINE	1805	BOERSCH	10/09/1187	SL		FILM
FLEISCH	ALEXANDRE	1830	MOLLAU	02/28/1854	PH		FILM
FLEITH	ANTOINE	1787	RIEDWIHR	10/12/1837	PH		FILM
FLEMMELEN	MATHIEU	1811	BALSCHWILLER	03/11/1842	NY		FILM
FLEUR	XAVIER	1829	DANJOUTIN	02/24/1848	NY		FILM
FLEURENT	MARGUERITE	1808	ETUEFFONT OR EITEMBS	08/31/1838	NO		FILM
FLEURY	JOSEPH	1827	LEPUIX	03/28/1846	PH		FILM
FLEURY	MARIE	1824	LEOUIX	05/14/1847	NY		FILM
FLEURY	SIMON	1812	ST DIZIER	03/09/1841	NY		FILM
FLEURY W W 4 CH	JEAN PIERRE	1801	FAVEROIS	02/24/1847	NY		FILM
FLEUT	XAVIER	1829	DANJOUTIN	02/24/1848	NY		FILM
FLICK	JAQUES	1850	NIEDERLAUTERBACH	01/01/1866	NY		PRIV
FLIEG	ANASTASIUS		ERLACH B	07/29/1849	A		FILM
FLIELLER	AUGUSTIN	1832	URBES	07/29/1854	TX		FILM
FLIELLER	JOSEPH	1792	KRUTH	01/24/1845	NY		FILM
FLIELLER CH 2	AUGUSTIN	1832	URBES	07/01/1854	TX	PRIN	PASS
FLIELLER D AUGUSTIN	BARBE	1852	URBES	07/01/1854	TX		PASS
FLIELLER D AUGUSTIN	CATHERINE	1849	URBES	07/01/1854	TX		PASS
FLIETZ OR FLEETZ	DAMIEN		GERMANY	04/17/1849	A		FILM
FLIETZ OR FLEETZ	FRANCISKA		GERMANY	04/17/1849	A		FILM
FLITZ OR FLEETZ	JEAN		GERMANY	04/17/1849	A		FILM
FLOR F OF 3	JOSEPH		ERCKARTSWILLER	01/01/1828	A		FILM
FLORANG	ANTOINE	1823	KATZENTHAL	10/20/1854	NO		FILM
FLORANG W W 5CH	ANTOINE	1809	KATZENTHAL	07/03/1854	NY		FILM
FLORAT	JEAN PIERRE	1821	MONTREUX VIEUX	01/30/1848	NY		FILM
FLORY W W	ANTOINE	1819	ATTENBACH	05/11/1854	NY		FILM
FLOTAT	JEAN PIERRE	1810	MEROUX	01/30/1844	NY		FILM
FLOTTAT	JACQUES	1826	GUEBWILLER	03/07/1854	NY		FILM
FLUG	ANDRE		MUELLENBACH B	08/23/1849	A		FILM
FLUHR	MARTIN	1795	BOLLWILLER	10/06/1847	NY		FILM
FLUHR W W 3CH	PIOTRE	1807	LAUW	10/06/1847	NY		FILM
FOERSCHEL	JOSEPH		HOERDT	02/28/1838	A		FILM
FOESS F OF 6	SALOMON		PFALZWEYER	01/01/1828	A		FILM
FOESSEL	ANDRE		WANTZENAU	03/07/1838	A		FILM
FOESSEL MN WILD	MADELAINE		WANTZENAU	03/07/1838	A		FILM
FOESSEL W W 3CH	ANTOINE		WANTZENAU	03/07/1838	A		FILM
FOESSEL W W WILD 3CH	ANTOINE		WANTZENAU	03/07/1838	A		FILM
FOGEL	FERDINAND		EDLINGEN B	09/01/1849	A		FILM
FOHRER	BARTHDEMY	1819	ST CROIX AUX MINES	07/15/1857	NY		FILM
FOHRER W W 2 CH	FRANCOIS ANTOI	1800	TRAUBACH LE HAUT	02/04/1839	NY		FILM

Lastname	Firstname	Birth Year	Birthplace	Emigration	De	Prof	Source
FOLLOT	FRANCOIS XAVIER	1815	OFFEMONT	04/02/1840	LV		FILM
FOLLOT	JOSEPH	1805	SERMAMAGNY TERR BELR	05/27/1846	NY		FILM
FOLTZ	BERNHARD	1851	DRACHENBRONN	01/01/1868	NY		NO.2
FOLTZ	JACQUES	1821	BOUXWILLER	07/06/1853	NY		FILM
FOLTZ	JOSEPH	1796	BOUXWILLER	04/22/1847	NY		FILM
FOLTZ	KARL		LANGENSOULTZBACH	01/01/1849	A		SUESS
FOLTZ	KARL		LAUTERBURG	01/01/1869	NY		NO.2
FOLTZ	MICHEL		LANGENSOULTZBACH	/ /	CA		SUESS
FOLTZ	MICHEL		LANGENSOULTZBACH	01/01/1868	A	FARR	SUESS
FOLTZ	THIEBAUT	1838	SENTHEIM	12/31/1865	NY		FILM
FOLTZENLOGEL	CATHERINA	1830	SURBOURG	01/01/1867	NY		NO.2
FONTAINE	JOSEF	1839	SOULTZ-SOUS-FORET	01/01/1867	NY	CARP	NO.2
FORST H CATHERINE CH	FRANCOIS JOSEPH	1805	KUTZENHAUSEN	12/01/1844	TX	CULT	SHIP
FORST MN MATHES	CATHERINE		KUTZENHAUSEN	12/01/1844	TX		SHIP
FOUNIER	JOSEPH			02/27/1857	A		FILM
FOURNIER	FRANCOIS	1808	BAS-RHIN	12/01/1844	TX	CULT	SHIP
FRANCK	PHILLIP	1849	RITTERSHOFEN	01/01/1868	NY		NO.2
FRANTZ	JACOB	1847	NIEDERBETSCHDORF	01/01/1866	A	FARM	NO.2
FREDERIC	JEAN	1820	RANSPACH	11/01/1843	TX	CULT	SHIP
FREIDRICH	JEAN			01/01/1843	TX		SHIP
FREUND	EMIL		MELLINGEN	/ /	LA		BULL
FREY H BRIGITTE CH 4	JAQUES		REGION OF STRASSBOUR	01/01/1854	TX		SHIP
FREY MN SCHOTT	BRIGITTE		REGION OF STRASBOURG	01/01/1854	TX		SHIP
FRICKER	JOSEPH	1828	BLODELSHEIM	10/01/1851	TX	CULT	PASS
FRICKER CH 1	JOSEPH	1801	NIEDERENTZEN	09/01/1846	TX	DAYL	PASS
FRICKER WW	PIERRE	1796	SOPPE-LE-HAUT	12/01/1844	TX	GWON	SHIP
FRIES	VALENTIN		ZINSWILLER	01/01/1817	A		NO.2
FRISON	CAROLINE	1860	OBERSEEBACH	01/01/1868	NY		NO.2
FRISON	GEORG	1852	OBERSEEBACH	01/01/1868	NY		NO.2
FRISON	JACOB	1868	OBERSEEBACH	01/01/1868	NY		NO.2
FRISON	MARIA ANNA	1851	OBERSEEBACH	01/01/1868	NY		NO.2
FRISON	MARIA EVA	1841	OBERSEEBACH	01/01/1868	NY		NO.2
FRISON	MARTIN	1839	OBERSEEBACH	01/01/1867	NY	FARM	NO.2
FRISON MN MAMOSER	ELISABETH		OBERSEEBACH	01/01/1868	NY		NO.2
FRISON W W 5 CH	PETER	1810	OBERSEEBACH	01/01/1868	NY		NO.2
FRITSCH	JOSEPH		LANGENSULTZBACH	01/01/1841	A		SUESS
FRITSCH	KARL FRIEDRICH		LANGENSULTZBACH	01/01/1843	A		SUESS
FRITSCH	LUDWIG		LANGENSULTZBACH	01/01/1839	A		SUESS
FRITSET W W 4CH	CHRISTOPHE		MACKWILLER	03/11/1817	A		FILM
FRITZ	JEAN	1844	KAIDENBURG	01/01/1866	NY	FARM	NO.2
FRITZ	LOUIS	1802	BRETTEN	12/01/1844	TX	CARP	SHIP
FRITZ	LUDWIG	1837	TRIEMBACH	01/01/1869	NY	FARM	NO.2
FRITZ	MAGDALENA	1843	TRIEMBACH	01/01/1867	NY		NO.2
FRITZ	SALOME	1189	NIEDERROEDERN	01/01/1868	NO		NO.2
FRITZ F OF 8	GEORGE		INGVILLER	01/01/1828	A		FILM
FRITZINGER	GEORG		DAMBACH	01/01/1817	A		NO.2
FRITZINGER	GEORG		ZINSWILLER	03/28/1817	A		FILM
FRITZINGER W W 4CH	CHRETIEN		OERMINGEN	03/23/1817	A		FILM
FROBE	JOSEPH	1816	SWISS	08/24/1866	NY		FILM
FROBE	JOSEPH	1811	SWISS	09/30/1866	NY		FILM

Lastname	Firstname	Year	Birthplace	Emigration	De	Prof	Source
FROCHLY	BERNARD	1821	FERRETTE	11/18/1851	NY		FILM
FROCHLY W 2 D	URSULA	1796	VIEUX FERETTE	04/07/1847	NY		FILM
FROEHLI	EMILE	1865	MULHOUSE	11/16/1865	NY		FILM
FROEHLI	THERESE	1844	MULHOUSE	11/12/1865	NY		FILM
FROEHLI W W 1 S	PIERRE	1830	MULHOUSE	11/12/1865	NY		FILM
FROEHLICH	MATHIAS	1837	OSTHEIM	03/21/1854	NY		FILM
FROEHLICH JR	MATHIAS	1825	OSTHEIM	08/25/1857	NY		FILM
FROEHLIG			GUMBRECHTSHOFEN	05/01/1818	A		FILM
FROEHLINGER W W 4CH	PIERRE		WINGEN	01/01/1828	A		FILM
FROEHLY W F	JOSEPH		VIEUX FERRETTE	/ /	NY		FILM
FROELA	MATHIEU	1825	OSTHEIM	05/19/1848	NY		FILM
FROELICH	MADELAINE	1832	OSTHEIM	02/02/1856	NY		FILM
FROELICH W SI	JACQUES	1833	OSTHEIM	02/02/1856	NY		FILM
FROLICH	CATHERINE	1827	OSTHEIM	04/13/1847	NY		FILM
FROMALD W W	PIERRE	1811	THANN	09/01/1845	PH		FILM
FROMM W W 4CH	ANDRE		MOLSHEIM	03/03/1817	A		FILM
FROMMER	JACQUES	1834	MITTELWIHR	03/11/1854	NY		FILM
FROMONT	FRANCOIS	1814	URCEREY	03/29/1852	NY		FILM
FROSCH	GEORG	1858	LEMBACH	01/01/1866	NY		NO.2
FROSSARD	JOSEPH	1823	FLORIMONT	09/01/1854	NO		FILM
FROTE	JOSEPH	1811	SWISS	09/30/1866	NY		FILM
FRUH	MICHEL	1821	COLMAR	08/04/1854	NY		FILM
FUCHS	AGATHE	1818	OLDEREN	11/04/1857	TX		FILM
FUCHS	ANNE-MARIE	1832	KRUTH	08/01/1860	TX	SERV	PASS
FUCHS	ANTON A FRANZIS	1817	RANSPACH	01/15/1846	A		FILM
FUCHS	CAROLINE	1833	ST HYPOLITE	03/03/1854	NY		FILM
FUCHS	CATHERINE	1815	MULHAUSEN	09/04/1845	NO		FILM
FUCHS	CATHERINE	1815	MULHAUSEN	01/29/1847	SL		FILM
FUCHS	FRANCOIS JOSEPH	1816	ZELLENBERG	05/10/1853	NY		FILM
FUCHS	FRANCOIS JOSEPH	1829	THANN	09/24/1856	NY		FILM
FUCHS	GEORGE		BADENWEYER (WEILER?B	06/20/1849	A		FILM
FUCHS	GEORGE		AUENHEIM	04/21/1849	NY		FILM
FUCHS	GEORGES	1802	IHRINGEN B	10/22/1847	NY		FILM
FUCHS	GEORGES W BR	1825	LIEPVRE	09/16/1847	NO		FILM
FUCHS	GERTRUDE		ROHRWILLER	03/12/1838	A		FILM
FUCHS	JACQUES		ALTECKENDORF	01/01/1828	A		FILM
FUCHS	JACQUES		ROHRWILLER	03/12/1838	A		FILM
FUCHS	JEAN		AUENHEIM	04/21/1849	NY		FILM
FUCHS	JOSEPH		FORSTHEIM	01/01/1817	A		NO.2
FUCHS	JOSEPH		SCHIRRHEIM	03/05/1838	A		FILM
FUCHS	JOSEPH	1826	HEITEREN	01/31/1852	NY		FILM
FUCHS	MARIE ANNE		ROHRWILLER	03/12/1838	A		FILM
FUCHS	MARTIN	1818	OBERGHERGHEIM	09/01/1846	TX	CULT	PASS
FUCHS	MARTIN	1818	OBERHERGHEIM	09/14/1846	TX		FILM
FUCHS	NICOLAS	1814	ODEREN	11/04/1857	TX		FILM
FUCHS	PIERRE MODESTE	1830	MUNTZEHEIM	11/11/1853	A		FILM
FUCHS	XAVIER	1856	ODEREN	04/11/1857	TX		FILM
FUCHS SEN	JACQUES		ROHRWILLER	03/12/1838	A		FILM
FUCHS CH 2	NICOLAS	1814	ODEREN	11/01/1857	TX	FOND	PASS
FUCHS CH 4	ANTOINE	1805	KRUTH	09/01/1854	TX	CULT	PASS

Lastname	Firstname	Birth Year	Birthplace	Emigration	De	Prof	Source
FUCHS D NICOLAS	MARIE	1852		11/01/1857	TX		PASS
FUCHS F OF 2	MCIHEL		WEISLINGEN	01/01/1828	A		FILM
FUCHS F OF 2	MICHEL		AUENHEIM	04/21/1849	NY		FILM
FUCHS F OF 4	ANTOINE		SCHWEIGHAUSEN	01/01/1828	A		FILM
FUCHS F OF 4	JEAN		ALTECKENDORF	01/01/1828	A		FILM
FUCHS H FRANCOISE	ANTOINE	1817	RANSPACH	11/01/1846	TX	PRIN	SHIP
FUCHS H MARIANNE CH3	JAQUES	1800	CERNAY	12/01/1844	TX		SHIP
FUCHS MN LARGER	AGATHE	1804		11/01/1857	TX		PASS
FUCHS S JAQUES	GEORGES	1830	CERNAY	12/01/1844	TX		SHIP
FUCHS S JAQUES	HENRI	1837	CERNAY	12/01/1844	TX		SHIP
FUCHS S JAQUES	JAQUES	1840	CERNAY	12/01/1844	TX		SHIP
FUCHS S NICOLAS	XAVIER	1848		11/01/1857	TX		PASS
FUCHS W 2CH	JACQUES	1803	CERNAY	11/09/1844	NY		FILM
FUCHS W ANTOINE	FRANCOISE	1819	RANSPACH	11/01/1846	TX		SHIP
FUCHS W D	NICOLAS A MARIA	1802	ODEREN	11/04/1957	TX		FILM
FUCHS W JAQUES	MARIANNE	1811	CERNAY	12/01/1844	TX		SHIP
FUCHS W W 4CH	ANTIONE	1805	KRUTH	09/06/1854	TX		FILM
FUELLENWARTH	FRIEDRICH		FROESCHWILLER	01/01/1881	A		SUESS
FUERSTENBERGER W W 6	ANTOINE		NIEDERHERGHEIM	09/12/1846	TX		FILM
FUGG W W A D	JEAN	1785	NEAWAY	08/11/1854	NY		FILM
FUGLER	BARTHELEMY	1825	RUSTENHART	11/01/1846	TX	TAYL	SHIP
FUHL	JOSEPH		MULLENBACH	08/23/1849	A		FILM
FUHLHABER W W 6CH	JEAN BAPTISTE	1799	OBERSAASHEIM	03/12/1852	NY		FILM
FUHRER	ANTOINE		PFOHREN B	08/21/1849	A		FILM
FUHRER	JACQUES		BALDENHEIM	03/06/1838	A		FILM
FUHRER W W 2CH	JEAN		OERMINGEN	03/23/1817	A		FILM
FUHRMANN	THIEBAUT		DIEMERINGEN W	03/03/1817	A		FILM
FUHRMANN F OF 6	GEORGES		MELSHEIM	01/01/1828	A		FILM
FUHRMANN F OF 8	JEAN		IMBSHEIM	01/01/1828	A		FILM
FUHS	PIERRE MODESTE	1830	MUNTZENHEIM	11/11/1853	NY		FILM
FULGRAF	ALPHONSE	1847	MARCKOLSHEIM	05/05/1866	NY		FILM
FULL F OF 4	PIERRE		ZITTERSHEIM	01/01/1828	A		FILM
FUNCK W W	VALENTIN	1827	ST AMARIN	04/25/1854	NY		FILM
FUND	JACOB		NIEDERBRONN	05/13/1738	A		FILM
FUND JR	JACOB		NIEDERBRONN	05/13/1738	A		FILM
FUNK	HENRY	1819	WERDENSCHWEIL SWISS	07/30/1845	A		FILM
FURLING	JEAN MICHEL	1822	HIRTZFELDEN	09/01/1852	TX	CULT	PASS
FURLING	PHILIPPE	1813	ROGGENHAUSEN	12/01/1847	NY		FILM
FURLING	THERESE	1832		02/01/1850	TX		PASS
FURLING	THERESE	1832	HIRTZFELDEN	02/07/1850	TX		FILM
FURLING A SI 3NEPHEW	JEAN MICHEL	1822	HIRTZFELDEN	09/23/1852	TX		FILM
FURRENBACHER	ANTOINE		SCHOTTERTHAL B	05/27/1849	A		FILM
FURRENBACHER	XAVIER		SCHOTTERTHAL B	05/27/1849	A		FILM
FURSTENBERGER CH 6	ANTOINE	1816	NIEDERHERGHEIM	09/01/1846	TX	CULT	PASS
FURSTENBERGER W W 5C	SEBASTIEN		HERRLISHEIM	11/24/1852	NO		FILM
FUSSER F OF 5	JEAN		MORSCHWILLER	03/04/1838	A		FILM
FUSSONG W W 4CH	PIERRE		ASSWILLER	03/03/1817	A		FILM

Lastname	Firstname	Birth Year	Birthplace	Emigration	De	Prof	Source
GABEL	BENEDIKT	1865	MUNCHHOUSE	01/01/1867	NY		NO.2
GABEL	CATHERINA	1849	MUNCHHOUSE	01/01/1867	NY		NO.2
GABEL	CATHERINA	1860	MUNCHHOUSE	01/01/1867	NY		NO.2
GABEL	HEINRICH	1866	MUNCHHOUSE	01/01/1867	NY		NO.2
GABEL	JOSEF	1844	SCHAFFHAUSEN	01/01/1865	NY		NO.2
GABEL	MAGDALENA		MUNCHHOUSE	01/01/1867	NY		NO.2
GABEL W W 3 CH	JOSEF	1829	MUNCHHOUSE	01/01/1867	NY	FARM	NO.2
GABEL W W 5CH	JACQUES		DRUSENHEIM	03/24/1838	A		FILM
GABERT	MARIE		PRINZBACH B	04/21/1849	A		FILM
GABLER	JEAN	1798	MUNWILLER	09/19/1846	A		FILM
GABLER	JOSEPH, SEBASTI	1831	ROUGEGOUTTE	09/09/1851	NY		FILM
GABRIEL	JOHANN	1836	SCHEIBENHARDT	01/01/1865	NY		NO.2
GABRIEL W W 4CH	MOISE	1811	NEUSTADT	08/09/1855	NY		FILM
GABRIEL W W F OF 7	JOSEPH		KURTZENHAUSEN	01/01/1828	A		FILM
GACKEL	BARBE		AUENHEIM	03/01/1838	A		FILM
GAECHLER	JEAN	1830	DANNEMAIRIE	08/12/1850	SF		FILM
GAENGER	JACQUES	1813	GRUNWETTERSBACH AREA	03/01/1837	A		FILM
GAERTNER F OF 7	JEAN		PETERSBACH	01/01/1828	A		FILM
GAESTEL	MICHEL	1819	HAUT-RHIN	12/01/1844	TX	CULT	SHIP
GAETZINGER W 1CH	MARGUERITTE		STEIN B	05/08/1849	A		FILM
GAHVILLER	JACOB	1820	OBERUZWIL	11/15/1846	TX		FILM
GAI W W 2CH	JOHANN CLAUDIUS	1812	ANJOUTEY	11/22/1843	TX		FILM
GAIBROIS 01011823	JACQUES		VENDELINCOURT SWISS	04/26/1848	NY		FILM
GAILLET	LOUIS	1813	BOUROGNE	03/10/1849	NY		FILM
GAIRIN	ELISABETH	1823	ST MARIE AUX MINES	10/20/1854	NO		FILM
GAITAN		1802	GIEDGEWOD	04/09/1844	TX		FILM
GAJELIN	CHARLES	1824	MULHOUSE	11/05/1849	NY		FILM
GALL F OF 5	JEAN MICHEL		KLEINGOEFT	01/01/1828	A		FILM
GALLAT	FRANCOIS XAVIER	1814	SENTHEIM	12/01/1844	TX	CULT	SHIP
GALLAT	XAVIER	1812	SENTHEIM	09/10/1844	NO		FILM
GALLIET W W 3 CH	JEAN PIERRE	1807	BOUROGNE	04/07/1845	NY		FILM
GALLISATH	ANNE MARIE	1830	EGUISHEIM	08/13/1853	NY		FILM
GALLMANN F OF 7	CHRETIEN		BRUMATH	01/01/1828	A		FILM
GALLWA W W 3 CH	JEAN		ETTENDORF	01/01/1828	A		FILM
GALLY	ALEXANDRIE	1806	MOLLAU	09/28/1844	NY		FILM
GALLY	BARNABE	1817	GEISHAUSEN	09/04/1845	NY		FILM
GALLY	JEANNE ELISABEH	1811	GIACHINOPOLI=NAPLES	04/26/1852	A		FILM
GALLY	JOSEPH	1813	ST AMARIN	05/07/1845	NY		FILM
GALLY W W 4CH	MARMENAUX	1800	RANSPACH	08/28/1844	NY		FILM
GAMBS	JEAN		STRASSBOURG	06/18/1817	A		FILM
GAME	JUSTIN	1821	SUARCE	01/10/1851	NY		FILM
GANG	JEAN BAPTISTE	1832	GUEBWILLER	04/16/1852	A		FILM
GANGLER	ANNE-MARIE	1786		06/01/1856	TX	DAYL	PASS
GANGLOFF	ANDRE		BRUMATH	01/01/1828	A		FILM
GANGLOFF	CATHERINE		ZUTZENDORFF	01/01/1828	A		FILM
GANGLOFF	FRANZ XAVER		NIEDERBRONN	01/01/1817	A		NO.2
GANGLOFF	JEAN FRANCOIS		ZUTZENDORF	01/01/1828	A		FILM
GANGLOFF	MARTHE		ZUTZENDORF	01/01/1828	A		FILM
GANGLOFF F OF 5	FRANC. JOSEPH		MORSCHWILLER	03/04/1838	A		FILM
GANGLOFF F OF 3	NICOLAS		PETERSBACH	01/01/1828	A		FILM

Lastname	Firstname	Birth Year	Birthplace	Emigration	De	Prof	Source
GANGLOFF F OF 4	JACQUES		NIEDERMODERN	01/01/1828	A		FILM
GANGLOFF F OF 5	PIERRE		NIEDERMODERN	01/01/1828	A		FILM
GANGLOFF F OF 7	JOSEPH		MORSCHWILLER	03/04/1838	A		FILM
GANTHER	CHARLES		KENZINGEN B	04/21/1849	A		FILM
GANTZ	FRANCOIS JOSEPH	1812	ANDLAU	01/13/1849	NY		FILM
GANTZ W W 2CH	JEAN	1818	MUNTZENHEIM	03/07/1854	CH		FILM
GARCHE	IGANCE	1829	INGERSHEIM	03/25/1852	NY		FILM
GARDNER	ROSINE		INGENHEIM	02/08/1828	A		FILM
GAREL W 2CH	MARIE ANNE	1824	SERMAMAGNY	06/28/1850	A		FILM
GARNER	IGANCE		SCHWEIGHAUSEN	01/01/1828	A		FILM
GARNER F OF 4	ANTOINE		SCHWEIGHAUSEN	01/01/1828	A		FILM
GARNIER F OF 5	JOSEPH		DAUENDORF	02/28/1838	A		FILM
GARNY	ANNA MARIA		NEHWILLER	01/01/1867	NY		NO.2
GARNY	APPOLONIA	1866	NEHWILLER	01/01/1867	NY		NO.2
GARNY	GEORG	1866	NEHWILLER	01/01/1867	A		NO.2
GARNY	MAGDALENA	1857	NEHWILLER	01/01/1867	NY		NO.2
GARNY W W 2 CH	CHRISTIAN	1837	NEHWILLER	01/01/1867	NY	FARM	NO.2
GARSTERSER H CATHERI	JEAN-BAPTISTE	1800	NIEDERENTZEN	09/01/1846	TX	DRIV	SHIP
GARTEISEN	JEAN BAPTISTE	1800	NIEDERENTZEN	09/07/1846	TX		FILM
GARTERSER CH 4	JEAN-BAPTISTE	1800	NIEDERENTZEN	09/01/1846	TX	CARM	PASS
GARTERSER D JEAN-BAP	MARIE-ANNE		NIEDERENTZEN	09/01/1846	TX		SHIP
GARTERSER MN ZURCHER	CATHERINE		NIEDERENTZEM	09/01/1846	TX		SHIP
GARTERSER S JEAN-BAP	ANTOINE FRANCOI		NIEDERENTZEN	09/01/1846	TX		SHIP
GARTERSER S JEAN-BAP	JEAN-BAPTISTE		NIEDERENTZEN	09/01/1846	TX		SHIP
GASPARY	HEINRICH	1841	LAUTERBURG	01/01/1866	NO	MERC	NO.2
GASPARY	SAMUEL	1841	LAUTERBURG	01/01/1866	NO	MERC	NO.2
GASPERMENT	JEAN FRANCOIS	1813	*LA BOUILLE	04/10/1839	PH		FILM
GASPERMENT	JOSEPH	1826	ST CROIX AUX MINES	11/24/1845	SL		FILM
GASRAS F OF 5	JEAN		GEUDERTHEIM	03/01/1838	A		FILM
GASROZZE	JOSEPH	1814	ALTKIRCH	07/23/1851	NY		FILM
GASS	ANNE		GEISWILLER	01/01/1820	A		FILM
GASS	CATHERINE		GEISWILLER	01/01/1828	A		FILM
GASS	GEORGE		GEISWILLER	01/01/1828	A		FILM
GASS	MADELAINE		GEISWILLER	01/01/1828	A		FILM
GASS	MARGUERITE		GEISWILLER	01/01/1828	A		FILM
GASS	MARIE		GERWILLER	01/01/1828	A		FILM
GASS	MICHEL		GEISWILLER	01/01/1828	A		FILM
GASS W W 2 CH	GEORGE		GEISWILLER	01/01/1828	A		FILM
GASSEN W W 4CH	DIDIER		WILLER	09/11/1851	NO		FILM
GASSENMEYER	HEINRICH		STEIN B	04/11/1849	A		FILM
GASSER	ANNE MARIE	1816	SIERENZ	05/03/1845	NY		FILM
GASSER	ANTOINE	1828	PFEFFERHAUSEN	02/03/1847	NY		FILM
GASSER	EUGENE		COLMAR	10/27/1851	NY		FILM
GASSER	FRANCOIS JOSEPH	1830	REGUISHEIM	11/06/1848	TX		FILM
GASSER	FRANCOIS-JOSEPH	1810	REGUISHEIM	11/01/1848	TX	DAYL	PASS
GASSER	JEAN BAPTISTE	1830	PFEFFERHAUSEN	09/21/1853	NY		FILM
GASSER	JEAN PIERRE	1835	PFEFFERHAUSEN	09/21/1853	NY		FILM
GASSER	MARTIN	1823	LAUWE	02/25/1852	NY		FILM
GASSER W W 1CH	FRANCOISE JOSEH	1816	NIEDERHAGENTHAL	10/09/1844	NY		FILM
GASSMANN	HENRIETTE	1849	SWISS	01/01/1866	A		FILM

```
                                Birth                                    79
Lastname            Firstname   Year  Birthplace        Emigration De Prof Source
--------------------------------------------------------------------------------
GAST W W 3CH        JOSEPH ANTOINE 1811 LIGSDORFF        02/09/1847 NY      FILM
GATTERWEYER W W 3CH ANDRE             NEUWILLER          /  /       A       FILM
GATZ                GEOFROID          BRUMATH            01/01/1828 A       FILM
GAUB                HENRY             DIEMERINGEN        03/03/1838 A       FILM
GAUBALT                               PARIS              04/09/1844 TX      FILM

GAUCHEL             ALEXIS      1806 DORANS              12/20/1837 NY      FILM
GAUCHET             FRANCOIS    1798 BELFORT             11/13/1844 PH      FILM
GAUCHET CH 1        FRANCOIS    1800 BRETTEN             12/01/1846 TX SHMA SHIP
GAUCHET D FRANCOIS  CATHERINE   1841 BRETTEN             12/01/1846 TX      SHIP
GAUCKLER            WILHELM     1840 WEISSENBURG         01/01/1866 NY CARP NO.2

GAUDEL              MARIE BARBE 1829 LA POUTROIE         03/14/1852 NO      FILM
GAUDEY              JEAN BAPTISTE 1812 HERIMONCOURT      07/26/1862 NY      FILM
GAUER               CATHERINE        BAERENDORFF        02/27/1838 A       FILM
GAUER W PAULUS ANTOI CATHERINE       BATZENDORFF        02/27/1838 A       FILM
GAUG                XAVIER           BAERENTHAL TYROL   09/30/1849 A       FILM

GAUG W W 4CH        MATHIEU          WEITERSWILLER      03/29/1817 A       FILM
GAUGLER             MARIE ANNE  1786 HOCHSTATT          06/20/1856 TX      FILM
GAUGLER W 5CH       MADELAINE   1791 RIMBACH            10/06/1846 NY      FILM
GAUJOT              PAUL        1852 WEISSENBURG         01/01/1869 NO MECH NO.2
GAULLE              GEORGE      1832 VALENTIGNEY         05/01/1865 NY      FILM

GAUSI               MARIE            SAUNOT             10/01/1862 NY      FILM
GAUSIN              MARIE       1839 SAUNOT             09/08/1862 NY      FILM
GAUTHER             EMILE            GERMANY            03/04/1849 NY      FILM
GAY H CATHERINE CH 2 JEAN-CLAUDE 1812 ANJOUTEY          11/01/1843 TX CULT SHIP
GAY S JEAN-CLAUDE   JOSEPH      1838 ANJOUTEY           11/01/1843 TX      SHIP

GAY S JEAN-CLAUDE   THEOBALD    1840 ANJOUTEY           11/01/1843 TX      SHIP
GAY W JEAN-CLAUDE   CATHERINE   1817 ANJOUTEY           11/01/1843 TX      SHIP
GCHIRNID            JEAN        1800 HINDLINGEN         02/01/1840 NY      FILM
GEANT W W 3CH       JEAN PIERRE 1805 ROUGEMONT          02/24/1840 PH      FILM
GEBEL               JOSEPH      1829 MASSEVAUX          01/04/1847 SL      FILM

GEBEL               LOUISE      1838 MASSEVAUX          05/20/1856 A       FILM
GEBER               JOSEPH      1806 ALTKIRCH           10/08/1844 NY      FILM
GEBHARDT            EUGENE      1818 RIQUEWIHR          08/21/1854 NY      FILM
GEBHARDT            FRANCOIS EMILE 1831 ST MARIE AUX MINES 07/03/1854 NO   FILM
GEBHARDT            GEORGES     1828 FORTSCHWIHR        02/18/1854 NO      FILM

GEEST   W W 2CH     JACQUES     1811 SCHLEITHAL         08/20/1847 NO      FILM
GEFSER W W 8CH      JACQUES          ROPPENTZWILLER     08/18/1854 A       FILM
GEHANT              FRANCOISE   1822 CHATENOIS          08/09/1844 A       FILM
GEHR                LOUIS       1826 BLOTZHEIM          05/31/1854 NY      FILM
GEIGENTASCH         FIDELE           HAIGERLOCH W       04/21/1849 A       FILM

GEIGER              AMBROIS     1811 BURNHAUPT          05/23/1840 NY      FILM
GEIGER              CHRETIEN         FRIEDENSTADT  W    10/15/1849 NY      FILM
GEIGER              JEAN BAPTISTE 1830 RIBEAUVILLE      05/14/1852 NO      FILM
GEIGER              JEAN IGNACE 1820 ST CROIX AUX MINES 10/19/1854 NO     FILM
GEIGER              LOUIS       1830 RIBEAUVILLE        05/21/1851 NY      FILM

GEIGER W W 2CH      ANTOINE          MALSCH B           05/01/1849 NY      FILM
GEIL                GEORGES     1817 OSTHEIM            03/21/1845 NY      FILM
GEINER                               GERMANY            04/05/1849 NY      FILM
GEISINGER           CHARLES          LEFFLINGEN B       08/05/1849 A       FILM
GEISS               SEBASTIEN   1798 UFFHEIM            02/06/1845 NY      FILM
```

Lastname	Firstname	Birth Year	Birthplace	Emigration	De	Prof	Source
GEISS FO OF 3	SEBASTIEN		MORSCHWILLER	04/03/1838	A		FILM
GEISS MN EISENSCHMIT			ROPPENHEIM	03/25/1852	AL		NO.1
GEISS W D	BARTHOLOME	1792	UFFHEIM	06/24/1854	A		FILM
GEISSER	CAROLINE	1844	ROPPENHEIM	01/01/1861	A		NO.1
GEISSERT	CAROLINE	1844		05/15/1861	A		PRIV
GEISSERT	ELISABETHA	1840	ROPPENHEIM	/ /	A		NO.1
GEISSERT	FRIEDRICH	1841	ROPPENHEIM	/ /	A		NO.1
GEISSERT	GEORG	1848		03/29/1864	A		PRIV
GEISSERT	GEORG	1848	ROPPENHEIM	03/29/1864	A		NO.1
GEISSERT	KATHARINA	1846		05/15/1861	A		PRIV
GEISSERT	KATHARINA	1846	ROPPENHEIM	05/15/1861	A		NO.1
GEISSERT 2 CH	JEAN FRIEDRICH		ROPPENHEIM	/ /	A		NO.1
GEISSERT CH 2	JEAN FRIEDRICH			/ /	A		PRIV
GEISSERT H ARNOLD5CH	FRIEDRICH	1814	ROPPENHEIM	/ /	A		NO.1
GEISSERT H ELISABETH	FRIEDRICH	1814		/ /	A		PRIV
GEISSERT MN ARNOLD	ELISABETHA	1820	ROPPENHEIM	/ /	A		NO.1
GEISSERT MN ARNOLDT	ELISABETH	1820		/ /	A		PRIV
GEISSERT W 9 CH	DANIEL	1790	ROPPENHEIM	03/25/1852	A		NO.1
GEISSMANN	JACQUES	1820	DORNACH	01/10/1852	NO		FILM
GEISTADT	GEOFFROI EMILE	1828	COLMAR	06/30/1854	NY		FILM
GELBHE	MADELAINE	1822	ST MARIE AUX MINES	08/03/1850	NO		FILM
GELBKE W W 3CH	FREDRIC	1791	SAXE	09/04/1851	NO		FILM
GELSCH	JOSEPH	1816	HIRSINGUE	04/20/1842	NY		FILM
GENEY	HENRI	1835	MULHOUSE	09/24/1856	NY		FILM
GENLOT	JULES	1833	BISCHWILLER	07/11/1853	NY		FILM
GENTIL	FREDERIC	1822	MONTBELLIARD	10/17/1862	NY		FILM
GENTIL	FREDERIC	1822	AUDINCOURT	10/17/1862	NY		FILM
GENTIL	JEAN LOUIS	1819	PARIS	11/22/1843	TX		FILM
GENTIö	PIERRE PERRAT	1840	MONTBELIARD	05/01/1865	NY		FILM
GEORG	CATHERINA	1862	MOTHERN	01/01/1869	NY		NO.2
GEORG	JOHANN	1865	MOTHERN	01/01/1869	NY		NO.2
GEORG	KARL	1867	MOTHERN	01/01/1869	NY		NO.2
GEORG	MICHEL		REICHSHOFFEN	01/01/1869	A		NO.2
GEORG	PETER	1865	MOTHERN	01/01/1869	NY		NO.2
GEORG	SOPHIE	1864	MOTHERN	01/01/1869	NY		NO.2
GEORG MN HOLLE	JOSEPHINE	1839	MOTHERN	01/01/1869	NY		NO.2
GEORG W W 5 CH	VALENTIN	1835	MOTHERN	01/01/1869	NY		NO.2
GEORGE	MARIE ANNE	1838	CHATENOIS	10/14/1854	NO		FILM
GEORGE W W 2CH	JACQUES		ALTWILLER	01/01/1817	A		FILM
GEORGES F OF 4	PAULUS		BERNOLSHEIM	03/03/1838	A		FILM
GERAL	SOPHIE	1811	STRASSBOURG	09/16/1850	NO		FILM
GERARD	JEAN BAPTISTE	1816	LIEPVRE	08/29/1846	NO		FILM
GERARD	JOSEPH	1804	LIEPVRE	08/29/2186	NO		FILM
GERARD	JOSEPH	1827	LäLLEMAND BOURBACH	08/24/1847	NY		FILM
GERARDIN	ANTOINE	1825	ST HYPOLITE	05/19/1849	NY		FILM
GERARDIN	HYPOLITE	1833	ST HYPOLITE	02/08/1853	A		FILM
GERBER	BARTHELEMI		ST JEAN DES CHAUX	01/01/1828	A		FILM
GERBER	BLAISE		WITTISHEIM	03/02/1838	A		FILM
GERBER	CATHERINE		WITTISHEIM	03/02/1838	A		FILM
GERBER	CHARLES	1819	ST MARIE AUX MINES	08/29/1848	NY		FILM

Lastname	Firstname	Year	Birthplace	Emigration	De	Prof Source
GERBER	CHRETIEN		DURSTEL	03/18/1838	A	FILM
GERBER	GEORGE		BETTWILLER	02/28/1838	A	FILM
GERBER	HEINRICH		NIEDERBRONN	05/13/1838	A	FILM
GERBER	HENRI	1826	KAYSERSBERG	02/13/1849	NO	FILM
GERBER	JACOB		NIEDERBRONN	05/13/1838	A	FILM
GERBER	JEAN PIERRE	1811	PFEFFERHOUSE H-R	02/28/1854	NY	FILM
GERBER	JOHN JACQUES		NIEDERBRON	05/13/1738	A	FILM
GERBER	JOSEPH ANTOINE	1824	KAYSERSBERG	02/13/1849	NO	FILM
GERBER	MICHEL		WITTISHEIM	03/02/1838	A	FILM
GERBER	NICOLAS		DURSTEL	03/18/1838	A	FILM
GERBER	PIERRE		DURSTEL	03/18/1838	A	FILM
GERBER	THERESE		WITTISHEIM	03/02/1838	A	FILM
GERBER	THERESE DAUGHTR		ST MARIE AUX MINES	10/15/1857	A	FILM
GERBER	XAVIER		WITTISHEIM	03/02/1838	A	FILM
GERBER F OF 6	LOUIS		ST JEAN DES CAHUX	01/01/1828	A	FILM
GERBER F OF 8	JEAN		ERCKARTSWILLER	01/01/1828	A	FILM
GERBER W CH	THERESE	1823	ST MARIE AUX MINES	10/15/1857	A	FILM
GERDES	ANNA	1816	WESTFALEN	09/17/1845	TX	FILM
GERDES	HERMANN	1842	WESTFALEN	09/17/1845	TX	FILM
GERDES	MARIA	1836	WESTFALEN	09/17/1845	TX	FILM
GERDES W W 2CH	JOHANN HEIMRICH	1809	WESTFALEN	09/17/1845	TX	FILM
GERHAUPT	XAVIER		MATZENHEIM	02/28/1834	A	FILM
GERIG	BENJAMIN	1842	PFASTATT	10/01/1860	NY	FILM
GERIG	SEBASTIEN	1839	PFASTATT	02/18/1857	NY	FILM
GERIG W S	BARBE		WINTZENHEIM	07/30/1838	NY	FILM
GERITZ	ROSINE		ERLACH B	08/21/1849	A	FILM
GERLING	GEORG		BUEHL	01/01/1834	A	SUESS
GERLINGER	PH.JACQUES		WEITERSWILLER	01/01/1828	A	FILM
GERMAIN	FRANCOIS		LIEPVRE	03/30/1839	NO	FILM
GERMAND	PAUL	1842	ARCEY	10/10/1865	NY	FILM
GERNIER	JEAN PIERRE	1833	MONTREUX VIEAUX	07/22/1857	NY	FILM
GEROLD	MARIE		ESCHBACH B	10/11/1849	A	FILM
GERS W W 6CH	HENRY		DIEDENDORF	03/20/1817	A	FILM
GERSCHEIMER	PHILIPPE		MACKWILLER	03/02/1838	A	FILM
GERSCHEIMER W W 3CH	JACQUES		RIMSDORF	03/29/1817	A	FILM
GERSEN	LEVY	1810	GUEBWILLER	08/14/1848	NY	FILM
GERST F OF 5	DANIEL		RUNTZENHEIM	01/01/1828	A	FILM
GERST F OF 8	HENRY		SESSENHEIM	02/23/1838	A	FILM
GERST W W 3CH	FREDERIC	1819	SCHLEITHAL	08/23/1847	NO	FILM
GERST W W AND 2CH	CHRETIEN	1829	SCHILTIGHEIM	02/05/1857	A	FILM
GERSTNER	LEIDGARD		HILPERTSAU B	09/28/1849	NY	FILM
GERT	CHRISTMANN		NIEDERBRONN	05/13/1738	A	FILM
GERT	HANS GEORG		NIEDERBRONN	05/13/1738	A	FILM
GERTH F OF 4	ANDRE		FORT LOUIS	01/01/1828	A	FILM
GERTHOFER	FRANCOIS JOSEPH	1812	BURNHAUPT	05/23/1846	NY	FILM
GERTHOFER W W 2CH	IGNACE	1814	BURNHAUTP	05/23/1846	NY	FILM
GERTHOFFER W W 5CH	JEAN	1786	BURNHAUPT	04/21/1847	NY	FILM
GERTZ	CATHERINE		NIEDERLAUTERBACH	01/01/1850	NO	PRIV
GERWIG	GEORG	1854	OBERBETSCHDORF	01/01/1854	NY	NO.2
GERWIG	GEORG HEINRICH		NIEDERBETSCHDORF	01/01/1817	A	NO.2

Lastname	Firstname	Birth Year	Birthplace	Emigration	De	Prof	Source
GERWIG W W 4CH	G. HENRY		NIEDERBETSCHDORF	03/28/1187	A		FILM
GESRAT	BAPTISTE CHARLE	1794	STRASSBOURG	08/01/1849	NY		FILM
GESSER W W 8CH	JACQUES	1797	ROPPENTZWILLER	08/19/1854	A		FILM
GETSCHY	DOMINIQUE	1845	STEINSELTZ	04/26/1847	NY		FILM
GETTLER	JEAN		NODSTAEDT W	04/13/1849	NY		FILM
GEUTZ W W 4CH	FRANCOIS JOSEPH	1812	ANDLAU	01/13/1849	NY		FILM
GEVENTHAL W 3CH		1814	BEAUCOURT	02/07/1842	NY		FILM
GEWISS CH 4	GASPARD	1808	KRUTH	08/01/1860	TX	CULT	PASS
GEWISS D GASPARD	CAROLINE	1845	KRUTH	08/01/1860	TX		PASS
GEWISS D GASPARD	JUSTINE	1842	KRUTH	08/01/1860	TX		PASS
GEWISS D GASPARD	SCHOLASTIQUE	1851	KRUTH	08/01/1860	TX		PASS
GEWISS MN SIFFERLEN	MARIE-ANNE	1820		08/01/1860	TX		
GEWISS MN SIFFERLEN	MARIE-ANNE	1820		08/01/1860	TX		PASS
GEWISS S GASPARD	FRANCOIS-ANTOIN	1834	KRUTH	08/01/1860	TX		PASS
GEYER	DAVID		BALBRONN	02/28/1838	A		FILM
GEYER	EVE		SCHALKENDORF	01/01/1828	A		FILM
GEYER	JEAN		ROESCHWOOG	01/01/1828	A		FILM
GEYER	NICOLAS		PUBERG	01/01/1828	A		FILM
GEYER F OF 3	PHILIPPE		PUBERG	01/01/1828	A		FILM
GEYER F OF 5	GEORGE		ERCKARTSWILLER	01/01/1828	A		FILM
GEYER F OF 5	PIERRE		RATZWILLER	01/01/1828	A		FILM
GEYER F OF 7	CHRETIEN		ROTZWILLER	01/01/1828	A		FILM
GEYER W W	JOSEPH		ROESCHWOOG	03/14/1817	A		FILM
GEYER W W 2CH	GEORGE		UHRWILLER	09/04/1819	A		FILM
GEYMANN	ALOYSE	1823	BIEDERTHAL	05/10/1185	NY		FILM
GEYMANN	JEAN	1827	BIEDERTHAL	04/17/1848	NY		FILM
GEYMANN	JEAN	1816	BIEDERTHAL	06/20/1850	NY		FILM
GEYMANN	JEAN	1826	BIEDERTHAL	03/31/1852	NY		FILM
GEYMANN W 4CH	JOSEPH	1819	BIEDERTHAL	06/13/1854	NY		FILM
GEYMARD	PHILIPPE	1835	ARCEY	10/10/1865	NY		FILM
GIESENREGEN F OF 7	GEORGE		INGWILLER	01/01/1828	A		FILM
GIESS	GEORGES		BERG	03/01/1838	A		FILM
GIGANDET	JEAN PIERRE	1798	MEROUX	07/02/1840	NY		FILM
GIGANDET	JOSPH	1818	SCHYNDEL	03/31/1853	NY		FILM
GIGANDET W W 3CH	FRANCOIS NICOLS	1815	MEROUX	04/16/1853	NY		FILM
GIGOS W W 1 CH	BLAISE	1798	BISEL	12/10/1839	NO		FILM
GILB	BERNARD		SCHOTTERTHAL	05/27/1849	A		FILM
GILGENKRANTZ	JEAN BAPTISTE	1806	SIGOLSHEIM	04/21/1840	NY		FILM
GILGER F OF 3	JEAN		DIERMINGEN	03/03/1838	A		FILM
GILGERT W W 3CH	ULRICH		BUTTEN	03/17/1817	A		FILM
GILLIET	JULIEN	1822	GIROMAGNY	11/05/1852	LV		FILM
GILLIG	DANIEL		SESSENHEIM	02/23/1838	A		FILM
GILLING	GEORGES		CLEEBOURG	01/01/1817	A		PRIV
GILLING	JACOB	1839	CLEEBURG	01/01/1868	NY		PRIV
GIMBEL F OF 2	HENRY		NEUWILLER	01/01/1828	A		FILM
GIMBEL F OF 3	MICHEL		NEUWILLER	01/01/1828	A		FILM
GINDER	JEAN		GERMANY	04/12/1849	NY		FILM
GINOT	ANTOINE	1811	MASSEVAUX	08/04/1847	NY		FILM
GIRADELLE W W 2CH	AMI	1824	NEUVILLERS	06/12/1855	NY		FILM
GIRALDIN F OF 7	CHARLES		HAGUENAU	01/03/1838	A		FILM

Lastname	Firstname	Birth Year	Birthplace	Emigration	De	Prof	Source
GIRAND	JOSEPH		GRANDVILLARS	04/25/1854	NY		FILM
GIRAND	PIERRE	1832	PEROUSA	09/27/1865	NY		FILM
GIRAND	URSULE	1791	DENNY	08/03/1856	NY		FILM
GIRARD	JOSEPH	1814	PETITE FONTAINE	11/24/1864	NY		FILM
GIRARDAT	ADELE	1830	BELFORT	06/13/1866	NY		FILM
GIRARDEY	BARBE	1791	ST AMARIN	07/24/1845	A		FILM
GIRARDEY	ISIDOR	1829	HIRSINGUE	09/06/1848	A		FILM
GIRARDEY A FAMILY	FRANCIS JOSEPH	1803	HIRSINGUE	03/07/1842	A		FILM
GIRARDEY W W 1CH	NICOLAS	1810	ROUGEGOUTTE	02/29/1840	NY		FILM
GIRARDEZ W W 2CH	JOSEPH	1819	ROUGEMONT	11/05/1844	PH		FILM
GIRARDIN	ANTOINE	1825	ST HYPOLITE	05/19/1849	NY		FILM
GIRARDIN	JACQUES	1820	ST MARIE AUX MINES	08/29/1848	NY		FILM
GIRARDIN	MARIE		BURBACH	03/02/1838	A		FILM
GIRARDOT	FRANCAIS	1800	FAVEROIS	05/20/1845	NO		FILM
GIRARDY CH 1	JOSEPH	1819	ROUGEMONT	10/01/1844	TX	CULT	PASS
GIRARDY W W	ALEXIS	1799	ROUGEGOUTTE	04/16/1851	NY		FILM
GIRODOT	CHRETIEN	1826	HEGENHEIM	02/04/1854	NY		FILM
GIROL	PIERRE	1841	ROPPE	03/10/1865	NY		FILM
GIROT	RICHARD	1826	PETIT FONTAINE	03/17/1849	NY		FILM
GIROT W W 3 S AND MO	PIERRE	1813	ROPPE	08/25/1856	NY		FILM
GIROT W W 3CH	PHILIPPE	1815	MASSEVAUX	09/04/1853	NY		FILM
GISSELBRAKT	JEAN MICHEL	1812	BALDENHEIM	03/28/1844	A		FILM
GISSLER W W 3H	SIMON		STRASSBOURG	05/27/1817	A		FILM
GISSY W W 1CH	CHARLES	1828	ST.AMARIN	08/11/1854	NY		FILM
GITTA	FRANCOIS JOSEPH	1816	LIBSDORFF	10/17/1849	NO		FILM
GLACK W W	JEAN GUILLAUME	1823	ALGOLSHEIM	02/17/1853	NY		FILM
GLADICIER W W 2CH	JEAN PIERRE	1810	VELLESCOT	08/05/1844	NY		FILM
GLADIERRE	PHILIPPE	1787	VELLESCOT	02/20/1845	NY		FILM
GLADIEUX W W 2CH	JEAN PIERRE	1810	VELLESCOT	08/05/1844	NY		FILM
GLASSER	ANTOINE	1835	OSTHEIM	05/29/1854	NY		FILM
GLATTFELDER	AUGUSTINE		APPENWEIER	08/11/1844	A		FILM
GLENTZINGER W W	GEORGE	1812	HATTSTATT	12/10/1851	NO		FILM
GLESIE	LUDWIG	1822	WEISSENBURG	01/01/1865	NY	BAKE	NO.2
GLOBECKLER	JEAN		TUTTLINGEN W	06/11/1849	A		FILM
GLORR	JACQUES		KEFFENAUCH	03/18/1817	A		FILM
GLOSS	FRANCOIS JOSEPH		DRUSENHEIM	03/24/1838	A		FILM
GLOSS W W 5CH	MATHIEU		DRUSENHEIM	03/24/1838	A		FILM
GLOSSIER	FRANCOISE	1825	MOLLAU	01/09/1849	A		FILM
GLOSSIER	IGNACE	1827	MOLLAU	01/09/1849	A		FILM
GLUCK	CHARLES	1860	NIEDERLAUTERBACH	01/01/1868	NY		PRIV
GLUCK	MARIE ANNE	1836	NIEDERLAUTERBACH	01/01/1868	NY		PRIV
GLUCK W W	JEAN GUILLAUME	1823	ALGOLSHEIM	02/17/1853	NY		FILM
GOCHSTATTER F OF 8	JEAN HENRY		BOUXWILLER	01/01/1828	A		FILM
GOCHWIND	DOMINIQUE	1827		03/02/1847	NY		FILM
GOCTURIND	DOMINIQUE	1827	PFEFFERHAUSEN	03/02/1847	NY		FILM
GODARD W 2 D	FRANCOIS	1793	LIEPVRE	07/04/1850	NY		FILM
GODEL	CAROLINE	1819	BARTENHEIM	08/14/1852	A		FILM
GOECHLER W W 4CH	GEORGES	1797	DONNEMARIE	09/08/1846	NY		FILM
GOEHLER	ELISABETH	1848	LEMBACH	01/01/1866	NY		NO.2
GOEHLER	LUISE	1848	LEMBACH	01/01/1866	NY		NO.2

Lastname	Firstname	Birth Year	Birthplace	Emigration	De	Prof	Source
GOEHRY	LUDWIG	1852	OBERBETSCHDORF	01/01/1854	NY		NO.2
GOEHRY	LUDWIG	1852	OBERBETSCHDORF	01/01/1868	NY		NO.2
GOELLER	JOHANN	1836	OBERLAUTERBACH	01/01/1865	NO		NO.2
GOELLER	MAGDALENA	1840	TRIEMBACH	01/01/1865	NY		NO.2
GOEPERT	CATHERINE	1833	ILLHAEUSERN	02/14/1855	NY		FILM
GOEPFERT	JEAN BAPTISTE	1830	SOPPE LE BAS	03/17/1854	NY		FILM
GOEPFERT	LEGER	1813	GUEMAR	06/28/1838	PH		FILM
GOEPFERT W W 2CH	JACQUES	1810	FFELDBACH	05/16/1845	NY		FILM
GOEPFORT	JEAN	1821	RIBEAUEVILLE	11/13/1848	NY		FILM
GOERGEN W W 6CH	HENRY		ERNOLSHEIM	03/18/1817	A		FILM
GOERIG	BARBE	1827	PFASTADT	09/09/1864	NY		FILM
GOERIG	CARBE	1857	PFASTADT	09/09/1864	NY		FILM
GOERIG	CHRETIEN	1855	PFASTATT	09/09/1864	NY		FILM
GOERIG	JOSEPH	1800	BOURG	03/05/1841	OH		FILM
GOERIG W W	CHRETIEN	1820	PFASTATT	09/09/1864	NY		FILM
GOESEL	JEAN GEORGES	1828	MULHOUSE	03/07/1857	SL		FILM
GOETTELMANN H THERES	JEAN-BAPTISTE	1813	ST. HIPPOLYTE	10/01/1843	TX	CULT	SHIP
GOETTELMANN S JEAN-B	CHARLES	1842	ST. HIPPOLYTE	10/01/1843	TX		SHIP
GOETTELMANN W JEAN-B	THERESE	1813	ST. HIPPOLYTE	10/01/1843	TX		SHIP
GOETTELMANN W W 1CH	JOHANN BAPTIST	1813	HYPOLETE	10/25/1843	TX		FILM
GOETTLER F OF 6	ANTOINE		DETTWILLER	01/01/1828	A		FILM
GOETZ	CHRETIEN		BRUMATH	01/01/1828	A		FILM
GOETZ	EDUARD	1828	ENSISHEIM	12/19/1853	NY		FILM
GOETZ	GEOFROID		BRUMATH	01/01/1828	A		FILM
GOETZ	GERTRUDE	1847	BITCHE LOTHRING	01/01/1866	NY		NO.2
GOETZ	JEAN	1812	ALTKIRCH	04/24/1840	NO		FILM
GOETZ	JOHANN	1807	BITCHE LOTHRING	01/01/1866	NY		NO.2
GOETZ	MARIE ANNE		BRUMATH	03/22/1838	A		FILM
GOETZ	MICHEL	1823	ENSISHEIM	01/12/1852	NO		FILM
GOETZ W 2CH	MARIE ANNE	1811	KAYSERSBERG	04/22/1856	NY		FILM
GOETZ W W 2CH	GEORGES JOSEPH	1812	RIBEAUVILLE	04/26/1847	NY		FILM
GOETZ A F	JOSEPH	1817	BANTZENHEIM	02/19/1853	NY		FILM
GOETZ F OF 4	DANIEL		BRUMATH	01/01/1828	A		FILM
GOETZ F OF 4	MICHEL		INGWILLER	01/01/1828	A		FILM
GOETZ F OF 6	AUGUSTIN		SESSENHEIM	02/23/1838	A		FILM
GOETZMANN	GEORG HEINRICH	1841	NIEDERBETSCHDORF	01/01/1866	OH	FARM	NO.2
GOETZMANN	GEORGES	1823	WALHEIM	09/10/1851	NY		FILM
GOETZMANN W W 2D	GEORGES	1797	BALLERSDORF	02/14/1853	NY		FILM
GOFFINET	FRANCOIS	1811	BARON	09/07/1838	NY		FILM
GOFFINET	JAM.	1828	PEROUSE	10/01/1866	NY		FILM
GOFFINET	JEAN CLAUDE	1822	PEROUSE	05/24/1854	NY		FILM
GOLDSCHMIDT	HENRY	1822	ST MARIE AUX MINES	04/11/1854	NY		FILM
GOLDSCHMIDT	JOSEPH	1809	ST MARIE AUX MINES	02/14/1839	OH		FILM
GOLDSCHMIDT	JULIE	1825	DORNACH	07/19/1848	NY		FILM
GOLDSCHMIDT W 2CH	ELISABETH		ST MARIE AUX MINES	01/27/1850	A		FILM
GOLDSCHMITT	JEAN	1809	MULHOUSE	02/11/1857	NY		FILM
GOLL	JEAN GEORGES	1833	MONTBELIARD	03/10/1866	NY		FILM
GOLLB	JOSEF	1840	MUNCHHOUSE	01/01/1868	NY		NO.2
GOLLET	ALOIS	1827	BISEL	02/02/1861	NY		FILM
GOLLY	JOSEPH	1816	FELLERINGEN	11/05/1844	NY		FILM

Lastname	Firstname	Birth Year	Birthplace	Emigration	De	Prof	Source
GOMMENZINGER W W 1CH	JOSEPH LOUIS	1801	ANDLAU	04/21/1847	NY		FILM
GORISSE	JOSEPH	1820	BELFORT	06/06/1866	NY		FILM
GORISSE	MARIE	1808	BELFORT	10/18/1766	NY		FILM
GORISSE	NICOLAS		BELFORT	09/05/1863	NY		FILM
GORNIUR	MARIE CATHERINE	1806	ST MARIE AUX MINES	04/08/1848	NY		FILM
GOSE W W 7CH	EMERISTE		EYWILLER	03/20/1817	A		FILM
GOSSE F OF 6	SEBASTIEN		UHLWILLER	03/03/1838	A		FILM
GOSSE F OF 9	FRANCOIS		ESCHWILLER	03/02/1838	A		FILM
GOSSE W W	PHILIPPE		EYWILLER	03/20/1817	A		FILM
GOTTAY F OF 9	MICHEL		HAGUENAU	03/01/1838	A		FILM
GOTTLOFSKI W W 3CH	PIERRE		RATZWILLER	03/03/1817	A		FILM
GOTZ	JEAN	1810	WALSDORF NASSAU	05/05/1840	NY		FILM
GOTZ	LAURENT		SOUFFLENHEIM	01/01/1828	A		FILM
GOTZ	MATHIEU		SOUFFLENHEIM	03/02/1838	A		FILM
GOTZ W W 6CH	MICHEL		SOUFFLENHEIM	03/02/1838	A		FILM
GOURES	LOUIS	1814	MONTECHEROUIL	02/07/1865	NY		FILM
GOURMET	FRANCOIS AUGUSTE	184	LA CHAPELLE SOUS ROM	02/23/1857	NY		FILM
GOUSE	MARGERITE		CHENEBIER	03/28/1863	A		FILM
GOUSE	MARGUERITE		CHENEBIER	03/28/1863	NY		FILM
GOUSE	MARGUERITE	1810	CHENEBIER	03/28/1863	NY		FILM
GOUSSET W W 7CH	JEAN PIERE	1803	ROUGEMONT	10/27/1846	PH		FILM
GOUTTERMANN W W 5CH	CHRISTISTONNE	1801	TROYE	03/25/1847	NO		FILM
GOZIGO	ETIENNE		RIMSDORF	03/17/1817	A		FILM
GRABER	CHARLES	1825	BESANCON	08/25/1866	NY		FILM
GRADWOHL	ABRAHAM		ZINSWILLER	01/01/1869	NY		NO.2
GRADWOHL	LEOPOLD		ZINSWILLER	01/01/1869	A		NO.2
GRAEBER W W 5CH	PIERRE		BURBACH	03/31/1817	A		FILM
GRAEFF F OF 7	JACQUES		BISCHWILLER	03/02/1838	A		FILM
GRAESSEL W SI 1CH	ALBERTINE	1826	MULHOUSE	09/01/1854	NO		FILM
GRAESSLE W W 2D	THEOPHILE	1820	BERNBACH	02/08/1850	NY		FILM
GRAF	C.		ULM	04/06/1849	NY		FILM
GRAF	JOSEPH		MUELLENBACH B	09/08/1849	A		FILM
GRAF	JOSEPHA		MUELLENBACH B	09/08/1849	A		FILM
GRAF	LUDWIG	1826	NEUFREISTETT B	10/25/1844	TX		FILM
GRAF W W 2 S	JACQUES		MULHAUSEN	01/01/1828	A		FILM
GRAF W W 2 S	JEAN		MULHOUSEN	01/01/1828	A		FILM
GRAFF	AUGUSTIN		MUELLENBACH B	04/13/1849	NY		FILM
GRAFF	GEORGES		EYWILLER	01/01/1828	A		FILM
GRAFF	GEORGES	1825	COLMAR	09/02/1850	NY		FILM
GRAFF	MARTIN	1799	SIGOLSHEIM	10/19/1853	A		FILM
GRAFF	MATHIAS	1798	COLMAR	09/11/1853	NO		FILM
GRAFF	MATHIAS	1808	COLMAR	01/22/1853	NO		FILM
GRAFF W W A S	FRANCOIS	1824	ACHENHEIM	05/14/1853	NY		FILM
GRAFFE	JACQUES	1831	WENTZWILLER	05/26/1866	NY		FILM
GRALL	DANIEL		LANGENSOULTZBACH	01/01/1840	A		SUESS
GRALL	PHILLIP		LANGENSOULTZBACH	01/01/1869	NY		NO.2
GRALL	PHILLIP		LAUTERBURG	01/01/1868	NY		NO.2
GRAMBACH	NICLOAS		SPARSBACH	01/01/1828	A		FILM
GRANDCLAUDE	JULES	1833	BAVILLIER	03/05/1852	SL		FILM
GRANDHEY W W 1CH	JOSEPH	1799	ROUGEMONT	08/08/1846	PH		FILM

Lastname	Firstname	Birth Year	Birthplace	Emigration	De	Prof	Source
GRANDJEAN	MARGUERITE	1803	ST CROIX AUX MINES	03/20/1857	NY		FILM
GRAS	GERTRUD	1818	HAMBACH	04/09/1844	TX		FILM
GRAS	GERTRUD	1818	HAMBACH	04/09/1844	TX		FILM
GRASBOILLOT	JEAN	1813	ST GERMAIN	02/08/1843	NY		FILM
GRASS F OF 5	JOSEPH		DAUENDORF	02/28/1838	A		FILM
GRASSELER W W 3CH	FRANCOIS XAVIER	1805	ROUGEGOUTTE	02/09/1839	NY		FILM
GRASSER	SEBASTIEN	1810	RIXHEIM	12/12/1849	NO		FILM
GRASTWOHL	ANDRE		REMLISDORFF W	04/20/1849	NY		FILM
GRAVEY	JEAN	1813	HECKEN	04/29/1852	NY		FILM
GRAVEY	NICOLAS	1815	SCHWEIGHAUSEN	04/26/1845	NY		FILM
GRAVIER	JEAN BAPTISTE	1795	OBERMICHELBACH	08/20/1847	A		FILM
GRAWAY W 2CH	JEAN PIERRE	1806	SOPPE LE BAS	11/25/1854	NY		FILM
GRAWEY W W 2CH	JEAN	1813	HECKEN	08/04/1846	NY		FILM
GREAUNINGER	PIERRE	1824	LAUTENBACH	03/17/1854	A		FILM
GREDER	MAGDELAINE	1783	ZINSWEILLER	02/16/1817	A		FILM
GREDY W 3CH	ANNE	1803	FELLERINGEN	03/28/1854	NY		FILM
GREETER	LOUIS	1825	HEGENHEIM	09/06/1847	NY		FILM
GREETER	LOUIS	1825	HEGENHEIM	09/06/1847	NY		FILM
GREGER	CHRISTINE	1821	HUNSPACH	01/01/1865	NY		NO.2
GREGER	MARIE	1820	HUNSPACH	01/01/1865	NY		NO.2
GREGER	MICHEL	1853	HUNSPACH	01/01/1865	NY		NO.2
GREGES	LEOPOLD	1823	FRAHIER	12/13/1865	NY		FILM
GREIBUEHL	EMIL	1868	ALTENSTADT	01/01/1869	NY		NO.2
GREIBUEHL	MARIA	1867	ALTENSTADT	01/01/1869	NY		NO.2
GREIBUEHL MN SCHNELO	MAGDALENA	1835	ALTENSTADT	01/01/1869	NY		NO.2
GREIBUEHL W W 2 CH	GEORG	1831	ALTENSTADT	01/01/1869	NY	FARM	NO.2
GREIN	JEAN GEORGE		NIEDERBETSCHDORF	03/21/1817	A		FILM
GREINEN	JACQUES		BOUXWILLER	01/01/1828	A		FILM
GREINER	GOERG	1844	NIEDERBETSCHDORF	01/01/1866	NY	FARM	NO.2
GREINER	GUSTAVE	1828	HUNAWIHR	02/29/1856	A		FILM
GREINER F OF 6	ADAM		RATZWILLER	01/01/1828	A		FILM
GREINER W W 2CH	JEAN	1800	MOUTRON	04/23/1840	NY		FILM
GREISS	JOHANN GEORG		NIEDERBETSCHDORF	01/01/1817	A		NO.2
GREISS W W 3CH	JEAN GEORGES		NIEDERBETSCHDORF	03/29/1817	A		FILM
GRELOT	MARIE ROSE	1818	SENONNES	03/21/1839	NO		FILM
GREMMEL	MATHIAS		ROSHEIM	09/06/1852	A		FILM
GRENALE W W 3CH	JEAN JACQUES	1802	OBERENTZEN	09/14/1846	NY		FILM
GRENIER		1810	MUHLBACK	10/21/1842	NY		FILM
GRENTZINGER	CELESTIN MODEST	1832	WALHEIM	08/22/1857	NY		FILM
GRENTZNING A F		1796	STEINSOULTZ	11/20/1841	NY		FILM
GRESCH W W 2 CH	VINCENT	1819	SOPPE LE BAS	08/18/1848	NY		FILM
GRESS F OF 6	PH. JACQUES		WEITERSILLER	01/01/1828	A		FILM
GRESS H MADELAINE	JEAN GEROGES		ROPPENHEIM	/ /	A		O.1
GRESS H MADELAINE1CH	JACOB	1799	ROPPENHEIM	/ /	A		NO.1
GRESS MN STREBLY	MADELAINE	1797	ROPPENHEIM	/ /	A		NO.1
GRESS S PHILIPPE	JACOB	1799		/ /	A		PRIV
GRESS W JEAN GEORGES	MADELAINE		ROPPENHEIM	/ /	A		NO.1
GRESS W W 2CH	MARTIN	1821	ROUGEGOUTTE	10/30/1852	SL		FILM
GRESS W W 3CH	DOMINIQUE	1822	ROUGEGOUTTE	10/30/1852	SL		FILM
GRESSEL W W 1CH	NICOLAS	1794	ULM	03/27/1852	NO		FILM

Lastname	Firstname	Birth Year	Birthplace	Emigration	De	Prof	Source
GRESSLE	HENRIE	1807	DURBACH B	04/26/1850	NO		FILM
GRESSLE 4 CH	BARBE	1811	COLMAR	11/26/1853	SL		FILM
GRESSOT	THIEBAUT	1826	COLMAR	04/09/1853	NY		FILM
GRETTER	ANTOINE	1800	BREITENBACH	10/18/1848	NY		FILM
GRETTER W 5CH	MARIE ANNE	1804	KAYSERSBERG	02/15/1849	NY		FILM
GRETZINGER	IGNACE	1819	RUMERSHEIM	11/29/1847	NY		FILM
GREVILLOT W W	ANDRE	1813	ST COSME	11/15/1850	NY		FILM
GRIEBEL	GEORGES		CLEEBOURG	01/01/1817	A		PRIV
GRIEDELMANN	FRANCOIS XAVIER	1814	MASSEVAUX	10/07/1847	SL		FILM
GRIEDELMANN W W A CH	FRANCOIS XAVIER	1835	ARCEY	10/10/1865	NY		FILM
GRIESEMANN W W 4CH	JEAN PIERRE	1802	BOUROGNE	04/07/1845	NY		FILM
GRIESHABER	JEAN		ENDERSBACH B	04/21/1849	A		FILM
GRIESS	JUSTINE AUGUSTE	1831	LANDAU	12/22/1854	NY		FILM
GRIESS W W 5CH	JACQUES		WINGEN	03/17/1817	A		FILM
GRIESSEMANN W W	CHRETIEN		ESCHBOURG	01/01/1828	A		FILM
GRIESSER	LOUIS	1817	THANN	05/21/1838	NY		FILM
GRIESSER W W	PIERRE	1795	ROUFFACH	04/14/1856	NY		FILM
GRIISSINGER	ANTOIN	1808	CARSPACH	12/24/1846	NY		FILM
GRILLE	PHILIPPE	1831	BELFORT	10/14/1865	NY		FILM
GRILLE W W 1CH	FRANCOIS XAVIER	1818	BELFORT	08/23/1847	NO		FILM
GRILLOT W W	FRANCOIS JOSEPH	1817	GRANDVILLAR	09/28/1846	NY		FILM
GRIMDELER W W 3CH	JEAN	1803	WIHR EN PLAIN	09/19/1848	NY		FILM
GRIME W W 5CH	PIERRE	1801	VELLESCOT	10/01/1844	NY		FILM
GRIMENWALD	JEAN	1832	MOOSCH	09/28/1854	NY		FILM
GRIMENWALD	JOSEPH	1813	KRUTZ	04/30/1850	NY		FILM
GRIMM W W CH	ANDRE	1817	NIEDERHERGHEIM	09/06/1849	A		FILM
GRIMOND W W 3CH	NICOLAS	1787	ETEIMBES	09/06/1847	NY		FILM
GRIMONT	JOSEPH	1838	SUARC	05/06/1857	NY		FILM
GRINGER W W 2CH	SERAPHIN	1812	OBERSASSHEIM	03/12/1852	NO		FILM
GRINI W W 1CH	THIBAUD FRANCOS	1814	MERXHEIM	01/13/1854	NY		FILM
GRINNER	PHILIPPE	1828	ST MARIE AUX MINES	10/07/1854	NY		FILM
GRIOT W W 3CH	PHILIPPE	1815	MASSEVAUX	04/09/1853	NY		FILM
GRISCH F OF 10	FRANCOIS JOSEPH		FORT LOUIS	01/01/1828	A		FILM
GRISCH F OF 2	ANTOINE		FORT LOUIS	01/01/1828	A		FILM
GRISCH THE SONS			FORT LOUIS	01/01/1828	A		FILM
GRISEZ	ADELE	1845	FRAHIER	12/07/1865	NY		FILM
GRISEZ	FRACNOIS FERREO	1832	PLANCHES	11/05/1852	LV		FILM
GRISEZ	NICOLAS	1823	LA CHAPELLE SOUS CHA	02/13/1845	NY		FILM
GRISEZ W W	CLAUDE PASCHAL	1784	ANDELAMANS	03/08/1847	NO		FILM
GRISEZ W W 4CH	FERRIOL	1811	PLANCHEZ	03/08/1847	NO		FILM
GRISSINGER	JOSEPH	1812	CARSPACH	11/05/1845	NY		FILM
GRISSMANN	AUGUSTE	1843	BOUROGNE	09/06/1866	NY		FILM
GRISSWEG	ANTOINE	1818	KIFFIS	04/05/1854	NY		FILM
GRISWARD W W 1 CH	JACQUES	1815	FERETTE	01/24/1849	NY		FILM
GRIVEL	CLAIRE EUGENIE	1828	LA POUTROISE	03/19/1852	SL		FILM
GROB	REGINE	1847	NIEDERLAUTERBACH	01/01/1866	NO		NO.2
GROB	REINE		NIEDERLAUTERBACH	01/01/1850	NO		PRIV
GROB	REINE	1847	NIEDERLAUTERBACH	01/01/1866	NO		PRIV
GROELL	JEAN CHARLES	1821	GUEMAR	03/09/1849	NY		FILM
GROELLY	ADAM	1809	BERENTZWILLER	03/20/1852	NY		FILM

Lastname	Firstname	Birth Year	Birthplace	Emigration	De	Prof	Source
GROFF	FRANCOIS JOSEPH	1813	SEPPOIS LE BAS	03/31/1852	NY		FILM
GROFF	GEORGE		FORT LOUIS	01/01/1828	A		FILM
GROFF	IGNACE		FORT LOUIS	01/01/1828	A		FILM
GROFF	MICHEL	1822	MUNWILLER	09/01/1851	TX	CULT	PASS
GROFF	MICHEL	1822	MUNZWILLER	09/17/1851	TX		FILM
GROFF CH 2	MICHEL	1822	MUNWILLER	09/01/1851			
GROFF F OF 3	ANTOINE		FORT LOUIS	01/01/1828	A		FILM
GROFF W W 5CH	ANTOINE	1800	DELLE	04/25/1850	NY		FILM
GROH	MICHEL		EPPINGEN B	05/12/1849	A		FILM
GROHMULLER	ROSINE	1808	LEMBACH	01/01/1866	NY		NO.2
GROISS W W 3CH	JEAN GEORGE		NIEDERBETSCHDORF	03/29/1817	A		FILM
GROLL	ELISABETH		PFAFFENHOFFEN	01/01/1828	A		FILM
GROLL	JACQUES		PFAFFENHOFFEN	01/01/1828	A		FILM
GRON W W 5CH	JEAN			03/17/1817	A		FILM
GRORS W W 5CH	JEAN		HERBITZHEIM	03/17/1817	A		FILM
GROS	CLAUDE AUGUSTE	1848	MONTBELIARD	11/17/1866	NY		FILM
GROS	JACQUES	1821	MAUTHIERMONT	03/08/1848	NO		FILM
GROS	PIE	1822	GUNDOLSHEIM	10/01/1848	TX	MECH	PASS
GROS W W 8CH	PIERRE	1798	VAUTHIERMONT	06/08/1846	NY		FILM
GROSBETTY	PIERRE	1829	THANN	07/01/1861	NY		FILM
GROSBOILLOT	MARIE	1845	ROUGEGOUTTE	05/01/1865	NY		FILM
GROSHAENY	CATHERINE	1835	LOGLENHEIM	02/11/1857	NY		FILM
GROSHAENY	CHRISTINE	1823	HALSHEIM	03/05/1846	NY		FILM
GROSJEAN	ETIENNE	1816	DORANS	03/02/1839	NY		FILM
GROSJEAN	JEAN BAPTISTE	1818	ST MARIE AUX MINES	04/13/1847	NO		FILM
GROSJEAN	JOSEPH		MORSCHWILLER	03/04/1838	A		FILM
GROSJEAN	JOSEPH NICOLAS	1822	NONTREUX VIEUX	01/30/1847	NY		FILM
GROSJEAN	JULIE	1840	VOLSCHWILLER	05/17/1866	NY		FILM
GROSJEAN	MICHEL	1824	BITSCHWILLER	03/13/1846	NY		FILM
GROSJEAN	NICOLAS	1829	ST MARIE AUX MINES	10/01/1857	A		FILM
GROSJEAN W W 2CH	PIERRE PAUL	1816	RORSCHWIHR	09/03/1847	A		FILM
GROSJEAN W W CH	FRANCOIS	1820	ST MARIE AUX MINES	10/27/1853	NO		FILM
GROSKOPF	ANTOINE	1836	HELFRANTZKIRCH	10/02/1866	NY		FILM
GROSMAN	JEAN APTISTE	1823	PULVERSHEIM	03/25/1853	NY		FILM
GROSMAN F OF 2	NICOLAS		WEISLINGERN	01/01/1828	A		FILM
GROSMAN F OF 8	GEORGE		WEISLINGEN	01/01/1828	A		FILM
GROSMAN W W	NICOLAS		WEISLINGEN	03/18/1187	A		FILM
GROSMANN	JEAN BAPTISTE	1823	PULVERSHEIM	03/25/1853	NY		FILM
GROSMANN W W 1CH	ANTOINE		WEISLINGEN	03/18/1817	A		FILM
GROSS	CAROLINE		STATTMATTEN	03/02/1838	A		FILM
GROSS	CHRETIEN		ZELL W	12/27/1849	A		FILM
GROSS	ELISABETH		BOUXWILLER	01/01/1828	A		FILM
GROSS	ELISABETH		STATTMATTEN	03/02/1838	A		FILM
GROSS	ERASME	1819	GUNDOLSHEIM	02/27/1852	A		FILM
GROSS	FELIX	1841	SOULTZ-SOUS-FORET	01/01/1865	NY		NO.2
GROSS	FELIX		ARTOLSHEIM	02/28/1838	A		FILM
GROSS	GUILLAUME	1816	ENSISHEIM	06/28/1849	NY		FILM
GROSS	JEAN	1823	SOPPE LE BAS	03/17/1854	NY		FILM
GROSS	JOSEPH	1825	COLMAR	10/29/1856	NY		FILM
GROSS	PAUL	1824	GUNDOLSHEIM	03/02/1852	A		FILM

Lastname	Firstname	Birth Year	Birthplace	Emigration	De	Prof	Source
GROSS	PIERRE	1826	GUNDOLSHEIM	10/20/1848	TX		FILM
GROSS	REINHARD		NIEDERBRONN	05/13/1838	A		FILM
GROSS	XAVIER	1816	GUNDOLSHEIM	11/01/1848	TX	CARP	PASS
GROSS F OF 3	GEORGE		ERCKARTSWILLER	01/01/1828	A		FILM
GROSS F OF 6	CHRISTOPHE		BOUXWILLER	01/01/1828	A		FILM
GROSS F OF 8	JACQUES		BRUMATH	01/01/1828	A		FILM
GROSS W W	JOSEPH	1787	DIEFMATTEN	01/29/1845	NY		FILM
GROSS W W 1CH	FREDERIC	1826	GUEBWILLER	05/17/1850	A		FILM
GROSS W W 1CH	XAVIER	1816	GUNDOLSHEIM	11/14/1848	TX		FILM
GROSS W W 2CH	MARTIN	1821	ROUGEGOUTTE	10/30/1852	SL		FILM
GROSS W W 3CH	DOMINIQUE	1822	GUNDOLSHEIM	10/30/1852	SL		FILM
GROSS W W 6 CH	RICHARD	1801	GUNDOLSHEIM	09/01/1851	NO		FILM
GROSS W W 6CH	GUILLAUME		WEYER	03/03/1817	A		FILM
GROSSENBACH	JOHANN	1828	BRANSHERALD	11/15/1846	TX		FILM
GROSSENBACH W W 6CH	JOHANN	1802		11/15/1845	TX		FILM
GROSSER	REINHARD		NIEDERBRONN	01/01/1838	A		FILM
GROSSJEAN	MARIE ANNE	1822	CHAVANNES LES GRANDS	07/19/1849	NY		FILM
GROSSMANN	AUGUSTE		DURLACH B	05/12/1849	NY		FILM
GROSSMANN	CHARLES AUGUSTE		DURLACH B	05/12/1849	NY		FILM
GROSSMANN	ELISE		DURLACH B	05/12/1849	A		FILM
GROSSMANN	GEORGE		FROHMUHL	01/01/1828	A		FILM
GROSSTEPHAN F OF 8	JACQUE		WALDOWISHEIM	01/01/1828	A		FILM
GROTH	LOUIS		HEIMBACH B	04/19/1849	NY		FILM
GROTS W W 6CH	ADAM		NEUHOFF	03/03/1817	A		FILM
GROTZINGER	ANSELM	1820	RUMERSHEIM	09/01/1849	NY		FILM
GROTZINGER	XAVIER	1822	RUMERSHEIM	09/01/1849	NY		FILM
GROTZINGER W W	JEAN		EMENDINGEN B	10/13/1849	A		FILM
GROTZINGER W W 3CH	JEAN	1795	RUMERSHEIM	09/04/1851	NO		FILM
GROTZINGER W W 5CH	GILLES	1815	RUMERSHEIM	09/01/1849	NY		FILM
GRUBER	LOUIS	1834	ST MARIE AUX MINES	10/24/1856	NO		FILM
GRUBER F OF 2	THIEBAUT		BOERSCH	02/26/1838	A		FILM
GRUBER W W 6CH	ANTOINE		BERNARDSWILLER	05/26/1817	A		FILM
GRUENEWALD	FRANZ	1813	URBIS	11/22/1843	TX		FILM
GRUENEWALD	FRANZ	1813	URBIS	11/22/1843	TX		FILM
GRUM W W 5CH	JEAN		BISLEY	02/26/1838	A		FILM
GRUMBACH	PIERRE		GUNGWILLER	02/03/1838	A		FILM
GRUN W W 1CH	THIEBAUD FRANC	1814	MERXHEIM	01/13/1854	NY		FILM
GRUNANVALD	CAROLINE	1834	MITZACH	07/18/1854	NY		FILM
GRUNDRICH W W 8CH	CHRETIEN		GUEMAR	03/17/1853	NY		FILM
GRUNEISEN	JOSEPH	1786	SOPPE LE BAS	09/21/1844	A		FILM
GRUNENWALD	MATHIAS	1820	KRUTH	09/01/1854	TX	DAYL	PASS
GRUNENWALD	MATHIAS	1820	KRUTH	09/14/1854	NY		FILM
GRUNENWALD CH 2	JOSEPH	1787		09/01/1859	TX	CULT	PASS
GRUNENWALD D JOSEPH	AGATHE	1828	KRUTH	09/01/1859	TX		PASS
GRUNENWALD D JOSEPH	THERESE	1838	KRUTH	09/01/1859	TX		PASS
GRUNENWALD W W 3CH	MATHIAS	1817	KRUTH	09/14/1854	TX		FILM
GRUNER	MICHEL	1845	SURBOURG	01/01/1866	NY		NO.2
GRUNI W W 5CH	JEAN	1784	RASTLEY	07/30/1849	NY		FILM
GRUNINGER	LAURENT	1812	COLMAR	08/27/1846	NY		FILM
GRUNINGER	MATHIAS	1808	COLMAR	10/31/1854	NY		FILM

Lastname	Firstname	Birth Year	Birthplace	Emigration	De	Prof	Source
GRUNSINGER-BURGER 8C	MADELAINE	1811	WITTELSHEIM	11/28/1854	TX		FILM
GRUNSINGERW 8 CH	MADELAINE	1813	WITTELSHEIM	11/28/1854	NY		FILM
GRUPP	JEAN PAUL	1829	GUEBWILLER	07/28/1849	NY		FILM
GRUPP	JEAN PAUL	1829	GUEBWILLER	04/03/1848	NY		FILM
GRUSENMEYER F OF 5	NICOLAS		SCHWEIGHAUSEN	01/01/1828	A		FILM
GRUSS	DOMINIQUE	1822	GUEMAR	09/14/1855	NY		FILM
GRUSS	JEAN BAPTISTE	1828	FESSENHEIM	07/20/1852	NO		FILM
GRUSS W W 5CH	ANTOINE	1804	VILVISHEIM	03/30/1839	NO		FILM
GRUSSENMEYER	JOSEF	1849	SURBOURG	01/01/1867	NY		NO.2
GRUSSER W 6CH	CATHERINE	1815	RIXHEIM	07/08/1857	NY		FILM
GRUSSI W W 2CH	JACQUES	1819	ROSTEIG B R	11/19/1846	NY		FILM
GRUSZ	MICHEL		STEINBOURG	01/01/1828	A		FILM
GSALTER	NICOLAS	1824	SCHWEIGHOUSE	08/16/1847	OH		FILM
GSCHWENDEN	HILESIE		BUEHLERTHAL B	04/19/1849	NY		FILM
GSCHWIND W 3CH	PIERRE	1813	FOLGENSBOURG	06/20/1845	NO		FILM
GSELL	BARBE	1823	KAYSERSBERG	02/28/1849	NO		FILM
GSELL	HENRY	1832	KAYSERSBERG	02/28/1849	NO		FILM
GSELL	MARIE ANNE	1823	OBERENTZEN	09/10/1851	TX		FILM
GSELL	MARIE-ANNE	1833	OBERENTZEN	09/01/1851	TX		PASS
GSELL	MICHEL	1827	KAYSERSBERG	06/11/1849	NO		FILM
GSELL A 4CH	MICHEL		OBERENSISHEIM	05/29/1844	TX		FILM
GSELL W W 3 CH	JACQUES		OBERHOFFEN	03/01/1838	A		FILM
GSELL H CATHERINE	MICHEL CH 8	1800	OBRENTZEN	04/01/1844	TX	CULT	SHIP
GSELL W W	LOUIS	1808	NIEDERENTZEN	01/10/1844	A		FILM
GSSCHWIND	JEAN MARCEL	1828	HINDLINGEN	02/06/1853	NO		FILM
GSTALDER	BERNHARD	1825	REININGUE	12/07/1853	NY		FILM
GSTALDER	HUBERT	1831	REININGUE	12/07/1853	NY		FILM
GTENGER	MARTIN	1820	COLMAR	07/09/1851	NY		FILM
GUCKERT W 4CH	MADELAINE	1806	HEITERSHEIM	04/14/1848	NY		FILM
GUEFFEMME	AMBROISE	1830	BOURGOGNE	08/01/1853	NY		FILM
GUELLER	JEAN BAPTISTE	1824	LIEPVRE	10/11/1854	NO		FILM
GUENAL	CHARLES	1822	PETIT CROIX	10/10/1157	SL		FILM
GUENAL	FRANCOISE	1831	MULHOUSE	10/10/1857	SL		FILM
GUENAL	HELENE	1836	MULHOUSE	10/10/1857	SL		FILM
GUENIG W W ANNE MARE	JOSEPH	1825	WITTENHEIM	07/17/1852	NY		FILM
GUENIN	FERDINAND	1812	DENDELINCOURT	09/30/1864	NY		FILM
GUENIN	W W 3CH		KESKASTEL	03/23/1803	A		FILM
GUENOT	JULES	1829	PAIX	09/06/1854	NY		FILM
GUENTHAL	ALISE	1849	MONTECHEROUIL	03/01/1865	NY		FILM
GUENTHAL	LEON	1857	MONTECHEROUIL	03/01/1865	NY		FILM
GUENTHAL	OCTOVE	1859	MONTECHEROUIL	03/01/1865	NY		FILM
GUENTHAL	STANIS	1848	MONTECHEROUIL	03/01/1865	NY		FILM
GUENTHER	ANNA LOUISA	1858	LAUTERBURG	01/01/1866	NO		NO.2
GUENTHER	ELISABETH		ERNOLSHEIM	01/01/1828	A		FILM
GUENTHER	ELISE	1865	LOBSANN	01/01/1866	NY		NO.2
GUENTHER	HEINRICH	1866	LOBSANN	01/01/1866	NY		NO.2
GUENTHER	JOSEPH	1852	LAUTERBURG	01/01/1866	NO		NO.2
GUENTHER	KARL	1865	LAUTERBURG	01/01/1866	NO		NO.2
GUENTHER	MAGDALENA	1845	LAUTERBURG	01/01/1866	NO		NO.2
GUENTHER	MAGDALENA	1864	LOBSANN	01/01/1866	NY		NO.2

Lastname	Firstname	Birth Year	Birthplace	Emigration	De	Prof	Source
GUENTHER	MARIE	1864	LAUTERBURG	01/01/1866	NO		NO.2
GUENTHER	ROSA	1853	LAUTERBURG	01/01/1866	MO		NO.2
GUENTHER	SCHOMAR		WUERTEMBERG	07/30/1849	A		FILM
GUENTHER F OF 2	CHARLES		LICHTENBERG	01/01/1828	A		FILM
GUENTHER W 3CH	MARIA	1835	LOBSANN	01/01/1866	NY	FARM	NO.2
GUENTHER W 6 CH	ANDREAS	1815	LAUTERBURG	01/01/1866	NO	MERC	NO.2
GUEPFERT	CATHERINE	1833	ILLHAUESERN	02/14/1855	NY		FILM
GUERIN	JEAN EDMOND	1822	NANTES	09/17/1845	A		FILM
GUERINGER	CATHERINE		WITTISHEIM	03/02/1838	A		FILM
GUERINGER	CATHERINE		WITTISHEIM	03/02/1838	A		FILM
GUERNINGUE W W S	BERNARD	1799	LEBETAIN	09/24/1854	NY		FILM
GUERRE W W 2 D	FRANCOIS XAVIER	1770	CHATENOIS	08/09/1849	A		FILM
GUERRING W W 5CH	BERNARD	1799	LEBETAIN	03/18/1847	NY		FILM
GUETHAL	ERNSEST	1861	MONTECHEROUIL	03/01/1865	NY		FILM
GUEUTHAL	ERNEST	1861	MONTECHEROUIL	01/03/1865	NY		FILM
GUGELMANN	CHARLES FRANCOI	1822	HUNINGEN	05/26/1855	NY		FILM
GUGERNUSS W W 9CH	FRANCOIS		NEUWILLER	03/31/1817	A		FILM
GUGGENMOOS F OF 5	SEBASTIEN		DURSTEL	03/18/1838	A		FILM
GUGIN	JEAN		KANSTATT W	06/21/1849	A		FILM
GUGIN	LOUIS		KANSTATT W	06/21/1849	A		FILM
GUIBERT	THE YOUNGER		FROESCHWILLER	/ /	A		SUESS
GUICHARD	MARIE	1796	SERMAMAGNY	09/28/1854	SL		FILM
GUIDAT	JEAN BAPTISTE	1824	ST MARIE AUX MINES	08/20/1847	NO		FILM
GUILLARD	FRANCOIS JOSPH	1828	MONTREUX VIEUX	02/04/1847	NY		FILM
GUILLARD	JEAN JACQUES	1814	DIEFMATTEN	03/12/1857	A		FILM
GUILLARD	LOUIS		MONTBELIARD	03/12/1863	NY		FILM
GUILLARD W W 2CH	JOSEPH	1812	DIEFFMATTEN	03/07/1854	NY		FILM
GUILLAUME	ANTOINE	1821	THANN	06/30/1845	NY		FILM
GUILLAUME	HENRY	1813	THANN	06/30/1845	NY		FILM
GUILLAUME	JOSEPH	1818	LIEPVRE	08/14/1838	NO		FILM
GUILLAUMEY	CELESTIN	1828	SERMAMAGNY	12/09/1846	SL		FILM
GUITTARD	MARIE CATHERINE	1825	MONTREUX VIEUX	01/30/1847	NY		FILM
GUITTARD W W 2CH	NICOLAS	1820	STERNENBERG	11/26/1851	A		FILM
GULDENSCHUE	LOUISE	1823	RANSPACH	09/05/1857	A		FILM
GULLAIN		1827	MONTBELIARD	04/11/1865	NY		FILM
GULLAIN		1842	MONTBELIARD	04/11/1865	NY		FILM
GULLING	CELESTINE	1826	BITSCHWILLER	04/21/1852	A		FILM
GULLY	BARBABE	1817	GEISHAUSEN	09/04/1845	NY		FILM
GULLY	IGNACE	1820	RANSPACH	08/22/1854	NO		FILM
GULLY	JEANNE ELISABEH	1811	GIOACHINOPOLI	04/26/1852	A		FILM
GULLY	JOSEPH		FELLERING	11/01/1844	TX	PRIN	PASS
GULLY	JOSEPH	1823	ST AMARIN	05/07/1845	NY		FILM
GULLY	KATHERINA	1822	RANSPACH	11/22/1843	TX		FILM
GULLY	MARIE		RANSBACH	08/01/1844	TX		PASS
GULLY	NICOLAS	1823	URBES	02/18/1850	A		FILM
GULLY	ROSINE	1818	ODEREN	11/04/1857	TX		FILM
GULLY D ANTOINE I	AGATHE	1841	FELLERING	05/01/1844	TX		SHIP
GULLY H CATHERINE C2	ANTOINE I	1800	FELLERING	05/01/1844	TX		SHIP
GULLY S ANTOINE I	ANTOINE II	1839	FELLERING	05/01/1844	TX		SHIP
GULLY W 2CH	MARIE	1814	SOULTZ	02/02/1850	PH		FILM

Lastname	Firstname	Birth Year	Birthplace	Emigration	De	Prof	Source
GULLY W ANTOINE I	CATHERINE	1800	FELLERING	05/01/1844	TX		SHIP
GULLY W W	VALENTIN	1816	MITZACH	04/24/1855	NY		FILM
GULLY W W 4CH	MARMENAUX	1800	RANSPACH	08/28/1844	NY		FILM
GULZWILLER	ANTOINE	1831	BIEDERTHAL	05/22/1866	NY		FILM
GUNDSCHACK W W 2 CH	MICHEL		GEUDERTHEIM	03/11/1817	A		FILM
GUNDY W W	JOSEPH	1798	FULLEREN	12/24/1846	A		FILM
GUNDY W W 8CH	SEBASTIEN	1806	FULLEREN	12/24/1846	A		FILM
GUNE	JOSEPH	1818	CARSPACH	10/25/1853	A		FILM
GUNER	MARTIN	1823	LAUW	02/25/1852	NY		FILM
GUNSETH F OF 5	CHRETIEN		WEITERSWILLER	01/01/1188	A		FILM
GUNTER	JOSEPH		DURCHHAUSEN W	05/23/1849	A		FILM
GUNTHER	ANDRE		LAUTERBOURG	01/01/1850	NO		PRIV
GUNTHER	CATHERINE		ERNOLSHEIM	01/01/1828	A		FILM
GUNTHER F OF 8	PIERRE		HERBITZHEIM	01/01/1828	A		FILM
GUNZBURGER	THEODORINE	1846	SIERENTZ	05/28/1865	NY		FILM
GURBA	PIERRE	1836	LIEBSDORF	07/04/1866	NY		FILM
GUSS	ADAM		WEITBRUCH	01/01/1828	A		FILM
GUTAPFEL	GEORGE		GEISWILLER	01/01/1828	A		FILM
GUTAPFEL	MADELAINE		GEISWILLER	01/01/1828	A		FILM
GUTAPFEL	MARIE		GEISWILLER	01/01/1828	A		FILM
GUTAPFEL	MICHEL		GEISWILLER	01/01/1828	A		FILM
GUTAPFEL F OF 5	VALENTIN		BOUXWILLER	01/01/1828	A		FILM
GUTAPFEL W W 2CH	MICHEL		GEISWILLER	01/01/1828	A		FILM
GUTAPFEL W W 3CH	GEORGES		BIOSSELSHAUSEN	01/01/1828	A		FILM
GUTAPFEL W W 4CH	JEAN		BOSSELSHAUSEN	01/01/1828	A		FILM
GUTH	FAVIER		SCHWEIGHAUSEN	01/01/1828	A		FILM
GUTHANS	JOSEF	1841	NIEDERLAUTERBACH	01/01/1865	NO		NO.2
GUTHANS	JOSEPH		NIEDERLAUTERBACH	01/01/1850	NO		PRIV
GUTHANS	JOSEPH	1837	NIEDERLAUTERBACH	01/01/1861	NO	BAKE	PRIV
GUTHMANN	FRACNOIS XAVIER	1819	FESSENHEIM	04/08/1847	NY		FILM
GUTHMULLER	FRIEDRICH	1826	LEMBACH	01/01/1866	NY		NO.2
GUTHNECK	CHARLES		DUPPIGHEIM	03/03/1838	A		FILM
GUTLEBEN	ANTOINE	1814	WEDENSOHLEN	04/05/1842	NO		FILM
GUTLEBEN W W	JEAN BAPTISTE	1805	WIDENSOHLEN	12/10/1838	NO		FILM
GUTTER F OF 4	JEAN		INGENHEIM	01/01/1828	A		FILM
GUTTER F OF 4	JEAN		INGENHEIM	01/01/1820	A		FILM
GUTZWILLER	JEAN ALOYSE	1817	BIEDERTHAL	01/04/1847	NY		FILM
GUTZWILLER	MATHIEU LOUIS	1826	FAGOLSHEIM	02/20/1852	NY		FILM
GUTZWILLER	XAVIER	1815	BIEDERTHAL	04/06/1847	NY		FILM
GUYER	CATHERINE	1842	ST MARIE AUX MINES	08/27/1857	NY		FILM
GUYER	ELISABETH	1841	ST MARIE AUX MINES	08/22/1857	NY		FILM
GUYER	SUSANNE	1836	ST MARIE AUX MINES	08/22/1857	NY		FILM
GWSCHIND W W CH	JEAN	1827	PFEFFERHOUSE	09/13/1852	NY		FILM
GWURTZ	NICOLAS	1805	FELLERINGEN	03/17/1842	NO		FILM

Lastname	Firstname	Birth Year	Birthplace	Emigration	De	Prof	Source
H				/ /			
HAAG	FRANCOIS JOSEPH		NIEDERLAUTERBACH	04/14/1838	A		FILM
HAAG	FRANCOIS JOSEPH		NIEDERLAUTERBACH	08/16/1837	A		FILM
HAAL	SERAPHIN	1835	LARIVIERE	02/18/1857	NY	FARM	FILM
HAAS	ANTOINE FRANC.	1793	TURCKHEIM	07/01/1853	OH	BUTC	FILM
HAAS	CHRETIEN		FREUDENSTADT W	04/20/1849	NY		FILM
HAAS	CHRISTINA	1818	MUNCHHOUSE	01/01/1868	NY		NO.2
HAAS	FLORIAN	1847	MUNCHHOUSE	01/01/1868	NY		NO.2
HAAS	FRANZ	1854	MUNCHHOUSE	01/01/1868	NY		NO.2
HAAS	GEORGE		DURSTEL	03/18/1838	A	DAYL	FILM
HAAS	IGNACE	1823	BURNHAUPT LE HAUT	06/12/1846	NY	DAYL	FILM
HAAS	JACOB	1822	CLIMBACH	01/01/1869	NY	FARM	NO.2
HAAS	JACQUES		STATTMATTEN	01/01/1828	A		FILM
HAAS	JEAN	1827	SAUSHEIM ? SANSHEIM	04/01/1857	NY		FILM
HAAS	JOSEF	1852	MUNCHHOUSE	01/01/1868	NY		NO.2
HAAS	JOSEPH	1842	NIEDERLAUTERBACH	01/01/1867	NO		PRIV
HAAS	MARIE ROSE	1816	RIMBACH	04/04/1840	NY		FILM
HAAS	MARTIN	1843	STEINSELTZ	01/01/1868	NY	FARM	NO.2
HAAS	PIERRE		DURSTEL	03/18/1838	A	WEAV	FILM
HAAS	ROSINA	1848	MUNCHHOUSE	01/01/1868	NY		NO.2
HAAS	SAALES		LAUDERTHAL SIGMARING	05/12/1849	A		FILM
HAAS	VALENTIN		ROTT	01/01/1817	A		NO.2
HAAS	WILHELMINE		FREUDENSTADT	04/20/1849	NY		FILM
HAAS W W 4 CH	JOSEF	1813	MUNCHHOUSE	01/01/1868	NY	FARM	NO.2
HAASS	JEAN	1835	BITSCHWILLER	09/27/1854	NY		FILM
HAASSER	JOSEPH		ROESCHWOOG	01/01/1828	A	LAYB	FILM
HABER	GEORGES		SCHILLERSDORF	01/30/1828	A		FILM
HABER	JACQUES		REINHARDSMUENSTER	01/01/1828	A	TAYL	FILM
HABER	MARIE		GEISWILLER	01/01/1828	A		FILM
HABER	PHILIPPE		SCHILLERSDORF	01/01/1828	A	FARM	FILM
HABER 1 CH	MARIE		REITWEILER	01/01/1828	A		FILM
HABER F OF 2	MICHEL		ERNOLSHEIM	01/01/1828	A		FILM
HABER F OF 6	GEORGES		INGENHEIM	01/01/1828	A		FILM
HABER W W 4 CH	JEAN		GRIESBACH	01/01/1828	A	DAYL	FILM
HABER W W 4CH	PHILLIPE		PRINTZHEIM	01/01/1832	A		FILM
HABERBUSCH W W 2CH	JEAN	1797	RAMERSHEIM	12/01/1847	NY	SHMA	FILM
HABERER	JOSEPH	1820	BERGHEIM	07/24/1851	A	WEAV	FILM
HABERKONN W W 2 CH	MICHEL		SOUFFLENHEIM	01/01/1828	A	FARM	FILM
HABERKORN	BENOIT		MARMOUTIER	01/01/1828	A		FILM
HABERLE	CATHERINA		BLAUFELDEN	06/21/1849	A		FILM
HABERSTOCK	CATHERINE	1802	OBERHERGHEIM	05/09/1849	PH	DAYL	FILM
HABERSTOCK	FRANCOIS JOSEPH	1798	OBERHERGHEIM	02/20/1847	PH	DAYL	FILM
HABERSTORK	JEAN	1823	ST. MARIE AUX MINES	09/13/1848	NY		FILM
HABERSTROH	JEAN	1824	ROPPEWILLER	07/19/1845	NO		FILM
HABERTHIER W W 2 CH	NICOLAS	1818	SCHWEIGHOUSE HAUT RH	04/23/1846	A		FILM
HABIS	CATHERINE		BLAUFELDEN W	06/21/1849	A		FILM
HABIS	CATHERINE		FREUDENSTADT W	09/29/1849	NY		FILM
HABISRITTINGER	SOPHIE		BAIERSBRONN	04/20/1849	NY		FILM
HABY	ANDREAS	1826	OBERENTZEN	11/15/1846	TX	FARM	FILM
HABY	CATHERINE	1806	OBERENTZEN	05/29/1844	TX		FILM

Lastname	Firstname	Birth Year	Birthplace	Emigration	De	Prof	Source
HABY	JACOB	1833	OBERENTZEN	05/29/1844	TX		FILM
HABY	JACOB	1796	OBERENSISHEIM	04/09/1844	TX		FILM
HABY	JACOB	1834	OBERENSISHEIM	04/09/1844	TX		FILM
HABY	JOSEPH	1813	OABERENZEN	11/22/1843	TX		FILM
HABY	JOSEPH	1820	OBERENTZEN	11/01/1843	TX	CULT	SHIP
HABY	JOSEPH	1822	OBERENTZEN	09/01/1851	TX	SHMA	PASS
HABY	LAURENT	1822	OBERENTZEN	09/01/1851	TX		PASS
HABY	LUDWIG PHILLIPE	1843	OBERENZEN	04/09/1844	TX		FILM
HABY	NICOLAS	1821	OBERENTZEN	11/01/1843	TX	CULT	SHIP
HABY	NIKOLAS	1817	OBERENZEN	11/22/1843		FARM	FILM
HABY 6 CH	FRANCOIS JOSEPH	1793	OBERENTZEN	09/14/1846	TX	FARM	FILM
HABY H MARIE ANNE	FRANCOIS-JOSEPH	1793	OBERNETZEN	09/01/1846	TX	CULT	SHIP
HABY H MARIE MARTHE	JACQUES	1796	OBERENTZEN	04/01/1844	TX	CULT	SHIP
HABY MN MEYER	ANNE MARIE		OBERENTZEN	09/01/1846	TX		SHIP
HABY W W 2 CH	JACOB	1796	OBERENTZEN	04/09/1844	TX		FILM
HACH	GILDEBERT		SINSHEIM B	04/14/1849	NY		FILM
HACHLER	PIERRE	1820	HAUT-RHIN	12/01/1844	TX	CULT	SHIP
HACHLER	PIERRE	1820	RHIN	01/01/1844	TX		SHIP
HACK	GEORGES	1819	CERNAY	09/03/1845	NY		FILM
HACK F OF 5	GEORGES		BRUMATH	01/01/1828	A		FILM
HACKEL F OF 4	JEAN		BRUMATH	01/01/1828	A		FILM
HACQUENOT	XAVIER	1827	VALDORE TERR BEL	12/31/1816	NY		FILM
HACUN	JEAN	1814	ROUFFACH	02/21/1852	TX	EXMI	FILM
HAEBERLIN	JEAN	1821	FORTSCHWIHR	09/17/1857	NY		FILM
HAECHLER	IGNACE	1795	SIGOLSHEIM	05/21/1842	NY		FILM
HAEFFELY	DANIEL	1817	PFASTATT	05/16/1849	NY	INGE	FILM
HAEFFNER	CATHERINE		BRETTEN B	06/21/1849	A		FILM
HAEFFNER	GEORGE		AUENHEIM	03/01/1838	A	FARM	FILM
HAEFFNER	MADELAINE	1825	ROPPENHEIM	01/01/1848	A		NO.1
HAEFFNER	MADELEINE	1825		01/01/1848	A		PRIV
HAEGELE	FANNY	1835	HUNINGUE	05/05/1857	NY		FILM
HAEGELE W W 5CH	JOSEPH		RUMERSHEIM	01/10/1848	NY		FILM
HAEGELIN	JACOB	1830	WITTELSHEIM	10/25/1843	TX		FILM
HAEGELIN	JOSEPH	1819	WITTELSHEIM	10/25/1843	TX		FILM
HAEGELIN	THERESE	1823	WITTELSHEIM	10/25/1843	TX		FILM
HAEGELIN MN ZINSMEYR	THERESE		WITTELSHEIM	01/01/1843	TX		SHIP
HAEGELIN WW AND CH	JOSEPH	1817	WITTELSHEIM	01/01/1843	TX		SHIP
HAEGI F OF 2	GEORGE		SUNDHAUSEN	03/02/1837	A		FILM
HAEHL W W 3 CH	SEBASTIEN		PFAFFENHEIM	/ /	NO	WINE	FILM
HAEHN MN MEYER	CATHERINE	1823	ESCHENBERG	05/05/1857	NY		FILM
HAEHN W W	JOSEF		ESCHENBERG	05/05/1857	NY		FILM
HAEHN W W 2 CH	JOSEF ANTOINE		SOULTZ	01/01/1816	PH		FILM
HAENDEL	FRANCOIS		DOSSENHEIM	02/27/1828	A	WEAV	FILM
HAENEL	CHRETIEN		REXINGEN	02/27/1828	A	WEAV	FILM
HAENEL	JEAN		CLEEBOURG	01/01/1855	NY		NO.2
HAENEL	MARGERITE		REXINGEN	02/27/1828	A		FILM
HAENN	ALEXANDRE	1831	RIBEAUVILLE	09/22/1854	PH		FILM
HAENN	JOSEF	1834	URSCHENHEIM	09/25/1854	NY		FILM
HAENNER	ANNE MARIE	1828	LEYMEN	06/24/1854	NY		FILM
HAENTZEL	JEAN	1824	ALTKIRCH	02/12/1852	NY		FILM

Lastname	Firstname	Birth Year	Birthplace	Emigration	De	Prof	Source
HAERRIG	EVA CATHERINA		BIETLENHEIM	01/01/1828	A		FILM
HAERRIG F OF 5	JEAN		HOERDT	01/01/1828	A	WEAV	FILM
HAERRIG F OF 7	CHRETIEN		GEUDERTHEIM	01/01/1828	A		FILM
HAESSIG	GEORG	1837	MERCKWILLER	01/01/1869	NY	FARM	NO.2
HAESSIG	GEORGE		ISSENHAUSEN	01/01/1828	A	TAYL	FILM
HAESSIG	HEIRNICH		NIEDERKUNTZENHAUSEN	01/01/1855	A		SUESS
HAESSIG	MICHEL	1854	MERCKWILLER	01/01/1869	NY		NO.2
HAESSLE	GUSTAVE	1828	RIMBACHZELL	10/11/1853	A		FILM
HAEVERLE W FAMILY	GEORGE	1802	DURRENENTZEN H.RHIN	03/25/1841	A		FILM
HAFFNER	JEAN		ST.JEAN DE CHAUX	01/01/1828	A		FILM
HAFFNER	JOSEPH		ST JEAN DE CHOUX	01/01/1828	A		FILM
HAFFNER	MADELEINE	1829		01/17/1856	NY		FILM
HAFFNER	PIERRE		SALENTHAL	01/01/1853	A		FILM
HAFFNER	ROSALIE		MORSCHWILLER	01/01/1828	A		FILM
HAFFNER	SEBASTIEN	1830	BURBACH LE BAS	12/02/1847	NY	SHMA	FILM
HAFNER	GEORGE		STADELHOFEN B	07/29/1849	A		FILM
HAFNER	JOSEPH	1841	OBERSTEINBACH	01/01/1865	NY		NO.2
HAG	ANTOINE	1835	WILDENSTEIN	10/11/1854	NY		FILM
HAG	GEOFROID		BRUMATH	01/01/1828	A	TAYL	FILM
HAG	MICHEL		SOUFFLENHEIM	01/01/1828	A		FILM
HAGELE WW AND CH 4	PIERRE		WITTELSHEIM	01/01/1845	TX		SHIP
HAGELE H MARIE ANNE	PIERRE CH 4	1816	WITTELSHEIM	01/01/1854	TX		SHIP
HAGENBACH W W 2 CH	MEINRAD	1812	MORSCHWILLER	04/01/1844	NO		FILM
HAGENMUELLER	JEAN	1828	OBERHERGHEIM	09/17/1846	TX		FILM
HAGENMUELLER	JOHANN	1828	OBERENTZEN	11/15/1846	TX		FILM
HAGENMULLER	JEAN	1828	OBERHERGHEIM	09/17/1846	TX		FILM
HAGENMüLLER	JEAN	1818	OBERHERGHEIM	11/01/1846	TX		SHIP
HAGER	AMBROISE	1803	SCHWEIGHAUSEN	05/21/1839	CN		FILM
HAGER	BENEDIKT	1866	MOTHERN	01/01/1869	NY		NO.2
HAGER	JOHANN	1835	MOTHERN	01/01/1867	NY		NO.2
HAGER	JOHANN	1860	MOTHERN	01/01/1869	NY		NO.2
HAGER	MARGARETHE	1861	MOTHERN	01/01/1869	NY		NO.2
HAGER	MARIA	1863	MOTHERN	01/01/1869	NY		NO.2
HAGER 4 CH	GEORG	1837	MOTHERN	01/01/1869	NY	FARM	NO.2
HAGER W W 2CH	GEORGE	1817	SCHWEIGHAUSEN	04/23/1846	OH	WEAV	FILM
HAGER W W 5 CH	JEAN THIEBAUD	1781	SCHWEIGHAUSEN	04/30/1846	OH		FILM
HAHN	LOUIS	1822	DORNACH	08/27/1850	NY	FARM	FILM
HAHN	MARGARETHA	1842	ROPPENHEIM	03/29/1845	A		NO.1
HAHN	PHILLIP HEINRIH	1844	ROPPENHEIM	03/29/1844	A		NO.1
HAHN	SALOME	1840	ROPPENHEIM	03/29/1845	A		NO.1
HAHN D JACOB	MARGARETHA	1842		03/29/1845	A		FILM
HAHN D JACOB	SALOME	1840		03/29/1845	A		FILM
HAHN F OF 8	JACQUES		BRUMATH	01/01/1828	A		FILM
HAHN H EVA ELISABETH	JACOB	1804		03/29/1845	A		FILM
HAHN H WOLFF 3 CH	JACOB	1804	ROPPENHEIM	03/29/1845	A		NO.1
HAHN MN WOLFF	EVA ELISABETH	1805		03/29/1845	A		FILM
HAHN MN WOLFF	JACOB	1805	ROPPENHEIM	03/29/1845	A		NO.1
HAHN S JACOB	PHILIPP HEINRIC	1844		03/29/1845	A		FILM
HAHNER	FRANCOIS		ESCHBACH B	05/12/1849	A		FILM
HAIDLE			KAUFFENHEIM	05/17/1856	A		FILM

Lastname	Firstname	Birth Year	Birthplace	Emigration	De	Prof	Source
HAINY WIDOW W 4CH	VEUVE		FROHMUHL	01/01/1817	A		FILM
HAISSY	JEAN			03/13/1852	NO		FILM
HAK	DANIEL		BURBACH	03/02/1838	A		FILM
HALBERSETZER	MARTIN	1827	KIENTZHEIM	06/14/1849	NY		FILM
HALBMEYER	JEAN	1806	COLMAR	11/26/1851	NO		FILM
HALDY	BENJAMIN	1842	ODEREM	11/15/1846	TX		FILM
HALDY	KATHARINA	1807	ODEREM	11/15/1846	TX		FILM
HALDY	KATHRIN	1839	ODEREM	11/15/1846	TX		FILM
HALDY	MARIA	1819	ODEREM	11/15/1846	TX		FILM
HALDY	MARIE JOSEPH	1846	ODEREM	11/15/1846	TX		FILM
HALDY F OF 6	MARIE		DEHLINGEN	01/01/1828	A		FILM
HALDY F OF 6	PHILLIPPE		DEHLINGEN	01/01/1828	A		FILM
HALDY F OF 9	LOUIS		HERBITZHEIM	01/01/1828	A		FILM
HALDY W W 1 CH	JOSEPH	1806	ESCHOLTZMATT	08/07/1846	NO		FILM
HALDY W W CH	JOSEPH	1807	ODEREM	11/15/1846	TX		FILM
HALFF	EMANUEL	1840	LAUTERBURG	01/01/1867	NY	PROF	NO.2
HALLEN	MICHEL	1819	FELLERINGEN	03/16/1842	NO		FILM
HALLER	AGATHE	1817	FELLERINGEN	11/04/1857	TX		FILM
HALLER	AMBROISE	1828	FELLERINGEN	11/09/1857	NY		FILM
HALLER	AMBROISE	1834	FELLERINGEN	11/23/1854	NY		FILM
HALLER	ANTOINE	1813	FELLERINGEN	05/06/1842	NO		FILM
HALLER	AUGUSTIN	1842	ODERN OR ODEREM	04/18/1844	TX		FILM
HALLER	BAPTISTE	1833	FELLERINGEN	06/24/1854	A	BUTC	FILM
HALLER	BARBE	1802	JEBSHEIM	08/20/1845	PH		FILM
HALLER	CHRETIEN		NEUWILLER	03/29/1817	A		FILM
HALLER	CHRISTIANE	1838	ODERN OR ODEREM	04/18/1844	TX		FILM
HALLER	CHRISTINE	1822	FELLERINGEN	10/30/1857	A		FILM
HALLER	CHRISTOPHE	1822	RANSPACH	11/15/1846	TX		FILM
HALLER	EMILIE	1837	RANSPACH	11/15/1846	TX		FILM
HALLER	EUSTACHE	1834	FELLERINGEN	08/25/1854	A		FILM
HALLER	FORTUNE	1822	FELLERINGEN	07/30/1844	NO	TAYL	FILM
HALLER	FRANZISKA	1796	RANSPACH	11/15/1846	TX		FILM
HALLER	FRIDOLIN	1829	FELLERINGEN	12/11/1852	NO		FILM
HALLER	GEORGE		NEUWILLER	01/01/1828	A	DAYL	FILM
HALLER	HUBERT	1813	MOOSCH	02/26/1851	NY	FARM	FILM
HALLER	JEAN ADAM		ESCHBOURG	01/01/1817	A		FILM
HALLER	JOHANN	1844	SCHOENBOURG	01/01/1869	NY	FARM	NO.2
HALLER	JOSEPH	1809	RANSPACH	11/01/1843	TX		SHIP
HALLER	JOSEPH	1812	RANSPACH	11/22/1843	TX	FARM	FILM
HALLER	JOSEPH	1833	FELLERINGEN	07/20/1852	PH		FILM
HALLER	MARIE ANN	1833	ODEREN	04/18/1844	TX		FILM
HALLER	MARIE ANNE	1808	ODERENKAUFMANN W W	04/18/1844	TX		FILM
HALLER	PAUL	1831	ODERN OR ODREM	04/18/1844	TX		FILM
HALLER	PIERRE		CLEEBOURG	01/01/1867	NY		PRIV
HALLER	REGINA	1839	ODERN OR ODEREM	04/18/1844	TX		FILM
HALLER	ROSALIE	1843	FELLERINGEN	11/04/1857	A		FILM
HALLER	THIEBAUD	1825	FELLERINGEN	06/28/1850	NY		FILM
HALLER	THOMAS	1831	PFEFFERHAUSEN	09/22/1853	A		FILM
HALLER	VALENTIN	1798	RANSPACH	11/15/1846	TX		FILM
HALLER WW AND CH	ANTOINE	1815	RANSPACH	12/01/1844	TX	CULT	SHIP

Lastname	Firstname	Birth Year	Birthplace	Emigration	De	Prof	Source
HALLER WW AND CH 6	JEAN	1805	ODEREN	11/01/1843	TX	CULT	SHIP
HALLER CH 1	RICHARD	1815	FELLERING	11/01/1857	TX		PASS
HALLER D JEAN	AUGUSTINE	1842	ODEREN	11/01/1843	TX		SHIP
HALLER D JEAN	CLEMENTINE	1838	ODEREN	11/01/1843	TX		SHIP
HALLER D JEAN	JOSEPHINE	1840	ODEREN	11/01/1843	TX		SHIP
HALLER D JEAN	MARIE ANNE	1833	ODEREN	11/01/1843	TX		SHIP
HALLER D JEAN	REGINE	1829	ODEREN	11/01/1843	TX		SHIP
HALLER D RICHARD	ROSALIE	1843	FELLERING	11/01/1857	TX		PASS
HALLER MN SPERISSER	FRANCOISE	1796	RANSPACH	11/01/1846	TX		SHIP
HALLER MN WILHELM	AGATHE		FELLERINGEN	01/01/1817	A		FILM
HALLER MN WILHELM	AGATHE	1817		11/01/1857	TX		PASS
HALLER S JEAN	PAUL	1831	ODEREN	11/01/1843	TX		SHIP
HALLER W JEAN	MARIE ANNE	1807	ODEREN	11/01/1843	TX		SHIP
HALLER W W 1 CH	FRANC.RICHARD	1815		10/15/1844	NO		FILM
HALLER W W 1 D	RICHARD	1815	FELLERINGEN	11/04/1857	TX		FILM
HALLER W W 4CH	PIERRE		CLEEBOURG	01/01/1817	A		FILM
HALLER W W 6 CH	JOHANN	1805	ODERN OR ODEREM	04/18/1844	TX	FARM	FILM
HALLER WW AND CH 3	ANTOINE	1798	RANSPACH	11/01/1846	TX		SHIP
HALLER WW AND CH 3	LOUIS		HT. RHIN	/ /	TX		SHIP
HALM	GEORGE		BRUMATH	01/01/1828	A		FILM
HALM	JOSEPH		SOUFFLENHEIM	01/01/1828	A		FILM
HALM W W 4 CH	JEAN		SOUFFLENHEIM	01/01/1828	A		FILM
HALM F OF 4	ANTOINE		SCHIRRHEIM	01/01/1828	A	DAYL	FILM
HALM F OF 4	CHRETIEN		WINGEN	01/01/1828	A		FILM
HALM F OF 8	ANDRE		SCHIRRHEIM	01/01/1828	A	FARM	FILM
HALMER	FRANCOIS		ESCHBACH B	05/12/1849	A		FILM
HALTER	GEORGE	1817	STRASSBOURG	01/01/1817	A	DAYL	FILM
HALTER F OF 2	LAMBERT		HAGUENAU	01/01/1828	A		FILM
HALTER F OF 3	SEBASTIEN		SCHIRRHEIM	01/01/1828	A	DAYL	FILM
HALTER F OF 4	JOSEPH		SCHIRRHEIM	01/01/1828	A		FILM
HALTER F OF 3	ANTOINE		SCHIRRHEIM	01/01/1828	A	FARM	FILM
HALTER F OF 4	LOUIS		SCHIRRHEIM	01/01/1828	A	DAYL	FILM
HALTER F OF 5	ANTOINE		SCHIRRHEIM	01/01/1828	A	FARM	FILM
HALTER F OF 5	JOSEPH		SCHIRRHOFFEN	01/01/1828	A		FILM
HALTER F OF 5	MICHEL		BURCKENWALDE	01/01/1828	A	FARM	FILM
HALTER F OF 6	LOUIS		SCHIRRHOFFEN	01/01/1828	A	FARM	FILM
HALTER F OF 8	MICHEL		SCHIRRHEIM	01/01/1828	A	WEAV	FILM
HALTER W W 3 CH	LOUIS		KALTENHOUSE	01/01/1817	A	DAYL	FILM
HALTERMEYER	ANTOINE		SINGRIST	01/01/1828	A	LAYB	FILM
HALTERMEYER	BERNHARD		SINGRIST	01/01/1828		LAYB	FILM
HALTERMYER W W	JAQUES		SCHILTIGHEIM	01/01/1828		DAYL	FILM
HALTERMYER W W 3CH	FRANCOIS		SCHILTIGHEIM	01/01/1828	A		FILM
HALTY MN HALLER	CATHERINE	1807	ODEREN	11/01/1846	TX		SHIP
HALTY WW AND CH 4	JOSEPH	1806	ODEREN	11/01/1846	TX		SHIP
HALTZEL F OF 9	PHILLIP GEORGE		SCHWEIGHAUSEN	01/01/1828	A	WEAV	FILM
HAM	GASPARD	1825	FELLERINGEN	01/06/1845	NY	LAYB	FILM
HAM	JEAN		PFULGRIESHEIM	01/01/1828	A		FILM
HAMALLE W W 1 CH	JEAN BAPTISTE	1819	NIFFER	09/21/1846	CH		FILM
HAMANN	ANTOINE		ST JEAN DES COUX	01/01/1828	A		FILM
HAMANN	CHARLES		ROMANSWILLER	01/01/1828	A	BUTC	FILM

Lastname	Firstname	Birth Year	Birthplace	Emigration	De	Prof	Source
HAMBARD W W 2 CH	XAVIER	1805	MONTREUX SWISS	11/05/1853	NY		FILM
HAMEL	BARBARA	1859	NEHWILLER	01/01/1867	NY		NO.2
HAMEL	ELISA	1861	NEHWILLER	01/01/1867	NY		NO.2
HAMEL	GEORG	1851	NEHWILLER	01/01/1867	NY		NO.2
HAMEL	HEINRICH	1856	NEHWILLER	01/01/1867	NY		NO.2
HAMEL	JAKOB	1853	NEHWILLER	01/01/1867	NY		NO.2
HAMEL	KARL	1867	NEHWILLER	01/01/1867	NY		NO.2
HAMEL	MADALENA	1857	NEHWILLER	01/01/1867	NY		NO.2
HAMEL	MAGDALENA	1825	NEHWILLER	01/01/1867	NY		NO.2
HAMEL W W 7 CH	JACOB	1820	NEHWILLER	01/01/1867	NY	FARM	NO.2
HAMIN F OF 3	VALENTIN		BISCHWILLER	03/02/1838	A		FILM
HAMM	FERDINAND		STRASSBOURG	07/11/1838	A		FILM
HAMM	PHILIPPE		KRAUTWILLER	02/27/1838	A		FILM
HAMM F OF 4	JEAN		GEUDERTHEIM	03/01/1838	A		FILM
HAMM F OF 8	MICHEL		INGENHEIM	01/01/1828	A		FILM
HAMM F OF 8	PHILIPPE		PLOBSHEIM	03/19/1838	A		FILM
HAMM W W 4 CH	FREDERIC		BUTTEN	03/17/1817	A	TAYL	FILM
HAMM WW AND CH 4	GEORGE		STRUTH	01/01/1817	A		FILM
HAMMANN	CHARLES		DETTWILLER	01/01/1832	A		FILM
HAMMANN F OF 5	JACQUES		SCHALKENDORF	01/01/1828	A		FILM
HAMMEL	ANTOINE	1843	DORNACH	07/26/1849	NY		FILM
HAMMEL	ISAAC	1823	THANN	04/11/1853	NO		FILM
HAMMEL	LOUIS		BALLBRONN	02/28/1838	A		FILM
HAMMERER	MADELEINE		HOLTZHAUSEN	10/11/1849	A		FILM
HAMMERSCHMIDT F OF 6	BERNARD		OTTERSTHAL	01/01/1828	A		FILM
HANASAUER WW CH 4	GEORGE		CLEEBOURG	03/28/1817	A		FILM
HANAUER	ANTOINE	1819	CERNAY	11/02/1844	TX		FILM
HANAUER	JACQUES	1823	HUNAWIHR	03/17/1847	NY		FILM
HANAUER	MARIA	1821	CERNAY	01/02/1844	TX		FILM
HANAUER	NANETTE	1843	CERNAY	01/02/1844	TX		FILM
HANAUER	VELTEN		NIEDERBRONN	05/13/1838	A		FILM
HANAUER WW AND CH	ANTOINE	1818	CERNAY	10/01/1843	TX		SHIP
HANHARD	JEAN DAVID	1812	BEBLENHEIM	04/13/1848	A		FILM
HANHARD	JEAN-DAVID	1818	BEBLENHEIM	04/01/1848	TX	WINE	PASS
HANHART	MICHEL	1809	WIHR-EN-PLAINE	05/23/1842	NY		FILM
HANN	ANJTOINE	1819	ROUFFACH	03/16/1852	TX		FILM
HANN	XAVIER	1822	ROUFFACH	02/01/1852	TX	EXPO	PASS
HANNS	ANTOINE		MINDERSHEIM	01/01/1828	A		FILM
HANOZ	JACQUES		WANGEN	01/01/1828	A		FILM
HANS	ANTOINE		ETTENDORF	10/29/1854	A		FILM
HANS	ELISABETH	1812	ODER	11/22/1843	TX		FILM
HANS	ELISABETH	1841	ODER	11/22/1843	TX		FILM
HANS	JUSTINE	1842	ODER	11/22/1843	TX		FILM
HANS	LEONHARD	1813	ODER	11/22/1843	TX		FILM
HANSBERGER	JOSEPH	1808	BITSCHWILLER	10/18/1845	NY		FILM
HANSER	FRANCOIS JOSEPH	1803	ALTKIRCH	02/12/1849	NY		FILM
HANSER F OF 4	PHILIPPE		SARRE UNION	01/01/1828	A		FILM
HANSKNACHT WW CH 1	WIDOW		ERNOLSHEIM	03/11/1817	A		FILM
HANSSAUER	GEORGES	1838	CLEEBOURG	01/01/1869	NY	TUMA	PRIV
HANSZ	JACQUES		WANGEN	01/01/1828	A		FILM

Lastname	Firstname	Birth Year	Birthplace	Emigration	De	Prof	Source
HANTER	FRANCOIS JOSEPH	1801	ALTKIRCH	04/13/1839	NY		FILM
HANTZ	DAVID	1835	MITTELWIHR	04/11/1857	NY		FILM
HANTZ	ELISABETH	1808	RECHESY	09/05/1845	NY		FILM
HANTZ	JEAN-JAQUES	1804	MITTELWIHR	06/01/1846	TX	DAYL	PASS
HANTZ CH 2	DENIS	1828	MITZACH	08/01/1860	TX		PASS
HANTZ CH 3	VALENTIN	1830	MITZACH	08/01/1860	TX		PASS
HANTZ D DENIS	JUSTINE	1860	MITZACH	08/01/1860	TX		PASS
HANTZ D VALENTIN	CAROLINE	1859	MITZACH	08/01/1860	TX		PASS
HANTZ D VALENTIN	JEANETTE	1856	MITZACH	08/01/1860	TX		PASS
HANTZ D VALENTIN	THERESE	1854	MITZACH	08/01/1860	TX		PASS
HANTZ MN GULLY	ROSINE	1823		08/01/1860	TX		PASS
HANTZ MN RINGENBACHR	SYBILLE	1830		08/01/1860	TX		PASS
HANTZ S DENIS	JUSTIN	1859	MITZACH	08/01/1860	TX		PASS
HANTZ WW AND CH 4	JEAN PIERRE	1806	RECHOTTE	08/14/1839	NY		FILM
HANTZ WW AND CH 5	JEAN JACQUES	1804	MITTELWIHR	06/27/1846	TX		PRIV
HANUSS	ANTOINE		MINVERSHEIM	01/01/1828	A		FILM
HARBAUER	FRANCOIS ANTOIN		NEUWILLER	01/01/1828	A		FILM
HARMAND	LUDWIG	1815	STRASSBOURG	01/01/1848	NO		PRIV
HARMANN	JACQUES	1835	MUNTZENHEIM	11/23/1854	CH		FILM
HARNIST	JEAN THIEBAUD	1815	WALHEIM	07/15/1852	NY		FILM
HARNY CH	MARIE ANNE	1819	WESTHALTEN	09/21/1850	NY		FILM
HARRER	BARBE	1825	WINTZENHEIM	05/21/1852	NO		FILM
HARRER	THERESE	1828	MUNTZENHEIM	01/19/1853	BU		FILM
HARTER H CATHERINE	FRANCOIS JOSEPH		KALTENHAUSEN	01/01/1828	A		FILM
HARTER W FRANCOIS	CATHERINE		KALTENHAUSEN	01/01/1828	A		FILM
HARTMANN	ANDRE	1802	KOCHENDORF	09/21/1846	NY		FILM
HARTMANN	CHRISTOPHE	1800	STUPFERICH	07/08/1854	NY		FILM
HARTMANN	EDOUARD	1815	MULHOUSE	04/15/1850	SF		FILM
HARTMANN	ELISABETH		KEHL	09/14/1898	A		FILM
HARTMANN	FRANCOIS JOSEPH	1814	STRASBOURG	03/01/1850	NY		FILM
HARTMANN	FRANCOIS JOSEPH	1820	CARSPACH	07/31/1847	NY		FILM
HARTMANN	FREDERIC NICOLA	1831	MULHOUSE	04/03/1849	SF		FILM
HARTMANN	GEORGES	1831	ENSCHINGEN	06/01/1850	CA		FILM
HARTMANN F OF 7	GEORGES		TIEFFENBACH	01/01/1828	A		FILM
HARTMANN F OF 7	NICOLAS		STRUTH	01/01/1828	A		FILM
HARTMANN H CLAESS	JACOB	1817	ROPPENHEIM	/ /	A		NO.1
HARTMANN H EVA ELISA	JACOB	1817		/ /	A		PRIV
HARTMANN MN CLAESS	EVA ELISABETH	1807		/ /	A		PRIV
HARTMANN WW AND CH 2	PIERRE	1818	ESCHENTZWILLER	09/05/1853	NY		FILM
HARTMANN WW CH 11	JEAN CLAUDE	1790	ROUGEMONT	10/27/1846	PH		FILM
HARY WW AND CH 2	MARTIN		BISSERT	03/06/1817	A		FILM
HASATTE	JACQUES	1805	SCHAUX	10/10/1865	NY		FILM
HASATTE	JEAN BAPTISTE	1817	PETIT MAGNY	06/20/1848	NY		FILM
HASCHAR F OF 6	JACQUES		WILLER	01/01/1828	A		FILM
HASCHER F OF 9	PHILIPPE		DASSENHEIM	01/01/1828	A		FILM
HASEL	CHRETIEN		STEINBACH	04/23/1849	A		FILM
HASENFORDER	GEORGES	1793	ST. LOUIS	11/11/1840	NY		FILM
HASENFRATH 2 CH	MARIE		ZEHRINGEN B	03/20/1828	A		FILM
HASENFRATZ CH 2	MARIE EVE		SOURBOURG	03/20/1828	A		FILM
HASER	ANDRE		SOUFFLENHEIM	03/02/1838	A		FILM

Lastname	Firstname	Birth Year	Birthplace	Emigration	De	Prof	Source
HASLI	FREDERIC		WIMMENAU	01/01/1828	A		FILM
HASLI	MICHEL		WIMMENAU	01/01/1828	A		FILM
HASSELBERGER	BERNARD		SCHIRRHOFF	03/01/1838	A		FILM
HASSELBERGER F OF 2	JEAN		SCHIRRHOFF	03/01/1838	A		FILM
HASSENFRATZ WW		1823	REICHSHOFFEN	12/30/1846	NY		FILM
HASSLE F OF 7	JACQUES		ERCKARDTSWILLER	01/01/1828	A		FILM
HASSLER	JOSEPH	1846	LAUTERBURG	01/01/1865	NY	DAYL	NO.2
HASSLER WW AND CH 2	JACQUES	1825	NIEDERLAUTERBACH	10/01/1851	NO		FILM
HASSMANN WW AND CH	ANTOINE FRANCOI	1815	STAUFFENBERG	07/28/1854	NY		FILM
HASTENBERGER	JOSEPH		HAGUENAU	03/01/1838	A		FILM
HASTENMANN	JEAN PIERRE	1834	ESSERT	03/29/1852	NO		FILM
HATIE MN FREYTAG	ALINE CH 2	1821	GUEWENHEIM	03/17/1854	NY		FILM
HATIE WW AND CH	CHRETIEN	1824	SENTHEIM	02/16/1846	NY		FILM
HATTENBERGER	GEORGES	1821	SOPPE-LE.HAUT	06/10/1840	NY		FILM
HATTENBERGER	JEAN JACQUES	1820	GUEWENHEIM	02/18/1850	NY		FILM
HAUBENNESTEL F OF 2	GEORGES		WASSELONE	01/01/1828	A		FILM
HAUBENNESTEL F OF 2	LOUIS		ERNOLSHEIM	01/01/1828	A		FILM
HAUBENNESTEL F OF 4	LAURENT		WASSELONNE	01/01/1828	A		FILM
HAUBERGUE	CATHERINE	1819	EGUENIGUE	06/03/1864	NY		FILM
HAUDISCHHAUSER	CHRETIEN		ETZINGEN	05/30/1849	NY		FILM
HAUERT	MATHIAS		SUNDHAUSEN	03/02/1837	A		FILM
HAUESBERGER	NICOLAS	1826	BELFORT	04/13/1866	NY		FILM
HAUFMANN	NICOLAS	1827	HERLISHEIM	09/15/1849	NO		FILM
HAUG	GEORGES	1823	VOGELSHEIM	02/03/1823	NY		FILM
HAUGERT	CHRISTOPH		SUNDHAUSEN	03/02/1837	A		FILM
HAUGERT	DANIEL		SUNDHAUSEN	03/02/1837	A		FILM
HAUMESSER	JEAN BAPTISTE	1821	GRUSSENHEIM	03/19/1857	NY		FILM
HAUMESSER WW CH 3	GEORGES	1800	AITZENHEIM	03/22/1850	NY		FILM
HAUMuLLER	IGNACE	1844	HEIMERSDORF	11/12/1865	NY		FILM
HAUMuLLER	MARIE ANNE	1832	HEIMERSDORFF	09/14/1857	NY		FILM
HAUPTMANN	JOSEPH	1819	SOULTZMATT	12/11/1847	NO		FILM
HAURY	FRANZ JOSEF		RIEDSELTZ	01/01/1868	A		NO.2
HAURY	GEORGE		RAUWILLER	03/07/1838	A		FILM
HAUS	CASPARD	1825	FELLERINGEN	01/06/1845	NY		FILM
HAUS	JACQUES		DRUSENHEIM	01/01/1828	A		FILM
HAUSEN	JOSEPH		SPAICHINGEN	04/21/1849	A		FILM
HAUSER	FELIX	1820	DURMENACH	07/03/1852	NY		FILM
HAUSER	FRANCOIS JOSPEH	1803	ALTKIRCH	02/12/1849	NY		FILM
HAUSER	FREDERIC		DANNINGEN	04/28/1849	A		FILM
HAUSER	JOSEPH	1822	OBERHERGHEIM	11/24/1852	NO		FILM
HAUSER F OF 4	PHILIPPE		SARRE UNION	01/01/1828	A		FILM
HAUSER W ARENER	CAROLINE	1832	MULHOUSE	02/14/1852	NY		FILM
HAUSHALTER	JOHANN GEORG		NIEDERBETSCHDORF	01/01/1817	A		NO.2
HAUSHALTER	MARGUERITE DORO		NIEDERBETSCHDORF	03/24/1855	A		FILM
HAUSHALTER WW CH 4	JEAN GEORGES		NIEDERBETSCHDORF	03/29/1817	A		FILM
HAUSKNECHT F OF 3	ADAM		ERNOLSHEIM	01/01/1828	A		FILM
HAUSKNECHT F OF 4	CHRETIEN		TIEFFENBACH	01/01/1828	A		FILM
HAUSMANN	DAVID		OBERHERGHEIM	04/08/1844	TX		FILM
HAUSMANN F OF 8			SCHUTTENWALD	04/06/1849	NY		FILM
HAUSS	MADELEINE	1822	KAYSERSBERG	10/24/1855	NY		FILM

Lastname	Firstname	Birth Year	Birthplace	Emigration	De	Prof	Source
HAUSS F OF 8	JACQUES JUN.		INGENHEIM	01/01/1828	A		FILM
HAUSSEN	GREGOR		GOSSHEIM	04/21/1849	A		FILM
HAUSSER	ROSALIE	1833	CERNAY	03/25/1857	PH		FILM
HAUSSHALTER	JEAN GEORGES		NIEDERBETSCHDORF	03/21/1817	A		FILM
HAUSSKNECHT	JEAN GEORGES		ASSWILLER	03/05/1838	A		FILM
HAUTBERGUE	MARGUERITE	1852	EGUENIGUE	06/03/1864	NY		FILM
HAUTENSCHELD	CATHERINE		BUESWILLER	01/01/1828	A		FILM
HAUTER	CHRETIEN		PFALZWEYER	01/01/1828	A		FILM
HAVAUER WW AND CH	SEBASTIEN	1814	SOULTZMATT	06/17/1847	NY		FILM
HAVON	JEAN	1814	ROUFFACH	02/21/1852	TX		FILM
HEBERLE	JOSEPH	1832	BITSCHWILLER	04/03/1852	NY		FILM
HEBERLE	MATHIAS	1824	DARNBACH	03/19/1852	NO		FILM
HEBRANCH	WOLFGANG		OBINGEN	04/17/1849	NY		FILM
HEBTEN	CATHERINE	1828	GUEWENHEIM	02/06/1852	NY		FILM
HECH	CATHERINE		BURBACH	03/02/1838	A		FILM
HECHINGER	GERRAIS	1815	NIEDERHERGHEIM	10/11/1852	TX		FILM
HECHINGER	SERVINS	1815	NIEDERHERGHEIM	10/01/1852	TX	CULT	PASS
HECHLER WW AND CH	DAVID	1823	MITTELWIHR	04/29/1853	NY		FILM
HECHT	AUGUSTE JACOB	1813	STRALFAND	03/20/1851	NY		FILM
HECHT	JOSEPH	1819	ROUFFACH	11/15/1843	A		FILM
HECK	CATHERINE	1822	LEPUIX	03/30/1847	NY		FILM
HECK	DANIEL		BURBACH	03/02/1838	A		FILM
HECK	GEORGE		LEUTESHEIM	04/21/1849	NY		FILM
HECK	MARGUERITE		BURBACH	03/02/1838	A		FILM
HECK F OF 16	DANIEL		BURBACH	03/02/1838	A		FILM
HECK WW AND CH 3	PIERRE		VOELLERDINGEN	03/23/1817	A		FILM
HECK F OF 7	PIERRE		SARREWERDEN	01/01/1828	A		FILM
HECKEL F OF 3	ANDRE		THAL	01/01/1828	A		FILM
HECKEL F OF 5	GEORGES		THAL	01/01/1828	A		FILM
HECKEL F OF 5	PIERRE		THAL	01/01/1828	A		FILM
HECKEL WW AND CH 5	NICOLAS		THAL	03/29/1817	A		FILM
HECKER	FRANCOIS JOSEPH	1832	PFETTENHAUSEN	09/26/1853	NY		FILM
HECKER	JOSEPH ANTOINE	1812	PFETTENHAUSEN	09/26/1853	NY		FILM
HECKLE	CHARLES		KRATZINGEN	05/24/1849	A		FILM
HECTORAL	GEORGES		VAUTHIERMONT	10/01/1844			PASS
HECTORAL	NICOLAS		VAUTHIERMONT	10/01/1844	TX		PASS
HEEL	THIEBAUD		KESKASTEL	01/01/1828	A		FILM
HEEPTING	MATHIAS		DEGGINGEN	06/04/1849	A		FILM
HEERGER	CATHERINBE		SCHLIERSTADT	05/12/1849	A		FILM
HEFFER	SEBASTIEN	1820	KINGERSHEIM	10/25/1851	NY		FILM
HEFFRE	MARGUERITE	1826	LIEPRE	08/21/1847	NY		FILM
HEFFRICH	GEORG	1837	SCHEIBENHARDT	01/01/1866	NY		NO.2
HEGY	ANDRE	1812	MERXHEIM	09/13/1852	LO		FILM
HEGY	SIGISMOND	1810	BURNHAUPT	03/13/1839	NY		FILM
HEIBERGER WW CH 6	JEAN	1805	TRAUBACH	08/21/1846	NY		FILM
HEID F OF 4	GEORGE		ALTENDORF	01/01/1828	A		FILM
HEIDEL	FRANCOIS XAVIER	1820	FELON	08/16/1844	NY		FILM
HEIDET	ANNA	1818	FELON	11/22/1843	TX		FILM
HEIDET	JOHANN CLAUDIUS	1811	FELON	11/22/1843	TX		FILM
HEIDMANN	NAPOLEON		MINVERSHEIM	01/01/1828	A		FILM

Lastname	Firstname	Birth Year	Birthplace	Emigration	De	Prof	Source
HEIDT	HENRI		SCHILLERSDORF	01/30/1828	A		FILM
HEIL	KARL	1851	WEISSENBURG	01/01/1869	NY		NO.2
HEILAND	CHARLES		SCHERTZHEIM	08/13/1849	A		FILM
HEILAND	JACQUES		SCHERTZHEIM	08/13/1849	A		FILM
HEILBRONN WW CH 6	CHRETIEN		OBENHEIM	03/10/1838	A		FILM
HEILI	BARTHELEMY		WANGENBOURG	01/01/1828	A		FILM
HEILMANN	JEAN MICHEL			04/14/1838	A		FILM
HEILMANN	JOSUE	1829	MULHOUSE	03/13/1849	NY		FILM
HEILMANN	MADELEINE	1778	ZINSWEILLER	02/16/1817	A		FILM
HEIM	JEAN		WINTZENHEIM	02/27/1838	A		FILM
HEIM	MICHEL		MARLENHEIM	01/01/1828	A		FILM
HEIM WW AND CH 2	GEORGES JUN.	1818	OSTHEIM	04/13/1847	NY		FILM
HEIMBURGER	ETIENNE	1813	COLMAR	09/04/1852	NY		FILM
HEIMBURGER F OF 10	GEORGES		MARLENHEIM	03/03/1838	A		FILM
HEIMBURGER F OF 5	FRANCOIS JOSEPH		MARLENHEIM	01/01/1828	A		FILM
HEIMBURGER F OF 7	JEAN		SCHWINDRATZHEIM	01/01/1828	A		FILM
HEIMBURGER WW CH 2	JEAN BAPTISTE	1826	COLMAR	08/04/1854	NY		FILM
HEIMLICH F OF 4	JEAN GEORGES		SESSENHEIM	02/23/1838	A		FILM
HEIMMAN	JEAN JAQUES	1824	HEGENHEIM	07/29/1850	NY		FILM
HEINHARDT WW	JEAN MICHEL	1832	KUNHEIM	07/06/1850	CH		FILM
HEINIMANN	JEAN JAQUES	1824	HEGENHEIM	07/29/1850	NY		FILM
HEINIS WW	FRANCOIS JOSEPH	1800	HABSHEIM	08/24/1841	NY		FILM
HEINRICH	ABRAHAM	1818	ILLZACH	08/25/1847	BO		FILM
HEINRICH	EDOUARD	1840	ST.MARIE AUX MINES	10/05/1854	NY		FILM
HEINRICH	JEAN		IMBSHEIM	01/01/1828	A		FILM
HEINRICH	LAURENT		IMBSHEIM	01/01/1828	A		FILM
HEINRICH	LOUIS	1831	WIHRAU VAL	12/07/1853	NY		FILM
HEINRICH	MICHEL		IMBSHEIM	01/01/1828	A		FILM
HEINRICH F OF 7	JAQUES		SESSENHEIM	02/23/1838	A		FILM
HEINRICH H GRESS 2CH	JAKOB		ROPPENHEIM	/ /	A		NO.1
HEINRICH H MARIE	JACOB			/ /			PRIV
HEINRICH H ROHR 2 CH	GEORG MICHAEL	1820	ROPPENHEIM	06/03/1852	AL		NO.1
HEINRICH MN GRESS	MARIE CATHERINE			/ /	A		PRIV
HEINRICH WW AND CH 2	JOSEPH	1814	MOOSCH	09/28/1854	NY		FILM
HEINRICH WW AND CH 3	THIEBAUD		OBERHOFFEN	03/01/1838	A		FILM
HEINTZ	BARBE		STATTMATTEN	03/02/1838	A		FILM
HEINTZ	HELENE	1812	RECHESY	09/05/1845	NY		FILM
HEINTZ	JAQUES	1823	STREITENHAST	03/15/1847	NY		FILM
HEINTZ	JEAN GEORGES		SESSENHEIJM	02/23/1838	A		FILM
HEINTZ	JOHANN	1850	NEHWILLER	01/01/1867	A		NO.2
HEINTZ	MARIE		NIEDERLAUTERBACH	01/01/1850	NO		PRIV
HEINTZ	ROSINA	1840	NEHWILLER	01/01/1866	A		NO.2
HEINTZ	VALENTIN	1841	VOGELSHEIM	01/01/1865	NY	DAYL	NO.2
HEINTZELMANN F OF 4	THEOPHILE		SCHWEIGHAUSEN	01/01/1828	A		FILM
HEINY WW AND CH 7	PIERRE		HIRSCHLAND	03/20/1817	A		FILM
HEIROMINUS F OF 5	MICHEL		SCHWINDRATZHEIM	01/01/1828	A		FILM
HEISLEN	LAURENT	1815	ROUFFACH	12/12/1844	JE		FILM
HEISLEN WW AND CH	PAUL	1818	ROUFFACH	12/15/1845	JE		FILM
HEISLEN MN MEYER CH	CATHERINE	1801	ROUFFACH	08/29/1854	SL		FILM
HEISSEL			LAUTERBOURG	01/01/1850	NO		PRIV

Lastname	Firstname	Birth Year	Birthplace	Emigration	De	Prof	Source
HEISSEL	ALBERT	1864	LAUTERBURG	01/01/1867	NO		NO.2
HEISSEL	EMIL	1866	LAUTERBURG	01/01/1867	NO		NO.2
HEISSEL MN KLOEPFER	SALOME	1837	LAUTERBURG	01/01/1867	NO		NO.2
HEISSEL W W 2CH	MICHEL	1835	LAUTERBURG	01/01/1867	NO	SHMA	NO.2
HEISSER	CATHARINA	1842	RIEDSELTZ	01/01/1868	NY		NO.2
HEISSER F OF 6	JEAN FREDERIC		BRUMATH	01/01/1828	A		FILM
HEISSERER	ANDRE		SCHIRRHEIN	03/05/1838	A		FILM
HEISSERER	GEORGE		SCHIRRHEIN	03/05/1838	A		FILM
HEISSERER F OF 3	LAURENT		SCHIRRHEIN	03/05/1838	A		FILM
HEISSERER F OF 4	NICOLAS		SCHIRRHEIN	03/05/1838	A		FILM
HEISSLER	MARTIN	1808	GUEWENHEIM	01/01/1869		DRIV	PASS
HEISSLER	MICHEL	1827	SIGOLSHEIM	03/11/1854	NY		FILM
HEIST	ANNE MARIE		BAIERBRONN	04/20/1849	NY		FILM
HEIST	AUGUSTE		BAIERBRONN	04/20/1849	NY		FILM
HEIST	CHRETIEN		BAIERBRONN	04/20/1849	NY		FILM
HEIST	FREDERIC		BAIERBRONN	04/20/1849	NY		FILM
HEIST	JAQUES		BAIERBRONN	04/20/1849	NY		FILM
HEIST	JUSTINE		BAIERBRONN	04/20/1849	NY		FILM
HEIST	RASINE		BAIERBRONN	04/20/1849	NY		FILM
HEIT F OF 5	HENRI		SCHILLERSDORF	01/01/1828	A		FILM
HEITEL	JOSEPHINE		DRUSENHEIM	03/24/1838	A		FILM
HEITEL	REINE		DRUSENHEIM	03/24/1838	A		FILM
HEITZ	AGATHE		NEUSTADT	08/21/1849	A		FILM
HEITZ	JEAN BAPTISTE	1822	KEMBAS	11/10/1847	NY		FILM
HEITZ	LAURENT	1822	MASEVAUX	10/01/1851	TX	TAYL	PASS
HEITZ F OF 9	JOSEPH		BRUMATH	01/01/1828	A		FILM
HEITZ WW AND CH 3	LAURENT	1812	FESSENHEIM	10/01/1851	TX		FILM
HEITZ WW AND CH 4	ANTOINE	1797	BURNHAUPT	09/23/1839	NY		FILM
HEITZLER WW AND CH 3	FRANCOIS JOSEPH		GRUSSENHEIM	10/25/1852	A		FILM
HEITZMANN	ANTOINE		MARCKOLSHEIM	02/26/1838	A		FILM
HEITZMANN	ANTOINE	1803	MARCKOLSHEIM	06/04/1849	NY		FILM
HEITZMANN	JACOB		GUTACH	04/03/1849	NY		FILM
HEITZMANN	JOSEPH		MARCKOLSHEIM	02/26/1838	A		FILM
HEITZMANN	LOUIS	1827	MAGNY	06/03/1845	NY		FILM
HEITZMANN	SALOME		OFFENBURG	04/20/1844	A		FILM
HEITZMANN	XAVIER	1819	SOULTZMATT	12/11/1847	NO		FILM
HEITZMANN	ZEPHIRIN	1835	WILDENSTEIN	10/11/1854	NY		FILM
HEIXLER CH	URSULA	1824	LEUTKIRCH	10/25/1844	NO		FILM
HELBING	FRIEDRICH		LANGENSULTZBACH	01/01/1843	A		SUESS
HELBLING	DAVID	1830	BITSCHWILLER	09/03/1852	NY		FILM
HELBY	GEORG		HATTEN III	01/01/1835	A		SUESS
HELD	BARBE	1841	OSTHEIM	08/06/1857	NY		FILM
HELD	JACOB		DEGGINGEN	06/04/1849	A		FILM
HELD	JEAN	1844	OSTHEIM	08/06/1857	NY		FILM
HELD B BARBE	JEAN	1844	OSTHEIM	08/06/1857	NY		FILM
HELD F OF 4	GEORGES		ESCHBOURG	01/01/1828	A		FILM
HELD WW	GEORGES	1824	OSTHEIM	03/25/1859	NY		FILM
HELDERLE	CATHERINE	1832	COLMAR	10/05/1854	NY		FILM
HELDT	BARBE		ROPPENHEIM	03/06/1838	A		FILM
HELDT	CAROLINE	1828	ROPPENHEIM	03/11/1851	A		NO.1

Lastname	Firstname	Birth Year	Birthplace	Emigration	De	Prof	Source
HELDT SI CAROLINE	MADELEINE	1823	ROPPENHEIM	03/11/1851	A		NO.1
HELENSTETTER	DANIEL		PFAFENHOFFEN	01/09/1838	A		FILM
HELGEN	ANTON	1807	OBERSTEINBRUNNEN	10/25/1843	TX		FILM
HELGEN WW AND CH	JOSEPH	1822	STEINBRUNN	01/31/1852	NY		FILM
HELL	GASPARD	1825	HELFRANTZKIRCH	05/06/1857	NY		FILM
HELL	GEORGES	1834	WITTERSDORF	04/19/1851	NO		FILM
HELL	JOSEPH	1795	HELFRANTZKIRCH	05/06/1857	NY		FILM
HELLER	ANTOINE		BADEN	10/11/1849	A		FILM
HELLER	CARL		FROESCHWILLER	01/01/1849	A		SUESS
HELLER	FRANCOIS		MARMOUTIER	01/01/1828	A		FILM
HELLER	GEORGE		FRIEDBERG B	01/01/1828	A		FILM
HELLER	GEORGE		WEITERSWILLER	10/11/1189	A		FILM
HELLER	JACQUES		ALTWILLER	01/01/1828	A		FILM
HELLER	JEAN		WISSEMBOURG	07/01/1820	A		FILM
HELLER	JEAN ADAM		ALTWILLER	01/01/1828	A		FILM
HELLER	JEAN JACQUES	1819	MITTELWIHR	07/05/1851	NY		FILM
HELLER	MADELAINE	1829	MITTELWIHR	06/04/1857	NO		FILM
HELLER F OF 4	HENRI		WEITERSWILLER	01/01/1828	A		FILM
HELLER MN PRISS	CATHERINE MADE	1790	BEBLENHEIM	06/04/1857	NO		FILM
HELLER S GEORG	CARL		FROESCHWILLER	01/01/1849	A		SUESS
HELLER W W 3CH	GEORGE		MOLSHEIM	03/03/1817	A		FILM
HELLER W W 4CH	HENRI	1792	OBERLESBACH	04/12/1847	NY		FILM
HELMER	JOSEPH		SOUFFLENHEIM	03/02/1838	A		FILM
HELMER	MICHEL		SOUFFLENHEIM	03/02/1838	A		FILM
HELMLINGER	GEORGES		PFAFFENHOFFEN	01/01/1828	A		FILM
HELMLINGER	JEAN	1814	INGWILLER	10/31/1854	NY		FILM
HELMLINGER	PHILIPPE		INGWILLER	01/01/1828	A		FILM
HELMLINGER F OF 2	LOUIS		ECKARTSWILLER	01/01/1828	A		FILM
HELMLINGER F OF 2	LOUIS		WIMMENAU	01/01/1828	A		FILM
HELMLINGER F OF 3	CHRETIAN		ERCKARTSWILLER	01/01/1828	A		FILM
HELMLINGER F OF 5	CHRETIEN		WIMMENAU	01/01/1828	A		FILM
HELMSTETTER	ADAM		PETERSBACH	01/01/1828	A		FILM
HELSLY W M 4CH	CATHERIN	1824	ST.CROIX AUX MINES	09/09/1852	NY		FILM
HELTEL W W 2CH	JOSEF		ZINSWILLER	02/20/1817	A		FILM
HEMBERGER	BARBARA	1847	WINTZENBACH	01/01/1847	NY		NO.2
HEMBERGER	BARBE		MOTHERN	01/01/1850	NO		PRIV
HEMMENDINGER	LEON	1838	SCHLETTSTADT	/ /	LA		BULL
HEMMERLE	MICHEL	1819	ROUFFACH	03/21/1845	A		FILM
HEMMERT F OF 4	NICOLAS		DEHLINGEN	01/01/1828	A		FILM
HEMMERT MN KOEPPEL	DOROTHEA		DEHLINGEN	01/01/1828	A		FILM
HEMSING	ANNA	1796	WESTFALEN	09/17/1845	A		FILM
HEMSING	ANNA MARIA	1823	WESTFALEN	09/17/1845	TX		FILM
HEMSING	BERNHARD	1837	WESTFALEN	09/17/1845	TX		FILM
HEMSING W W 2CH	BERNHARD	1794	WESTFALEN	09/17/1845	TX		FILM
HENCK F OF 4	PHILIPPE		SUNDHAUSEN	01/23/1827	A		FILM
HENCKY W F	JEAN	1814	RIQUEWIHR	04/06/1837	NY		FILM
HENEK	PHILIPPE		SUNDHAUSEN	03/02/1837	A		FILM
HENNECKER W W 1CH	JEAN		DOSSENHEIM	03/31/1817	A		FILM
HENNECKER W W CH	JEAN		DOSSENHEIM	03/31/1817	A		FILM
HENNEL	HENRI		ERNOLSHEIM	01/01/1828	A		FILM

Lastname	Firstname	Birth Year	Birthplace	Emigration	De	Prof	Source
HENNEL	MICHEL		ERNOLSHEIM	01/01/1828	A		FILM
HENNEMAN W W 2CH	JACQUES	1805	LEVAL	11/23/1855	A		FILM
HENNEMAN W W A NEPH	GEORGES	1779	ROUGEGOTTE	05/02/1839	NY		FILM
HENNINGER	BARGE		BACKNANG W	07/30/1849	A		FILM
HENNINGER	FERDINAND		ETTENHEIM B	08/21/1849	A		FILM
HENNINGER	JEAN		BADEN	06/27/1833	A		FILM
HENNOT	CONSTANT	1840	FRAHIER	09/29/1865	NY		FILM
HENNY	JOSEPH		OBINGEN	05/16/1849	A		FILM
HENNY W W 2CH	CHRETIEN	1818	OSTHEIM	04/04/1849			FILM
HENRI W 5CH	MARGUERITE	1811	LIEPVRE	10/11/1854	A		FILM
HENRISSAT	JOSEPH	1831	CHAVANNES LES GRANDS	02/06/1855	NY		FILM
HENRY	JEAN	1818	FELLERING	08/01/1854	TX	BRLA	PASS
HENRY	JEAN BAPTISTE	1817	LIEPVRE	09/02/1847	NO		FILM
HENRY	JEAN PHILIPPE	1825	LIEPVRE	11/29/1848	NO		FILM
HENRY	JEAN PIERRE			09/26/1854	NO		FILM
HENRY	JEAN PIERRE	1839	LIEPVRE	01/13/1857	NO		FILM
HENRY	JEAN PIERRE			09/26/1854	NO		FILM
HENRY W 2CH	CONRAD AUGUSTE	1813	THANN	01/08/1845	NY		FILM
HENRY W 3CH	MARIE MADELAINE	1800	LIEPVRE	09/05/1854	NO		FILM
HENRY W D AND S	MARIE CATHERINE	1815	LIEPVRE	03/13/1857	NO		FILM
HENTZ	FRANCOIS JEAN	1820	OBERHERGHEIM	12/27/1851	A		FILM
HENTZ	JEAN BAPTISTE	1828	OBERHERGHEIM	11/19/1852	A		FILM
HENTZ W W 2CH	GEORGE		REICHSHOFFEN	03/27/1817	A		FILM
HENZLER	GEORGES	1800	WOLFERSHOFFEN B	11/07/1854	A		FILM
HEOLZER	LUGARDE		GERMANY	04/01/1849	NY		FILM
HEPP	FRANCOISE		HAGUENAU	03/01/1838	A		FILM
HEPP MN FOISSET	MARIE MADELAINE	1812	UEBERACH	03/02/1851	NO		FILM
HEPPE	AGATHE	1818	MEZIRE	04/01/1866	NY		FILM
HERB W W 2CH	HENRI		ENDINGEN B	05/29/1852	NY		FILM
HERBELIN	EMELIE	1843	BELFORT	03/17/1866	NO		FILM
HERBERT	MARTIN		PIRMASENZ	09/28/1849	A		FILM
HERBETTE W W 3CH	FRANCOISE	1806	BERMONT	04/11/1855	A		FILM
HERBRECHT	ANTOINE	1832	TAGOLSHEIM	09/21/1852	NY		FILM
HERBRICH	JEAN	1829	KIENTZHEIM	10/24/1854	NO		FILM
HERBST W W 1CH	ANDRE	1812	GUEWENHEIM	08/23/1847	NY		FILM
HERBST W W 3CH	NICOLAS		LA PETIT	/ /	07		FILM
HERBSTER	PHILIPPE	1823	MASSEVAUX	09/14/1847	NY		FILM
HERD W W M AND BR	THIEBAUT		BETTENDORF	/ /	NY		FILM
HERGER	CATHARINE		SCHLIERDORF B	05/12/1849	A		FILM
HERIGOTT	AUGUSTIN	1828	LAUTENBACH	03/15/1854	NY		FILM
HERMANN	BABETTE	1809	ALTENSTADT BA	02/29/1848	NY		FILM
HERMANN	FRANCOIS ANTOIN	1828	MARMOUTIER	01/01/1828	A		FILM
HERMANN	GEORG	1843	LEMBACH	01/01/1866	NY	BAKE	NO.2
HERMANN	JEAN	1821	MULHOUSE	09/01/1846	TX	FILE	PASS
HERMANN	JEAN GREGOIRE	1821	REICHSHOFFEN	09/16/1846	TX		FILM
HERMANN	JOSEPH	1791	WINTZENHEIM	07/28/1852	NY		FILM
HERMANN	MARGUERITE		ZUTZENDORFF	01/01/1828	A		FILM
HERMANN	NICOLAS	1830	MUNTZENHEIM	08/14/1852	A		FILM
HERMIG	FREDERIQUE	1828	KEHL B	09/12/1849	NY		FILM
HERMY	FRANCOIS XAVIER	1817	BERNARDSWILLER	02/12/1846	NO		FILM

Lastname	Firstname	Birth Year	Birthplace	Emigration	De	Prof	Source
HERN	DOMINIQUE	1806	MEYENHEIM	12/20/1851	TX		FILM
HERN	PAUL	1830	MEYENHEIM	12/20/1851	TX		FILM
HERNUNG	GEORGES	1816	MUNSTER	06/03/1854	NY		FILM
HERO	CESAR	1833	WOLSCHWILLER	04/19/1853	NY		FILM
HEROLD	BARBE	1824	KAYSERSBERG	07/23/1847	NO		FILM
HEROLT	JEAN	1819	KAYSERSBERG	09/25/1841	NO		FILM
HERR	JEANNE CLAUDE	1824	VESOUL	04/25/1848	NO		FILM
HERR	THEODORE	1788	COLMAR	07/02/1847	NY		FILM
HERR F OF 5	PHILIPPE		WEITERSWILLER	01/01/1828	A		FILM
HERR F OF 6	CHRETIEN		BOUXWILLER	01/01/1828	A		FILM
HERRENBERGER W W 7CH	MICHEL	1796	MULHOUSE	10/11/1853	A		FILM
HERRENSCHMIDT	CATHERINE		OERMINGEN	01/01/1828	A		FILM
HERRENSCHMIDT	FREDERIC		STRASSBOURG	01/01/1828	A		FILM
HERRGOTT	AUGUSTIN	1828	LAUTENBACH	03/15/1854	NY		FILM
HERRGOTT	PIERRE	1835	MITZACH	10/05/1854	NY		FILM
HERRGOTT W W 2CH	AUGUSTIN	1820	MITZACH	09/06/1854	NY		FILM
HERRMAN MN HOLTZER	CAROLINE	1825	MOTHERN	01/01/1867	NY		NO.2
HERRMANN	ELISABETH	1858	MOTHERN	01/01/1867	NY		NO.2
HERRMANN	IGNACE	1829	SCHLESTADT	04/16/1852	NY		FILM
HERRMANN	JACQUES	1835	MUNTZENHEIM	11/23/1854	CH		FILM
HERRMANN	JEAN	1808	MULHOUSE	08/05/1847	A		FILM
HERRMANN	JEAN	1832	BURNHAUPT LE BAS	03/11/1854	NY		FILM
HERRMANN	JEAN BAPTISTE	1832	SELESTAT	11/14/1851	NY		FILM
HERRMANN	JOHANN	1865	MOTHERN	01/01/1867	NY		NO.2
HERRMANN	MAGDALENA	1856	MOTHERN	01/01/1867	NY		NO.2
HERRMANN W 2CH	CATHERINE		REITWEILER	02/27/1838	A		FILM
HERRMANN W W	PHILIPPE		GUMBRECHTSHOFFEN	04/28/1819	A		FILM
HERRMANN W W 3 CH	ALOYSIUS	1825	MOTHERN	01/01/1867	NY		NO.2
HERRSCHE W W 3CH	ANDRE	1811	VOLGELSHEIM	05/10/1851	NY		FILM
HERSCHBERGER W W 3CH	GEORGES	1794	OSTHEIM	04/13/1847	NY		FILM
HERSCHBERGER W W 5CH	FREDERIC	1800	OSTHEIM	08/10/1854	NY		FILM
HERSCHER	JEAN	1821	OSTHEIM	03/10/1849	NY		FILM
HERTEL	SEBASTIEN	1810	ELBACH	04/22/1853	NY		FILM
HERTEL	THIEBAUD	1820	ELBACH	02/25/1851	NY		FILM
HERTENSTEIN	ANDRE		KIPPENHEIMWEILER	08/17/1849	NY		FILM
HERTENSTEIN	ANNA MARIE		KIPPENHEIMWEILER B	08/17/1849	NY		FILM
HERTINGEN	JEAN BAPTISTE	1827	ROPPE	01/25/1856	NY		FILM
HERTLER	CATHERINE PHILI	1832	PARIS	06/18/1850	NY		FILM
HERTZ	N.M.		BALBRONN	02/28/1838	A		FILM
HERZ	MICHEL	1851	NIEDERROEDERN	01/01/1869	NY		NO.2
HERZOG	AMBROISE	1814	THANNENKIRCH	10/16/1852	NY		FILM
HERZOG MN BALD. 4CH	ELISABETH	1810	THANNENKIRCH	10/31/1854	NO		FILM
HERZOG W S	FRIDOLIN	1821	THANNENKIRCH	10/16/1852	NY		FILM
HESIN	BARBARA		GUMBRECHTSHOFFEN	10/15/1826	OH		FILM
HESS	HENRI		CLEEBOURG	01/01/1855	A		PRIV
HESS	JOSEPH	1825	RODEREN	02/17/1847	A		FILM
HESS W W 5CH	FRANCOIS ANTOIN		INGWILLER	03/23/1817	A		FILM
HESSEMANN	CHARLES FRANCOS	1824	SERMAMAGNY	04/09/1853	NY		FILM
HESSLER	PETER	1820	WINTZENBACH	01/01/1868	NY	FARM	NO.2
HESTERICH F OF 2	ALOISE		WEISLINGEN	01/01/1828	A		FILM

Lastname	Firstname	Birth Year	Birthplace	Emigration	De	Prof	Source
HESTIN W W 1CH	JOSEPH	1817	ROMBACH	10/23/1846	NO		FILM
HETTEL	GREGOR		BEDIGHEIM	04/21/1849	A		FILM
HETTEL	JOSEPH	1782	ZINSWILLER	02/16/1817	A		FILM
HETTERICH	PHILLIP		HOHWILLER	01/01/1817	NY		NO.2
HETTERLIN	JOSEPH	1808	HEIMERSDORF	01/26/1846	NY		FILM
HETTIER	FRANCOIS JOSEPH		AUENHEIM	03/14/1817	A		FILM
HETTINGER	BARBARA	1838	BREMMELBACH	01/01/1866	NY		NO.2
HETZEL W W 3CH	JOSEF		ZINSWILLER	02/20/1817	A		FILM
HETZEL W W 3CH	JOSEPH ?SAME?		BAS RHIN FRANCE	01/01/1817	A		FILM
HETZMANN	FRANCOIS	1819	ST. COSME	02/28/1844	NY		FILM
HEUBACH	DOROTHE		NORTINGEN W	05/12/1849	A		FILM
HEUCHEL W W	FRANCOIS JOSEPH	1831	CERNAY	08/13/1852	SL		FILM
HEUECK F OF 4	PHILIPPE		SUNDHAUSEN	03/02/1837	A		FILM
HEUSSERER	GERTRUDE		ROHRWILLER	03/12/1838	A		FILM
HEYBERGER	JOSEPH	1822	TRAUBACH LE BAS	02/18/1854	NY		FILM
HEYBERGER W 3D	MARIE ANNE		ILLHAEUSERN	02/14/1855	NY		FILM
HEYBERGER W W 1CH	JEAN BAPTISTE	1821	VOEGTLINSHOFFEN	05/08/1850	SL		FILM
HEYDT	MARGARETHE	1840	NIEDERROEDERN	01/01/1868	NO		NO.2
HEYER W W 5 CH	JOSEPH ANTOINE	1812	PFEFFERHAUSEN	03/02/1847	NY		FILM
HEYGEL	JOSEPH		WANTZENAU	03/07/1838	A		FILM
HEYGEL SENIOR	JOSEPH		WANTZENAU	03/07/1838	A		FILM
HEYLAND	GUSTAVE ADOLPHE	1812	HUNAWIHR	09/11/1846	NY		FILM
HEYLANDT W D		1810	MUHLBACH	10/21/1842	NY		FILM
HEYLANDT W W A GRASO	LOUIS	1785	HUNAWIHR	10/03/1846	NY		FILM
HEYMANN	FRIEDRICH	1798	OBERBETSCHDORF	01/01/1864	NY		NO.2
HEYMANN	JULIA	1841	NIEDERROEDERN	01/01/1868	NO		NO.2
HEYMANN	JULIE		NIEDERROEDERN	01/01/1866	NO		PRIV
HEYMANN	VALENTIN		MALZENHEIM	02/28/1838	A		FILM
HEYTIN W W	JEAN GEORGES	1823	LIEPVRE	08/27/1851	NO		FILM
HIBON	LUDWIG	1849	CLIMBACH	01/01/1869	NY		NO.2
HICKEL	MARIE		KURTZENHAUSEN	03/03/1838	A		FILM
HICKEL F OF 6	THIEBAUT		GRIES	02/28/1838	A		FILM
HICKEL F OF4	ANDRE		BISWILLER	03/02/1838	A		FILM
HIEBEL	PHILLIP	1831	SCHLEITHAL	01/01/1866	NY		NO.2
HIEBLER	FLORENT		THAL	01/01/1828	A		FILM
HIEBLER F OF 4	PIERRE		THAL	01/01/1828	A		FILM
HIEGEL	MICHEL		UHLWILLER	03/03/1838	A		FILM
HIGEL	ALOYSE	1821	ROHLING	07/10/1849	NY		FILM
HIGEL	JEAN HENRY	1821	GROS-RECHERCHING	02/12/1853	NY		FILM
HIGEL	THIEBAUT		KUTTOLSHEIM	04/14/1841	A		FILM
HILD	PIERRE		WINGEN	01/01/1828	A		FILM
HILD	XAVIER			02/27/1857	A		FILM
HILD F OF 3	FRANCOIS JOSEPH		LICHTENBERG	01/01/1828	A		FILM
HILD F OF 3	GASPARD		SILTZHEIM	01/01/1828	A		FILM
HILD W W 3CH	FRANCOIS		WINGEN	01/01/1828	A		FILM
HILD W W A D	XAVIER	1798	MULHOUSE	02/27/1857	SL		FILM
HILDENBRAND	CHRETIEN		DETTWILLER	01/01/1828	A		FILM
HILDENBRAND	LEON	1834	MUSBACH	02/09/1852	NY		FILM
HILDT F OF 2	MARGUERITE		FORT LOUIS	01/01/1828	A		FILM
HILDY				/ /			

Lastname	Firstname	Birth Year	Birthplace	Emigration	De	Prof	Source
HILDY	NICLAS	1836	MULHOUSE	01/01/1836	NY		FILM
HILDY W W 2CH	JOSEPH	1813	ILLFURTH	09/08/1853	NY		FILM
HILEMANN	JEAN GOERGES		BOUXWILLER	02/25/1828	A		FILM
HILL F OF 6	GEORGE		BRUMATH	01/01/1828	A		FILM
HILL W W 5CH	MICHEL		BOERSCH	03/18/1817	A		FILM
HILLENBRUND	BALTHAZARD	1813	UNTERHALBEN	11/13/1844	NY		FILM
HILLENMEYER	XAVIER	1784	WATTWILLER	09/15/1851	NY		FILM
HILLENMEYER W W		1815	WATTWILLER	08/07/1840	NY		FILM
HILLER	GEORG	1850	RITTERSHOFEN	01/01/1869	NY		NO.2
HILS F OF 3	PHILIPPE		BOUXWILLER	01/01/1828	A		FILM
HILTENBRAND	RICHARD	1819	BUHL	03/17/1854	A		FILM
HILTY	PIERRE	1818	FLORIMONT	09/13/1852	NY		FILM
HIMBERT W W	JOSEPH	1791	ASPACH	03/16/1841	NY		FILM
HIMGER W S	GUILLAUME	1795	LAXENFELDEN	11/21/1848	NY		FILM
HIMMLER	MARCEL	1888	GUNDERSHOFFEN	/ /		LA	BULL
HINDELANG	JOSEF	1821	SCHLEITHAL	01/01/1866	NO		NO.2
HINDELANG	JOSEPH		SCHLEITHAL	01/01/1850	NO		PRIV
HINDERER	IGNACE	1836	WINGERSHEIM	01/01/1828	A		FILM
HINDERER	JACQUES	1816	REININGUE	07/29/1852	NY		FILM
HINDERMANN W W	JEAN JACQUES	1816	HARBOURG	04/13/1847	NY		FILM
HINDERMANN W W 3CH	JACQUES	1826	HORBOURG	05/01/1844	NY		FILM
HINDRELET W W 2CH	JOSEPH	1796	GRANDVILLARS	02/15/1851	NY		FILM
HINGUE W 4CH	MARIE THERESE	1791	LA CHAPELLE SOUS CHX	02/09/1847	OH		FILM
HINTERMEYER F OF 9	MICHEL		SCHWEIGHAUSEN	01/01/1828	A		FILM
HINZINGER W 6CH	THERESE	1794	FOUCHY	10/09/1839	NO		FILM
HIRLEMANN F OF 5	JEAN MICHEL		BOUXWILLER	01/01/1828	A		FILM
HIRLENMANN	JACOB		NIEDERKUTZENHAUSEN	01/01/1852	A		SUESS
HIRN	ELISABETH	1821	ILLHAEUSERN	07/06/1857	NY		FILM
HIRONIMUS W W 5CH	JACQUES		UHRWILLER	04/09/1819	A		FILM
HIROT	GREGOIRE	1822	THANNENKIRCH	04/15/1847	NY		FILM
HIRSCH	ALFONS	1840	NIEDERROEDERN	01/01/1868	NY		NO.2
HIRSCH	ALPHONSE		NIEDERROEDERN	01/01/1866	NO		PRIV
HIRSCH	BENJAMIN HEINR	1867	DRACHENBRONN	01/01/1868	NY		NO.2
HIRSCH	CHARLES LEOPOLD	1849	HATTSTATT	07/20/1866	NY		FILM
HIRSCH	CHARLOTTE	1845	NIEDERROEDERN	01/01/1864	NY		NO.2
HIRSCH	DAVID	1852	WOELFLINGEN	01/01/1866	NY		NO.2
HIRSCH	ISIDORE	1846	HATTEN	01/01/1865	NY	MERC	NO.2
HIRSCH	JACOB	1843	HATTEN	01/01/1865	NY		NO.2
HIRSCH	JULIE	1852	HATTEN	01/01/1865	NY		NO.2
HIRSCH	LEVY	1826	SOULTZMATT	06/24/1852	NY		FILM
HIRSCH	LINA		RENINGEN W	04/18/1849	NY		FILM
HIRSCH	NANETTE	1844	HATTEN	01/01/1865	NY		NO.2
HIRSCH	SOPHIE	1850	WEISSENBURG	01/01/1866	NY		NO.2
HIRSCH	THEOPHILE	1847	HATTEN	01/01/1865	NY		NO.2
HIRSCH F OF 7	CHARLES		SAVERNE	01/01/1828	A		FILM
HIRSCH MN LEVY	SARA	1838	DRACHENBRONN	01/01/1868	NY		NO.2
HIRSCH W W 1 SON	BENJAMIN	1842	DRACHENBRONN	01/01/1868	NY		NO.2
HIRSCHBERGER	HELENE		ICHENHAUSEN	04/25/1849	NY		FILM
HIRSCHBERGER	ISRAEL		ICHENHAUSEN	04/25/1849	NY		FILM
HIRTH W S	CATHERINE	1788	SOPPE LE BAS	05/06/1840	NY		FILM

```
HIRTZ MN LEVY W 1CH   ANNE             1814 GUEBWILLER        10/25/1849 PH        FILM
HIRTZ W W 1CH         LEMANN           1806 GUEBWILLER        04/27/1850 PH        FILM
HIRTZEL               SIMON            1827 BALDENHEIM        01/19/1855 NY        FILM
HIRTZEL F OF 5        CHRETIEN              SUNDHAUSEN        03/02/1837 A         FILM
HIRTZLIN W W 3CH      JOSEPH           1802 NEUWILLER         10/14/1845 A         FILM

HISSER W W 2CH        SEBASTIEN        1815 KAYSERSBERG       08/10/1849 A         FILM
HISSLER W W 6CH       MARTIN           1796 HAGENTHAL LE BAS  07/06/1849 NY        FILM
HISSUNG               CATHERINE             PETERSBACH        01/01/1828 A         FILM
HISSUNG               PIERRE                PETERSBACH        01/01/1828 A         FILM
HISSUNG F OF 2        MADELAINE             STRUTH            01/01/1828 A         FILM

HISSUNG W W 3CH       NICOLAS               STRUTH            03/03/1817 A         FILM
HITTENBRANT           FRANCIS JOSEPH   1820 MURBACH           02/09/1852 NY        FILM
HITZEL                CATHERINE        1811 ZINSWEILER        02/16/1817 A         FILM
HITZEL                ELISABETH        1815 ZINSWEILER        02/16/1817 A         FILM
HITZEL                MADELAINE             ZINSWEILER        02/16/1817 A         FILM

HITZEL                MARGUERITE       1789 ZINSWEILLER       02/16/1817 A         FILM
HITZEL                MARIE ANNE       1813 ZINSWEILER        02/16/1817 A         FILM
HITZEL W W 3CH A MO   JOSEPH           1786 ZINSWEILER        02/16/1817 A         FILM
HOBLER  F OF 4        CHRETIEN              HAMBACH           01/01/1828 A         FILM
HOBLER F OF 4         GEORGE                HAMBACH           01/01/1828 A         FILM

HOBLER W W 1CH        GEORGE                LA PETIT PIERRE   03/03/1817 A         FILM
HOCH F OF 5           HENRI                 OERMINGEN         01/01/1828 A         FILM
HOCH WW 3CH           CASIMIR          1822 DOLMETINGEN       02/14/1855 NY        FILM
HOCHDERFER W W 5CH    PIERRE                NEHWILLER         03/11/1817 A         FILM
HOCHENEDEL            MICHEL                REUTENHEIM        03/01/1838 A         FILM

HOCHENWEL             MICHEL                LEUTENHEIM        03/01/1838 A         FILM
HODAPP                FRANCOIS              STADELHOFEN B     07/29/1849 A         FILM
HODAPP                WENDELIN              STADELHOFEN B     07/29/1849 A         FILM
HOECHAR W W F OF 6    JACQUES               WILLER            01/01/1828 A         FILM
HOECKELSWEILER        GEORGES          1827 JEBSHEIM          04/12/1854 NY        FILM

HOEFFLIGER            VALENTIN         1810 GUEBWILLER        04/29/1842 NY        FILM
HOEFFLIGER W 6CH      VALENTIN         1809 GUEBWILLER        04/11/1845 PH        FILM
HOEFLER               CATHERINE        1814 ZINSWEILLER       02/16/1817 A         FILM
HOEFLER               MARIE ANNE       1787 ZINSWEILLER       02/16/1817 A         FILM
HOEHN                 BARBE                 SESSENHEIM        02/23/1838 A         FILM

HOEHN                 CHRETIEN              RUNTZENHEIM       01/01/1828 A         FILM
HOEHN                 MADELAINE             RUNTZENHEIM       01/01/1828 A         FILM
HOEHN                 MARIE EVE             SESSENHEIM        02/23/1838 A         FILM
HOEHN                 MICHEL                RUNTZENHEIM       01/01/1828 A         FILM
HOEHN                 PIERRE                RUNTZENHEIM       01/01/1828 A         FILM

HOEHN                 TOBI                  AUENHEIM          01/13/1828 A         FILM
HOEHN                 VALENTIN              RUNTZENHEIM       01/01/1828 A         FILM
HOEHN D JEAN GEORGES  MADELAINE             ROPPENHEIM        04/18/1847 A         NO.1
HOEHN F OF 11         JEAN GEORGE           RUNTZENHEIM       01/01/1828 A         FILM
HOEHN F OF 5          GEORGE                RUNTZENHEIM       01/01/1828 A         FILM

HOEHN F OF 5          HENRI                 RUNTZENHEIM       01/01/1828 A         FILM
HOEHN F OF 8          JEAN                  RUNTZENHEIM       01/01/1828 A         FILM
HOEHN H SALOME        JEAN GEORGES          ROPPENHEIM        04/12/1847 A         NO.1
HOEHN W JEAN GEORGES  SALOME                ROPPENHEIM        04/12/1847 A         NO.1
HOELLER               CONRAD           1832 WEISSENBURG       01/01/1866 NY WINE   NO.2
```

Lastname	Firstname	Birth Year	Birthplace	Emigration	De	Prof	Source
HOELTZEL	JOHANN HEINRICH		LANGENSOULTZBACH	01/01/1817	A		NO.2
HOELTZEL	JOHANN HEINRICH		LAUTERBURG	01/01/1817	A		NO.2
HOELTZEL	THIEBAUT		PETERSBACH	01/01/1828	A		FILM
HOELTZEL F OF 4	PHILIPPE GEORGE		SCHWEIGHAUSEN	01/01/1828	A		FILM
HOELTZEL F OF 4	PIERRE		SCHWEIGHAUSEN	01/01/1828	A		FILM
HOELTZEL W W 4CH	JEAN JACQUES		GOERSDORF	03/22/1817	A		FILM
HOELZEL W W 7 CH	G.HENRY		LANGENSOULTZBACH	03/03/1817	A		FILM
HOENIG F OF 2	ANDRE		WEINBOURG	01/01/1828	A		FILM
HOFEN	MEDERD		OENSBACH B	04/08/1849			FILM
HOFER	FRANCOISE	1823	FELLERING	09/24/1852	PH		FILM
HOFER	JOSEPH	1810	BETTLACH	11/15/1846	TX		FILM
HOFER MN KUNG W 1CH	MARIE ELISABETH	1818	NIEDERWYL SWISS	11/06/1847	NY		FILM
HOFERER	FRANCOISE	1830	RIBEAUVILLE	09/25/1855	NO		FILM
HOFERT	MICHEL	1836	DURRENENTZEN	11/10/1854	A		FILM
HOFERT	SALOME	1832	DURRENENTZEN	02/02/1856	CH		FILM
HOFERT W W	JEAN	1831	DURRENENTZEN	02/02/1856	CH		FILM
HOFF	CHRISTMANN		NIEDERBRONN	05/13/1838	A		FILM
HOFF	GEORGE		MARMOUTIER	01/01/1828	A		FILM
HOFF	HANS ADAM		NIEDERBRONN	05/13/1838	A		FILM
HOFF	JOSEPH		REINHARDSMUNSTER	04/11/1853	A		FILM
HOFFART	JOHANN	1846	NEHWILLER	01/01/1867	NY		NO.2
HOFFART	JOSEPH	1834	SCHLEITHAL	03/20/1857	NO		FILM
HOFFART F OF 3	BERNHARD	1837	OBERMODERN	01/01/1828	A		FILM
HOFFER	HEINRICH		BUEHL	01/01/1840	A		SUESS
HOFFER	JOSEPH	1824	OSTHEIM	05/24/1854	NY		FILM
HOFFER W W 9CH	CHRETIEN		PETIT PIERRE	03/20/1817	A		FILM
HOFFERT	ANTOINE	1825	OSTHEIM	04/15/1854	NY		FILM
HOFFERT	JACQUES	1826	MUNTZENHEIM	01/11/1847	NY		FILM
HOFFERT	JACQUES	1833	DURRENENTZEN	08/17/1852	CH		FILM
HOFFERT W W 2CH	JACQUES	1812	ALGOLSHEIM	03/11/1854	NY		FILM
HOFFMANN	ALOYSE		DANNEMARIE	02/13/1849	NY		FILM
HOFFMANN	AUGUSTIN	1030	LUTTERBACH	03/15/1854	NY		FILM
HOFFMANN	GEORGE	1842	DAMBACH	03/12/1856	A		FILM
HOFFMANN	JEAN		OBERMODERN	01/01/1828	A		FILM
HOFFMANN	JOACHIM	1805	ZUNIKON SWISS	04/30/1857	NY		FILM
HOFFMANN	JOHANN PETER	1845	STEINSELTZ	01/01/1866	NY	MERC	NO.2
HOFFMANN	KARL	1834	SELTZ	01/01/1867	WA		NO.2
HOFFMANN	VALENTIN		DAMBACH	03/12/1856	A		FILM
HOFFMANN W W 2CH	GERMAIN	1815	HUTTEN B	07/29/1853	NY		FILM
HOFFMANN W W 5CH	FREDERIC		PETERSBACH	03/17/1817	A		FILM
HOFFMANN W W 6CH	GASPARD		LIPSHEIM	05/27/1817	A		FILM
HOFFMEYER	FRANCOIS JOSEPH	1799	HIRTZFELDEN	11/01/1850	TX		PASS
HOFFMEYER	SEBASTIEN	1821	OBERHERGHEIM	01/31/1852	NY		FILM
HOFFMEYER W W 4CH	JOSEPH	1804	ROUFFACH	06/08/1847	A		FILM
HOFFMEYER W W 6CH	BERNARD	1806	ROUFFACH	10/13/1843	A		FILM
HOFFNER	AGATHE	1822	GEISHAUSEN	08/11/1854	NY		FILM
HOFFSCHIRR	MADELAINE	1807	SCHWEIGHAUSEN	08/16/1847	A		FILM
HOFSTETTER MN MEYER	SALOME	1824	ST.CROIX AUXMIES	09/25/1857	NY		FILM
HOFSTETTER W W 1S	JOSEPH	1819	ST.CROIX AUX MINES	09/25/1857	NY		FILM
HOHL	BABETTE		MERCHENTHAL W	07/31/1849	A		FILM

Lastname	Firstname	Birth Year	Birthplace	Emigration	De	Prof	Source
HOHLER	FRANCOIS ANTOIE	1821	NIFTER	04/07/1854	NY		FILM
HOHMANN	JEAN BAPTISTE		HAGUENAU	03/01/1838	A		FILM
HOHN	ANTOINE		SOUFFLENHEIM	03/02/1838	A		FILM
HOIGNEY	PIERRE	1842	ROUGEGOUTTE	05/19/1865	NY		FILM
HOIGNI	JEAN JACQUES	1815	VELLESCOT	04/08/1840	NY		FILM
HOLD	JOHANN PAUL	1845	SALMBACH	01/01/1866	NO	BAKE	NO.2
HOLDER	LOUIS LUCIEN	1833	GIROMAGNY	02/21/1857	NY		FILM
HOLINGER	RENE	1825	ALGOLSHEIM	11/11/1853	NY		FILM
HOLINGER F OF 3	GASPARD		MUTTERHOLTZ	04/05/1838	A		FILM
HOLL	JEAN	1774	RIESPACH	12/14/1843	NY		FILM
HOLL F OF 6	JOSEPH		LICHTENBERG	01/01/1828	A		FILM
HOLLE	KARL	1844	MOTHERN	01/01/1866	NY	CARP	NO.2
HOLLENDER	GEORG	1846	SURBOURG	01/01/1868	NY	SHMA	NO.2
HOLLENDER	JOSEF	1849	SURBOURG	01/01/1866	NY	DAYL	NO.2
HOLLIGER	ANDRE	1827	OBERHERGHEIM	11/01/1848	TX	TAYL	PASS
HOLLIGER W W 2CH	JEAN	1791	BONISWIL SWISS	02/09/1849	A		FILM
HOLLINGER	DAVID	1818	ALGOLSHEIM	03/09/1853	NY		FILM
HOLLINGER W W 4CH	ALOYSE	1808	ST.MARIE AUX MINES	03/27/1848	NY		FILM
HOLM	LOUIS	1822	DORNACH	08/27/1850	NY		FILM
HOLNUG	ELISABETH		SOULZ W	04/03/1849	NY		FILM
HOLSTEIN	JOSEPH ANTOINE	1817	DOLTEREN	06/27/1849	NY		FILM
HOLSTEIN W W	JOSEPH ANTOINE	1818	DOLTERNE	05/01/1854	NY		FILM
HOLSTERN	CHRETIEN		BETRA SIGMARINEN	05/02/1849	NY		FILM
HOLTZ	JEAN	1811	MULHAUSEN B	07/20/1838	NY		FILM
HOLTZER	JOSEPH		GUNDERSHOFFEN	01/01/1869	NY		NO.2
HOLTZER	MARGARETHE	1847	MOTHERN	01/01/1869	NY		NO.2
HOLTZMANN	GEORG	1866	NIEDERBETSCHDORF	01/01/1868	NY		NO.2
HOLTZMANN	JACQUES		NIEDERBETSCHDORF	05/03/1856	A		FILM
HOLTZMANN	PHILLIP	1867	NIEDERBETSCHDORF	01/01/1868	NY		NO.2
HOLTZMANN	SALOME	1840	NIEDERBETSCHDORF	01/01/1868	NY		NO.2
HOLTZMANN	SALOME	1865	NIEDERBETSCHDORF	01/01/1868	NY		NO.2
HOLTZMANN W W 3 CH	THEOBALD	1826	NIEDERBETSCHDORF	01/01/1868	NY	DAYL	NO.2
HOLZER W W 2CH	JOSEPH		GUNDERSHOFFEN	03/11/1817	A		FILM
HOLZUMNTH W W 6CH	THIEBAUD	1808	WITTERSDORF	04/19/1851	NO		FILM
HOMEL W W	WENDELIN		KILSTETT	03/03/1838	A		FILM
HOMEL MN HERMANN	MARIE EVE		KILSTETT	03/03/1838	A		FILM
HOMMEL W 5CH	WENDELIN		KILSTETT	03/03/1838	A		FILM
HOOG CH 4	JOSEPH	1809	RIXHEIM	11/01/1851	TX		PASS
HOOG W W 2CH	JOSEPH	1809	RIXHEIM	11/18/1851	TX		FILM
HOPP W W 3CH	JEAN		NEHWILLER	03/11/1817	A		FILM
HORARSBERGER W W 2CH	JEAN	1822	MUNTZENHEIM	09/01/1854	CH		FILM
HORN	ANNE MARIE	1827	LEYMAN	03/19/1852	NY		FILM
HORN	DOMINIQUE	1806	MEYENHEIM	12/01/1851	TX	CULT	PASS
HORN	PAUL	1830	MEYENHEIM	12/20/1851	TX		FILM
HORNECKER	CHRETIEN FREDEC	1829	MITTELWIHR	03/31/1848	NY		FILM
HORNECKER	GE LUC		NEUHOFF	03/03/1817	A		FILM
HORNECKER	MARGUERITE		NEUHOFF	03/03/1817	A		FILM
HORNECKER	MICHEL		PLOBSHEIM	03/19/1838	A		FILM
HORNECKER MN BUCK			NEUHOFF	03/03/1817	A		FILM
HORNECKER MN BUCK	WIDOW		NEUHOFF	03/03/1817	A	DAYL	FILM

Lastname	Firstname	Birth Year	Birthplace	Emigration	De	Prof	Source
HORNER	CATHERINA	1846	SURBOURG	01/01/1867	NO		NO.2
HORNER	JACQUES	1819	WOLFERSDORF	04/19/1847	NY		FILM
HORNSTEIN	SEBASTIEN	1835	THANN	03/25/1856	NY		FILM
HORNUNG	JEAN	1816	WOLSCHWILLER	05/02/1846	NY		FILM
HORNUNG	LUCAS		BEDIGHEIM	04/21/1849	A		FILM
HORNUNG	MARIE		BEDIGHEIM	04/21/1849	A		FILM
HORNY	JEAN	1818	FELLERINGEN	08/23/1854	TX		FILM
HORNY CH 4	NICOLAS	1822	KRUTH	10/01/1859	TX	TISS	PASS
HORNY D NICOLAS	MARIE-ROSE	1859	KRUTH	10/01/1859	TX		PASS
HORNY MN FISCHER	CATHERINE			10/01/1859	TX		PASS
HORNY S NICOLAS	CELESTIN	1855	KRUTH	10/01/1859	TX		PASS
HORNY S NICOLAS	ERASME	1851	KRUTH	10/01/1859	TX		PASS
HORNY W W 2 CH	SEBASTIEN	1806	GUEBWILLER	04/04/1839	NY		FILM
HORSTMANN	JEAN LOUIS FRED		HERBITZHEIM	12/25/1820	A		FILM
HORTER	NICOLAS	1831	EGUISHEIM	02/25/1852	NO		FILM
HORTH	JACQUES		SOUFFLENHEIM	03/02/1838	A		FILM
HORUMMEL	ANTOINE		KENTZINGEN B	04/21/1849	A		FILM
HOSATTE	JULIE	1845	SCHAUX	10/10/1865	NY		FILM
HOSATTE	LOUIS	1837	CHAUX	12/04/1855	NO		FILM
HOSCHAR F OF 8	NICOLAS		HERLITZHEIM	01/01/1828	A		FILM
HOSENLOP	JEAN	1827	BUEHL	05/01/1848	NY		FILM
HOST W W	MICHEL		ZITTERSHEIM	03/11/1817	A		FILM
HOTAT	GEORGES	1829	GRANDVILLARS	09/10/1850	NY		FILM
HOTZ	CATHERINE		NIEDERLAUTERBACH	01/01/1850	NO		PRIV
HOTZ	CATHERINE	1849	NIEDERLAUTERBACH	01/01/1867	NO		NO.2
HOTZ	REGINA	1840	NIEDERLAUTERBACH	01/01/1868	NY		NO.2
HOUBRE	ALEXIS	1811	ROUFFACH	02/19/1854	NO		FILM
HOUBRE	LOUIS	1837	SERMAMAGNY	10/04/1855	NO		FILM
HOUDE F OF 6	ETIENNE		MORSCHWILLER	03/04/1838	A		FILM
HOUMAIRE	EUGENE	1836	FRAHIER	04/06/1866	NY		FILM
HOUMARD	DAVID LOUIS	1808	CHAMPUX	04/09/1844	TX		FILM
HOWALD	MICHEL	1834	OBERSEEBACH	01/01/1867	NY	FARM	NO.2
HUBELNOERLIN	SEBASTIEN	1817	LARGITZEN	05/06/1850	NY		FILM
HUBEN	A		OPPENAU	03/31/1849	NY		FILM
HUBER	ADAM		WIMPENAU	01/01/1828	A		FILM
HUBER	ANTOINE		APPENWEIER B	11/02/1849	A		FILM
HUBER	BARBE	1814	RIBEAUVILLE	10/14/1854	NO		FILM
HUBER	ELISABETH		APPENWEIER B	11/02/1849	A		FILM
HUBER	FRANCOIS		ENGENTHAL	03/06/1838	A		FILM
HUBER	JACQUES		REINHARDSMUNSTER	01/01/1828	A		FILM
HUBER	JOSEPH		MUNICH	06/01/1849	A		FILM
HUBER	LAURENT		RAUWILLER	03/07/1838	A		FILM
HUBER	LOUIS	1827	ZELLENBERG	02/08/1856	NY		FILM
HUBER	PHILIPPE		MUTTERHOLTZ	04/05/1838	A		FILM
HUBER	THEOPHILE	1828	MULHOUSE	10/30/1848	SL		FILM
HUBER W W 5CH A SI	MARTIN		BINZGEN	05/23/1853	A		FILM
HUBER F OF 2	JEAN		INGENHEIM	01/01/1828	A		FILM
HUBER W 1CH	MARGARETHA		UNTER ACHERN B	06/11/1849	A		FILM
HUBER W 3CH	MARIE		DURRBACH	04/27/1849	A		FILM
HUBER W W 4CH	JEAN		ST.MARIE AUX MINES	01/01/1828	A		FILM

Lastname	Firstname	Birth Year	Birthplace	Emigration	De	Prof	Source
HUBERSTRICH W W 2CH	LAMBERT	1808	ALTKIRCH	01/22/1849	A		FILM
HUBLAIRE	ADOLPHE	1844	ROPPE	04/30/1866	NY		FILM
HUBLER	AUGUSTE		THAL	01/01/1828	A		FILM
HUBLER	BERNARD		THAL	01/01/1828	A		FILM
HUBLER	FLORENT		THAL	01/01/1828	A		FILM
HUBLER F OF 4	PIERRE		THAL	01/01/1828	A		FILM
HUBRY	JEAN PIERRE	1828	SUARCE	02/27/1851	NY		FILM
HUBSCHWERLIN	FRANCOIS	1811	HIRSINGUE	04/27/1842	NY		FILM
HUBSTENBERGER F OF 5	JOSEPH		ROESCHWOOG	01/01/1828	A		FILM
HUBY W W	JACQUES	1816	OBERHERGHEIM	09/10/1851	TX		FILM
HUCK	JACQUES		BISCHWILLER	03/02/1838	A		FILM
HUCK	JOSEPH		ROESCHWOOG	01/01/1828	A		FILM
HUCK	MICHEL		SCHWEIGHAUSEN	01/01/1828	A		FILM
HUCK W W 2CH	JOSEPH	1810	ZIMMERBACH	01/24/1852	NY		FILM
HUCK F OF 3	JOSEF		ROESCHWOOG	01/01/1828	A		FILM
HUCK W W 4CH	JEROME		DRUSENHEIM	03/24/1838	A		FILM
HUCK W W 4CH	PIERRE		DRUSENHEIM	03/24/1838	A		FILM
HUCKEL F OF 4	JEAN		BRUMATH	01/01/1828	A		FILM
HUEBER	FRANCOIS JOSEPH	1810	BERRWILLER	09/16/1850	NO		FILM
HUEBER W W	THIEBAUT		RODEREN	/ /	NY		FILM
HUESCHLE	ANTOINE		ZEIL B	07/31/1849	A		FILM
HUESCHLE	JOSEPH		ZEIL B	07/21/1849	A		FILM
HUFF	ANTOINE	1798	FRIESSEN	11/11/1846	NY		FILM
HUFF	CATHERINE		BRETTEN B	06/21/1849	A		FILM
HUG	DOROTHE		NIEDERHEIM B	04/23/1849	A		FILM
HUG	FERDINAND	1824	MULHAUSEN	10/15/1846	NY		FILM
HUG	JEAN JACQUES	1829	JEBSHEIM	03/22/1849	NY		FILM
HUG	JOSEPH EDUARD	1809	HABSHEIM	05/31/1851	TX		FILM
HUG	JOSEPH,EDUARD	1809	WITTELSHEIM	04/01/1851	TX	PRIE	PASS
HUG	MARIE		WITTISHEIM	03/02/1838	A		FILM
HUG W W 2CH	JEAN	1811	HERRLISHEIM	03/09/1852	NY		FILM
HUG CH 2	FRANCOIS JOSEPH	1807	KRUTH	08/01/1860	TX	CULT	PASS
HUG MN WELKER	ANNE-MARIE	1813		08/01/1860	TX		PASS
HUGEL	CAROLINE		KEHL	04/07/1849	NY		FILM
HUGEL W W	JOSEPH		SCHOENBOURG	01/01/1828	A		FILM
HUGEL W W 1CH	LOUIS		SCHOENBOURG	01/01/1828	A		FILM
HUGONT W W 2CH	JEAN PIERRE	1805	CHAVANNES SUR LéTANG	08/28/1843	NY		FILM
HUGUENEL	LOUIS	1823	ST.MARIE AUX MINES	10/14/1854	NO		FILM
HUGUENOT	CATHERINE	1827	MORVILLARS	10/23/1855	NY		FILM
HUGUENOT	JACQUES	1808	ISSENHEIM	06/08/1854	NY		FILM
HUGUET	JOSEPH	1836	CHAVANNES LES GRANDS	06/01/1865	NY		FILM
HUID			RENINGEN W	08/18/1849	NY		FILM
HUJEL			GERMANY	04/12/1849	A		FILM
HUKLE	CHARLES		KRATZINGEN B	05/24/1849	A		FILM
HUL F OF 5	HENRI		SCHILLERSDORFF	01/01/1828	A		FILM
HULIER	GUILLAUME		GROSSWEIER	10/11/1849	A		FILM
HUMANN	CHARLES	1822	OSTHEIM	01/20/1849	NY		FILM
HUMANN	MICHEL		IMBSHEIM	01/01/1828	A		FILM
HUMANN F OF 3	GEORGE		FESSENHEIM	02/27/1838	A		FILM
HUMBERT	JACQUES JULIEN	1843	COUTAVON	05/17/1866	NY		FILM

Lastname	Firstname	Birth Year	Birthplace	Emigration	De	Prof	Source
HUMBERT W M 4CH	MARIE ANN	1825	THANNENKIRCH	09/15/1855	A		FILM
HUMBRECHT	ALOYSE	1828	ST. HYPOLITE	10/14/1852	PH		FILM
HUMBRECHT	JOSEPH	1812	MULHOUSE	09/01/1846	TX	CULT	PASS
HUMBRECHT W W 1CH	JOSEPH	1809	ODEREN	09/17/1846	TX		FILM
HUMEL W W 5CH	JOSEPH		SOUFFLENHEIM	03/02/1838	A		FILM
HUMELEUR	FERDINAND	1833	BREBOTTE	03/23/1855	NO		FILM
HUMMEL	BONIFACE		KIRCHENHOFEN B	06/01/1849	A		FILM
HUMMEL	CATHERINE	1817	BERGEHEIM	08/31/1842	PH		FILM
HUMMEL	GEORGE		SPARSBACH	01/01/1828	A		FILM
HUMMEL	NICOLAS		SPARSBACH	01/01/1828	A		FILM
HUMMERER W W 2CH	JEAN BAPTISTE	1834	GUEBWILLER	01/02/1849	NY		FILM
HUND	BERNARD		NUSSBACH B	09/30/1849	A		FILM
HUND	CHARLES		NUSSBACH B	09/30/1849	A		FILM
HUNGER MN HELLER	URSULE	1798	BRUEBACH	02/02/1850	NY		FILM
HUNGER W F	CHRETIEN	1802	SACHSENFELD	03/31/1854	NY		FILM
HUNHARDT W W	JEAN MICHEL	1832	KUNNHEIM	07/06/1850	CH		FILM
HUNNINQUE	CLEMENCE	1836	SAUNOT	10/01/1862	NY		FILM
HUNSINGER	JEAN JACQUES	1817	KUNHEIM	03/30/1846	NY		FILM
HUNSINGER	JEAN JACQUES	1817	KUNNHEIM OR KUNHEIM	03/25/1841	NY		FILM
HUNSINGER	PIERRE		WEISLINGEN	01/01/1828	A		FILM
HUNSINGER F OF 3	PIERRE		WEISLINGEN	01/01/1828	A		FILM
HUNTZINGER	GEORGE		PETERSBACH	01/01/1828	A		FILM
HUNTZINGER	JACQUES	1794	ST. MARIE AUX MINES	02/14/1853	NY		FILM
HUNTZINGER	MARGERITE		PETERSBACH	01/01/1828	A		FILM
HUNTZINGER	PHILIPPE		PETERSBACH	01/01/1828	A		FILM
HUNTZINGER F OF 7	JEAN JACQUES		BOUXWILLER	01/01/1828	A		FILM
HUNZINGER	ADAM		HATTEN III	01/01/1837	A		SUESS
HUOT	ALEXIS	1831	EVETTE	06/07/1847	NY		FILM
HUOT	JEAN BAPTISTE	1797	EVETTE	06/26/1847	NY		FILM
HUPGEN	ARNOLD	1827	EUPEN	11/15/1846	TX		FILM
HUPGEN	HELENE	1798	EUPEN	11/15/1846	TX		FILM
HUPGEN	JOHANN HUBERT	1785	EUPEN	11/15/1846	TX		FILM
HUPGEN	MARIE	1825	EUPEN	11/15/1846	TX		FILM
HUPGEN	NIKOLAUS	1843	EUPEN	11/15/1846	TX		FILM
HUSER	MARIE CATHERINE	1806	HARBOURG	02/15/1844	NY		FILM
HUSS	MARTIN	1848	KAIDENBURG	01/01/1866	NY		NO.2
HUSS	SOPHIE	1853	KAIDENBURG	01/01/1866	NY		NO.2
HUSS	WENDELIN	1856	KAIDENBURG	01/01/1866	NY		NO.2
HUSS MN BECKER	MARIA ANNA	1817	KAIDENBURG	01/01/1866	NY		NO.2
HUSS W W 3 CH	KARL	1817	KAIDENBURG	01/01/1866	NY	FARM	NO.2
HUSSE W 2CH	URSULE	1805	COLMAR	09/16/1848	NY		FILM
HUSSER	ANNE MARIE	1807	SUNDHOFFEN	07/20/1854	NO		FILM
HUSSER	JACQUES	1820	MUNTZENHEIM	03/29/1847	NY		FILM
HUSSER	MARIE	1827	MUNTZENHEIM	11/22/1854	CH		FILM
HUSSER	MARIE MADELAINE	1837	MUNTZENHEIM	08/30/1852	A		FILM
HUSSER	MATHIAS	1810	MUNTZENHEIM	11/22/1854	CH		FILM
HUSSER	PHILIPPE	1814	MUNTZENHEIM	04/19/1841	NY		FILM
HUSSER W 4CH	JOSEPH	1790	WITTELSHEIM	12/17/1847	NY		FILM
HUSSLER	CAROLINE	1837	BISCHWILLER	09/09/1857	NY		FILM
HUSSLER	MADELAINE	1806	RIQUEWIHR	03/25/1856	NY		FILM

Lastname	Firstname	Birth Year	Birthplace	Emigration	De	Prof	Source
HUSSONG	CHRETIEN		HAMBACH	03/08/1838	A		FILM
HUSSONG W W 4 CH	PIERRE		HAMBACH	03/06/1817	A		FILM
HUTH	ALBERT	1822	NEUFREISTETT B	11/15/1846	TX		FILM
HUTH	DAVID		NUREMBERG	05/03/1849	A		FILM
HUTH	LUDWIG	1813	NEUFREISTETT B	10/25/1843	TX		FILM
HUTHER	JOSEPH		ILLKIRCH	03/05/1838	A		FILM
HUTHINGER	MARTINE	1806	IFELSHEIM B	03/05/1853	NY		FILM
HUTT	JULIE	1845	NIEDERROEDERN	01/01/1867	NY		NO.2
HUTTLER F OF 2	GEORGES		DAUENDORF	02/28/1838	A		FILM
HUTZLER	ANTOINE	1805	NIEDERENTZEN	09/01/1846	TX	CULT	PASS
HUTZLER	AUGUSTIN		OBERENTZEN	/ /			FILM
HUTZLER	MICHEL	1831	OBERENTZEN	02/06/1852	TX		FILM
HUTZLER	MICHEL	1831	OBERENTZEN	09/01/1850	TX	BRLA	PASS
HUTZLER CH 3	AUGUSTIN	1812	OBERENTZEN	09/01/1846	TX	DAYL	PASS
HUTZLER W W 4CH	MICHEL	1796	OBERENTZEN	02/06/1852	TX		FILM
HUTZLER W W 3CH	AUGUSTIN	1808	OBERENTZEN	09/07/1846	TX		FILM
HUTZLER W W 6CH	ANTOINE	1805	OBERENTZEN	09/05/1846	TX		FILM
HUWILLER F OF 7	ANTOINE		MORSCHWILLER	03/04/1838	A		FILM
HUY F OF 8	JACQUES		COSSWILLER	03/01/1838	A		FILM
HUY W 2CH	MARIE ANNE	1817	BENDORF	11/20/1852	NO		FILM

Lastname	Firstname	Birth Year	Birthplace	Emigration	De	Prof	Source
ICHLEN W W 8CH	THIEBAUD	1787	GUEBWILLER	04/28/1838	NY		FILM
IDOUX	FRANCOIS JOSEPH	1820	SALMBACH	10/25/1843	TX		FILM
IDOUX	MARIE		SALMBACH	10/25/1843	TX		FILM
IDOUX W W 4CH	FRANCOIS JOSEPH	1797	SALMBACH	10/05/1843	TX		FILM
IFFENECKER	JEAN	1822	BRECHAUMONT	10/04/1844	NO		FILM
IHLER	CHARLES	1827	MASSEVAUX	10/09/1847	NO		FILM
IHLER	MARTIN	1802	ROUFFACH	11/15/1843	A		FILM
IHLER W W 2CH	PAUL	1803	ROUFFACH	11/15/1843	A		FILM
ILBACH	IMPHA		SINSHEIM B	10/04/1849	A		FILM
ILG	CRESCENTZ		DURBACH B	04/21/1849	A		FILM
ILLIG	CATHERINE		NIEDERLAUTERBACH	01/01/1850	NO		PRIV
ILLIG	CATHERINE	1838	NIEDERLAUTERBACH	01/01/1861	NO		PRIV
ILLIG	EKISABETH		NIEDERLAUTERBACH	01/01/1850	NO		PRIV
ILLIG	GEORG	1847	NIEDERLAUTERBACH	01/01/1865	NY	FARM	NO.2
ILLIG	GEORGES		NIEDERLAUTERBACH	01/01/1850	NO		PRIV
ILLIG	GEORGES	1843	NIEDERLAUTERBACH	01/01/1861	NO		PRIV
ILLIG	JEAN	1824	NIEDERLAUTERBACH	01/01/1868	NY	EXMI	PRIV
ILLIG	JOHANN		KUTZENHAUSEN	01/01/1817	A		NO.2
ILLIG	PIERRE		NIEDERLAUTERABCH	01/01/1850	NO		PRIV
ILLIG	PIERRE	1849	NIEDERLAUTERBACH	01/01/1866	NO		PRIV
ILTER	MADELAINE	1823	LAUW	07/12/1850	OH		FILM
ILTI	FRANCOISE	1825	SEWEN	10/13/1847	TX		FILM
ILTIS	FRANCOISE	1825	LEYMEN	10/01/1847	TX	TISS	PASS
ILTIS	JEAN BAPTISTE	1817	HATTSTATT	06/04/1845	NY		FILM
ILTIS W W 2CH	JEAN ANTOINE	1822	SEWEN	05/05/1854	NY		FILM
ILTU	FRANCOISE	1825	SEWEN	10/13/1847	TX		FILM
IMBER	GEORGES	1793	MULHOUSEN	05/14/1844	NY		FILM
IMBERNOTH	M.LOUISE	1838	KAYSERSBERG	11/06/1856	NO		FILM
IMBES F OF 6	ANTOINE	1805	WOLSCHWILLER	05/18/1842	NY		FILM
IMBS F OF 3	AUGUST		GOTTENHAUSEN	01/01/1828	A		FILM
IMMELE	FRANCOIS LOUIS	1827	HATTSTATT	05/20/1857	A		FILM
IMMELE W W 3CH	ANTOINE	1810	OBERMARSCHWILLER	04/08/1852	NY		FILM
IND	ALOIS	1849	RANSPACH	05/31/1859	NY		FILM
IND	ANNE	1808	RANSPACH	05/31/1859	NY		FILM
IND	ANNE	1834	RANSPACH	05/31/1859	NY		FILM
IND	JOSEPH	1842	RANSPACH	05/31/1859	NY		FILM
IND	MARIE	1837	RANSPACH	05/31/1859	NY		FILM
IND	MORAND	1811	RANSPACH	05/31/1859	NY		FILM
IND W W A 4CH	MORAND		RANSPACH	05/31/1859	A		FILM
INGOLD	DOMINIQUE NAPOL	1806	SOULTZ	09/04/1845	NY		FILM
IODRE	MICHEL	1825	GRANDVILLARS	12/14/1844	OH		FILM
IRR F OF 4	MICHEL		UHLWILLER	03/03/1838	A		FILM
IRR F OF 6	ANTOINE		WINGERSHEIM	01/01/1828	A		FILM
ISAAC WITH SI	PAULINE	1822	SOULTZ	10/11/1854	NY		FILM
ISRAEL F OF 3	MICHEL		DETTWILLER	01/01/1828	A		FILM
ISSEMANN F OF 8	SEBASTIEN		SCHIRHOFF	03/01/1838	A		FILM
ISSENMAN F OF 5	JACQUES		BUESWILLER	01/01/1828	A		FILM
ISSENMAN F OF5	GEORGE		BUESWILLER	01/01/1828	A		FILM
ISSENMANN	BERNHARD		GERMANY	04/03/1849	NY		FILM
ISSINGER	CONRAD		MOTHERN	01/01/1850	NO		PRIV

Lastname	Firstname	Birth Year	Birthplace	Emigration	De	Prof	Source
ITTEL	ANNE MARIE	1825	HORBOURG	11/03/1865	CH		FILM
ITTEL	DAVID	1804	SUNDHOFFEN	06/12/1840	NY		FILM
ITTEL	GEORGES	1828	HORBOURG	04/12/1855	NY		FILM
ITTEL	MARIE SALOME	1814	HORBOURG	04/02/1842	NY		FILM
ITTEL W W AND DAU	GEORGES	1793	HORBOURG	04/02/1842	NY		FILM

Lastname	Firstname	Birth Year	Birthplace	Emigration	De	Prof	Source
JACKLE	AUGUSTE	1837	COLMAR	01/09/1855	NO		FILM
JACOB	ANDRE		WOELLENHEIM	02/27/1838	A		FILM
JACOB	FLORENT		WOELLENHEIM	02/27/1838	A		FILM
JACOB	FRANCOIS JOSEPH		BURCKENWALD	01/01/1828	A		FILM
JACOB	HENRI	1814	KRUTH	01/24/1845	NY		FILM
JACOB	JACQUES		INGENHEIM	01/01/1828	A		FILM
JACOB	JOSEPH		ESCHBOURG	03/03/1817	A		FILM
JACOB	MARGARETHE	1846	BITCHE LOTHRING	01/01/1866	NY		NO.2
JACOB	MARIE ANNE		WOELLENHEIM	02/27/1838	A		FILM
JACOB	MARIE ANNE	1830	THANNENKIRCH	03/27/1855	SL		FILM
JACOB	MARIE CATHERINE		WOELLENHEIM	02/27/1838	A		FILM
JACOB	MICHEL		INGENHEIM	01/01/1828	A		FILM
JACOB	MICHEL		KIRRWILLER	01/01/1828	A		FILM
JACOB	THIEBAUT		INGENHEIM	01/01/1828	A		FILM
JACOB F OF 2	MADELAINE		DURSTEL	03/18/1838	A		FILM
JACOB F OF 9	JOSEPH		LOCHWILLER	01/01/1828	A		FILM
JACOB H MADELEINE	RAOUL CH 5			07/12/1847	A		PRIV
JACOB MN SCHATZ	ANNE MARIE		KRUTH	02/27/1838	A		FILM
JACOB W 4 DAU A 5 S	AGATHE	1813	KRUTH	11/10/1855	TX		FILM
JACOB W W 1CH	GEORGES		BADEN	06/27/1833	A		FILM
JACOB W W 2CH	JEAN BAPTISTE	1799	LA CHAPELLE SOUS ROE	05/09/1855	A		FILM
JACOB W W AND CH	FLORENT		KRUTH	02/27/1838	A		FILM
JACOBI	AJCQUES		INGVILLER	01/01/1828	A		FILM
JACOBI F OF 5	PIERRE		STEINBOURG	01/01/1828	A		FILM
JACOBI F OF 6	GEORGE		INGWILLER	01/01/1828	A		FILM
JACOBI W W 3CH	PIERRE		STEINBOURG	03/29/1817	A		FILM
JACOBS	PHILIPPE GEORGE		SESSENHEIM	02/23/1838	A		FILM
JACQUA3T	FRANCOIS	1827	BELFORT	01/16/1863	NY		FILM
JACQUEMIN	FRANCOIS XAVIER	1822	VEZELOIS	04/24/1845	NY		FILM
JACQUEMIN	JEAN BAPTISTE	1833	ST.CROIX AUX MINES	10/19/1854	SL		FILM
JACQUEMIN	MARIE	1823	MEROUX	04/13/1855	NY		FILM
JACQUEMIN	NICOLAS EMILE	1817	SENONES	04/06/1840	NY		FILM
JACQUEMIN	PIERRE LOUIS	1825	FOUSSEMAGNE	04/24/1846	NY		FILM
JACQUEMIN W W 4CH	JEAN BAPTISTE	1809	SENONES	09/10/1845	A		FILM
JACQUENIN W W 3CH	EMILE	1816	SONONES	07/29/1854	NY		FILM
JACQUENOT	MADELAINE	1823	VALDOIE TERR BELFORT	10/28/1857	NY		FILM
JACQUENOT	MADELAINE	1824	VALDOIE TERR BEL	09/20/1852	NY		FILM
JACQUES	SIMON	1824	WINTZENHEIM	08/20/1856	NY		FILM
JACQUES	WITH SISTER	1838	HATTSTATT	11/07/1855	NY		FILM
JACQUILLARD	ANDRE		STRUTH	01/01/1828	A		FILM
JACQUILLARD	JEAN NICOLAS		HARSKIRCHEN	01/01/1828	A		FILM
JACQUOT	CHARLES	1840	MONTBELIARD	04/14/1866	NY		FILM
JACQUOT	CLEMENT	1838	FRAHIER	07/16/1865	NY		FILM
JACQUOT	FRANCOIS JOSEPH	1837	ESSERT	06/04/1857	NY		FILM
JACQUOT	HENRIETTE	1843	MONTBELIARD	04/14/1866	NY		FILM
JACQUOT	JULES	1849	FRAHIER	02/08/1866	NY		FILM
JACQUOT	JULIE	1847	FRAHIER	09/29/1865	NY		FILM
JACQUOT	PHILIBERT	1835	FRAHIER	04/04/1866	NY		FILM
JACQUOT	PIERRE JOSEPH	1830	MENOUCOURT	04/22/1852	NY		FILM
JACQUOT W D	MARIE CATHERINE	1823	LIEPVRE	05/12/1846	NO		FILM

Lastname	Firstname	Birth Year	Birthplace	Emigration	De	Prof	Source
JACQUOT W W	JOSEPH	1801	LIEPVRE	03/30/1839	NO		FILM
JACQUOT W W 1CH	PIERRE	1803	OBERMICHELBACH	08/20/1847	A		FILM
JACQUOT W W 3CH	NICOLAS	1819	ST CROIX AUX MINES	04/07/1855	NY		FILM
JADIN	FRANCOISE	1820	BELFORT	03/09/1849	NY		FILM
JAECK	GOTTFRIED		SCHWANN W	05/12/1849	A		FILM
JAEG	MICHEL		WITTERNHEIM	02/28/1838	A		FILM
JAEGER	ANTOINE		RASTATT B	09/20/1849	A		FILM
JAEGER	CHARLES	1825	ST MARIE AUX MINES	10/28/1848	NO		FILM
JAEGER	ELISABETH	1823	ST MARIE AUX MINES	10/20/1854	NO		FILM
JAEGER	FRANZ	1839	STUNDWILLER	01/01/1868	NY	FARM	NO.2
JAEGER	JOSEPH		ICHENHEIM	04/23/1849	NY		FILM
JAEGER	JOSEPH		SCHILLERSDORF	01/01/1828	A		FILM
JAEGER	MADELAINE		ICHENHEIM	08/24/1849	A		FILM
JAEGER	MADELAINE	1784	MASSEVAUX	10/01/1851	A		FILM
JAEGER	MARIE		ICHENHEIM B	08/24/1849	A		FILM
JAEGER	MICHAEL		NIEDERBRONN	05/13/1838	A		FILM
JAEGER W F	JEAN		WANGEN	01/01/1828	A		FILM
JAEGER W W	JOSEPH MATHIEU	1809	MASSEVAUX	03/31/1847	NY		FILM
JAEGER W W 2CH	LOIUS		SARRE	03/06/1817	A		FILM
JAEGGY	MARC	1815	HIRTZFELDEN	11/29/1850	TX		FILM
JAEGLE	FRANC.JOSEPH	1821	AMMERSCHWIHR	05/08/1848	NY		FILM
JAEGLE	JACQUES		FORT LOUIS	01/01/1828	A		FILM
JAEGLE	JEAN BAPTISTE		FORT LOUIS	01/01/1828	A		FILM
JAEGY	ANDRE	1820	ST CROIX EN PLAINE	04/24/1852	NY		FILM
JAEGY	JEAN	1818	RIESPACH	04/04/1840	NY		FILM
JAEN	XAVIER	1834	BENDORF	10/07/1865	NY		FILM
JAGER	THERESE	1835	OBERHERGHEIM	02/21/1856	NO		FILM
JAGER W W 7CH	JOSEPH	1807	UFFHEIM	07/30/1850	NY		FILM
JAGLIN	MEINRAD	1828	PFEFFERHAUSEN	01/23/1847	NY		FILM
JAKOB	NICOLAS		SASSOLSHEIM	01/01/1828	A		FILM
JAMET	JOSEPH	1815	HARTMANNSWILLER	10/31/1848	OH		FILM
JAMIN	NICOLAS		STRUTH	01/01/1828	A		FILM
JANCKER	NICOLAS		PUBERG	01/01/1828	A		FILM
JANITZKE	EDMUND	1823	KLAWOTZTH	12/01/1851	NY		FILM
JANNES F OF 8	ADAM		ESCHBOURG	01/01/1828	A		FILM
JANTZ F OF 13	JACQUES		KIRRBERG	01/01/1828	A		FILM
JAPY	LOUISE EMILIE	1843	MONTBELLIARD	11/26/1864	NY		FILM
JARDON	AUGUSTE	1839	CHALLONVILLARS	05/07/1866	NY		FILM
JARDON	MELANIE	1844	CHALLONVILLARD	02/17/1864	NY		FILM
JARDON	RENE	1824	ESCHAVANNE	04/08/1866	NY		FILM
JARDON W W 2CH	JEAN CLAUDE		SALBERT	/ /	NO		FILM
JAUDER	CRISTA	1840	MORVILLARD	05/24/1865	NY		FILM
JAUGLEN W CH	MRS.	1826	GUEBWILLER	11/29/1848	LV		FILM
JEACQUOT	JEAN BAPTISTE	1809	ST.CROIX AUX MINES	10/28/1846	SL		FILM
JEAGLEN	JEAN	1815	GALFINGUE	05/22/1840	NY		FILM
JEAGLEN W 1CH	MARIE	1826	GUEBWILLER	11/29/1848	LV		FILM
JEAGLIN	DOMINIQUE	1833	PFEFFERHAUSEN	11/16/1853	NY		FILM
JEAN	BLANC ABEL	1864	BENDORF	10/07/1865	NY		FILM
JEAN BLANC	ALEXANDRE	1852	HAUTE SAONE	03/07/1866	NY		FILM
JEAN BLANC	CHARLES	1829	FRAISSE HAUTE SAONE	03/07/1866	NY		FILM

Lastname	Firstname	Birth Year	Birthplace	Emigration	De	Prof	Source
JEAN BLANC	CONSTANT	1859	FRAISEE HAUT SAONE	03/07/1866	NY		FILM
JEAN BLANC	JOSEPH	1862	FRAISSE HAUTE SAONE	03/07/1866	NY		FILM
JEAN JOSEPH				/ /			
JEAN PIERRE 1 CH	MARIE LOUISE	1818	SERVANCE	02/14/1844	NY		FILM
JEANETTE	MICHEL	1826	LIEPVRE	09/06/1854	NO		FILM
JEANMAIRE W SI	ALEXANDRE	1817	CHALVRAINE	09/22/1857	SF		FILM
JEANMAIRE	MARIE LOUISE	1839	MULHOUSE	09/22/1857	SF		FILM
JEANNEY	ADELE	1840	GROSMAGNY	03/03/1865	NY		FILM
JEANNEZ	JOSEPH	1819	BRETAGNE	04/02/1839	NY		FILM
JEANNEZ	MARIE JEANNE	1819	MEROUX	05/03/1850	NY		FILM
JEANPIERRE	JOSEPH	1824	FAVEROIS	03/07/1854	NO		FILM
JEANPIERRE W W 2CH	FRANCOIS	1796	KEHL	09/12/1849	NY		FILM
JECKERT W W 1CH	MICHEL	1823	OBERSAASHEIM	10/02/1854	NY		FILM
JEGGY	JEAN	1795	NAMBSHEIM	01/17/1852	NY		FILM
JEGLIN	JEAN	1823	PFETTERHOUSE	03/22/1855	NY		FILM
JEHL	FRIDOLIN		ARTOLSHEIM	02/28/1838	A		FILM
JEHL	JEAN BAPTISTE	1831	GUEMAR	04/03/1857	NY		FILM
JEHLY	JEAN ADAM		ZENSWILLER	/ /		PA	FILM
JELSCH	FORTAIN	1842	GRANVILLARD	03/03/1866	NY		FILM
JELSCH	FRANCOISE ANTOI	1804	HIRSINGEN	06/29/1840	NY		FILM
JELSCH	JOSEPH	1816	HIRSINGEN	04/20/1842	NY		FILM
JEMELEN	JEAN	1832	EGLINGUE	11/30/1853	NY		FILM
JENCK	JEAN		AUENHEIM	03/14/1817	A		FILM
JENCK	JEAN		AUENHEIM	03/14/1817	A		FILM
JENN	MARIE AGATHE	1815	MOLLAU	03/11/1845	OH		FILM
JENN W W 1 S	APPOLINAIRE	1815	NIEDERBRUCK	03/29/1851	OH		FILM
JENNY	ANTOINE	1827	GUEBWILLER	07/28/1849	NY		FILM
JENNY	FRANCOIS JOSEPH	1827	GUEBWILLER	08/03/1848	NY		FILM
JENNY	JEAN	1819	ESCHOLZMATT	03/22/1855	NY		FILM
JENNY	JEAN GEORGES	1823	KIENTZHEIM	05/02/1850	NO		FILM
JENNY	LOUIS	1824	KIENTZHEIM	08/02/1854	NO		FILM
JENTER	JOHANN		SCHLEITHAL	01/01/1821	A		NO.2
JENTHER	JACQUES		ALTWILLER	01/01/1828	A		FILM
JENTZER F OF 8	HENRY		SARREWERDEN	01/01/1828	A		FILM
JERMANN	FRANCOIS	1820	RIESPACH	09/26/1853	NY		FILM
JERR W W 2CH	JEAN BAPTISTE	1825	MITTELWIHR	03/11/1854	TX		FILM
JESSEL	FRANCOIS GILLES	1809	ST PIERREBOIS	01/11/1849	NY		FILM
JESSER	JOSEPHINE		ROHRWILLER	01/01/1828	A		FILM
JESSLEN	FRANCOIS JOSEPH	1819	BERRWILLER	01/31/1852	NO		FILM
JETZER	JOSEPH	1819	HEGENHEIM	08/07/1850	NY		FILM
JEUNE W W 1CH	MARTIN		KIECHLINSBERG	05/07/1833	A		FILM
JEUNER W W 4CH	JEAN		DUPPIGHEIM	03/28/1817	A		FILM
JIGON	MARGERUTHE	1820	CHEVENEZ	02/25/1864	NY		FILM
JIGON M.	HENRY	1840	CHEVENEZ	02/25/1864	NY		FILM
JIGON M.	JOSEPH	1821	CHEVENEZ	02/25/1864	NY		FILM
JOA	PHILIPP	1808	FELDREINACH	11/22/1843	TX		FILM
JOCKERLT	JAKOB		WILLSTAEDT	07/30/1849	TX		FILM
JODER	BABETTE	1836	ATTENSCHWILLER	08/16/1865	NY		FILM
JODER	CATHERINE	1798	MORVILLARS	03/12/1857	NY		FILM
JODER	CATHERINE	1781	MORVILLARS	02/08/1857	CD		FILM

Lastname	Firstname	Birth Year	Birthplace	Emigration	De	Prof	Source
JODER	CHRETIEN	1821	LARGITZEN	12/18/1841	NY		FILM
JODER	GREGOIRE	1828	MORTZWILLER	08/20/1847	NY		FILM
JODER	JEAN	1846	ATTENSCHWILLER	08/16/1865	NY		FILM
JODER	JOSEPH	1821	TAGSDORFF	12/09/1841	NY		FILM
JODER	MARIE	1849	ATTENSCHWILLER	08/16/1865	NY		FILM
JODER W 2 C	JACQUES	1791	HIRSINGUE	03/19/1841	NY		FILM
JODER W W	SIMON		DANJOUTIN	/ /	NY		FILM
JODER W W 3CH	JEAN	1796	STEINBACH	03/18/1845	NY		FILM
JODER W W 5CH	JEAN	1786	MORVILLARS	02/08/1857	CD		FILM
JODRE	MICHEL	1825	GRANDVILLARS	12/14/1844	OH		FILM
JODREY	FREDERIC	1846	ETOBON	08/23/1866	NY		FILM
JODREY	JULIE	1848	ETOBON	08/23/1866	NY		FILM
JOERGER	BARTHELEMI		ROESCHWOOG	01/01/1828	A		FILM
JOHLEG SCHLEG	PAUL		ZIEROLSHOFEN	07/31/1849	A		FILM
JOHO	MATHIAS	1811	KUENHEIM	05/15/1850	CH		FILM
JOLIAT	LOUIS	1827	BEAUCOURT	02/26/1851	NY		FILM
JOLIDON W W 6 CH	FRANCOIS	1806	VAUTHIERMONT	06/06/1846	NY		FILM
JONAS F OF 3	CHRETIEN		REIPERTSWILLER	01/01/1828	A		FILM
JONAS F OF 2	THOMAS		REIPERTSWILLER	01/01/1828	A		FILM
JONASSE W W 2CH	BALTHASAR		LA PETIT PIERRE	08/03/1817	A		FILM
JONNET	JOSEPH	1817	KINGERSHEIM	03/13/1855	NY		FILM
JONTE	JEAN PIERRE	1814	BELLEMAGNY	02/03/1839	NY		FILM
JONVEAUX	L		SOULTZ-SOUS-FORETS	01/01/1850	NO		PRIV
JOOS	ELISABETH	1830	MITTELWIHR	11/01/1854	TX	SERV	PASS
JORDAN	AGNES	1827	HOUSSEN	09/07/1850	NY		FILM
JOSEPH	CHARLES	1824	GUEBWILLER	05/19/1852	NY		FILM
JOSS	ADAM		WITTENDORF OR DORNHE	05/12/1849	A		FILM
JOSS	ELISABETH	1830	ST. HIPPOLYTE	11/03/1854	TX		FILM
JOST	DONAT		ALTSCHWEIER	09/30/1849	A		FILM
JOST	FRANCOIS THOMAS		ROESCHWOOG	01/01/1828	A		FILM
JOST	JOSEPH			06/05/1836	A		FILM
JOST W W 2 S	CHARLES FREDERC	1823	MUNSTER	05/29/1854	NY		FILM
JOSTE	CATHERINE	1772	ZINSWEILLER	02/16/1817	A		FILM
JOTTER	CATHERINE	1831	HIRTZBACH	03/22/1855	NY		FILM
JOUDAIN	MICHEL	1815	OFFEMONT	11/09/1846	NY		FILM
JOURDAIN	ARMAND	1841	BADEVELLE	02/15/1864	NY		FILM
JOURDAIN	CALESTIA	1835	EGUENIGUE	02/12/1853	NY		FILM
JOURDAIN	CELESTINE	1801	FRANCE	06/01/1861	NY		FILM
JOURDAIN	EMELIE	1840	BEDEVELLE	02/15/1864	NY		FILM
JUCHS	JOSEPH		FROESCHWEILER	01/01/1817	A		NO.2
JUD	ALOISE	1849	RANSPACH	05/31/1859	NY		FILM
JUD	ANNE		RANSPACH	05/31/1859	NY		FILM
JUD	JOSEPH		RANSPACH	05/31/1859	NY		FILM
JUD	JOSEPHINE		RANSPACH	05/31/1859	NY		FILM
JUD	MOISE		RANSPACH	05/31/1859	NY		FILM
JUD	MORAND	1818	RANSPACH	05/31/1859	NY		FILM
JUD F OF 3	MICHEL		INGWILLER	01/01/1828	A		FILM
JUDAS	FRANCOIS DAMIEN	1815	BLODELSHEIM	10/01/1851	TX	DAYL	PASS
JUDLIN	FRANCOIS	1820	BELFORT	09/03/1849	NY		FILM
JUDLIN	JEAN	1838	GRANDVILLARS	08/09/1855	NO		FILM

Lastname	Firstname	Birth Year	Birthplace	Emigration	De	Prof	Source
JUDLIN	JOSEPH	1813	THANN	04/28/1847	NY		FILM
JUDLIN	JOSEPH	1813	THANN	11/16/1851	NY		FILM
JUEKER W W 4CH	PAUL		POLOGNE	03/29/1817	A		FILM
JUELICH	HANSS ADAM		NIEDERBRONN	05/13/1838	A		FILM
JUEN	ANNE MARIE	1821	WOLSCHWILLER	05/18/1842	NY		FILM
JUEN	JOSEPH	1823	WOLSCHWILLER	05/02/1846	NY		FILM
JUEN	XAVIER	1834	BENDORF	11/07/1865	NY		FILM
JUENN W W 4CH	CHRISTIAN	1786	SCHRUNTZ	03/10/1838	A		FILM
JUIDE	ADOLPHE	1813	STRASSBOURG	09/03/1850	NY		FILM
JUIF	MARIE	1823	COLMAR	04/13/1855	NY		FILM
JUILLARD	CATHERINE	1839	VALENTIGNEY	12/20/1864	NY		FILM
JUILLARD	CATHERINE	1812	VALENTIGNEY	10/05/1866	NY		FILM
JUILLARD	EMELIE	1842	VALENTIGNEY	12/20/1864	NY		FILM
JUILLARD	EMILE	1840	VALENTIGNEY	10/05/1866	NY		FILM
JUILLARD	LOUIS	1835	MONTBELIARD	05/15/1863	NY		FILM
JUILLARD W W 5CH	NICOLAS	1798	OSTHEIM	04/24/1844	NY		FILM
JUILLERAT	JEAN PIERRE	1837	CHEVENEZ	02/24/1864	NY		FILM
JUILLET	JULES	1849	FRAHIER	02/03/1866	NY		FILM
JUIT	MARIE	1823	MEROUX	04/18/1855	NY		FILM
JUKER OR TUKER	FRANCOIS LOUISE	1824	BLODELSHEIM	06/03/1852	NY		FILM
JULIEN				/ /			
JULIEN	DANIEL FRANCOIS	1828	AUDINCOURT	03/27/1852	NY		FILM
JULLERAD W W 1CH	JEAN PIERRE	1793	MAGNY	07/02/1831	NY		FILM
JUNCKER	JEAN JACQUES	1794	RIGUEWIHR	03/20/1848	NY		FILM
JUNCKER W W 8CH	CHRETIEN		BAERENDORF	03/18/1817	A		FILM
JUND	VICTOIRE		WANTZENAU	01/01/1828	A		FILM
JUND F OF 7	MICHEL		INGWILLER	01/01/1828	A		FILM
JUNG	ADAM		PETERSBACH	01/01/1828	A		FILM
JUNG	CATHERINE		PETERSBACH	01/01/1828	A		FILM
JUNG	CATHERINE	1779	ZINSWEILLER	02/16/1817	A		FILM
JUNG	CHARLES		PETERSBACH	01/01/1828	A		FILM
JUNG	CHRETIEN		STRUTH	01/01/1828	A		FILM
JUNG	CHRISTIAN		LANGENSOULTZBACH	01/01/1845	A		SUESS
JUNG	FRIEDRICH		LANGENSULTZBACH	01/01/1857	A		SUESS
JUNG	GEORGE		BRUMATH	01/01/1828	A		FILM
JUNG	HENRI		ESCHBOURG	01/01/1828	A		FILM
JUNG	JEAN ADAM		PFALZWEYER	01/01/1828	A		FILM
JUNG	MARIE ANNE		HAGUENAU	01/01/1828	A		FILM
JUNG	MARIE ANNE		LEUTENHEIM	01/01/1828	A		FILM
JUNG	NICOLAS		PETERSBACH	01/01/1828	A		FILM
JUNG	PHILIPP		WEISLINGEN	01/01/1828	A		FILM
JUNG	PHILIPPE JACQUS	1794	ST. MARIE AUX MINES	03/11/1817	A		FILM
JUNG	QUINTIN		LUPSTEIN	01/01/1828	A		FILM
JUNG F OF 2	JACQUES		BISCHWILLER	01/01/1828	A		FILM
JUNG F OF 2	LAURENT		BISCHWILLER	01/01/1828	A		FILM
JUNG F OF 8	FRANCOIS JOSEPH		LEUTENHEIM	01/01/1828	A		FILM
JUNG MN BALLIG	CHRISTINA		LANGENSULTZBACH	01/01/1857	A		SUESS
JUNG S FRIEDRICH	PHILLIP		LANGENSULTZBACH	01/01/1857	NY		SUESS
JUNG W PHILLIP			LANGENSULTZBACH	01/01/1842	NY		SUESS
JUNG W W 2CH	GASPARD		OTTWILLER	03/03/1817	A		FILM

Lastname	Firstname	Birth Year	Birthplace	Emigration	De	Prof	Source
JUNG W W 2CH	PHILIPPE		PETERSBACH	03/11/1817	A		FILM
JUNG W W 4CH	CHRETIEN		LA PETIT PIERRE	03/03/1817	A		FILM
JUNGBLATT	JOSEF		SUNDHOFFEN	03/03/1838	A		FILM
JUNGBLATT W W 4CH	ANDRE		LA PETIT PIERRE	01/01/1828	A		FILM
JUNKER	CHRETIEN		BAERENDORF	01/01/1828	A		FILM
JUNKER	JEANETTE		BAERENDORF	01/01/1828	A		FILM
JUNKER	MADELAINE		BAERENDORF	01/01/1828	A		FILM
JUNKER	THERESE		BAERENDORF	01/01/1828	A		FILM
JUNKER CH 2	JEAN JAQUES	1805	THANN	01/01/1843	TX	SERR	PASS
JUNUELE W W 1S	JOSEPH	1794	HATTSTADT	08/23/1851	NO		FILM
JURY	JOSEPHINE	1807	DOLLENDORF	10/26/1843	TX		FILM
JURY	XAVER	1803	DOLLENDORF	10/26/1843	TX		FILM
JUSTER	JOSEPH	1832	VALDOIE	01/04/1851	NY		FILM

Lastname	Firstname	Birth Year	Birthplace	Emigration	De	Prof	Source
KABIS W W 1CH	JOSEPH	1816	KAYSERSBERG	04/13/1847	NY		FILM
KABLE	FERDINAND		SARREWERDEN	01/01/1828	A		FILM
KACHLER	CATHERINE		SOPPE-LE-BAS	11/01/1844	TX		PASS
KACHLER	CATHERINE	1820	GUEWENHEIM	11/18/1844	PH		FILM
KACHLER	DIDAMUS	1818	BALSCHWILLER	05/14/1847	NY		FILM
KADERLY	JACQUES	1823	CHAMPAUX	04/09/1844	TX		FILM
KADERLY	JEAN	1826	CHAMPAUX	04/09/1844	TX		FILM
KAEHL F OF 7			DOSSENHEIM	01/01/1828	A		FILM
KAEMMERLEN	JEAN BAPTISTE	1828	ST AMARIN	06/14/1847	A		FILM
KAEMPF	JOSEPH		ICHENHEIM	04/23/1849	NY		FILM
KAEPPELE	STEPHAN		BINDLINGEN B	09/30/1849	A		FILM
KAEPPELIN	AIME ANTOINE	1829	MULHAUSEN	04/26/1847	NY		FILM
KAERCHER F OF 2	GEORGES		DETTWILLER	01/01/1828	A		FILM
KAERCHER F OF 4	JACQUES		DETTWILLER	01/01/1828	A		FILM
KAERCHER F OF 6	MICHEL		DETTWILLER	01/01/1828	A		FILM
KAETZEL	PHILIPPE		STRUTH	01/01/1828	A		FILM
KAETZEL F OF 6	PHILIPPE		STRUTH	01/01/1828	A		FILM
KAETZEL F OF 2	GEOFROI		STRUTH	01/01/1828	A		FILM
KAETZEL F OF 2	NICOLAS		STRUTH	01/01/1828	A		FILM
KAETZEL F OF 6	GEOFROI		STRUTH	01/01/1828	A		FILM
KAEUFFER	JEAN BAPTISTE	1807	OBERSAASHEIM	04/03/1844	NY		FILM
KAFFER	MATHEUS		BILLINGEN W	06/01/1849	A		FILM
KAFNER F OF 6	JACQUES		MACKWILLER	03/02/1838	A		FILM
KAFTLER W W 3CH	MICHEL	1806	RIBEAUVILLE	08/04/1845	NY		FILM
KAH W S	VERONIQUE	1821	MOTHERN	11/06/1852	NY		FILM
KAHL	HEINRICH	1866	BRUEHL	01/01/1866	NY		NO.2
KAHL	SALOME	1867	BRUEHL	01/01/1866	NY		NO.2
KAHL 2 CH HEINR,SALO	ELISE	1839	BUEHL	01/01/1868	NY		NO.2
KAHN	ABRAHAM	1847	LAUTERBURG	01/01/1866	NY		NO.2
KAHN	ABRAHAM	1850	NIEDERBRONN	01/01/1866	NY		NO.2
KAHN	BARBARA		HERMERSWEILER	01/01/1865	NY		NO.2
KAHN	HEINRICH	1834	RIEDSELTZ	01/01/1864	NY		NO.2
KAHN	MOISE	1830	HATTSTATT	04/29/1852	NY		FILM
KAHN	ROSALI	1851	RIEDSELTZ	01/01/1868	NY		NO.2
KAISER	EVE		OBERHOFFEN	03/01/1838	A		FILM
KAISER	OTTO		KENTZINGEN B	04/21/1849	A		FILM
KAISER	SALOME	1846	MERCKWILLER	01/01/1869	NY		NO.2
KAISER	SEBASTIEN	1830	MULHOUSE	10/21/1854	NY		FILM
KAISER W W	CONRAD		GERMANY	04/12/1849	A		FILM
KAISER W W 1CH	CHRETIEN		OBERHOFFEN	01/03/1838	A		FILM
KALB F OF 7	JEAN		BRUMATH	01/01/1828	A		FILM
KALTENBACH	LOUIS	1817	RUELISHEIM	05/21/1845	A		FILM
KALTENBACH	MARTIN		SCHELINGEN B	04/14/1849	NY		FILM
KALTENBACH W W 1 S	MAXIMILIEN		STAFFELFELDEN	04/17/1852	A		FILM
KAMERITZ	JEAN	1825	COLMAR	08/23/1848	NO		FILM
KAMMER	JACQUES		WEITERSWILLER	01/01/1828	A		FILM
KAMMERER	ADELE	1825	ILLZACH	03/18/1856	SF		FILM
KAMMERER	KILIAN	1822	SIGOLSHEIM	02/09/1852	NO		FILM
KAMMERER W 2S	MICHEL	1820	RIBEAUVILLE	10/31/1854	NY		FILM
KAMPMANNN F OF 7	ERNEST THIM		BRUMATH	03/02/1838	A		FILM

Lastname	Firstname	Birth Year	Birthplace	Emigration	De	Prof	Source
KANDEL F OF 5	IGNACE		DAUENDORF	02/28/1838	A		FILM
KANIGSTEIN	CATHARINA		HOMBOURG	07/29/1849	A		FILM
KANNES F OF 5	JEAN		DETTWILLER	01/01/1828	A		FILM
KANTZ	CATHERINE		SCHERTZHEIM	08/13/1849	A		FILM
KANTZ	DAVID		SCHERTZHEIM	08/13/1849	A		FILM
KAPFER	JOSEPH		SCHWEIGHAUSEN	01/01/1828	A		FILM
KAPFER F OF 5	DAVID		SCHWEIGHAUSEN	01/01/1828	A		FILM
KAPFER F OF 4	NICOLAS		SCHWEIGHAUSEN	01/01/1828	A		FILM
KAPFER OR KAPPER	JOSEPH		SCHWEIGHAUSEN	01/01/1828	A		FILM
KAPP	XAVIER		KIENHEIM	04/01/1837	A		FILM
KAPPEL W W 4CH	JEAN LOUIS		TIEFFENBACH	03/29/1817	A		FILM
KAPPER	JOSEPH		SCHWEIGAHSUEN	01/01/1828	A		FILM
KAPPER F OF 4	NICOLAS		SCHWEIGHAUSEN	01/01/1828	A		FILM
KAPPER F OF 5	ANDRE		SCHWEIGHAUSEN	01/01/1828	A		FILM
KAPPLER W W 2CH	BALTHASAR		WINGEN	03/17/1817	A		FILM
KARCH	ROSINE		NIDERLAUTERBACH	01/01/1850	NO		PRIV
KARCH	XAVIER	1817	OSENBACH	01/17/1852	NY		FILM
KARCHER	ANTOINE	1837	COLMAR	08/02/1854	NY		FILM
KARCHER	EDOUARD	1826	COLMAR	03/06/1849	NY		FILM
KARCHER	HENRY		OFFWILLER	03/03/1817	A		FILM
KARCHER	JEAN	1825	COLMAR	02/28/1852	NY		FILM
KARCHER	MATHIEU	1832	COLMAR	08/02/1854	NY		FILM
KARCHER	NICOLAS		DEHLINGEN	03/03/1817	A		FILM
KARCHER F OF6	MICHEL		INGENHEIM	01/01/1828	A		FILM
KARCHER W W	LOUIS	1823	NEUWILLER	03/31/1857	NY		FILM
KARCHER W W CH	PHILIPPE	1831	COLMAR	08/02/1854	A		FILM
KARL	HENRI		DIEDENDORF	01/01/1817	A		FILM
KARL	LOUIS		HIRSCHLAND	01/01/1817	A		FILM
KARLE	ANDRE	1833	NIEDERENTZEN	02/01/1852	TX	DAYL	PASS
KARLE	ANDRE	1833	NIEDERENTZEN	02/06/1852	TX		FILM
KARLE CH 2	FRANCOIS JOSEPH	1806	NIEDERENTZEN	11/01/1854	TX	DAYL	PASS
KARLE W W	FRANC JOSEPH		ST CROIX EN PLAINE	11/07/1854	TX		FILM
KARM	FRANCOIS ANTOIN	1834	OBERENTZEN	09/01/1853	TX	DAYL	PASS
KARM	GEORGES	1826	OBERENTZEN	09/01/1857	TX	DAYL	PASS
KARM	JEANNE	1818	HAMBOURG	01/17/1852	NY		FILM
KARM W F	GEORGES	1820	OBERENTZEN	09/10/1850	TX		FILM
KARRER	JEANNE	1819	SOPPE LE HAUT	05/04/1838	NY		FILM
KARRER	PHILIPPE	1824	MEYENEIM	09/01/1850	TX	CULT	PASS
KARRER	THERESE	1823	MEYENHEIM	02/01/1852	TX	TAYL	PASS
KARSCH	ROSINE	1851	NIEDERLAUTERBACH	01/01/1866	NO		PRIV
KASPAR W W AND D	LAUDDIN		HASLACH B	05/22/1849	A		FILM
KASSEL	NICOLAS		ZITTERSHEIM	01/01/1828	A		FILM
KASSEL F OF 4	ADAM		ZITTERSHEIM	01/01/1828	A		FILM
KAST	ANNE MARIE		AMMERSCHWIHR	11/18/1854	A		FILM
KASTENDEICH	JEAN		HIRSINGEN	01/01/1828	A		FILM
KASTENDEICH	JEAN NICOLAS		DIEDENDORF	03/03/1838	A		FILM
KASTLER W W 3CH	MICHEL		RIBEAUVILLE	04/08/1845	NY		FILM
KATTNER F OF 9	GEORGE		DETTWILLER	01/01/1828	A		FILM
KATZ	JOSEPH	1822	CERNAY	08/11/1851	NO		FILM
KATZEL F OF 2	PIERRE		STRUTH	01/01/1828	A		FILM

Lastname	Firstname	Birth Year	Birthplace	Emigration	De	Prof	Source
KAUFAMNN	WOLF		NIEDERROEDERN	01/01/1866	NO		PRIV
KAUFFMAN	CHRETIEN		HIRTZBACH	03/23/1838	NY		FILM
KAUFFMAN W W	ELISE	1832	BELFORT	01/01/1866	NY		FILM
KAUFFMANN	BARBARA	1847	TRIEMBACH	01/01/1868	NO		NO.2
KAUFFMANN	BARBE		TRIMBACH	01/01/1850	NO		PRIV
KAUFFMANN	CATHERINE	1823	MASSEVAUX	06/07/1847	NY		FILM
KAUFFMANN	ESTHER	1843	TRIEMBACH	01/01/1865	LV		NO.2
KAUFFMANN	GEORGE		SCHILLERSDORF	01/01/1828	A		FILM
KAUFFMANN	IGNACE	1804	RAIMERSWILLER	06/21/1852	NY		FILM
KAUFFMANN	JACQUES	1817	HEITERER	09/14/1846	TX		FILM
KAUFFMANN	JACQUES		SCHILLERSDORF	01/01/1828	A		FILM
KAUFFMANN	LAURENT	1807	RIPPI	06/14/1848	NY		FILM
KAUFFMANN	LORENZ	1837	SCHWABWILLER	01/01/1837	NY		NO.2
KAUFFMANN	M	1842	ANDELMANS	03/14/1864	NY		FILM
KAUFFMANN	MARIE ANNE		SCHWABWILLER	04/17/1860	A		FILM
KAUFFMANN	MICHEL	1832	BERGHEIM	07/20/1854	NY		FILM
KAUFFMANN	MOSES	1850	TRIEMBACH	01/01/1867	NO		NO.2
KAUFFMANN	NICOLAS	1829	BLODELSHEIM	10/01/1851	TX	DAYL	PASS
KAUFFMANN	THERESE	1847	TRIEMBACH	01/01/1865	LV		NO.2
KAUFFMANN	VALENTIN		DAMBACH	03/12/1856	NY		FILM
KAUFFMANN F OF 4	MARIE		HATTMATT	01/01/1828	A		FILM
KAUFFMANN W 1CH	NICOLAS	1816	KAYSERSBERG	09/02/1849	NY		FILM
KAUFFMANN W W 4CH	JACQUES	1800	HUIENPACH	03/23/1838	NY		FILM
KAUFMANN	AGATHE	1827	ROUFFACH	03/31/1857	PH		FILM
KAUFMANN	ANNE		HATTMATT	01/01/1828	A		FILM
KAUFMANN	DANIEL	1827	BETTENDORFF	06/01/1845	OH		FILM
KAUFMANN	JACOB	1816	HEITEREN	11/15/1846	TX		FILM
KAUFMANN	JOSEPH	1824	LEVONCOURT	01/25/1845	OH		FILM
KAUFMANN	JOSEPH	1809	ROUFFACH	01/24/1856	PH		FILM
KAUFMANN	KARL	1852	ELSASS	/ /	LA		BULL
KAUFMANN	SALOMON		NIEDERROEDERN	01/01/1866	NO		PRIV
KAUFMANN	SALOMON	1849	NIEDERROEDERN	01/01/1867	NO		NO.2
KAUFMANN	WOLF	1845	NIEDERROEDERN	01/01/1869	NY	MERC	NO.2
KAUFMANN F OF 3	MICHAEL		HATTMATT	01/01/1828	A		FILM
KAUFMANN W W 7CH	CHRISTIEN		HALLEN	10/01/1846	A		FILM
KAUTZ OR KANTZ	DAVID		SCHERTZHEIM	08/13/1849	A		FILM
KAUTZ OR KANTZ	DOROTHE		SCHERTZHEIM	08/13/1849	A		FILM
KAYSER	JACQUES		PFULLINGEN ? W	09/04/1849	NY		FILM
KAYSER	JEAN		SESSENHEIM	01/01/1828	A		FILM
KAYSER	JOSEPH	1815	SAINT ULRICH	05/26/1845	NY		FILM
KAYSER	LAURENT		SESSENHEIM	01/01/1828	A		FILM
KAYSER	PIERRE		WILWISHEIM	01/01/1828	A		FILM
KEATIG	JOHN			01/01/1880	PH		FILM
KEBLER	JEAN BAPTISTE	1823	GEISHOUS = GEISHAUSE	04/09/1845	NY		FILM
KECH	FERDINAND	1808	LINTHAL	02/28/1840	NY		FILM
KECK	CATHERINE		AUENHEIM	04/21/1849	NY		FILM
KECK	FRANCOIS	1831	CERNAY	11/18/1851	NY		FILM
KECK	MICHAEL		AUENHEIM	04/21/1849	NY		FILM
KECK	PHILIPPE		ROESCHWOOG	01/01/1828	A		FILM
KEGREIS	JEAN	1843	RIQUEWIHR	07/29/1857	CH		FILM

Lastname	Firstname	Birth Year	Birthplace	Emigration	De	Prof	Source
KEGREIS	JEAN JACQUES	1840	RIQUEWIHR	07/29/1857	CH		FILM
KEGREIS W W 1CH	JEAN JACQUES	1817	MUNSTER	05/22/1854	NY		FILM
KEHR	JOSEPH	1835	ODEREN	07/03/1854	NY		FILM
KEHRES	FRANZ SEBASTIAN	1816	RUNTZENHEIM	01/01/1852	A		PRIV
KEHRES MN HEINTZMANN	BARBARA	1825	AUENHEIM	01/01/1852	A		PRIV
KEHRES S SEBASTIAN	AUGUST	1840	RUNTZENHEIM	01/01/1852	A		PRIV
KEIFER W W	JEAN		BUHLERTHAL	04/18/1849	NY		FILM
KEIFLIN W W 1CH	CHARLES	1804	VIEUX FERRETTE	12/23/1839	NY		FILM
KEIM	FREDERIC CHRETN	1826	MASSEVAUX	12/30/1853	NY		FILM
KEIMENBERGER	JEAN GEORGES	1822	POTHRAU OR POTHRAN	03/30/1847	NY		FILM
KEISER	MATHIAS	1817	ILLFURTH	05/07/1851	NY		FILM
KELDEN F OF 5	JEAN		HAEGEN	01/01/1828	A		FILM
KELLER	ANDREAS	1819	OBERENSISHEIM	11/22/1843	TX		FILM
KELLER	APOLINAIRE	1830	BURNHAUPT LE BAS	02/13/1857	NY		FILM
KELLER	EVE		VOELLERDINGEN	01/01/1828	A		FILM
KELLER	FRANCOIS	1826	NIEDERENTZEN	09/01/1846	TX	DAYL	PASS
KELLER	FRANCOIS	1826	OBERENTZEN	09/07/1846	NY		FILM
KELLER	FRANCOIS-JOSEPH	1805	NIEDERHERGHEIM	09/01/1846	TX	CULT	PASS
KELLER	GEORGES		REINHARDSMUENSTER	04/11/1853	A		FILM
KELLER	JEAN	1812	RIXHEIM	11/04/1851	NY		FILM
KELLER	JEAN PAUL	1833	COLMAR	08/02/1854	NY		FILM
KELLER	LOUIS	1823	BRUNSTATT	03/13/1847	NY		FILM
KELLER	MARIANNE	1825	OBERENZEN	11/15/1846	TX		FILM
KELLER	MICHEL	1819	COLMAR	09/08/1852	NY		FILM
KELLER	SOPHIE	1811	STRASSBOURG	09/16/1850	NO		FILM
KELLER	URSULE	1798	BRUEBACH	02/02/1850	NY		FILM
KELLER F OF 6	LAURENT		ST. JEAN DES CHOUX	01/01/1828	A		FILM
KELLER MN MANN	ANNE			09/01/1846	TX		PASS
KELLER W W 3CH	FRANCOIS JOSEPH	1807	NIEDERHERGHEIM	09/08/1846	TX		FILM
KELLER W W 3CH	GUSTAVE	1815	CHAUX	08/03/1844	NO		FILM
KELLERMANN	CHRETIEN CHARLE	1805	ST MARIE AUX MINES	07/13/1840	NO		FILM
KEMMERLIN	FERDINAND	1832	RANSPACH	01/01/1868	TX		PASS
KEMPF	ANTOINE	1775	MEYENHEIM	09/01/1846	TX	CARP	PASS
KEMPF	ANTOINE	1775	MEYENHEIM	11/22/1843	TX		FILM
KEMPF	ANTON	1807	MEYENHEIM	11/22/1843	TX		FILM
KEMPF	AUGUSTE	1844	LUTTER	06/22/1865	NY		FILM
KEMPF	BENJAMIN	1829	NIEDERENTZEN	11/01/1850	TX	CARP	PASS
KEMPF	CATHERINE	1806	OBERENSISHEIM	04/09/1844	TX		FILM
KEMPF	CECILE	1795	NIEDERENTZEN	02/01/1850	TX		PASS
KEMPF	CHARLES ALBERT	1826	GUEBWILLER	08/21/1848	NY		FILM
KEMPF	JAKOB	1834	OBERENSISHEIM	04/09/1844	TX		FILM
KEMPF	JEAN	1824	ALTENACH	02/15/1847	NO		FILM
KEMPF	JEAN	1834	VEBERSTRASS	08/07/1852	NY		FILM
KEMPF	JEAN THIEBAUT	1813	UEBERSTRASS	04/04/1840	NY		FILM
KEMPF	JOSEPH	1843	MEYENHEIM	11/22/1843	TX		FILM
KEMPF	JOSEPH	1822	NIEDERENTZEN	02/13/1850	TX		FILM
KEMPF	LUDWIG PHILIPP	1843	OBERENSISHEIM	04/09/1844	TX		FILM
KEMPF	MARIE AGATHE	1820	UEBERSTRASS	05/10/1845	OH		FILM
KEMPF	MARTHA	1805	OBERENZEN	05/29/1844	TX		FILM
KEMPF	MARTHA	1805	OBERENSISHEIM	09/04/1844	TX		FILM

128

Lastname	Firstname	Birth Year	Birthplace	Emigration	De	Prof	Source
KEMPF	SERAPHIN	1823	WALHEIM	07/14/1852	A		FILM
KEMPF	THERESE	1841	MEYENHEIM	11/22/1843	TX		FILM
KEMPF	THERESE	1829	WALHEIM	07/14/1852	A		FILM
KEMPF 3 CH	CECILE	1795	NIEDERENTZEN	02/13/1850	TX		FILM
KEMPF CH 2	THERESE	1790	NIEDERENTZEN	09/01/1855	TX		PASS
KEMPF W 2 D 1 NEPHEW	CATHERINE	1793	NIEDERENTZEN	02/13/1852	TX		FILM
KEMPF W THERESE	JOSEPH	1809	MEYENHEIM	11/22/1843	TX		FILM
KEMPF W W 2 CH	JOSEPH	1809	MEYENHEIM	11/15/1843	TX		FILM
KEMPF W W 6CH	LEONARD	1804	NIEDERENTZEN	02/10/1848	A		FILM
KEMPFF	JEAN BAPTISTE	1828	NIEDERENTZEN	12/23/1845	A		FILM
KEMPFF W 2 D	THERESE	1790	NIEDERENTZEN	09/07/1855	TX		FILM
KENTZEL F OF 4	CHARLES		DURSTEL	01/01/1828	A		FILM
KENTZINGER	FRANCOIS	1836	ST HYPOLITE	03/17/1857	PH		FILM
KERN	ANTOINE		BREITHAL	09/23/1849	A		FILM
KERN	BONNART		BUEHLERTHAL	04/19/1849	NY		FILM
KERN	DOMINIQUE		MEYENHEIM	12/20/1851	TX		FILM
KERN	MICHEL		SPARSBACH	01/01/1828	A		FILM
KERN	PAUL	1830	MEYENHEIM	12/01/1851	TX	DAYL	PASS
KERN F OF 2	JEAN		INGENHEIM	01/01/1828	A		FILM
KERN F OF 9	CHRETIEN		SPARSBACH	01/01/1828	A		FILM
KERN W W 8CH	XAVIER	1811	RAMMERSMATT	11/22/1843	NY		FILM
KERNE	JOSEPH	1811	LIEPVRE	08/23/1850	NO		FILM
KERNER	ANTON	1840	SCHAFFHAUSEN	01/01/1865	NY		NO.2
KERNER	JOSEF	1837	SCHAFFHAUSEN	01/01/1868	NY		NO.2
KERNER	PETER	1841	SELTZ	01/01/1865	NY	FARM	NO.2
KERNER	THERESE	1844	SCHAFFHAUSEN	01/01/1868	NY		NO.2
KERNMANN F OF 2	CHARLES		BRUMATH	01/01/1828	A		FILM
KEROL	LEOPOLD	1833	NEW ORLEANS	05/24/1849	NO		FILM
KERSCHENMANN	MADELAINE		SCHERTZHEIM	08/13/1849	A		FILM
KERSTINY	ANNA	1809		09/17/1845	TX		FILM
KERSTINY	HEINRICH	1844		09/17/1845	TX		FILM
KERSTINY	HERMANN	1837		09/17/1845	TX		FILM
KERSTINY W W 2CH	HEINRICH	1809		09/17/1845	TX		FILM
KERTH	BERNARD	1819	LANDAU	08/25/1854	A		FILM
KESLER	CATHERINE	1842		02/27/1857	A		FILM
KESLER	ROSE	1802		02/27/1857	A		FILM
KESLER MN LECRILLE	MARGUERITE	1800		02/27/1857	A		FILM
KESSEL W 3CH	JEAN JACQUES	1808	MITTELWIHR	03/27/1848	NY		FILM
KESSELER	ISIDOR	1878	MERTZWILLER	/ /	LA		BULL
KESSLER	AUGUSTIN	1814	RANSPACH	08/01/1844	TX	TOUR	PASS
KESSLER	GEORGE		STRASSBOURG	01/01/1835	A		FILM
KESSLER	JEAN	1796	RANSPACH	08/01/1844	TX	FACT	PASS
KESSLER	JOSEPH		BISCHWILLER	01/01/1828	A		FILM
KESSLER	JULIE	1836	BITSCHWILLER	05/24/1852	NY		FILM
KESSLER	MARIE LOUISE	1831	HERICOURT	09/01/1851	NY		FILM
KESSLER	SARAH		ELSASS	/ /	LA		BULL
KESSLER	VALENTIN	1826	ST. AMARIN	09/01/1856	TX	FACT	PASS
KESSLER W 3CH	BLAISE	1771	OTTINGUE	12/23/1839	NY		FILM
KESSLER W 4CH	AUGUSTIN	1814	RANSPACH	08/28/1844	NY		FILM
KESSLER-KAHN	MATHILDE	1864	ELSASS	/ /	LA		BULL

Lastname	Firstname	Birth Year	Birthplace	Emigration	De	Prof	Source
KESSLER-STERNFELS	CARIE	1869	ELSASS	/ /	LA		BULL
KETTENRING	JACQUES	1824	HOCHSTETT	03/29/1848	NY		FILM
KETTENRING MN MEYER	DOROTHE	1779	TRULBEN	11/19/1850	PH		FILM
KETTENRING W W	LOUIS	1827	HOCHSHILL	01/30/1849	PA		FILM
KETTERER	EVA	1850	OBERBETSCHDORF	01/01/1868	NY		NO.2
KETTERER	FRIEDRICH	1846	OBERBETSCHDORF	01/01/1867	NY		NO.2
KETTERER	JACOB	1847	OBERBETSCHDORF	01/01/1867	NY		NO.2
KETTERER	JOSEPH		HOCHSTETTEN	12/05/1849	A		FILM
KETTERER	MARIE-ANNE	1835	HERRLISHEIM	11/01/1855	TX	SERV	PASS
KETTERER	SISTER OF MARIE	1837	HERRLISHEIM	11/29/1855	TX		FILM
KETTERLIN W 5CH	MARIE LOUISE	1810	MICHELBACH LE BAS	12/13/1856	A		FILM
KEUN	DOMINIQUE		KIGLINSBERGEN	04/07/1849	NY		FILM
KEYSER F OF 4	JACQUES		DETTWILLER	01/01/1831	A		FILM
KICKK	JEAN GEORGE		INGENHEIM	01/01/1828	A		FILM
KIEBELEBER	JEAN GEORGE	1814	ST MARIE AUX MINES	10/06/1854	NY		FILM
KIEFER W 46 OTHER EG	ADAM		ALSACE	10/09/1836	A		FILM
KIEFFER	ANTOINE		MORSCHWILLER	01/01/1828	A		FILM
KIEFFER	FRANCOIS ANTOIE	1829	WALHEIM	03/18/1857	A		FILM
KIEFFER	GEORGE ADAM		SOUFFLENHEIM	01/01/1828	A		FILM
KIEFFER	GEORGES		SALLENTHAL	04/09/1853	A		FILM
KIEFFER	JEAN		UHRWILLER	04/09/1819	A		FILM
KIEFFER	JEAN THIEBAUD	1820	THANN	06/13/1854	NY		FILM
KIEFFER	JOSEPH		SOUFFLENHEIM	01/01/1838	A		FILM
KIEFFER	JOSEPH		RODEREN CAN DE THANN	04/09/1847	A		FILM
KIEFFER	LEGER	1823	TAGOLSHEIM	09/17/1851	NY		FILM
KIEFFER	MICHEL	1817	KUTZENHAUSEN	09/10/1845	NY		FILM
KIEFFER	THOMAS		BURCKENWALD = BIRCKE	01/01/1828	A		FILM
KIEFFER	XAVIER	1824	SOPPE LE HAUT	03/28/1854	NO		FILM
KIEFFER F OF 5	GEOFFROI		INGWILLER	01/01/1828	A		FILM
KIEFFER F OF 5	MARTIN		GRIES	01/01/1828	A		FILM
KIEFFER W 5 CH	CATHERINE		ASPACH LE HAUT	09/26/1849	NY		FILM
KIEFFER W W 4CH	MICHEL		UHRWILLER	04/09/1819	A		FILM
KIEFFER W W 7CH	ANTOINE		SOUFFLENHEIM	01/01/1828	A		FILM
KIEFFER W W 8CH	JOSEPH		SOUFFLENHEIM	01/01/1828	A		FILM
KIEFFREITER	MARGUERTE		DURSTEL	01/01/1828	A		FILM
KIEHL W FAMILY	GEORGE		ROTHBACH	01/01/1817	A		FILM
KIELSCH W W 4CH	ANTOINE	1803	LIXHAUSEN	04/15/1847	PA		FILM
KIEMER	LUDWIG	1836	SELTZ	01/01/1865	NY	SHMA	NO.2
KIENE	ANDRE	1822	UBERKUMMEN	01/25/1847	NY		FILM
KIENE	ANTOINE	1809	UBERKUMMEN	03/17/1847	NY		FILM
KIENE	AUGUSTE	1818	ROUFFACH	09/12/1846	NY		FILM
KIENE	CATHERINE	1828	MONTREUX JEUNE	09/10/1850	NY		FILM
KIENE	JOSEPH	1807	WEKIMMERL?	05/24/1851	NY		FILM
KIENE W W 2CH	JEAN	1805	UEBERKUMMEN	01/25/1847	NY		FILM
KIENER	JOSEPH	1802	NIEDERENTZEN	09/01/1846	TX	CULT	PASS
KIENER W W 5CH	JOSEPH	1802	NIEDERENTZEN	09/07/1847	TX		FILM
KIENLEN	BERNARD	1827	HOUSSEN	09/29/1856	NY		FILM
KIENLEN	MAURICE	1832	HOUSSEN	05/29/1857	NY		FILM
KIENSELE	FERDINAND		FRIESENHEIM	08/05/1849	A		FILM
KIENTZEL	CHARLES JOSEPH		HAGUENAU	03/01/1838	A		FILM

Lastname	Firstname	Birth Year	Birthplace	Emigration	De	Prof	Source
KIENTZY CH 4	HUBERT	1822	KRUTH	08/01/1860	TX	CULT	PASS
KIENTZY D HUBERT				/ /			
KIENTZY D HUBERT	ANNE-MARIE	1855	KRUTH	08/01/1860	TX		PASS
KIENTZY D HUBERT	MARIE-ANNE	1859	KRUTH	08/01/1860	TX		PASS
KIENTZY MN HEGRICH	ANNE-MARIE	1825		01/01/8180	TX		PASS
KIENTZY S HUBERT	SEVERIN	1853	KRUTH	08/01/1860	TX		PASS
KIENZLE	FRIEDEL	1817		10/25/1843	NY		FILM
KIESTNER W W CH			UNSHURST	05/24/1849	A		FILM
KIETZLER	JOSEPH	1831	KIFTIS	05/21/1866	NY		FILM
KILCKRE	JACQUES	1819	CHAVANATTE	04/03/1851	NY		FILM
KILHOFFER	FRANCOIS ANTOIE		REINHARDSMUENSTER	04/11/1853	A		FILM
KIMMENAUER	NICOLAS		REINHARDSMUENSTER	01/01/1852	A		FILM
KIMPFLIN	REME	1825	BOLLWILLER	10/12/1853	NY		FILM
KIMPFLIN W W	ANDRE	1822	MERXHEIM	12/10/1852	NO		FILM
KING	JEAN	1816	MULHOUSE	08/29/1851	NY		FILM
KINGUE W 4CH	MARIE THERESE	1786	LA CHAPELLE SOU CHAX	02/09/1842	OH		FILM
KINTZLER	MADELAINE	1822	ST MARIE AUX MINES	03/03/1850	NO		FILM
KIRCH XERFFER	PAUL		SOUFFLENHEIM	01/01/1828	A		FILM
KIRCHBERGER F OF 6	CHARLES		BOUXWILLER	01/01/1828	A		FILM
KIRCHER	FRANCOIS JOSEPH		MARLENHEIM	01/01/1828	A		FILM
KIRCHER	FREDERIC		WEINBOURG	01/01/1828	A		FILM
KIRCHER	JACQUES	1816	BURNHAUPT	05/13/1839	NY		FILM
KIRCHER F OF 8	MICHEL		MARLENHEIM	01/01/1828	A		FILM
KIRCHHOFF	JOSEPH	1827	NIEDERMORSCHWIHR	09/30/1848	NY		FILM
KIRCHHOFF W W	JEAN LEON	1831	NIEDERMORSCHWIHR	01/05/1854	NY		FILM
KIRCHMEYER	DOMINIQUE	1817	THANN	09/03/1845	NY		FILM
KIRCHNER	CHRISTOPHE		LANGENSOULTZBACH	01/01/1817	A	SHMA	NO.2
KIRCHNER	CHRISTOPHE		LAUTERBURG	01/01/1817	A	SHMA	NO.2
KIRCHNER W W 4CH	CHRISTOPHE		WUERTEMBERG	02/26/1817	A		FILM
KIRSCH	JOSEPH		SINGRIST	01/01/1828	A		FILM
KIRSCHBAUM	BARTHELEMY		DIERMINGEN	03/03/1817	A		FILM
KIRSCHER	FRANCOIS JOSEPH	1807	BURNHAUPT	04/06/1839	NY		FILM
KIRSCHER	FRANCOIS JOSEPH	1808	BURNHAUPT	05/04/1840	NY		FILM
KIRSCHER	FRANCOIS JOSEPH	1799	BURNHAUPT	05/04/1840	NY		FILM
KIRSCHER W W 5CH	JOSEPH	1782	BURNHAUPT	04/21/1840	NY		FILM
KIRTZINGER	ANNE		RENNINGEN W	04/18/1849	NY		FILM
KIRY	MICHEL	1818	BATTENHEIM	02/07/1849	NY		FILM
KISLER	GEORGE		WEITERSWILLER	01/01/1828	A		FILM
KISSEL	ADELE	1831	MUTZIG	03/05/1853	NY		FILM
KISTNER	GUSTAVE		OBERKIRCH	04/06/1849	NY		FILM
KISTNER	MARIE		OBERKIRCH	04/06/1849	NY		FILM
KITTENBRANDT	FRANCOIS JOSEPH	1820	MURBACH	02/09/1852	NY		FILM
KITTLER	JACQUES	1820	SAUSHEIM	07/28/1849	A		FILM
KITTLER	REINE	1825	MEYENHEIM	08/28/1855	NY		FILM
KLAPPENBACH	AUGUSTE		BARR	02/27/1838	A		FILM
KLAPPENBACH	JACQUES		BARR	02/27/1838	A		FILM
KLEFFER	APPOLONIA	1863	MUNCHHOUSE	01/01/1867	NY		NO.2
KLEFFER	ELISABETH	1865	MUNCHHOUSE	01/01/1867	NY		NO.2
KLEFFER	FRANZISKA	1837	MUNCHHOUSE	01/01/1867	NY		NO.2
KLEFFER	MARGARETHA	1864	MUNCHHOUSE	01/01/1867	NY		NO.2

Lastname	Firstname	Birth Year	Birthplace	Emigration	De	Prof	Source
KLEFFER	MARTIN	1859	MUNCHHOUSE	01/01/1867	NY		NO.2
KLEFFER	SABINE	1865	MUNCHHOUSE	01/01/1867	NY		NO.2
KLEFFER	STEFAN	1861	MUNCHHOUSE	01/01/1867	NY		NO.2
KLEFFER MN HORNUNG	FRANCISCA	1836	MUNCHHOUSE	01/01/1867	NY		NO.2
KLEFFER W W 2CH	FRANZ JOSEF	1838	MUNCHHOUSE	01/01/1867	NY	FARM	NO.2
KLEFFER W W 4 CH	PANTALEON	1827	MUNCHHOUSE	01/01/1867	NY	FARM	NO.2
KLEIBER	ALOIS	1835	STRASSBOURG	11/22/1843	TX		FILM
KLEIBER	EMIL	1839	STRASSBOURG	11/22/1843	TX		FILM
KLEIBER	JOSEPH	1833	STRASSBOURG	11/22/1843	TX		FILM
KLEIBER	KATHARINA	1841	STRASSBOURG	11/22/1843	TX		FILM
KLEIBER	THERESE	1803	STRASSBOURG	11/22/1843	TX		FILM
KLEIBER W W 5 CH	JOHANN GEORG	1801	STRASSBOURG	11/22/1843	TX		FILM
KLEIN	ADAM		KESKASTEL	01/01/1828	A		FILM
KLEIN	ANDRE	1828	BERGHOLTZ	04/23/1850	NY		FILM
KLEIN	ARTHUR	1847	SURBOURG	01/01/1865	NY		NO.2
KLEIN	BARBE	1826	MITTELWIHR	03/27/1848	NY		FILM
KLEIN	CHRETIEN		HAMBACH	03/08/1838	A		FILM
KLEIN	DAVID W W 9CH	1812	OSTHEIM	06/27/1854	NY		FILM
KLEIN	ETIENNE	1813	NEUKIRCH	09/05/1849	NO		FILM
KLEIN	FRANCOIS		GUTHENBERG BOHEMIA	07/31/1849	A		FILM
KLEIN	FRED		GERMANY	04/05/1849	NY		FILM
KLEIN	FREDERIC		BITSCHWILLER	02/03/1838	A		FILM
KLEIN	JACQUES	1778	STRUTH	08/12/1846	NO		FILM
KLEIN	JEAN		MELSHEIM	01/01/1828	A		FILM
KLEIN	JOSEPH	1857	NIEDERLAUTERBACH	01/01/1866	NO		NO.2
KLEIN	LOUIS	1818	GUEBWILLER	09/01/1849	PH		FILM
KLEIN	MAGDALENA	1840	NIEDERLAUTERBACH	01/01/1866	NO		NO.2
KLEIN	MARGARETHA	1859	NIEDERLAUTERBACH	01/01/1866	NO		NO.2
KLEIN	MARIE	1826	WEILLER	02/29/1856	NO		FILM
KLEIN	MARX	1852	HATTEN	/ /	LA		BULL
KLEIN	PAUL	1824	OBERSASSHEIM	06/28/1852	NY		FILM
KLEIN	PHILLIP JACOB		ROTBACH	01/01/1817	A		NO.2
KLEIN	PIERRE		NIEDERLAUTERBACH	01/01/1850	NO		PRIV
KLEIN	PIERRE	1840	NIEDERLAUTERBACH	01/01/1866	NO	BRLA	PRIV
KLEIN	PIERRE		HAMBACH	08/03/1838	A		FILM
KLEIN	RENE		HAMBACH	03/08/1838	A		FILM
KLEIN	THERES	1803	SIERENTZ	09/04/1857	NY		FILM
KLEIN	THIEBAUD	1815	STRUTH	10/24/1835	NY		FILM
KLEIN W 2 CH	ANNE ELISABETH	1812	ADAMSWILLER	12/02/1851	PH		FILM
KLEIN W W 4CH	ANDRE		DRUSENHEIM	01/01/1828	A		FILM
KLEIN F OF 3	JACQUES		HATTMATT	01/01/1828	A		FILM
KLEIN F OF 3	JACQUES		BISCHWILLLER	03/02/1838	A		FILM
KLEIN F OF 3	LAURENT		MARTENHEIM	01/01/1828	A		FILM
KLEIN F OF 4	JACQUES		MUTTERSHOLTZ	04/05/1838	A		FILM
KLEIN F OF 4	NICOLAS		KESKASTEL	01/01/1828	A		FILM
KLEIN F OF 5	GEORGES		MELSHEIM	01/01/1828	A		FILM
KLEIN F OF 5	NICOLAS JEAN		WEISLINGEN	01/01/1828	A		FILM
KLEIN F OF 6	JACQUES		SESSENHEIM	02/23/1838	A		FILM
KLEIN F OF 6	JEAN		ERCKARTSWILLER	01/01/1828	A		FILM
KLEIN F OF 6	JEAN GEORGE		GEUDERTHEIM	03/01/1838	A		FILM

Lastname	Firstname	Birth Year	Birthplace	Emigration	De	Prof	Source
KLEIN W 6 CH	ADAM		OERMINGEN	03/23/1817	A		FILM
KLEIN W F			KASKASTEL	03/23/1803	A		FILM
KLEIN W F	PHILIPPE JACQUS		ROTHBACH	01/01/1817	A		FILM
KLEIN W GR.D.	DAVID SENIOR	1786	OSTHEIM	02/08/1856	NY		FILM
KLEIN W W 2 CH	PETER		NIEDERLAUTERBACH	01/01/1866	NO		NO.2
KLEIN W W 2CH	ANTOINE		ESCHBOURG	03/17/1817	A		FILM
KLEIN W W 2CH	MATHIAS		OSTHEIM	04/13/1847	NY		FILM
KLEIN W W 2CH	NICOLAS		WEISLINGEN	03/23/1817	A		FILM
KLEIN W W 4CH	HENRY		HAMBACH	03/20/1817	A		FILM
KLEIN W W 5 CH	GEORGE		PFLAZWEYER	03/24/1817	A		FILM
KLEIN W W 5CH	LAURENT		BISSERT	06/03/1817	A		FILM
KLEIN W W 5CH	NICOLAS		WEISLINGEN	03/23/1817	A		FILM
KLEIN W W 5CH	PHILIPPE		KESKASTEL	01/01/1817	A		FILM
KLEIN W W 7CH	MICHEL		HAMBACH	03/17/1817	A		FILM
KLEIN-WEIGEL	JOSEPH		NIEDERLAUTERBACH	01/01/1850	NO		PRIV
KLEIN-WEIGEL	MADELAINE		NIEDERLAUTERBACH	01/01/1850	NO		PRIV
KLEIN-WEIGEL	MARGUERITE		NIEDERLAUTERBACH	01/01/1850	NO		PRIV
KLEIN-WEIGEöL				/ /			
KLEINELAUS	MICHEL		ETTENDORFF	01/01/1828	A		FILM
KLEINFELD W W	JOSEPH	1806	GUEBWILLER	05/25/1839	NY		FILM
KLEINHAUS	JEAN		ZIMMERSHEIM	07/05/1854	NY		FILM
KLEINPETER	ANNE MARIE		WANTZENAU	03/07/1838	A		FILM
KLEINRICHERT	JEAN	1796	RICHWILLER	12/30/1851	A		FILM
KLEINSCHMIDT F OF 2	MATHIEU		STRASSBOURG	09/01/1832	A		FILM
KLEISS F OF 3	GEORGES		ESCHBOURG	01/01/1828	A		FILM
KLEITZ F OF 5	JACQUES		DETTWILLER	01/01/1828	A		FILM
KLEITZ F OF 5	JACQUES		DOSSENHEIM	01/01/1828	A		FILM
KLEM	FRANCOIS ANTOIE	1835	HIRSINGEN	05/01/1857	NY		FILM
KLEM	GEORGES	1809	GUNDOLSHEIM	11/12/1852	SL		FILM
KLEM	JOSEPH	1833	HIRSINGUE	02/22/1851	NY		FILM
KLEM	PAUL	1824	OBERSAASHEIM	01/28/1852	NY		FILM
KLENCK	MARIE		KORK	04/21/1849	NY		FILM
KLENERT	GUILLAUME HENRI		DURLACH B	05/12/1849	NY		FILM
KLETT	JACQUES		DUSSLINGEN W	06/18/1849	A		FILM
KLETT	JEAN		DUSSLINGEN W	06/18/1849	A		FILM
KLING	DAVID	1848	HATTEN	/ /	LA		BULL
KLING	FLORENT		SINGRIST	01/01/1828	A		FILM
KLING	FRANCOISE		HOHENGROEFT	01/01/1828	A		FILM
KLING	GEORGE		PETERSBACH	01/01/1828	A		FILM
KLING	LAURENT		PETERSBACH	01/01/1828	A		FILM
KLING W SI	JOSEPH		HOHENGOEFT	01/01/1828	A		FILM
KLINGER	JEAN	1817	HOUSSEN	04/24/1845	NY		FILM
KLINGER W 3 S	MARIE ANNE	1809	BATZENHEIM	12/19/1850	SL		FILM
KLINGER W W 4CH	MAURICE	1811	HOUSSEN	03/30/1853	NY		FILM
KLINGMANN	JOS. PIERRE		HAGUENAU	03/01/1838	A		FILM
KLINTZ W 1CH	ANNE MARIE	1821	INGERSHEIM	05/20/1848	A		FILM
KLIPFEL W W 5CH	HENRY		NEHWILLER	03/11/1817	A		FILM
KLIPFFEL	AUGUST ANTOINE	1827	BARR	10/20/1854	A		FILM
KLOEPFER	SALOME		LAUTERBOURG	01/01/1850	NO		PRIV
KLOETZLEN	JOSEPH	1807	STRUETH	03/18/1865	NY		FILM

Lastname	Firstname	Birth Year	Birthplace	Emigration	De	Prof	Source
KLOPFENSTEIN	ANNE	1827	LEYMEN	02/28/1766	NY		FILM
KLOPFENSTEIN	ANNE	1851	LEYMEN	08/04/1865	NY		FILM
KLOPFENSTEIN	BABETTE	1860	LEYMEN	08/04/1865	NY		FILM
KLOPFENSTEIN	BENJAMIN	1839	LEYMEN	06/16/1865	NY		FILM
KLOPFENSTEIN	CATHERINE	1841	GUNDELDINGEN	04/08/1865	NY		FILM
KLOPFENSTEIN	CATHERINE	1833	LEYMEN	09/09/1856	NY		FILM
KLOPFENSTEIN	CHRETIEN	1842	LEYMEN	06/16/1865	NY		FILM
KLOPFENSTEIN	CHRETIEN	1837	LEYMEN	04/08/1865	NY		FILM
KLOPFENSTEIN	CHRETIEN	1862	GUNDELFINGEN	02/14/1855	NY		FILM
KLOPFENSTEIN	DANIEL	1833	ANDELNANS	02/10/1853	NY		FILM
KLOPFENSTEIN	ELISABETH		WIMMENAU	01/01/1828	A		FILM
KLOPFENSTEIN	GEORGE		ERCKARTSWILLER	01/01/1828	A		FILM
KLOPFENSTEIN	JEAN	1817	LEYMEN	04/08/1185	NY		FILM
KLOPFENSTEIN	JEAN	1858	LEYMEN	04/08/1865	NY		FILM
KLOPFENSTEIN	JEAN	1788	FLORIMONT	04/14/1841	NY		FILM
KLOPFENSTEIN	JOSEPH	1829	LEYMEN	06/16/1865	NY		FILM
KLOPFENSTEIN	JOSEPH	1829	LEYMEN	03/02/1852	NY		FILM
KLOPFENSTEIN	JOSEPH	1850	LEYMEN	04/08/1866	NY		FILM
KLOPFENSTEIN	LIDIE	1845	LEYMEN	04/08/1866	NY		FILM
KLOPFENSTEIN	MARIE	1857	LEYMEN	08/04/1866	NY		FILM
KLOPFENSTEIN	MICHEL	1843	LEYMEN	04/08/1866	NY		FILM
KLOPFENSTEIN W W 7CH	CHARLES	1805	BELFORT	01/26/1847	NY		FILM
KLOPFSTEIN	CHRETIEN	1820	BELFORT	09/17/1839	NY		FILM
KLOPFSTEIN	J	1841	CHAVANNES LES GRANDS	06/06/1865	NY		FILM
KLOPFSTEIN	JEAN	1807	LEYMEN	03/18/1846	NY		FILM
KLOPFSTEIN	MICHEL	1835	GUNDELFINGEN SWISS	03/03/1854	NY		FILM
KLOTZ	ELISE	1851	LAUTERBURG	01/01/1869	NY		NO.2
KLOTZ	JULIA	1847	SOULTZ-SOUS-FORET	01/01/1866	NY		NO.2
KLOTZ	SALOMON	1854	UHRWILLER	/ /	LA		BULL
KLOTZ MN ABRAHAM	JULIA		REICHSHOFFEN	/ /	LA		BULL
KLUMPP	CAROLINE	1840	ROPPENHEIM	07/12/1847	A		NO.1
KLUMPP	DANIEL		ROPPENHEIM	05/02/1850	A		SUESS
KLUMPP	GEORG	1844	ROPPENHEIM	07/12/1847	A		NO.1
KLUMPP	GEORGES	1829	ROPPENHEIM	10/05/1848	A		NO.1
KLUMPP	MARGARETHA SALE	1843	ROPPENHEIM	07/12/1847	A		NO.1
KLUMPP	THEODORE	1841	ROPPENHEIM	07/12/1847	A		NO.1
KLUMPP H RINCKEL 5CH	KARL	1813	ROPPENHEIM	07/12/1847	A		NO.1
KLUMPP H SALOMEA	KARL	1813		07/12/1847	A		PRIV
KLUMPP MN RINCKEL	SALOME ELISABEH	1816	ROPPENHEIM	07/12/1747	A		NO.1
KLUR	CHARLES	1829	INGERSHEIM	09/17/1846	NY		FILM
KLUSS F OF 4	JEAN		VOLKSBER	01/01/1828	A		FILM
KNAB W 3CH	JEANNE	1823	BERGHEIM	07/20/1854	NY		FILM
KNAL	JOSEPH	1842	KUHLENDORF	01/01/1869	NY	FARM	NO.2
KNAPP F OF 5	MICHEL		MENCHHOFFEN	01/01/1828	A		FILM
KNAUB	MARIE ANNA	1849	MOTHERN	01/01/1869	NY		NO.2
KNAUB	MARTIN		MOTHERN	01/01/1850	NO		PRIV
KNAUB	MARTIN	1840	MOTHERN	01/01/1869	A		NO.2
KNAUSS F OF 5	JEAN		DETTWILLER	01/01/1828	A		FILM
KNAUSS W W 2CH	GEOFFROI	1792	COLMAR	04/15/1846	NY		FILM
KNAUSS W W 4CH	JEAN FREDERIC	1787	MITTELWIHR	07/04/1846	NY		FILM

Lastname	Firstname	Birth Year	Birthplace	Emigration	De	Prof	Source
KNECHT	JOSEPHINE	1824	SENTHEIM	12/04/1847	NY		FILM
KNITTEL W W 1CH	FRANCOIS JOSEPH	1822	BENNWIHR	04/26/1854	NY		FILM
KNITTEL W F	ANTOINE	1789	BENNWIHR	04/26/1854	NY		FILM
KNITTEL W W 5CH	PIERRE LOUISE	1792	BENNWIHR	04/11/1846	CH		FILM
KNOBEL W 3 CH	MRS		MULHOUSE	04/26/1852	SL		FILM
KNOCHEL W SI 1CH	GEORGE		GUMBRECHTSHOFFEN	09/04/1849	A		FILM
KNODEL F OF 2	GEOFROID		ROMANSWILLER	01/01/1828	A		FILM
KNODERER W W 3CH	ANDRE		STRASSBOURG	05/12/1817	A		FILM
KNOEBEL	ANTOINE		EHRENSTAETEN B	12/26/1849	A		FILM
KNOEBEL	JEAN		EHRENSTAETEN B	12/26/1849	A		FILM
KNOELL	EUGENE		OBERSTEINBACH	01/01/1850	NO		PRIV
KNOEPFLE	JEAN	1797	COLMAR	12/11/1847	NO		FILM
KNOEPFLE W 4CH	MARGUERITE	1806	COLMAR	04/25/1848	CH		FILM
KNOERR	MARTIN	1841	MUNCHHOUSE	01/01/1868	NY	DAYL	NO.2
KNOLK	PETER		OBENHEIM	08/01/1854	NO		FILM
KNOLL	GEORGES		OBENHEIM	03/10/1838	A		FILM
KNOLL	JEAN BAPTISTE	1798	LIEPVRE	08/14/1838	NO		FILM
KNOLL	LEB		HORGEN W	05/24/1849	A		FILM
KNOLL W S	CATHERINE	1800	LIEPVRE	09/30/1854	NO		FILM
KNOLL W S AND D	CECILE	1805	LIEPVRE	11/05/1856	NO		FILM
KNOLL W W CH	JOSEPH	1834	OBENHEIM	03/10/1838	A		FILM
KNUTZ W W 8 CH	CHARLES		BAERENDORF	03/18/1817	A		FILM
KOB W W	JOSEPH	1828	SOULTZ	10/01/1850	TX		FILM
KOBEL W W 1CH	NICOLAS		HIRSCHLAND	03/20/1817	A		FILM
KOBERLE	LOUIS	1828	ST HYPOLITE	02/08/1853	A		FILM
KOBLENTZER	VALENTIN		RETSCHWILLER	01/01/1817	A		NO.2
KOBLER	CHRISTIAN		HATTEN III	01/01/1836	A		SUESS
KOBLER F OF 7	PIERRE		PFAFFENHOFFEN	01/01/1828	A		FILM
KOBLER SO PHILLIP	PHILLIP		HATTEN III	01/01/1836	A		SUESS
KOBLER W 2 SONS	PHILLIP		HATTEN III	01/01/1836	A		SUESS
KOCH	ANTOINE	1811	LIEPVRE	04/06/1839	NO		FILM
KOCH	FERDINAND	1841	MONTBELIARD	11/20/1865	NY		FILM
KOCH	FRANCOIS	1812	ZINSWEILLER	02/16/1817	A		FILM
KOCH	FRANCOIS ANTOIE	1822	EGUISHEIM	10/20/1865	NO		FILM
KOCH	JEAN GEORGES	1818	LIEPVRE	09/10/1838	NO		FILM
KOCH	JEAN GEORGES	1816	ZINSWEILLER	02/16/1817	A		FILM
KOCH	JOHANNA SOPHIE	1800	MUIDEN NETHERLANDS	04/09/1844	TX		FILM
KOCH	JOSEPH	1817	ZINSWEILLER	02/16/1817	A		FILM
KOCH	JOSEPH		GERMANY	05/04/1849	NY		FILM
KOCH	MICHEL		ESCHBOURG	03/03/1817	A		FILM
KOCH	NICOLAS	1828	MULHOUSE	03/03/1852	NY		FILM
KOCH	PHILIPPE	1797	GUEBWILLER	02/11/1841	NY		FILM
KOCH	XAVIER	1836	EGUISHEIM	09/18/1854	NY		FILM
KOCH W 1CH	CATHERINE		CERNAY	/ /	PH		FILM
KOCH F OF 3	ANDRE		SILTZHEIM	01/01/1828	A		FILM
KOCH F OF 3	PHILIPPE		BUST	03/01/1838	A		FILM
KOCH F OF 4	JEAN		SILTZHEIM	01/01/1828	A		FILM
KOCH W W 1CH	JEAN BAPTISTE	1806	LIEPVRE	05/16/1839	NO		FILM
KOCH W W 3CH	MARTIN		ZINSWILLER	02/20/1817	A		FILM
KOCH W W 3CH	MARTIN	1787	ZINSWEILLER	02/16/1817	A		FILM

Lastname	Firstname	Birth Year	Birthplace	Emigration	De	Prof	Source
KOCHELL			GERMANY	03/31/1849	A		FILM
KOCHER	GEORG	1838	OBERROEDERN	01/01/1869	NY	FARM	NO.2
KOCHER	MAGDALENA	1851	FORSTFELD	01/01/1868	NY		NO.2
KOCHER F OF 3	ANTOINE		ROESCHWOOG	01/01/1828	A		FILM
KOCHER F OF 4	LAUREN		ROESCHWOOG	01/01/1828	A		FILM
KOCHERLEIN W W 5CH	GUILLAUME	1812	NIEDERRAD	02/24/1854	NY		FILM
KOCHERT	JOSEPH	1851	EBERBACH	01/01/1867	NY		NO.2
KOCHHOFFER	MADELAINE	1823	WINGEN	07/02/1849	NY		FILM
KOCHL F OF 6	HENRY		BOUXWEILER	01/01/1828	A		FILM
KOCHLIN	GUSTAVE	1812	MULHAUSEN	07/15/1841	NY		FILM
KOCHLY	LOUIS	1829	BERGHEIM	06/16/1854	A		FILM
KOCHNIG	JEAN		WEISLINGEN	01/01/1828	A		FILM
KOCHNIG	PHILIPPE		WEISLINGEN	01/01/1828	A		FILM
KOEBEL	BARBARA	1864	OBERSEEBACH	01/01/1865	NY		NO.2
KOEBEL W CH	KATHERINA	1833	OBERSEEBACH	01/01/1865	NY	DAYL	NO.2
KOEBELING	FREDERIC	1839	RIBEAUVILLE	12/07/1855	NY		FILM
KOEBELL			GERMANY	03/31/1849	A		FILM
KOECHLIN	FERDINAND	1821	MULHOUSE	10/21/1853	NY		FILM
KOECHLIN	JACQUES	1813	PARIS	04/12/1850	SL		FILM
KOEGLER	JACQUES	1825	ST ULRICH	03/17/1853	NY		FILM
KOEGLER	JOSEPH	1820	ALTENACH	01/02/1847	NO		FILM
KOEGLER W W 3CH	ETIENNE	1798	FULLEREN	12/23/1846	A		FILM
KOEHL	JEAN MARTIN	1810	ST AMARIN	02/18/1848	NO		FILM
KOEHL	MARIE ANNE	1789	BERRWILLER	07/17/1856	NY		FILM
KOEHL F OF 7	ANTOINE		ESCHBOURG	01/01/1828	A		FILM
KOEHL W 3CH	MARIE ANNE	1811	BERRWILLER	09/14/1854	NO		FILM
KOEHL WW 5CH	HENRI		REIPERTSWILLER	01/01/1817	A		FILM
KOEHLER	BASTIEN		TAUDENBACH B	09/08/1849	A		FILM
KOEHLER W W	ANTOINE		STEINBACH B	10/04/1849	A		FILM
KOEHLHOFFER	PHILLIP HEINRIC	1847	RITTERSHOFEN	01/01/1866	NY	MERC	NO.2
KOENIG	ANTOINE	1823	ODEREN	11/01/1857	TX	FACT	PASS
KOENIG	BARBE		DIEMERINGEN	01/01/1828	A		FILM
KOENIG	BERNHARD		INGVILLER	01/01/1828	A		FILM
KOENIG	CHARLES	1830	GUEBWILLER	01/30/1849	NY		FILM
KOENIG	CHARLES LOUIS		BOUXWILLER	01/01/1828	A		FILM
KOENIG	ELISABETHE	1786	ZINSWEILLER	02/16/1817	A		FILM
KOENIG	GEORGE	1808	CARSPACH	01/08/1842	PH		FILM
KOENIG	JEAN		SCHERTZHEIM	08/13/1849	A		FILM
KOENIG	JOSEF		REICHSHOFFEN	01/01/1817	A		NO.2
KOENIG	JOSEPH	1793	BERRWILLER	09/16/1850	NO		FILM
KOENIG	MARAND	1813	OBERMORSCHWILLER B R	01/17/1852	NY		FILM
KOENIG	MICHEL		REICHSHOFFEN	01/01/1817	A		NO.2
KOENIG	NICOLAS		DIEMERINGEN	03/03/1838	A		FILM
KOENIG	PIERRE		DIEMERINGEN	03/03/1838	A		FILM
KOENIG	ROSINE	1818	ODEREN	11/04/1857	TX		FILM
KOENIG W CH	VALENTIN	1816	SOULTZ	09/12/1850	NY		FILM
KOENIG W W 2CH	SECHER ROMAIN		ROUFFACH	12/18/1843	PH		FILM
KOENIG F OF 4	ANDRE		BOUXWILLER	01/01/1828	A		FILM
KOENIG F OF 5	JACQUES		INGVILLER	01/01/1828	A		FILM
KOENIG W W 3 D	ANTOINE	1815	WINTZFELDEN	11/04/1857	TX		FILM

Lastname	Firstname	Birth Year	Birthplace	Emigration	De	Prof	Source
KOENIG W W 3 D	CHARLES FREDRIC	1823	ST MARIE AUX MINES	08/08/1857	A		FILM
KOENIG W W 4CH	GEORGE		MULHAUSEN	01/01/1828	A		FILM
KOENINGER	GEORGE		KAPPEL RODECK	07/23/1849	A		FILM
KOEPPEL	CHRISTINE		DEHLINGEN	01/01/1828	A		FILM
KOEPPEL	DOROTHEE		DEHLINGEN	01/01/1828	A		FILM
KOEPPEL	PIERRE		HAMBACH	08/03/1838	A		FILM
KOEPPEL F OF 5	PHILIPPE		HAMBACH	08/03/1838	A		FILM
KOEPPLER	LOUIS	1818	COLMAR	06/28/1847	NY		FILM
KOESTER	LORENT		BETTWILLER	02/28/1838	A		FILM
KOFFREITER	MARGUERITE		DURSTEL	03/18/1838	A		FILM
KOHLER			WERENTZHAUSEN	04/11/1866	NY		FILM
KOHLER	ALOYSE	1804	WURZACH W	06/03/1857	NY		FILM
KOHLER	ANTOINE	1823	KRUTH	08/01/1860	TX	TISS	PASS
KOHLER	AUGUSTE	1822	COLMAR	03/27/1845	NO		FILM
KOHLER	CATHERINE	1838	HERENTZHAUSEN	04/11/1866	NY		FILM
KOHLER	CATHERINE	1825	KUNHEIM	12/28/1854	NY		FILM
KOHLER	CATHERINE		ROTHENBURG W	09/05/1849	NY		FILM
KOHLER	CLOTHILDE		AUENHEIM B	03/05/1849	A		FILM
KOHLER	GANGOLF	1832	GUEBWILLER	03/09/1849	NY		FILM
KOHLER	JEAN		LAUCCHERTHAL	05/12/1849	A		FILM
KOHLER	JEAN JACQUES		SOULTZ W	06/23/1849	A		FILM
KOHLER	JOSEPH	1825	BISEL	10/11/1851	NY		FILM
KOHLER	LOUIS	1859	WERENTZHAUSEN	04/11/1866	NY		FILM
KOHLER	MORAND	1825	OBERMORSCHWILLER	06/22/1852	NY		FILM
KOHLER F OF 10	CHARLES		RANWILLER	03/07/1838	A		FILM
KOHLER F OF 4	JOSEPH.		DAUENDORF	02/28/1834	A		FILM
KOHLER F OF 7	PIERRE		PFAFFENHOFFEN	01/01/1828	A		FILM
KOHLER F OF 9	JEAN		DETTWILLER	01/01/1828	A		FILM
KOHLER MN GEWISS	AGATHE	1820		08/01/1860	TX	TISS	PASS
KOHLER W W 3 BR	FRIEDRICH	1818	EGG TYROL	07/26/1848	A		FILM
KOHLMANN W W	LUDWIG		STEIN B	08/05/1849	A		FILM
KOHLY	GEORGE	1829	RIQUEWIHR	11/26/1853	NO		FILM
KOHN	ANTOINE		RHINAU	01/04/1855	A		FILM
KOLB	GASPARD	1825	ROMMERSMATT	10/24/1845	NY		FILM
KOLB	GEORG	1846	RIEDSELTZ	01/01/1867	NY	FARM	NO.2
KOLB	JOSEPH	1820	SOULTZ	10/01/1850	TX		PASS
KOLL	JACQUES	1809	WATTWILLER	08/14/1846	A		FILM
KOLLER	ANTOINE	1825	HERRLISHEIM	11/10/1851	NO		FILM
KOLLER	DOROTHEE		FREUDENSTADT W	04/20/1849	NY		FILM
KOLLER	NICOLAS	1830	HERRLISHEIM	01/03/1852	NO		FILM
KOLLIGE	ANDRE	1827	OBERHERGHEIM	11/11/1848	TX		FILM
KOLLMANN	BARTH		KERRHOFFEN B	05/26/1849	NY		FILM
KOMENBERG	JOSEPH	1828	SWITZERLAND	09/30/1866	NY		FILM
KONIG	JOSEPH		REICHSHOFFEN	03/28/1817	A		FILM
KONIG	MICHEL		REICHSHOFFEN	03/28/1817	A		FILM
KONMAN MN HUTR. W D	MARTINE		IFELSHEIM B	05/03/1853	NY		FILM
KONTZINGER	ANDRE	1828	ST. HYPOLITE	03/05/1852	PH		FILM
KOOG W W 2CH	JOSEPH	1789	RIXHEIM	11/18/1851	TX		FILM
KOOI VAN DER	MAAS BOOKEN	1809	MUIDEN NETHERLAND	04/09/1842	TX		FILM
KOOS	JOSEPH	1814	RAMERSMATT	09/07/1846	NY		FILM

Lastname	Firstname	Birth Year	Birthplace	Emigration	De	Prof	Source
KOOS	MARIE ANNE	1787	RAMMERSMATT	10/21/1845	NY		FILM
KOPF	MICHEL		INGENHEIM	01/01/1828	A		FILM
KOPF	THIEBAUT		INGENHEIM	01/01/1828	A		FILM
KOPF	XAVIER	1822	CARSPACH	10/01/1851	NY		FILM
KOPF F OF 2	GUILLAUME		BOUXWILLER	01/01/1828	A		FILM
KOPP	FRANCOISE	1831	MULHOUSE	10/10/1857	SL		FILM
KOPP W W 3CH	JEAN MICHEL		PLOBSHEIM	05/12/1817	A		FILM
KOPPEL	LOUIS		HERBITZHEIM	01/01/1828	A		FILM
KORB	CHARLES XAVIER	1826	THANN	07/10/1847	NO		FILM
KORB	JOSEPH THIEBAUD	1833	THANN	04/26/1852	NY		FILM
KOSER F OF 5	MICHEL		WEISLINGEN	01/01/1828	A		FILM
KOSH	JEAN		BITTELSBRONN W	04/23/1849	A		FILM
KOSSLER W W CH	JEAN	1795	RANSPACH	08/28/1844	NY		FILM
KOSSMAUS	SIGEBERT		ROTHENFELS B	08/09/1849	A		FILM
KRAEHLING	ANTOINE		ICHENHEIM	04/23/1849	NY		FILM
KRAEMER	CHARLES		BERG	03/01/1838	A		FILM
KRAEMER	JEAN		OBERLAUTERBACH	01/01/1850	NO		PRIV
KRAEMER	JOHANN	1830	OBERLAUTERBACH	01/01/1865	NO	FARM	NO.2
KRAEMER	LAZARE		INGENHEIM B	01/01/1828	A		FILM
KRAEMER	MADELEINE		OBERLAUTERBACH	01/01/1850	NO		PRIV
KRAEMER	MARIE		DURBACH B	05/11/1849	A		FILM
KRAEMER	XAVIER		GRIESHEIM B	10/11/1849	A		FILM
KRAEMER F OF 4 JUNIO	JACQUES		INGENHEIM	01/01/1828	A		FILM
KRAEMER F OF 5 SENIR	JACQUES		INGENHEIM	01/01/1828	A		FILM
KRAEMER F OF 6	ANTOINE		WALDOWISHEIM	01/01/1828	A		FILM
KRAFFT	MARC	1800	RAEDERSHEIM	12/13/1853	NO		FILM
KRAFFT	PIERRE		FORT LOUIS	01/01/1828	A		FILM
KRAFFT	VICTOIRE		FORT LOUIS	01/01/1828	A		FILM
KRAFT	JOSEPH ANDRE	1817	CERNAY	11/29/1845	NO		FILM
KRAFT	LAURENT		RAEDERSHEIM	04/12/1843	NY		FILM
KRAFT F OF 6	JACQUES		NEUWILLER	01/01/1828	A		FILM
KRAFT F OF 2	FRANCOIS		ROESCHWOOG	01/01/1828	A		FILM
KRAFT W F	JOSEPH	1812	LUTTERBACH	07/25/1854	NY		FILM
KRAFT W W	JEAN		AUENHEIM	01/01/1817	A		FILM
KRAINK	CHARLES	1804	THANN	01/05/1857	NY		FILM
KRAINK	FREDERIQUE	1833	BASTE	03/30/1855	NY		FILM
KRAINK	JEAN GEORGE	1835	THANN	02/23/1853	NY		FILM
KRAMBS F OF 8	HENRY		SAVERNE	01/01/1828	A		FILM
KRAMCH	SUSANNE ELISABE		THANN	03/17/1845	NY		FILM
KRANIK W 2CH	SUZANNE ELISABE		THANN	03/17/1845	NY		FILM
KRANNER	AMBROISE		ZELL B	09/30/1849	A		FILM
KRAPF	JOSEPH	1841	ROSHEIM	10/01/1860	NY		FILM
KRAPF	SUSETTE	1839	ROSHEIM	10/01/1860	NY		FILM
KRAPP W W 2CH	BALTHASAR		LANGENSOULTZBACH	02/26/1817	A		FILM
KRATZMEYER	CHARLES	1826	LANGENSOULTZBACH	03/14/1838	A		FILM
KRATZMEYER	ELISABETH	1834	LANGENSOULTZBACH	03/14/1838	A		FILM
KRATZMEYER	GEORGE	1829	LANGENSOULTZBACH	03/14/1838	A		FILM
KRATZMEYER	SALOME	1810	LANGENSOULTZBACH	03/14/1838	A		FILM
KRATZMEYER W W 5 CH	JEAN GEORGE		LANGENSOULTZBACH	03/14/1838	A		FILM
KRAUNEN	CARL		KIGLINGSBERGER	04/07/1849	NY		FILM

Lastname	Firstname	Birth Year	Birthplace	Emigration	De	Prof	Source
KRAUS	JOHANNA		MALSCH B	09/30/1849	A		FILM
KRAUSHAAR	EMMANUEL	1824	GUEBWILLER	09/08/1846	A		FILM
KRAUT F OF 5	MATHIAS		DAUENDORF	02/28/1838	A		FILM
KRAUTH	MATHIAS		TROSSINGEN W	04/28/1849	A		FILM
KRAUTZ F OF 3	CHRETIEN		DETTWILLER	01/01/1828	A		FILM
KREBER	FRANCOIS	1816	LIEGEN	05/17/1848	NY		FILM
KREBNEL	JEAN	1800	BLAMONT	05/01/1860	NY		FILM
KREBS	BLAISE	1821	ACHEN	05/12/1849	A		FILM
KREBS	PIERRE	1828	BINNING	06/26/1851	NY		FILM
KREIGER F OF 6	MICHEL		BOUXWILLER	01/01/1828	A		FILM
KREIS	JACQUES		KIRRBERG	03/12/1838	A		FILM
KREITMANN F OF 7	JACQUES		BRUMATH	01/01/1828	A		FILM
KREMBLER	FRANCOIS XAVIER	1823	LA CHAPELLE SUR CHAX	07/24/1845	NO		FILM
KREMER	JOHANN	1838	OBERLAUTERBACH	01/01/1866	NO	FARM	NO.2
KREMER	MAGDALENA	1844	OBERLAUTERBACH	01/01/1866	NO		NO.2
KRESPACH W W 7CH	NICOLAS		AUENHEIM	03/01/1838	A		FILM
KRESS	FREDERIC		AUENHEIM	03/01/1838	A		FILM
KRESS F OF 7	ALOYSE		KILSTETT	05/12/1817	A		FILM
KRESSER W F	JEAN ADAM		GUNGWILLER	04/14/1854	NY		FILM
KRETZ F OF 3	JEAN		NOTHALTEN	01/01/1838	A		FILM
KREUTZBERGER	FREDERIC GUILLA	1824	GUEBWILLER	08/14/1848	PH		FILM
KREUTZER	HENRY		DIEMERINGEN	07/03/1817	A		FILM
KREY	FRANCOIS IGNACE	1813	BIESHEIM	05/27/1848	NY		FILM
KREYBULL W W 3CH	JACQUES	1803	DOMPIERRE	03/22/1839	NY		FILM
KREYBULL W W 4CH	JEAN	1794	ST SUSANNE	03/22/1839	NY		FILM
KREYENBUHL W F	JEAN	1805	DURRENENTZEN	05/06/1842	NY		FILM
KREYSEHR	ELISABETH	1814	ST MARIE AUX MINES	02/22/1849	NO		FILM
KRIEB			REININGEN W	04/18/1849	NY		FILM
KRIEG	JOSEPH		ZINSWILLER	03/28/1817	A		FILM
KRIEG F OF 5	JEAN		BRUMATH	01/01/1828	A		FILM
KRIEGELSTEIN	JEAN		BOUXWILLER	01/01/1828	A		FILM
KRIEGER	JOSEPH		OSTWALD	05/12/1817	A		FILM
KRIEGER F OF 3	FRANCOIS		HAGUENAU	03/01/1838	A		FILM
KRIEGER F OF 4	JACQUES		ZOEBERSDORF	01/01/1828	A		FILM
KRIEGER W	MARIA		ECKENDORF W	06/21/1849	A		FILM
KRIEGER W W	ANORE	1819	WILLGOTTHEIM	03/29/1855	NO		FILM
KRIMM	FLORENT		ENGENTHAL	01/01/1828	A		FILM
KRINTZ F OF 3	JEAN		NEUWILLER	01/01/1828	A		FILM
KRIPPLEBER F OF 10	MICHEL		BRUMATH	01/01/1828	A		FILM
KRIPS	JACQUES		REINHARDSMUNSTER	04/11/1853	A		FILM
KROETTNER F OF 8	CHRETIEN		DETTWILLER	01/01/1828	A		FILM
KROH	GEORG		LEMBACH	01/01/1844	A	COOP	SUESS
KROMER W W 2CH	ANTOINE	1825	BALDENHEIM	12/19/1850	A		FILM
KRON	MARGUERITE		RATZWILLER	01/01/1828	A		FILM
KROPF W W 3CH	JACQUES		BALDENHEIM	02/22/1819	A		FILM
KROPP	BALTHAZAR		LANGENSOULTZBACH	01/01/1817	A	WAMA	NO.2
KROPP W W 2CH	BALTHASAR		LANGENSOULTZBACH	02/26/1817	A		FILM
KRUG F OF 5	JACQUES		MACKWILLER	03/02/1838	A		FILM
KRUGLEN W W CH	NAR		SCHWEIGHAUSEN	/ /	A		FILM
KRUST	THIEBAUD	1816	ASPACH LE BAS	08/14/1840	NO		FILM

Lastname	Firstname	Birth Year	Birthplace	Emigration	De	Prof	Source
KRUTZER	PIERRE		DIEMERINGEN	03/03/1817	A		FILM
KUBLER	JACQUES	1820	COLMAR	09/21/1854	NO		FILM
KUBLER	JEAN MATHIAS	1825	RODEREN	11/07/1853	NY		FILM
KUBLER W W 5CH	JEAN		BADEN	06/22/1833	A		FILM
KUCHEL	MARIE SALOME	1820	OSTHEIM	12/24/1853	NY		FILM
KUCHEL	SALOME	1815	OSTHEIM	02/12/1856	NY		FILM
KUCK	JACQUES		BISCHWILLER	03/02/1838	A		FILM
KUEHNLE	CATHERINE		DURLACH B	05/12/1849	NY		FILM
KUEN W W 2CH	JEAN	1810	HERRLISHEIM	12/30/1852	SL		FILM
KUEN W W 2CH	MATHIAS	1820	MULHOUSEN	03/25/1847	NY		FILM
KUEN W W 4CH	JOSEPH	1816	HERRLISHEIM	09/03/1852	NY		FILM
KUENEMANN	PIERRE	1813	MORTZWILLER	02/26/1840	A		FILM
KUENEMANN	THIEBAUT	1816	MORTZWILLER	03/27/1852	NY		FILM
KUENEMANN W 8CH	THIEBAUT	1803	RAMMERSMATT	06/18/1846	NY		FILM
KUENEMANN W W	FRANCOIS JOSEPH	1814	BURNHAUPT LE BAS	10/25/1850	SL		FILM
KUENT	PAUL	1837	MEYENHEIM	01/16/1858	TX		FILM
KUENTZ	JACQUES		BOUXWILLER	04/20/1841	NY		FILM
KUENTZ	LAURENT	1833	SIEGEN	08/29/1854	NY		FILM
KUENTZ	PAUL	1835	MEYENHEIM	01/01/1856	TX	SADD	PASS
KUENTZ	SEBASTIEN	1823	MEYENHEIM	02/01/1852	TX	CULT	PASS
KUESTNER			UNHURST B	05/24/1849	A		FILM
KUESTNER	ANTOINE		RENCHEN B	10/27/1849	A		FILM
KUESTNER	FRANCOIS ANTOIN		RENCHEN B	10/27/1849	A		FILM
KUFFLER	MARIE ELISABETH		HERBITZHEIM	01/01/1828	A		FILM
KUGEL W W 4CH	MICHEL		KIRRBERG	03/20/1817	A		FILM
KUGLER	JACQUES		BISCHWILLER	02/03/1838	A		FILM
KUGLER F OF 4	JACQUES		BISCHWILLER	03/02/1838	A		FILM
KUGLER F OF 4	PIERRE		BISCHWILLER	03/02/1838	A		FILM
KUGLER F OF 5	JEAN ADAM		SESSENHEIM	02/23/1838	A		FILM
KUHLMANN	JEAN BAPTISTE		SCHLESTADT	03/02/1838	A		FILM
KUHN	EVA	1841	SCHOENBOURG	01/01/1865	NY		NO.2
KUHN	FRANCOIS	1794	RUESTENHART	06/12/1846	A		FILM
KUHN	GEORG	1845	LOBSANN	01/01/1867	NY		NO.2
KUHN	LAMBRECHT		REICHSHOFFEN	01/01/1869	A		NO.2
KUHN	LOUIS		GOTTENHAUSEN	01/01/1828	A		FILM
KUHN F OF 9	JOSEPH		RUNTZENHEIM	01/01/1828	A		FILM
KUHN W W 2CH	BERNHARD		STRASSBOURG	06/04/1817	A		FILM
KUHNER	AMBROISE	1829	MALMERSPACH	10/20/1854	NO		FILM
KUIN W W A S A D IL	JOSEPH	1807	ERSTEIN	10/05/1849	NO		FILM
KUNDERMANN	LOUISE		BRETTEN B	06/21/1849	A		FILM
KUNEGEL	NICOLAS	1837	ARTZENHEIM	11/27/1856	NY		FILM
KUNEMANN	ARMANDE	1825	CERNAY	06/23/1855	NY		FILM
KUNG W 1CH	MARIE ELISABETH	1818	NIEDERWYL	11/06/1847	NY		FILM
KUNRAD	LORENZ		ALTSCHWEIER	09/30/1849	A		FILM
KUNTZ	FERDINAND VICTR	1832	COLMAR	06/03/1856	NY		FILM
KUNTZ	HEINRICH	1838	BRUEHL	01/01/1867	NY		NO.2
KUNTZ	JACQUES HENRI		DOSSENHEIM	01/01/1828	A		FILM
KUNTZ	JEAN	1837	BERGHEIM	04/11/1855	NY		FILM
KUNTZ	JOSEPH		WANTZENAU	01/03/1838	A		FILM
KUNTZ	PHILLIP	1843	WEILER	01/01/1865	NY	TAYL	NO.2

Lastname	Firstname	Birth Year	Birthplace	Emigration	De	Prof	Source
KUNTZ	SOPHIE	1850	WEILER	01/01/1865	NY		NO.2
KUNTZ F OF 5	JACQUES		DOSSENHEIM	01/01/1828	A		FILM
KUNTZ F OF 4	CHRETIEN		DOSSENHEIM	01/01/1828	A		FILM
KUNTZEL	CHARLES JOSEPH		HAGUENAU	03/01/1838	A		FILM
KUNTZMANN F OF 6	ANDRE		FORT LOUIS	01/01/1828	A		FILM
KUNZ	JOHANN JACOB		NIEDERBRONN	05/13/1838	A		FILM
KUONY	JEAN BAPTISTE		SOPPE LE BAS	10/30/1851	NY		FILM
KUPFERLE			LAUTERBOURG	01/01/1850	NO		PRIV
KUPFERSCHMIED			GERMANY	04/01/1849	NY		FILM
KUPP	MADELAINE		GERMANY	04/01/1849	NY		FILM
KUPPELMEYER	JEAN LOUIS	1786	LAUTENBOURG	05/18/1840	NY		FILM
KUPPER	CATHERINA	1824	OBERSTEINBACH	/ /	A		PRIV
KUPPER	MAGDALENA	1814	OBERSTEINBACH	/ /	A		PRIV
KUPPINGER W 1 CH	ELISABETH		STEIN B	05/08/1849	A		FILM
KURG	MADELAINE	1819	KOETZINGUE	10/02/1854	NY		FILM
KURRUS	MADELAINE		BADEN	05/10/1833	A		FILM
KURRUS	MARIE		BADEN	05/10/1833	A		FILM
KURTZ W W	ANTOINE		REICHSHOFFEN	03/22/1817	A		FILM
KURTZ F OF 3	MICHEL		PETERSBACH	01/01/1828	A		FILM
KURTZ F OF 6	PIERRE		FROHMUHL	01/01/1828	A		FILM
KURTZ W W 6 CH	ARMAND		STRUTH	03/03/1817	A		FILM
KURTZEMANN	ALEXANDRE	1822	HUSSEREN	07/20/1854	NY		FILM
KURTZEMANN	JEAN	1819	MOOSCH	08/01/1844	TX	FACT	PASS
KURTZEMANN CH 3	VALENTIN	1823	ST. AMARIN	08/01/1860	TX	DRIV	PASS
KURTZEMANN D VALENTN	CAROLINE	1860	ST. AMARIN	08/01/1860	TX		PAS
KURTZEMANN D VALENTN	CATHERINE	1857	ST. AMARIN	08/01/1860	TX		PASS
KURTZEMANN S VALENTN	CHARLES	1856	ST. AMARIN	08/01/1860	TX		PASS
KURTZMANN	JEAN	1819	MOOSCH	08/28/1844	NO		FILM
KURZMANN W W 7CH	MARTIN	1806	RANSPACH	07/16/1846	A		FILM
KUSSEL W W 7CH	ANTOINE		ROESCHWOOG	07/16/1846			FILM
KUSSLER	MADELAINE		RIQUEWIHR	09/20/1852	NY		FILM
KUTTLER W W 2CH	SEBASTIEN	1806	STERNENBERG	04/02/1840	NY		FILM
KUTZEMANNMNBOBENRIET	CATHERINE	1827		08/01/1860	TX		PASS

Lastname	Firstname	Birth Year	Birthplace	Emigration	De	Prof	141 Source
L<'HOMME	MARGUERITE	1830	DORNACH	11/04/1853	NY		FILM
LA BRELLE	AUGUSTIN	1833	GILDWILLER	03/12/1854	BU		FILM
LABICHE	ALFRED	1835	ENSISHEIM	10/31/1853	NY		FILM
LABICHE	HENRY	1826	ENSISHEIM	06/06/1849	PH		FILM
LABIGOUL WW AND CH 6				/ /			
LABIGOUL WW ANDCH 6	LOUIS		HARSKIRCHEN	03/06/1817	A		FILM
LABLOTIER	JULES	1841	BREBOTTE	04/09/1863	NY		FILM
LABLOTIERE	JEAN BAPTISTE	1835	MERROUX	03/07/1854	NY		FILM
LABLOTTER	JULES		BREBOTTE	04/09/1863	NY		FILM
LABONTE WW AND CH 1	PHILIPPE		HAMBACH	03/20/1817	A		FILM
LABONTE WW AND CH 7	MARTIN		WIMMENAU	01/01/1817	A		FILM
LABOUEBE	EMILE	1844	MONTREUX	06/16/1866	NY		FILM
LABOUEBE	JOSEPH	1822	LUTRAN	02/25/1853	NY		FILM
LABOUEBE	PIERRE JOSEPH	1828	LUTRAN	03/08/1851	NY		FILM
LABOUEBE	PIERRE JOSEPH	1828	LUTRAN	04/09/1847	NO		FILM
LACHENAL	ANDRE	1835	PREVESSIN	11/04/1864	NY		FILM
LACHER	THOMAS LOUIS	1825	GUEBWILLER	07/28/1849	NY		FILM
LACOLOMBE	CHARLES	1849	BELFORT	08/24/1866	NY		FILM
LADER	PANTALEON	1828	KRUTH	09/14/1854	TX		FILM
LAEDERLE	AUGUSTE		OFFENBURG	11/10/1849	A		FILM
LAEDLIN	ADELE	1856	WEISSENBURG	01/01/1866	NY		NO.2
LAEDLIN	AMALIE	1849	WEISSENBURG	01/01/1866	NY		NO.2
LAEDLIN	AUGUST	1858	WEISSENBURG	01/01/1866	NY		NO.2
LAEDLIN	BAPTIST	1852	WEISSENBURG	01/01/1866	NY		NO.2
LAEDLIN	HENRIETTE	1865	WEISSENBURG	01/01/1866	NY		NO.2
LAEDLIN	PHILIPP	1854	WEISSENBURG	01/01/1866	NY		NO.2
LAEDLIN MN TILLIE	ADELE	1831	WEISSENBURG	01/01/1866	NY		NO.2
LAEDLIN W W 6 CH	THOMAS	1820	WEISSENBURG	01/01/1866	NY		NO.2
LAEMELEN	JACQUES	1826	RIXHEIM	12/13/1848	NO		FILM
LAEMLE	MATHIAS	1831	BREIZENBACH	07/05/1854	PH		FILM
LAEMLEN	JACQUES	1826	RIXHEIM	12/13/1848	NO		FILM
LAENGER	FERDINAND	1823	GUEMAR	12/17/1851	NY		FILM
LAENGER	SEBASTIEN	1828	GUEMAR	02/23/1857	NY		FILM
LAEUFER	JOHANN JACOB		WOERTH	01/01/1847	A		SUESS
LAFONGE	ABEL	1865	FRAISSE	03/06/1866	NY		FILM
LAFONGE	ALEXANDRE	1835	FRAISSE	03/06/1866	NY		FILM
LAFONGE	APOLINE	1843	FRAISSE	03/06/1866	NY		FILM
LAFONGE	AUGUSTIN	1864	FRAISSE	03/06/1866	NY		FILM
LAFONGE	CELESTINE	1836	FRAISSE	03/06/1866	NY		FILM
LAFONGE	CONSTANCE	1859	FRAISSE	03/06/1866	NY		FILM
LAFONGE	CONSTANCE	1864	FRAISSE	03/06/1866	NY		FILM
LAFONGE	CONSTANT	1866	FRAISSE	03/06/1866	NY		FILM
LAFONGE	DELPHIN	1852	FRAISSE	03/06/1866	NY		FILM
LAFONGE	FELECIE	1850	FRAISSE	03/06/1866	NY		FILM
LAFONGE	FELECIE	1864	FRAISSE	03/06/1866	NY		FILM
LAFONGE	FELICIE	1845	FRAISSE	03/06/1866	NY		FILM
LAFONGE	FERDINAND	1833	FRAISSE	03/06/1866	NY		FILM
LAFONGE	FERDINAND	1866	FRAISSE	03/06/1866	NY		FILM
LAFONGE	FRAISINE	1840	FRAISSE	03/06/1866	NY		FILM
LAFONGE	FRANCOIS ARSENE	1864	FRAISSE	03/06/1866	NY		FILM

Lastname	Firstname	Birth Year	Birthplace	Emigration	De	Prof	Source
LAFONGE	FRANCOIS PIERRE	1821	FRAISSE	03/06/1866	NY		FILM
LAFONGE	FRANCOISE EUGEN	1862	FRAISSE	03/06/1866	NY		FILM
LAFONGE	JOSEPH	1801	FRAISSE	03/06/1866	NY		FILM
LAFONGE	JOSEPH	1839	FRAISSE	03/06/1866	NY		FILM
LAFONGE	JOSEPH	1866	FRAISSE	03/06/1866	NY		FILM
LAFONGE	JOSEPZH	1832	FRAISSE	03/06/1866	NY		FILM
LAFONGE	LUDIVINE	1859	FRAISSE	03/06/1866	NY		FILM
LAFONGE	MARIANNE	1803	FRAISSE	03/06/1866	NY		FILM
LAFONGE	MARIE	1829	FRAISSE	03/06/1866	NY		FILM
LAFONGE	MARIE	1836	FRAISSE	03/06/1866	NY		FILM
LAFONGE	MARIE	1864	FRAISSE	03/06/1866	NY		FILM
LAFONGE	XAVIER FRANCOIS	1823	FRAISSE	03/06/1866	NY		FILM
LAGUESSE	JEAN DOMINIQUE	1808	ROMBACH	08/24/1838	NY		FILM
LAIBE	JEAN PIERRE	1814	FAREROIS	04/06/1847	NY		FILM
LAIBE	JOSEPHINE	1832	ST. DIZIER	01/02/1855	NO		FILM
LALLEMENT	HENRI	1797	MAGNY	02/08/1844	NY		PRIV
LAMA WW AND CH 2	JEAN CHRISTOPHE		STRASBOURG	05/27/1817	A		FILM
LAMBELIN	MARGUERITE FLOR	1830	SERMAMAGNY	01/22/1853	NO		FILM
LAMBELIN	PIERRE	1798	ROUGEMONT	02/24/1840	PH		PRIV
LAMBELIN WW AND CH 6	PIERRE	1798	ROUGEMONT	02/24/1840	PH		FILM
LAMBERT	LOUIS	1800	ODRATZHEIM,	02/17/1852	NO		FILM
LAMBERT	LOUIS PHILIPPE	1830	AUXELLES-HAUT	09/19/1850	NO		FILM
LAMBERT F OF 6	JOSEPH		SCHIRRHEIN	03/05/1838	A		FILM
LAMBLEC	AUGUSTE	1831	CERNAY	03/07/1854	NY		FILM
LAMBLIN	JOSEPH	1839	ROUGEMONT	09/28/1866	NY		FILM
LAMBOLE	FRANCOIS JOSEPH	1826	ANGEOT	02/28/1846	CT		FILM
LAMBOUR	HUBERT		BURCKENWALD	01/01/1828	A		FILM
LAMBOUR	LOUIS		BURCKENWALD	01/01/1828	A		FILM
LAMBRECHT	FERDINAND	1839	GUEBWILLER	09/30/1857	NY		FILM
LAMEY	GEORGES	1817	GRIESBACH	08/23/1853	NY		FILM
LAMEY	MARIE ANNE		GOTTENHAUSEN	01/01/1828	A		FILM
LAMGE	HENRY			09/26/1854	NO		FILM
LAMS WW AND CH 3	GEORGE		DUNTZENHEIM	01/01/1828	A		FILM
LAMS D GEORGE	CATHERINE		DUNTZENHEIM	01/01/1828	A		FILM
LAMS D GEORGE	MARGUERITE		DUNTZENHEIM	01/01/1828	A		FILM
LAMS H CATHERINE	GEORGE		DUNTZENHEIM	01/01/1828	A		FILM
LAMS S GEORGE	SEBASTEIN		DUNTZENHEIM	01/01/1828	A		FILM
LAMS W GEORGE	CATHERINE		DUNTZENHEIM	01/01/1828	A		FILM
LAMY F OF 7	GEORGES		DIEDENDORF	03/03/1838	A		FILM
LANDSEE	JOSEPH		GERMANY	04/05/1849	NY		FILM
LANDWERLEN WW AND CH	JEAN	1832	BALDERSHEIM	09/18/1854	NY		FILM
LANG	BARUCH	1833	DURMENACH	10/25/1853	NY		FILM
LANG	CATHERINE		NEUSATZ	07/13/1849	A		FILM
LANG	DAVID	1832	DURMENACH	06/29/1853	NY		FILM
LANG	DAVID	1832	DURMENACH	09/09/1851	NO		FILM
LANG	GEORGES		BUHL	05/24/1837	A		FILM
LANG	JACQUES		UHRWILLER	04/30/1839	A		FILM
LANG	JOHANN		UHRWILLER	01/01/1817	A		NO.2
LANG	JOHANN	1850	NEHWILLER	01/01/1868	A		NO.2
LANG	JOSEF	1865	MOTHERN	01/01/1866	NY		NO.2

Lastname	Firstname	Birth Year	Birthplace	Emigration	De	Prof	Source
LANG	JPSEPH		MOTHERN	01/01/1850	NO		PRIV
LANG	MARGUERITE		ZUTZENDORFF	01/01/1828	A		FILM
LANG	SALOMON	1821	RIBEAUVILLE	11/07/1855	NY		FILM
LANG	SCOLASTIQUE		HAEGEN	01/01/1828	A		FILM
LANG	SIXTE	1839	OBERLAUTERBACH	07/11/1857	PH		FILM
LANG	SOPHIE		RUST	05/12/1849	A		FILM
LANG F OF 5	ARON		STRUTH	01/01/1828	A		FILM
LANG MN BEYER	MARIA	1843	MOTHERN	01/01/1866	NY		NO.2
LANG W MICHEL		1803	MULHOUSE	11/05/1835	NY		FILM
LANG WW	MICHEL	1805	MULHOUSE	11/05/1835	NY		FILM
LANG WW AND CH 4	JEAN		UHRWILLER	03/11/1817	A		FILM
LANG WW AND CH 4	JEAN		UHRWILLER	04/09/1819	A		FILM
LANGARD WW AND CH	JOSEPH	1795	CHAUX	02/10/1840	NY		FILM
LANGBRONN	MAGDALENA	1844	NIEDERBETSCHDORF	01/01/1868	NY		NO.2
LANGE	FRANCOIS			09/26/1854	NO		FILM
LANGE	JEAN PIERRE			09/26/1854	NO		FILM
LANGEL	ANDRES		MOMMENHEIM	02/28/1838	A		FILM
LANGENACHER	PETER		HENTZINGEN	04/21/1849	A		FILM
LANGENACKER	PETER		NIEDERBRONN	05/13/1738	A		FILM
LANGENBACH	BENJAMIN		KENTZINGEN(B)	04/21/1849	A		FILM
LANGENFELD	MARTIN	1813	WIEDENSOHLEN	02/16/1839	PH		FILM
LANT	CHARLES		SCHERTZHEIM	08/13/1849	A		FILM
LAPORTE VVE				02/01/1844	TX		PASS
LAPP F OF 10	JEAN		IMBSHEIM	01/01/1828	A		FILM
LAPP WW AND CH 9	MICHEL	1805	STRASBOURG	07/19/1847	A		FILM
LARGER	JOSEPH	1808	FELLERINEG	/ /			PRIV
LARGER	JOSEPH	1808	FELLERINGEN	08/07/1844	NY		FILM
LARGER	NICOLAS	1811	FELLERINGEN	08/07/1844	NY		FILM
LARGER W FUCHS NICOL	AGATHE	1818	ODEREN	11/04/1857	TX		FILM
LARGER WW AND CH	JEAN	1811	KRUTH	09/01/1854	NY		FILM
LASCHE	ANTOINE	1813	GUEMAR	03/26/1841	PH		FILM
LASCHE	REMI	1828	GUEMAR	08/26/1857	NO		FILM
LASSIAT	JOSEPH	1834	LIEPRE	09/30/1854	NO		FILM
LASSIAT	SEABSTIEN	1816	LIEPRE	08/14/1838	NO		FILM
LATSCH WW	ETIENNE SEBASTI	1810	SEWEN	04/04/1846	NY		FILM
LATSCHA WW	JOSEPH	1833	BISEL	04/29/1851	NY		FILM
LATSCHA WW AND CH 3	GEORGES	1819	OTTINGEN	03/11/1854	DE		FILM
LATZARUS	ANTOINE JUN.		DETTWILLER	01/01/1828	A		FILM
LAUBACHER F OF 3	JOSEPH		MINVERSHEIM	01/01/1828	A		FILM
LAUBACHER F OF 3	LOUIS		ESCHBOURG	01/01/1828	A		FILM
LAUBACHER F OF 4	NICOLAS		MINVERSHEIM	01/01/1828	A		FILM
LAUBACHER WW	JOSEPH		ESCHBOURG	01/01/1828	A		FILM
LAUBACKER	LOUIS MATHIAS		ESCHBOURG	03/03/1817	A		FILM
LAUBER	CATHERINE	1837	BOURGFELDEN	04/20/1865	NY		FILM
LAUBER	JACQUES	1839	BORUGFELDEN	04/20/1865	NY		FILM
LAUBER	JACQUES	1864	BOURGFELDEN	04/20/1865	NY		FILM
LAUBER H JOSEPHINE	SEBASTIEN	1827	WALBACH	11/03/1854	NY		FILM
LAUBER W SEBASTIEN	JOSEPHINE	1828	WALBACH	11/03/1854	NY		FILM
LAUBSER	JOSEPH	1813	SELESTAT	06/07/1847	NY		FILM
LAUBY	JOSEPH ANTOINE	1833	HAVRE	04/01/1853	NY		FILM

Lastname	Firstname	Birth Year	Birthplace	Emigration	De	Prof	Source
LAUDREE	JOSEPH		GERMANY	04/05/1849	NY		FILM
LAUER	JEAN ANTOINE PH		HAGUENAU	01/01/1828	A		FILM
LAUER F OF 2	PHILIPPE		MENCHHOFFEN	01/01/1828	A		FILM
LAUP WW AND CH 4	JACQUES		KESKASTEL	01/01/1817	A		FILM
LAURENT		1791	BELFORT	02/28/1863	NY		FILM
LAURENT	CATHERINE	1829	ROPPE	12/30/1864	NY		FILM
LAURENT	FRANCOIS	1861	CHATENOIS	11/17/1863	NY		FILM
LAURENT	FRANCOISE	1844	CHATENOIS	11/17/1863	NY		FILM
LAURENT	JACQUES	1805	CHATENOIS	11/17/1863	NY		FILM
LAURENT	JEANNE	1818	GRANDVILLARS	02/21/1849	NY		FILM
LAURENT	JOSEPH		FELON	08/16/1844	NY		FILM
LAURENT	JOSEPH	1816	GRANDVILLARS	01/25/1851	NY		FILM
LAURENT	JOSEPH	1833	VRIMENIL	09/29/1854	NY		FILM
LAURENT	MARIE APPOLINE	1820	PARIS	/ /	NY		FILM
LAURENT MN PALAT	MARIE CH 5	1797	GROSNE	12/31/1851	NY		FILM
LAUT	MADELEINE		ANNWEILER	06/03/1849	A		FILM
LAUTENSCHLAG AND CH	ELISABETH	1819	MULHOUSE	09/07/1848	NY		FILM
LAUTER CH 4	DENIS	1781	RIEDISHEIM	10/01/1843	TX	TONM	PASS
LAUTER WW AND CH	DENICE	1781	RIEDISHEIM	10/03/1843	NY		FILM
LAUTERBACH	DOROTHE	1844	SOULTZ-SOUS-FORET	01/01/1868	NY		NO.2
LAUTH	JACQUES		BRUMATH	05/28/1817	A		FILM
LAUTHER	CATHERINA	1846	SELTZ	01/01/1868	NY		NO.2
LAUTHER	JOSEF	1844	SELTZ	01/01/1868	NY	CARP	NO.2
LAUX WW AND CH 4	JACQUES		KESKASTEL	01/01/1817	A		FILM
LAVAL	FRANCOIS	1829	GRANDVILLARS	04/26/1854	NY		FILM
LAVAL WW AND CH 3	JEROME	1806	CHAUX	02/27/1846	NO		FILM
LAVALLE	BERNARD	1841	NIEDERLAUTERBACH	01/01/1864	NY	MERC	PRIV
LAVON	M.ANGELIQUE	1846	NIEDERLAUTERBACH	01/01/1866	NO		PRIV
LE COMPTE DE LUSY	AUGUSTE WW CH 3		MEUSE	04/08/1844	TX		FILM
LE COMPTE DE LUSY	JEAN BAPTISTE	1843	MEUSE	04/08/1844	TX		FILM
LE COMPTE DE LUSY	MARIE EMILIE	1839	MEUSE	04/08/1844	TX		FILM
LE COMPTE DE LUSY	MARIE JEANNE P	1808	MEUSE	04/08/1844	TX		FILM
LE COMPTE DE LUSY	STEPHANIE	1841	MEUSE	04/08/1844	TX		FILM
LE COMTE DE LUSY	AUGUSTE		MEUSE	04/09/1844	CL		FILM
LE COMTE DE LUSY	EMILIE	1839	MEUSE	04/09/1844	CL		FILM
LE COMTE DE LUSY	JEAN BAPTISTE	1843	MEUSE	04/09/1844	CL		FILM
LE COMTE DE LUSY	STEPHANIE	1841	MEUSE	04/09/1844	CL		FILM
LEATZ WW AND CH 4	JACQUES		STRUTH	03/03/1817	A		FILM
LEBERRECHT	QUIRIN	1823	KRAUTERGERSHEIM	02/22/1851	NY		FILM
LECONTE	GUILLAUME		GERSTHEIM	03/03/1838	A		FILM
LECRILIE	MARGUERITE	1800		02/27/1857	A		FILM
LECUREUX	EDMOND		BLUSSENGEAUX	02/17/1866	NY		FILM
LECUREUX	EMILE		BLUSSENGEAUX	02/17/1866	NY		FILM
LECUREUX	LOUIS		BLUSSENGEAUX	02/17/1866	NY		FILM
LECUREUX	MARIE		BLUSSENGEAUX	02/17/1866	NY		FILM
LECUREUX	PAUL		BLUSSENGEAUX	02/17/1866	NY		FILM
LECUREUX	PIERRE		BLUSSENGEAUX	02/17/1866	NY		FILM
LEDAGAR F OF 6	BERNHARD		PFAFFENHOFFEN	01/01/1828	A		FILM
LEDDERMANN WW CH 6	PIERRE		ALTWILLER	01/01/1817	A		FILM
LEDERLE	RUBERT		AITORN	09/30/1849	A		FILM

LEDERMANN F OF 3   JEAN   DETTWILLER   01/01/1828 A   FILM
LEDERMANN WW CH 6   PIERRE   ALTWILLER   01/01/1817 A   PRIV
LEDIG   MICHEL   1845 GOERSDORF   01/01/1867 NY WAGO NO.2
LEDOGAR   PIERRE   PFAFFENHOFFEN   01/01/1828 A   FILM
LEDOGAR F OF 6   BERNHARD   PFAFFENHOFFEN   01/01/1828 A   FILM

LEDS   CHARLES LOUIS   1835 BEAUCOURT   10/11/1854 NO   FILM
LEEMEL F OF 2   JEAN   IMBSHEIM   01/01/1828 A   FILM
LEFERRE AND CH   HYPOLITE   1804 ST. HYPOLITE   09/29/1846 NY   FILM
LEFERRE MN BADER   MARIE ANNE CH 3 1803 HOMMERT   10/15/1850 NO   FILM
LEFFLER WW AND CH 3   JEAN   BAERENDORF   03/23/1817 A   FILM

LEGAISSE WW AND CH 5 ALEXANDRE   1802 THANNENKIRCH   12/11/1846 CH   FILM
LEHARDT   LOUIS AUGUSTIN 1821 ST. LOUIS   02/22/1851 NY   FILM
LEHMANN   FANNY   1813 SURBOURG   01/01/1867 NY   NO.2
LEHMANN   FREDERIC   1820 RIQUEWIHR   03/31/1848 NY   FILM
LEHMANN   GEORG   1850 MUNCHHOUSE   01/01/1867 NY   NO.2

LEHMANN   JEAN   OBENHEIM   03/10/1838 A   FILM
LEHMANN   JEAN DAVID   1831 MITTELWIHR   04/03/1848 NY   FILM
LEHMANN   MARIE ANNE   LEUTENHEIM   03/01/1838 A
LEHMANN   MARX   1842 FROESCHWEILER 01/01/1865 A MERC NO.2
LEHMANN   MICHEL   DRUSENHEIM   03/24/1838 A   FILM

LEHMANN   PHILIPP   GUNSTETT   01/01/1817 A WEAV NO.2
LEHMANN   REGINA   1847 SCHLEITHAL   01/01/1868 NY   NO.2
LEHMANN CH 2   CATHERINE   1806 OBERLAUTERBACH 08/21/1854 NY   FILM
LEHMANN D JEAN GEORG   1848 ANDOLSHEIM   02/04/1856 SL   FILM
LEHMANN F OF 4   JOSEPH   SCHIRRHEIN   03/05/1838 A   FILM

LEHMANN F OF 4   NICOLAS   SCHIRRHEIN   03/05/1838 A   FILM
LEHMANN F OF 5   MICHEL   SCHIRRHEIN   03/05/1838 A   FILM
LEHMANN MN BAUER   MADELEINE   1823   04/21/1856 SL   FILM
LEHMANN S JEAN GEORG   1850 ANDOLSHEIM   02/04/1856 SL   FILM
LEHMANN S JEAN GEORG   1852 ANDOLSHEIM   02/04/1856 SL   FILM

LEHMANN W JEAN GEORG   1823 ANDOLSHEIM   02/04/1856 SL   FILM
LEHMANN WW   PHILIPPE   OBENHEIM   03/10/1838 A   FILM
LEHMANN WW AND CH 3   JEAN GEORGES   1819 ANDOLSHEIM   02/04/1856 SL   FILM
LEHMANN WW AND CH 4   PHILIPPE   1806 BOFTZHEIM   02/26/1851 CH   FILM
LEHMES   JEAN   1816 KOESTLACH   12/16/1839 NO   FILM

LEHR   MICHEL   1822 PULVERSHEIM   11/14/1848 NY   FILM
LEIDERMANN WW CH 6   PIERRE   ALTWILLER   01/01/1817 A   FILM
LEINFURTH   JOHANNES   NIEDERBRONN   05/13/1838 A   FILM
LEINGE   FRANCOIS   09/26/1854 NO   FILM
LEINHARD   HANSS   UHRWILLER   05/13/1838 A   FILM

LEINIGER   ELISABETH   WIMMENAU   01/01/1828 A   FILM
LEINIGER F OF 2   JACQUES   PUBERG   01/01/1828 A   FILM
LEININGER   GEORGE   DURSTEL   03/18/1838 A   PRIV
LEININGER   PHILIPPE   WIMMENAU   01/01/1828 A   FILM
LEININGER   PIERRE   SIEWILLER   03/18/1838 A   PRIV

LEININGER F OF 7   JACQUES   MENCHHOFFEN   01/01/1838 A   FILM
LEININGER F OF 7   PIERRE   HIRSCHLAND   03/03/1838 A   FILM
LEINNINGER   ANNE MARIE   1812 ZINSWEILLER   02/16/1817 A   FILM
LEINNINGER   JOSEPH   1810 ZINSWEILLER   02/16/1817 A   FILM
LEINNINGER   MATHIEU   1815 ZINSWEILLER   02/16/1817 A   FILM

Lastname	Firstname	Birth Year	Birthplace	Emigration	De	Prof	Source
LEINNINGER MN DAULE	MARGUERITE		ZINSWEILLER	02/16/1817	A		FILM
LEINNINGER WW CH 3	MICHEL	1782	ZINSWEILLER	02/16/1817	A		FILM
LEINS AND CH	JOSEPHINE	1801	WEITINGEN	10/10/1845	NY		FILM
LEISCHNER	DOMINIQUE	1814	RUELISHEIM	11/09/1848	NY		FILM
LEISY	JEAN	1820	COLMAR	09/21/1841	NO		FILM
LEISY	JEAN	1820	COLMAR	10/21/1847	NO		FILM
LEISY	JEAN	1820	COLMAR	10/26/1846	NO		FILM
LEJAL WW			SCHILTIGHEIM	01/01/1828	A		FILM
LEJEAL	JEAN BAPTISTE		HAGUENAU	03/01/1838	A		FILM
LEJEAL	LOUIS		HAGUENAU	03/01/1838	A		FILM
LEMAIRE	DOMINIQUE	1816	PEXONNE	09/20/1849	NY		FILM
LEMAIRE	JEAN CLAUDE	1820	REGUISHEIM	08/07/1848	NO		FILM
LEMAIRE	JOSEPHINE	1824	BATTENHEIM	10/14/1854	NY		FILM
LEMAIRE WW	JEAN BAPTISTE	1834	LIEPRE	09/30/1854	NY		FILM
LEMAIRE WW AND CH	JOSEPH	1817	PEXONNE	04/26/1847	NY		FILM
LEMAJELET	GASPARD	1824	VALDIEU	02/28/1849	NY		FILM
LEMANN	MARIE ANNE		LEUTENHEIM	03/01/1838	A		FILM
LEMBLE MN LIMACHER	ANNE MARIE	1830	LEIMBACH	05/26/1856	NY		FILM
LEMMEL	ANTOINE		MOMMENHEIM	02/28/1838	A		FILM
LENEZ	EUGENE	1834	PHAFFANS	04/09/1863	NY		FILM
LENEZ D PIERRE FRANC		1833	PHAFFANS	08/25/1856	NY		FILM
LENEZ D PIERRE FRANC		1835	PHAFFANS	08/25/1856	NY		FILM
LENEZ S PIERRE FRANC		1837	PHAFFANS	08/25/1856	NY		FILM
LENEZ W PIERRE FRANC		1806	PHAFFANS	08/25/1856	NY		FILM
LENEZ WW AND CH 3	PIERRE FRANCOIS	1802	PHAFFANS	08/25/1856	NY		FILM
LENHARDT	JEAN ADAM	1814	WINGEN	04/06/1840	NY		FILM
LENHERR	JEANNE	1825	ST. LOUIS	07/01/1846	TX	TAYL	PASS
LENHERR	JEANNE	1825	ST.LOUIS	07/03/1846	TX		FILM
LENMIELET	GASPARD	1824	VALDIEU	02/28/1849	NY		FILM
LENN WW AND CH 3	THIEBAUD	1813	BOURBACH-LE-BAS	04/26/1845	NY		FILM
LENNBLEC	AUGUSTE	1831	CERNAY	03/07/1854	NY		FILM
LENTZ	JACQUES			03/03/1817	A		FILM
LENTZ	JEAN		RIMSDORF	03/17/1817	A		FILM
LENTZ	JOSEPH	1828	UEBERKUMEN	10/21/1844	NO		FILM
LENTZ	MARIE ANNE	1829	BRECHAUMONT	01/18/1847	NY		FILM
LENTZ	MICHEL		THAL	01/01/1828	A		FILM
LENTZ	NICOLAS		PUBERG	01/01/1828	A		FILM
LENTZ F OF 3	JEAN		HERBITZHEIM	01/01/1828	A		FILM
LENTZ F OF 5	JACQUES		OBERMODERFN	01/01/1828	A		FILM
LENTZ F OF 7	JEAN		MELSHEIM	01/01/1828	A		FILM
LENTZ F OF 7	MICHEL		ZUTZENDORF	01/01/1828	A		FILM
LENTZ F OF 8	JACQUES		ZUTZEMDORF	01/01/1828	A		FILM
LENTZ WW AND CH 2	GEORGE		LA PETITE PIERRE	03/03/1900	A		FILM
LENTZ WW AND CH 3	JEAN GEORGE		KILSTETT	05/28/1817	A		FILM
LEOFFLER	CHRETIEN FREDER	1816	GRUNWETTERSBACH	03/11/1837	A		FILM
LEONHARD	EDUARD		REICHSHOFFEN	01/01/1869	A		NO.2
LEONHART F OF 4	JACQUES		SUNDHAUSEN	03/02/1837	A		FILM
LERCH	MICHEL		MARMOUTIER	01/01/1828	A		FILM
LERCH	QUIRIN		HAEGEN	01/01/1828	A		FILM
LERCH F OF 4	ETIENNE		HAEGEN	01/01/1828	A		FILM

Lastname	Firstname	Birth Year	Birthplace	Emigration	De	Prof	Source
LERETZ WW AND CH 4	JEAN	1813	MULHOUSE	01/26/1849	NY		FILM
LERNINGER	GEORGE		DURSTEL	03/18/1838	A		FILM
LEROMAIN CH 2	MARIE	1811	ST. CROIX AUX MINES	09/20/1854	NO		FILM
LEROMAIN CH 5	MARGUERITE	1811	LIEPVRE	11/11/1854	NO		FILM
LEROMAIN WW AND CH	ALEXANDRE	1808	LIEPVRE	05/02/1839	NO		FILM
LEROMAIN WW AND CH 5	JOSEPH	1810	ROMBACH	10/11/1854	NO		FILM
LESSER	JACQUES		SUNDHAUSEN	03/02/1837	A		FILM
LESSER	MADELEINE		SUNDHAUSEN	03/02/1837	A		FILM
LESSER	PHILIPPE		SUNDHAUSEN	03/02/1837	A		FILM
LESSIN WW AND CH	FRANCOIS XAVIER		ROBERTSAU	06/04/1817	A		FILM
LESTER	FRANCOIS NICOLA		GUEWENHEIM	/ /	NY		FILM
LETIQUE	MARIE THERESE	1820	ST. CROIX AUX MINES	10/16/1846	SL		FILM
LETSCHER	ADAM		PETERSBACH	01/01/1828	A		FILM
LETTERMANN	GREGOR		ETTENHEIM	09/30/1849	A		FILM
LETZ	FREDERIC		PFAFFENHOFFEN	01/01/1828	A		FILM
LETZ	JACQUES		PFAFFENHOFFEN	01/01/1828	A		FILM
LETZKUS	JOSEPH		DEUTSCHLAND	04/06/1849	NY		FILM
LETZLER	CATHERINE		DEHLINGEN	01/01/1828	A		FILM
LETZLER	EVE		DEHLINGEN	01/01/1828	A		FILM
LETZLER WW CH 5	JACQUES	1820	EYWILLER	01/23/1857	CI		FILM
LETZLER WW F OF 6	NICOLAS		DEHLINGEN	01/01/1828	A		FILM
LEUMAS MN BLOCH	CAROLINE		ZABERN	/ /	LA		BULL
LEURACELAT	GASPARD	1824	VALDIEU	02/28/1849	NY		FILM
LEUTZ WW AND CH 4	NICOLAS		VOLSBURG	03/06/1817	A		FILM
LEUVREUX	EDMOND	1860	BLUSSENGEAUX	02/17/1866	NY		FILM
LEUVREUX	EMILE	1858	BLUSSENGEAUX	02/17/1866	NY		FILM
LEUVREUX	LOUIS	1863	BLUSSENGEAUX	02/17/1866	NY		FILM
LEUVREUX	MARIE	1852	BLUSSENGEAUX	02/17/1866	NY		FILM
LEUVREUX	PAUL	1856	BLUSSENGEAUX	02/17/1866	NY		FILM
LEUVREUX	PIERRE	1855	BLUSSENGEAUX	02/17/1866	NY		FILM
LEUVREUX F OF 6	MARIE		BLUSSENGEAUX	02/17/1866	NY		FILM
LEVAUER	CATHERINE	1825	KUNHEIM	12/29/1854	NY		FILM
LEVEQUE	EDUARD		ST LOUIS	07/23/1846	A		FILM
LEVEQUE	MARIE ALBERT FE	1809	ST. LOUIS	07/23/1846	A		FILM
LEVI	GERT		INGVILLES	01/01/1828	A		FILM
LEVI	GOTTSCHON		INGVILLER	01/01/1828	A		FILM
LEVI	HENRI		INGVILLER	01/01/1828	A		FILM
LEVI	JULIUS		LANGENSOULTZBACH	01/01/1867	A		SUESS
LEVY	A		SURBOURG	01/01/1850	NO		PRIV
LEVY	AARON	1849	RIEDSELTZ	01/01/1867	NY		NO.2
LEVY	ABRAHAM	1831	GOERSDORF	01/01/1867	NY		NO.2
LEVY	ABRAHAM	1841	HIRSINGEN	06/04/1857	NY		FILM
LEVY	ADELE	1847	SURBOURG	01/01/1869	NO		NO.2
LEVY	AMALIE	1845	SURBOURG	01/01/1869	NO		NO.2
LEVY	ARON		FEGERSHEIM	05/28/1817	A		FILM
LEVY	ARON	1830	THANN	07/18/1854	NY		FILM
LEVY	ARON	1845	SURBOURG	01/01/1865	NY		NO.2
LEVY	BABETTE	1796	SURBOURG	01/01/1796	NY		NO.2
LEVY	BERNHARD	1844	SCHLEITHAL	01/01/1866	NY		NO.2
LEVY	BORACH	1851	TRIEMBACH	01/01/1867	NY		NO.2

Lastname	Firstname	Birth Year	Birthplace	Emigration	De	Prof	Source
LEVY	CAROLINE	1829	SURBOURG	01/01/1866	NY		NO.2
LEVY	CAROLINE	1843	RIEDSELTZ	01/01/1864	NY		NO.2
LEVY	EDOUARD	1827	MULHOUSE	08/30/1850	NY		FILM
LEVY	G.	1847	NIEDERROEDERN	01/01/1869	NY		NO.2
LEVY	GABRIEL	1847	NIEDERROEDERN	01/01/1865	NY	MERC	NO.2
LEVY	GUSTAF	1864	NIEDERROEDERN	01/01/1868	NO		NO.2
LEVY	HEINRICH	1850	RIEDSELTZ	01/01/1867	NY		NO.2
LEVY	HENRIETTE		WISSEMBOURG	01/01/1869	NO		PRIV
LEVY	HERMANN	1833	HATTEN	01/01/1867	NY	TAYL	NO.2
LEVY	ISAAC		RENINGEN	04/18/1849	NY		FILM
LEVY	ISRAEL	1841	SURBOURG	01/01/1865	NY		NO.2
LEVY	JACOB	1865	SURBOURG	01/01/1865	NY	TAYL	NO.2
LEVY	JACQUES	1842	CERNAY	03/31/1857	PH		FILM
LEVY	JOHANN	1856	SURBOURG	01/01/1866	NY		NO.2
LEVY	JULIE	1846	TRIEMBACH	01/01/1865	NY		NO.2
LEVY	LISETTE	1848	GOERSDORF	01/01/1867	NY		NO.2
LEVY	MARIA	1857	SURBOURG	01/01/1866	NY		NO.2
LEVY	MARIE	1843	NIEDERROEDERN	01/01/1869	NY		NO.2
LEVY	MARX	1866	NIEDERROEDERN	01/01/1868	NO		NO.2
LEVY	MOISE	1824	SOULTZMATT	07/02/1852	NY		FILM
LEVY	MOISE	1847	LAUTERBURG	01/01/1865	NY	BAKE	NO.2
LEVY	RACHEL	1847	SURBOURG	01/01/1867	NY		NO.2
LEVY	ROSALIE	1819	BIESHEIM	07/14/1842	NY		FILM
LEVY	SALOMON	1838	NIEDERROEDERN	01/01/1865	NY	MERC	NO.2
LEVY	SALOMON	1862	NIEDERROEDERN	01/01/1868	NO		NO.2
LEVY	SAMUEL		OBERSEEBACH	02/09/1866	A		FILM
LEVY	SIMON`	1844	NIEDERROEDERN	01/01/1844	NY	MERC	NO.2
LEVY	SIMON	1846	SURBOURG	01/01/1866	NY	MERC	NO.2
LEVY	SIMON	1863	SURBOURG	01/01/1866	NY		NO.2
LEVY	ZACHARIAS	1858	SURBOURG	01/01/1866	NY		NO.2
LEVY MN HIRTZ	ANNE CH	1814	GUEBWILLER	04/27/1850	PH		FILM
LEVY B HENRIETTE	JACQUES	1825	CERNAY	03/31/1857	PH		FILM
LEVY S SAMUEL	ELIAS		FROESCHWILLER	01/01/1870	A		SUESS
LEVY SI JACQUES	HENRIETTE	1840	CERNAY	03/31/1857	PH		FILM
LEVY W W 4 CH	JOHANN	1823	SURBOURG	01/01/1866	NY		NO.2
LEVY WW 3 CH	MOSES	1822	NIEDERROEDERN	01/01/1868	NO		NO.2
LEWY	PIERRE	1840	MERTZEN	01/20/1857	NY		FILM
LEXAUER	CATHERINE	1825	KUNHEIM	12/28/1854	NY		FILM
LEY	ANNE MARIE	1828	WOLSCHWILLER	11/15/1852	NY		FILM
LEY	CESAR	1831	WOLSCHWILLER	09/03/1852	NY		FILM
LEY	FRANCOIS CLAUDE	1820	KIENTZHEIM	04/24/1850	NO		FILM
LEY	FRANCOIS JOSEPH	1818	GUEMAR	04/05/1853	NY		FILM
LEYENBERGER	JAYQUES		RAUWILLER	03/07/1838	A		FILM
LEYNENBERG WW CH 5	FRANCOIS		KIRRBERG	03/29/1817	A		FILM
LHOTE	CLAUDE FRANCOIS		ARGIESANS	01/10/1852	NO		FILM
LIBSIG WW AND CH 2	ANTOINE	1803	NEUWILLER	12/04/1845	CI		
LICHTLE WW AND CH 3	MARTIN	1818	HERBLISHEIM	03/09/1852	NY		FILM
LICKEL	JOSEF	1849	WEILER	01/01/1866	NY		NO.2
LICKEL F OF 9	GEORGE		SCHILLERSDORF	01/01/1828	A		FILM
LIEB F OF 4	JACQUES		ALTWILLER	01/01/1828	A		FILM

Lastname	Firstname	Birth Year	Birthplace	Emigration	De	Prof	Source
LIEBELIN WW	JOSEPH	1815	CHAUX	10/06/1846	NY		FILM
LIEBELIN WW AND CH 4	JACQUES		CHAUX	10/27/1846	NO		FILM
LIEBER WW	DOMINIQUE	1817	WITTELSHEIM	11/13/1844	TX		FILM
LIEBERT WW AND CH 3	LOUIS	1824	COLMAR	08/16/1852	NO		FILM
LIECHARD	CHARLES		GENGENBACH	06/28/1849	A		FILM
LIECHARD	JOSEPH		GENGENBACH	06/28/1849	A		FILM
LIECHLY CH 4	JACQUES	1777	LANGEOIS	04/11/1857	NY		FILM
LIECHTLY CH	JACQUES	1813	BETTENDORF	03/01/1841	NY		FILM
LIECHTY WW AND CH 3	PIERRE	1822	ALLENJOIE	02/24/1854	NY		FILM
LIEDE	JACQUES CHRISTO		DURLACH	05/12/1849	NY		FILM
LIEHT	MADELEINE		HOLTZHAUSEN	10/11/1849	A		FILM
LIENHARD	JOSEPH		ESCHBOURG	03/03/1817	A		FILM
LIENHARD F OF 5	PHILIPPE		BISCHOLTZ	01/01/1828	A		FILM
LIENHARD F OF 9	JACQUES		BISCHHOLTZ	01/01/1828	A		FILM
LIENHARD MN BERNHARD	CATHERINE	1802	CERNAY	07/30/1856	NY		FILM
LIENHARDT	ANTOINE		REINHARDSMUNSTER	01/01/1828	A		FILM
LIENHARDT	GEORGES	1832	DUNTZENHEIM	09/08/1852	A		FILM
LIENHARDT	HANSS GEORG		UHRWILLER	05/13/1838	A		FILM
LIENHARDT	JACQUES	1834	DUNTZENHEIM	09/08/1852	A		FILM
LIENHARDT F OF 2	MADELAINE		BISCHWILLER	03/02/1838	A		FILM
LIENHARDT S JACQUES	GEORGE	1833	DUNTZENHEIM	09/08/1852	A		FILM
LIENHART	GEORGES	1822	REINHARDSMUNSTER	11/26/1851	NO		FILM
LIENHART	PETER		FROESCHWILLER	01/01/1846	A		SUESS
LIENHART	PETER S JACOB		FROESCHWILLER	01/01/1846	A		SUESS
LIESCH	SALOME		SCHERTZHEIM	08/13/1849	A		FILM
LILLER	FRANCOIS	1824	GUEWENHEIM	03/11/1854	NY		FILM
LIMACHER W LEMBLE JO	ANNE MARIE	1830	BOURBACH-LE-BAS	05/26/1856	NY		FILM
LIMMENDINGER MN WIRA	ANNE MARIE CH 4	1855	PFETTERHOUSE	/ /	NY		FILM
LINCK	MARTIN		RIEDSELTZ	01/01/1868	A		NO.2
LINCK F OF 7	MADELAINE		SCHIRRHEIN	03/05/1838	A		FILM
LINCK F OF 8	ANTOINE		SCHIRRHEIN	03/05/1838	A		FILM
LINCK F OF 8	LOUIS		SCHIRHOFF	03/01/1838	A		FILM
LINCK F OF 8	LOUIS		SCHIRHOFF	03/05/1838	A		FILM
LINCK WW AND CH 2	JACQUES	1795	OSTHEIM	03/17/1845	NY		FILM
LINDAUER	BENEDICT		JEBENHAUSEN	05/03/1849	A		FILM
LINDAUER	FANNY		JEBENHAUSEN	05/03/1849	A		FILM
LINDECKER	JEAN THIEBAUD	1814	HECHEN	03/19/1850	WA		FILM
LINDECKER CH 3	ANNE MARIE	1814	PFAFFENHEIM	04/29/1853	NY		FILM
LINDEMANN	JACOB		GRIESBACH	01/01/1817	A		NO.2
LINDEMANN	PETER		GUNDERSHOFFEN	01/01/1817	A		NO.2
LINDEMANN	THOMAS		SCHWALDORF	05/03/1849	NY		FILM
LINDEMANN WW CH 2	JACQUES		GRIESBACH	03/17/1817	A		FILM
LINDEN	APPOLONIA		KIGLINGSBERGEN	04/07/1849	NY		FILM
LINDENTHALER WW CH 2	JOSEPH ALOYSE	1816	KAPPEL	02/20/1852	NY		FILM
LINDER	ADELE	1833	WOLSCHWILLER	09/26/1856	NY		FILM
LINDER	ANNE		WILWISHEIM	01/01/1828	A		FILM
LINDER	FRANCOISE	1826	BATTENHEIM	08/29/1854	NY		FILM
LINDER	JEAN	1817	MUESPACH-LE-BAS	04/10/1847	NY		FILM
LINDER	LUISE	1850	WEISSENBURG	01/01/1865	NY		NO.2
LINDERMANN WW AND CH	PIERRE		GUNDERSHOFFEN	03/17/1817	A		FILM

Lastname	Firstname	Birth Year	Birthplace	Emigration	De	Prof	Source
LINGELSER WW	ANDRE		OHNENHEIM	03/06/1817	A		FILM
LINGRUN	JOSEPH	1801	BATTENHEIM	09/21/1846	TX		FILM
LINK	FRANZ		BADEN	07/30/1849	A		FILM
LINK	JOSEPH		AITORN	09/30/1849	A		FILM
LINSENMEYER	ADAM	1841	OBERSEEBACH	01/01/1841	NY	FARM	NO.2
LINSENMEYER	MARIA ANNA	1843	OBERSEEBACH	01/01/1868	NY		NO.2
LINSMEISTER	HUBERT	1815	BILTZHEIM	09/07/1846	TX		FILM
LINTZENBOLTZ	ANASTASE	1817	KRAUTERGERSHEIM	08/20/1845	AL		
LINZENMEYER WW CH 3	ANTOINE	1802	COLMAR	09/19/1846	A		FILM
LIONIN	FOLVERIN	1833	BEAUCOURT	03/11/1863	NY		FILM
LIROT	ANDRE	1817	THANNENKIRCH	10/11/1852	A		FILM
LIROT	MAXIMIN	1824	THANNENKIRCH	12/14/1846	CH		FILM
LISCHER	JEAN JACQUES	1817	KUNHEIM	04/13/1841	A		FILM
LISCHER MN LETZLER	CATHERINE		DEHLINEGN	01/01/1828	A		FILM
LISCHER WW	PIERRE		DEHLINGEN	01/01/1828	A		FILM
LISCHY	EDOUARD	1821	ILLZACH	05/22/1848	NY		FILM
LISSE	CATHERINE	1864	BADEVEL	09/20/1866	NY		FILM
LISSE	CHARLES	1866	BADEVEL	09/20/1866	NY		FILM
LISSE	JACQUES	1838	BADEVEL	09/20/1866	NY		FILM
LISSE	JULIE	1840	BADEVEL	09/20/1866	NY	F	FILM
LITIQUE	NICOLAS	1817	ST.CROIX AUX MINES	05/11/1846	SL		FILM
LITOT	XAVIER	1817	AUXELLES BAS	09/30/1851	NY		FILM
LITSCHE	ELISE		EISINGEN	04/11/1849	A		FILM
LITTERI	LAURENT	1822	HAGUENAU (BAS-RHIN)	04/22/1852	NY		FILM
LITTIG	PHILIPPE		BISCHWILLER	03/02/1838	A		FILM
LITTNER WW AND CH 7	JEAN		HIRSCHLAND	03/20/1817	A		FILM
LITZLER	JEAN	1801	FRANCKEN	02/02/1848	NY		FILM
LITZLER	MEINRAD	1822	OBERDORFF	03/03/1846	NY		FILM
LOCHARD	VEUVE	1832	BLUSSENGEAUX	02/17/1866	NY		FILM
LOCHERT			RIEDSELTZ	01/01/1850	NO		PRIV
LOCHERT	CATHERINE		NIEDERLAUTERBACH	01/01/1850	NO		PRIV
LOCHERT	CATHERINE	1846	NIEDERLAUTERBACH	01/01/1866	NO		PRIV
LOCHERT	ELISABETH	1843	NIEDERLAUTERBACH	01/01/1866	NO		PRIV
LOCHERT	EMIL	1849	NIEDERLAUTERBACH	01/01/1865	NO		NO.2
LOCHERT	EMILE		NIEDERLAUTERABCH	01/01/1850	NO		PRIV
LOCHERT	JOHANN	1816	RIEDSELTZ	01/01/1866	NO		NO.2
LOCHERT	JOSEPH		NIEDERLAUTERBACH	01/01/1850	NO		PRIV
LOCHERT	JOSEPH	1850	NIEDERLAUTERBACH	01/01/1866	NO		PRIV
LOCHERT	LOUISE	1850	NIEDERLAUTERBACH	01/01/1866	NO		PRIV
LOCHERT	MARGARETHE	1797	LAUTERBURG	01/01/1865	NY		NO.2
LOCHERT	REGINE	1849	NIEDERLAUTERBACH	01/01/1866	NO		NO.2
LOCHERT	REINE		NIEDERLAUTERBACH	01/01/1850	NO		PRIV
LOCKERT F	JEAN	1819	LUTTENBACH	05/24/1854	NY		FILM
LODS	ADELE		HERICOURT	06/20/1863	NY		FILM
LODS	ADELE	1855	HERICOURT	10/02/1863	NY		FILM
LODS	EMILIE	1852	HERICOURT	10/02/1863	NY		FILM
LODS	EMILIE		HERICOURT	06/20/1863	NY		FILM
LODS	ERNELIE	1826	HERICOURT	03/13/1865	NY		FILM
LODS	FELICIE	1843	HERICOURT	12/07/1865	NY		FILM
LODS	FERDINAND	1843	HERICOURT	12/07/1865	NY		FILM

Lastname	Firstname	Birth Year	Birthplace	Emigration	De	Prof	Source
LODS	GEROGES LOUIS	1853	VALERIE	07/28/1849	NY		FILM
LODS	JULES		HERICOURT	06/20/1863	NY		FILM
LODS	JULES	1845	HERICOURT	10/02/1863	NY		FILM
LODS	JULES EMILE	1852	HERICOURT	03/12/1865	NY		FILM
LODS	PIERRE	1840	COISEVAUX	01/29/1866	NY		FILM
LODS	THEODORE		HERICOURT	06/20/1863	NY		FILM
LODS	THEODORE	1846	HERICOURT	10/07/1865	NY		FILM
LODS	THEODORE	1847	HERICOURT	10/02/1863	NY		FILM
LOEB	AARON	1846	LEMBACH	01/01/1866	NY	MERC	NO.2
LOEB	FELIX LION		REICHSHOFFEN	01/01/1869	A		NO.2
LOEBENSTEIN	LISETTE		LAUBHEIM	05/16/1849	A		FILM
LOEBS	KAIM		DETTWILLER	01/01/1828	A		FILM
LOECHER	JOSEPH	1830	CERNAY	03/07/1854	NY		FILM
LOEFFEL	APPOLINAIRE	1802	VIEUX-THANN	12/07/1844	NY		FILM
LOEGLES	CHRETIEN	1805	ARTZENHEIM	05/15/1851	NY		FILM
LOEMEL F OF 7	JEAN		IMBSHEIM	01/01/1828	A		FILM
LOERACHER	FREDERIC	1820	MITTELWIHR	06/11/1856	NY		FILM
LOERSCH	CATHERINE		BADEN	10/11/1849	A		FILM
LOESCHER	DAVID	1813	SUNDHOFFEN	03/31/1852	NY		FILM
LOESVENGUTH W W		1817	SCHWABWILLER	01/16/1849	NY		FILM
LOEW	ALOYSE	1827	RIBEAUVILLE	09/23/1846	NO		FILM
LOEWEL	THEODORE		INGENHEIM	01/01/1828	A		FILM
LOEWENGUTH	GEORGES	1815	SCHWABWILLER	07/18/1845	NY		FILM
LOFFER	LUCIA		GERMANY	04/06/1849	NY		FILM
LOHMULLER			KRUTH	09/01/1854	NY		FILM
LOHMULLER	JULES		NORDSTAEDT	04/13/1849	NY		FILM
LOHR	DANIEL		DAMBACH	01/01/1817	A		NO.2
LOHR	GILBERT		ROESCHWOOG	01/01/1828	A		FILM
LOHRENTZ	GEORGE		WEITERSWILLER	01/01/1828	A		FILM
LOHRENTZ	JACQUES		WEITERSWILLER	01/01/1828	A		FILM
LOILLIER	CHARLES JOSEPH	1828	COURCELLES	04/10/1847	NY		FILMN
LOMBART MN PARISOT	MARIE	1793	FRESSE (HAUT SAON)	10/23/1855	SL		FILM
LOPINAT WW AND CH	JACQUES	1782	GRANDVILLARS	08/23/1854	NO		FILM
LOPINOT	ANTOINE	1815	GRANDVILLARS	03/22/1851	NO		FILM
LOPINOT	FRANCOIS	1818	GRANDVILLARS	05/17/1845	NY		FILM
LOPINOT WW AND CH 4	JOSEPH	1820	GRANDVILLARS	09/10/1850	NO		FILM
LORBER	IGNACE JUN.	1836	RIBEAUVILLER	08/22/1857	NY		FILM
LORBER	JOSEPH	1806	KAYSERSBERG	10/17/1851	NO		FILM
LORBER	JOSEPH	1831	ST.BLAISE LA ROCHE	09/11/1851	NO		FILM
LORENTZ	BASRUABE		BADEN	09/21/1849	A		FILM
LORENTZ	FORTINUITE	1830	MOOSCH	11/23/1854	NY		FILM
LORENTZ	FRANCOIS JOSEPH	1810	SENTHEIM	09/10/1844	NO		FILM
LORENTZ	FREDERIC	1838	SIERENTZ	08/09/1855	NY		FILM
LORENTZ	GENEVIEVE	1842	SIERENTZ	09/04/1857	NY		FILM
LORENTZ	JACQUES	1830	HUSSEREN	03/12/1852	NO		FILM
LORENTZ	JEAN	1773	FURDENEHEIM(BAS RHIN	03/08/1828	A		FILM
LORENTZ	JOSEPH	1816	STERNENBERG	04/02/1840	NY		FILM
LORENTZ	JOSEPH	1835	SIERENTZ	02/05/1857	NY		FILM
LORENTZ F OF 2	FRANCOIS JOSEPH		MARMOUTIER	01/01/1828	A		FILM
LORENTZ F OF 5	PHILIPPE		ESCHBOURG	01/01/1828	A		FILM

Lastname	Firstname	Birth Year	Birthplace	Emigration	De	Prof	Source
LORENTZ F OF 8	ANTOINE		SINGRIST	01/01/1828	A		FILM
LORENTZ WW AND CH	JOSEPH	1822	MORTZWILLER	03/28/1849	NY		FILM
LORENTZ WW AND CH 5	JEAN	1795	STERNENBERG	02/27/1846	NY		FILM
LORENZ	FREDERIC		GERMANY	04/12/1849	NY		FILM
LORENZ	JEAN		SINGRIST	01/01/1828	A		FILM
LORENZ F OF 2	REMY		SINGRIST	01/01/1828	A		FILM
LORETZ WW AND CH 4	JEAN	1813	MULHOUSE	01/26/1844	NY		FILM
LORINE CH	PIERRE RAOUL		STRASBOURG	05/12/1817	A		FILM
LORRAINE WW AND CH 3	NICOLAS	1792	PETITMAGNY	12/10/1851	NY		FILM
LOSEL CH MN RATH	ELISABETH	1829	ST. MARIE AUX MINES	10/11/1854	NO		FILM
LOSINGER CH 3	BARBE	1800	COLMAR	09/20/1854	NY		FILM
LOTHAUNER CH 8	THIEBAUD	1808	GUEWENHEIM	04/20/1854	NY		FILM
LOTRINGER	JOSEPH	1814	SOULTZ	03/25/1853	NY		FILM
LOTZ F OF 5	LAURENT		PLOBSHEIM	03/19/1838	A		FILM
LOUIS	FRANTZ	1817	BOUROGNE	12/30/1846	NY		FILM
LOUIS WW AND CH 5	JACQUES	1807	DENNEY	09/02/1846	NY		FILM
LOURENGUTH	IGNACE	1810	SCHWABWILLER	11/22/1849	NY		FILM
LOUTERBACH	DAVID	1811	ST.MARIE AUX MINES	02/28/1853	NY		FILM
LOUVENGUTH	GEORGES	1815	SCHWABWILLER	07/18/1845	NY		FILM
LUDASCHER	JEAN		SCHWOBSHEIM	03/04/1838	A		FILM
LUDER	PANTALEON	1828	KRUTH	09/01/1854	TX	DRIV	PASS
LUDER	PANTALEON	1828	KRUTH	09/14/1854	TX		FILM
LUDER CH 9	NICOLAS	1807	KRUTH	09/01/1860	TX	BELL	PASS
LUDER D NICOLAS	ADELAIDE	1842	KRUTH	09/01/1860	TX		PASS
LUDER D NICOLAS	ANNE-MARIE	1832	KRUTH	09/01/1860	TX		PASS
LUDER D NICOLAS	ANTOINETTE	1853	KRUTH	09/01/1860	TX		PASS
LUDER D NICOLAS	CHRISTINE	1836	KRUTH	09/01/1860	TX		PASS
LUDER MN ARNOLD	ANNE-MARIE			/ /			
LUDER S NICOLAS	AUGUSTE	1847	KRUTH	09/01/1860	TX		PASS
LUDER S NICOLAS	AUGUSTIN	1840	KRUTH	09/01/1860	TX		PASS
LUDER S NICOLAS	EDOUARD	1851	KRUTH	09/01/1860	TX		PASS
LUDER S NICOLAS	MARC	1831	KRUTH	09/01/1860	TX		PASS
LUDER S NICOLAS	THIEBAUD	1855	KRUTH	09/01/1860	TX		PASS
LUDERER	CHARLES		APPENWEIER	10/31/1849	A		FILM
LUDINGEN	GUSTAVE		WEISSENBORN	09/30/1849	A		FILM
LUDINGEN	HERMANN		WEISSENBORN	09/30/1849	A		FILM
LUDMANN WW AND CH 7	NICOLAS		BERG	03/29/1817	A		FILM
LUDMANN WW AND CH 9	JEAN		EYWILLER	03/20/1817	A		FILM
LUDNER MNH SECK	MADELEINE CH 2	1809	THANN	03/03/1845	A		FILM
LUDORF F OF 4	GUILLAUME		SAVERNE	01/01/1828	A		FILM
LUDWIG	ANTON		KUHLENDORF	01/01/1817	A		NO.2
LUDWIG	CATHERINE	1826	JEBSHEIM	03/21/1857	NY		FILM
LUDWIG	FRANCOIS JOSEPH		KUHLENDORF	03/28/1817	A		FILM
LUDWIG	FRANZ JOSEPH		KUHLENDORF	01/01/1817	A		NO.2
LUDWIG	JEAN		KUHLENDORF	03/28/1817	A		FILM
LUDWIG	JEAN G.		KUHLENDORF	03/28/1817	A		FILM
LUDWIG	JOHANN		KUHLENDORF	01/01/1817	A		NO.2
LUDWIG	JOHANN GEORG		KUHLENDORF	01/01/1817	A		NO.2
LUDWIG	THIEBAUT		INGENHEIM	01/01/1828	A		FILM
LUDWIG CH 3	MADELAINE	1814	MITTELWIHR	03/15/1856	NY		FILM

Lastname	Firstname	Birth Year	Birthplace	Emigration	De	Prof	Source
LUDWIG CH 4	CATHERINE		HERRLISHEIM	11/19/1847	NO		FILM
LUDWIG D FRANZ	JOSEPHINE	1846	HEISSEREN	11/15/1846	TX		FILM
LUDWIG D ZACHARIAS	JOSEPHINE	1842	HUSSEREN	11/22/1843	TX		FILM
LUDWIG F OF 7	CHARLES GOTTLIE		BOUXWILLER	01/01/1828	A		PRIV
LUDWIG S FRANZ	JOSEPH	1832	HEISSEREN	11/15/1846	TX		PRIV
LUDWIG S MADELAINE	FREDERIC	1837	MITTELWIHR	03/15/1856	NY		FILM
LUDWIG S MADELAINE	JACQUES	1842	MITTELWIHR	03/15/1856	NY		FILM
LUDWIG S ZACHARIAS	FELIX	1838	HUSSEREN	11/22/1843	TX		FILM
LUDWIG W FRANZ	MARIANNE	1799	HEISSEREN	11/15/1846	TX		FILM
LUDWIG W ZACHARIAS	ROSINE	1815	HUSSEREN	11/22/1843	TX		FILM
LUDWIG WW AND CH 2	FRANZ	1812	HEISSEREN	11/15/1846	TX		FILM
LUDWIG WW AND CH 2	JACQUES	1823	JEBSHEIM	08/21/1854	NY		FILM
LUDWIG WW AND CH 2	ZACHARIAS	1814	HUSSEREN	11/22/1843	TX		FILM
LUDWIG WW AND CH 3	ANTOINE		KUHLENDORF	03/28/1817	A		FILM
LUDWIG WW AND CH 3	JEAN	1808	HERLISHEIM	10/12/1849	NO		FILM
LUHMANN CH 6	THERESE	1809	GUEBWILLER	04/11/1845	PH		FILM
LUHR	MADELEINE		HOLTZHAUSEN	10/11/1849	A		FILM
LUISENBOLTZ WW CH 2	JEAN	1801	KRAUTERGERSHEIM	04/16/1840	NY		FILM
LUMSTEIN F OF 7	GEORGES		BOUXWILLER	01/01/1828	A		FILM
LURY	JEAN	1820	COLMAR	09/21/1841	NO		FILM
LUSTENBERGER	FLORENT		WANGENBOURG	01/01/1828	A		FILM
LUSTENBERGER	LOUIS		WANGENBOURG	01/01/1828	A		FILM
LUSTIG	JACOB		REICHSHOFFEN	01/01/1869	A		NO.2
LUSTIG	JACOB		RIEDSELTZ	01/01/1868	NY		NO.2
LUTHER F OF 8	JEAN		HERBITZHEIM	01/01/1828	A		FILM
LUTHRINGER	BALTHAZARD	1820	MITZACH	05/05/1844	NY		FILM
LUTHRINGER	DENIS	1824	FELLERINGEN	09/14/1848	NY		FILM
LUTHRINGER	FERDINAND	1818	ST. AMARIN	09/01/1859	TX	CULT	PASS
LUTHRINGER	JOSEPH	1835		09/14/1854	NY		FILM
LUTHRINGER WW AND CH	MAURICE	1796	MITZACH	07/18/1854	NY		FILM
LUTIUQE	GEORGES	1791	BREITENAU	03/30/1839	NY		FILM
LUTRINGER	JOSEPH	1818	RANSPACH	11/22/1843	TX		FILM
LUTRINGER	JOSEPH	1828	FELLERINGEN	04/13/1852	PH		FILM
LUTRINGER	MARIE ANNE	1820	HUSSEREN	05/09/1840	A		FILM
LUTT	CATHERINE		DUNTZENHEIM	01/01/1828	A		FILM
LUTT W JACQUES	MARIE		DUNTZENHEIM	01/01/1828	A		FILM
LUTTENBACHER	AGNES	1817	ODEREN	11/04/1857	TX		FILM
LUTTENBACHER	JOSEPH	1817	ODEREN	11/01/1857	TX	FACT	PASS
LUTTENBACHER W JOSEP	AGNES MN WILHEL	1817	FELLERINGEN	11/04/1857	TX		FILM
LUTTENBACHER WW CH 2	ANDRE	1805	GUEBWILLER	04/04/1839	NY		FILM
LUTTENBACHER WW CH 4	JOSEPH	1817	FELLERINGEN	11/04/1857	TX		FILM
LUTTENSCHLAGER	LEGER	1810	SENTHEIM	09/18/1844	NO		FILM
LUTTERINGER	DENIS	1824	FELLERING	09/19/1848	NY		FILM
LUTTERINGER WW CH 5	FRANCOIS JOSEPH	1806	ST. AMARIN	04/28/1855	NY		FILM
LUTZ		1844	URBES	01/01/1869	TX	PRIN	PASS
LUTZ	JACQUES		HAMBACH	03/08/1838	A		FILM
LUTZ	JEAN		INGVILLER	01/01/1828	A		FILM
LUTZ	JEAN GEORGE	1816	NURTH	04/13/1848	NY		FILM
LUTZ	MADELEINE	1837	SONDERSDORFF	05/17/1866	NY		FILM
LUTZ	VALENTIN JUN.		DETTWILLER	01/01/1828	A		FILM

Lastname	Firstname	Birth Year	Birthplace	Emigration	De	Prof	Source
LUTZ WW AND CH 6	JOSEPH		ETTENDORF	01/01/1828	A		FILM
LUTZ F OF 4	FRANCOIS JOSEPH		MORSCHWILLER	03/04/1838	A		FILM
LUTZ F OF 5	FREDERIC		MENCHHOFFEN	01/01/1828	A		FILM
LUTZ WW AND CH 4	FRANCOIS ANTOIN		GRAND DUCHY OF BADEN	05/07/1833	A		FILM
LUX	CHRETIEN		WINGEN	01/01/1828	A		FILM
LUX	EMIL	1866	ALTENSTADT	01/01/1868	NY		NO.2
LUX	GEORG		HATTEN OR LEYN	01/01/1836	A		SUES
LUX	GUILLAUME		SIEWILLER	03/02/1838	A		FILM
LUX	JOSEPH	1868	ALTENSTADT	01/01/1868	NY		NO.2
LUX	LOUIS		SARENNE	01/01/1828	A		FILM
LUX	MADELEINE		WINGEN	01/01/1828	A		FILM
LUX	MARIA	1860	ALTENSTADT	01/01/1868	NY		NO.2
LUX	MICHEL		SCHIRRHEIN	03/05/1838	A		FILM
LUX	PETER	1844	ALTENSTADT	01/01/1868	NY	BLSM	NO.2
LUX WW AND CH 2	CHRETIEN		WINGEN	01/01/1828	A		FILM
LUX 3 CH	FRIEDRICH	1846	ALTENSTADT	01/01/1868	NY	BLSM	NO.2
LUX F OF 8	IGNACE		SCHIRHOFF	03/01/1838	A		FILM
LUXENAIRE	JOSEPH	1826	LIEPVRE	05/11/1854	NY		FILM
LUY	JOHANN HUBERT	1819	HAMBACH	04/09/1844	TX		FILM
L'EURE CH	FRANCOIS	1783	FRESNE	02/13/1844	NY		FILM
L'HEURE	FRANCOIS	1783	FRESNE	02/13/1844	NY		FILM
L'HOLE	AMBROISE	1825	URCEREY	10/22/1847	NY		FILM
L'HOMME	MARGUERITE	1830	DORNACH	11/04/1853	NY		FILM
L'HOMME	MARIE JULIE	1826	CHAUX	09/19/1850	NO		FILM
L'HOMME	MARIE JULIE		CHAUX	09/19/1850	NO		FILM
L'HOMME WW AND CH 6	NICOLAS	1804	SERMAMAGNY	11/06/1840	NO		FILM
L'HOMME WW AND CH 6	NICOLAS	1804	SERMAMAGNE	11/06/1846	A		
L'HOTE	AMBROISE	1825	URCEREY	10/22/1847	NY		FILM
L'HOTE	BALTHAZARD	1832	ARGIESANS	03/12/1852	NY		FILM
L'HOTE	BALTHAZARD	1832	ARGIESANS	03/12/1852	NY		FILM
LÖBENSTEIN	JAKOB		NEHWEILLER(BAS RHIN)	10/15/1826	A		FILM
LÖWENSTEIN	JAKOB		NEHWILLER BAS RHIN	10/15/1826	OH		FILM

Lastname	Firstname	Birth Year	Birthplace	Emigration	De	Prof	Source
M . JARDON	IGNACE	1847	CHALONVILLARS	02/17/1864	NY		FILM
MAAG	MARIE	1816	SUSSIEN	04/05/1851	NY		FILM
MAAS	LOUIS	1820	KAYSERSBERG	07/18/1853	NY		FILM
MAAS	TOBIAS		POLAND	/ /	LA		BULL
MAAS MN WEILL	MARIE	1831	SCHIRRHOFEN	/ /	LA		BULL
MABISSE	JAQUES FREDERIC		AUDINCOURT	04/28/1865	NY		FILM
MACHARD	CATH.A VERONIQU		VAULHIESMON	02/23/1857	NY		FILM
MACHLING F OF 10	PHILIPPE		BRUMATH	01/01/1828	A		FILM
MACK	FRANCOIS	1814	PFASTATT	08/28/1849	NY		FILM
MACK	JAQUES	1840		04/22/1856	NY		FILM
MACK	JEAN BAPTISTE	1828	KLIENTZHEIM	03/22/1850	CH		FILM
MACK	JEAN FREDERIC		KAYSERSBERG	04/22/1850	NY		FILM
MACK	JEAN FREDERIC	1810	KIENTZHEIM	08/26/1854	NY		FILM
MACK	JEAN JAQUES	1815	KIENTZHEIM	09/14/1854	NY		FILM
MACK	JOSEPHINE	1811		04/22/1856	NY		FILM
MACK	MADELEINE	1828	HAGUENAU	08/19/1852	NY		FILM
MACK AND CH	JEAN JAQUES	1815	KIENTZHEIM	04/29/1856	NY		FILM
MACK MN GOETZ	MARIE ANNE	1811		04/22/1856	NY		FILM
MACK S JEAN FREDERIC	EDOUARD	1853		02/02/1856	NY		FILM
MACK WW AND CH 4	FRANCOIS	1785	HAGUENAU	05/05/1851	NY		FILM
MADER AND CH	JEAN		STRASBOURG	06/04/1817			FILM
MADHEUX	CHARLES	1841	RECHESY	10/01/1865	NY		FILM
MADRU	FRANCOIS	1795	ANGEOT	02/19/1846	A		FILM
MADRU	JEAN BAPTISTE	1809	ANGLOT	05/05/1845	A		FILM
MADRU	JEAN BAPTISTE	1825	ANGLOT	03/19/1853	NY		FILM
MAECHLER	MARIE ANNE	1833	KAYSERSBERG	02/16/1849	NY		FILM
MAEDER WW AND CH 5	NICOLAS		UHLWILLER	03/14/1817	A		FILM
MAENNER	ANTOINE	1815	BOERSEN	02/17/1848	NY		FILM
MAENNLING	NICOLAS		BETTWILLER	02/28/1838	A		FILM
MAESER	MICHEL	1827	MUNCHHAUSEN	09/22/1851	NY		FILM
MAFFEY	LUDAN	1809	MARLENHEIM	10/09/1840	NY		FILM
MAFFEY F OF 6	JEAN		MARLENHEIM	01/01/1828	A		FILM
MAGER	JEAN ADAM		KESKASTEL	01/01/1828	A		FILM
MAGER	MELCHIOR	1815	ST.MARIE AUX MINES	03/17/1847	NY		FILM
MAGER	VALENTIN		NIEDERHAUSBERGEN	01/01/1828	A		FILM
MAGER	VALENTIN		NIEDERHAUSBERGEN	03/08/1838	A		FILM
MAGLER	CHRETIEN		HAMBACH	03/08/1838	A		FILM
MAGLER	NICOLAS		HAMBACH	03/08/1838	A		FILM
MAGLER	PIERRE		HAMBACH	03/08/1838	A		FILM
MAGNUS	FRANCOIS HENRY		STRASBOURG	05/12/1817	A		FILM
MAHLER	CATHERINE	1814	MIETESHEIM	01/16/1838	A		FILM
MAHLER F OF 2	MICHEL		SESSENHEIM	02/23/1838	A		FILM
MAIER	CONRAD		SCHWENNINGEN	05/24/1849	A		FILM
MAIER	JACOB		BACKNANG	07/30/1849	A		FILM
MAIER	LERY		OBERNDORF	06/21/1849	A		FILM
MAIGRAT	FRANCOIS	1823	BORON	01/25/1847	NY		FILM
MAIGRET	CHARLES	1856	DALLES	06/10/1865	NY		FILM
MAIGRET	GEORGES	1813	DALLES	06/10/1865	NY		FILM
MAIGRET	GEORGES	1844	DALLES	06/10/1865	NY		FILM
MAIGRET	JEAN	1861	DALLES	06/10/1865	NY		FILM

Lastname	Firstname	Birth Year	Birthplace	Emigration	De	Prof	Source
MAIGRET	JULES	1848	DALLES	06/10/1865	NY		FILM
MAIGRET	LOUIS	1847	DALLES	06/10/1865	NY		FILM
MAIGRET	MALVINA	1857	DALLES	06/10/1865	NY		FILM
MAIGRET	MARANE	1851	DALLES	06/10/1865	NY		FILM
MAIGRET	MARIANNE	1821	DALLES	06/10/1865	NY		FILM
MAIGRET	PIERRE	1842	DALLES	06/10/1865	NY		FILM
MAIGRET	SUSANE	1839	DALLES	06/10/1865	NY		FILM
MAILLARD	ANTOINE	1816	BRETAGNE	02/02/1844	NY		FILM
MAILLARD	HENRY	1816	BRETAGNE	02/10/1844	NY		FILM
MAILLARD	MARIE	1821	BRETAGNE	02/02/1844	NY		FILM
MAILLARD AND CH 2	JEAN PIERRE	1804	BRETAGNE	02/20/1845	NY		FILM
MAILLARD WW AND CH	LOUIS	1795	BRETAGNE	02/12/1845	NY		FILM
MAILLOT	CHERIN	1843	ARCAY	10/06/1865	NY		FILM
MAIRED EGLISE	FRANCOIS		CHENEBIER	03/28/1863	NY		FILM
MAIRED WW AND CH	EGLISE FRANCOIS		FORT LOUIS	01/01/1828	NY		FILM
MAISSE F OF 5	JEAN		FORT LOUIS	01/01/1828	A		FILM
MAITRE	EUGENIE	1831	FAVEROIS	08/21/1855	NO		FILM
MAITRE	FRANCOIS LAUREN	1827	FAVEROIS	03/28/1846	NO		FILM
MAITRE	PAULINE	1835	FAVEROIS	08/12/1857	NO		FILM
MAITRE WW AND CH 2	JOSEPH	1806	EBAUVILLER	03/29/1847	NY		FILM
MAJOR WW AND CH 3	MELCHIOR		OTTWILLER	03/03/1817	A		FILM
MALBLANC	ADELE	1864	VALENTIGNEY	02/19/1866	NY		FILM
MALBLANC	CATHERINE	1824	VALENTIGNEY	02/19/1866	NY		FILM
MALBLANC	EMILE	1823	VALENTIGNEY	02/19/1866	NY		FILM
MALBLANC	FREDERIC	1831	VALENTIGNEY	02/19/1866	NY		FILM
MALBLANC	FRITZ	1856	VALENTIGNEY	02/19/1866	NY		FILM
MALBLANC	LOUISE	1858	VALENTIGNEY	02/19/1866	NY		FILM
MALBLANC	PIERRE	1825	PLANCHET	10/06/1865	NY		FILM
MALENDA	MADELAINE	1850	CLEEBOURG	01/01/1867	NY	TAYL	PRIV
MALHIR WW AND CH 3	NICOLAS		HERBITZHEIM	03/17/1817	A		FILM
MALIN	CATHERINE	1836	BATTENHEIM	10/28/1866	NY		FILM
MALIN	GEORGES	1866	BATTENHEIM	10/28/1866	NY		FIM
MALLET	JEAN		COLMAR	04/20/1852	NY		FILM
MALLET	JEAN	1810	COLMAR	04/20/1852	NY		FILM
MALLINGER WW	GEORGE LUCIEN		NIEDERBRONN	02/26/1817	A		FILM
MALLO	CHRETIEN		WIMMENAU	01/01/1828	A		FILM
MALLS	GEORGES		STATTMATTEN	01/01/1828	A		FILM
MALO WB	MICHEL	1828	ORBEY	09/20/1851	NY		FILM
MALONVET	FRANCOIS	1834	MEROUX	04/16/1853	NO		FILM
MALOURET	FRANCOIS	1834	MEROUX	04/16/1853	NO		FILM
MANDEL	CHARLOTTE	1846	TRIEMBACH	01/01/1867	NY		NO.2
MANDEL	FRANCOIS	1849	TRIEMBACH	01/01/1866	NY		NO.2
MANDEL	JOSEPH	1849	TRIEMBACH	01/01/1867	NY		NO.2
MANDEL	JULIE	1849	TRIEMBACH	01/01/1866	NY		NO.2
MANDEL	LEOPOLD	1847	TRIEMBACH	01/01/1866	NY		NO.2
MANDEL	SAMUEL	1840	TRIEMBACH	01/01/1866	NY		NO.2
MANG	CLAUDE JAQUES	1800	GIROMAGNY	06/24/1854	BU		FILM
MANGEL	MADELEINE		KIGLINGSBERGEN	04/07/1849	NY		FILM
MANGLER	JEAN		ZINSWEILLER	02/16/1817	A		FILM
MANGOLD	ALOISE	1834	LUTTER	05/01/1861	NY		FILM

Lastname	Firstname	Birth Year	Birthplace	Emigration	De	Prof	Source
MANGOLD	JOSEPH	1827	LUTHER	05/04/1865	NY		FILM
MANGOLD	LOUIS		MERDINGEN	10/12/1849	A		FILM
MANGOLD	MARTIN	1836	LUTTER	09/14/1856	NY		FILM
MANGOLD F OF 5	JAQUES		SCHWEIGHAUSEN	01/01/1828	A		FILM
MANGOLD WSI	MARIE ANNE	1824	LUTTER	03/20/1854	NY		FILM
MANGOLD WW	ANTOINE	1893	NIEDERMEUSPACH	06/26/1847	NY		FILM
MANHARDT	SALOME		BALBRON	02/28/1838	A		FILM
MANHARDT F OF 5	GEORGE		BALBRON	02/28/1838	A		FILM
MANK	JEAN ANDRE		HAGUENAU	03/01/1838	A		FILM
MANN	ANNE MARIE	1835	OBERHERGHEIM	02/21/1856	NO		FILM
MANN	ANTOINE	1811	OBERHERGHEIM	12/19/1850	NY		FILM
MANN	CATHERINE	1820	OBERHERGHEIM	08/30/1849	A		FILM
MANN	FRANCOIS JOSEPH	1830	OBERENTZEN	11/01/1850	TX	SHEP	PASS
MANN	FRANCOIS JOSEPH	1830	OBERENTZEN	12/05/1850	TX		FILM
MANN	FRANCOIS JOSEPH	1831	OBERHERGHEIM	10/11/1854	NO		FILM
MANN	JEAN LOUIS	1827	OBERENTZEN	09/14/1846	TX		FILM
MANN	JEAN-LOUIS	1825	OBERENTZEN	09/01/1846	TX	SHEP	PASS
MANN	LOUIS	1821	OBERENTZEN	02/01/1852	TX	DAYL	PASS
MANN MN AHR	MADELAINE			02/01/1852	TX		PASS
MANN WW AND CH	LOUIS	1821	OBERENTZEN	02/06/1852	TX		FILM
MANNE WW AND CH 4	JEAN GUILLAUME	1819	ST.CROIX AUX MINES	09/08/1852	NO		FILM
MANNHART	MAGRARETHE	1815	LAUTERBURG	01/01/1866	NY		NO.2
MANNHEIMER	SARA	1848	SOUTZ-SOUS-FORET	01/01/1866	NY		NO.2
MANNY	MATHIAS	1838	OSTHEIM	05/20/1854	NY		FILM
MANUELL	EMMANUEL	1847	TRIEMBACH	01/01/1865	NY		NO.2
MARC	ANTON	1817	KRUTH	04/09/1844	TX		FILM
MARCH	ANTOINE	1798	LAUTENBACHZELL	11/02/1847	TX		FILM
MARCH	BENAVENTURE	1826	WITTENHEIM	05/22/1848	NY		FILM
MARCHAL	JEAN BAPTISTE	1828	LIEPRE	08/21/1847	NY		FILM
MARCHAL	JOSEPH	1834	LIEPRE	10/14/1854	NO		FILM
MARCHAL	MARIE	1825	LAGRANGE	04/08/1851	NY		FILM
MARCHAL	PIERRE JOSEPH	1809	SUARCE	04/14/1841	NY		FILM
MARCHAL AND CH 4	FRANCOIS	1803	ETTUEFFORT HAUT	10/23/1842	A		FILM
MARCHAL WW	NICOLAS	1808	LUBINE	08/02/1854	NO		FILM
MARCHAL WW AND CH	PIERRE JOSEPH	1826	LAGRANGE	12/03/1853	NY		FILM
MARCHAND	ALEXIS	1821	SERMAMAGNY	11/08/1851	NO		FILM
MARCHAND	ANTOINE	1816	CHATENOIS	02/21/1839	NY		FILM
MARCHAND	CATHERINE	1834	ROUGEMONT	12/08/1855	NY		FILM
MARCHAND	JAQUES	1814	ROUGEMONT	08/25/1852	NY		FILM
MARCHAND	JOSEPH	1813	BORON	08/29/1845	NY		FILM
MARCHAND	JUSTIN DESIREE	1822	LA CHAPELLE SOUS CHO	03/05/1846	NO		FILM
MARCHAND	LOUIS	1834	HERRLISHEIM	01/03/1852	A		FILM
MARCHAND	VINCENT	1819	VALDORE	03/16/1849	NY		FILM
MARCHAND MN CHANEY	MARIE AND CH	1817	BRETAGNE	03/03/1846	NY		FILM
MARCHAND WW	JOSEPH	1796	HERRLISHEIM	02/22/1848	A		FILM
MARCK	ANTOINE	1798	ENISHEIM	11/01/1847	TX	DRIV	PASS
MARCONNET AND CH 2	SUZANNE ELISABE		THANN	03/17/1845	NY		FILM
MARCONNOT	MARIE	1844	VETRIGNE	04/19/1866	NY		FILM
MARCY	CHARLES		ROPPENHEIM	03/06/1838	A		FILM
MARER	JEAN	1841	FOLGENSBURG	05/01/1866	NY		FILM

Lastname	Firstname	Birth Year	Birthplace	Emigration	De	Prof	Source
MAREY H BOSTET.A.9CH	PHILIPPE	1792	ROPPENHEIM	/ /		A	NO.1
MAREY MN BOSTETTER	MADELEINE		ROPPENHEIM	/ /		A	NO.1
MARGOT	JOSEPH	1810	LIEPRE	03/17/1849	NO		FILM
MARGOT	JOSEPH	1810	LIEPRE	11/16/1841	NO		FILM
MARGRAFF	JACOB		SALMBACH	01/01/1860	A		NO.2
MARIE	FERDINAND	1836	CHAUX	12/06/1854	NY		FILM
MARIE	LOUIS	1833	SERMAMAGNY	01/09/1856	NO		FILM
MARIE	LOUISE	1848	SERMAMAGNY	10/02/1865	NY		FILM
MARIE	VINCENT ISIDORE	1826	SERMAMAGNY	03/04/1852	NO		FILM
MARIE AND CH	LOUIS JEAN PIER	1818	SERVANCE	02/14/1844	NY		FILM
MARIE WW AND CH 2	FRANCOIS XAVIER	1819	CHAUX	02/09/1847	NO		FILM
MARION	MARIE FRANCOISE	1829	ANJOUTEY	02/08/1856	NY		FILM
MARK	ANTOINE		DURRENBACH	06/24/1854	A		FILM
MARKOLFF	JEAN		WOLSCHHEIM	01/01/1828	A		FILM
MARQUIS AND CH 2	MARIE ANNE	1795	MERWILLIERS	04/09/1844	TX		FILM
MARQUIS AND CH 3	JEAN JOSEPH	1794	MERWILLEIRS	04/09/1844	TX		FILM
MARQUIS D JEAN JOSEP	LEONORE	1822	MERWILLIERS	04/09/1844	TX		FILM
MARQUIS S JEAN JOSEP	ALEXIS	1827	MERWILLIERS	04/09/1844	TX		FILM
MARQUIS S MARIE ANNE	ALEXIS		MERWILLIERS	04/09/1844	TX		FILM
MARQUIS S MARIE ANNE	HENRI	1836	MERWILLIERS	04/09/1844	TX		FILM
MARSOT	ALEXIS	1791	CHAUX	08/20/1845	NO		FILM
MARSOT	CELESTIN	1815	BORON	04/01/1843	NY		FILM
MARSOT	CHERIN	1823	BORON	04/01/1843	NY		FILM
MARSOT	FRANCOIS	1799	PUIX	02/24/1844	NY		FILM
MARSOT	PHILIPPE	1800	LA COTE	05/05/1840	A		FILM
MARSOT	XAVIER	1831	ETTUEFONT HAUT	06/19/1854	NY		FILM
MARSOT WW AND CH 2	JOSEPH	1806	SERMAMAGNY	04/07/1847	NO		FILM
MARTER WW AND CH	LOUIS	1814	BEINHEIM	08/23/1850	NY		FILM
MARTERER	ELISE	1846	WEISSENBURG	01/01/1865	NY		NO.2
MARTERER	PHILIPP	1810	WEISSENBURG	01/01/1865	NY		NO.2
MARTIN	ANTOINE		SCHIRRHEIN	03/05/1838	A		FILM
MARTIN	CHRISTINE	1859	MUNCHHOUSE	01/01/1868	NY		NO.2
MARTIN	EUGENIE GENEREU	1819	ST.URSANNE	03/13/1848	NY		FILM
MARTIN	FRANCOIS	1822	JONCHERY	10/08/1853	NO		FILM
MARTIN	FRANCOIS JOSEPH	1802	RETZWILLER	05/05/1845	A		FILM
MARTIN	GEORGES		LEUTENHEIM	03/01/1838	A		
MARTIN	JEAN	1821	BESANCON	01/06/1866	NY		FILM
MARTIN	JEAN	1823	SENTHEIM	09/11/1851	NY		FILM
MARTIN	JEAN GUSTAVE	1835	KEHL	11/09/1857	SL		FILM
MARTIN	JOSEPH ANTOINE		HAGUENAU	03/08/1838	A		FILM
MARTIN	MADELEINE	1821	LOBSANN	08/11/1849	NO		FILM
MARTIN	MAGDALENA	1851	MUNCHHOUSE	01/01/1851	NY		NO.2
MARTIN	MICHEL		ERNOLSHEIM	01/01/1828	A		FILM
MARTIN	MICHEL	1847	OBERSEEBACH	01/01/1867	NY		NO.2
MARTIN	NICOLAS		HOERDT	02/28/1838	A		FILM
MARTIN	NICOLAS		STRUTH	01/01/1828	A		FILM
MARTIN	NICOLAS	1827	MOOSCH	12/26/1854	NY		FILM
MARTIN	PETER	1854	MUNCHHOUSE	01/01/1868	NY		NO.2
MARTIN	PHILIPINE		SOUFFLENHEIM	03/02/1838	A		FILM
MARTIN	PIERRE		STRUTH	01/01/1828	A		FILM

Lastname	Firstname	Birth Year	Birthplace	Emigration	De	Prof	Source
MARTIN	REGINA	1864	MUNCHHOUSE	01/01/1868	NY		NO.2
MARTIN	VALENTIN	1824	ST.GERMAIN	06/25/1850	A		FILM
MARTIN	WENDELIN		LEUTENHEIM	03/01/1838	A		FILM
MARTIN MN GABEL	ROSINA	1829	MUNCHHOUSE	01/01/1868	NY		NO.2
MARTIN MN HINZINGER	THERESE CH 6	1794	FOUCHY	10/09/1839	NO		FILM
MARTIN W W 4 CH	MICHEL	1822	MUNCHHOUSE	01/01/1868	NY		NO.2
MARTIN WW	BLAISE		SOUFFLENHEIM	03/02/1838	A		FILM
MARTIN WW	SIMON	1821	RANSPACH	09/18/1844	NY		FILM
MARTIN WW AND CH 2	ANTOINE	1809	RETZWILLER	10/27/1846	NY		FILM
MARTINGE	XAVIER		FORT LOUIS	01/01/1828	A		FILM
MARTINHANG			PFAFFENHEIM	04/29/1853	NY		FILM
MARTINHANG	ANNE MARIE	1814	PFAFFENHEIM	04/29/1853	NY		FILM
MARTINHANG CH 3	ANNE MARIE	1814	PFAFFENHEIM	04/29/1853	NY		FILM
MARTOT	PHILIPPE	1800	LA COTE	05/05/1840	CI		FILM
MARTY	ANDRE	1818	OBERHERGHEIM	08/25/1852	PH		FILM
MARTY	JOSEPH	1831	OBERHERGHEIM	08/25/1852	PH		FILM
MARTY	MICHEL	1823	OBERHERGHEIM	02/01/1852	TX	CULT	PASS
MARTY	SEBASTEIN	1830	OBERHERGHEIM	10/24/1854	TX		FILM
MARTY	SEBASTIEN	1830	OBERHERGHEIM	10/01/1854	TX	BAKE	PASS
MARTZ	ERNST		GERMANY	04/01/1898	NY		FILM
MARTZ F MICHEL	MICHEL		SCHWEIGHAUSEN	01/01/1828	A		FILM
MARTZ S MICHEL	MICHEL		SCHWEIGHAUSEN	01/01/1828	A		FILM
MARTZLOF	JEAN ADAM		ADAMSWILLER	02/27/1838	A		FILM
MARTZOFF	MARGUERITE		SIEWILLER	03/02/1838	A		FILM
MARTZOLFF	JEAN		WOLSCHHEIM	01/01/1828	A		FILM
MARUQIS D JEAN JOSEP	SERAPHINE	1833	MERWILLIERS	04/09/1844	TX		FILM
MARX	DAVID	1837	WINTZENBACH	01/01/1864	NY	FARM	NO.2
MARX	ELISABETH	1818	PFAFFENHEIM	08/18/1843	A		FILM
MARX	GERGARD	1847	KUTZENHAUSEN	01/01/1865	NY	TAYL	NO.2
MARX	MARGUERITE		BRUMATH	06/02/1866	A		FILM
MARX	MARTIN	1808	BETTENDORF	08/07/1850	NY		FILM
MARX	MARX	1815	RIBEAUVILLE	07/20/1857	NY		FILM
MARX	MATHIAS		STEINBOURG	01/01/1828	A		FILM
MARX WW	JOSEPH	1824	RIBEAUVILLE	02/08/1855	NY		FILM
MARXEY WW AND CH 7	JEAN		REICHSHOFFEN	03/22/1817	A		FILM
MARZLOFF	JEAN		ADAMSWILLER	02/27/1838	A		FILM
MARZLOFF	JEAN JAQUES		ERNOLSHEIM	03/11/1817	A		FILM
MARZLOFF	PIERRE		ADAMSWILLER	02/27/1838	A		FILM
MARZLOFF CH 2	CATHERINE MARGU		WEYER	03/03/1817	A		FILM
MARZLOFF WW AND CH	NICOLAS		ALTWILLER	01/01/1817	A		FILM
MARZLOFF WW AND CH 4	DAVID		HIRSCHLAND	03/20/1817	A		FILM
MARZOLF	MARGUERITE		WIMMENAU	01/01/1828	A		FILM
MASQUELET	MAURICE		WESTHAUSEN	01/01/1828	A		FILM
MASSEN WW AND CH 4	NICOLAS	1808	COLROY-LA-GRANDE	09/30/1854	NO		FILM
MASSEY	LUCLAN	1809	MARLENHEIM	10/09/1840	NY		FILM
MASSON	NICOLAS	1792	FRELAND	04/19/1829	PH		FILM
MASSON WW AND CH 4	NICOLAS	1808	COLROY-LA-GRANDE	09/30/1854	NO		FILM
MASSOT	JOSEPH	1821	CHAUX	02/20/1845	NO		FILM
MAST	NICOLAS	1797	RANSPACH	06/29/1844	A		FILM
MATHER WW AND CH 5		1808	OSTHEIM	03/25/1853	NY		FILM

Lastname	Firstname	Birth Year	Birthplace	Emigration	De	Prof	Source
MATHER WW AND CH 5	JEAN DE LOUIS	1806	OSTHEIM	04/13/1847	NY		FILM
MATHEY	CLAUDE FRANCOIS	1834	SALBERT	10/10/1852	NY		FILM
MATHEY	FRANCOIS	1800	SALBERT	03/31/1857	DE		FILM
MATHEY	JUSTIN	1843		10/01/1862	NY		FILM
MATHIA	JAQUES		INGVILLERS	01/01/1828	A		FILM
MATHIA	NICOLAS		PUBERG	01/01/1828	A		FILM
MATHIA	PHILIPPE		RATZWILLER	01/01/1828	A		FILM
MATHIA WW AND CH 8	JEAN		HAMBACH	03/20/1817	A		FILM
MATHIAR WW AND CH 2	JAQUES		HAMBACH	03/06/1817	A		FILM
MATHIAS	JEAN MICHEL	1821	OBERENTZEN	09/29/1851	TX		FILM
MATHIAS	JEAN-MICHEL	1821	OBERENTZEN	09/01/1851	TX	CULT	PASS
MATHIAS	PHILIPP	1848	EBERBACH	01/01/1867	NY		NO.2
MATHIEU	JEAN CLAUDE	1821	ST. GERMAIN	04/08/1851	NY		FILM
MATHIEU	LOUISE	1828	ST. CROIX AUX MINES	10/14/1846	SL		FILM
MATHIEU	MARIE	1824	BITSCHE	05/11/1857	PH		FILM
MATHIEU	MARIE ANNE	1824	ST.CROIX AUX MINES	11/10/1845	SL		FILM
MATHIEU	REINHARD		NIEDERBETSCHDORF	03/21/1817	A		FILM
MATHIEU WW AND CH	FRANCOIS		HAMBACH	03/12/1817	A		FILM
MATHIEU WW AND CH 2	JEAN PIERRE	1810	ST.MARIE AUX MINES	12/05/1846	SL		FILM
MATHIEU WW AND CH 4	JEAN DOMINIQUE	1804	RAMBACH	03/30/1854	SL		FILM
MATHIS	CHARLES	1868	ROPPENHEIM	/ /	AF		NO.1
MATHIS	FRIEDRICH	1871	ROPPENHEIM	/ /	AF		NO.1
MATHIS	GASPARD		SCHOTTERTHAL	05/27/1849	A		FILM
MATHIS	JOSEPH	1833	COLMAR	08/12/1854	NY		FILM
MATHIS	MADELEINE	1867	ROPPENHEIM	/ /	AF		NO.1
MATHIS WM	BARBE	1828	DETTWILLER	03/06/1851	LO		FILM
MATHIS H BOSTETTER3C	FREDERIC CHARLE	1840	ROPPENHEIM	/ /	AF		NO.1
MATHIS MN BOSTETTER	CATHERINE	1839	ROPPENHEIM	/ /	AF		NO.1
MATHIS MN VOGEL CH 3	CATHERINE	1800	RIBEAUVILLE	10/07/1854	NY		FILM
MATOUILLET WW	FRANCOIS	1799	LEBETAIN	03/18/1847	NY		FILM
MATT	AUGUSTIN		MULLENBACH	08/23/1849	A		FILM
MATT	JEAN			/ /			
MATT	JEAN		MULLENBACH	08/23/1849	A		FILM
MATT	JOSEPH		OBENAU	07/23/1844	A		FILM
MATT AND CH	XAVIER	1792	RICKTE	10/27/1854	NY		FILM
MATT WW AND CH	JEAN GEORGES	1826	VIEUX THANN	08/11/1854	NY		FILM
MATT WW AND CH 5	JEAN	1810	FISCHENBACH	10/01/1846	SL		FILM
MATTER	ANTOINE		ROESCHWOOG	01/01/1828	A		FILM
MATTER	CHRISTMANN		ALTECKENDORF	01/01/1828	A		FILM
MATTER	GEORGES	1821	MUNTZENHEIM	02/06/1852	NY		FILM
MATTER	JEAN		ALTECKENDORF	01/01/1828	A		FILM
MATTER	JEAN		KIRRWILLER	01/01/1828	A		FILM
MATTER	JEAN GEORGES		ALTECHENDORF	01/01/1828	A		FILM
MATTER	MICHEL		ALTECHENDORF	01/01/1828	A		FILM
MATTER	MICHEL		KIRRVILLER	01/01/1828	A		FILM
MATTER	MICHEL		OBERMODERN	01/01/1828	A		FILM
MATTER	PIERRE		ROESCHWOOG	01/01/1828	A		FILM
MATTER WW AND CH 2	JAQUES		RINGENDORF	01/01/1828	A		FILM
MATTERN H LANG	VALENTIN		BUEHL	01/01/1830	A		SUESS
MATTERN H LANG CATH	VELENTIN		BUEHL	01/01/1830	A		SUESS

Lastname	Firstname	Birth Year	Birthplace	Emigration	De	Prof	Source
MATTERN MN LANG	CATHERINA		BUEHL	01/01/1830	A		SUESS
MATTHIS	JEAN		DETTWILLER	01/01/1828	A		FILM
MATTLER W AND CH 5	JOSEPH	1799	DURLINSDORFF	04/04/1843	NY		FILM
MATTLER WW AND CH 4	JEAN	1805	DURLINSDORFF	10/01/1848	NO		FILM
MATTLER WW AND CH 5	JEAN	1808	DURLINSDORFF	10/17/1849	NO		FILM
MATTS	GEORGE		STATTMATTEN	03/02/1828	A		FILM
MAUDREUX	JEAN JAQUES	1816	MOVAL	03/30/1838	NY		FILM
MAUER	REGINE		EHRENSTETTEN	12/26/1844	A		FILM
MAUER WW AND CH 2	NICOLAS		STRUTH	01/01/1817	A		FILM
MAUERN MN UNGEREN	FRANCOISE	1786	DRACHENBRONN	09/03/1849	A		FILM
MAUGLER D JEAN HENRY	MARGUERITE ELIS	1812	ZINSWEILLER	02/16/1817	A		FILM
MAUGLER H MARGUERITE	JEAN HENRY	1787	ZINSWEILLER	02/16/1817	A		FILM
MAUGLER MN SCHLEITEN	MARGUERITHE		ZINSWEILLER	02/16/1817	A		FILM
MAUHLER	IGNACE	1795	SEGOLSHEIM	05/21/1842	NY		FILM
MAULER	TOBIE	1812	MITTELWIHR	03/12/1852	NY		FILM
MAUN	BARTHELEMY	1829	OBERHERGHEIM	03/07/1854	A		FILM
MAUR	CONRAD		SCHWENNINGEN	05/24/1844	A		FILM
MAURER	AUGUSTIN	1809	NIEDERHERGHEIM	09/07/1855	NY		FILM
MAURER	DOMINIQUE	1825	NIEDERENTZEN	02/01/1852	TX	CULT	PASS
MAURER	DOMINIQUE	1825	NIEDERHERGHEIM	02/07/1852	TX		FILM
MAURER	FELIX		ENGENTHAL	03/06/1838	A		FILM
MAURER	FLAURENT		SUNDHAUSEN	03/02/1837	A		FILM
MAURER	FRANCOIS JOSEPH	1821	NIEDERHERGHEIM	02/09/1852	TX		FILM
MAURER	FRANCOIS-JOSEPH	1821	SAINTE-CROIX-AUX-MIN	02/01/1852	TX	CHAR	PASS
MAURER	GEORGES	1831	ROMBACH	10/08/1847	NO		FILM
MAURER	JAQUES		KESKASTEL	01/01/1828	A		FILM
MAURER	JAQUES	1807	RIQUEWIHR	03/09/1837	CH		FILM
MAURER	JEAN	1817	ST.MARIE AUX MINES	04/07/1854	NY		FILM
MAURER	JOSEPH	1817	ST. ULRICH	08/27/1846	NY		FILM
MAURER	JOSEPH	1826	BIESHEIM	08/20/1856	NY		FILM
MAURER	NICOLAS		KESKASTEL	01/01/1828	A		FILM
MAURER	PIERRE	1815	DRACHENBRUNN	04/15/1848	CH		FILM
MAURER CH 3	AUGUSTIN VALENT	1808	NIEDERHERGHEIM	06/12/1847	NY		FILM
MAURER D JOSEPH		1838	ST. MARIE AUX MINES	10/30/1855	NO		FILM
MAURER S JOSEPH		1833	ST. MARIE AUX MINES	10/30/1855	NO		FILM
MAURER W JOSEPH		1803	ST. MARIE AUX MINES	10/30/1855	NO		FILM
MAURER WW AND CH 2	FORTUNE	1811	ST. ULRICH	05/14/1847	NY		FILM
MAURER WW AND CH 2	JOSEPH	1792	ST. MARIE AUX MINES	10/30/1855	NO		FILM
MAURICE	AGATHE	1834	LIEPRE	09/01/1854	NO		FILM
MAURICE	GERMAIN	1822	MERWILLIERS	04/09/1844	TX		FILM
MAURY	PAUL	1833	MULHOUSE	02/23/1857	NO		FILM
MAUSCH	NICOLAS		PUBERG	01/01/1828	A		FILM
MAUSY WW AND CH 4	ANTOINE	1802	WITTENHEIM	04/13/1855	NY		FILM
MAUZER	AUGUSTIN VALENT	1808	NIEDERHERGHEIM	07/12/1847	NY		FILM
MAYER	BABETTE	1851	DRACHENBRONN	01/01/1864	NY		NO.2
MAYER	CARL		ETTENHEIM	09/02/1849	A		FILM
MAYER	JOSEPH	1838	SCHWEIZ	03/03/1866	NY		FILM
MAYER	MARGUERITE	1827	NIEDERHERGHEIM	02/09/1852	TX		FILM
MAYER	THIEBAUD	1831	THANN	11/22/1851	NY		FILM
MAYER	VALENTIN		NIEDERHAUSBERGEN	01/01/1828	A		FILM

Lastname	Firstname	Birth Year	Birthplace	Emigration	De Prof	Source
MAYLER	CHRETIEN		HAMBACH	03/08/1838 A		FILM
MAYLER	NICOLAS		HAMBACH	03/08/1838 A		FILM
MAYLER	PIERRE		HAMBACH	03/08/1838 A		FILM
MAZZEL	JOHANN	1817	YVONAND	11/15/1846 TX		FILM
MECK WW	JEAN JAQUES	1826	LUTTENBACH	05/20/1854 NY		FILM
MEEDER	CARL	1836	ROPPENHEIM	07/12/1841 A		NO.1
MEEDER	CAROLINE			05/02/1850 A		PRIV
MEEDER	PHILIPP	1839	ROPPENHEIM	07/12/1841 A		NO.1
MEEDER	PHILIPP GEORG	1838	ROPPENHEIM	07/12/1841 A		NO.1
MEEDER BR CAROLINE	PHILIPPE GEORGE	1828		10/05/1848 A		PRIV
MEEDER SI PHIL GEOR	CAROLINE		ROPPENHEIM	05/02/1850 A		NO.1
MEEDER BR PHILIPPE	FRIEDRICH	1825		07/12/1847 A		PRIV
MEEDER BR. CAROLINE	FRIEDRICH	1825	ROPPENHEIM	07/12/1847 A		NO.1
MEEDER BR.FRIEDRICH	PHILLIP GEORGE	1828	ROPPENHEIM	07/12/1847 A		NO.1
MEEDER H ARNOLD 3 CH	PHILLIPPE	1800	ROPPENHEIM	07/12/1841 A		NO.1
MEEDER H MAGDALENA	PHILIPPE	1800		07/12/1841 A		PRIV
MEEDER MN ARNOLDT	MAGDALENA	1811		07/12/1841 A		PRIV
MEEDER MN ARNOLDT	MAGDALENE	1811	ROPPENHEIM	07/12/1841 A		NO.1
MEEDER S PHILIPPE	CARL	1836		07/12/1841 A		PRIV
MEEDER S PHILIPPE	PHILIPP	1839		07/12/1841 A		PRIV
MEEDER S PHILIPPE	PHILIPP GEORG	1838		07/12/1841 A		PRIV
MEERKAM	DAVID		COSSWILLER	01/01/1828 A		FILM
MEERTRAM	DAVID		COSSWILLER	01/01/1828 A		FILM
MEHL	GEORGE		ISSENHAUSEN	01/01/1828 A		FILM
MEHL	HENRY		HATTMATT	01/01/1828 A		FILM
MEHL	JEAN		INGENHEIM	01/01/1828 A		FILM
MEHL	SALOME		HATTMATT	01/01/1828 A		FILM
MEHL WW AND CH 3	JAQUES		HERBITZHEIM	03/17/1817 A		FILM
MEHL WW AND CH 3	JEAN		BOSSELSHAUSEN	01/01/1828 A		FILM
MEHL WW AND CH 6	ADAM		BOSSELSHAUSEN	01/01/1828 A		FILM
MEHL WW AND CH 6	JAQUES		RIEDHEIM	01/01/1828 A		FILM
MEHRLE	LOUISE		RASTADT	09/20/1849 A		FILM
MEICH	JEAN BAPTISTE	1833	ST. MARIE AUX MINES	08/04/1854 NO		FILM
MEINRAD	LORENZ		ALTSCHWEYER	09/30/1849 A		FILM
MEINSOHN	FRANCOIS JOSEPH	1811	CERNAY	06/12/1846 NO		FILM
MEINSOHN	JEAN BAPTISTE	1822	CERNAY	06/17/1846 NO		FILM
MEINSOHN	JEAN BAPTISTE	1822	CERNAY	10/21/1847 NO		FILM
MEISBURGER WW CH 5	ERASM	1794	HATTSTATT	02/22/1848 A		FILM
MEISE	AGATHE	1811	BLOTZHEIM	12/16/1844 NO		FILM
MEISSERT	FRANCISKA	1847	MUNCHHOUSE	01/01/1867 NY		NO.2
MEISSERT	SUSANNA	1849	MUNCHHOUSE	01/01/1868 NY		NO.2
MEISTER	ANTOINE	1819	ROEDERSDORF	08/11/1851 NY		FILM
MEISTER	FRANCOIS XAVIER	1822	BISEL	03/22/1847 NY		FILM
MEISTER	GEORGE	1802	ST. AMARIN	03/01/1852 NY		FILM
MEISTER	MARGUERITE	1820	BAEDERSDORF	02/20/1852 NY		FILM
MEISTER AND CH 2	MARIE ANNE	1817	BENDORF	11/20/1852 NO		FILM
MEISTERKNECHT	SALOME		ROOPENHEIM	03/06/1838 A		FILM
MEIXNER	JAQUES	1807	NUSSLACH	10/07/1837 A		FILM
MELCHER SI LENTZ JEA	ELISABETH		KILLSTETT	05/28/1817 A		FILM
MELIS	GEORGE		HAMBACH	03/06/1817 A		FILM

MELLECKER   JOSEPH   1824 GUERENATTEN   04/20/1846 NY   FILM
MELLECKER   XAVIER   1802 GUERENATTEN   06/17/1851 NY   FILM
MENAGER   MAURICE   1807 BELFORT   03/01/1847 NY   FILM
MENCHHOEFFER   GEORGE   SCHILLERSDORF   01/01/1828 A   FILM
MENCHHOEFFER   JAQUES   SCHILLERSDORF   01/30/1828 A   FILM

MENCHHOEFFER   PHILIPPE   INGVILLER   01/01/1828 A   FILM
MENCHHOFFER WW CH   JAQUES   BOSSELSHAUSEN   01/01/1828 A   FILM
MENEGAY   JULES MARCEL   1834 FROIDEFONTAINE   02/16/1852 NY   FILM
MENEGLER AND CH 2   MARIE JOSEPHINE 1823 ST.LOUIS   08/25/1853 PH   FILM
MENEGUEY   1806 BOUROGNE   12/22/1863 NY   FILM

MENEGUY   JOSEPH   1791 FROIDEFONTAINE   02/21/1849 NO   FILM
MENETRE   FRANCOIS XAVIER 1838 PEROUSE   08/06/1855 NY   FILM
MENETRE WW AND CH 2 ANTOINE   1804 LIEPRE   03/30/1839 NO   FILM
MENETREZ   CATHERINE   1830 FAVEROIS   05/10/1850 NO   FILM
MENETREZ   JEAN CLAUDE   1824 MAGNY   11/13/1844 NY   FILM

MENETREZ   JEAN PIERRE   1822 MAGNY   03/20/1840 NY   FILM
MENGER   ANTOINE   DETTWILLER   01/01/1828 A   FILM
MENIGOT   MARGUERITE   1840 MONTBELIARD   05/01/1865 NY   FILM
MENNINGER   FRANCOIS JOSEPH 1816 BALDERSHEIM   10/08/1844 A   FILM
MENTZER   JEAN   INGENHEIM   01/01/1828 A   FILM

MENY   CHARLES   1838 FELLERINGEN   06/24/1854 NY   FILM
MENY   EUSTACHE   1826 FELLERINGEN   09/20/1853 DE   FILM
MENY   JEAN THIEBAUD   1819 FELLERING   09/01/1854 TX HAIR PASS
MENY   JOSEPH   1844 URBES   11/12/1865 NY   FILM
MENY   RENE   1830 FELLERINGEN   06/24/1854 NY   FILM

MENY   VALENTIN   1830 FELLERING   03/01/1861 TX PRIN PASS
MENY WW AND CH 4   JEAN THIEBAUD   1819 FELLERING   09/01/1854 TX   FILM
MERAT   JEAN PIERRE   1812 GRANDVILLARS   02/13/1849 NY   FILM
MERAT   JEAN PIERRE   1812 GRANDVILLARS   09/16/1850 NO   FILM
MERAT WW AND CH 4   JOSEPH   1820 BREBOTTE   07/18/1854 NY   FILM

MERCHLING   PHILIPPE   UTTWILLER   01/01/1828 A   FILM
MERCHLINGER   CHRISTOPHE FRED 1801 GRUNWETTERSBACH   03/01/1837 A   FILM
MERCHLINGER   DAVID   1810 GRUNWETTERSBACH   03/01/1837 A   FILM
MERCHLINGER   JEAN DAVID   GRUNWETTERSBACH   03/01/1837 A   FILM
MERCHLöIN   CATHERINE   IMBSHEIM   01/01/1828 A   FILM

MERCHLöINGER   JAQUES   1815 GRUNWETTERSBACH   03/01/1837 A   FILM
MERCHY   MARIE SALOME   1827 BEBLENHEIM   08/26/1850 NY   FILM
MERCHY H MADELEINE FREDERIQUE   1837   03/15/1856 NY   FILM
MERCIER   ELISABETHE   1799 VALENTIGNEY   02/14/1866 NY   FILM
MERCIER   JOSEPH   1820 GRANDVILLARS   08/09/1855 NO   FILM

MERCIER   JOSEPH   1842 VAL ST. DIZIER   10/11/1865 NY   FILM
MERCIER AND CH   FELIX   1825 URCEREY   04/11/1857 NY   FILM
MERCIER S FELIX   1854 URCEREY   04/11/1857 NY   FILM
MERCIER WW AND CH 2 PIERRE   1830 GRANDVILLARS   07/17/1854 NY   FILM
MERCIER WW AND CH 3 DOMINIQUE   1802 BOUROGNE   03/26/1844 NY   FILM

MERCIER WW AND CH 3 PIERRE   1813 GRANDVILLARS   08/23/1854 NO   FILM
MERCIOLE   JEAN BAPTISTE   1807 LIEPRE   08/14/1838 NO   FILM
MERCK   MAGDALENA   1849 ALTENSTADT   01/01/1869 NY   NO.2
MERCK   MARGARETHA   1832 BREMMELBACH   01/01/1868 NY   NO.2
MERCKEL   JOSEPH   LEUTENHEIM   01/01/1828 A   FILM

Lastname	Firstname	Birth Year	Birthplace	Emigration	De	Prof	Source
MERCKEL	PIERRE		MALSHEIM	01/01/1828	A		FILM
MERCKER	PHILIPPE		INGWILLER	01/01/1828	A		FILM
MERCKLE	GEORGES		GUNDERSHOFFEN	04/09/1817	A		FILM
MERCKLE	JEAN	1831	FELLERINGEN	01/28/1850	NY		FILM
MERCKLEN	FRANCOIS XAVIER	1832	THANN	10/11/1865	NY		FILM
MERCKLEN	THIEBAUD HENRI	1795	THANN	04/01/1844	NY		FIM
MERCKLEN D WALBURGE	ANETTE	1854	RANSPACH	09/05/1857	A		FILM
MERCKLEN MN WISSANG	WALBURGE CH	1823	RANSPACH	09/05/1857	A		FILM
MERCKLIN	GEORGE		IMBSHEIM	01/01/1828	A		FILM
MERCKLIN	MICHEL		IMBSHEIM	01/01/1828	A		FILM
MERCKLIN WW	HENRI		MULHAUSEN	01/01/1828	A		FILM
MERCKLIN WW AND CH 6	JAQUES		MULHAUSEN	01/01/1828	A		FILM
MERCKLING	JEAN		HATTMATT	01/01/1828	A		FILM
MERCKLING	JEAN GEORGE		BRUMATH	01/01/1828	A		FILM
MERGAIN	HENRY	1824	CHEVENEZ	03/05/1864	NY		FILM
MERGLE	BARBARA	1813	RIEDISHEIM	10/25/1843	TX		FILM
MERGLE	EMILE	1838	RIEDISHEIM	10/25/1843	TX		FILM
MERGLE	JAKOB	1836	RIEDISHEIM	10/25/1843	TX		FILM
MERGLE	KARL	1842	RIEDISHEIM	10/25/1843	TX		FILM
MERGLE	PETER	1811	RIEDISHEIM	10/25/1843	TX		FILM
MERGY	JEAN HENRI	1829	GRENZINGEN	09/14/1865	NY		FILM
MERHLEN	AMBROISE	1828	FELLERINGEN	08/22/1854	TX		FILM
MERIAN	JEAN	1817	OBERENTZEN	11/01/1848	TX	BRLA	PASS
MERION	JEAN	1817	OBERNETZEN	11/04/1848	TX		FILM
MERKEL	JOSEF	1844	SURBOURG	01/01/1867	NY	CARP	NO.2
MERKLEN	AMBROISE	1828	FELLERING	08/01/1854	TX	PRIN	PASS
MERKLEN	MONRAD	1843	MITZACH	01/01/1869	TX	BRLA	PASS
MERLET MN BROMLER	MARIE	1815	MANINGEN	07/05/1854	NY		FILM
MERLOT	CHRISTOPHE ADOL	1824	BELFORT	02/03/1852	PH		FILM
MERMAT WW AND CH	PIERRE	1820	BELFORT	06/29/1841	NY		FILM
MERMIER AND CH	FRANCOISE	1795	ANJOUTEY	07/09/1850	A		FILM
MEROTH	FERDINAND		ETTENHEIM	07/13/1849	A		FILM
MERTZ			ETTLINGEN	04/27/1849	A		FILM
MERTZ	JEAN		BUST	03/01/1838	A		FILM
MERTZ	MICHEL		AUENHEIM	05/03/1849	A		FILM
MERTZ	NICOLAS		BUST	03/01/1838	A		FILM
MERZ	CATHERINA		DUERINGEN	04/11/1849	NY		FILM
MESSANG	JOSEPH		BURCKENWALD	01/01/1828	A		FILM
MESSNER	ANTOINE		LEUTENHEIM	01/01/1828	A		FILM
MESSNER WW AND CH 2	ANTOINE		SOUFFLENHEIM	01/01/1828	A		FILM
METROT	GINGER	1817	JONCHEREY	03/06/1847	NY		FILM
METTREZ	HENRI	1842	MONTBELIARD	09/30/1865	NY		FILM
METZ	BARBE	1843	NIEDERLAUTERBACH	01/01/1869	NY	DAYL	PRIV
METZ	GEORGE		PUBERG	01/01/1828	A		FILM
METZ	JOSEPH		NIEDERBUEHL	09/20/1849	A		FILM
METZ WW AND CH 4	JAQUES		ROSTEIG	03/11/1817	A		FILM
METZE WW AND CH	PIERRE DAVID	1818	LAIRE	06/20/1848	NY		FILM
METZGER	BONIFACIUS		LE HAVRE	04/12/1849	NY		FILM
METZGER	EVE		SESSENHEIM	01/01/1828	A		FILM
METZGER	JAQUES	1821	BENNWIHR	08/13/1849	NY		FILM

Lastname	Firstname	Birth Year	Birthplace	Emigration	De	Prof	Source
METZGER	JAQUES JUN.		SESSENHEIM	01/01/1828	A		FILM
METZGER	JEAN		DETTWILLER	01/01/1828	A		FILM
METZGER	JEAN		GERMANY	04/12/1849	NY		FILM
METZGER	JEAN JAQUES		MULHOUSE	02/06/1854	NY		FILM
METZGER	JEAN JAQUES	1834	MULHOUSE	02/06/1854	NY		FILM
METZGER	JOSEPH	1809	KINTZHEIM	08/19/1850	NY		FILM
METZGER	JOSEPH	1810	KIENTZHEIM	02/21/1852	NY		FILM
METZGER	MICHEL		SCHILLERSDORF	01/01/1828	A		FILM
METZGER	MICHEL		SCHILLERSDORF	01/30/1828	A		FILM
METZINGER	GEORGE	1830	GUEBWILLER	07/02/1849	NY		FILM
METZLER	FREDERIC		ST. JEAN DES CHOUX	01/01/1828	A		FILM
METZLER	NICOLAS		SCHIRRHEIN	01/01/1828	A		FILM
METZLER	PIERRE		SOUFFLENHEIM	01/01/1828	A		FILM
MEUNIER	FRANCOIS JOSEPH	1807	DANNEMARIE	09/07/1854	NY		FILM
MEURDEFAIN	GUSTAVE	1840	ARCEY	11/04/1862	NY		FILM
MEURET	FREDERIC JERME	1800	ROUFFACH	02/01/1851	TX	MERC	PASS
MEURET	FREDERIC JEROME	1800	FOLGENBOURG	02/26/1851	TX		FILM
MEUSBURGER	JEAN CONRAD	1813	KAYSERSBERG	02/16/1850	NY		FILM
MEXER	ANNE-MARIE	1826	OBERENTZEN	11/01/1848	TX	SERV	PASS
MEY WW AND CH	JH. JAQUES		NEUHOFF	03/03/1817	A		FILM
MEYEDR MN HENRY CH 2	MARIE CATHERINE	1815	LIEPRE	03/13/1857	NO		FILM
MEYER	ADAM		SOUFFLENHEIM	03/02/1838	A		FILM
MEYER	ALEXANDRE		ST. AMARIN	08/07/1850	A		FILM
MEYER	ANDRE	1798	COLMAR	03/19/1852	NO		FILM
MEYER	ANNE MARIE	1820	OBERENTZEN	11/04/1842	TX		FILM
MEYER	ANTOINE		HAEGEN	01/01/1828	A		FILM
MEYER	ARBOGAST	1829	OBERENTZEN	09/01/1851	BRLA	PASS
MEYER	BATHOLOMAEUS	1801	SPERICHER	11/15/1846	TX		FILM
MEYER	BERNARD		OBERNAI	02/27/1838	A		FILM
MEYER	BERNARD	1840	ASCHBACH	01/01/1867	NY		NO.2
MEYER	BLASIUS	1831	OBERENSISHEIM	04/09/1844	TX		FILM
MEYER	BLASIUS	1857	MOTHERN	01/01/1867	NY		NO.2
MEYER	CATHERINE	1831	OSTHEIM	09/16/1856	NY		FILM
MEYER	CHRETIEN		SUNDHAUSEN	03/02/1837	A		FILM
MEYER	DINA	1811	NIEDERROEDERN	01/01/1869	NY		NO.2
MEYER	EMILE	1839	MULHOUSE	09/05/1855	NY		FILM
MEYER	EUSTACHE	1835	ST. AMARIN	08/22/1854	NO		FILM
MEYER	FRANCOIS		SARENNE	01/01/1828	A		FILM
MEYER	FRANCOIS ANTOIN	1813	NIEDERLANG	09/13/1837	PH		FILM
MEYER	FRANCOIS JOSEPH	1828	SONDERSDORF	04/08/1847	NY		FILM
MEYER	FRANCOIS JOSEPH	1832	URBES	01/10/1853	SF		FILM
MEYER	FRANCOISE	1824	OBERENTZEN	09/01/1846	TX	SERV	PASS
MEYER	FRANCOISE	1824	OBERENTZEN	09/19/1846	TX		FILM
MEYER	FRANZ	1812	BUTTEN	01/02/1844	TX		FILM
MEYER	GEORGE		OBERMODERN	01/01/1828	A		FILM
MEYER	GEORGE		ROESCHWOOG	01/01/1828	A		FILM
MEYER	GEORGE		TIEFFENBACH	01/01/1828	A		FILM
MEYER	GEORGE	1822	OBENBRUCK	05/02/1854	CI		FILM
MEYER	GERTRUD	1831	NIEDERROEDERN	01/01/1868	NO		NO.2
MEYER	GREGOIRE	1820	INGERSHEIM	01/28/1852	NO		FILM

166

Lastname	Firstname	Birth Year	Birthplace	Emigration	De	Prof	Source
MEYER	GUSTAVE	1823	ALTKIRCH	07/15/1847	A		FILM
MEYER	HENRI	1823	BISEL	10/08/1851	NY		FILM
MEYER	HENRIETTE	1824	MULHAUSEN	07/02/1846	TX		FILM
MEYER	HENRIETTE	1849	NIEDERSEEBACH	01/01/1866	OH		NO.2
MEYER	HENRIETTE^	1824	MULHOUSE	07/01/1846	TX		
MEYER	IGNACE		BOUXWILLER	01/01/1828	A		FILM
MEYER	IGNACE	1816	BOUXWILLER	09/30/1854	NO		FILM
MEYER	JACOB		FROESCHWEILER	01/01/1817	A	WEAV	NO.2
MEYER	JAQUES		ALTECKENDORF	01/01/1828	A		FILM
MEYER	JAQUES		BISCHWILLER	03/02/1838	A		FILM
MEYER	JAQUES		SUNDHAUSEN	03/02/1837	A		FILM
MEYER	JAQUES	1784	OBERENTZEN	09/01/1851	TX	BRLA	PASS
MEYER	JEAN	1807	WICKERSCHWIHR	10/05/1837	PH		FILM
MEYER	JEAN	1816	OSTHEIM	03/21/1845	NY		FILM
MEYER	JEAN	1818	COLMAR	08/29/1854	CH		FILM
MEYER	JEAN	1820	OSTHEIM	03/12/1847	NY		FILM
MEYER	JEAN	1828	CERNAY	06/20/1849	NY		FILM
MEYER	JEAN BAPTISTE	1828	BIESHEIM	01/12/1852	TX		FILM
MEYER	JEAN BAPTISTE	1830	WINTZENHEIM	02/28/1852	SL		FILM
MEYER	JEAN-BAPTISTE	1828	MEYENHEIM	01/01/1852	TX		PASS
MEYER	JOHANN GEORG	1808	STILL	11/22/1843			FILM
MEYER	JOSEPH	1809	BERGHEIM	12/29/1846	NO		FILM
MEYER	JOSEPH	1811	HAGUENAU	03/03/1848	NY		FILM
MEYER	JOSEPH	1826	BLOTZHEIM	10/01/1851	A		FILM
MEYER	JOSEPH	1827	BERNANDORF	02/02/1849	NY		FILM
MEYER	JOSEPH	1834	OBERENSISHEIM	04/09/1844	TX		FILM
MEYER	JOSEPH JUN.		BURCKENWALD	01/01/1828	A		FILM
MEYER	JOSEPH SEN.		BURCKENWALD	01/01/1828	A		FILM
MEYER	LOUIS		STRUTH	01/01/1828	A		FILM
MEYER	LOUIS	1841	DURMENACH	10/01/1860	NY		FILM
MEYER	LUDWIG	1819	SELESTAT	01/01/1845	A		PRIV
MEYER	M		EUDINGEN	04/03/1849	NY		FILM
MEYER	MADELEINE	1828	STRUTH	04/19/1851	A		FILM
MEYER	MADELEINE	1830	NIFTER	02/21/1849	NY		FILM
MEYER	MAGDALENA	1858	MOTHERN	01/01/1867	NY		NO.2
MEYER	MARGARETHE	1795	NIEDERROEDERN	01/01/1864	NY		NO.2
MEYER	MARGARITE	1827	NIEDERHERGHEIM	02/01/1852	TX		PASS
MEYER	MARGUERITE		TIEFFENBACH	01/01/1828	A		FILM
MEYER	MARIE ANNE	1835	OBERENSISHEIM	04/09/1844	TX		FILM
MEYER	MARTIN	1834	BREITENBACH	04/19/1856	NY		FILM
MEYER	MICHEL		NEHWILLER	01/01/1868	NY		NO.2
MEYER	MICHEL	1799	NIEDERROEDERN	01/01/1864	NY	FARM	NO.2
MEYER	MICHEL	1822	MARMONTIER	09/16/1853	A		FILM
MEYER	MINETTE	1848	NIEDERROEDERN	01/01/1847	NO		NO.2
MEYER	NARCISSE	1818	OSTHEIM	03/21/1845	NY		FILM
MEYER	PANTALEON		MEMMELSHOFFEN	01/01/1817	A		NO.2
MEYER	PHILIPPE	1813	ALTKIRCH	09/03/1849	NO		FILM
MEYER	PHILIPPE HENRI		ASCHBACH	06/21/1838	A		FILM
MEYER	ROSINA		KIECHLINGSBERG	05/24/1849	A		FILM
MEYER	SEBASTEIN	1826	STRUTH	02/15/1851	PH		FILM

Lastname	Firstname	Birth Year	Birthplace	Emigration	De	Prof	Source
MEYER	SEBASTIEN		HOLTZHEIM	03/01/1838	A		FILM
MEYER	THIEBAUD	1815	MICHELBACH	02/03/1852	NY		FILM
MEYER WW AND CH 2	JEAN	1816	SONDERNACH	04/19/1845	NY		FILM
MEYER WW AND CH 4	FRANCOIS	1808	BURNHAUPT-LE-HAUT	04/21/1847	NY		FILM
MEYER WW AND CH 4	LUDAU		LIPSHEIM	05/27/1817	A		FILM
MEYER CH	ANNE MARIE		WEILER	06/18/1849	A		FILM
MEYER CH 7	JOSEPH	1800	WITTELSHEIM	11/01/1844	TX	CULT	PASS
MEYER D MARIE CATHER		1840	LIEPRE	03/13/1857	NO		FILM
MEYER MN HEISLER	CATHERINE	1801	ROUFFACH	08/29/1854	SL		FILM
MEYER MN HUG	ANNA		NEU-BREISACH	01/01/1845	NO		PRIV
MEYER MN KELTENRING	DOROTHEE	1809	TRULBEN	11/19/1850	PH		FILM
MEYER MN WEISS	THERESE	1797	BERGHEIM	03/25/1856	NY		FILM
MEYER S CATHERINE	MARIE	1834	OSTHEIM	09/16/1856	NY		FILM
MEYER S MARIE	CATHERINE	1831	OSTHEIM	09/16/1856	NY		FILM
MEYER S MARIE CATHER		1843	LIEPRE	03/13/1857	NO		FILM
MEYER W 2 CH	JOSEF	1828	MOTHERN	01/01/1867	NY		NO.2
MEYER W HAEHN JOSEPH	CATHERINE	1823	ENSCHENBERG	05/05/1857	NY		FILM
MEYER W HOFSTETTER J	SALOME	1824	HOLTZHEIM	09/25/1857	NY		FILM
MEYER WW	FRANCOIS ULRICH	1810	ST. AMARIN	05/30/1845	NY		FILM
MEYER WW	JAQUES	1784	OBERENTZEN	09/10/1851	TX		FILM
MEYER WW	SEBASTIEN	1821	ST. AMARIN	02/08/1854	CI		FILM
MEYER WW	TRUDBERT		MOLSHEIM	03/03/1817	A		FILM
MEYER WW AND CH	ANTOINE	1822	DESSENHEIM	03/15/1853	NY		FILM
MEYER WW AND CH	DOMINIQUE	1794	WATTWILLER	11/13/1854	NY		FILM
MEYER WW AND CH	JEAN BAPTISTE	1819	BOLLWILLER	04/27/1850	NO		FILM
MEYER WW AND CH 2	ANTOINE		SOUFFLENHEIM	03/02/1838	A		FILM
MEYER WW AND CH 3	JEAN	1821	TRAUBACH-LE-BAS	04/11/1855	NY		FILM
MEYER WW AND CH 3	JOSEPH	1802	TURCKHEIM	11/19/1844	NO		FILM
MEYER WW AND CH 4	CLAUDE		LA PEITIE PIERRE	03/03/1817	A		FILM
MEYER WW AND CH 4	ETIENNE	1806	FULLEREN	12/24/1846	A		FILM
MEYER WW AND CH 4	JOSEPH	1788	BOURBACH-LE-BAS	11/21/1847	NY		FILM
MEYER WW AND CH 5	AMARIN	1810	DIDENHEIM	09/05/1854	NY		FILM
MEYER WW AND CH 6	JOSEPH	1805	BOURBACH	10/08/1844	NY		FILM
MEYER WW AND CH 6	PHILIPPE	1813	WURMLINGEN	03/11/1854	BU		FILM
MEYER WW AND CH 7	JOSEPH	1800	WITTELSHEIM	11/11/1844	NO		FILM
MEYER WW AND CH 7	SEBASTIEN	1802	BOURBACH-LE-BAS	11/17/1845	NY		FILM
MEYLING	JOSEPH	1817	SOULTZ	06/17/1847	NY		FILM
MEYUNG	ANTOINE	1842	WALDIGHOFEN	12/13/1865	NY		FILM
MICHEL	ANTOINE		WILWISHEIM	01/01/1828	A		FILM
MICHEL	EILISA		LEUTESHEIM	04/21/1849	NY		FILM
MICHEL	GEORGES		SCHILTIGHEIM	01/01/1828	A		FILM
MICHEL	JAQUES		MARLENHEIM	01/01/1828	A		FILM
MICHEL	JEAN		INGENHEIM	01/01/1828	A		FILM
MICHELAT H JULIE GEN	ALOISIUS	1838	ST.DIZIER	10/01/1865	NY		FILM
MICHELAT W ALOISIUS	JULIE GENEVIEVE	1843	ST.DIZIER	10/01/1865	NY		FILM
MICHELI	PHILIPPE		WEINBOURG	01/01/1828	A		FILM
MICLO	JEAN NICOLAS	1825	ORBEY	03/16/1851	NY		FILM
MICLO MN PATRY	BARBE	1820	ORBEY	06/28/1855	A		FILM
MIEGEL	ADAM		DIEMERINGEN	03/03/1838	A		FILM
MIEGEL	CATHERINE		DIEMERINGEN	03/03/1838	A		FILM

Lastname	Firstname	Birth Year	Birthplace	Emigration	De	Prof	Source
MIEGEL	CHERTIEN		DIEMERINGEN	03/03/1838	A		FILM
MIEGEL	PHILIPPE		DIEMERINGEN	03/03/1838	A		FILM
MIGG MN FEGER CH	PAULINE	1824	ZELL	08/23/1850	NY		FILM
MIGNEREZ	JEAN NICOL	1803	ETOBONS	07/01/1863	NY		FILM
MILHOT	GEORGES	1831	FRAISSE	03/06/1866	NY		FILM
MILIUS	GUILLAUME		OTTENBOURG	08/11/1849	A		FILM
MILLER	BARBE	1830	BELFORT	09/01/1852	A		FILM
MILLER	CHRISTINE		WEISLINGEN	01/01/1828	A		FILM
MILLER	JOSEPH	1821	CHARANATTE	01/30/1840	NY		FILM
MILLER	PHILIPPE JEAN		WEISLINGEN	01/01/1828	A		FILM
MILLER	PHILIPPE JUN.		WEISLINGEN	01/01/1828	A		FILM
MILLER	PHILIPPE SEN.		WEISLINGEN	01/01/1828	A		FILM
MILLES	JAQUES		RUNTZENHEIM	01/01/1828	A		FILM
MILLES	PIERRE		RUNTZENHEIM	01/01/1828	A		FILM
MILLET	JOSEPH	1836	BOTANS	04/28/1852	NY		FILM
MILLET WW AND CH 3	FRANCOIS	1811	BOTANS	04/29/1853	NY		FILM
MILLET WW AND CH 4	JEAN CLAUDE	1806	BOTANS	04/29/1853	NY		FILM
MILTENBREI	ANNA		AUENHEIM	05/03/1849	A		FILM
MINEMEYER	PHILIPPE		PFALZWEYER	01/01/1828	A		FILM
MINGER	PETER	1820	HAINFELD	04/09/1844	TX		FILM
MINKE	SAMUEL		FROHMUHL	01/01/1828	A		FILM
MINKER CH 4	VEUVE		FROHMUHL	01/01/1817	A		FILM
MINNEMEYER	NICOLAS		BUST	03/01/1838	A		FILM
MINNEMEYER WW CH 4	PIERRE		SCHOENBURG	01/01/1828	A		FILM
MINNI	GEORGES		DETTWILELR	01/01/1828	A		FILM
MISCHLER	ANNE MARIE	1835	BENNWIHR	06/24/1854	NY		FILM
MISCHLER	MADELEINE	1831	BENNWIHR	12/13/1856	NY		FILM
MISSLAND	JEAN	1821	BITSCHWILLER	10/18/1845	NY		FILM
MISSLAND	MARIE ANNE	1822	WILLER	01/01/1846	NY		FILM
MISSLIN WW AND CH 4	JOSEPH		GRANDDUCHY OF BADEN	06/27/1833	A		FILM
MITSCHLER	JOSEF		REICHSHOFFEN	01/01/1817	A		NO.2
MITTNACHT	JEAN JAQUES	1812	HUNAWIHR	08/28/1848	NY		FILM
MJULLER S LAURENT	LAURENT		ZINSWEILLER	02/16/1817	A		FILM
MMUHLHEIM	MARIE		OBERMODERN	01/01/1828	A		FILM
MOCH	ADELE	1846	HAGUENAU	01/01/1869	NY		NO.2
MOCHRINGER	JOSEPH	1830	ALTKIRCH	01/19/1849	CI		FILM
MOCK	BABETTE	1815	HATTEN	01/01/1865	NY		NO.2
MOCKEL	HENRI		MUTTERSHOLTZ	04/05/1838	A		FILM
MOEGLIN	SEBASTIEN	1819	MEYENHEIM	11/01/1851	TX	CULT	PASS
MOELLINGER	JOSEPH	1831	WELLOLSHEIM	06/30/1854	NY		FILM
MOELLINGER WW	GEORGE LOUIS		NIEDERBRONN	01/01/1817	A		FILM
MOERCH WW AND CH	SIMON		GRANDDUCHY OF BADEN	06/27/1833	A		FILM
MOERSCHFELDER	CHRETIEN		PFALZWEYER	01/01/1828	A		FILM
MOGLIN	SEBASTIEN	1819	MEYENHEIM	11/04/1851	TX		FILM
MOGNAT	CLOTILDE	1844	ARCEY	10/07/1865	NY		FILM
MOHN	JOSEPH	1818	HIRSINGEN	04/20/1852	NY		FILM
MOHN	MORAND	1824	THANN	02/22/1851	NY		FILM
MOINAT	CATHERINE	1823	ST. DIZIER	04/16/1847	NY		FILM
MOINAT H MARIE	VALENTIN	1827	ST. DIZIER	10/01/1865	NY		FILM
MOINAT MN PROUKER	MARIE W VALENT		ST. DIZIER	10/01/1865	NY		FILM

Lastname	Firstname	Birth Year	Birthplace	Emigration	De	Prof	Source
MOINAT S OR D VALENT		1859	ST. DIZIER	10/01/1865	NY		FILM
MOINAT S VALENTIN	AUGUSTE	1862	ST. DIZIER	10/01/1865	NY		FILM
MOINAT S VALENTIN	PIERRE	1851	ST.DIZIER	10/01/1865	NY		FILM
MOINE CH	PIERRE	1782	BORON	03/02/1847	NY		FILM
MOINET	FRANCOIS	1796	DENNEY	03/06/1838	NY		FILM
MOINET WW AND CH 3	PIERRE	1800	DENNEY	08/21/1855	A		FILM
MOLINART WW AND CH 6	DANIEL		WINGEN	01/01/1817	A		FILM
MOLL	ANTOINE	1845	RAEDERSDORF	10/26/1865	NY		FILM
MOLL	CHARLES		DIEDENDORF	03/03/1838	A		FILM
MOLL	EMILE	1842	NIEDER-HAGENTHAL	10/06/1865	NY		FILM
MOLL	HENRY		DIEDENDORF	03/03/1838	A		FILM
MOLL	JEAN	1819	RAEDERSDORF	03/01/1861	NY		FILM
MOLL	JOSEPHINE		GERMANY	04/17/1849	A		FILM
MOLLINGER WW	GEORGE LUCIEN		NIEDERBRONN	02/26/1817	A		FILM
MOLLY	ANTOINE	1810	COLMAR	01/05/1842	NY		FILM
MOMMER	JOSEPH		THAL	01/01/1828	A		FILM
MOMMER	PIERRE		THAL	01/01/1828	A		FILM
MONDRUX	FRANCOIS	1811	MOVAL	10/22/1841	A		FILM
MONIER	THIEBAUD	1829	BESONCOURT	09/26/1865	NY		FILM
MONNIER	CELESTIN	1837	SUARCE	12/01/1865	NY		FILM
MONNIER	FRANCOIS	1810	FAVEROIS	08/21/1855	NO		FILM
MONNIER	FRANCOIS XAVIER	1795	SUARCE	04/21/1841	NY		FILM
MONNIER	JEAN	1799	ANJOUTEY	01/15/1852	LO		FILM
MONNIER	JEAN BAPTISTE	1815	ETUEFFONT HAUT	03/09/1840	NY		FILM
MONNIER	JEAN PIERRE	1797	CHEVREMONT	11/06/1846	NY		FILM
MONNIER	MARIE	1848	BAVEREL	09/30/1866	NY		FILM
MONNIER AND CH 2	JEAN CLAUDE	1803	COLMAR	01/23/1854	NY		FILM
MONNIER D NICOLAS F	MARGUERITE	1847	ANJOUTEY	02/03/1857	NO		FILM
MONNIER H MARIE	HENRY	1800	GROSMAGNY	03/03/1865	NY		FILM
MONNIER MN GIRARD	URSULE	1791	DENNEY	03/08/1856	NY		FILM
MONNIER S NICOLAS		1847	ANJOUTEY	02/03/1857	NO		FILM
MONNIER S NICOLAS F		1851	ANJOUTEY	02/03/1857	NO		FILM
MONNIER S NICOLAS F		1853	ANJOUTEY	02/03/1857	NO		FILM
MONNIER S NICOLAS F		1855	ANJOUTEY	02/03/1857	NO		FILM
MONNIER W HENRY	MARIE	1804	GROSMAGNY	03/03/1865	NY		FILM
MONNIER W NICOLAS F		1821	ANJOUTEY	02/03/1857	NO		FILM
MONNIER WW	FRANCOIS	1830	FAREROIS	08/21/1855	NO		FILM
MONNIER WW AND CH 3	JOSEPH	1803	ROPPE	11/22/1853	NY		FILM
MONNIER WW AND CH 5	NICOLAS FERDINA	1821	ANJOUTEY	02/03/1857	NO		FILM
MONNIN	FRANCOIS	1807	ARGIESANS	07/13/1847	NY		FILM
MONNIN	XAVIER	1819	LEBETAIN	11/10/1854	NY		FILM
MONNIOT	ACHILLE	1854	ARCEY	03/26/1864	NY		FILM
MONNIOT	FRINGUE	1861	ARCEY	03/26/1864	NY		FILM
MONNIOT	HYPOLITE	1828	ARCEY	03/26/1864	NY		FILM
MONNIOT	JUSTINA	1857	ARCEY	03/26/1864	NY		FILM
MONNIOT	MATIDE	1864	ARCEY	03/26/1864	NY		FILM
MONNIOT	PHILIBERT	1824	ARCEY	03/26/1864	NY		FILM
MONSCHE	THIEBAUD	1836	MUNSTER	06/13/1854	NY		FILM
MONSCHEIN WW	AUGUSTIN	1804	OSTHEIM	04/18/1846	NY		FILM
MONSCHEIN WW AND CH2	MICHEL	1811	OSTHEIM	04/23/1844	NY		FILM

Lastname	Firstname	Birth Year	Birthplace	Emigration	De	Prof	Source
MONTAGNON	XAVIER	1825	CHAVANNES-SUR-L`ETAN	05/29/1848	NY		FILM
MONTANDON WW AND CH6	FRANCOIS JOSEPH	1807	PORRENTRUY	03/23/1855	SL		FILM
MONTARON	GUSTAVE	1845	ROUGEMONT	10/08/1866	NY		FILM
MONTARON WW AND CH 5	SEBASTIEN	1790	ROUGEMONT	10/22/1844	PH		FILM
MONTENDON	FRANCOIS XAVIER	1804	LEPUIX	08/09/1853	NY		FILM
MONTRE	JEANNE	1866	GRANDVILLARS	08/28/1866	NY		FILM
MOOG	ALFRED	1852	NIEDERROEDERN	01/01/1869	NY		NO.2
MOOG	CAROLINE		NIEDERROEDERN	01/01/1866	NO		PRIV
MOOG	CAROLINE	1851	NIEDERROEDERN	01/01/1867	NO		NO.2
MOOG	CHARLES		NIEDERROEDERN	01/01/1866	NO		PRIV
MOOG	CHARLOTTE	1845	NIEDERROEDERN	01/01/1865	NO		NO.2
MOOG	CLEMENCIA	1849	NIEDERROEDERN	01/01/1869	NY		NO.2
MOOG	GEORG	1866	WINTZENBACH	01/01/1866	NY		NO.2
MOOG	JOHANETTA	1853	NIEDERROEDERN	01/01/1869	NY		NO.2
MOOG	M.	1847	NIEDERROEDERN	01/01/1867	NO	SHMA	NO.2
MOOG	MEYER		NIEDERROEDERN	01/01/1866	NO		PRIV
MOOG AND CH 3	ELISABETH	1799	SCHLEITHAL	07/18/1854	NY		FILM
MOOG MN TROMTER	EVA	1841	WINTZENBACH	01/01/1866	NO		NO.2
MOOG W W 1CH	JOHANN	1838	WINTZENBACH	01/01/1864	NY		NO.2
MORAND MN DIETTMANN	MADELAINE		WITTERSDORFF	03/25/1856	A		FILM
MOREL WW	SAMUEL	1805	THANN	04/03/1849	NY		FILM
MORGEN			LAUTERBOURG	01/01/1850	NO		PRIV
MORGEN	MICHEL	1838	LAUTERBURG	01/01/1867	NO	FARM	NO.2
MORITZ	ANNE		ZUTZENDORFF	01/01/1828	A		FILM
MORITZ	BARBE	1840	GUEBWILLER	04/15/1857	NY		FILM
MORITZ	JEAN BAPTISTE	1832	FRIESEN	09/20/1853	NY		FILM
MORITZ	LEONARD		PFAFFENHOFFEN	01/01/1828	A		FILM
MORITZ	STANISLAUS	1828	KRUTH	06/12/1854	NY		FILM
MORITZ WW AND CH	JEAN ADAM		PFAFFENHOFFEN	10/13/1842	A		FILM
MORKARSCH	JOSEPH		HONGRIE	08/11/1849	A		FILM
MORLOCH AND CH			OELBRONN	04/11/1849	A		FILM
MORLOT WW	CHRISTOPHE ADOL	1824	BELFORT	02/03/1852	PH		FILM
MORTEAU	ANTOINE	1833	DANJOUTIN	02/06/1849	NY		FILM
MORTEAU AND CH	MARIANNE	1821	DANJOUTIN	08/26/1847	NO		FILM
MOSACK	MICHEL		SOUFFLENHEIM	03/02/1838	A		FILM
MOSATT	LOUIS	1837	CHAUX	12/04/1855	NO		FILM
MOSCHENROSCH	MICHEL		BISCHWILLER	03/02/1828	A		FILM
MOSCHENROSS	IGNACE		HAGUENAU	03/01/1838	A		FILM
MOSER	BENOIT	1800	BOLLWILLER	03/23/1843	NY		FILM
MOSER	CHRETIEN	1829	BOLLWILLER	02/28/1853	NY		FILM
MOSER	GEORG	1839	DUERRENBACH	01/01/1866	NY		NO.2
MOSER	GEORGE		GERMANY	04/01/1849	NY		FILM
MOSER	JEAN		SPEIHINGEN	05/23/1849	A		FILM
MOSER	JOHANN		KUHLENDORF	01/01/1817	A		NO.2
MOSER CH 3	JEAN CHRETIEN		MOLSHEIM	03/08/1838	A		FILM
MOSER MN ROTH CH 6	ELISABETH	1807	LA CROIX AUX MINES	02/24/1854	NY		FILM
MOSER WW AND CH	FREDERIC CONRAD	1826	GUEBWILLER	08/26/1854	NY		FILM
MOSER WW AND CH 4	JEAN		KUHLENDORF	03/28/1817	A		FILM
MOSSELER	MADELEINE		WEISLINGEN	01/01/1828	A		FILM
MOSSER	ELISABETH	1810	MECHE	12/31/1851	NY		FILM

Lastname	Firstname	Birth Year	Birthplace	Emigration	De	Prof	Source
MOSSER	GEORGES		SCHIRRHEIN	04/30/1838	A		FILM
MOSSER	JACQUES		BISWILLER	03/02/1838	A		FILM
MOSSER	MATHIEU		SOUFFLENHEIM	03/02/1838	A		FILM
MOSSER	THIEBAUD	1820	GUEWENHEIM	01/17/1852	NY		FILM
MOSSER WW	FIDELE	1813	ROFFACH	12/11/1843	JE		FILM
MOSSER WW AND CH 2	JEAN		FROHMUHL	03/06/1817	A		FIM
MOSSER WW AND CH 3	CHRETIEN		HEMMERSWILLER	03/29/1817	A		FILM
MOSSER WW AND CH 7	JOSEPH		SOUFFLENHEIM	03/02/1838	A		FILM
MOSSLER F OF 3	BRIGITTE		DETTWILLER	01/01/1833	A		FILM
MOSSMANN	FREDERIC		NEUWILLER	01/01/1828	A		FILM
MOST	LAURENT	1821	ZILLISHEIM	06/13/1853	NY		FILM
MOST	NICOLAS	1832	THANN	04/20/1857	NY		FILM
MOSTER	JULIENNE		KANDELI	04/23/1849	NY		FILM
MOTHFRISCH	MICHEL		LUPSTEIN	01/01/1828	A		FILM
MOTSCH	ETIENNE	1829	MERXHEIM	04/17/1849	NO		FILM
MOTTET WW AND CH 6	XAVIER	1815	ROPPE	11/22/1853	NY		FILM
MOUGENOT	AUGUSTIN	1820	CHALONVILLARD	03/05/1865	NY		FILM
MOUGEOT	LOUIS FRANCOIS	1829	ST.MARIE AUX MINES	07/26/1847	NO		FILM
MOUGIN	XAVIER	1846	CHALONVILLARS	02/13/1866	NY		FILM
MOUILLESAEAUX	JOSEPH	1815	BOERSEN	02/17/1848	NY		FILM
MOUILLESEAUX	MARIE	1822	ANDEL	02/22/1847	NY		FILM
MOUILLESEAUX CH	MARIE ANNE	1794	ANDELNANS	02/25/1848	NY		FILM
MOULIEN WW AND CH 2	PIERRE	1816	ROUGEMONT	02/24/1840	PH		FILM
MOULIN WW AND CH 4	JEAN PIERRE	1788	ROUGEMONT	02/24/1840	PH		FILM
MOUNIEN	FREDERIC	1824	BEAUCOURT	04/26/1854	NY		FILM
MOUNIER	FRANCOIS XAVIER	1800	SUARCE	04/21/1841	NY		FILM
MOUNIER	MARIE	1848	BADEVEL	09/30/1866	NY		FILM
MOUONIER	FRANCOIS	1832	ROMAGNY	03/04/1865	NY		FILM
MOUREAUX	JACQUES	1814	DELLE	04/06/1840	NY		FILM
MOURNE CH 3	MARIE ANNE	1819	VEZELOIS	03/19/1847	NO		FILM
MOUTH	MICHEL	1820	LEMBACH	01/01/1866	NY		NO.2
MOUTRE	JULIE	1838	VELESCOT	08/22/1861	NY		FILM
MOYNOT	CLOTILDE	1844	ARCEY	10/07/1865	NY		FILM
MOZER	AUGUSTIN	1835	CHAMPAGNEY	03/02/1860	NY		FILM
MUCHER	JOSEF KARL	1830	SURBOURG	01/01/1867	NO	MERC	NO.2
MUCKENSTURM	ANTOINE		WOMMENHEIM	02/28/1838	A		FILM
MUECHLER WW AND CH	IGNACE	1820	SIGOLSHEIM	04/09/1845	NY		FILM
MUELLER			WITTENDORF	05/12/1849	NY		FILM
MUELLER	ANTOINE		WILLENGEN	05/02/1849	NY		FILM
MUELLER	BARBE		STADELHOFEN	07/29/1849	A		FILM
MUELLER	CECILIA		MUELHAUSEN	04/28/1849	A		FILM
MUELLER	CHERTIEN		KORK	04/21/1849	NY		FILM
MUELLER	CHRISITAN		WITTENDORF	05/12/1849	A		FILM
MUELLER	CHRISTIAN		BACKNANG	07/30/1849	A		FILM
MUELLER	CHRISTINA		WITTENDORF	05/12/1849	A		FILM
MUELLER	FELIX		DURBACH	09/05/1849	A		FILM
MUELLER	FRIEDRICH		WITTENDORF	05/12/1849	A		FILM
MUELLER	GEORG	1806	ROHRSCHWIHR	10/25/1843	TX		FILM
MUELLER	GOTTLIEB		WITTENDORF	05/12/1849	A		FILM
MUELLER	HEINRICH	1808	FRANKFURT A.MAIN	11/22/1843	TX		FILM

Lastname	Firstname	Birth Year	Birthplace	Emigration	De	Prof	Source
MUELLER	JEAN		WITTENDORF	05/12/1844	A		FILM
MUELLER	JOH.JACQUES		NIEDERBRONN	05/13/1838	A		FILM
MUELLER	JOSEPH		NIEDERLAUTERBACH	01/01/1850	NO		PRIV
MUELLER	JOSEPH		NIEDERLAUTERBACH	01/01/1866	NO		PRIV
MUELLER	JULES		NIEDERLAUTERBACH	01/01/1850	NO		PRIV
MUELLER	MARIE		ENDERSBACH	04/21/1849	A		FILM
MUELLER	MARIE		NIEDERLAUTERBACH	01/01/1850	NO		PRIV
MUELLER	MARIE		WITTENDORF	05/12/1849	A		FILM
MUELLER	REGINE		ENDERSBACH	04/21/1849	A		FILM
MUELLER	ROSALIE		NIEDERLAUTERBACH	01/01/1850	NO		PRIV
MUELLER	ROSINA		HEIDELBERG	06/01/1849	A		FILM
MUELLER	THEODORE	1812	ELFELD	10/25/1843	TX		FILM
MUELLER	THEODORE	1812	ELFELD(NASSAU)	10/25/1843	TX		FILM
MUELLER	WENDELIN		STADELHOFEN	07/29/1849	A		FILM
MUELLER WW AND CH 3	MARTIN	1809	ERSCHWIL (SS)	05/29/1844	TX		FILM
MUELLER D CHRETIEN	BARBE		KORK	04/21/1849	NY		FILM
MUELLER D CHRETIEN	CHRISITNE		KORK	04/21/1849	NY		FILM
MUELLER D CHRETIEN	ELISE		KORK	04/21/1849	NY		FILM
MUELLER D CHRETIEN	MARIE		KORK	04/21/1849	NY		FILM
MUELLER D MARTIN	FLORENTIN	1844	ERSCHWIL(SW)	05/29/1844	TX		FILM
MUELLER D MARTIN	ROSE DOMINIKA	1841	ERSCHWIL(SW)	05/29/1844	TX		FILM
MUELLER D MARTIN	ROSE DOMINIKA	1841	ERSCHWILL	04/09/1844	TX		FILM
MUELLER H MARIE	CHRETIEN		KORK	04/21/1849	NY		FILM
MUELLER MN BAUER	MAGDALENA	1811	ERSCHWILL	04/09/1844	TX		FILM
MUELLER MN KLENK	MARIE		KORK	04/21/1849	NY		FILM
MUELLER S CHRETIEN	JEAN		KORK	04/21/1849	NY		FILM
MUELLER S MARTIN	FLORENTIN	1844	ERSCHWILL	04/09/1844	TX		FILM
MUELLER S MARTIN	WILHELM	1837	ERSCHWIL(SW)	05/29/1844	TX		FILM
MUELLER S VALENTIN	BERNHARD		BUEHL	01/01/1841	A		SUESS
MUELLER S VALENTIN	GEORG		BUEHL	01/01/1841	A	TAYL	SUESS
MUELLER WW AND CH 2	MARTIN	1809	ERSCHWILL	04/09/1844	TX		FILM
MUELLERLEILE F OF 6	CATHERINE		LAHN	09/30/1849	A		FILM
MUENCH	BERNHARD	1793	HATTSTATT	11/15/1846	CL		FILM
MUENCH	BERNHARD	1793	HATTSTATT	11/15/1846	TX		FILM
MUENCH	ERASMUS	1812	FELLERINGEN	04/09/1844	CL		FILM
MUENCH	ERASMUS	1812	FELLERINGEN	04/09/1844	TX		FILM
MUENCHER	KATHARINA	1818	WESTFALEN	09/17/1845	TX		FILM
MUENCHNER	KATHARINA	1818	WESTFALEN	09/17/1845	CL		FILM
MUETH	JEAN	1818	BISEL	04/28/1842	NY		FILM
MUGEL	NICOLAS		BOUXWILLER	01/01/1828	A		FILM
MUGEL F OF 7	GEORGES		WEINBOURG	01/01/1828	A		FILM
MUGEL WW AND CH 7	CHARLES		ALTWILLER	01/01/1817	A		FILM
MUGLER	PHILIPPE		DEMENINGEN	03/03/1838	A		FILM
MUGLER	PHILIPPE		DEMERINGEN	01/01/1828	A		FILM
MUHL F OF 2	GEORGE		GEUDERTHEIM	03/01/1838	A		FILM
MUHLBERGER D LUDWIG	MARIE LOUISE		HATTEN	01/01/1846	A		SUESS
MUHLER	BARBE		CHATEMOIS	03/08/1838	A		FILM
MUHLER	FRANCOIUSE		CHATENOIS	03/08/1838	A		FILM
MUHLER D JEAN	BARBE		CHATENOIS	03/08/1838	A		FILM
MUHLER D JEAN	FRANCOISE		CHATENOIS	03/08/1838	A		FILM

Lastname	Firstname	Birth Year	Birthplace	Emigration	De	Prof	Source
MUHLER D JEAN	MARIE ANNE		CHATENOIS	03/08/1838	A		FILM
MUHLER MN WENNERT	CATHERINE		CHATENOIS	03/08/1838	A		FILM
MUHLER S JEAN	JEAN		CHATENOIS	03/08/1838			FILM
MUHLER WW AND CH 5	JEAN		CHATENOIS	03/08/1838	A		FILM
MULET	XAVIER	1824	AUXELLES-BAS	07/11/1853	NO		FILM
MULHEINN F OF 4	MARIE		OBERMODERN	01/01/1828	A		FILM
MULLER			LAUTERBOURG	01/01/1850	NO		PRIV
MULLER	ANNE MARIE		HORNBERG	06/11/1849	A		FILM
MULLER	ANTOINE	1808	KAYSERSBERG	08/28/1844	NO		FILM
MULLER	ANTON	1838	LAUTERBURG	01/01/1867	NO	FARM	NO.2
MULLER	AUGUSTE THEODOR	1805	COLMAR	10/10/1840	SL		FILM
MULLER	CHARLES	1811	TINSWEILLER	02/16/1817	A		FILM
MULLER	CONRAD		LANGENSOULTZBACH	01/01/1817	A	DAYL	NO.2
MULLER	ELISABETH	1824	MOTHERN	01/01/1867	NY		NO.2
MULLER	EMILE	1822	THANN	09/30/1856	NY		FILM
MULLER	EMILE	1838	THANN	07/29/1857	CI		FILM
MULLER	FRANCOIS JOSEPH		BERRWILLER	01/01/1857	TX		PASS
MULLER	FRANCOIS JOSPEH	1818	FALKWILLER	09/10/1844	NO		FILM
MULLER	FRANCOIS LEON	1834	MULHOUSE	02/09/1852	NY		FILM
MULLER	FRANCOISE	1831	THANN	08/05/1848	RI		FILM
MULLER	FRIEDRICH		LANGENSOULTZBACH	01/01/1817	A		NO.2
MULLER	GEORG	1845	WEISSENBURG	01/01/1865	NY		NO.2
MULLER	ISISDOR	1847	DEHLINGEN	/ /	LA		BULL
MULLER	JACQUES		LOHR	01/01/1828	A		FILM
MULLER	JACQUES		RATTENWEILER	05/24/1849	A		FILM
MULLER	JACQUES	1803	NEUWILLER	10/04/1845	CI		FILM
MULLER	JACQUES	1839	RIEDSELTZ(BR)	10/02/1855	NY		FILM
MULLER	JEAN		BIRCKENWALD	01/01/1828	A		FILM
MULLER	JEAN	1805	NIEDERENTZEN	01/20/1844	JE		FILM
MULLER	JEAN	1820	KAYSERSBERG	06/30/1843	NO		FILM
MULLER	JEAN BAPTISTE	1828	FERRETTE	02/10/1847	NY		FILM
MULLER	JOSEPH		BIRKENWALD	01/01/1828	A		FILM
MULLER	JOSEPH		COLMAR	04/20/1852	NY		FILM
MULLER	JOSEPH		NIEDERLAUTERBACH	01/01/1850	NO		PRIV
MULLER	JOSEPH		REIPERTSWILLER	01/01/1817	A		FILM
MULLER	JOSEPH	1823	MOÖÖAU	12/11/1848	NO		FILM
MULLER	JOSEPH	1826	BANTZENHEIM	04/15/1854	A		FILM
MULLER	JOSEPH	1828	TESSENHEIM	06/01/1852	NO		FILM
MULLER	JULIUS	1856	NIEDERLAUTERBACH	01/01/1866	NO		NO.2
MULLER	LOUIS			01/01/1856	NY		FILM
MULLER	LOUIS	1817	BERGHEIM	12/29/1854	NO		FILM
MULLER	LOUIS ERNEST	1824	WILDBERG (W)	08/23/1848	NY		FILM
MULLER	MARGUERITE		NIEDERMODERN	01/01/1828	A		FILM
MULLER	MARIE		NIEDERLAUTERBACH	01/01/1850	NO		PRIV
MULLER	MARIE	1844	NIEDERLAUTERBACH	01/01/1866	NO		NO.2
MULLER	MARIE ANNE	1831	ILLHAUSEN	09/07/1857	NY		FILM
MULLER	MARIE ELISABETH	1831	ECHENTZWILLER	08/20/1857	NO		FILM
MULLER	MEINRAD	1820	STRUTH	11/25/1846	PH		FILM
MULLER	MICHEL		THAL(KANTON MARMOUT)	01/01/1828	A		FILM
MULLER	MICHEL	1814	WITTELSHEIM	11/13/1844	TX		FILM

Lastname	Firstname	Birth Year	Birthplace	Emigration	De	Prof	Source
MULLER	MICHEL JUN.			/ /			
MULLER	NICOLAS	1835	ORSCHWIHR	08/17/1854	PH		FILM
MULLER	PANTALEON	1825	MULHAUSEN	11/03/1846	NY		FILM
MULLER	PETER		GUNDERSHOFFEN	01/01/1869	NY		NO.2
MULLER	PIERRE		CLEEBOURG	01/01/1817	NY		PRIV
MULLER	PIERRE		SELESTAT	02/22/1819	A		FILM
MULLER	ROSALIE	1848	NIEDERLAUTERBACH	01/01/1866	NO		NO.2
MULLER	SEBASTIEN		REICHSHOFFEN	01/01/1817	A		NO.2
MULLER	SEBASTIEN	1815	MEYENHEIM	11/01/1848	TX	CULT	PASS
MULLER	SEBASTIEN	1815	MEYENHEIM	11/13/1848	TX		FILM
MULLER	THIEBAUD	1799	ROUFFACH	04/26/1843	NO		FILM
MULLER	THIEBAUD	1833	THANN	03/27/1852	NO		FILM
MULLER F OF 3	JOSEPH	1833	BOTANS	04/10/1857	NY		FILM
MULLER MN KOEHL C 3	MARIE ANNE	1811	BERRWILLER	09/14/1854	NO		FILM
MULLER WW	PHILIPPE	1813	DEERFELDEN	04/22/1848	NY		FILM
MULLER WW AND CH 4	LOUIS		WEISLINGEN	03/23/1817	A		FILM
MULLER WW AND CH 5	GEORGE		GOERSDORF	03/11/1817	A		FILM
MULLER WW AND CH 7	JACQUES		WIMMENAU	01/01/1817	A		FILM
MULLER BR EMILE	FRANCOIS		THANN	09/30/1856	NY		FILM
MULLER CH 2	VICTOR	1810	MOLLAU	09/01/1851	TX	PRIN	PASS
MULLER CH 7	JEAN		KÖLN	03/29/1817	A		FILM
MULLER F	JOSEPH	1809	BERRWILLER	09/24/1857	NO		FILM
MULLER F OF 2	CHARLES		SAVENNE	01/01/1828	A		FILM
MULLER F OF 2	CHRIST.	1848	ANDELMANS	04/10/1857	NY		FILM
MULLER F OF 2	MICHEL JUN.		DETTWILLER	01/01/1828	A		FILM
MULLER F OF 4	FRANCOIS	1811	EVERSBERG	09/30/1856	NY		FILM
MULLER F OF 4	JACQUES		NEUWILLER	01/01/1828	A		FILM
MULLER F OF 4	JACQUES		SCHWINDRATZHEIM	01/01/1828	A		FILM
MULLER F OF 5	ANTOINE		SESSENHEIM	02/23/1838	A		FILM
MULLER F OF 5	MICHEL SEN.		WEITERSWILLER	01/01/1828	A		FILM
MULLER F OF 5	PIERRE		BOUXWILLER	01/01/1828	A		FILM
MULLER F OF 5	PIERRE		HERBITZHEIM	01/01/1828	A		FILM
MULLER MN FILWEBER	MARIE ANNE			01/01/1856	NY		FILM
MULLER MN GULLY CH 2	MARIE	1814	SOULTZ	02/02/1850	PH		FILM
MULLER MN HENRY CH 3	MARIE MADELEINE	1800	LIEPRE	09/05/1854	NO		FILM
MULLER MN ROBERT C 3	MARIE MADELEINE	1806	COLMAR	09/01/1852	SL		FILM
MULLER MN TRAUTH	FRANCOISE		ZINSWEILER	02/16/1817	A		FILM
MULLER S LAURENT	CHARLES		ZINSWEILER	02/16/1817	A		FILM
MULLER W 3 CH	JOSEPH	1816	NIEDERLAUTERBACH	01/01/1866	NO	SHMA	NO.2
MULLER W W	JEAN		CHATENOIS	01/01/1838	A		FILM
MULLER WW	FREDERIC		LANGENSOULTZBACH	03/17/1817	A		FILM
MULLER WW AND CH	ANDRE	1814	THANN	10/09/1852	RI		FILM
MULLER WW AND CH	FRANCOIS JOSEPH	1802	TURCKHEIM	11/09/1844	NO		FILM
MULLER WW AND CH	HENRY		LANGENSOULTZBACH	01/01/1817	A		FILM
MULLER WW AND CH	HENRY		LANGENSOULTZBACH	02/26/1817	A		FILM
MULLER WW AND CH	JOSEPH	1817	RICHWILLER	02/18/1850	NY		FILM
MULLER WW AND CH	SEBASTIEN		REICHSHOFFEN	03/29/1817	A		FILM
MULLER WW AND CH 2	JEAN	1807	RIBEAUVILLE	03/06/1855	NO		FILM
MULLER WW AND CH 2	JEAN BAPTISTE	1811	LIEPRE	09/02/1847	NO		FILM
MULLER WW AND CH 2	JEAN JACQUES		LANGENSOULTZBACH	01/01/1817	A		FILM

Lastname	Firstname	Birth Year	Birthplace	Emigration	De	Prof	Source
MULLER WW AND CH 2	JEAN JACQUES		LANGENSOULTZBACH	02/26/1817	A		FILM
MULLER WW AND CH 2	LAURENT	1786	ZINSWEILLER	02/16/1817	A		FILM
MULLER WW AND CH 2	VICTOR	1814	MOLLAU	09/11/1855	TX		FILM
MULLER WW AND CH 3	ANTOINE		RATZWILLER	03/03/1817	A		FILM
MULLER WW AND CH 3	CHRETIEN		STRASBOURG	03/01/1819	A		FIM
MULLER WW AND CH 3	DANIEL		LANGENSOULTZBACH	01/01/1817	A		FILM
MULLER WW AND CH 3	DANIEL		LANGENSULTZBACH	02/26/1817	A		FILM
MULLER WW AND CH 3	FRANCOIS	1810	BISEL	09/11/1852	NY		FILM
MULLER WW AND CH 3	GEORGE	1816	JEBSHEIM	02/07/1846	NY		FILM
MULLER WW AND CH 3	IGNACE	1813	RUMERSHEIM	01/03/1848	NY		FILM
MULLER WW AND CH 3	JOSEPH		ESCHBOURG	03/23/1817	A		FILM
MULLER WW AND CH 3	MICHEL		REIPERTSWILLER	01/01/1817	A		FILM
MULLER WW AND CH 3	PIERRE		GUNDERSHOFFEN	03/11/1817	A		FILM
MULLER WW AND CH 4	GEORGE		INGWILLER	03/29/1817	A		FILM
MULLER WW AND CH 4	JOSEPH	1785	LEBINE (VOSGES)	05/07/1840	NY		FILM
MULLER WW AND CH 5	JACQUES		WOLFSKIRCHEN	03/31/1817	A		FILM
MULLER WW AND CH 5	JEAN		DUPPIGHEIM	03/03/1817	A		FILM
MULLER WW AND CH 6	CHRETIEN		LAHR	03/06/1817	A		FILM
MULLER WW AND CH 6	PIERRE	1814	BELFORT	05/31/1853	NY		FILM
MULLER WW AND CH 7	GEORGE HENRI		LANGENSOULTZBACH	01/01/1817	A		FILM
MULLER WW AND CH 7	GEORGE HENRY		LANGENSOULTZBACH	02/26/1817	A		FILM
MULLER WW AND CH 7	JOSEPH JUN.		REIPERTSWILLER	01/01/1817	A		FILM
MULLIERE	ALEXANDRE	1830	FRAHIER	02/20/1866	NY		FILM
MULLIERE	JOSEPH	1834	BELFORT	04/24/1866	NY		FILM
MULLLER	DANIEL		LANGENSOULTZBACH	01/01/1817	A	SHMA	NO.2
MULLLER	GEORG HEINRICH		LANGENSOULTZBACH	01/01/1817	A	CARP	NO.2
MULLLER	HEINRICH	1817	LANGENSOULTZBACH	01/01/1817	A	DAYL	NO.2
MULLLER	JACOB		LANGENSOULTZBACH	01/01/1817	A	SHMA	NO.2
MULLLER MN WERNER	CATHERINE		CHATENOIS	03/08/1838	A		FILM
MULLR WW AND CH 2	PIERRE		WINGEN	01/01/1817	A		FILM
MULTHAUP	HENRI	1816	VOERDEN	11/04/1848	NY		FILM
MUNCH	ANNE MARIE	1829	HEIMERSDORFF	02/19/1851	NY		FILM
MUNCH	BERNARD	1794	MARCKOLSHEIM	09/24/1846	TX		FILM
MUNCH	JEAN	1831	HEIMERSDORF	11/25/1851	A		FILM
MUNCH WW AND CH	ANDRE	1825	GUEWENHEIM	03/12/1852	NY		FILM
MUNCH WW AND CH	LOUIS		LA PETITE PIERRE	03/03/1817	A		FILM
MUNICH	LOUIS		LA PETITE PIERRE	01/01/1828	A		FILM
MUNIER	JEAN DOMINIQUE	1827	LIEPRE	09/02/1847	NO		FILM
MUNSCH	ADAM		ERCKARTSWILLER	01/01/1828	A		FILM
MUNSCH	ADAM SEN.		ERCKARTSWILLER	01/01/1828	A		FILM
MUNSCH	ANDRE	1834	OBERENTZEN	11/01/1857	TX	FACT	PASS
MUNSCH	ANDRE	1834	ODEREN	11/01/1857	TX	FACT	PASS
MUNSCH	ANDRE	1834	ODEREN	11/04/1857	TX		FILM
MUNSCH	AUGUSTIN	1836	ODEREN	11/01/1857	TX	FACT	PASS
MUNSCH	AUGUSTIN	1836	ODEREN	11/04/1857	TX		FILM
MUNSCH	CAROLINE		LOHR	01/01/1828	A		FILM
MUNSCH	ERASME	1823	KRUTH	03/21/1844	NO		FILM
MUNSCH	EUGENE	1841	MULHOUSE	05/01/1860	NY		FILM
MUNSCH	FRANCOIS JOSEPH	1826	MOOSCH	08/23/1853	NO		FILM
MUNSCH	JEAN THIEBAUD	1830	MOOSCH	09/05/1848	NO		FILM

Lastname	Firstname	Birth Year	Birthplace	Emigration	De	Prof	Source
MUNSCH	JOSEPH	1800	ODEREN	03/01/1860	TX	CULT	PASS
MUNSCH	LOUIS		LOHR	01/01/1828	A		FILM
MUNSCH	MAURICE JUN.	1836	MOOSCH	08/11/1854	NY		FILM
MUNSCH	MICHEL	1834	ODEREN	11/01/1857	TX	FACT	PASS
MUNSCH	MICHEL	1834	ODEREN	11/04/1857	TX		FILM
MUNSCH	MTHIAS	1822	MOOSCH	02/14/1848	NO		FILM
MUNSCH	NICOLAS	1805	FELLERING	08/01/1855	TX	GWON	PASS
MUNSCH WW AND CH 2	NICOLAS	1821	MOOSCH	09/28/1854	NY		FILM
MUNSCH F OF 2	ELISABETH		ERCKARTSWILLER	01/01/1828	A		FILM
MUNSCH F OF 3	ADAM		ERCKARTSWILLER	01/01/1828	A		FILM
MUNSCH F OF 3	CHRISTINE	1824	ERCKARTSWILLER	01/01/1828	A		FILM
MUNSCH F OF 3	GEORGES		HAMBACH	01/01/1828	A		FILM
MUNSCH F OF 6	NICOLAS		HAMBACH	03/08/1838	A		FILM
MUNSCH WW	NICOLAS	1805	ODEREN	08/06/1855	TX		FILM
MUNSCH WW AND CH	PIERRE	1809	MOOSCH	04/27/1850	NO		FILM
MUNSCH WW AND CH 2	ANDRE	1819	ODEREN	04/10/1855	NY		FILM
MUNSCH WW AND CH 2	FORTUNE	1810	HEIMERSDORFF	01/22/1840	OH		FILM
MUNSCH WW AND CH 2	GEORGES		ERCKARTSWILLER	03/23/1817	A		FILM
MUNSCH WW AND CH 2	JEAN	1820	MOOSCH	09/28/1854	NY		FILM
MUNSCH WW AND CH 3	ANTOINE	1803	ODEREN	09/28/1854	NY		FILM
MUNSINGER	MADELEINE	1808	KUENHEIM	02/22/1856	CH		FILM
MUNTZINGER	JOSEPH		LEUTENHEIM	03/01/1838	A		FILM
MUNWILLER	LAURENT	1836	MEYENHEIM	01/01/1852	TX	CULT	PASS
MURA	AUGUSTE	1827	HUSSEREN	09/02/1853	NY		FILM
MURA	FRANCOIS ANTOIN	1822	MOOSCH	04/29/1853	NO		FILM
MURA	FRANCOIS ANTOIN	1822	MOOSCH	09/15/1848	NO		FILM
MURA	FRANCOIS ANTOIN	1832	MOOSCH	10/01/1852	JE		FILM
MURA	JEAN	1825	HUSSEREN	09/23/1854	NY		FILM
MURA	THIEBAUD	1831	MOOSCH	10/27/1854	NY		FILM
MURA	VALENTIN	1825	MOOSCH	09/28/1854	TX		FILM
MURA	VALENTIN	1835	MOOSCH	08/11/1853	NO		FILM
MURA	VALENTIN	1835	MOOSCH	09/01/1854	TX	DAYL	PASS
MURA	WALBOURG	1825	ST, AMARIN	07/22/1852	PH		FILM
MURA W ARNOLD ANTOIN	CATHERINE			10/01/1859	TX		PASS
MURA WW AND CH 4	ANTOINE	1811	MOOSCH	11/11/1854	NY		FILM
MURBACH	HENRI	1832	MUNSTER	09/30/1854	NY		FILM
MURBACH	JEAN DAVID	1822	SUNDHOFFEN	09/02/1854	CH		FILM
MURBACH F	JEAN	1802	KUNHEIM	03/25/1841	NY		FILM
MURBACH WW AND CH	JACQUES	1800	KUENHEIM	09/23/1853	CH		FILM
MURBEIS	GUILLAUME		LAHN(B)	09/30/1849	A		FILM
MURE	JEAN BAPTISTE	1826	WATTWILLER	03/17/1857	NY		FILM
MURER	GUILLAUME	1819	BURNHAUPT-LE-BAS	02/21/1840	NY		FILM
MURINGER WW AND CH 5	THIEBAUD	1800	STEINBACH	11/02/1847	NY		FILM
MURRMANN F OF 4	DANIEL		BRUMATH	01/01/1828	A		FILM
MUSCH	OUIS		ESCHBOURG	01/01/1828	A		FILM
MUSSELMANN	ELISABETH		WISLOCH	05/12/1849	A		FILM
MUSSER CH 4	MADELEINE	1813	MUNSTER	04/02/1856	NO		FILM
MUSSLIN	SEBASTIEN	1800	RIXHEIM	10/01/1847	TX	DAYL	PASS
MUSSLIN WW AND CH 6	SEBASTIEN	1800	RIXHEIM	10/28/1847	TX		FILM
MUSULMANN	ELISABETH		WISLOCH	05/12/1849	A		FILM

Lastname	Firstname	Birth Year	Birthplace	Emigration	De	Prof	Source
MUTH	JACQUES	1824	SEPPOIS-LE-BAS	01/25/1845	PH		FILM
MUTH	MAURICE	1824	SEPPOIS-LE-BAS	04/24/1849	PH		FILM
MUTHER WW AND CH 5	JEAN	1808	OSTHEIM	03/25/1853	NY		FILM
MUTSCHLER	DANIEL	1841	LAMPERTSLOCH	01/01/1866	NY	FARM	NO.2
MUTTER	JOSEPH	1825	OBERHAGENTHAL	10/25/1847	CI		FILM
MUTTER	JOSEPH	1827	OBERHAGENTHAL	03/22/1849	CI		FILM
MUTZIG F OF 4	LAURENT		HALBRONN	02/28/1838	A		FILM
MUTZIGER	MADELEINE	1825	OSTHEIM	02/19/1852	NO		FILM
MUTZIGER	MARIE ANNE	1835	OSTHEIM	03/18/1856	NY		FILM
MUTZIGER	NICOALS	1832	OSTHEIM	10/11/1856	NY		FILM
MuCKLI	HENRI		PFALZWEYER	01/01/1828	A		FILM
MuGEL	NICOLAS		BOUXWILLER	01/01/1828	A		FILM
MuHL F OF 2	GEORGE		GEUDERTHEIM	03/01/1838	A		FILM
MuHL F OF 6	GEORGE		GEUDERTHEIM	03/01/1838	A		FILM
MuHLBERGER F FO 6	FREDERIC		BRUMATH	01/01/1828	A		FILM
MuHLER	JEAN		CHATENOIS	03/08/1838	A		FILM
MuHLER D JEAN	BARBE		CHATENOIS	03/08/1838	A		FILM
MuHLER D JEAN	FRANCOISE		CHATENOIS	03/08/1838	A		FILM
MuHLER D JEAN	MADELEINE		CHATENOIS	03/08/1838	A		FILM
MuHLER D JEAN	MARIE ANNE		CHATENOIS	03/08/1838	A		FILM
MuHLER F BARBE	JEAN		CHATENOIS	03/08/1838	A		FILM
MuHLER S JEAN	BARBE		CHATENOIS	03/08/1838	A		FILM
MuHLER S JEAN	FRANCOIS		CHATENOIS	03/08/1838	A		FILM
MuHLER S JEAN	JEAN		CHATENOIS	03/08/1838	A		FILM
MuHLER W JEAN	CATHERINE		CHATENOIS	03/08/1838	A		FILM
MuHLER WW AND CH 5	JEAN		CHATENOIS	03/08/1838	A		FILM
MuHLHEISER	BENOIT		SCHIRRHEIN	03/05/1838	A		FILM
MuHLHEISER	LOUIS		SCHIRRHEIN	03/05/1838	A		FILM
MuLHAUPT	XAVIER	1833	SOULTZMATT	11/12/1865	NY		FILM
MuLLER	ADAM		STRUTH	01/01/1828	A		FILM
MuLLER	ADELHARD	1842	URBES	11/12/1865	A		FILM
MuLLER	ANNE MARIE		WORNBERG	06/11/1849	A		FILM
MuLLER	ANTOINE	1808	KAYSERSBERG	08/28/1844	NO		FILM
MuLLER	AUGUSTE THEODOR	1805	COLMAR	10/10/1840	SL		FILM
MuLLER	CHARLES	1811	ZINNSWILLER	02/16/1817	A		FILM
MuLLER	EMILE	1838	THANN	07/29/1857	OH		FILM
MuLLER	FRANCOIS JOSEPH	1818	FALKWILLER	09/10/1844	NO		FILM
MuLLER	FRANCOIS LEON	1834	MULHOUSE	02/09/1852	NY		FILM
MuLLER	FRANCOISE	1811	EVERSBERG	09/30/1856	NY		FILM
MuLLER	FRANCOISE	1831	THANN	08/05/1848	A		FILM
MuLLER	FREDERIC	1835	BEBLENHEIM	03/31/1857	NY		FILM
MuLLER	MARIE URSULE	1793	SEPPOIS-LE-BAS	05/02/1840	NY		FILM
MuLLER	MATHIAS	1836	LIEBENSWILLER	09/04/1866	NY		FILM
MuLLER	SAMUEL		STRUTH	01/01/1828	A		FILM
MuLLER	SEBASTIEN		REICHSHOFFEN	03/21/1817	A		FILM
MuLLER F OF 2	CHARLES		SARENNE	01/01/1828	A		FILM
MuLLER F OF 7	SERAPHIN		MARMOUTIER	01/01/1828	A		FILM
MuLLER BR EMILE	FRANCOIS		EVERSBERG	09/30/1856	NY		FILM
MuLLER F CHARLES	LAURENT		ZINSWEILLER	02/16/1817	A		FILM
MuLLER F CHRISTIEN	JOSEPH		ANDELSMANS	04/10/1857	NY		FILM

Lastname	Firstname	Birth Year	Birthplace	Emigration	De	Prof	Source
MÜLLER F OF 2	CHARLOTTE		STRUTH	01/01/1828	A		FILM
MÜLLER F OF 3	FREDERIC		INGVILLER	01/01/1828	A		FILM
MÜLLER F OF 5	ANDRE		MARCKOLSHEIM	02/26/1838	A		FILM
MÜLLER F OF 5	ANTOINE		SESSENHEIM	02/23/1838	A		FILM
MÜLLER F OF 6	FREDERIC		BRUMATH	03/22/1838	A		FILM
MÜLLER F OF 6	NICOLAS		WOLFSKIRCHEN	01/01/1828	A		FILM
MÜLLER F OF 8	ANTOINE		DAUENDORF	02/28/1838	A		FILM
MÜLLER S JOSEPH	CHRISTIEN	1848	ANDELSMANS	04/10/1857	NY		FILM
MÜLLER SI FRANCOIS	EMILE	1822	EVERSBERG	09/30/1856	NY		FILM
MÜLLER WW	FREDERIC		LANGENSOULTZBACH	03/17/1817	A		FILM
MÜLLER WW	PIERRE		ESCHBOURG	01/01/1828	A		FILM
MÜLLER WW AND CH	ANDRE	1812	THANN	10/09/1852	RI		FILM
MÜLLER WW AND CH	FRANCOIS JOSEPH	1802	TURCKHEIM	11/09/1844	NO		FILM
MÜLLER WW AND CH 3	ANTOINE		RATZWILLER	03/03/1817	A		FILM
MÜLLER WW AND CH 3	CHRETIEN		STRASBOURG	03/01/1819	A		FILM
MÜLLER WW AND CH 3	DANIEL		LANGENSOULTZBACH	01/01/1817	A		FILM
MÜLLER WW AND CH 3	FRANCOIS	1810	BISEL	09/11/1852	NY		FILM
MÜLLER WW AND CH 3	GEORGE	1816	KOENIGSOCHESHAUSEN	02/07/1846	NY		FILM
MÜLLER WW AND CH 4	GEORGE		INGWILLER	03/29/1817	A		FILM
MÜLLER WW AND CH 5	GEORGE		GOERSDORF	03/11/1817	A		FILM
MÜLLER WW AND CH 6	CHRETIEN		LAHR	03/06/1817	A		FILM
MÜLLER WW AND CH 7	GEORGE HENRI		LANGENSOULTZBACH	01/01/1817	A		FILM
MÜLLER WW F OF 6	PHILIPP		DEHLINGEN	01/01/1828	A		FILM
MUNCH			DEUTSCHLAND	03/31/1849	A		FILM
MUNCH	ACHILLE	1864	COURTARON	05/17/1866	NY		FILM
MUNCH	ALOYSE	1840	LUTTER	07/17/1864	NY		FILM
MUNCH	JOSEPH	1803	LUTTER	05/17/1866	NY		FILM
MUNCH	MARIE URSULE	1843	LUTTER	05/17/1866	NY		FILM
MUSSLIN	LOUIS	1837	HAGENHEIM	08/17/1866	NY		FILM
MÜHLHAUPT	XAVIER	1833	SOULTZMATT	11/12/1865	NY		FILM
MÜHLHEISER	BENOIT		SCHIRRHEIN	03/05/1838	A		FILM
MÜHLHEISER	LOUIS		SCHIRRHEIN	03/05/1838	A		FILM
MÜLLER		1844	URBES	11/12/1865	NY		FILM
MÜLLER	ADAM		STRUTH	01/01/1828	A		FILM
MÜLLER	ADELHARD	1842	URBES	11/12/1865	NY		FILM
MÜLLER	FREDERIC	1835	BEBLENHEIM	03/31/1857	NY		FILM
MÜLLER	JACQUES		INGVILLER	01/01/1828	A		FILM
MÜLLER	JEAN BAPTISTE	1851	LIEBENSWILLER	09/04/1866	NY		FILM
MÜLLER	JOSEPH		MINVERSHEIM	01/01/1828	A		FILM
MÜLLER	LAURENT		DÜRCKHEIM	02/27/1817	A		FILM
MÜLLER	LAURENT	1813	ZINSWEILLER	02/16/1817	A		FILM
MÜLLER F OF 7	LAURENT		GEUDERTHEIM	03/01/1838	A		FILM
MÜLLER FOF 5	ANDRE		MARCKOLSHEIM	02/26/1838	A		FILM
MÜLLER F LAURENT	LAURENT		ZINSWEILLER	02/16/1817	A		FILM
MÜLLER F OF 11	JEAN		LICHTENBERG	01/01/1828	A		FILM
MÜLLER F OF 2	CHARLOTTE		STRUTH	01/01/1828	A		FILM
MÜLLER F OF 3	FREDERIC		INGVILLER	01/01/1828	A		FILM
MÜLLER F OF 5	JACQUES		BRUMATH	01/01/1828	A		FILM
MÜLLER F OF 6	FREDERIC		BRUMATH	03/22/1838	A		FILM
MÜLLER F OF 6	HENRI		INGVILLER	01/01/1828	A		FILM

Lastname	Firstname	Birth Year	Birthplace	Emigration	De	Prof	Source
MÜLLER F OF 6	HENRI		WOLFSKIRCHEN	01/01/1828	A		FILM
MÜLLER F OF 8	ANTOINE		DAUENDORF	02/28/1838	A		FILM
MÜLLER F OF 9	JACQUES		WOLFSKIRCHEN	01/01/1828	A		FILM
MÜLLER FOF 5	JEAN		BOUXWILLER	01/01/1828	A		FILM

Lastname	Firstname	Birth Year	Birthplace	Emigration	De	Prof	Source
NAAS	BARBE		RUNTZENHEIM	01/01/1828	A		FILM
NAAS	JACQUES		SESSENHEIM	02/23/1838	A		FILM
NAAS	MATHIEU		RUNTZENHEIM	01/01/1828	A		FILM
NABLO	JACQUES		PFALZWEYER	01/01/1828	A		FILM
NACHBAUR	PIERRE	181		/ /			
NACHBAUR	PIERRE	1801	CERNAY	03/16/1843	NY		FILM
NADELHOTTER	THEORDORE	1816	COLMAR	06/22/1848	LO		FILM
NAEGELEN	SARAPHIN	1838	SICKERT	09/09/1852	NO		FILM
NAEGELEN	VALENTIN	1820	BOURBACH-LE-BAS	04/26/1852	NY		FILM
NAEGELIN	MICHEL I			/ /			
NAEGELIN CH 6	MICHEL I	1809	HIRTZFELDEN	09/01/1846	TX	CULT	PASS
NAGELE	CATHERINE	1813	HUNTINGUE	05/31/1859	NY		FILM
NAGELIN WW AND CH 6	MICHEL	1809	HIRTZFELDEN	09/21/1846	TX		FILM
NAGEOTTE	LOUIS	1831	VAUJANCOURT	09/07/1847	NY		FILM
NAGLER	HENRI (FILS)	1824	RANSPACH	08/01/1844	TX	BAKE	PASS
NAGLER	HENRY	1824	RANSPACH	08/28/1844	NY		FILM
NAGLER	JACQUES		RANSPACH	07/27/1853	NY		FILM
NAGLER D CHARLES	FREDERIQUE	1832	RANSPACH	07/27/1853	NY		FILM
NAGLER MN REISSER	CATHERINE		RANSPACH	07/27/1853	NY		FILM
NAGLER S CHARLES	JACQUES		RANSPACH	07/27/1853	NY		FILM
NAGLER WW AND CH 2	CHARLES	1819	RANSAPCH	07/27/1853	NY		FILM
NAHL	SALOME		KAUFFENHEIM	05/17/1856	A		FILM
NANSE	JOSEPH	1826	ALTKIRCH	06/20/1848	PH		FILM
NANZ F OF 10	JACQUES		SESSENHEIM	02/23/1838	A		FILM
NARDIN	ADELE	1826	HERICOURT	05/05/1866	NY		FILM
NARDIN	ALFRED	1851	HERICOURT	05/05/1866	NY		FILM
NARDIN	EMILE	1823	HERICOURT	05/05/1866	NY		FILM
NARDIN	GEORGES	1854	HERICOURT	05/05/1866	NY		FILM
NASS	AUGUSTIN	1810	BERRWILLER	02/03/1845	NO		FILM
NATH WW	ERHARD		KIGLINGSBERGEN	04/07/1849	NY		FILM
NATH WW AND CH	SEBASTIEN		KIGLINGSBERGEN	04/07/1849	NY		FILM
NATHAN	SALOMON	1846	SURBOURG	01/01/1867	NY	MERC	NO.2
NATHERN	JEAN		BERSTHEIM	03/03/1838	A		FILM
NATHISEN WW AND CH 5	LUDAU		LIPSHEIM	05/27/1817	A		FILM
NATTER CH 4	JOSEPH	1804	RIXHEIM	11/01/1851	TX		PASS
NATTERN WW AND CH 4	JOSEPH	1824	RIXHEIM	11/18/1851	TX		FILM
NATZGER WW	PIERRE	1806	WALHEIM	03/01/1841	NY		FILM
NAUERT	JACQUES		MULHOUSE	05/11/1857	NY		FILM
NAUERT	JEAN	1844	MULHOUSE	05/11/1857	NY		FILM
NAUERT	NICOLAS	1834	MULHOUSE	05/11/1857	NY		FILM
NAUERT	PIERRE	1849	MULHOUSE	05/11/1857	NY		FILM
NAUERT MN SIMON	MARIE	1809	MULHOUSE	05/11/1857	NY		FILM
NAUSE	ELISABETH	1829	ALTKIRCH	04/17/1849	PH		FILM
NAUSE	JOSEPH	1826	ALTKIRCH	06/20/1848	PH		FILM
NECK	GEORGES	1813	LIEPVRE	03/30/1839	NO		FILM
NECKHAUS F OF 3	JACQUES		DURSTEL	03/18/1838	A		FILM
NEDER	MICHEL	1849	KEFFENBACH	01/01/1868	NY	FARM	NO.2
NEEDER F OF 4	GEROGE MICHEL		ROPPENHEIM	03/06/1838	A		FILM
NEEFZ	CONRAD		DURBACH	04/08/1849	A		FILM
NEFF	DOMINIQUE	1793	BERWILLER	08/26/1854	NY		FILM

Lastname	Firstname	Birth Year	Birthplace	Emigration	De	Prof	Source
NEFF	MATERNE	1836	BERRWILLER	04/12/1854	NY		FILM
NEHLIG	ANDRE		DEHLINGEN	01/01/1828	A		FILM
NEHLIG F OF 4	PHILIPPE		WILLER	01/01/1828	A		FILM
NEHR WW AND CH 2	JOSEPH	1798	ST, AMARIN	10/12/1846	TX		FILM
NEHR WW AND CH 2	JOSEPH	1799	ST.AMARIN	02/15/1851	NO		FILM
NEIBEL	ANNE	1828	RAPPERSWIL	11/15/1846	TX		FILM
NEIHARD	LUDWIG		WINGEN	01/01/1817	A	FARM	NO.2
NERHARD WW	LOUIS		WINGEN	03/03/1817	A		FILM
NESSEL WW AND CH 6	LOUIS		DRUSENHEIM	03/24/1838	A		FILM
NETTER	ABRAHAM	1828	HARTMANNSWILLER	01/20/1857	NY		FILM
NETTER	JOSEPH	1832	HARTMANNSWILLER	11/09/1857	PH		FILM
NETTER SI ABRAHAM	PAULIN	1836	HARTMANNSWILLER	01/20/1857	NY		FILM
NETZ S JOSEPH	JOHANN	1827	MITZACH	11/15/1846	TX		FILM
NETZ W JOSEPH	WALBURGA	1806	MITZACH	11/15/1846	TX		FILM
NETZ WW AND CH	JOSEPH	1797	MITZACH	11/15/1846	TX		FILM
NEU F	BERNARD CAON	1815	RIBEAUVILLE	08/26/1854	NY		FILM
NEUBAUER	CAROLINE		PETERSBACH	01/01/1828	A		FILM
NEUBAUER	CATHERINE	1823	LEMBACH(BR)	06/10/1846	NY		FILM
NEUBAUER	CHRISTINE		PETERSBACH	01/01/1828	A		FILM
NEUBAUER	JEAN	1818	LEMBACH(BR)	05/01/1848	NO		FILM
NEUBUR F OF 3	JACQUES		ESCHBOURG	01/01/1828	A		FILM
NEUBURGER	JOSEPH		MAUCKRATH	06/21/1849	A		FILM
NEUBURGER	MARN		MAUCKRATH	06/21/1849	A		FILM
NEUCKLER	THERESE		ROTHENBOURG	04/06/1849	NY		FILM
NEUHART	MICHEL	1820	KUTZENHAUSEN	09/03/1845	NY		FILM
NEUMAEYER S MARTIN	MARTIN	1837	ROUFFACH	11/28/1843	JE		FILM
NEUMANN	THEODOR		ROESCHWOOG	01/01/1828	A		FILM
NEUMANN F OF 4	GEORGE		IMBSHEIM	01/01/1828	A		FILM
NEUMAYER	THOMAS		HASLACH	05/12/1849	A		FILM
NEUMEYER D MARTIN	ANNE MARIE	1834	ROUFFACH	11/28/1843	JE		FILM
NEUMEYER MN SINGER	MARIE W MARTIN		ROUFFACH	11/28/1843	JE		FILM
NEUMEYER WW AND CH 2	MARTIN		ROUFFACH	11/28/1843	JE		FILM
NEUTASCHER	ROBERT		KENTZINGEN	05/03/1849	NY		FILM
NEY MN FEY CH 2	MADELEINE	1800	DORNACH	10/06/1851	PI		FILM
NEYBERGER	BERNARD		ICHENHAUSEN	04/25/1849	NY		FILM
NEYER	JOSEPH	1818	RETZWILLER	03/26/1844	NY		FILM
NICAISE WW AND CH 5	JACQUES		BISSERT	03/06/1817	A		FILM
NICKLAES	PIERRE		REXINGEN	03/31/1828	A		FILM
NICKLAES CH			REXINGEN	03/31/1828	A		FILM
NICLAIS	PIERRE		BERG	03/01/1838	A		FILM
NICLAUS	CHARLES		DEUTSCHLAND	04/05/1849	NY		FILM
NICLAUS	PIERRE		STRUTH	01/01/1828	A		FILM
NICO	JOSEPH	1817	ESCHENTZWILLER	07/26/1849	LY		FILM
NICOLA	FRANCOIS		NEUWILLER	01/01/1828	A		FILM
NICOLAI CH	AMELIE	1817	MULHOUSE	08/12/1854	NY		FILM
NICOLAS MN PETITAT	MARIE GENEREUSE	1797	FAHY(SW)	03/13/1855	NY		FILM
NICOT	MARTIN	1818	TURCKHEIM	09/10/1846	NY		FILM
NICOULIN	ALINE	1857	SWISS	03/31/1866	NY		FILM
NICOULIN	ANA	1865	SWISS	03/31/1866	NY		FILM
NICOULIN	CONSTANT	1861	SWISS	03/06/1866	NY		FILM

Lastname	Firstname	Birth Year	Birthplace	Emigration	De	Prof	Source
NICOULIN	HENRY	1858	SWISS	03/31/1866	NY		FILM
NICOULIN	JEAN PIERRE	1829	SWISS	03/31/1866	NY		FILM
NICOULIN	JEAN PIERRE	1829	SWISS	04/01/1866	NY		FILM
NICOULIN	JOSEPH	1841	SWISS	04/01/1866	NY		FILM
NICOULIN	JOSEPH	1862	SWISS	04/01/1866	NY		FILM
NICOULIN	MARIE	1844	SWISS	03/31/1866	NY		FILM
NICOULIN	MARIE	1859	SWISS	04/01/1866	NY		FILM
NICOULIN	PHILOMENE	1861	SWISS	04/01/1866	NY		FILM
NICOULIN	PIERRE	1858	SWISS	04/01/1866	NY		FILM
NICOULIN F OF 8	ARSENE	1859	SWISS	03/31/1860	NY		FILM
NICOULIN S JEAN PIER	CHARLES	1864	SWISS	04/01/1866	NY		FILM
NIDERGANG	GEORGES	1829	GUEBWILLER	10/21/1856	NY		FILM
NIDERGANG	GEORGES	1830	GUEBWILLER	02/13/1854	NY		FILM
NIEBER WW AND CH 7	JACQUES		SIEWILLER	03/29/1817	A		FILM
NIEDERGANG	LEON GUILLAUME	1834	RIBEAUVILLE	08/14/1855	NY		FILM
NIEDERHAMMER	MARIE LOUISE		ZELL	08/01/1849	A		FILM
NIEFERGALE	JEAN	1819	DURMENACH	11/14/1846	NY		FILM
NIER WW AND CH 8	VALENTIN		DRULINGEN	03/03/1817	A		FILM
NIERENGARTEN	LOUISE	1828	WINGEN	10/09/1850	NY		FILM
NIESS	FRIEDERICH	1841	HOFFEN	01/01/1869	NY		NO.2
NIESS	GEORGE JUN.		BOSSELSHAUSEN	01/01/1828	A		FILM
NIESS SI GEORGE	CATHERINE		BOSSENHAUSEN	01/01/1828	A		FILM
NIFENBECKER	JULIE		HERICOURT	10/02/1863	NY		FILM
NIFENECKER	JULIE	1823	HERICOURT	06/20/1863	NY		FILM
NIPPERT	GEORGE		INGVILLER	01/01/1828	A		FILM
NISSLE F OF 2	HENRI		ERSTEIN	11/08/1837	A		FILM
NITSCHELM WW	FREDERIC	1829	MUNSTER	07/29/1854	NY		FILM
NIW	BENOIT	1827	RIBEAUVILLE	11/18/1851	SL		FILM
NOBLAT	JEAN PIERRE	1823	VELESCOT	12/18/1843	NY		FILM
NOEL	MAGDALENA	1846	SELTZ	01/01/1866	WA		NO.2
NOEL	NICOLAS		WINGEN	01/01/1828	A		FILM
NOETH	JEAN LOUIS	1827	GUEBWILLER	07/19/1848	NY		FILM
NOETZ	MICHEL		NEUWILLER	01/01/1828	A		FILM
NOILAND D CHARLES	XA	1835	ESSERT	09/03/1857	BU		FILM
NOILAND D CHARLES XA		1833	ESSERT	09/03/1857	BU		FILM
NOILAND D CHARLES XA		1835	ESSERT	09/03/1857	BU		FILM
NOILAND D CHARLES XA		1838	ESSERT	09/03/1857	BU		FILM
NOILAND D CHARLES XA		1844	ESSERT	09/03/1857	BU		FILM
NOILAND MN PERRIN	ADELAIDE	1803	ESSERT	09/03/1857	BU		FILM
NOILAND WW AND CH 5	CHARLES XAVIER	1797	ESSERT	09/03/1857	BU		FILM
NOLD	FRANCOISE	1827	SALMBACH	09/03/1857	NY		FILM
NOLD	JEAN-PAUL		SALMBACH	01/01/1850	NO		PRIV
NOLL	THERESE		DURBACH(B)	04/08/1849	A		FILM
NOLLINGER	GEORGES	1830	WITTERSDORFF	01/23/1852	NY		FILM
NOLLINGER WW CH 3	DAVID	1804	ILLFURTH	08/04/1849	NO		FILM
NOLTE	GEORG		WOERTH	01/01/1840	A		SUESS
NONDMANN	JACQUES	1796	HAGENTHAL	08/06/1865	NY		FILM
NONDMANN	SARA	1802	HAGNETHAL	08/06/1865	NY		FILM
NOPPET	BERNARD	1854	LAUTERBURG	01/01/1865	NY		NO.2
NOPPET	JOSEF	1856	LAUTERBURG	01/01/1865	NY		NO.2

Lastname	Firstname	Birth Year	Birthplace	Emigration	De	Prof	Source
NOPPET	MARGARTHE	1829	LAUTERBURG	01/01/1865	NY		NO.2
NOPPET	MICHEL	1865	LAUTERBURG	01/01/1865	NY		NO.2
NOPPET	PETER	1860	LAUTERBURG	01/01/1865	NY		NO.2
NOPPET W W 4 CH	BERNARD	1828	LAUTERBURG	01/01/1865	NY	BRLA	
NORD	KARL	1858	NIEDERLAUTERBACH	01/01/1865	NO		NO.2
NORDMANN	JOSEPH	1843	HAGENHEIM	08/07/1866	NY		FILM
NORROT	DOMINIQUE	1817	BOUROGNE	06/12/1838	NY		FILM
NORTZ	MARTIN		ROTHENBOURG	05/09/1849	NY		FILM
NOTER W RUFF XAVIER	MARIE	1815	MULHOUSE	02/22/1856	NO		FILM
NOTTER	LOUIS		WALDOLWISHEIM	01/01/1828	A		FILM
NOTTER CH 4	JOSEPH	1804	RIXHEIM	11/01/1851	TX		PASS
NOTTER MN BROGLY	FRANCOISE			11/01/1851	TX		PASS
NUDELHOFFER WW	JEAN	1818	OSTHEIM	03/25/1845	NY		FILM
NUEFFER	AUGUSTE	1832	GUEBWILLER	04/20/1852	NY		FILM
NUFER			ETTENHEIM	04/03/1849	NY		FILM
NUFFER WW AND CH 2	ANTOINE		KESKASTEL	03/03/1817	A		FILM
NUHLAUS F OF 3	JACQUES		DURSTEL	03/18/1838	A		FILM
NULLRT	JEAN GEORGES	1842		03/03/1866	NY		FILM
NUN WW AND CH 3	JOSEPH	1806	THANN	09/02/1846	NY		FILM
NUSBAUM F OF 5	LAURENT		GOTTENHAUSEN	01/01/1828	A		FILM
NUSBAUM WW AND CH 2	JOSEPH	1825	BOURBACH-LE-BAS	02/12/1852	NY		FILM
NUSS	CLAIRE MARIE	1819	KIENTZHEIM	08/10/1849	NY		FILM
NUSSBAUMER		1825	GACHLIEVIL	11/15/1846	CL		FILM
NUSSBAUMER		1827	GACHLIEVIL	11/15/1846	CL		FILM

Lastname	Firstname	Birth Year	Birthplace	Emigration	De Prof	Source
OBAETS WW AND CH 2	FRANCOIS JOSEPH		OHNENHEIM	03/06/1817	A	FILM
OBDORFF	JACQUES	1820	GUEBWILLER	04/06/1840	NY	FILM
OBERFELD	GUILLAUME		RENCHEN	05/31/1844	A	FILM
OBERHOLTZ F OF 2	PIERRE		SARENNE	01/01/1828	A	FILM
OBERLAND	MARIE HENRY VIC	1820	BELFORT	09/12/1847	NY	FILM
OBERLE	CHRETIEN		HORNBERG	10/03/1849	A	FILM
OBERLEND	VICTOR	1820	BELFORT	09/13/1852	NY	FILM
OBERLIN	ANDRE	1822	HOLTZWIHR	03/07/1854	NY	FILM
OBERLIN	AUGUSTINE		FRIESENHEIM(B)	08/05/1849	A	FILM
OBERLIN	FRANCOIS ANTOIN	1823	HOLTZWIHR	02/13/1854	NY	FILM
OBERLIN	FREDERIQUE		FRIESENHEIM	08/05/1849	A	FILM
OBERLIN	JACQUES	1807	JEBSHEIM	02/17/1853	NY	FILM
OBERLIN	LOUISE		FRIEDENHEIM(B)	08/05/1849	A	FILM
OBERLIN WW AND CH	JACQUES	1830	JEBSHEIM	11/11/1854	NY	FILM
OBERST	JEAN	1812	SEPPOIS-LE-HAUT(BR)	03/17/1847	NY	FILM
OBERZUSSER CH	ELISABETH	1825	SUNDHOFFEN	09/14/1853	NY	FILM
OBLIGSCHLAGER S ALEX	JOSEPH	1843	DUEREN(P)	04/09/1844	TX	FILM
OBLIGSCHLAGER W ALEX	MARIE ANNA	1818	DUEREN(P)	04/09/1844	TX	FILM
OBLIGSCHLAGER WW CH	ALEXANDER	1818	DUEREN(P)	04/09/1844	TX	FILM
OBRECHT	ANDRE		STADELHOFEN(B)	07/29/1849	A	FILM
OBRECHT	JACQUES	1812	JEBSHEIM	03/14/1839	PH	FILM
OBRECHT	JEAN JACQUES	1828	KUNHEIM (HR)	06/13/1854	CH	FILM
OBRECHT	JEAN MICHEL	1834	ANDOLSHEIM	02/09/1856	SL	FILM
OBRECHT	MADELAINE	1823	COLMAR	03/04/1839	A	FILM
OBRECHT	VALENTIN	1832	ANDOLSHEIM	03/30/1855	SL	FILM
OBRECHT F	JEAN GEORGES	1813	JEBSHEIM	08/21/1854	NY	FILM
OBRECHT F OF 3	JEAN	1818	JEBSHEIM	04/11/1854	NY	FILM
OBRECHT WW AND CH 5	MICHEL	1803	JEBSHEIM	03/22/1842	NY	FILM
OBRY WW AND CH	PELAGE	1824	COLMAR	03/27/1850	NY	FILM
OCHLHAFFEN	JOSEPH ISIDOR	1820	GRUSSENHEIM	10/20/1852	NY	FILM
OCHLHAFFEN	MARIE ANNE	1824	GRUSSENHEIM	10/25/1853	NY	FILM
OEHLER	ANDRE	1806	ST. MARIE AUX MINES	09/26/1854	NY	FILM
OEHLHAFFEN	JOSEPH ISIDOR	1820	GRUSSENHEIM	10/20/1852	NY	FILM
OEHLINGER	CATHERINE	1820	MULHOUSE	02/23/1857	NO	FILM
OERTEL	GEORGE	1808	BISCHOFFSHEIM AM RH	04/09/1844	CL	FILM
OERTEL F	JACQUES		UHRWILLER	04/25/1818	A	FILM
OERTEL WW AND CH 4	MATHIAS		OSTWALD	03/31/1817	A	FILM
OERTEL WW AND CH 5	BERARD		OSTWALD	03/31/1817	A	FILM
OERTLE	FREDERIC	1828	MULHOUSE	11/20/1851	NO	FILM
OERTLIN WW	MATHIAS	1823	SUNDHOFFEN	09/01/1854	CH	FILM
OESTER	JEAN	1809	MUNSTER	07/05/1854	NY	FILM
OETH	GEORGES		GUNDERSHOFFEN	04/09/1817	A	FILM
OEURRARD	JACQUES	1824	MEROUX	03/28/1854	NY	FILM
OEURRARD D CATHERINE		1824	MEROUX	03/04/1857	NY	FILM
OEURRARD D CATHERINE		1828	MEROUX	03/04/1857	NY	FILM
OEURRARD D CATHERINE		1836	MEROUX	03/04/1857	NY	FILM
OEURRARD MN BIGEARD	CATHERINE CH 4	1798	MEROUX	03/04/1857	NY	FILM
OEURRARD S CATHERINE		1853	MEROUX	03/04/1857	NY	FILM
OFFENBURGER F OF 2	JEAN		WITTISHEIM	03/02/1838	A	FILM
OFFERLE	GEORGE		BALDENHEIM	03/06/1838	A	FILM

Lastname	Firstname	Birth Year	Birthplace	Emigration	De	Prof	Source
OFFERLE F OF 3	CHRETIEN		MUTTERSHOLTZ	04/05/1838	A		FILM
OFFNER	LUDWIG	1850	OBERLAUTERBACH	01/01/1866	NO		NO.2
OFFNER	MARIE		OBERLAUTERBACH	01/01/1850	NO		PRIV
OGE F OF 3	VENDELIN		DETTWILLER	01/01/1828	A		FILM
OGEL	ELISABETH	1791	CLEEBOURG	01/01/1864	NY		PRIV
OHL F OF 2	THIEBAULT		MOMMENHEIM	02/28/1838	A		FILM
OHL F OF 3	CHRETIEN		TIEFFENBACH	01/01/1828	A		FILM
OHL F OF 6	ANTOINE		MOMMENHEIM	02/28/1838	A		FILM
OHLINGER CH 4	ANNE AMRIE	1800	DORNACH	08/31/1838	A		FILM
OHLMANN	BARBE		WANTZENAU	03/07/1838	A		FILM
OHLMANN	IGNACE		OHLUNGEN	03/01/1838	A		FILM
OHLMANN	MARIE ANNE		OHLUNGEN	03/01/1838	A		FILM
OHLMANN	MAX	1847	SURBOURG	01/01/1865	NY		NO.2
OHLMANN WW AND CH 4	MICHEL		WANTZENAU	03/07/1838	A		FILM
OHLMANN MN ZAHN	GERTRUDE		WANTZENAU	03/07/1838	A		FILM
OHNMACHT	WALBURGA		BAUGENDORF	06/04/1849	A		FILM
OHRESSER	FELIX		SCHWEIGHAUSEN	01/01/1828	A		FILM
OHZLING	JEAN		REICHSHOFFEN	03/22/1817	A		FILM
OLAND	JOSEF	1840	SELTZ	01/01/1865	NY		NO.2
OLEYER	FRANZ	1842	ALTENSTADT	01/01/1869	NY		NO.2
OLEYER	REGINA	1840	ALTENSTADT	01/01/1869	NY		NO.2
OLFF MN BECK CH 4	SARA	1811	REGUISHEIM	07/25/1853	NY		FILM
ORGAST	FRANCOISE	1827	HERICOURT	10/01/1866	NY		FILM
ORIEZ WW AND CH	ALEXIS	1809	CHAUX	01/06/1844	PH		FILM
ORIEZ WW AND CH 3	PIERRE	1800	LA CHAPELLE SOUS CHA	10/31/1844	NY		FILM
ORLIEB	MICHEL	1854	MITTELWIHR	06/04/1857	NO		FILM
ORLIEB	SALOME	1852	MITTELWIHR	06/04/1857	NO		FILM
ORLIEB MN HELLER	MADELAINE	1829	MITTELWIHR	06/04/1857	NO		FILM
ORRIEZ F OF 3	FRANCOIS	1819	SERMAMAGNY	02/06/1847	NO		FILM
ORTH	MICHEL	1832	SCHLEITHAL	11/23/1850	PH		FILM
ORTH	PIERRE	1833	SCHLEITHAL	10/20/1851	NY		FILM
ORTH	WILHELM		WEISSENBURG	01/01/1865	NY		NO.2
ORTH MN MOOG CH 3	ELISABETH	1799	SCHLEITHAL	07/18/1854	NY		FILM
ORTH WW AND CH 4	CHRETIEN PHILIP	1776	LOERRACH(B)	05/09/1840	NY		FILM
ORTLIEB	MARIE BARBE	1836	OSTHEIM	01/20/1854	NY		FILM
ORTLIEB	MICHEL	1824	MITTELWIHR	03/10/1855	NY		FILM
ORTLIEB D JACQUES		1842	BEBLENHEIM	07/28/1856	NY		FILM
ORTLIEB W JACQUES		1802	BEBLENHEIM	07/28/1856	NY		FILM
ORTLIEB WW AND CH	JACQUES	1812	BEBLENHEIM	07/28/1856	NY		FILM
ORTLIEB WW AND CH	PAUL	1801	BEBLENHEIM	03/28/1855	NY		FILM
ORTLOFF	MARIE ANNE	1830	ISSENHEIM	06/08/1854	NY		FILM
ORTSCHEID	JEAN	1843	SONDERSDORFF	07/11/1857	NY		FILM
ORTSCHEID	JEAN	1843	VIEUX FERRETTE	07/11/1857	NY		FILM
ORTSCHEID	MADELAINE	1840	VIEUX FERRETTE	07/11/1857	NY		FILM
ORTSCHEID	MADELEINE	1840	SONDERSDORFF	07/11/1857	NY		FILM
ORTSCHEID MN BLIND	MARIE CH 2	1801	SONDERSDORFF	07/11/1857	NY		FILM
ORTSCHEIDT	ANDRE	1810	VIEUX FERRETTE	01/23/1840	NY		FILM
ORVEZ CH 3	ALEXIS	1800	LA CHAPELLE/CHAUX	10/01/1844	TX	CULT	PASS
OSCHGER MN HELSBY	LEON CH 4	1824	ST. CROIX AUX MINES	09/09/1852	NY		FILM
OSER	CORNELIE		UNSHURST	05/03/1849	A		FILM

Lastname	Firstname	Birth Year	Birthplace	Emigration	De	Prof	Source
OSSER	JACQUES	1810	BIEDERTHAL	03/23/1840	NY		FILM
OSSWALD	JACQUES		DETTWILLER	02/28/1838	A		FILM
OSSWALD F OF 2	GEORGES		RATZWILLER	01/01/1828	A		FILM
OSSWALT F OF 7	HENRY		RATZWILLER	01/01/1828	A		FILM
OSTER	THIEBAUD		ESCHBOURG	01/01/1828	A		FILM
OSTER F OF 5	ADAM		ESCHBOURG	01/01/1828	A		FILM
OSTERDAG	ANNE MARIE	1820	TRAUBACH-LE-BAS	03/06/1848	NY		FILM
OSTERMEYER	JOSEPH LOUIS	1820	COLMAR	03/01/1852	NO		FILM
OSWALD	JACOB		BUBENHEIM(BA)	09/30/1849	NY		FILM
OSWALD F OF 3	GEORGES		INGENHEIM	01/01/1828	A		FILM
OTH F CATHERINE	GEORGE		ZINSWEILLER	02/16/1817	A		FILM
OTH D GEORGE	CATHERINE	1806	ZINSWEILLER	02/16/1817	A		FILM
OTH D GEORGE	MARGUERITE	1808	ZINSWEILLER	02/16/1817	A		FILM
OTH D GEORGE	MARIE ANNE	1810	ZINSWEILLER	02/16/1817			FILM
OTH D GEORGE	ODILE	1816	ZINSWEILLER	02/16/1817	A		FILM
OTH WW AND CH 4	GEORGE	1780	ZINSWEILLER	02/16/1817	A		FILM
OTT		1865	HERICOURT	08/30/1866	NY		FILM
OTT	JEAN	1798	BERENTZWILLER	01/13/1849	BU		FILM
OTT	JOSEPH		ROTHENBOURG(W)	04/06/1849	NY		FILM
OTT	JOSEPH	1828	BERENTZWILLER	05/23/1851	NY		FILM
OTT	MICHEL		RUNTZENHEIM	01/01/1828	A		FILM
OTT	THOMAS		ROTHENBOURG(W)	04/06/1849	NY		FILM
OTT F OF 3	LAURENT		BALDENHEIM	03/06/1838	A		FILM
OTT F OF 4	GEORGE		BALDENHEIM	03/06/1838	A		FILM
OTT F OF 6	JEAN		ST. JEAN DES CHOUX	01/01/1828	A		FILM
OTT F OF 8	JACQUES		BALDENHEIM	03/06/1838	A		FILM
OTT MN VOLLMER	CATHERINE		ROTHENBOURG (W)	04/06/1849	NY		FILM
OTT WW	MICHEL		MUNTZENEHEIM	02/23/1853	CH		FILM
OTT WW	SEBASTEIN		ROESCHWOOG	03/14/1817	A		FILM
OTT WW AND CH 3	FIDELE		ROTHENBOURG(W)	04/06/1849	NY		FILM
OTT WW AND CH 3	NICOLAS		VOLSBOURG	03/06/1817	A		FILM
OTTER	THERESE	1833	RIBEAUVILLER	08/22/1857	NY		FILM
OTTERMANN	CATHERINE		ESCHBOURG	01/01/1828	A		FILM
OTTERMANN WW CH 2	CHRETIEN		ESCHBOURG	03/18/1817	A		FILM
OTTMANN	GEORGE		WANTZENAU	03/01/1838	A		FILM
OTTMANN F OF 6	GEORGE		GEUDERTHEIM	03/01/1838	A		FILM
OTTMANN F OF 6	JEAN		BRUMATH	01/01/1828	A		FILM

Lastname	Firstname	Birth Year	Birthplace	Emigration	De	Prof	Source
PAAIS WW AND CH 8	JOSEPH	1809	ROMBACH	10/11/1854	NO		FILM
PABST	LAURENT		SCHIRRHEIN	03/05/1838	A		FILM
PABST F OF 4	JOSEPH		SCHIRRHEIN	03/05/1838	A		FILM
PACAUT	FRANCOIS HENRI	1837	FONTAINE	06/23/1857	NY		FILM
PACAUT	MARIE ANNE	1832	FONTAINE	11/09/1857	NY		FILM
PACK	JOSEPH	1830	COLMAR	09/01/1854	NY		FILM
PACLET WW AND CH 3	FRANCOIS	1812	ESSERT	03/29/1852	NY		FILM
PAFRY	MARIE BARBE	1820	ORBEY	06/28/1855	LO		FILM
PAGNARD	NICOLAS	1803	CHAVANNE-SUR-L`ETANG	05/27/1848	NY		FILM
PAICHEUR WW AND CH 6	FRANCOIS	1800	BOUROGNE	03/26/1849	NY		FILM
PAIRIR	NICOLAS	1820	ST.CROIX AUX MINES	11/03/1847	NO		FILM
PAIRIS	NICOLAS	1836	LIEPRE	03/07/1857	NY		FILM
PALM	THOMAS	1817	ALTENSTADT	08/22/1854	NY		FILM
PALME	JACQUES	1804	SERMAMAGNY	02/22/1856	NO		FILM
PALME	VINCENT	1829	SCHYNDEL	03/30/1853	NO		FILM
PANS WW AND CH 3	PIERRE	1812	ECHENAIS	08/23/1847	NO		FILM
PANTALEON	SIMON	1821	MOLLAY	05/11/1844	NY		FILM
PANTHER	MAGDALENA		STADELHOFEN(B)	07/29/1849	A		FILM
PAPIER	XAVIER	1845	CHALONVILLARD	04/28/1863	NY		FILM
PAPON	MARIE		VAULTHIERMONT	08/01/1844	TX		PASS
PAPON WW AND CH 2	FRANCOIS	1798	ANGEOT	09/20/1847	JA		FILM
PAQUOT	PIERRE FRANCOIS	1785	BETHONVILLIER	07/15/1837	NY		FILM
PARIS	LOUIS	1824	ALTKIRCH	06/06/1849	NY		FILM
PARISET	ANTOINE		BUCHENWALD	01/01/1828	A		FILM
PARISOT	BERNARD		BURCKENWALD	01/01/1828	A		FILM
PARISOT D MARIE		1823	FRESSE(HAUT SAONE)	10/23/1855	SL		FILM
PARISOT MN LOMBARD	MARIE CH	1893	FRESSE(HAUT SAONE)	10/23/1855	SL		FILM
PARISOT WW	ANTOINE	1813	CHAUX	02/01/1854	NO		FILM
PARMENTIER	BARBE	1836	COLMAR	04/23/1857	NY		FILM
PARMENTIER	CATHERINE	1828	MUNSTER	11/22/1856	SL		FILM
PARRET	JEAN BAPTISTE		PUIX	02/14/1844	NY		FILM
PARROT	FREDERICH		BARRANS	/ /	NY		FILM
PARROT	GEORGES	1810	BARANS	02/16/1866	NY		FILM
PARROT	GEORGES	1826	VALENTIGNEY	03/27/1865	NY		FILM
PARROT	JACQUES	1844	AUDINCOURT	04/30/1864	NY		FILM
PARROT	LOUIS	1842	AUDINCOIURT	04/30/1864	NY		FILM
PARROT	LOUISE	1848	MONTBELIARD	03/31/1865	NY		FILM
PARROT	LOUISE CAROLINE	1808	MONTBELIARD	03/08/1866	NY		FILM
PARROT	SUZANNE	1812	BARBAS	02/16/1866	NY		FILM
PASCAL	MARIE JEANNE	1808	MEUSE	04/09/1844	CL		FILM
PATAT	CONSTANT	1822	SOPPE-LE-BAS	01/30/1851	CA		FILM
PATAT CH 5	MARIE	1797	GROSNE	12/31/1851	NY		FILM
PAUL	DANIEL		WINDSTEIN	01/01/1869	A	WEAV	NO.2
PAUL D DANIEL	ROSINE	1815	WINDSTEIN	02/20/1817	A		FILM
PAUL F OF 3	JOSEPH		FORT LOUIS	01/01/1828	A		FILM
PAUL F OF 5	MICHEL		SARENNE	01/01/1828	A		FILM
PAUL S DANIEL	CHRETIEN	1811	WINDSTEIN	02/20/1817	A		FILM
PAUL S DANIEL	DANIEL	1807	WINDSTEIN	02/20/1817	A		FILM
PAUL S DANIEL	PHILIPPE	1813	WINDSTEIN	02/20/1817	A		FILM
PAUL WW	DANIEL	1776	WINDSTEIN	02/20/1817	A		FILM

Lastname	Firstname	Birth Year	Birthplace	Emigration	De	Prof	Source
PAUL WW AND CH 4	DANIEL		WINDSTEIN	02/26/1817	A		FILM
PAUL WW AND CH 4	DANIE6		WINDSTEIN	01/01/1817	A		FILM
PAULEN	J.		DUNTZENHEIM	01/01/1828	A		FILM
PAULEN	SEBASTIEN		DUNTZENHEIM	01/01/1828	A		FILM
PAULEN F OF 3	THIEBAUD		INGENHEIM	01/01/1828	A		FILM
PAULEN D JACQUES	CATHERINE		DUNTZENHEIM	01/01/1828	A		FILM
PAULEN D LAMS GEORGE	MARGUERITE		DUNTZENHEIM	01/01/1828	A		FILM
PAULEN F OF 3	THIEBAUD SEN.		INGENHEIM	01/01/1828	A		FILM
PAULEN F OF 4	GEORGES SEN.		INGENHEIM	01/01/1828	A		FILM
PAULEN F OF 5	MICHEL		BOUXWILLER	01/01/1828	A		FILM
PAULEN F OF 6	JEAN		INGENHEIM	01/01/1828	A		FILM
PAULEN F OF 7	JACQUES		INGENHEIM	01/01/1828	A		FILM
PAULEN MN LUTT	MARIE		DUNTZENHEIM	01/01/1828	A		FILM
PAULEN S JACQUES	JACQUES		DUNTZENHEIM	01/01/1828	A		FILM
PAULEN W LAMS GEORGE	CATHERINE		DUNTZENHEIM	01/01/1828	A		FILM
PAULEN WW AND CH 2	JACQUES		DUNTZENEHEIM	01/01/1828	A		FILM
PAULI F OF 4	GEORGES		DETTWILLER	01/01/1828	A		FILM
PAULIN WW AND CH 6	STANISLAS	1803	MOOSCH	01/22/1847	NY		FILM
PAULIN WW AND CH 7	XAVIER	1806	KRUTH	05/13/1845	NY		FILM
PAULUS	ANTOINE		HAGUENAU	03/01/1838	A		FILM
PAULUS	JOHANN HEINRICH		LANGENSOULTZBACH	01/01/1817	A	WEAV	NO.2
PAULUS F OF 4	GEORGES		BERNOLSHEIM	03/03/1838	A		FILM
PAULUS D ANTOINE	MARIE		BATZENDORFF	02/27/1838	A		FILM
PAULUS S ANTOINE	ANTOINE		BATZENDORFF	02/27/1838	A		FILM
PAULUS WW AND CH 2	ANTOINE		BATZENDORFF	02/27/1838	A		FILM
PAULY	FREDERIC		AUENHEIM	03/01/1838	A		FILM
PAULY	GEORGE		RUNTZENHEIM	01/01/1828	A		FILM
PAUTLER	MICHEL	1838	BREMMELBACH	01/01/1868	NY	FARM	NO.2
PAYER WW AND CH 6	JOSEPH	1810	ROPPE	11/22/1853	NY		FILM
PAYOT WW AND CH 6	JEAN CLAUDE	1797	ROPPE	08/03/1846	SA		FILM
PBERT	XAVIER		SELLBACH(B)	05/27/1849	A		FILM
PEBUS W WENDELIN	KATHARINA		THANN	10/25/1843	CL		FILM
PEBUS WW	WENDELIN	1797	THANN (HR)	10/25/1843	CL		FILM
PECHIN	CELESTIN	1825	JONCHEREY	02/22/1847	NY		FILM
PECHLING F OF 9	JEAN		SCHILLERSDORF	01/01/1828	A		FILM
PEGUIGNOT	JEAN BAPTISTE	1822	ERRERET(HAUT SAONE)	05/17/1847	NY		FILM
PELLETIER CH 3	FRANCOISE	1809	RIBEAUVILLE	09/22/1854	NO		FILM
PELTIER	JACQUES	1797	CHAPELLE SOUS CHAUX	10/27/1846	OH		FILM
PELTIER	JEAN BAPTISTE	1814	ERETTE	03/05/1852	HO		FILM
PELTIER	VEINCENT		ERETTE	03/05/1852	HO		FILM
PELTIER WW AND CH 4	ETIENNE	1792	SALBERT	03/06/1838	NO		FILM
PELTZER	JOHANN NIKOLAUS	1795	EUPEN(BE)	11/15/1846	CL		FILM
PENQUEL WW AND CH 3	ANTOINE	1788	OFFEMONT	09/30/1847	NY		FILM
PENQUET	FRANCOIS	1822	OFFEMONT	11/10/1846	NY		FILM
PENQUET	PIERRE	1826	OFFEMONT	11/10/1846	NY		FILM
PEQUIGNOT	JULES	1844	BEAUCOURT	06/05/1865	NY		FILM
PEQUIGNOT	MARIE	1839	EVETTE	03/09/1866	NY		FILM
PEQUIGNOT WW AND CH	CONSTANT	1824	GIROMAGNY	09/03/1852	NY		FILM
PEQUIGUOT	AUGUSTIN	1832	CHATELIER	01/22/1865	NY		FILM
PEQUINGRIST		1832	FRAYS	06/22/1864	NY		FILM

Lastname	Firstname	Birth Year	Birthplace	Emigration	De	Prof	Source
PERCHEL	LOUISE		RASENWILLER	06/01/1866	A		FILM
PERCY	FRANCOIS JOSEPH	1832	RIERRESCEMONT	09/01/1854	NY		FILM
PERCY	MATHIAS	1831	PIERRESCEMONT	02/22/1856	PA		FILM
PEREZ	MARIE ANNE	1828	ETUEFFONT-BAS(HR)	11/26/1851	MI		FILM
PERIOTAT	ANTOINE		HOCHFELDEN	01/01/1828	A		FILM
PERIOTAT	CESAR		HOCHFELDEN	01/01/1828	A		FILM
PERIOTAT	LOUISE		HOCHFELDEN	01/01/1828	A		FILM
PERIOTAT	MARIE ANNE		HOCHFELDEN	01/01/1828	A		FILM
PERIOTAT	VERONIQUE		HOCHFELDEN	01/01/1828	A		FILM
PERLET	CAROLINE		GERMANY	04/01/1849	NY		FILM
PERLET	SAMUEL	1848	BADEREL	08/13/1866	NY		FILM
PERNE	BERNARD	1828	GUEBWILLER	04/21/1847	NY		FILM
PEROLLA	ANNE MARIE	1815	THANN	07/26/1849	A		FILM
PEROT	FRANCOIS		SERMAMAGNY	11/11/1851	SL		FILM
PEROT	JACQUES SIMON	1829	SERMAMAGNY	10/08/1849	NO		FILM
PEROT	JULIE	1830	CHAUX	08/11/1854	NO		FILM
PEROT WW	FRANCOIS XAVIER	1823	VALDOIE	06/25/1847	NO		FILM
PEROT WW	PIERRE	1808	BREBOTTE	02/14/1844	NY		FILM
PERREY	PIERRE	1827	VETRIGNE	09/22/1866	NY		FILM
PERREZ	MARGUERITE	1813	OFFEMONT	02/04/1840	LO		FILM
PERRIN	ADELAIDE	1803	ESSERT	09/03/1857	BU		FILM
PERRIN	JOHANN	1837	ALTENSTADT	01/01/1867	NY		NO.2
PERRIN	PIERRE	1830	DENNEY	03/04/1852	SL		FILM
PERRIN CH 6	ETIENNE	1801	MASEVAUX	09/01/1847	TX	CULT	PASS
PERRIN WW AND CH 6	ETIENNE	1801	LA BRESSE (VOSGES)	09/27/1847	TX		FILM
PERROD	FRANCOIS JOSEPH	1832	ROUGEGOUTTE	11/15/1852	NY		FILM
PERROD	PIERRE	1830	ROUGEGOUTTE	10/30/1852	NY		FILM
PERROT	FERDINAND FRANC	1821	SERMAMAGNY	09/26/1845	NY		FILM
PERROT	FRANCOIS JOSEPH	1801	ROUGEGOUTTE	08/26/1846	NY		FILM
PERROT	GEORGES	1841	MONTBELIARD	08/14/1866	NY		FILM
PERROT	GEORGES EUGENE	1822	VESCEMONT	04/27/1849	NY		FILM
PERROT	JEAN JOSEPH	1814	PUIX	09/03/1852	NY		FILM
PERROT	THIEBAUD	1829	MOOSCH	09/28/1854	NY		FILM
PERSON F OF 2	PIERRE		DASSENHEIM	01/01/1828	A		FILM
PETDAT CH 2	MARIE GENEREUSE	1797	FAHY(SW)	05/13/1855	NY		FILM
PETEL	FRANCOIS	1821	CERNAY	08/18/1843	NY		FILM
PETER	ANNE-MARIE	1815	MALMERSPACH	10/01/1846	TX	TAYL	PASS
PETER	ANTOINE	1814	MOOSCH	08/01/1844	TX	FACT	PASS
PETER	CHARLOTE		WEISLINGEN	01/01/1828	A		FILM
PETER	CHRETIEN		DURSTEL	03/18/1838	A		FILM
PETER	FRANCOIS FIDELE	1834	LAPOUTRIE	04/14/1856	NY		FILM
PETER	FRANCOIS JOSEPH		DRUSENHEIM	03/24/1838	A		FILM
PETER	FRANCOIS JOSEPH	1825	MOOSCH	08/11/1853	NO		FILM
PETER	GEORGES		BISCHHOLTZ	01/01/1828	A		FILM
PETER	HENRI		TIEFFENBACH	01/01/1828	A		FILM
PETER	HENRY	1835	RIESPACH	12/15/1854	NY		FILM
PETER	JACQUES JUN.		BOSSELSHAUSEN	01/01/1828	A		FILM
PETER	JEAN		MULHAUSEN	01/01/1828	A		FILM
PETER	JEAN	1806	FELDBACH	12/16/1843	NY		FILM
PETER	JOSEPH		MULHOUSE	11/16/1865	NY		FILM

Lastname	Firstname	Birth Year	Birthplace	Emigration	De	Prof	Source
PETER	JOSEPH	1814	HAMBACH(P)	04/09/1844	CL		FILM
PETER	JOSEPH	1820	FASSENHEIM	06/01/1852	NO		FILM
PETER	JOSEPH	1820	FELDBACH	02/03/1857	NO		FILM
PETER	JOSEPH	1839	RIESPACH	08/16/1865	NY		FILM
PETER	JOSEPH	1840	RIESPACH	05/31/1859	NY		FILM
PETER	JOSEPH	1861	RIESPACH	11/16/1865	NY		FILM
PETER	JUSTINE	1836	ODEREN	11/04/1857	TX		FILM
PETER	LEON ANTOINE	1814	MOOSCH	08/28/1844	NO		FILM
PETER	MARGUERITE		MULHOUSE	01/01/1828	A		FILM
PETER	MARIE	1865	MULHOUSE	11/16/1865	NY		FILM
PETER	MARIE ANNE	1814	HALMERSPACH	10/03/1846	TX		FILM
PETER	NICOLAS		HAMBACH	03/08/1838	A		FILM
PETER	NICOLAS		WEISLINGEN	01/01/1828	A		FILM
PETER	PHILIPPE		DURSTEL	03/18/1838	A		FILM
PETER	PIERRE	1809	MOOSCH	04/27/1850	NO		FILM
PETER F OF 8	FRANCOISE ANTOI		NEUWILLER	01/01/1828	A		FILM
PETER S JOSPEH	PETER		MULHOUSE	11/16/1865	NY		FILM
PETER D JOSEPH	MARIE		MULHOUSE	11/16/1865	NY		FILM
PETER F OF 13	MARIE		SUNDHAUSEN	03/02/1837	A		FILM
PETER MN KOEPPEL	CHRISTINE W THI		DEHLINGEN	01/01/1828	A		FILM
PETER S JOSEPH	JOSEPH		MULHOUSE	11/16/1865	NY		FILM
PETER W JOSEPH	MADELAINE		MULHOUSE	11/16/1865	NY		FILM
PETER WW	THEIBAUD		DEHLINGEN	01/01/1828	A		FIM
PETER WW AND CH	JEAN		RIEGEL(B)	09/16/1898	NY		FILM
PETER WW AND CH 4	JOSEPH	1831	MULHOUSE	11/16/1865	NY		FILM
PETERLI	MARIA	1818	FELLERINGEN(HR)	11/22/1843	CL		FILM
PETERLI	MARIE	1818	FELLERINGEN	11/22/1843	TX		FILM
PETERS F	FIDELE		OOS(B)	04/03/1849	NY		FILM
PETERS JOSEPH	EMILE		MULHOUSE	11/16/1865	NY		FILM
PETERSCHMILL	CHRETIEN	1821	RUSTENHART	07/25/1854	NY		FILM
PETERSCHMITT	JEAN	1826	NAMBSHEIM	03/15/1854	NY		FILM
PETERSCHMITT	JOSEPH	1829	NAMBSHEIM	03/15/1854	NY		FILM
PETET	ADELE	1824	RONCHAMP	03/17/1865	SF		FILM
PETET	ANTOINE	1823	RONCHAMP	03/17/1865	SF		FILM
PETHER	JOSEPH	1812	FLORIMOND	08/14/1847	NY		FILM
PETIT	FRANCOIS	1821	CERNAY	08/18/1843	NY		FILM
PETIT MN WAGNER		1782	MULHOUSE	05/17/1842	SL		FILM
PETIT DEMARGE	JOSEPH	1825	ST.MARIE AUX MINES	02/19/1855	NY		FILM
PETIT JEAN WW CH 3	JEAN PIERRE	1810	ROUGEMONT	02/24/1840	PH		FILM
PETIT MN COLLIN	JUSTINE	1812	LUCELLE	05/30/1854	NY		FILM
PETIT WW AND CH	JEAN BAPTISTE	1818	ESSERT	04/22/1852	NY		FILM
PETITAL CH 2	MARIE GENEREUSE	1797	FAHY (SW)	03/13/1855	NY		FILM
PETITJEAN	FRANCOIS	1831	ETEUFFONT HAUT	05/15/1851	NY		FILM
PETITJEAN	JEAN CLAUDE	1827	SERMAMAGNY	01/28/1853	NO		FILM
PETITJEAN	MARIE	1814	BELFORT	11/07/1863	NY		FILM
PETITJEAN F	JOSEPH		RAEDERSHEIM	11/14/1851	NY		FILM
PETREMONT	EMILE	1819	ST.CROIX AUX MINES	11/07/1846	SL		FILM
PETRI F OF 5	JACQUES		BOUXWILLER	01/01/1828	A		FILM
PETTER	MATHIAS		MOMMENHEIM	02/28/1838	A		FILM
PEYER WW AND CH 4	JACQUES	1803	MAGNY	05/27/1853	NY		FILM

Lastname	Firstname	Birth Year	Birthplace	Emigration	De	Prof	Source
PEYRONNET MN BIELLER	BARBE W PIERRE	1822	CHAZELLES, CHARONTE	04/15/1857	IL		FILM
PEYRONNET S PIERRE	JOSEPH	1856	CHAZELLES, CHARONTE	04/15/1857	IL		FILM
PEYRONNET WW AND CH	PIERRE	1824	CHAZELLES,CHARONTE	04/15/1857	IL		FILM
PFAFF			HASLACH(B)	05/12/1849	A		FILM
PFAFF	ELISABETH		KENTZINGEN(B)	04/21/1849	A		FILM
PFAFF	JOHANN GEORG	1844	EBERBACH	01/01/1867		FARM	PRIV
PFAFF	JOSEPH		HAGUENAU	03/01/1838	A		FILM
PFAFF	JOSEPH	1849	EBERBACH	01/01/1867	NY		PRIV
PFAFF WW AND CH 5	NICOLAS	1796	KEMBS	10/20/1847	NO		FILM
PFAHL	JOSEPH		MULLENBACH	08/31/1849	A		FILM
PFAHL	MARIANNE		MULLENBACH	08/31/1849	A		FILM
PFANNER	JEAN GREGOIRE	1803	ALTKIRCH	09/13/1849	NO		FILM
PFARRER	BENEDICT	1820	BREMENTHAL	11/15/1846	CL		FILM
PFARRER	ELISABETH	1825	BREMENTHAL	11/15/1846	CL		FILM
PFAU	ANDRE	1808	KLAENTHOF(W)	10/10/1843	NY		FILM
PFAU	DOROTHEE		REMLISDORF (W)	04/20/1849	NY		FILM
PFAU	LOUIS	1818	RIBEAUVILLE	12/31/1854	NO		FILM
PFAU WW AND CH 2	JEAN MICHEL	1831	BEBLENHEIM	12/13/1853	NO		FILM
PFEFFER	SEBASTIAN		REMINGEN(W)	04/18/1849	NY		FILM
PFEIFER	PIERRE SIMON	1826	BUHL	04/22/1848	NY		FILM
PFEIFER S H.BALTHAZA	HANS MARTIN		PREUSCHDORF	01/01/1729	A		SUESS
PFEIFFER	CHRETIEN		ENDINGEN(W)	06/11/1849	A		FILM
PFEIFFER	FRANCOIS JOSEPH	1823	REICHSHOFFEN(BR)	03/16/1853	NY		FILM
PFEIFFER	GASPARD	1799	LANGENSCHLEITEL(BR)	12/23/1847	NY		FILM
PFEIFFER	JACQUES	1818	GEISHAUSEN	06/28/1850	NY		FILM
PFEIFFER	JEAN		SIEWILLER	03/18/1817	A		FILM
PFEIFFER	JEAN ADAM	1830	REICHSHOFFEN(BR)	04/22/1852	NY		FILM
PFEIFFER	JOSEPH	1811	GUEBWILLER	08/08/1851	NY		FILM
PFEIFFER	PIERRE CASIMIR	1821	REICHSHOFFEN(BR)	03/19/1853	NY		FILM
PFEIFFER	PIERRE LOUIS	1826	SARRELOUIS (P)	04/07/1855	NY		FILM
PFEIFFER	SEBASTIEN	1823	REGUISHEIM	08/02/1854	NO		FILM
PFEIFFER WW AND CH	MATHIAS	1817	BOURGFELDEN	08/11/1854	NY		FILM
PFEIFFER MN METZ	ANNA MARIA		PREUSCHDORF	01/01/1729	A		SUESS
PFENNIG F OF 7	GEORGE		KIRRWILLER	01/01/1828	A		FILM
PFERSCH F OF 4	JACQUES		DASSENHEIM	01/01/1828	A		FILM
PFETZER	MARIE JOSEPHINE		RENCHEN (BADEN)	10/27/1849	A		FILM
PFEW	JEAN JACQUES	1829	BEBLENHEIM	12/12/1853	NO		FILM
PFISTER	ANTOINE	1825	OSTHEIM	02/17/1848	NY		FILM
PFISTER	IGNACE	1817	OSTHEIM	08/16/1847	NY		FILM
PFISTER	JACQUES	1834	OSTHEIM	05/16/1854	NY		FILM
PFISTER	JEAN CHERTIEN	1809	BEBLENHEIM	04/30/1832	NY		FILM
PFISTER	JOSEPH	1800	TRAUBACH-LE-BAS	10/01/1846	NY		FILM
PFISTER	JOSEPH	1820	OSTHEIM	02/01/1848	NY		FILM
PFISTER F OF 5	GEORGE		BALDENHEIM	03/06/1838	A		FILM
PFISTER MN DESCH CH	MARIE ANNE	1818	RAEDERSHEIM	12/21/1852	NO		FILM
PFISTEREN	M.		OBERKIRCH (BADEN)	04/06/1849	NY		FILM
PFITZENMAIER	CHARLES		BACKNANG (W)	07/30/1849	A		FILM
PFLEGER WW AND CH 2	JEAN	1817	FRIESSEN	03/09/1846	NY		FILM
PFLUG	SALOME	1849	OBERHOFEN	01/01/1867	NY		NO.2
PFLUG H HALLER	FREDERIC	1827	CLEEBOURG	01/01/1867	NY	TAYL	PRIV

Lastname	Firstname	Birth Year	Birthplace	Emigration	De	Prof	Source
PFLUG MN HALLER	MARGUERITE	1837	CLEEBOURG	01/01/1867	NY		PRIV
PFLUM	CHRETIEN		KENTZINGEN (BADEN)	04/21/1849	A		FILM
PFOHL	FRANCISKA	1836	SURBOURG	01/01/1867	NY		NO.2
PFOHL	PIERRE	1820	SOURBOURG (BR)	02/03/1857	NY		FILM
PFOHL	PIERRE	1828	SOURBOURG (BR)	02/27/1857	NY		FILM
PFRIMMER WW F OF 4	CHRETIEN		REITWEILER	02/27/1838	A		FILM
PFROMMER	LOUIS		DENNACH (W)	04/10/1849	A		FILM
PFUESTER WW AND CH 6	JOSEPH	1782	OSTHEIM	03/17/1845	NY		FILM
PFUFF	EMILIE		ALBIRSBACH(W)	05/12/1849	A		FILM
PFUFF	SIEGFRIES		ALBIRSBACH(W)	05/12/1849	A		FILM
PHEMLPIN	CLAIRE	1849	FRAHIER(HS)	07/16/1865	NY		FILM
PHERSCH F OF 5	HENRY		HERBITZHEIM	01/01/1828	A		FILM
PHILIPP	ALOIS	1839	OBERROEDERN	01/01/1869	NY		NO.2
PHILIPP	BABETTE	1818	MUEHLHAUSEN(HR)	10/25/1843	TX		FILM
PHILIPP D VINZENZ	JOSEPHINE	1841	MUEHLHAUSEN(HR)	10/25/1843	TX		FILM
PHILIPP WW AND CH	VINZENZ	1810	MUEHLHAUSEN(HR)	10/25/1843	TX		FILM
PHILIPPE	FRANCOIS	1808	L`ALLEMAND ROMBACH	10/02/1854	NO		FILM
PHILIPPE	JACQUES	1820	HINDLINGEN	04/27/1849	NY		FILM
PHILIPPE	LUDWIG	1841	WINGEN	01/01/1866	NY	FARM	NO.2
PHILIPPE	SOPHIE	1820	DU MENIL (VOSGES)	05/15/1856	SF		FILM
PHILIPPE	THIEBAUT	1815	FRIESEN(HR)	01/18/1847	NY		FILM
PHILIPPI F OF 8	JEAN ADAM		KESKASTEL	01/01/1828	A		FILM
PHILIPPS F OF 14	BERNARD		THAL	01/01/1828	A		FILM
PHILIPPS F OF 6	NICOLAS		RAUWILLER	01/01/1828	A		FILM
PHILLIPS	FERDINAND	1840	STUNDWILLER	01/01/1867	NY	MILL	NO.2
PHILLIPS	JOSEPHINE	1848	BRUEHL	01/01/1867	NY		NO.2
PHITER MN DESCH CH	MARIE ANNE	1818	ROEDERSHEIM	12/31/1852	NO		FILM
PICCARD	MATHILDE		RENNINGEN(W)	04/18/1849	NY		FILM
PICCARD	SALOMON		RENNINGEN(W)	04/18/1849	NY		FILM
PIERCON CH 3	MADELEINE	1806	BRETAGNE	10/08/1847	NY		FILM
PIEROST	LOUIE	1848	OFFEMONT	04/19/1866	NY		FILM
PIEROT	FRANCOISE	1812	SERMAMAGNY	11/27/1851	SL		FILM
PIEROT CH 2	MARIE ANNE	1788	CHAUX	01/30/1847	NO		FILM
PIERRE	CELESTINE	1834	CHENEBIER	/ /			
PIERRE	CELESTINE	1834	CHENEBIER	03/28/1863	NY		FILM
PIERRE	JEAN GEORGES	1828	LIEPRE	09/13/1847	NO		FILM
PIERRE	SEBASTIEN	1836	LIEPRE	08/12/1854	NO		FILM
PIERRE WW AND CH 4	PHILIPPE		HERBITZHEIM	04/17/1817	A		FILM
PIERREL WW AND CH 3	MAURICE	1796	ST. MAURICE	10/20/1854	NY		FILM
PIERRERELCIN W JEAN		1828	LAPOUTROIE	10/20/1856	NY		FILM
PIERRERELCIN WW	JEAN JOSEPH CH	1826	LAPOUTROIE	10/20/1856	NY		FILM
PIERRIN	MARIE THEOPHILE	1811	ST.CROIX AUX MINES	05/18/1848	A		FILM
PIETET	JEAN JACQUES MA	1818	SUARCE	02/26/1851	NY		FILM
PIETTE	ALEXANDRE	1824	ST.CROIX AUX MINES	04/15/1848	NO		FILM
PINCE	FRANCOIS	1826	ROPPE	03/24/1846	NY		FILM
PINEL	FRANCOIS DELORE	1796	ST,MARIE AUX MINES	10/25/1853	NO		FILM
PINGENAT	LOUIS	1812	SOPPE-LE-BAS	09/28/1854	NY		FILM
PINGENOT	JEAN NICOLAS	1799	BRETTEN	10/10/1844	NO		FILM
PINGENOT WW	PIERRE FRANCOIS	1810	BRETTEN	10/10/1844	NO		FILM
PINT	JEAN		RIMSDORF	03/17/1817	A		FILM

Lastname	Firstname	Birth Year	Birthplace	Emigration	De	Prof	Source
PIOT	ANTOINE	1835	RIERESCEMONT	08/26/1854	A		FILM
PIQUENEZ WW AND CH 5	JEAN CLAUDE	1787	GRANDVILLARS	02/04/1851	CH		FILM
PIQUEREZ	MARIE ANNE	1822	MEROUX	05/04/1846	NY		FILM
PIQUEREZ WW AND CH 2	FRANCOIS	1813	ANDELNANS	03/19/1847	NO		FILM
PIQUET	JACQUES JOS.		HAGUENAU	01/01/1828	A		FILM
PIQUET	VICTOR	1834	ST.AMARIN	10/16/1852	A		FILM
PIQUET WW AND CH	MATHIAS	1811	DANNEMARIE	04/16/1852	NY		FILM
PIRSOM F OF 8	J. ADAM		HIRSCHLAND	01/01/1828	A		FILM
PIRSON	NICOLAS		KIRRBERG	01/01/1828	A		FILM
PIRSON	PIERRE		KIRRBERG	01/01/1828	A		FILM
PISCATOR F OF 5	FREDERIC		HAMBACH	01/01/1828	A		FILM
PISTER	CAROLINE		WINGEN	01/01/1828	A		FILM
PISTONIUS WW AND CH2	FRANCOIS JOSEPH	1813	VOLLE	10/20/1851	NO		FILM
PISTZENTHALER WW CH4	MICHEL	1810	HOLTZWIHR	12/04/1852	NY		FILM
PLANSON	PIERRE	1842	VALENTIGNAY	05/06/1865	NY		FILM
PLATTNER	JOHANN	1819	RUYGOLDWIL	11/15/1846	TX		FILM
PLUMBERG	ANTOINE	1821	DELLE	08/13/1844	NY		FILM
POEPPELE	ANTOINE		MULLENBACH B	08/23/1849	A		FILM
POERSCHEL	JOSEPH		HOERDT	02/28/1838	A		FILM
POETE	FRANCOIS XAVIER	1826	GRANDVILLARS	02/25/1853	NY		FILM
POETE	PIERRE JOSEPH	1831	GRANDVILLARS	09/08/1853	NY		FILM
POIL	JEAN	1836	HAGENHEIM	08/17/1866	NY		FILM
POINCOT	JEAN BAPTISTE	1824	FRESSE	09/26/1850	NO		FILM
POIRE	CELESTIN	1831	FRAIS	01/26/1852	NO		FILM
POIRE	HENRI	1830	FRAIS	01/26/1852	NO		FILM
POIRE	HENRI LOUIS	1835	FRAIS	01/26/1852	NO		FILM
POIRE	JOSEPH	1833	FRAIS	01/26/1852	NO		FILM
POIRIER	ALEXIS	1843	ANJOUTEY	02/03/1857	NO		FILM
POIRIER	MARGUERITE	1847		02/03/1857	NO		FILM
POIROT WW AND CH 5	ALEXANDRE	1809	OFFEMONT	05/31/1853	NY		FILM
POISSON F OF 4	CLAUDE		ROESCHWOOG	01/01/1828	A		FILM
POLIN	JEAN BAPTISTE	1822	PUIX	09/03/1852	NY		FILM
POLY	THERESE	1844	FRAHIER	04/06/1866	NY		FILM
POMMIER	ANNE	1811	CHAUX	03/04/1865	NY		FILM
POMMIER	GEORGES	1851	CHAUX	03/04/1865	NY		FILM
POMMIER	JOSEPH	1811	CHAUX	02/10/1840	NY		FILM
POMMIER	JOSEPH	1828	CHAUX	03/04/1865	NY		FILM
POMMIER	PHILOMENE	1848	CHAUX	03/04/1865	NY		FILM
POMMIER	ROSE	1839	CHAUX	03/04/1865	NY		FILM
POMMIER	VINCENT	1804	CHAUX	03/04/1865	NY		FILM
POMMIER	VINCENT	1841	CHAUX	03/04/1865	NY		FILM
PONCE	FRANCOIS	1826	ROPPE	03/24/1846	NY		FILM
PORCHEUR	FRANCOIS	1836	MORVILLARCH	05/26/1865	NY		FILM
PORICARTE	ELIZABETH			06/14/1819	A		FILM
POSTE	MADELEINE	1785	ZINSWEILLER	02/16/1816	A		FILM
POSTE	MADELEINE	1810	ZINSWEILLER	02/16/1817	A		FILM
POSTE	MADELEINE	1813	ZINSWEILLER	02/16/1817	A		FILM
POSTE	MARGUERITE	1782	ZINSWEILLER	12/16/1817	A		FILM
POUCHET	JOSEPH	1829	BELFORT	01/07/1863	NY		FILM
POUCHOT	FELISIE	1797	BELFORT	01/07/1863	NY		FILM

Lastname	Firstname	Birth Year	Birthplace	Emigration	De	Prof	Source
POUCHOT	JULES	1837	BELFORT	01/07/1863	NY		FILM
POUCHOT	JULES JOSEPH		BELFORT	01/07/1863	NY		FILM
POUCHOT WW AND CH 7	JOSEPH	1814	ESSERT	03/25/1852	NY		FILM
POURCHE	FERDINAND	1823	PEROUSE	04/17/1841	NY		FILM
POURCHOT WW AND CH 2	JACQUES FREDERC	1799	BEAUCOURT	09/18/1847	NY		FILM
POURVOURVILLE	ADOLPHE	1811	MULHAUSEN	01/22/1840	TX		FILM
POUSING	CATHERINE		BURBACH	01/01/1828	A		FILM
POUTH F			KIEHHEIM	01/01/1828	A		FILM
POUTIER	PIERRE		BURCKENWALD	01/01/1828	A		FILM
PRAEFKE CH	ALBERT	1796	BREMEN	10/24/1839	NO		FILM
PREFRIED	M. KATHERINA	1786	ROPPENHEIM	/ /	HU		NO.1
PREISS	CATHERINE	1830	RIQUEWIHR	11/26/1856	NY		FILM
PREISSER	ANTOINE	1821	APPENWIHR	05/23/1849	NY		FILM
PREISSIG	CHARLES	1823	ST.MARIE AUX MINES	05/01/1855	A		FILM
PRELLY	MATIAS	1819	HOMBOURG(HR)	04/14/1854	NY		FILM
PRENAT	AUGUSTE	1828	VILLARS LE SEE	09/12/1846	NY		FILM
PRENAT	CONSTANT	1828	VILLARS LE SEE	02/16/1846	NY		FILM
PRENAT	FLORENTIN	1828	VILLARS LE SEE	02/16/1846	NY		FILM
PRENAT	JEAN BAPTISTE	1828	VILLARS LE SEE	09/04/1847	NY		FILM
PRENAT	XAVIER	1828	VILLARS LE SEE	09/12/1846	NY		FILM
PRENOT	JULES	1836	MONTBELIARD	04/23/1863	NY		FILM
PRENOT CH 2	MARIE ANNE	1788	CHAUX	01/30/1847	NO		FILM
PRETAL		1843	SUARCE	12/01/1865	NY		FILM
PREVOD	PIERRE	1816	CHAUX	03/10/1840	NY		FILM
PREVOST	FRANCOIS	1810	BAVILLIERS	03/03/1832	SL		FILM
PREVOST WW AND CH 2	PIERRE	1795	LIXHEIM	09/13/1844	SL		FILM
PREVOT	XAVIER	1829	SCHYNDEL	03/30/1853	NY		FILM
PREVOT WW AND CH 2	JEAN LOUIS	1811	CHAUX	02/05/1847	NO		FILM
PRICH	JOHANN BAPTIST	1826	ROUFFACH	11/15/1846	TX		FILM
PRICHARD	SIMON	1817	BRETAGNE	08/25/1853	A		FILM
PRIFF	JACQUES	1811	SOPPE-LE-BAS	10/08/1844	A		FILM
PRIFT CH	RAOUL	1787	SOPPE-LE-HAUT	11/04/1844	NO		FILM
PRINTZ	J.A.		RITTERSHOFEN	01/01/1817	A		NO.2
PRIOS	MICHEL	1831	MITTELWIHR	04/11/1857	NY		FILM
PRISCH	JEAN ADAM		RIFFERSHOFFEN	03/21/1817	A		FILM
PRISS	CATHERINE		MITTELWIHR	06/04/1857	NO		FILM
PRISS	CATHERINE MADEL	1790	BEBLENHEIM	06/04/1857	NO		FILM
PRISS	JOAN	1827	MITTELWIHR	04/25/1856	NY		FILM
PRIULIX	JEAN ADAM		RITTERSHOFFEN	03/29/1817	A		FILM
PROBST	CELESTIN	1847	LUTHER (HR)	05/04/1865	NY		FILM
PROBST	FRANCOIS BARNAB	1816	ROUFFACH	12/29/1842	A		FILM
PROBST	JEAN	1825	ROUFFACH	11/15/1843	A		FILM
PROBST	JOSEPH JUN.	1812	ROUFFACH	11/15/1843	A		FILM
PROBST WW AND CH	ARBOGAST	1826	TRAUBACH-LE-BAS	03/21/1854	NY		FILM
PROHASCA WW	JOSEPH		NEUWILLER	03/17/1817	A		FILM
PROHLHUETER	FRIEDRICH	1841	RITTERSHOFEN	01/01/1868	NY		NO.2
PRONEZ	SEBASTIEN	1828	JONCHERY	03/06/1847	NY		FILM
PRONQUE	MARIE	1811	JONCHERY	03/06/1847	NY		FILM
PROTH WW AND CH 3	CHRETIEN		BERRWILLER	04/12/1855	NY		FILM
PROUKER	MARIE	1830	ST.DIZIER	10/01/1865	NY		FILM

Lastname	Firstname	Birth Year	Birthplace	Emigration	De	Prof	Source
PRUDHOMME	L.JOSEPH AUGUST	1822	ROUFFACH	11/15/1846	TX		FILM
PRUDHOMME	LOUIS JOSEPH	1823	WASSELONNE(BR)	10/31/1846	A		FILM
PUEGER	JOSEPH	1808	LEYMEN	09/27/1852	NY		FILM
PULCHER	CLAUDE JACQUES	1776	CHAUX	01/25/1843	NY		FILM
PULCHER WW	JEAN BAPTISTE	1804	CHAUX	06/15/1853	NY		FILM
PULCHER WW AND CH 7	MARTIN	1806	CHAUX	08/19/1839	NY		FILM
PUNDT	CATHERINE	1798	KAYSERSBERG	08/20/1852	NO		FILM
PUTH F OF 5	ANTOINE		WESTFALEN	01/01/1828	A		FILM
PUTHER WW AND CH 7	MARTIN	1806	CHAUX	08/19/1839	NY		FILM
PUTTER	ALOYSE	1822	SENTHEIM	09/13/1847	NY		FILM
PY	JOSEPH	1788	LEBETAIN	08/09/1837	NY		FILM
PY	PIERRE	1828	FRAHIER	04/04/1866	NY		FILM
PY WW AND CH 6	JEAN PIERRE	1799	EGUENIQUE	08/09/1837	NY		FILM

Lastname	Firstname	Birth Year	Birthplace	Emigration	De	Prof	Source
QUALLIN	FRANCOIS	1791	JOUY	10/05/1843	TX		FILOM
QUALLIN CH 4	FRANZ	1795	CERNAY	10/25/1843	A		FILM
QUALLIN D FRANZ	CHRISTINE	1821	CERNAY	10/25/1843	TX		FILM
QUALLIN D FRANZ	CLARINE	1820	CERNAY	10/25/1843	TX		FILM
QUALLIN D FRANZ	JULIE	1825	CERNAY	10/25/1843	TX		FILM
QUALLIN D FRANZ	THERESE	1831	CERNAY	10/25/1843	TX		FILM
QUALLINE	AUGUST	1826	CERNAY	10/25/1843	TX	MECH	FILM
QUANE W W 3CH	JOSEPH	1812	COURTE LE VANT	03/26/1844	NY		FILM
QUERRY W W 1CH	JEAN PIERRE	1815	FAVEROIS	01/15/1844	NY	FARR	FILM
QUICKERT	ANTOINE	1816	OBERHERGHEIM	10/21/1847	NY	BRLA	FILM
QUICKERT	LEGER	1810	OBERHERGHEIM	10/21/1847	NY	BRLA	FILLM
QUICKERT	XAVIER		OBERHERGHEIM	10/14/1847	NY	SHMA	FILM
QUICKERT W W 3CH	*ONRAD	1803	OBERHERGHEIM	10/14/1847	NY		FILM
QUINTUS	CATHERINE	1825	GRUBWILLER	08/14/1848	A	MIER	FILM
QUINTUS	EMILE	1827	GRUBWILLER	10/13/1843	A	SERR	FILM
QUINTZLER F OF 4	JEAN		WEITBRUCH	02/26/1838	A	JOIN	FILM
QUIQUEREZ	JOSEPH	1842	ROUGEGOUTTE	05/19/1865	NY		FILM
QUIRIN	FREDERIC		KESKASTEL	01/01/1828	A	TAYL	FILM
QUIRINS	NICOLAS		BERG	03/01/1838	A	DAYL	FILM

```
---------------------------------------------------------------------------------------
RABENSCHANTZ          NIKOLAUS     1815 MITZACH (E)          11/15/1846 TX DAYL FILM
RABRECHT              ROBERT       1816 NIEDERHERGHEIM       02/01/1852 TX CULT PASS
RABY                  LOUIS        1813 PARIS                09/17/1845 TX      FILM
RACK                  JEAN         1812 MULHOUSE             09/02/1852 NY      FILM
RAEDELSBERGER         DAVID        1827 ILLHAEUSERN          04/13/1841 NY      FILM

RAEKS WW              JEAN BAPTISTE 1807 CERNAY              06/26/1839 NY      FILM
RAESSLER              GASPARD      1825 BITSCHWILLER         08/30/1853 NY      FILM
RAETER W W            JEAN BAPTISTE 1807 CERNAY              06/26/1839 NY      FILM
RAETTICH WW CH 2      FRANCOIS JOSEPH 1817 STAFFELFELDEN     04/09/1847 A       FILM
RAHERT                JEAN         1828 COLMAR               08/28/1855 NY      FILM

RAINICHE W W          FRANCOIS JOSEPH 1814 CHAUX            04/01/1854 NO      FILM
RAIS W W              CHRETIEN          GUMBRECHTSHOFFEN     04/16/1819 A  TAYL FILM
RALLAY     CH         MARIE ELISE  1821 MALBOUHANS (H-SAONE) 06/12/1855 NY     FILM
RALY                  LOUIS        1812 PARIS                09/17/1845 A       FILM
RAMESIN               JACQUES      1785 EGUENIGUE            02/28/1844 PH      FILM

RAMINGER              MARTIN       1825 DUFFENHEIM           12/13/1848 NO      FILM
RAMSEIN CH7           BARBE        1806 LUCERNE (SW)         04/17/1855 NY      FILM
RAMSER                ROSINA            RIEGEL (B)           06/04/1849 NY      FILM
RAMSTEIN              JOSEPH       1823 GUEWENHEIM           06/17/1852 NY      FILM
RAMSTEIN WW CH 3      THIEBAUT     1801 WATTWILLER           11/10/1855 NY      FILM

RANTZEN               JACOB             GUMBRECHTSHOFFEN(BR) 10/15/1826 OH      FILM
RAOUL H CLAUSS 5 CH   JACOB             ROPPENHEIM           07/12/1847 A       NO.1
RAOUL MN CLAUSS       MADELAINE         ROPPENHEIM           07/12/1847 A       NO.1
RAPINE                MARIE MADELEINE 1830 VILLARS LE SEE    07/10/1847 NY      FILM
RAPP                  CHRISTINE         WEINBOURG            01/01/1828 A       FILM

RAPP                  DANIEL            BOOFZHEIM            02/25/1838 A       FILM
RAPP                  JACQUES           WEINBOURG            01/01/1828 A       FILM
RAPP                  JEAN         1813 DURRENENTZEN         08/13/1852 CH      FILM
RAPP F OF 8           JEAN              SUNDHAUSEN           03/02/1838 A       FILM
RAPP WW AND CH 3      ANDRE        1818 SONDERSDORFF         03/02/1847 NY      FILM

RAPPERT WW CH 3       CONRAD            BUTTEN               04/17/1817 A       FILM
RAPPOLL               MADELEINE         KUHLENDORF           03/28/1817 A       FILM
RAPPOLT               MAGDALENA         KUHLENDORF           01/01/1817 A       NO.2
RASCHUNG              JOSEPH       1841 SENTHEIM             12/31/1865 NY      FILM
RATH CH               ELISABETH    1809 ST.MARIE AUX MINES   10/11/1854 NY      FILM

RATHERN               JEAN              BERSTHEIM            03/03/1838 A       FILM
RATTLICH              FRANCOIS JOSEPH 1813 STAFFELFELDEN     04/09/1847 A  LAYB FILM
RAU                   JEAN              SCHWENNINGEN(W)      05/24/1849 A       FILM
RAU    W GOETZ        ANNE MARIE        BRUMATH              03/22/1838 A       FILM
RAUL                  SEBASTIAN    1806 WINTZENHEIM(HR)      04/09/1844 TX      FILM

RAUSCHER F OF 4       GEORGE            PUBERG               01/01/1828 A       FILM
RAUSCHER F OF 6       NICOLAS           DIEMERINGEN          03/03/1838 A       FILM
RAUSCHER MN LEHMANN   CATHERINE CH 2 1805 OBERLAUTERBACH(BR) 08/21/1854 NY     FILM
RAUSCHER WW CH2       MARCEL            ALTWILLER            01/01/1817 A       FILM
RAUSS WW              JEAN DAVID   1782 HAIDERBACH(W)        05/25/1847 NO      FILM

RAVEY                 FRANCOIS     1826 ISLE SUR LE DOUBS    10/10/1865 NY      FILM
RAYNAL WW CH 2        CHARLES NAPOLEO 1806 STRASBOURG        05/31/1851 NY      FILM
RAYOT                 CATHERINE    1840 BAR                  02/07/1865 NY      FILM
RAYOT                 LOUISE       1849 VALENTIGNEY          02/16/1865 NY      FILM
RAYOT                 PIERRE       1828 VALENTIGNEY          03/22/1865 NY      FILM
```

Lastname	Firstname	Birth Year	Birthplace	Emigration	De	Prof	Source
RE F OF 3	JEAN NICOLAS		KESKASTEL	01/01/1828	A		FILM
REBENACK W F			HARSKIRCH	03/23/1803	A		FILM
REBER	JOSEPH	1827	UFFHEIM	02/20/1847	NY		FILM
REBERT	MARIE MADELEINE	1806	COLMAR	09/01/1852	SL		FILM
REBERT CH 5	HENRIETTE	1814	COLMAR	04/14/1851	CI		FILM
REBHAN WW AND CH 6	MATHIAS	1800	GUEWENHEIM	02/19/1846	NY		FILM
REBHOLZ WW CH	JOSEPH		BETRA (SIGMARIN)	04/29/1849	A		FILM
REBISCHON	THIEBAUD	1799	VILLEFRANCHE	06/23/1847	A		FILM
REBISCHUNG	NICOLAS		MITZACH	10/02/1846	TX		FILM
REBJOCK WW AND CH 3	ANTOINE		WINGEN	01/01/1817	A		FILM
REBRASSIE	MARIE	1795	BRETAGNE(T OF BELFO)	09/25/1844	A		FILM
RECHE	JEAN PIERRE	1821	JONCHEREY	01/13/1849	NY		FILM
RECHT	BENJAMIN		SCHAFFHAUSEN	09/19/1852	A		FILM
RECHT	JOSEPH		SCHAFFHAUSEN	01/01/1828	A		FILM
RECHTENSTEIN	LOUISE		DETTWILLER	01/01/1828	A		FILM
RECK	HENRI	1796	ILLZACH	07/01/1857	NY		FILM
RECK	JEAN		DORNACH	07/01/1857	NY		FILM
RECK	JEAN JACQUES	1805	ST.MARIE AUX MINES	08/31/1848	NY		FILM
RECKETH	ELISABETH	1836	WECKERSCHWILLER	05/11/1857	NY		FILM
REDELLE	FRANCOIS ALEXAN	1812	GRANDVILLARS	03/02/1847	NY		FILM
REDELSPERGER	ANNE MARIE	1832	MOOSCH	03/25/1852	NO		FILM
REDELSPERGER	CHARLES	1809	ST.MARIE AUX MINES	03/14/1854	NY		FILM
REDELSPERGER	FRANCOIS	1835	ST,MARIE AUX MINES	11/10/1854	NO		FILM
REDELSPERGER	GEORGES	1822	ST.MARIE AUX MINES	03/15/1856	NY		FILM
REDELSPERGER	JACQUS	1826	ST.MARIE AUX MINES	11/23/1854	NY		FILM
REDELSPERGER	THERESE	1833	MOOSCH	06/06/1854	NY		FILM
REDERSDORFF WW CH 7	JEAN	1816	KETTLACH	09/21/1844	OH		FILM
REEB	JEAN NICOLAS		KESKASTEL	01/01/1828	A		FILM
REEB	THIEBAUD		KESKASTEL	01/01/1828	A		FILM
REECH	GEORG		LANGENSOULTZBACH	01/01/1856	A		SUESS
REES	MICHEL	1807	BELSEN(W)	08/30/1850	NY		FILM
REFFE	JEAN		BAERENDORF	03/01/1838	A		FILM
REGMANN	LEGER	1832	RIXHEIM	08/09/1852	TX		FILM
REGNAULT	CONSTANT	1842	AUDINCOURT	02/19/1866	NY		FILM
REGNAULT	GEORGES	1818	VALENTIGNEY	12/20/1864	NY		FILM
REHM	ADELE CAROLINE		NIEDERBETSCHDORF	/ /	A		NO.1
REHM	CHARLES	1863	NIEDERBETSCHDORF	/ /	A		NO.1
REHM	GUSTAVE	1835		/ /	A		PRIV
REHM	JACQUES		HATTMATT	01/01/1828	A		FILM
REHM	JEAN	1832	WINTZENHEIM	08/20/1841	A		FILM
REHM	SALOME ADELE	1864	NIEDERBETSCHDORF	/ /	A		NO.1
REHM CH	REINHARD		STRASBOURG	05/27/1817	A		FILM
REHM WW AND CH 6	JACQUES		DARENTZEN	02/10/1853	CH		FILM
REHM F OF 2	MARTIN		HATTMATT	01/01/1828	A		FILM
REHM H WEBER 3CHI	GUSTAVE	1835	NIEDERBETSCHDORF	/ /	A		NO.1
REHM MN WEBER	SALOME		NIEDERBETSCHDORF	/ /	A		NO.1
REHM WW AND CH 2	CHRETIEN		FROHMUHL	03/06/1817	A		FILM
REHM WW AND CH 4	JEAN		FROHMUHL	01/01/1817	A		FILM
REIBEL WW AND CH 4	ARMAND		ST.MAURICE	03/16/1838	A		FILM
REICH	AUGUSTIN	1828	NIEDERMICHELBACH	03/23/1852	BU		FILM

Lastname	Firstname	Birth Year	Birthplace	Emigration	De	Prof	Source
REICH	JACQUES	1809	SIEGEN(BR)	12/09/1843	PH		FILM
REICH	SAMUEL	1813	BADEN	03/01/1837	A		FILM
REICH CH	PIERRE	1784	SALMBACH (BR)	11/07/1845	NO		FILM
REICHERT	ELISABETH		NEUHAEUSEL	03/20/1838	A		FILM
REICHERT	FREDERIC		EPPINGEN(B)	06/04/1849	A		FILM
REICHMANN	ELISE		MUELHAUSEN(W)	04/28/1849	A		FILM
REICHMANN	JOSEPHINE		OEFFINGEN(W)	05/08/1849	A		FILM
REICHMANN	MARGUERITA		OEFFINGEN(W)	05/08/1849	A		FILM
REICHMANN	THERESE		OEFFINGEN(W)	05/08/1849	A		FILM
REIF	ELISE		KORK	04/21/1849	NY		FILM
REIMAND	CATHERINE		DRUSENHEIM	03/24/1838	A		FILM
REIMAND	JACQUES		DRUSENHEIM	03/24/1838	A		FILM
REIN	AARON	1841	SIERENTZ(HR)	05/28/1865	NY		FILM
REIN	JACQUES		DURSTEL	03/18/1838	A		FILM
REINAGEL	FRANCOIS JOSEPH		SCHWEIGHAUSEN	01/01/1828	A		FILM
REINAGEL F OF 6	JEAN		SCHWEIGHAUSEN	01/01/1828	A		FILM
REINBERGER	GEORGE		PETERSBACH	01/01/1828	A		FILM
REINBERGER	JACQUES		PETERSBACH	01/01/1828	A		FILM
REINBERGER	NICOALS		PETERSBACH	01/01/1828	A		FILM
REINERT	MICHEL		STEINBOURG	03/29/1817	A		FILM
REINHARD	GEORGE		ECKARDTSWILLER	01/01/1828	A		FILM
REINHARD	HENRI	1819	ILLZACH	11/03/1840	NO		
REINHARD	JEAN	1844	RIESBACH(HR)	03/12/1866	NY		FILM
REINHARD	JEAN ULRIC	1807	ILLZACH	03/25/1843	A		FILM
REINHARD	JOSEPH	1841		02/14/1857	NY		FILM
REINHARD	MATHIS		NIEDERBETSCHDORF	01/01/1817	A		NO.2
REINHARD	ULRIC	1811	ILLZACH	10/27/1845	NY		FILM
REINHARD CH4	MARIE		ESCHBOURG	03/31/1817	A		FILM
REINHARD F OF 5	GEORGE		SCHILLERSDORFF	01/01/1828	A		FILM
REINHARD F OF 8	MICHEL		ECKARDTSWILLER	01/01/1828	A		FILM
REINHARD WW AND CH 2	DAVID		ALGOLSHEIM	01/29/1842	NY		FILM
REINHARD WW AND CH 2	MATHIEU		NIEDERBETSCHDORF	03/29/1817	A		FILM
REINHARD WW AND CH 3	FIDELE		PETITE PIERRE	03/31/1817	A		FILM
REINHARD WW AND CH 3	FREDERIC		OSTEIM	04/12/1854	NY		FILM
REINHARD WW AND CH 3	LAURENT	1814	OSTHEIM	08/10/1854	NY		FILM
REINHARD WW AND CH 4	JEAN		03171817	/ /			FILM
REINHARD WW CH 2	JACQUES	1816	OSTHEIM	08/26/1856	NY		FILM
REINHARDT	ALBERT EMILE	1824	STRASBOURG	02/02/1857	NY		FILM
REINHARDT	CAMILLE	1835	ILLZACH	10/26/1854	NY		FILM
REINHARDT	GEORGE	1813	KINHARDT(W)	/ /	TX		FILM
REINHARDT	JOSEPH	1840	ST.MARIE AUX MINES	07/01/1857	NY		FILM
REINHARDT F OF 5	JACQUES		OBERMODERN	/ /	A		FILM
REINHARDT MN VOGT	SALOME CH 5	1806	LIESTEL	10/09/1857	NY		FILM
REINHARDT WW AND CH4	HENRY	1820	ILLZACH	/ /	NY		FILM
REINHART	JOSEPH	1833	RIESPACH	08/16/1865	NY		FILM
REINICHE	FRANCOIS VICTOR	1834	ETTUEFFORT HAUT	06/29/1854	NY		FILM
REINICHE	THIEBAUD	1830	ETTUEFFORT HAUT	06/13/1854	NY		FILM
REINICHE F OF 7	JACQUES		INGVILLER	01/01/1828	A		FILM
REINOLD	JOH. ABRAHAM		GERMANY	04/12/1849	NY		FILM
REINSCHMITT	CAROLINE	1849	WEISSENBURG	01/01/1866	NY		NO.2

Lastname	Firstname	Birth Year	Birthplace	Emigration	De	Prof	Source
REINSCHMITT	LUISE	1852	WEISSENBURG	01/01/1866	NY		NO.2
REIS MN SCHOETTEL	CH 7	1800	STRASBOURG	07/29/1841	NO		FILM
REISACHER WW	HEINRICH EDOUAR	1818	FRIESSEN (HR)	10/25/1843	TX		FILM
REISCHER	EUGENIE	1847	WEISSENBURG	01/01/1866	NY		NO.2
REISEL WW AND CH 2	JOSEPH		CHAVANNES LES GRANDS	08/05/1844	NY		FILM
REISER	CHARLES		GEISINGEN(W)	05/12/1849	A		FILM
REISER	GUILLAUME		GEISINGEN(W)	05/12/1849	A		FIL
REISS	JACQUES	1793	BOUXWILLER(BR)	09/23/1839	A		FILM
REISS F OF 8	LAURENT		WESTHOFFEN	01/01/1828	A		FILM
REISS WW	CHRETIEN		GAMBERTSHOFFEN	06/23/1819	A		FILM
REISSER	CATHERINE		RANSPACH	07/27/1853	NY		FILM
REISSER	JOSEPH	1827	GUEBWILLER	12/06/1847	NY		FILM
REISSINGER	JACQUES		OBENHEIM	03/10/1838	A		FILM
REISSINGER	MICHEL		OBENHEIM	03/10/1838	A		FILM
REISZ	JOSEPH		ERLOCH(B)	07/29/1849	A		FILM
REISZ	VICTORIA		ERLOCH(B)	07/19/1849	A		FILM
REITTER	JACQUES	1822	HUNAWIHR	05/05/1846	NY		FILM
REITZ	CHARLOTTE		WINGEN	01/01/1828	A		FILM
REITZER	AMBROISE	1830	MASEVAUX	08/01/1853	TX	CULT	PASS
REITZER	AMBROISE	1833	NIEDERBRUCK	08/20/1853	TX		FILM
REITZER SI AMBROISE	FRANCOISE		NIEDERBRUCK	08/20/1853	TX		FILM
REITZER WW AND CH 3	AMBROISE	1804	NIEDERBRUCK	08/20/1853	TX		FILM
RELING WW AND CH 3	JEAN BAPTISTE	1826	L`ALEMAND ROMBACH	09/02/1854	NO		FILM
RELL	JOHANN	1841	NIEDERROEDERN	01/01/1865	NY	DAYL	NO.2
RELL	M.MAGDALENA	1850	NIEDERROEDERN	01/01/1865	NY		NO.2
RELL	MARGARETHA	1847	NIEDERROEDERN	01/01/1865	NY		NO.2
RELL	MONIKA	1843	NIEDERROEDERN	01/01/1865	NY		NO.2
RELLINGER WW AND C2	PHILIPPE		SOUFFLENHEIM	01/01/1828	A		FILM
RELLY	MATHIAS	1819	HOMBOURG(HR)	04/14/1854	NY		FILM
REMDA	SEBASTIAN	1804	RIXHEIM	09/20/1844	NY		FILM
REMI	WILLIS	1812	GUEBWILLER	07/26/1849	NY		FILM
REMI WW AND CH 6	PIERRE		DOSSENHEIM	03/31/1817	A		FILM
REMICIEUX	ANTOINE	1820	ERETTE	05/17/1847	NY		FILM
REMINGER	JEAN	1819	ZIMMERSHEIM	02/11/1849	NO		FILM
REMINGER	JOSEPH	1821	PFAFFENHEIM	11/03/1849	NO		FILM
REMMING MN DIDIERJEA	VIRGINIE	1821	ORBEY	03/18/1856	NY		FILM
REMUS	HENRI	1830	BITSCHWILLER	04/07/1851	NY		FILM
REMY WW AND CH 3	PHILIPPE	1819	ST.MARTIN	10/31/1854	NY		FILM
RENAUD	ANNE MARIE	1809	BITSCHE	04/25/1856	NY		FILM
RENAUD	JEAN	1836	AUDINCOURT	02/19/1866	NY		FILM
RENAUD	JULES	1843	HERICOURT	10/27/1866	NY		FILM
RENAUD F FO 2	GASPARD		SARENNE	01/01/1828	A		FILM
RENCK	JACQUES	1814	MITTELWIHR	02/25/1848	NY		FILM
RENGGER F OF 10	ETIENNE		LICHTENBERG	01/01/1828	A		FILM
RENIL	CHR.		VALSCH(B)	07/31/1849	A		FILM
RENIL	JOSEPH		VALSCH(B)	07/31/1849	A		FILM
RENNIE F OF 4	JACQUES		LICHTENBERG	01/01/1828	A		FILM
RENNSTEIN WW CH	JACQUES	1802	BLEICHEISEN	10/20/1854	NO		FILM
RENSING WW	HEINRICH	1805	WESTFALEN	09/17/1845	TX		FILM
RENSING WW AND CH	JOHANN GERHARD	1818	WESTFALEN	09/17/1845	TX		FILM

Lastname	Firstname	Birth Year	Birthplace	Emigration	De	Prof	Source
RENTSCHLER	JACQUES		LEGELHARST(B)	06/04/1849	A		FILM
RENTSCHLER	JEAN		LEGELSHART(B)	06/04/1849	A		FILM
RENZ	FERDINAND	1810	SAULGAU(W)	05/15/1834	A		FILM
RENZ	JOHANN MICHEL	1808	SAULGAU(W)	05/15/1834	A		FILM
RENZ	JOSEPH	1816	SAULGAU(W)	05/15/1834	A		FILM
REPPERT	DANIEL		WINGEN	01/01/1828	A		FILM
RESCET	FRANCOIS	1800	CHARMOIS	02/13/1840	NY		FILM
RESCOEBER	ANTOINE	1821	ROPPENTZWILLER	01/10/1845	PH		FILM
RESPILAIRE	PIERRE	1843	RONCHAMP	02/03/1866	NY		FILM
RESSE	MARIE JULIE			01/09/1854	NY		FILM
RESSERT	JACQUES FRANCOS	1814	CHAUX	02/17/1845	NO		FILM
RESSERT	JOSEPH	1813	CHAUX	05/07/1851	NO		FILM
REST WW AND CH	VALENTIN	1817	MALMERSPACH	08/22/1854	NO		FILM
RESTLE	LEGER	1828	WUENHEIM	11/14/1851	NY		FILM
RESTLY	JEAN	1813	MULHAUSEN	05/27/1845	CI		FILM
RESWEBER	ANTOINE	1821	ROPPERTZWILLER	01/28/1845	PH		FILM
RETSED	CH 4		ERCKARTSWILLER	03/11/1817	A		FILM
RETTIG	ELISABETH		STATTMATTEN	03/02/1838	A		FILM
RETTIG	EVE		STATTMATTEN	01/01/1828	A		FILM
RETTIG F OF 6	FREDERIC		SESSENHEIM	02/23/1838	A		FILM
RETTIG F OF 3	MICHEL		STATTMATTEN	02/03/1838	A		FILM
RETZEL	JACOB AUGUSTIN	1836	COLMAR	09/03/1857	NY		FILM
REUILLARD	JEAN PIERRE	1819	ROUGEMONT	10/17/1857	IO		FILM
REUSS	JACQUES		SOUFFLENHEIM	01/01/1828	A		FILM
REUTH	ARBOGAST		SOUFFLENHEIM	03/02/1828	A		FILM
REUTTER	ANTOINE	1824	OSTHEIM	10/07/1851	NO		FILM
REUTZ	CATHERINE		WANTZENAU	03/07/1838	A		FILM
REVELLE	LUCIE	1849	VALDOIE	03/03/1865	A		FILM
REY	JACQUES JOSEPH	1820	BOUXWILLER	10/17/1850	NY		FILM
REY	MARIE CATHERINE	1806	ST.MARIE AUX MINES	04/08/1848	NY		FILM
REY	THIEBAUD	1822	PFEFFERHAUSEN	03/24/1847	NY		FILM
REYBACH	DOMINIQUE	1831	GUNDOLSHEIM	03/17/1853	NO		FILM
REYDEL	ANDRE F OF 6		HAEGEN	01/01/1828	A		FILM
REYDEL	CATHERINE		HAEGEN	01/01/1828	A		FILM
REYDEL	CATHERINE		HAEGEN	01/01/1828	A		FILM
REYMANN	JOSEPH	1796	HIRTZFELDEN	06/01/1852	TX	TISS	PASS
REYMANN	JOSEPH	1798	MUNCHHAUSEN	06/21/1852	TX		FILM
REYMANN	LEGER	1832	RIXHEIM	08/01/1852	TX	CULT	PASS
REYMANN	LEGER	1830	RIXHEIM	08/09/1857	A		FILM
REYMANN CH6	CATHERINE	1823	RIXHEIM	07/08/1859	CI		FILM
RHEIN WW			SCHILITGHEIM	01/01/1828	A		FILM
RHEINERT	MADELEINE CH	1804	HUNAWIHR	12/09/1854	NY		FILM
RHEINSCHMIDT	CATHERINE		BUEHLERTHAL(B)	04/19/1849	NY		FILM
RHEINSCHMIDT	LUCAS		BUEHLERTHAL(B)	04/19/1849	NY		FILM
RIAL	EMILIE	1864	CHEVENEZ	03/14/1864	NY		FILM
RIAL	JACQUES	1838	CHEVENEZ	03/14/1864	NY		FILM
RIAL	JULIE	1844	CHEVENEZ	03/14/1864	NY		FILM
RIBER	CATHERINE	1845	MEYENHEIM	11/10/1854	TX		FILM
RIBER	EDOUARD	1843	MEYENHEIM	11/10/1854	TX		FILM
RIBER	FRANCOIS JOSEPH	1820	MEYENHEIM	09/05/1846	TX		FILM

Lastname	Firstname	Birth Year	Birthplace	Emigration	De	Prof	Source
RIBER	FRANCOIS JOSEPH	1814	MEYENEHEIM	02/07/1850	TX		FILM
RIBER	GEORGES	1839	MEYENHEIM	11/10/1854	TX		FILM
RIBER	JEAN	1818	MEYENHEIM	09/05/1846	TX		FILM
RIBER	SEBASTIAN	1809	MEYENHEIM	11/25/1848	TX		FILM
RIBSTIM	JEAN	1826	MUNTZENHEIM	02/26/1853	BU		FILM
RICH	BARBE CH 7	1806	LUCERNE(SW)	04/17/1855	NY		FILM
RICH	JACQUES	1821	BOUXWILLER	10/12/1840	NY		FILM
RICH	JEAN BAPTISTE	1833	OBERENTZEN	09/10/1851	TX		FILM
RICH	JEAN-BAPTISTE	1819	OBERENTZEN	09/01/1851	TX	SHMA	PASS
RICH	MADELAINE	1804	MULHOUSE	05/01/1860	NY		FILM
RICH	MARIE-ANNE	1814	ORSCHWIHR	11/01/1847	TX	HOWI	PASS
RICH	PIERRE	1796	NEUWILLER	04/14/1843	NY		FILM
RICH WW AND CH 3	JACQUES	1808	RUNDERBACH	11/04/1849	NY		FILM
RICH CH 3	JEAN	1824	ST.JACQUES(SW)	03/08/1856	NY		FILM
RICH WF	DANIEL	1819	RIESPICH	04/23/1851	NY		FILM
RICHARD	CHARLES	1797	MULHOUSE	03/13/1843	NO		FILM
RICHARD	FRANCOIS	1818	FEVEROIS	04/06/1847	NO		FILM
RICHARD	FRANCOIS	1818	FAVEROIS	08/21/1855	NO		FILM
RICHARD	FREDERIC	1828	COURCELLES	03/31/1865	NY		FILM
RICHARD	FREDRIC	1799	MITTELWIHR	09/22/1848	NY		FILM
RICHARD	HENRI	1814	FAVEROIS	04/23/1844	NY		FILM
RICHARD	JOSEPH	1845	FAVEROIS	10/20/1857	NO		FILM
RICHARD	JULIE	1848	FAVEROIS	08/20/1857	NO		FILM
RICHARD	KARL	1797	MUELHAUSEN	01/01/1845	NO	MERC	PRIV
RICHARD	M JULES	1846	PEROUSE	02/17/1864	NY		FILM
RICHARD	MARIE ANNE	1802	FAVEROIS	08/20/1857	NO		FILM
RICHARD	SIMON	1827	BRETAGNE	/ /	NY		FILM
RICHARD W W 6CH	JACQUES	1798	WOLFERSDORF	04/19/1847	NY		FILM
RICHARD W W 6CH	JOSEPH	1815	BLAMONT	10/10/1853	NY		FILM
RICHARD W W A S	FERIOL	1816	EVELLE16	05/01/1853	NY		FILM
RICHARDT	JOSEPH	1825	BOUXWILLER	04/24/1847	NY		FILM
RICHART W W 3CH	JACQUES	1816	HECKEN	03/30/1850	NY		FILM
RICHE	DIZIER	1809	ST.DIZIER	11/07/1854	NO		FILM
RICHE	JEAN PIERE	1821	JONCHEREY	01/13/1849	NY		FILM
RICHER	SEBASTIEN	1824	NIEDERENTZEN	10/01/1848	TX	BRLA	PASS
RICHERT	ALOIS		NEHWILLER	01/01/1868	A		NO.2
RICHERT	ANNE	1825	FUELLERSEN	02/24/1848	NY		FILM
RICHERT	ANTOINE		MARLENHEIM	01/01/1828	A		FILM
RICHERT	CATHERINE		GEUDERTHEIM	01/01/1828	A		FILM
RICHERT	GEORGE	1821	DUERRENENTZEN	02/17/1846	NY		FILM
RICHERT	GEORGES		MARLENHEIM	01/01/1828	A		FILM
RICHERT	JACQUES		ZUTZENDORFF	01/01/1828	A		FILM
RICHERT	JEAN THIEBAUD	1826	FULLEREN	12/18/1846	A		FILM
RICHERT	MARIE		ADELSHOFEN B	04/21/1849	NY		FILM
RICHERT	MICHEL		HATTMATT	01/01/1828	A		FILM
RICHERT W W 4CH	GEORGES	1802	ZELLENBERG	09/17/1856	NY		FILM
RICHLY W 2CH	JACQUES	1812	RIQUEWIHR	03/15/1854	CH		FILM
RICHTER	MICHEL		HERBITZHEIM	01/01/1828	A		FILM
RICHTER F OF 12	FREDERIC		SCHOPPERTEN	01/01/1828	A		FILM
RICK	ANNE	1821	MULHAUSEN	03/12/1839	NY		FILM

Lastname	Firstname	Birth Year	Birthplace	Emigration	De	Prof	Source
RICKEL	HENRIETTE	1824	COLMAR	09/14/1855	NO		FILM
RIEBEL	ANDRE		KUHLENDORF	03/28/1817	NY		FILM
RIEBEL	ANTOINE		KUHLENDORF	03/28/1817	A		FILM
RIEBEL	ANTON		KUHLENDORF	01/01/1817	A		NO.2
RIEBER	FRANCOIS JOSEPH	1829	MEYENHEIM	02/01/1850	TX	CULT	PASS
RIEBER	JOHANN	1818	MEYENHEIM	11/15/1846	TX		FILM
RIEBER	JOSEPH	1820	MEYENHEIM	11/15/1846	TX		FILM
RIEBER	SEBASTIEN	1809	MEYENHEIM	11/01/1848	TX	CULT	PASS
RIEBER BR EDOUARD	GEORGES	1839	MEYENHEIM	11/01/1854	TX		PASS
RIEBER BR GEORGES	EDOUARD	1842	MEYENHEIM	11/01/1854	TX		PASS
RIEBER SI GEORGES	CATHERINE	1845	MEYENHEIM	11/01/1854	TX		PASS
RIEBLE W CH	CHRISOTOME		STEINACH B	04/21/1849	A		FILM
RIEBSTEIN W W 3CH	JEAN	1806	TURCKHEIM	03/05/1853	NY		FILM
RIEDE	LOUIS		DURLACH B	05/12/1849	NY		FILM
RIEDEN W W 2CH	JEAN	1799	ZILLISHEIM	10/17/1844	A		FILM
RIEDINGER	ANNE	1842	KANDEL BA	04/23/1849	NY		FILM
RIEDINGER	BARBE	1849	KANDEL BA	04/23/1849	NY		FILM
RIEDINGER	CATHERINE	1844	KANDEL BA	04/23/1849	NY		FILM
RIEDINGER	LOUIS	1847	KANDEL BA	04/23/1849	NY		FILM
RIEDINGER	MARGUERITH		REIPERTSWILLER	01/01/1828	A		FILM
RIEDINGER	MICHEL	1843	KANDEL BA	04/23/1849	NY		FILM
RIEDINGER F OF 3	JEAN GEORGE		HOERDT	01/01/1828	A		FILM
RIEDINGER F OF 4	FRANCOIS		FROHMUHL	01/01/1828	A		FILM
RIEDINGER F OF 4	FREDERIC		GRIES	01/01/1828	A		FILM
RIEDINGER F OF 4	JEAN		NIEDERSOULTZBACH	01/01/1828	A		FILM
RIEDLING	IGNACE		DAUENDORF	01/01/1828	A		FILM
RIEFF	JOSEPH ANTOINE	1815	COURTARON	08/18/1853	A		FILM
RIEFF	XAVIER	1836	RIBEAUVILLE	10/14/1854	NY		FILM
RIEFFER	GEORGES		SALENTHAL	04/09/1853	A		FILM
RIEG F OF 4	JEAN		BALDENHEIM	03/06/1838	A		FILM
RIEGEL	CAROLINE	1818	OSWALD	10/17/1849	A		FILM
RIEGER	JOSEPH	1837	ODEREN	10/07/1854	NY		FILM
RIEGERT CH 8	NICOLAS		HOMBOURG	04/01/1844	TX	CULT	PAS
RIEGERT W W 5CH	ANTOINE		SCHWEIZHAUSEN	01/01/1828	A		FILM
RIEGERT W W 8CH	NICOLAS	1801	HOMBOURG	04/23/1844	NY		FILM
RIEGGER	JEAN NEPONNIENE	1820	ZEPFENHORN W	11/19/1842	NY		FILM
RIEH	SCOLASTIQUE		LAUTENHEIM	03/01/1838	A		FILM
RIEHEL	LAURENT		WANGEN	01/01/1828	A		FILM
RIEHERT F OF 4	JACQUES		ZUTZENDORFF	01/01/1828	A		FILM
RIEHL	BERNARDE		LEUTENHEIM	03/01/1838	A		FILM
RIEHL	ELISABETH		LEUTENHEIM	03/01/1838	A		FILM
RIEHL	GEORGES		MULHAUSEN	01/01/1828	A		FILM
RIEHL	JEAN		MULHAUSEN	01/01/1828	A		FILM
RIEHL F OF 3	JEAN		INGENHEIM	01/01/1828	A		FILM
RIEHL W 4CH	JACQUES		MULHOUSEN	01/01/1828	A		FILM
RIEHö	DANIEL	1811	STRASBOURG	05/25/1847	NY		FILM
RIEKHIR	XAVIER	1823	DANNEMAREE	05/26/1851	NY		FILM
RIEMEN F OF 6	THIEBAUD		KESKASTEL	01/01/1828	A		FILM
RIEMER	JOSEPH		MINVERSHEIM	01/01/1828	A		FILM
RIENER W W 2CH	JOHANN MARX		NEUWILLER	03/17/1817	A		FILM

Lastname	Firstname	Birth Year	Birthplace	Emigration	De	Prof	Source
RIESLE	GOTTFRIED		SIMONSWALD B	08/21/1849	A		FILM
RIESS	JACQUES	1813	VOGELSHEIM	05/10/1851	NY		FILM
RIESSER	JEAN JACQUES	1813	VOGELSHEIM	02/20/1852	A		FILM
RIEST	GENOFEVA		NIEDERSARSBACH B	05/24/1849	A		FILM
RIESZ W W 5CH	GEORGE		OERMINGEN	03/23/1817	A		FILM
RIETH W S	JOSEPH	1808	RAMMERSMATT	05/13/1850	NY		FILM
RIETHMILLER W 2CH	MARIANNE	1811	LAUTENBACH ZELL	10/19/1854	A		FILM
RIETSCH	JOSEPH	1826	MUNCHHAUSEN	09/20/1851	NY		FILM
RIFF	ALOISE	1855	MOERNACH MULHOUSE	10/01/1860	NO		FILM
RIFF	GEORGES	1820	EINSIHEIM	10/20/1842	A		FILM
RIFF	JACQUES	1811	SOPPE LE RAC	10/08/1844	A		FILM
RIFF	JOSEPH	1830	MOERNACH MULHOUSE	10/01/1860	NO		FILM
RIFF	JOSEPH	1831	MARNACH HR	04/11/1866	NY		FILM
RIFF	PIERRE	1854	MOERNACH	10/01/1860	NO		FILM
RIFF	RAOUL	1787	SOPPE LE HAUT	11/04/1844	NO		FILM
RIFF	THERESE		MOERNACH	10/01/1860	NO		FILM
RIFFART W W 3CH	CHARLES ETIENNE	1795	RHEINFELD	06/25/1840	NY		FILM
RIGEL	JEAN BAPTISTE	1826	MEYENHEIM	10/27/1854	NY		FILM
RIGEL	LAURENT	1817	MEYENHEIM	12/01/1851	TX	CULT	PASS
RIGLY	PIERRE	1818	ILLHAEUSERN	08/27/1842	A		FILM
RIHN	MADELAINE	1833	OBERBRONN	08/13/1857	NY		FILM
RIHN	MADELEINE	1833	DORNACH	08/01/1857	TX		PASS
RIHN	MICHEL		WESTHAUSEN CANT MARU	01/01/1828	A		FILM
RIMBOLD	JOSEPH	1821	LEVAL	02/24/1840	A		FILM
RIMBOLD CH 6	FRANCOIS	1803	ROUGEMONT	10/01/1856	TX	CULT	PASS
RIMOLD W W 2 S	FRANCOIS		ROUGEMONT	10/24/1856	TX		FILM
RINCK	BARTHOLEMI		ROESCHWOOG	01/01/1828	A		FILM
RINCK	LOUIS		FORT LOUIS	01/01/1828	A		FILM
RINCK	MARTIN		LEUTENHEIM	03/01/1838	A		FILM
RINCK F OF 5	FRANCOIS LOUIS		ROESCHWOOG	01/01/1828	A		FILM
RINCKEL	ROSINE		KAUFFENHEIM	03/05/1838	A		FILM
RINCKEL H VIX S.A5CH	ANDREAS	1793	FORSTFELD	07/12/1847	A		NO.1
RINCKEL MN VIX A.5CH	SALOME	1794	ROPPENHEIM	07/12/1847	A		FILM
RINCKEL S ANDREAS	FRIEDRICH		ROPPENHEIM	04/28/1844	A		NO.1
RINCKER	FRANCOIS ANT.	1806	OBERMICHELBACH	01/06/1866	NY		FILM
RINCKER	JOSEPH	1800	OBERMICHELBACH	04/21/1857	NY		FILM
RINDERLE	THERESE		STEINBOURG	01/01/1828	A		FILM
RINDS	FREDERIC		BOUXWILLER	01/01/1828	A		FILM
RINGEISEN	FRANCOIS JOSEPH		HERBSHEIM	02/25/1838			FILM
RINGENBACH W CH 3	FRANCOIS JOSEPH	1819	SEWEN	05/02/1854	NY		FILM
RINGENBACH WW CH2	JEAN ANTOINE	1810	SEWEN	05/02/1854	NY		FILM
RINGENBACHER	MONIQUE	1843	MITZACH	01/01/1869	TX		PASS
RINGENWALD	ALOYSE	1845	VIEUX FERRETTE	02/22/1866	NY		FILM
RINGIESSEN F OF 9	ANTOINE		BINDERNHEIM	02/28/1866	NY		FILM
RINGLOF	FRANCOISE		SCHWARZACH, BADEN	07/31/1849	A		FILM
RINGLOF	FRED		SCHWARZACH, BADEN	07/31/1849	A		FILM
RINKER	JEAN JACQUES	1798	HERTMANNSWILLER	10/03/1844	NY		FILM
RINNE	LUISE	1849	WEISSENBURG	01/01/1865	NY		NO.2
RINSSEL	CHARLES	1822	MULHAUSEN	11/07/1843	NO		FILM
RIODY WW CH 2	JEAN		SCHWARZACH, BADEN	07/31/1849	A		FILM

Lastname	Firstname	Birth Year	Birthplace	Emigration	De	Prof	Source
RIOTTE	JOSEPH	1835	L`ALTEMAND ROMBACH	11/25/1854	NO		FILM
RIOTTE WW CH 4	JEAN PIERRE	1810	ST. CROIX-SUR-MINES	11/03/1847	NO		FILM
RIPON WW AND CH	JACQUES	1810	OFFEMONT	01/30/1840	A		FILM
RIPP	ALOISE	1833	VIGNERON	10/31/1854	NY		FILM
RIPP	JOSEPH		OHLUNGEN	01/03/1838	A		FILM
RIPPERT	GEORGES	1829	RIQUEWIHR	06/12/1854	NY		FILM
RIPS W 8 PERS	JACQUES		DIRSHEIM, BADEN	10/31/1849	A		FILM
RISACHER	MARTIN	1834	MOOSCH	09/01/1853	NY		FILM
RISBECK	SIMON	1832	DAHN, BAVIERE RH.	07/01/1856	A		FILM
RISCH W CH 2	CHRETIEN	1811	OBERMICHELBACH	04/27/1865	NY		FILM
RISCHER	ANNE MARIE	1844	OBERMICHERLBACH	04/27/1865	NY		FILM
RISLER	JEREMIE	1806	MULHOUSE	05/11/1854	NY		FILM
RISS	IGNACE	1820	SENTHEIM	06/12/1847	NY		FILM
RISS F OF 5	MOISE		OBERNAI	02/27/1847	NY		FILM
RISSER	DAVID	1826	GUEBWILLER	10/02/1847	NY		FILM
RISSER	GREGOIRE XAVIER	1818	RIBENUVILLE	11/03/1854	NO		FILM
RISSER	JEAN		VOELLERDINGEN	01/01/1828	A		FILM
RITSCH	FRANCOIS	1822	THANN	09/06/1847	NY		FILM
RITSCH	JOPSEPH	1832	THANN	08/05/1848	A		FILM
RITTER	ANTOINE		ENGENTHAL	01/01/1828	A		FILM
RITTER	ANTOINE		SCHAFFHAUSEN	01/01/1828	A		FILM
RITTER	CATHERINE		BERSTETT	01/01/1828	A		FILM
RITTER	FLORENT		ENGENTHAL	01/01/1828	A		FILM
RITTER	JACQUES		MOLSHEIM	03/31/1817			FILM
RITTER	JEAN		HUTTENDORF	01/01/1828	A		FILM
RITTER	JEAN BAPTISTE	1814	MEYENHEIM	03/05/1849	TX		FILM
RITTER	JOSEPH		ENGENTHAL	01/01/1828	A		FILM
RITTER	JOSEPH	1815	LAUTENBACH	09/02/1848	A		FILM
RITTER	JOSEPHINE		ROTHENBURG W	05/03/1849	NY		FILM
RITTER F OF 5	FREDERIC		ENGENTHAL	01/01/1828	A		FILM
RITTERBECK F OF8	JOSEPH		WEITERSWILLER	01/01/1828	A		FILM
RITTERER	GEORG	1843	REIMERSWILLER	01/01/1866	NY		NO.2
RITTIMANN W W 7CH	JEAN	1800	OBERENTZEN	09/14/1846	TX		FILM
RITTLER	JEAN-BAPTISTE	1814	MEYENHEIM	03/05/1849	TX	SADD	PASS
RITTMANN	FREDERIC		BONNWEILER W	04/10/1869	A		FILM
RITTMANN CH 7	JEAN	1800	OBERENTZEN	09/01/1846	TX	CULT	PASS
RITTNER	JEAN	1817	ANDOLSHEIM	06/29/1841	NY		FILM
RITTNER 2 S	ANDRE	1786	MUNTZENHEIM	09/28/1737	NY		FILM
RITTNER W D	MATHIAS	1793	JEBSHEIM	09/27/1854	NY		FILM
RITZENTHALER	CATHERINE	1824	JEBSHEIM	09/14/1857	NY		FILM
RITZENTHALER	MADELAINE	1834	JEBSHEIM	01/15/1857	NY		FILM
RIVE	LEONARD	1807	COLAR	07/22/1848	NO		FILM
RIVEZ	ESTLLE	1842	VSöFPOR	04/18/1866	NY		FILM
RIVEZ	FRANCOIS G.	1808	CHAUX	03/14/1840	NY		FILM
RIVIERE	FRANCOIS	1811	CORMARANCHE	03/08/1847	NY		FILM
ROAY	MARIE	1842	BADEREL	09/25/1866	NY		FILM
ROBAY W 4 CH	JEAN PIERRE	1799	ST. GERMAIN	07/30/1842	NY		FILM
ROBERT	JEAN	1835	DORNACH/MULHOUSE	05/29/1854	NY		FILM
ROBIN		1842	VESOUL	01/06/1866	NY		FILM
ROBISCHON	CHRISOSTOME	1823	SEPPOIX-LE-BAS	10/13/1852	NY		FILM

205

Lastname	Firstname	Birth Year	Birthplace	Emigration	De	Prof	Source
ROCK W W	JOSEPH	1805	OBERSTERBACH	03/30/1839	NY		FILM
ROCKENBACH F OF 4	CHRETIEN		GERSTHEIM	03/03/1838	A		FILM
ROCKLY W W 3 CH	MEINRAD	1807	HIRTZBACH	07/26/1847	NY		FILM
RODE	GEORGES	1821	GUEBWILLER	08/31/1848	NY		FILM
ROEGLER	MICHEL	1847	MEMMELSHOFFEN	01/01/1866	NY	WAMA	NO.2
ROEHM	JEAN		GERSTHEIM	03/03/1838	A		FILM
ROEHRI	MARIE ANNE		KALTENHAUSEN	01/01/1828	A		FILM
ROEHRIG	ELISABETH	1847	SCHLEITHAL	01/01/1866	NY		NO.2
ROEHRIG	JOSEF	1848	MUNCHHOUSE	01/01/1865	NY		NO.2
ROEHRIG	MARGERITE	1842	TRIEMBACH	01/01/1867	NY		NO.2
ROEHRIG S PHILLIP R	N.		HATTEN	01/01/1845	A		SUESS
ROESCH	FRANCOIS-JOSEPH	1823	EGUISHEIM	01/12/1854	NY		FILM
ROESCH	LOUIS	1833	GUERMAR	01/10/1938	PH		FILM
ROESCH	PROTHAIA	1809	GUERMAR	07/10/1838	PH		FILM
ROESCH F OF 6	JOSEPH		DETTWILLER	01/01/1832	A		FILM
ROESCH W F	GASPARD	1812	ALTENACH	10/17/1850	NY		FILM
ROESCHARD W W 1 CH	JEAN GEORGES	1809	WEIL/BADEN	06/26/1844	PH		FILM
ROESER	CHRISTINE		BETTWILLER	02/28/1838	A		FILM
ROESER	PIERRE		BETTWILLER	02/28/1838	A		FILM
ROESER F OF 4	PHILIPPE		HAMBACH	03/08/1838	A		FILM
ROESER F OF 4	JACQUES		BETTWILLER	01/28/1838	A		FILM
ROESER F OF 4	NICOLAS		BETTWILLER	02/28/1838	A		FILM
ROESER F OF 4	PHILIPPE		BETTWILLER	02/28/1838	A		
ROESH	FRANCOIS LOUS	1820	GUERMAR	03/26/1841	PH		FILM
ROESS	JEAN	1821	WINTZENHEIM	03/30/1843	NY		FILM
ROESS 5 CH	ELISABETH	1814	WURTZENHEIM	09/20/1853	NY		FILM
ROESSER	HENRY		BERG	03/01/1838	A		FILM
ROESSER	NICOLAS		ESCHBOURG	01/01/1828	A		FILM
ROESSER F OF 4	PHILIPPE		BUST	01/01/1829	A		FILM
ROFUBSCH F OF 8	JEAN		INGENHEIM	01/01/1828	A		FILM
ROGENMUSER	JOSEPH	1822	ALKIRCH	04/24/1847	NY		FILM
ROHE	CASPAR	1828	OBERSEEBACH	01/01/1867	NY	FARM	NO.2
ROHEFRITSCH	ROCHE		MONSWILLER	01/01/1828	A		FILM
ROHMER	JOSEPH	1819	KIENTZHEIM	03/13/1849	NY		FILM
ROHMER	MARTIN	1804	ST. HYPOLITE	07/16/1850	NY		FILM
ROHNBACHER F OF 8	MICHEL		LICHTENBERG	01/01/1828	A		FILM
ROHRBACH	DOROTHEA		HATTEN	01/01/1845	A		SUESS
ROHRBACHER	HEINRICH	1842	HATTEN	01/01/1868	NY	FARM	NO.2
ROLAND	ALPHONSE	1817	DELLE TERR DE BELFOR	05/18/1840	NY		FILM
ROLAND	HENRI EDOUARD	1829	KEYSERSBERG	01/22/1851		NY	FILM
ROLL	BERNARD	1805	VIEUX FERRETTE	02/22/1866	NY		FILM
ROLL	FRANCOIS	1841	VIEUX FERRETTES	02/22/1866	NY		FILM
ROLL	MARTIN	1804	KIFFIS	03/09/1844	NY		FILM
ROLL	XAVIER	1822	MASSERAUX	12/12/1848	NY		FILM
ROLL 1 CH	THERESE	1808	KIFFIS	03/08/1844	NY		FILM
ROLL F OF 5	JOSEPH		SARERNE	01/01/1828	A		FILM
ROLL F OF 12	JEAN		DETTWILLER	01/01/1832	A		FILM
ROLL F OF 3	MARIE MADELEINE	1824	MASSERAUX	04/26/1852	SL		FILM
ROLL F OF 4	JOSEPH		DETTWILLER	01/01/1830	A		FILM
ROLL F OF 6	CASPARI		DETTWILLER	01/01/1828	A		FILM

Lastname	Firstname	Birth Year	Birthplace	Emigration	De	Prof	Source
ROLL F OF 9	IGNACE		DETTWILLER	01/01/1832	A		FILM
ROLLACK	LEOPOLD	1835	SIERENTZ	12/08/1853	NY		FILM
ROLLIN	FRANCOIS	1838	BUFFALO	12/31/1862	NY		FILM
ROLLING	JOSEPH		SEE BIRKENWALD	01/01/1828	A		FILM
ROLLING F OF 5	FRANCOIS		SEE BIRKENWALD	01/01/1828	A		FILM
ROMINGER	BENOIT	1822	BERGHOLTZ	11/25/1854	NY		FILM
ROMOND	JEAN CLAUDE C.	1824	URCEREY	10/07/1847	NY		FILM
ROMONT	EMILE FRANCOIS	1834	URCEREY	08/11/1854	NY		FILM
ROMONT	FRANCOIS	1826	URCEREY	10/21/1851	NY		FILM
RONDEY	EMILE	1847	COURCHATON, FRANCE	11/05/1866	NY		FILM
RONNBACH*	JEAN		WASSELONNE	01/01/1838	A		FILM
RONNECKER	FRANCOIS TH.		FORT LOUIS	01/01/1828	A		FILM
RONNIE F OF 10	ETIENNE		LICHTENBERG	01/01/1828	A		FILM
RONNIE F OF 4	JACQUES		LICHTENBERG	01/01/1828	A		FILM
ROOP	MARIE	1850	DURRNTZEN, HAUT-RHIN	02/02/1856	A		FILM
ROOS	ACHILLE	1849	WEISSENBURG	01/01/1866	NY	MERC	NO.2
ROOS	CELESTIN	1849	WEISSENBURG	01/01/1866	NY		NO.2
ROOS	DANIEL		NIEDERROEDERN	01/01/1866	NO		PRIV
ROOS	DANIEL	1846	NIDERROEDERN	01/01/1865	NO		NO.2
ROOS	EDOUARD	1818	MASSRAUX	04/18/1838	NY		FILM
ROOS	EVA	1846	NIEDERROEDERN	01/01/1866	NY		NO.2
ROOS	JOHANN	1850	NIEDERROEDERN	01/01/1866	NY		NO.2
ROOS	JOSEPH	1822	WILLER	11/13/1845	PH		FILM
ROOS	LUDWIG	1843	NIEDERROEDERN	01/01/1866	NY		NO.2
ROOS	SEBASTIAN		GERMANY	04/06/1849	NY		FILM
ROOS	VIKTOR	1847	WEISSENBURG	01/01/1866	NY	MERC	NO.2
ROOS F OF 8	JACQUESS		DETTWILLER	01/01/1828	A		FILM
ROOS F OF 9	JEAN		DETTWILLER	01/01/1828	A		FILM
ROOS H DOROTHE	JACOB		HATTEN III	01/01/1835	A		SUESS
ROOS MN HUNZINGER	DOROTHEA		HATTEN III	01/01/1837	A		SUESS
ROOS W CH 5	CONRAD	1790	MASSERAUX	05/04/1838	NY		FFILM
ROOSZ	NANSEDUS	1818	BURNHAUPT-BAS	05/05/1840	NY		FILM
ROPP	CAROLINE	1848	DURRENTZEN, HAUT-RH.	02/02/1856	A		FILM
ROPP	JEAN GEORGE		ALTECKENDORF	01/01/1828	A		FILM
ROPP	MARIE	1850	DURRENENTZEN	02/02/1856	CH		FILM
ROPP 6 CH	JOSEPH	1798	LUEMACHWILLER	04/13/1853	CD		FILM
ROPPI	JEAN		BIRKENWALD	03/01/1862	A		FILM
ROSENBACH F OF 7	JEAN		WASSELONNE	01/01/1828	A		FILM
ROSENBLATT	AUGUSTE	1834	OBERDORF	01/27/1866	NY		FILM
ROSENECKER	A.		OPPENAU	04/06/1849	NY		FILM
ROSENFELDER	CATHERINE	1850	ROPPENHEIM	09/11/1853	A		NO.1
ROSENFELDER	FRIEDRICH	1846	ROPPENHEIM	09/11/1853	A		NO.1
ROSENFELDER	SALOME	1844	ROPPENHEIM	09/11/1853	A		NO.1
ROSENFELDER W FRIED	BARBARA			09/11/1853	A		PRIV
ROSENFELDER D FRIEDR	CATHERINE	1850		09/11/1853	A		PRIV
ROSENFELDER D FRIEDR	SALOME	1844		09/11/1853	A		PRIV
ROSENFELDER H KIRCHB	FRIEDRICH 4CH	1814	ROPPENHEIM	09/11/1853	A		NO.1
ROSENFELDER MN KIRCB	BARBARA		ROPPENHEIM	09/11/1853	A		NO.1
ROSENFELDER S FRIEDR	FRIEDRICH	1846		09/11/1853	A		PRIV
ROSENFELDER S FRIEDR	PHILIPPE HEINRI	1848		09/11/1853	A		PRIV

Lastname	Firstname	Birth Year	Birthplace	Emigration	De	Prof	Source
ROSENFELDER WW	FRIEDRICH	1814		09/11/1853	A		PRIV
ROSENTHAL	CAROLINE	1847	TRIEMBACH	01/01/1866	NY		NO.2
ROSENTHAL	ESTHER	1842	TRIEMBACH	01/01/1866	NY		NO.2
ROSIER	ETIENNE	1822		/ /			FILM
ROSIER	GEORGES	1834	OFFEMONT	03/11/1853	NY		FILM
ROSIER	JEAN BAPTISTE	1819	OFFEMONT	05/10/1847	NY		FILM
ROSIER WW AND CH	JEAN PIERRE	1806	VETRIGNE	03/05/1847	NY		FILM
ROSS	JEAN		KEHL, BADEN	09/14/1849	A		FILM
ROSSE	*CELESTIN	1832	ROUGEGOUTTE	11/12/1852	NY		FILM
ROSSE	AMBROISE	1817	ARGISON	04/13/1866	NY		FILM
ROSSE	CONSTANT	1851	ARGISON	04/13/1866	NY		FILM
ROSSE	ELISABETHE	1821	ARGISON	04/13/1866	NY		FILM
ROSSE	FRANCOIS	1848	ARGISON	01/13/1866	NY		FILM
ROSSE	JEAN PIERRE	1836	CHAVNNES LES GRANDS	05/06/1865	NY		FILM
ROSSE	JULES	1857	ARGISON	04/13/1866	NY		FILM
ROSSE	MARIE JULIE	1837	DELLE	09/01/1854	NY		FILM
ROSSE W CH 3	CATHERINE	1807	BRETAGNE, TERR DE B.	09/05/1844	NY		FILM
ROSSEE	MARIE ANNE	1825	CHEVENNES LES GRANDS	09/10/1850	NY		FILM
ROSSELOT	FRANCOIS	1825	DANJOUTIN	09/20/1853	NY		FILM
ROSSELOT	JEAN PIERRE	1802	VOURVENANS	04/28/1838	NY		FILM
ROSSELOT W W 6CH	HENRY	1798	ANDELNONS	03/10/1838	NY		FILM
ROSSER	GEORGE		SCHWEIGHAUSEN	01/01/1828	A		FILM
ROSSEY	JOSEPH	1814	GIROMAGNY	08/27/1849	NY		FILM
ROSSEZ	CELESTIN	1833	MONTREUX H R	10/15/1853	NY		FILM
ROSSEZ	F. XAVIER	1834	BAVILLIERS	12/11/1866	NY		FILM
ROSSEZ	PIERRE DESIRE	1832	URCEREY	05/15/1852	NY		FILM
ROSSIER	CATHERINE	1827	MORVILLARS	10/02/1865	NY		FILM
ROSSIER	CHARLES	1823	MORVILLARS	10/02/1865	NY		FILM
ROSSIER	CHARLES	1864	MORVILLARS	01/01/1865	NY		FILM
ROSSIER	EMILE	1853	OFFEMONT	12/14/1865	NY		FILM
ROSSIER	FRANCOIS	1851	MORVILLARS	10/02/1865	NY		FILM
ROSSIER	JEAN PIERRE	1849	MORVILLARS	10/02/1865	NY		FILM
ROSSIER	JOSEPH	1854	MORVILLARS	10/02/1865	NY		FILM
ROSSIGNOL	CLAUDE ACHILLE	1862	ANNECY	05/05/1865	NY		FILM
ROSSIGNOL	ELISE	1829	ANNECY	05/06/1864	NY		FILM
ROSSIGNOL W W A S	CLAUDE	1833	ANNECY HAUTE SAVOIE	05/06/1865	NY		FILM
ROSSNER W W 2CH	GEORGE		SCHWEIZHAUSEN	11/07/1867	A		FILM
ROSSWAG	CONSTANTIN		ENDINGEN B	07/31/1839	A		FILM
ROST W W A CH	VALENTIN	1817	MALMERSPACH	08/22/1854	NO		FILM
ROTH	ANDRE		GRIESHEIM	01/01/1828	A		FILM
ROTH	ANDRE	1822	OLTINGEN	01/02/1840	NY		FILM
ROTH	ANDRE	1836	MULHOUSE	04/07/1854	NY		FILM
ROTH	ANNE	1803	LA CROIX AUX MINES	02/14/1857	NY		FILM
ROTH	BARBE	1818	BRUNSTATT	03/18/1846	NY		FILM
ROTH	CHRETIEN		ALTWILLER	01/01/1828	A		FILM
ROTH	CHRETIEN	1806	DORNACH	07/11/1837	NY		FILM
ROTH	CHRETIEN		BOLLWILLER	04/12/1844	NY		FILM
ROTH	CHRETIEN	1828	WITTELSHEIM	07/17/1856	NY		FILM
ROTH	CHRISTINE		VOLKSBERG	01/01/1828	A		FILM
ROTH	CHRISTOPHE	1808	EXINCOURT DOUBS	01/04/1844	NY		FILM

Lastname	Firstname	Birth Year	Birthplace	Emigration	De	Prof	Source
ROTH	DAVID		BARR	02/27/1838	A		FILM
ROTH	FLORENT		WESTHAUSEN	01/01/1828	A		FILM
ROTH	GEOFROI		BARR	02/27/1838	A		FILM
ROTH	GUILLAUME		MUEHLBOURG B	08/05/1849	A		FILM
ROTH	HEINRICH	1844	TRIEMBACH	01/01/1865	NY	TAYL	NO.2
ROTH	HENRY		ALTWILLER	01/01/1828	A		FILM
ROTH	JACQUES	1825	BRUNSTAETT	04/22/1852	A		FILM
ROTH	JACQUES		ALTWILLER	01/01/1828	A		FILM
ROTH	JEAN	1792	PULVERSHEIM	03/05/1838	NY		FILM
ROTH	JEUNE	1819	KIRCHEBERG	07/26/1845	NY		FILM
ROTH	KARL	1845	TRIEMBACH	01/01/1866	NY	FARM	NO.2
ROTH	LAURENT		MENCHHOFFEN	01/01/1828	A		FILM
ROTH	LEONARD		KAPPEL RODECK B	07/23/1849	A		FILM
ROTH	LOUIS		ALTWILLER	01/01/1828	A		FILM
ROTH	MADELAINE	1840	GLAY	02/16/1856	NY		FILM
ROTH	MARIE	1824	PFASTATT	02/10/1849	OH		FILM
ROTH	MARIE	1830	MONTBELIARD	02/25/1852	NY		FILM
ROTH	NICOLAS	1820	DORNACH	02/14/1839	OH		FILM
ROTH	NICOLAS	1814	REMBERVILLE	03/08/1839	NY		FILM
ROTH	PHILLIP		UHRWILLER	01/01/1817	A		NO.2
ROTH	PIERRE	1810	DAMBLAY	04/01/1844	NY		FILM
ROTH	PIERRE	1832	MONTBELIARD	04/16/1852	NY		FILM
ROTH	PIERRE	1833	ASPACH	08/28/1851	A		FILM
ROTH	SERAPHIN	1831	THANNENKIRCH	11/16/1853	NY		FILM
ROTH F OF 5	JEAN HENRY		BISCHOLTZ	01/01/1828	A		FILM
ROTH W 3CH	PHILIPPE		RUST B	05/12/1849	A		FILM
ROTH W FAMILY	JOSEPH	1794	FELDBACH	03/03/1852	NO		FILM
ROTH W W 3CH	PHILIPPE		UHRWILLER	03/02/1817	A		FILM
ROTH W W 7CH	DAGOBERT	1818	STERNHEIM	07/27/1847	NY		FILM
ROTH W W A 4CH	CHRETIEN	1804	LORGUIN MEURTH	04/08/1839	NY		FILM
ROTH F OF 4	JACQUES		NIEDERSOULTZBACH	01/01/1828	A		FILM
ROTH W	JOSEPH	1831	BOLLWILLER	08/30/1855	NY		FILM
ROTH W 4CH	PHILIPPE		UHRWILLER	04/09/1819	A		FILM
ROTH W 5CH	ELISABETH	1807	WURTZENHEIM	09/20/1853	NY		FILM
ROTH W 6 CH	ELISABETH	1807	LA CROIX AUX MINES	02/24/1854	NY		FILM
ROTH W W 3CH	HENRY	1808	BOURBACH LE BAS	11/27/1847	NY		FILM
ROTH W W 3CH	JEAN	1798	BALE	05/30/1840	NY		FILM
ROTH W W 3CH	JEAN BAPTISTE	1802	ST CROIX AUX MINES	10/18/1853	SL		FILM
ROTH W W 3CH	NICOLAS		ALTWILLER	01/01/1817	A		FILM
ROTH W W 3CH	PHILIPP		RUST B	05/12/1849	A		FILM
ROTH W W 4CH	NICOLAS	1786	POLVERSHEIM	01/03/1840	OH		FILM
ROTH W W 5CH	LAURENT		SOUFFLENHEIM	01/01/1828	A		FILM
ROTH W W 9CH	JACQUES	1795	HESINGUE	04/13/1848	NY		FILM
ROTHACKER	JOSEPH		BALDENHEIM	03/03/1819	A		FILM
ROTHANN	ANTOINETTE	1823	ALTKIRCH	05/01/1857	NO		FILM
ROTHENBURGER	JACQUES		DURLACH B	05/12/1849	NY		FILM
ROTHENBURGER	JEAN BAPTISTE	1807	ROUFFACH	07/04/1840	A		FILM
ROTHENBURGER W W 3CH	GEORGES	1819	BERGHOLTZ ZELL	12/15/1852	NY		FILM
ROTHENFLUEH	GEORGES	1830	BERRWILLER	09/14/1854	NO		FILM
ROTHFELDER	CHERESE		ROTHENBURG W	05/09/1849	NY		FILM

Lastname	Firstname	Birth Year	Birthplace	Emigration	De	Prof	Source
ROTHFELDER	XAVIER	1825	CERNEY	08/17/1848	NY		FILM
ROTHFUSS	ANNE MARIE		REMLISDORFF W	04/20/1849	NY		FILM
ROTHMUND	JOSEPH	1796	MULHAUSEN B	04/08/1841	NY		FILM
ROTHMUND	MARIE ANNE	1822	GUEBWILLER	09/23/1847	A		FILM
ROTHMUND	PIERRE	1814	GUEBWILLER	09/15/1845	A		FILM
ROTT	MARTIN	1836	BIRLENBACH	01/01/1866	NY	FARM	NO.2
ROTTEMANN	CATHERINE	1816	WULHEIM	07/25/1850	NY		FILM
ROTTENMAIER	JOSEPH		GERMANY	04/01/1849	NY		FILM
ROTTER	GEORGE		SCHWEIGHAUSEN	01/01/1828	A		FILM
ROTTER F OF 3	NICOLAS		SCHWEIGHAUSEN	01/01/1828	A		FILM
ROTTMANN	FRANCOIS	1849	LUEMSCHWILLER	06/01/1861	NY		FILM
ROTZELEUR	JOSEPH	1825	FAVEROIS	04/26/1845	NY		FILM
ROUECHE	FRANCOIS	1823	ANGEOT	06/04/1847	NY		FILM
ROUECHE	JEAN PIERRE	1819	BREBOTTE	07/29/1840	NY		FILM
ROUECHE	PIERRE FRANCOIS	1822	BREBOTTE	07/29/1840	NY		FILM
ROUECHE	RICHARD NICOLAS	1811	ANGEOT	04/05/1845	A		FILM
ROUECHE	THEOPHILE	1825	BREBOTTE	01/15/1844	NY		FILM
ROUECHE W W 2CH	JACQUES RICHARD	1803	ANGEOT	02/19/1846	A		FILM
ROUNECKER	FRANCOIS THOMAS		FORT LOUIS	01/01/1828	A		FILM
ROUSSEL	CHARLES	1822	MULHOUSE	11/07/1843	NO		FILM
ROUX	ETIENNE JOSEPH	1806	PARIS	11/22/1843	TX		FILM
ROY	AUGUSTE	1839	BADEVEL	09/25/1866	NY		FILM
ROY	NICOLAS	1824	ANGEOT	03/07/1846	A		FILM
ROY	NICOLAS	1824	ANGEOT	10/04/1847	A		FILM
ROY	PIERRE JOSEPH	1796	ESSERT	09/07/1855	NY		FILM
ROY	PIERRE JOSEPH	1796	ESSERT	09/11/1856	NY		FILM
ROY W W 5CH	JOSEPH	1800	ESSERT	05/21/1852	NO		FILM
ROYER	BARBE		SOUFFLENHEIM	01/01/1828	A		FILM
ROYER	FRANCOIS JOSEPH	1811	BAVILLIERS	04/30/1846	NY		FILM
ROYER	FRANCOIS JOSEPH	1813	SOUFFLENHEIM	10/21/1850	NY		FILM
ROYER	PHILIPPE		SOUFFLENHEIM	01/01/1828	A		FILM
ROYER	REMIE		SOUFFLENHEIM	01/01/1828	A		FILM
ROYER WW AND CH 4	NICOLAS		SOUFFLENHEIM	01/01/1828	A		FILM
RUB	GEORG	1848	RETSCHWILLER	01/01/1866	NY		NO.2
RUB	HEINRICH	1847	RETSCHWILLER	01/01/1866	NY		NO.2
RUB	MICHEL	1852	RETSCHWILLER	01/01/1866	NY		NO.2
RUB	SALOME	1849	RETSCHWILLER	01/01/1866	NY		NO.2
RUBEL	EDUARD	1850	NIEDERROEDERN	01/01/1866	NY		NO.2
RUBERT	ELISABETH		GOTTENHAUSEN	01/01/1828	A		FILM
RUBERT	JACQUES		GOTTENHAUSEN	01/01/1828	A		FILM
RUBLE	CHRISOSTOME		STEINACH (B)	04/21/1849	A		FILM
RUBRECHT	ANTOINE	1829	NIEDERHERGHEIM	02/09/1852	TX		FILM
RUBRECHT	ROBERT	1816	NIEDERHERGHEIM	02/09/1852	TX		FILM
RUCH			RENCHEN (B)	04/06/1849	NY		FILM
RUCH	ADAM		DOSSENHEIM	01/01/1828	A		FILM
RUCH	CHRETIEN		BOUXWILLER	01/01/1828	A		FILM
RUCH	CHRETIEN	1826	ST. MARIE AUX MINES	10/24/1854	NY		FILM
RUCH	GEORGES		MERTZWILLER	04/09/1817	A		FILM
RUCH	JACQUES P.		BOUXWILLER	01/01/1828	A		FILM
RUCH	JEAN		ALTECHENDORF	01/01/1828	A		FILM

Lastname	Firstname	Birth Year	Birthplace	Emigration	De	Prof	Source
RUCH	JEAN		DUNTZENHEIM	01/01/1828	A		FILM
RUCH	JEAN	1807	ALTECKENDORF	03/18/1828	A		FILM
RUCH F OF 8	MICHEL		ALTECKENDORF	01/01/1828	A		FILM
RUCK	THEIBAUD		BUESWILLER	01/01/1828	A		FILM
RUCKSTUHT WW,CH 4	JEAN		STOSSWIHR	04/13/1855	NO		FILM
RUCTERSCHTULLE	EMILE	1847	ANJOUTEY	01/01/1866	NY		FILM
RUDINGER WW CH 5	JOSEPH	1797	HEITEREN	10/24/1846	A		FILM
RUDIO F OF 5	PIERRE		EYWILLER	01/01/1828	A		FILM
RUDLER	ANTOINE	1824	BITTSCHWILLER	08/29/1845	NY		FILM
RUDLER	JOSEPH	1826	BITTSCHWILLER	05/02/1854	NY		FILM
RUDOLF		1821	ENISHEIM	11/18/1856	A		FILM
RUDOLF	BARBE		PLOBSHEIM	01/01/1828	A		FILM
RUDOLF F OF 3	MICHEL		PLOBSHEIM	01/01/1828	A		FILM
RUDOLF WW AND CH 2	GEOGES	1799	BATTENHEIM	12/18/1854	NY		FILM
RUDOLPH	JEAN	1820	WEIDA SAXE	03/07/1853	NY		FILM
RUDOLPH WW AND CH 3	JEAN	1821	OSTHEIM	03/24/1848	NY		FILM
RUDY	GEORGES		SCHWEIGHAUSEN	01/01/1828	NY		FILM
RUEB	BARBE	1793	RIBEAUVILLE	09/25/1855	NO		FILM
RUEDINGER	ELISABETH	1827	HESSEREN	11/15/1846	TX		FILM
RUEDINGER	JOHANN	1827	HESSEREN	11/15/1846	TX		FILM
RUEDINGER	JOSEPH	1897	HESSEREN	11/15/1846	TX		FILM
RUEDINGER	JOSEPH	1829	HESSEREN	11/15/1846	TX		FILM
RUEDINGER	MARIA	1795	HESSEREN	11/15/1846	TX		FILM
RUEDINGER	MARIA	1821	HESSEREN	11/15/1846	TX		FILM
RUEDINGER	THERESE	1835	HESSEREN	11/15/1846	TX		FILM
RUEDOLFF	MARTIN	1825	ENISHEIM	03/27/1849	PH		FILM
RUEFF	LAZARE	1826	HERRLISHEIM	01/17/1849	NY		FILM
RUENTZ WW	SEBASTIAN	1823	MEYENHEIM	02/12/1852	TX		FILM
RUEST	GENAFERA		NIEDERSARSBACH(B)	05/24/1849	A		FILM
RUEZ	ELOIE	1818	VENEMONT	05/04/1853	CA		FILM
RUF	AUGUSTE	1826	RIBEAUVILLE	09/18/1856	NO		FILM
RUF	CHARLES		GERMANY	04/17/1849	A		FILM
RUF	JACOB		GERMANY	04/17/1849	A		FILM
RUF F OF 16	JEAN GEORGES		GERMANY	04/17/1849	A		FILM
RUFF	CHRISTMANN		OBERMODERN	01/01/1828	A		FILM
RUFF	ELIE	1823	PFASTATT	05/07/1851	NY		FILM
RUFF	JEAN		STUNDWILLER	01/01/1850	NO		PRIV
RUFF WW CH 5	JEAN GEORGES		NIEDERBRONN LES BAIN	03/17/1187	A		FILM
RUFF D XAVIER		1836	COURTELEVANT	02/22/1856	A		FILM
RUFF D XAVIER		1845	COURTELEVANT	02/22/1856	A		FILM
RUFF MN NOTER	MARIE	1805	COURTELEVANT	02/22/1856	A		FILM
RUFF S XAVIER		1838	COURTELEVANT	02/22/1856	A		FILM
RUFF S XAVIER		1843	COURTELEVANT	02/22/1856	A		FILM
RUFF WW	MAURICE	1820	SEPPOIS LE BAS	03/17/1849	NO		FILM
RUFF WW CH4	XAVIER	1807	COURTELEVANT	02/22/1856	A		FILM
RUFF WW CH 3	MICHEL		BASSETSHAUSEN	01/01/1828	A		FILM
RUHLAND	JEAN	1827	MUNSTER	05/24/1854	NY		FILM
RUHLMANN CH2	MARIE	1811	ST.CROIX AUX MINES	09/20/1854	NO		FILM
RUHR	CLMENT	1806	BERGHEIM	12/15/1853	CI		FILM
RUITH CH	JOSEPH	1808	RAMMERSMATT	05/13/1850	NY		FILM

Lastname	Firstname	Birth Year	Birthplace	Emigration	De	Prof	Source
RUMMEL	CHARLES		ETTLINGEN(B)	06/21/1849	A		FILM
RUMMEL	EDOUARD		ETTLINGEN (B)	06/21/1849	A		FILM
RUMMEL	GUILLAUME		ETTLINGEN (B)	06/21/1849	A		FILM
RUMMEL	JULIUS		ETTLINGEN (B)	06/21/1849	A		FILM
RUMMEL	MARIANNE		ETTLINGEN(B)	06/21/1849	A		FILM
RUMMEL	RODOLPH		ETTLINGEN(B)	06/21/1849	A		FILM
RUMMELHART	JOSEPH	1822	STERNENBERG	02/17/1846	CD		FILM
RUMPLER F OF 7	PHILIPPE		MARLENHEIM	01/01/1828	A		FILM
RUMSTEIN	JOSEPH	1824	GUEWENHEIM	03/01/1855	NY		FILM
RUNDA	SEBASTEIN	1804	RIXHEIM	09/20/1844	NY		FILM
RUNDER CH 4	BENOIT		RIXHEIM	09/01/1844	TX	DACU	PASS
RUNDER WW AND CH 3	BENOIT	1807	RIXHEIM	10/09/1844	NY		FILM
RUNSER	NICOLAS		STRASBOURG	06/18/1817	A		FILM
RUNSER WW AND CH 6	PHILIPPE	1810	FOLGENSBURG	01/27/1846	NY		FILM
RUNTZ	MARKUS		FORSTHEIM	01/01/1817	A	DAYL	NO.2
RUNTZLER	JOSEPH	1845	HERMERSWEILER	01/01/1866		FARM	NO.2
RUPP	CHRETIEN	1818	REINBECK LANGHALTEN	12/14/1839	NY		FILM
RUPP	G.	1824	STUNDWILLER	01/01/1865	NO	FARM	NO.2
RUPP	JEAN	1780	ORSCHWEYER(B)	03/06/1838	NY		FILM
RUPP	JOSEPH		STRASSBOURG	03/30/1819	A		FILM
RUPP	MARTIN	1846	STEINSELTZ	01/01/1869	NY		NO.2
RUPP	SAMUEL		STRASSBOURG	05/12/1817	A		FILM
RUPPE	ANDRE APPOLINAE	1784	THANN	09/14/1846	NY		FILM
RUPPRECHT	CHARLES		BISCHWILLER	01/17/1828	A		FILM
RUSCH F OF 3	JACQUES		OBERMODERN	01/01/1828	A		FILM
RUSCH F OF 5	JOSEPH		KUETTOLSHEIM	01/01/1828	A		FILM
RUTHENMANN	C AND D		KIGLINSBERGEN B	07/04/1849	NY		FILM
RUTSCHMANN F OF 5	HENRY		BOUXWILLER	01/01/1828	A		FILM
RUYER	MARIE SARA	1811	LIEPVRE	08/14/1838	NO		FILM

Lastname	Firstname	Birth Year	Birthplace	Emigration	De	Prof	Source
SAAS	ANDRE	1806	MUNSTER	05/20/1854	NY		FILM
SAAS WW AND CH	JEAN	1832	MUNSTER	08/05/1854	NY		FILM
SACHALSKI	JEAN		ESCHBOURG	03/03/1817	A		FILM
SACHERER D GABRIEL	ELISE	1835	MUEHLHAUSEN(HR)	11/22/1843	TX		FILM
SACHERER D GABRIEL	LOUISE	1838	MUEHLHAUSEN	11/22/1843	TX		FILM
SACHERER D GABRIEL	MARIE	1839	MUEHLHAUSEN(HR)	11/22/1843	TX		FILM
SACHERER S GABRIEL	EMIL	1842	MUEHLHAUSEN(HR)	11/22/1843	TX		FILM
SACHERER W GABRIEL	MARIE ANNE	1810	MUEHLHAUSEN(HR)	11/22/1843	TX		FILM
SACHERER WW AND CH 4	GABRIEL	1806	MUEHLHAUSEN(HR)	11/22/1843	TX		FILM
SACHS	KASPAR LEO	1799	OBERWYL(SW)	04/09/1844	CL		FILM
SAEGER	ANTOINE	1800	STERNBERG(BA)	09/03/1857	NY		FILM
SAEGER	ELSIABETH	1823	ST. MARIE AUX MINES	10/20/1854	NO		FILM
SAEMANN	GEORGE		HAMBACH	03/08/1838	A		FILM
SAEMANN F OF 5	PHILIPP		HAMBACH	03/08/1838	A		FILM
SAENGLE	AGNES		FREUDENSTADT	04/20/1849	NY		FILM
SAEUBERLICH	AGATHE		REICHENBACH(B)	04/27/1849	A		FILM
SAGER	JOSEPH ANTOINE	1800	STERNBERG(BA)	07/26/1848	NY		FILM
SAGER WW AND CH 3	PHILIPPE HENRY		INGWILLER	03/29/1817	A		FILM
SAGER WW AND CH 5	MELCHIOR	1799	SERMAMAGNY	04/01/1847	NO		FILM
SAISER	MICHEL	1826	OSTHEIM	12/19/1848	NY		FILM
SALATHE F OF 2	ANDRE		SUNDHAUSEN	03/02/1837	A		FILM
SALATHE F OF 4	DAVID		BALDENHEIM	03/06/1838	A		FILM
SALBACH	DAMIAN		GRIESHEIM(B)	10/11/1849	A		FILM
SALCHRATH	APPOLINE	1823	GUEBWILLER	02/21/1849	PH		FILM
SALCHRATH WW AND CH	JOSEPH	1803	GUEBWILLER	09/10/1844	JE		FILM
SALEVEY	CAROLINE	1838	MOTHERN	01/01/1869	NY	FARM	NO.2
SALEVEY	JOHANN	1807	MOTHERN	01/01/1869	NY		NO.2
SALEVEY	JOHANN	1841	MOTHERN	01/01/1869	NY		NO.2
SALI	RENE		ENGENTHAL	01/01/1828	A		FILM
SALIM	THIEBAUD	1821	FRIESEN	04/27/1849	NY		FILM
SALINGER	BERNHARD		SELTZ	/ /	NY	FARM	NO.2
SALINGER	CHRETIEN		FROHMUHL	01/01/1828	A		FILM
SALINGER	MADELEINE		FROHMUHL	01/01/1828	A		FILM
SALINGER F OF 3	ANTOINE		PETERSBACH	01/01/1828	A		FILM
SALOMON	ISAAK		TIEFFENBACH	01/01/1828	A		FILM
SALOMON	JEAN BAPTISTE	1828	BERNWILLER	04/16/1852	NO		FILM
SALTZGER	GUILLAUME		DEUTSCHLAND	04/05/1849	NY		FILM
SALTZMANN	MICHEL		OSTHEIM	07/29/1854	NY		FILM
SALTZMANN WW CH 2	JEAN JACQUES	1828	SIGOLSHEIM	02/08/1853	NY		FILM
SALVEY	HELENE	1866	MOTHERN	01/01/1868	NY		NO.2
SALVEY	LUDWIG	1867	MOTHERN	01/01/1868	NY		NO.2
SALVEY MN BAUMANN	CAROLINE	1829	MOTHERN	01/01/1868	NY		NO.2
SALVEY W W 2 CH	SEBASTIEN	1830	MOTHERN	01/01/1868	NY	FARM	NO.2
SALZMANN	FREDERIC JUN.	1819	RIBEAUVILLE	09/18/1854	NY		FILM
SALZMANN	FREDERIC JUN.	1820	RIBEAUVILLE	08/13/1853	NO		FILM
SAMENFINK	VINCENT		MARLEN(B)	09/30/1849	A		FILM
SAMUEL	HENRIETTE	1823	BIESHEIM	07/01/1852	NY		FILM
SAMUEL	THERESE	1823	BIESHEIM	07/01/1852	NY		FILM
SAND	ADAM		DOSSENHEIM	01/01/1828	A		FILM
SAND F OF 7	JEAN SEN.		BRUMATH	01/01/1828	A		FILM

Lastname	Firstname	Birth Year	Birthplace	Emigration	De	Prof	Source
SANDEL	FREDERICKE		ROPPENHEIM	06/13/1847	A		NO.1
SANDEL	FREDERIKE			06/13/1847	A		PRIV
SANDEL H MADELEINE	JEAN GEORGES			07/12/1847	A		PRIV
SANDEL H MADELEINE	JEAN GEORGES		ROPPENHEIM	07/12/1847	A		NO.1
SANDEL MN BOSTETTER	MADELEINE	1810		07/12/1847	A		FILM
SANDEL MN BOSTETTER	MADELEINE	1810	ROPPENHEIM	07/12/1847	A		NO.1
SANDHAS	ADOLPHE		HASLACH	07/30/1849	A		FILM
SANDROCK	GEORGE		ROPPENHEIM	01/01/1828	A		FILM
SANDSCHIPPER	JOHANN	1810		09/17/1845	TX		FILM
SANDSCHIPPER	MARIA	1815		09/17/1845	TX		FILM
SARAZIN	MARIE CATHERINE	1828	AUXELLES BAS	09/30/1851	NO		FILM
SARBACH	AUGUSTIN		HERBITZHEIM	01/01/1828	A		FILM
SARSELIE	BARBE		FORT LOUIS	01/01/1828	A		FILM
SATTER	JACQUES	1806	AITZENHEIM	12/11/1852	NY		FILM
SATTLER	ALEXANDRE	1826	TURCKHEIM	10/01/1849	A		FILM
SATTLER	GREGOIRE	1827	TURCKHEIM	04/25/1849	NY		FILM
SATTLER F OF 4	MARTIN		SESSENEHIM	01/01/1828	A		FILM
SAUER	PETRONELLE		GERMANY	04/17/1849	A		FILM
SAUER WW	PIERRE		GERMANY	04/17/1849	A		FILM
SAUGIER	THERESE	1832	GRANDVILLARS	09/10/1850	NO		FILM
SAUGIER WW	JOSEPH	1800	GRANDVILLARS	09/03/1855	NO		FILM
SAUR	CATHERINE	1802	GRANDVILLARS	09/10/1850	NO		FILM
SAUSOTTE WW AND CH 8	FRANCOIS	1799	ETUEFFONT HAUT	04/03/1840	NY		FILM
SAUTER W W 1CH	DIONYSIUS	1783	RIEDISHEIM	10/25/1843	TX		FILM
SAUTHER	MAGDALENA		MUELHAUSEN	04/28/1849	A		FILM
SAUVAGENT	JACQUES	1820	LA MADELAINE	09/28/1839	NY		FILM
SAUVAGEOT	MARIE ANNE	1823	FONTAINE	08/02/1854	NY		FILM
SAUVAGEOT	XAVIER	1825	LA MADELAINE	06/21/1843	NY		FILM
SAUZIER WW	JOSEPH	1800	GRANDVILLARS	09/03/1855	NO		FILM
SAX WW AND CH 4	ETIENNE		HUNGARY	03/17/1817	A		FILM
SAXMANN WW	NICOLAS		LOHR	03/29/1817	A		FILM
SCHAAB	MICHEL	1817	LINGOLSHEIM	05/12/1817	A		FILM
SCHAAB WW	JOSEPH	1804	RIXHEIM	09/17/1846	TX		FILM
SCHAAD	CHRETIEN	1824	ESSERT	04/11/1857	NY		FILM
SCHAAD	JOSEPH	1840	GEISPOLSHEIM	04/11/1857	NY		FILM
SCHABTAG CH	CARTHERINE	1824	ST.MARIE AUX MINES	/ /	NO		FILM
SCHABUTZ	JACQUES	1838	SONDERSDORF	05/01/1861	NY		FILM
SCHACH F OF 6	BARTHELEMI		SCHWEIGHAUSEN	01/01/1828	A		FILM
SCHACHERER	JOSEPH	1804	TRAUBACH-LE-HAUT	07/12/1838	NY		FILM
SCHACK	LOUIS		HAGUENAU	01/01/1828	A		FILM
SCHADERER	JEAN	1837	HINDLINGEN	06/27/1856	NY		FILM
SCHAEBEL F OF 6	BARTHELEMI		SCHWEIGHAUSEN	01/01/1828	A		FILM
SCHAEDELE	MAGDALENA	1828	ALTENSTADT	01/01/1865	NY		NO.2
SCHAEFER D NIKOLAUS	CATHERINA BARB	1757	LAMPERTSLOCH	01/01/1765	A		SUESS
SCHAEFER F OF 6	NICOLAS		BUTTEN	01/01/1828	A		FILM
SCHAEFER M BILBIS	ELISABETH		LAMPERTSLOCH	01/01/1765	A		SUESS
SCHAEFER S NIKOLAUS	GEORG HEINRICH	1764	LAMPERTSLOCH	01/01/1765	A		SUESS
SCHAEFER W ELISABETH	NIKOLAUS		LAMPERTSLOCH	01/01/1765	A		SUESS
SCHAEFFALL	JEAN BAPTISTE	1807	RIBEAUVILLE	06/27/1846	NY		FILM
SCHAEFFEL	ANTOINE	1856	ILLHAEUSERN	07/06/1857	NY		FILM

Lastname	Firstname	Birth Year	Birthplace	Emigration	De	Prof	Source
SCHAEFFEL	JEAN BAPTISTE	1807	RIBEAUVILLE	06/27/1846	NY		FILM
SCHAEFFEL MN HIRN	ELISABETH	1821	ILLHAUSEN	07/06/1857	NY		FILM
SCHAEFFEL S GAETAN	ANTOINE	1855	ILLHAUSEN	07/06/1857	NY		FILM
SCHAEFFEL S GAETAN	GAETAN	1849	ILLHAUSEN	07/06/1857	NY		FILM
SCHAEFFEL WW AND CH2	GAETAN	1821	ILLHAUSEN	07/06/1857	NY		FILM
SCHAEFFER			THAL	01/01/1828	A		FILM
SCHAEFFER	ADAM		DURSTEL	01/01/1828	A		FILM
SCHAEFFER	ALPHONSE		HAGUENAU	01/01/1828	A		FILM
SCHAEFFER	BARBE		GERSTHEIM	03/03/1838	A		FILM
SCHAEFFER	BERNARD		MARLENHEIM	01/01/1828	A		FILM
SCHAEFFER	CATHERINE		STEIN(B)	05/08/1849	A		FILM
SCHAEFFER	CHARLES		STUTTGART(W)	08/17/1849	A		FILM
SCHAEFFER	CHARLES		STEIN(B)	05/08/1849	A		FILM
SCHAEFFER	DONATIER		SPEIHINGEN(W)	05/23/1849	A		FILM
SCHAEFFER	IGNAZ		GUNSTETT	01/01/1817	A	WEAV	NO.2
SCHAEFFER	JEAN BAPTISTE		ROESCHWOOG	01/01/1828	A		FILM
SCHAEFFER	JOSEF	1850	NIEDERROEDERN	01/01/1867	NY		NO.2
SCHAEFFER	JOSEPH		HAGUENAU	01/01/1828	A		FILM
SCHAEFFER	PAUL		IFFETSHEIM	04/06/1849	NY		FILM
SCHAEFFER	PIERRE PHILIPPE	1830	DASLE	04/09/1850	NY		FILM
SCHAEFFER	SEBASTEIN	1811	OBERHERGHEIM	02/25/1847	PH		FILM
SCHAEFFER	THEODORE		MARLENHEIM	01/01/1828	A		FILM
SCHAEFFER F OF 3	JEAN GEORGE		BRUMATH	03/22/1838	A		FILM
SCHAEFFER F OF 6	THIEBAUT		BIETLENHEIM	01/01/1828	A		FILM
SCHAEFFER F FO 7	NICOLAS		NEUWILLER	01/01/1828	A		FILM
SCHAEFFER F OF 6	ANDRE		MARLENHEIM	01/01/1828	A		FILM
SCHAEFFER W W A CH 4	FREDERIC PIERRE		HAMBACH	05/23/1817	A		FILM
SCHAEFFER WW CH 6	NICOLAS		HIRSCHLAND	03/20/1817	A		FILM
SCHAEFFOLDT	JEAN BAPTISTE	1806	RIBEAUVILLE	02/13/1843	NY		FILM
SCHAEFOLT	JEAN BAPTISTE	1807	RIBEAUVILLE	03/06/1856	NY		FILM
SCHAEPPLE	CHRETIEN		OFFENBOURG	04/20/1849	A		FILM
SCHAEPPLE	JACOB		OFFENBOURG	04/20/1849	A		FILM
SCHAERE	XAVIER	1823	DELLE	04/10/1852	NO		FILM
SCHAEUFFELE	SALOME	1841	OBERBETSCHDORF	01/01/1841	NY		NO.2
SCHAFFENECKER	JEAN	1823	MASSEVAUX	03/29/1848	NY		FILM
SCHAFFER	JOSEF	1846	NIEDERROEDERN	01/01/1867	NY	FARR	NO.2
SCHAFFER	MUNRAD	1822	NIEDERLARG(HR)	11/24/1851	NY		FILM
SCHAFFNER	GOTTFRIED		GOESSDORF	01/01/1857	A		SUESS
SCHAGENE WW AND CH 2	JOSEPH	1814	SOPPE LE HAUT	06/06/1844	NY		FILM
SCHAI	FRIDERICH		KANSTATT(W)	06/21/1849	A		FILM
SCHALCKHAMMER WW CH	ANTOINE		STRASBOURG	05/27/1817	A		FILM
SCHALER WW AND CH 4	ANDRE		DUPPIGHEIM	03/23/1817	A		FILM
SCHALHAUNN	PIERRE		SALENTHAL	04/09/1853	CA		FILM
SCHALHOLTZ	KILIAN RUDOLF	1848	LAUTERBURG	01/01/1868	NY	DAYL	NO.2
SCHALL F OF 4	ANDRE		HAGUENAU	01/01/1828	A		FILM
SCHALLENBERGER	JACQUES	1806	VOEGTLINSHOFFEN	02/23/1846	NY		FILM
SCHALLER	FRIEDRICH	1848	WOERTH	01/01/1866	NY	WAMA	NO.2
SCHALLER	JACQUES	1842	MITTELWIHR	03/15/1856	NY		FILM
SCHALLER	MADELAINE	1814	MITTELWIHR	03/15/1856	NY		FILM
SCHALLER	SALOME	1842	WOERTH	01/01/1866	NY		NO.2

Lastname	Firstname	Birth Year	Birthplace	Emigration	De	Prof	Source
SCHALLER	SEBASTIEN		ROESCHWOOG	01/01/1828	A		FILM
SCHALLER CH	ANNE MARIE	1820	MITTELWIHR	12/08/1855	NY		FILJM
SCHALLER D ANNE MARI	LOUISE	1835	MITTELWIHR	12/08/1855	NY		FILM
SCHALLER F	DAVID	1825	MITTELWIHR	03/27/1852	NY		FILM
SCHALLER S ANTON	MICHEL		FROESCHWILLER	01/01/1875	A		SUESS
SCHALLER S GEORG	KARL		FROESCHWILLER	01/01/1875	A	CARP	SUESS
SCHALLER S GEORG	MICHEL	101	FROESCHWILLER	01/01/1882	A		SUESS
SCHALLER WW	CHRETIEN	1824	MITTELWIHR	03/27/1848	NY		FILM
SCHALLER WW AND CH	GEORGES	1805	MICHELBACH	05/14/1847	NY		FILM
SCHALLER WW AND CH	JEAN JACQUES	1788	MITTELWIHR	04/07/1846	NY		FILM
SCHALLER WW AND CH 3	MICHEL JACQUES	1787	MITTELWIHR	03/16/1848	NY		FILM
SCHALLER WW AND CH 8	JEAN BAPTISTE	1815	PFETTERHAUSEN	02/08/1854	NY		FILM
SCHALTENBRAND	MEINRAD	1820	PFEFFERHAUSEN	10/29/1854	NY		FILM
SCHAMBER F OF 9	ETIENNE		KIRRBERG	01/01/1828	A		FILM
SCHAMBERGER	MATHIAS	1836	ASPACH-LE-BAS	03/21/1854	NY		FILM
SCHAMER	FRANCOIS CHARLE	1833	SIGOLSHEIM	03/12/1855	NY		FILM
SCHAMON	HEINRICH	1804	SEGERSDORF	04/09/1844	TX		FILM
SCHAMW	FRANCOIS CHARLE	1833	SIGOLSHEIM	03/12/1855	NY		FILM
SCHANDEL	CHRETIEN		SCHIRHOFF	01/01/1828			FILM
SCHANDEL F OF 2	MICHEL		SCHIRRHOFF	01/01/1828	A		FILM
SCHANDEL F OF 3	JEAN		SCHIRRHOFF	01/01/1828	A		FILM
SCHANDEL F OF 6	PHILIPPE		SCHIRRHOFF	01/01/1828	A		FILM
SCHANDEL FOF 4	JEAN		SCHIRRHEIN	01/01/1828	A		FILM
SCHANDELMAYER	CATHERINE		NUNENHEYER B	10/06/1849	A		FILM
SCHANDELMEYER			NUNENHEYER(B)	10/06/1849	A		FILM
SCHANDELMEYER	GEORGE		DURBACH(B)	04/08/1849	A		FILM
SCHANDELMEYER	JACQUES		NUNENHEYER B	10/06/1849	A		FILM
SCHANNO	JOSEPH JUN.	1838	SIGOLSHEIM(HR)	06/03/1856	NY		FILM
SCHANNO F	EMILIE	1840	SIGOLSHEIM	06/03/1856	NY		
SCHANNO F EMILIE	JOSEPH		SIGOLSHEIM	06/03/1856	NY		FILM
SCHANTZ	DANIEL	1814	ARLESHEIM SWISS	10/25/1853	A		FILM
SCHANTZ	JOSEPH	1811	ARLESHEIM(SW)	10/25/1853	BU		FILM
SCHARDT	LOUI AUGUSTIN	1821	ST.LOUIS(HR)	02/22/1851	NY		FILM
SCHATT WW AND CH 5	BLAISE	1801	BLODELSHEIM	10/24/1851	TX		FILM
SCHATTENBRAND	LEOPOLD	1828	PFEFFERHAUSEN	03/02/1847	NY		FILM
SCHATTENBRAND	MEINRAD	1833	PFEFFERHAUSEN	09/21/1853	NY		FILM
SCHATTER	JOSEPH	1812	RICHWILLER	03/14/1839	A		FILM
SCHATZ	ANNE MARIE		WOELLENHEIM	01/01/1828	A		FILM
SCHAUB			NIEDERBRONN	02/22/1817	A		FILM
SCHAUB	CARL		ORSCHWIER(B)	04/23/1849	A		FILM
SCHAUB	CHARLES	1828	RIXHEIM	10/23/1849	NY		FILM
SCHAUB	FRANZ ANTON		NIEDERBRONN	01/01/1817	A		NO.2
SCHAUB	JOSEPH	1804	MULHOUSE	09/01/1846	TX	DAYL	PASS
SCHAUB	MARTIN		NECHARDENSHEIGEN(W)	06/21/1849	A		FILM
SCHAUB F OF 6	VALENTIN SEN.		INGENHEIM	01/01/1828	AU		FILM
SCHAUB WW	FRANCOIS		NIEDERBRONN	02/26/1817	A		FILM
SCHAUFELE	AUGUSTE		BETTEN(B)	06/21/1849	A		FILM
SCHAUL F FO 2	ULRICH		FORT LOUIS	01/01/1828	A		FILM
SCHAUTZ	DANIEL	1816	ARLESHEIM(SW)	10/25/1857	BU		FILM
SCHAVANNE	IGNACE	1825	ASPACH	01/17/1847	NY		FILM

Lastname	Firstname	Birth Year	Birthplace	Emigration	De	Prof	Source
SCHEBELEN	JOSEPH	1833	ASPACH LE HAUT	12/31/1856	NY		FILM
SCHEBEN	JOSEPH		REINHARDSMUNSTER	01/01/1828	A		FILM
SCHEER	MARTIN	1845	NEHWILLER	01/01/1866	A	CARP	NO.2
SCHEER	MICHEL		MINVERSHEIM	01/01/1828	A		FILM
SCHEHIN	ROSE	1843	FELLERING	09/01/1860	TX	WORK	PASS
SCHEHRER MN DULEY	ELISABETH		KALTENHAUSEN	01/01/1828	A		FILM
SCHEHRER W W DUTEY E	ANTOINE		KALTENHAUSEN	01/01/1828	A		FILM
SCHEHRER WW AND CH 2	ANTOINE		KALTENHAUSEN	01/01/1828	A		FILM
SCHEIBEL	MARTIN	1831	MOOSCH	08/26/1854	NY		FILM
SCHEIBEL MN BOBENRIE	ANNE MARIE CH 6	1800	RANSPACH	07/16/1846	NY		FILM
SCHEIBER F OF 8	JACQUES		SCHIRRHEIN	01/01/1828	A		FILM
SCHEIBLE	JEAN	1795	LAKINGEN(B)	01/29/1844	A		FILM
SCHEIBLE WW AND CH	FERDINAND	1823	SOULTZ	09/01/1854	A		FILM
SCHEICHER	SEBASTIEN	1848	RIEDSELTZ	01/01/1867	NY	FARM	NO.2
SCHEID	FRANZ	1843	SCHOENBOURG	01/01/1865	NY	WAMA	NO.2
SCHEIDAKER F OF 5	MARTIN		BALINGEN(B)	05/03/1849	A		FILM
SCHEIDECKER	JEAN	1818	DORNACH	02/12/1844	NY		FILM
SCHEIDER	ADAM		WEISLINGEN	01/01/1828	A		FILM
SCHEIDER	FRANCOISE PAULI	1834	NANCY	06/25/1856	NY		FILM
SCHEIDER	GEORGES		EYWILLER	01/01/1828	A		FILM
SCHEIDER	JEAN		HOCHSTETT	01/01/1828	A		FILM
SCHEIDER W 1CH	CHRISTINE	1826	STEINBACH	04/21/1854	A		FILM
SCHEIGERT W W 1CH	CHARLES	1829	ST CROIX AUX MINES	07/23/1851	NO		FILM
SCHEITZ WW AND CH 5	JOSEPH	1781	RIEDISHEIM	10/06/1843	TX		FILM
SCHEL	MARTIN	1849	OBERSEEBACH	01/01/1866	NY		NO.2
SCHELCHER	EDOUARD	1834	NEUF BRISACH	03/31/1857	NY		FILM
SCHELEN	JOSEPH		REINHARDSMUNSTER	01/01/1828	A		FILM
SCHELL	JACOB		BITTERSHEIM(BA)	09/30/1849	A		FILM
SCHELL WW AND CH 2	NICOLAS		REIPERTSWILLER	01/01/1817	A		FILM
SCHELL WW AND CH2	GEORGE		DRUSENHEIM	01/01/1828	A		FILM
SCHELLHORN	ELISABETH	1842	SCHLEITHAL	01/01/1866	NY		NO.2
SCHEMERBER	JOSEPH	1797	HOCHSTADT	11/15/1846	TX		FILM
SCHEMERBER	MARIA	1802	HOCHSTADT	11/15/1846	TX		FILM
SCHEMI WW AND CH 4	ANTOINE	1805	HERRLISHEIM	08/30/1849	NO		FILM
SCHENAL	THERESE		LAUBHEIM	05/16/1849	A		FILM
SCHENCBERG	PIERRE	1819	RECOUVRANCE	02/20/1843	NY		FILM
SCHENCH WW AND CH 4	ANTOINE	1805	HERRLISHEIM	08/30/1849	NO		FILM
SCHENCK	DAVID	1809	DELEMONT(SW)	04/17/1855	NY		FILM
SCHENCK	FRANZISKA	1807	BRUEHL	01/01/1865	NY		NO.2
SCHENCK	JOSEPH	1842	BRUEHL	01/01/1865	NY		NO.2
SCHENCK	MAGDALENA	1841	LOBSANN	01/01/1866			NO.2
SCHENCK BR VERONIQE	JOSEPH	1817	HELFRANTZKIRCH	06/04/1857	NY		FILM
SCHENCK SI JOSEPH	VERONIQUE	1838	HELFRANTZKIRCH	06/04/1857	NY		FILM
SCHENCK WW	GEORGES	1821	MULHOUSE	03/17/1854	NY		FILM
SCHENEBERG	PIERRE	1819	RECOURRANCE	02/20/1843	NY		FILM
SCHENKENWITZ	AUGUSTE		BADEN(B)	10/11/1849	A		FILM
SCHENNEBERG	ALEXANDRE	1832	BREBOTTE	09/16/1850	NO		FILM
SCHEPP	PHILLIP	1848	WEISSENBURG	01/01/1866	NY		NO.2
SCHER			GERMANY	03/31/1849	A		FILM
SCHERB	FRANCOIS JOSEPH	1826	ROUFFACH	02/17/1853	NO		FILM

Lastname	Firstname	Birth Year	Birthplace	Emigration	De	Prof	Source
SCHERB	JACQUES	1833	ROUFFACH	01/03/1853	NO		FILM
SCHERB	MOYSE MICHEL	1824	ROUFFACH	02/17/1853	NO		FILM
SCHERB BR ALOYSE	LOUIS		ROUFFACH	05/19/1856	NY		FILM
SCHERB BR LOUIS	ALOYSE		ROUFFACH	05/19/1856	NY		FILM
SCHEREN	ELISE		NIEDERHEIM(B)	04/23/1849	A		FILM
SCHERER	JEAN		ESCHBOURG	03/03/1817	A		FILM
SCHERER	JOSEPH	1797	SENTHEIM	11/15/1846	TX		FILM
SCHERER	MARIE ANNE	1834	GUEBWILLER	03/07/1854	SL		FILM
SCHERER F OF 7	HENRY		RAUWILLER	01/01/1828	A		FILM
SCHERER WW AND CH 3	JEAN	1808	JEBSHEIM	03/15/1854	NY		FILM
SCHERIQUE	JOSEPH	1825	CABROQUE(VOSGES)	03/15/1854	NY		FILM
SCHERLEN	MICHEL	1822	FELLERINGEN	08/27/1844	NY		FILM
SCHERLEN	PIERRE	1824	FELLERINGEN	08/27/1844	NY		FILM
SCHERLEN WW AND CH	MELCHIOR	1793	FELLERINGEN	02/22/1850	NO		FILM
SCHERNER	MADELAINE	1814	TRAUBACH-LE-HAUT	03/08/1845	NY		FILM
SCHERRER	EDOUARD	1859	OBERDORF	02/27/1866	NY		FILM
SCHERRER	FRANCOIS JOSEPH	1831	BRUNSTADT	10/23/1855	NY		FILM
SCHERRER	JACQUES	1811	SOPPE LE BAS	09/21/1844	CO		FILM
SCHERRER	JEAN	1821	RIECHEN(SW)	12/03/1847	NY		FILM
SCHERRER	JEAN THIEBAUD	1819	THANN	07/28/1854	BU		FILM
SCHERRER	JOSEPH	1817	RIEBENINGUE(B)	12/22/1853	NY		FILM
SCHERRER	JOSEPH	1862	OBERDORF	02/27/1866	NY		FILM
SCHERRER	MADELAINE	1814	TRAUBACH LE HAUT	03/08/1845	NY		FILM
SCHERRER	MADELAINE	1827	TRAUBACH LE HAUT	05/20/1854	NY		FILM
SCHERRER	THEOBALD	1823	LUTTERBACH	06/04/1857	NY		FILM
SCHERRER D JACOB	THERESE	1841	THANN	10/25/1843	TX		FILM
SCHERRER D JEAN	MADELAINE		OBERDORF	02/27/1866	NY		FILM
SCHERRER D JEAN	VIRGINIE		OBERDORF	02/27/1866	NY		FILM
SCHERRER S JACOB	AUGUST	1833	THANN	10/25/1843	TX		FILM
SCHERRER S JACOB	JAKOB	1828	THANN	10/25/1843	TX		FILM
SCHERRER S JACOB	JOSEPH	1830	THANN	10/25/1843	TX		FILM
SCHERRER S JEAN	EDOUARD		OBERDORF	02/27/1866	NY		FILM
SCHERRER W JACOB	ANNA MARIA	1800	THANN (HR)	10/25/1843	TX		FILM
SCHERRER W JEAN	VERONIQUE		OBERDORF	02/27/1866	NY		FILM
SCHERRER W JEAN	VIRGINIE	1833	OBERDORF	02/27/1866	NY		FILM
SCHERRER WW AND CH 3	PAUL	1808	TRAUBACH LE HAUT	12/16/1847	NY		FILM
SCHERRER WW AND CH 4	JEAN	1842	OBERDORF	02/27/1866	NY		FILM
SCHERRER WW AND CH 5	JOSEPH	1778	WOLFERSDORFF	10/14/1846	NY		FILM
SCHERRER WW AND CH 5	JOSEPH	1813	TRAUBACH LE HAUT	12/02/1847	NY		FILM
SCHERRER WW AND CH 8	JEAN	1800	TRAUBACH LE HAUT	10/11/1854	WA		FILM
SCHERRER WW AND CH5	JACOB	1801	THANN	10/25/1843	TX		FILM
SCHERTZ	JOHANN	1824	RIEDISHEIM	10/25/1843	TX		FILM
SCHERTZ	JOSEPH	1811	RIEDISHEIM	10/25/1843	TX		FILM
SCHERTZ	JOSEPH	1820	RIEDISHEIM	10/25/1843	TX		FILM
SCHERTZ	SEBASTIAN	1821	RIEDISHEIM	10/25/1843	TX		FILM
SCHERTZ F OF 9	JOSEPHE		KESKASTEL	01/01/1828	A		FILM
SCHERTZ MN GOLDSCHMI	ELISABETH CH 2	1819	ST, MARIE AUX MINES	06/27/1850	CI		FILM
SCHERTZ WW AND CH	CHARLES	1816	RIEDISHEIM	07/29/1847	NO		FILM
SCHERTZ WW AND CH 5	JOSEPH	1781	RIEDISHEIM	10/06/1843	TX		FILM
SCHERY	JOSEF	1832	SELTZ	01/01/1866	NY	SHMA	NO.2

Lastname	Firstname	Birth Year	Birthplace	Emigration	De	Prof	Source
SCHERZER	ANTOINE		ETTENDORF	10/29/1854	A		FILM
SCHETTLY WW AND CH 6	JEAN	1800	FALKWILLER (HR)	04/21/1840	NY		FILM
SCHETZ	CHARLES	1816	RIEDISHEIM	12/30/1844	NO		FILM
SCHETZ	JOHANN	1814	RIEDISHEIM	10/25/1843	TX		FILM
SCHEUBY F OF 4	PHILIPPE		HAMBACH	01/01/1828	A		FILM
SCHEUCH	LOUIS		OERMINGEN	01/01/1828	A		FILM
SCHEUCH	PHILIPPE		OERMINGEN	01/01/1828	A		FILM
SCHEUR	NICOLAS		WIMMENAU	01/01/1828	A		FILM
SCHEURER	ALEXIS		UNZHURST(B)	08/14/1849	A		FILM
SCHEURER	ANDRE		REXINGEN	01/01/1828	A		FILM
SCHEURER	CATHERINE		UNZHURST	01/01/1828	A		FILM
SCHEURER	JOSEPH		UNZHURST(B)	08/14/1849	A		FILM
SCHEURER F OF 7	GEORGE		FORT LOUIS	01/01/1828	A		FILM
SCHEURER WW AND CH	FRANCOIS	1816	ST, CROIX AUX MINES	10/16/1846	SL		FILM
SCHEURER WW AND CH 5	CHARLES		BERG	03/29/1817	A		FILM
SCHEURER WW AND CH 7	GEORGES		HIRSCHLAND	01/01/1828	A		FILM
SCHEURICH	LORENZ		SCHLIERSTADT(B)	05/12/1849	A		FILM
SCHEUZEL	MICHEL		WEISLINGEN	01/01/1828	A		FILM
SCHIBI	JOSEPH		HENGWILLER	01/01/1828	A		FILM
SCHICH	GASPARD	1818	ZIHENTHAL	04/25/1848	NY		FILM
SCHICKHAUS			BAS RHIN	07/15/1826	NY		FILM
SCHICKLE WW AND CH 4	JOHANN		EISINGEN(B)	04/11/1849	A		FILM
SCHICKLIN CH 2	URSULE	1851	VIEUX FERRETTE	/ /	NY		FILM
SCHIEB MN KUNEMANN	ARMANDE	1825	CERNAY	06/23/1855	NY		FILM
SCHIEDLE	PETER	1774	REGENBURG	04/09/1844	TX		FILM
SCHIENBERG	CASPARD	1834	OBERBRUIK	09/07/1853	CI		FILM
SCHIERK	ANNE MARIE	1813	SEPPOIS-LE-BAS	04/24/1849	PH		FILM
SCHIFFERSTEIN	JOSEPH		MOMMENHEIM	01/09/1838	A		FILM
SCHIFFNUCCHER CH	LEONARD	1793	SCHEIBENHARD(BR)	11/08/1845	NO		FILM
SCHIGAND	GUILLAUME	1822	DURMENACH	02/20/1847	NY		FILM
SCHILDER	MARTIN	1826	HERRLISHEIM	06/05/1845	A		FILM
SCHILL	ALBERT	1861	OBERDORFF(HR)	10/17/1865	NY		FILM
SCHILL	ANNE MARIE	1837	OBERDORFF(HR)	10/17/1865	NY		FILM
SCHILL	ANTOINE	1837	OBERDORFF(HR)	10/17/1865	NY		FILM
SCHILL	CATHERINE	1865	OBERDORFF(HR)	10/17/1865	NY		FILM
SCHILL	ELISABETH		HILPERTSAU(B)	09/28/1849	NY		FILM
SCHILL WW AND CH 2	JEAN BAPTISTE	1807	WALDIGHOFEN	05/17/1845	NY		FILM
SCHILLER	ANDRE		SCHIRRHEIN	01/01/1828	A		FILM
SCHILLER	HENRIETTE	1824	COLMAR	09/14/1855	NO		FILM
SCHILLER F OF 6	GEORGE		SCHIRRHEIN	01/01/1828	A		FILM
SCHILLER F OF 4	SALOME		SCHIRRHEIN	01/01/1828	A		FILM
SCHILLING	ANDRE		DOMFESSEL	01/01/1828	A		FILM
SCHILLING	CHARLES	1815	FELLERINGEN	09/28/1844	NY FILM		FILM
SCHILLING	FRANCOIS JOSEPH	1827	MOOSCH	09/10/1853	NO		FILM
SCHILLING	JOSEPH	1840	MOOSCH	06/23/1854	NY FILM		FILM
SCHILLING WW AND CH4	BERNARD	1819	SIEGUE	04/26/1853	NY		FILM
SCHILLING WW CH 3	JEAN JACQUES	1818	FELLERINGEN	09/08/1853	DE		FILM
SCHILLINGER	AGATHE		KIECHLINGSBERGEN	05/24/1849	A		FILM
SCHILLINGER	FERDINAND	1833	WITTENHEIM	06/15/1852	PH		FILM
SCHILLINGER	NICOLAS	1828	BLODELSHEIM	06/26/1855	NY		FILM

Lastname	Firstname	Birth Year	Birthplace	Emigration	De	Prof	Source
SCHIM	MICHEL		HATTMATT	01/01/1828	A		FILM
SCHINDLER	ANTOINE		ERLACH(B)	08/21/1849	A		FILM
SCHINDLER	BENEDICT		ERLACH(B)	07/29/1849	A		FILM
SCHINDLER	M		OBERKIRCH	04/06/1849	NY		FILM
SCHINDLER	XAVIER	1825	TRAUBACH LE HAUT	05/27/1845	CD		FILM
SCHINI F OF 7	JEAN		ZUTZENDORF	01/01/1828	A		FILM
SCHINN WW AND CH 4	JEAN		SCHILTIGHEIM	01/01/1828	A		FILM
SCHIRCH	CHRETIEN	1831	SCHIRMECH(VOSGES)	03/17/1854	NY		FILM
SCHIRCK	ANNE MARIE	1816	SEPPOIS-LE-BAS	04/24/1846	NY		FILM
SCHIRCK	JEAN	1819	HINDLINGEN	06/10/1850	NY		FILM
SCHIRCK F OF 5	JACQUES		MUTTERSHOLTZ	04/05/1838	A		FILM
SCHIRM W W 4CH	JEAN		SCHILTIGHEIM	01/01/1828	A		FILM
SCHIRMER	CATHERINE	1790	DORNACH	07/24/1849	A		FILM
SCHIRMER	DONAT	1830	SOULTZMATT	11/20/1854	A		FILM
SCHIRMER	LOUIS	1809	NIEDERSTEINBRUNN	03/26/1847	NY		FILM
SCHIRMER	MARIE ANNE	1821	SOULTZMATT	08/02/1847	NY		FILM
SCHITL	JOSEPH		WEISLINGEN	01/01/1828	A		FILM
SCHITT WW AND CH 6	JEAN		SOUFFLENHEIM	01/01/1828	A		FILM
SCHITTLY WW AND CH 6	JEAN	1800	FALKWILLER(HR)	04/21/1840	NY		FILM
SCHLATTER	BENJAMIN		DORNACH	01/12/1852	NY		FILM
SCHLATTER	BENOIT	1810	RICHWILLER	12/15/1851	NY		FILM
SCHLATTER	JOSEPH	1816	HEIDWILLER	01/21/1846	NY		FILM
SCHLATTER	SEBASTIEN	1819	RICHWILLER	10/11/1839	OH		FILM
SCHLATTER W W 3CH	BENOIT	1816	RICHWILLER	07/20/1852	NY		FILM
SCHLATTER W W 5CH	CHRETIEN	1794	RICHWILLER	07/26/1852	NY		FILM
SCHLECHT			RENCHEN B	03/31/1849	NY		FILM
SCHLECHT	ANDRE		BOUXWILLER	01/01/1828	A		FILM
SCHLEG	PAUL		ZIEROLSHOFEN B	07/31/1849	A		FILM
SCHLEGEL W 5CH	JEAN	1798	ROUFFACH	09/08/1853	NY		FILM
SCHLEGEL W W 2CH	JOSEPH	1809	FROENINGEN	06/19/1854	NY		FILM
SCHLEGEL W W 3 D	CHRETIEN	1811	MULHOUSE	02/11/1857	NY		FILM
SCHLEGER	ANDRE		ST. MAERGEN B	12/05/1849	A		FILM
SCHLEGIC	NICOLAS	1809	FROENINGEN	03/04/1839	NY		FILM
SCHLEIFEN	MARGUERITHE		ZINSWEILLER	02/16/1817	A		FILM
SCHLEIFER	JACOB HEINRICH		NIEDERBRONN	01/01/1817	A	WEAV	NO.2
SCHLEIFFER			NIEDERBRONN	02/22/1817	A		FILM
SCHLEIFFER	JOHANNES		MERTZWILLER	12/01/1837	A		FILM
SCHLEIFFER W W	JEACQUES HENRY		NIEDERBRONN	02/26/1817	A		FILM
SCHLEISSEN	CATHERINE	1817	ZINSWEILLER	02/16/1817	A		FILM
SCHLEISSEN	JACUQES	1813	ZINSWEILLER	02/16/1817	A		FILM
SCHLEISSEN	JEAN GOERGES	1805	ZINSWEILLER	02/16/1817	A		FILM
SCHLEISSEN	MARGUERTE	1809	ZINSWEILLER	02/16/1817	A		FILM
SCHLEISSEN 4CH	PHILIPPE	1791	ZINSWEILLER	02/16/1817	A		FILM
SCHLEISSEN W W 4CH	PHILLIPE		ERKARTSWILLER	11/03/1817	A		FILM
SCHLEMMER	MARGUERITHE		ERCKARTSWILLER	01/01/1828	A		FILM
SCHLEMMER F OF 8	PIERRE		ERCKARTSWILLER	01/01/1828	A		FILM
SCHLEN	DAVID	1810	ETUFFENT LE HAUT	11/22/1843	TX		FILM
SCHLETZER	ELISABETH		ST MARIE AUX MINES	08/03/1850	NO		FILM
SCHLETZER W 2CH	ELISABETH	1814	ST MARIE AUX MINES	02/22/1841	NO		FILM
SCHLEXTTER	BENOIT	1810	RICHWILLER	04/03/1848	NY		FILM

```
SCHLEY F OF 3         JACQUES             GEUDERTHEIM       01/01/1828 A    FILM
SCHLICHT              CHRISTOPHE          SCHWANN W         08/21/1849 A    FILM
SCHLIMMER             GEORGE              ERCKARTSWILLER    01/01/1828 A    FILM
SCHLINGER                                 HAUT RHIN         01/28/1866 NY   FILM
SCHLOSSER                                 RENCHEN B         03/31/1849 NY   FILM

SCHLOSSER             JEAN                                  04/14/1838 A    FILM
SCHLOSSER W W 5CH     PIERRE         1806 BOURBACH LE BAS   10/21/1844 NY   FILM
SCHLOTTER W W 2CH     JEAN                SOULEZ W          06/23/1849 A    FILM
SCHLOTTER W W 5CH     CHRETIEN       1794 RICHWILLER        07/26/1852 NY   FILM
SCHLOTTERBACK         MATHEUS             SOULEZ W          06/23/1849 A    FILM

SCHLOYEL              LOUIS               REINHARDSMUNSTER  01/01/1828 A    FILM
SCHLUMBERGER          ADOLPHE        1831 GUEBWILLER        09/27/1853 NO   FILM
SCHLUMBERGER          CAROLINE       1829 MULHOUSE          02/13/1852 NY   FILM
SCHLUMBERGER          JULES          1837 GUEBWILLER        02/04/1857 NY   FILM
SCHMAL  F OF 7        JEAN                BRUMATH           01/01/1828 A    FILM

SCHMALTZ                                  LAUTERBOURG       01/01/1850 NO   PRIV
SCHMALTZ              MARIA ANNA     1845 NEHWILLER         01/01/1866 NO   NO.2
SCHMALTZ              MARIE               NEEWILLER         01/01/1850 NO   PRIV
SCHMANN               CATHERINE           BURBACH           01/01/1828 A    FILM
SCHMATZ               JOHANN         1835 LAUTERBURG        01/01/1869 NY   NO.2

SCHMAUCH W 3CH        MARIE ANNE          OTTERSTHAL        01/01/1828 A    FILM
SCHMBER F OF 9        ETIENNE             KIRRBERG          01/01/1828 A    FILM
SCHMECK               DOROTHEA            SCHAMBERG         08/21/1849 A    FILM
SCHMELGLE             CHARLES             ENDINGEN B        09/07/1849 A    FILM
SCHMELTZ W W 1S       FRANCOI ANTOINE 1816 WILLE BAS RHIN   04/28/1838 NY   FILM

SCHMELZLE W 2CH       MARGUERITHE         FREUDENSTADT W    09/02/1849 NY   FILM
SCHMERBER             JOSEPH         1797 HOCHSTATT         10/01/1846 TX   FILM
SCHMERBER             MORAND         1819 RIXHEIM           09/29/1843 TX   FILM
SCHMERBER             MORAND         1817 RIXHEIM           10/25/1843 TX   FILM
SCHMERBER 1CH         ELISABETH      1801 MULHOUSEN         12/06/1844 NO   FILM

SCHMERLES             JOSEPH         1797 HOCHSTATT         10/01/1846 TX   FILM
SCHMID                DOMINIQUES     1835 MERXHEIM          12/18/1852 A    FILM
SCHMID                MICHEL              FREUDENSTADT W    05/30/1849 NY   FILM
SCHMIDR               EMILE          1860 BLOTZHEIM         05/01/1861 NY   FILM
SCHMIDT               ANTOINE             KOEGENHEIM        02/25/1838 A    FILM

SCHMIDT               BABY           1861 BLOTZHEIM         05/01/1861 NY   FILM
SCHMIDT               CATHERINE      1807 MERXHEIM          04/17/1849 A    FILM
SCHMIDT               CHARLES             HARSKIRCHEN       01/01/1828 A    FILM
SCHMIDT               CHRETIEN       1833 BLOTZHEIM         05/01/1861 NY   FILM
SCHMIDT               CHRETIEN            WEISLINGEN        01/01/1828 A    FILM

SCHMIDT               CONRAD              WOLFSKIRCHEN      01/01/1828 A    FILM
SCHMIDT               DOMINIQUE      1835 MERXHEIM          12/18/1852 A    FILM
SCHMIDT               FERDINAND      1838 RANSPACH          11/22/1843 TX   FILM
SCHMIDT               FRANCOIS JOSEPH 1828 MULHOUSE         08/14/1848 NY   FILM
SCHMIDT               FRANZ ANTON    1844 SURBOURG          01/01/1865 NY   NO.2

SCHMIDT               FREDERIC       1828 RIQUEWIHR         11/22/1853 NY   FILM
SCHMIDT               HENRI               WOLFSKIRCHEN      01/01/1828 A    FILM
SCHMIDT               HENRY               WISSEMBOURG       01/01/1869 NO   PRIV
SCHMIDT               JACQUES             COSSWILLER        01/01/1828 A    FILM
SCHMIDT               JACQUES             BRUMATH           01/01/1828 A    FILM
```

Lastname	Firstname	Birth Year	Birthplace	Emigration	De	Prof	Source
SCHMIDT	JAKOB	1815	HAMBACH PRUSSIA	04/09/1844	TX		FILM
SCHMIDT	JEAN	1827	WALDIGHOFEN	09/19/1848	NY		FILM
SCHMIDT	JEAN	1861	BLOTZHEIM	05/01/1861	NY		FILM
SCHMIDT	JEAN ADAM		HIRSCHLAND	03/03/1838	A		FILM
SCHMIDT	JEAN MARTIN	1818	NEUWILLER	09/04/1845	NO		FILM
SCHMIDT	JOSEPH	1835	RANSPACH	11/22/1843	TX		FILM
SCHMIDT	JOSEPH		FRIESENHEIM B	08/05/1849	A		FILM
SCHMIDT	JOSEPH	1810	DITTENHEIM	09/09/1854	PH		FILM
SCHMIDT	JOSEPH	1794	GUEBWILLER	09/28/1854	NY		FILM
SCHMIDT	JOSEPH	1807	RANSPACH	11/22/1843	TX		FILM
SCHMIDT	JOSEPH		FRIESENHEIM B	08/05/1849	A		FILM
SCHMIDT	MARGARETHE	1821	HUNSPACH	01/01/1868	NY		NO.2
SCHMIDT	MARIA	1813	RANSPACH	11/22/1843	TX		FILM
SCHMIDT	PIERRE		HIRSCHLAND	01/01/1828	A		FILM
SCHMIDT	SEVERIN	1818	RANSPACH	11/22/1843	TX		FILM
SCHMIDT	THERESE	1836	GUEBWILLER	03/31/1857	NY		FILM
SCHMIDT	THERESE	1835	BLOTZHEIM	05/01/1861	NY		FILM
SCHMIDT	VALENTIN		BRUMATH	01/01/1828	A		FILM
SCHMIDT W W 1 CH	JEAN MARTIN	1818	NEUWILLER	09/04/1845	NO		FILM
SCHMIDT F OF 3	FREDERIC		SESSEHEIM	01/01/1828	A		FILM
SCHMIDT F OF 7	GEORGES		DIEMERINGEN	03/03/1838	A		FILM
SCHMIDT W 3CH	GEORGES	1798	MERXHEIM	10/19/1854	A		FILM
SCHMIDT W W 1CH	JOSEPH	1804	STERNENBERG	02/08/1845	NY		FILM
SCHMIDT W W 3CH	GEORGES	1798	MERXHEIM	10/19/1854	A		
SCHMIDT W W 4CH	CHARLES AUGUSTE	1814	STRASSBOURG	03/14/1852	NY		FILM
SCHMIDT W W 4CH	JACQUES		STRASSBOURG	05/12/1817	A		FILM
SCHMIDT W W 5CH	GEORG		NEHWILLER	03/11/1817	A		NO.2
SCHMIED F OF 3	FREDERIC		SESSENHEIM	02/23/1838	A		FILM
SCHMIEDLE	PETER	1774	REGENBURG SWISS	04/09/1844	TX		FILM
SCHMILLER W 3 CH	MICHEL		HERMERSWILLER	03/29/1817	A		FILM
SCHMIT W W 4CH	FRANCOIS ANTOIE	1817	GUEWENHEIM	02/16/1846	NY		FILM
SCHMITHS	JEAN		LA PETIT PIERRE	03/03/1817	A		FILM
SCHMITHS W W 1CH	JEAN		LA PETIT PIERE	03/03/1817	A		FILM
SCHMITT	ALEXANDRE		ROESCHWOOG	03/14/1817	A		FILM
SCHMITT	ANDRE		ILLHAEUSERN	02/17/1847	NY		FILM
SCHMITT	ANT ?		OFFENBURG	04/20/1849	A		FILM
SCHMITT	ANTOINE		KOEGENHEIM	02/25/1838	A		FILM
SCHMITT	ANTOINE	1838	OBERENTZEN	01/14/1850	TX		FILM
SCHMITT	ANTOINE	1833	OBERENTZEN	02/13/1850	TX		FILM
SCHMITT	ANTON		OFFENBOURG	04/20/1849	A		FILM
SCHMITT	AUGUSTE	1828	FELLERINGEN	07/08/1852	PH		FILM
SCHMITT	BARBE		HERBITZHEIM	01/01/1828	A		FILM
SCHMITT	BARBE		KIRCHHEIM UNTER TECK	05/23/1849	A		FILM
SCHMITT	CATHERINE		MULHAUSEN	01/01/1828	A		FILM
SCHMITT	CONRAD	1819	OBERDORFF	11/27/1839	NY		FILM
SCHMITT	DANIEL		LORENTZEN	01/01/1828	A		FILM
SCHMITT	EMMA	1851	WEISSENBURG	01/01/1865	NY		NO.2
SCHMITT	ERASME		REINHARDSMUENSTER	01/01/1828	A		FILM
SCHMITT	ETIENNE		UNVERSHEIM	01/01/1828	A		FILM
SCHMITT	FRANCOIS	1836	NIEDERLAUTERBACH	01/01/1868	NO	MERC	PRIV

Lastname		Firstname	Birth Year	Birthplace	Emigration	De	Prof	Source
SCHMITT		FRANCOIS	1823		02/27/1857	A		FILM
SCHMITT		FRANCOIS JOSEPH		MINVERSHEIM	01/01/1828	A		FILM
SCHMITT		FRANCOIS XAVIER		HUTTENHEIM	02/27/1838	A		FILM
SCHMITT		FRANCOIS.JOSEPH	1834	OBERENTZEN	10/01/1854	TX	CULT	PASS
SCHMITT		GEORG		NEEWILLER	01/01/1850	NO		PRIV
SCHMITT		GEORG	1844	NEHWILLER	01/01/1866	NO FARR		NO.2
SCHMITT		HANS GEORG		PREUSCHDORF	01/01/1740	A		SUESS
SCHMITT		HEINRICH WILHEL	1831	WEISSENBURG	01/01/1869	NO BREW		NO.2
SCHMITT		IGANCE		HAGUENAU	03/01/1838	A		FILM
SCHMITT		JACQUES		OERMINGEN	03/23/1817	A		FILM
SCHMITT		JEAN		BADEN	05/10/1833	A		FILM
SCHMITT		JEAN	1813	MUTTELMUESBACH	03/09/1840	NY		FILM
SCHMITT		JEAN	1811	LUNDLINGER	12/26/1846	NY		FILM
SCHMITT		JEAN	1820	SOULTZEREN	05/24/1854	A		FILM
SCHMITT		JEAN	1831	THANN	07/28/1854	A		FILM
SCHMITT		JEAN MICHEL		DRUSENHEIM	08/25/1837	A		FILM
SCHMITT		JEAN MICHEL		OBERENTZEN	01/01/1825	TX		FILM
SCHMITT		JEAN PAUL	1826	OSTHEIM	12/26/1848	NY		FILM
SCHMITT		JEAN PIERRE	1820	JONCHERRY	05/26/1845	NY		FILM
SCHMITT		JEAN.MICHEL	1835	OBERENTZEN	09/01/1846	TX	DAYL	PASS
SCHMITT		JOSEPH		MORSCHWILLER	03/04/1838	A		FILM
SCHMITT		JOSEPH		HAGUENAU	03/01/1838	A		FILM
SCHMITT		JOSEPH	1816	WALDIGHOFEN	07/20/1838	NY		FILM
SCHMITT		JOSEPH		KOEGENHEIM	02/25/1838	A		FILM
SCHMITT		JOSEPH	1811	GUEBWILLER	05/04/1839	A		FILM
SCHMITT		JOSEPH	1817	WALDIGHOFEN	12/19/1839	NY		PRIV
SCHMITT		JOSEPH	1819	FULLEREN	12/18/1846	A		FILM
SCHMITT		JOSEPH	1811	ROGGENBURG	04/28/1855	NY		FILM
SCHMITT		KARL	1855	WEISSENBURG	01/01/1866	NY		NO.2
SCHMITT		MADELAINE	1819	FELLERINGEN	08/07/1844	NY		FILM
SCHMITT		MARGUERITE		MULHOUSEN	01/01/1828	A		FILM
SCHMITT		MARIA ANNA	1847	NEHWILLER	01/01/1866	NO		NO.2
SCHMITT		MARIE	1797	MULHOUSE	07/15/1857	NY		FILM
SCHMITT		MARIE		NEEWILLER	01/01/1850	NO		PRIV
SCHMITT		MARIE AMDELAINE	1832	MULHOUSE	09/13/1853	TX		FILM
SCHMITT		MARIE ANNE	1830	SOPPE LE HAUT	05/02/1851	A		FILM
SCHMITT		MARIE ROSE	1830	SOULTZ	04/20/1852	CA		FILM
SCHMITT		MARIE-MADELEINE	1832	MUNTZENHEIM	09/01/1853	TX	SERV	PASS
SCHMITT		MICHEL			/ /			
SCHMITT		NICOLAS	1831	OBERENTZEN	09/01/1851	TX	CULT	PASS
SCHMITT		NICOLAS		WINVERSHEIM	01/01/1828	A		FILM
SCHMITT		PIERRE	1814	OBERDORFF	12/16/1839	NY		FILM
SCHMITT		PIERRE	1801	THEDING	07/18/1184	NY		FILM
SCHMITT		ROSINE		BRUMATH	03/22/1838	A		FILM
SCHMITT		SALOME	1853	WEISSENBURG	01/01/1865	NY		NO.2
SCHMITT		SEBASTIEN	1815	BERGHEIM	08/18/1853	NO		FILM
SCHMITT	F OF 3	RENE		RHEINHARSMUNSTER	01/01/1828	A		FILM
SCHMITT	F OF 5	CHRISTINE		SCHILLERSDORF	01/01/1828	A		FILM
SCHMITT	F OF 8	HENRY DANIEL		BRUMATH	01/01/1828	A		FILM
SCHMITT	W W 1CH	MATHIEU	1823	ROESCHWOOG	09/14/1853	NY		FILM

Lastname	Firstname	Birth Year	Birthplace	Emigration	De	Prof	Source
SCHMITT W W 8CH	JACQUES		LA PETIT PIERRE	03/03/1817	A		FILM
SCHMITT CH 2	FRANCOIS JOSEPH	1803	OBERENTZEN	09/01/1855	TX	CULT	PASS
SCHMITT CH 3	XAVIER	1811	OBERENTZEN	09/31/1846	TX		PASS
SCHMITT CH 6	NICOLAS	1804	RANSPACH	08/01/1844	TX	DRIV	PASS
SCHMITT F OF 11	MICHEL		WEITERSWILLER	01/01/1828	A		FILM
SCHMITT F OF 3	CHRETIEN		RUNTZENHEIM	01/01/1828	A		FILM
SCHMITT F OF 3	JEAN		ISSENHAUSEN	01/01/1828	A		FILM
SCHMITT F OF 4	GEORGE		HERBITZHEIM	01/01/1828	A		FILM
SCHMITT F OF 4	GEORGE		REIPERTSWILLER	01/01/1828	A		FILM
SCHMITT F OF 6	CHRETIEN		SUNDHAUSEN	03/02/1837	A		FILM
SCHMITT F OF 6	GEORGE		SAVERNE	01/01/1828	A		FILM
SCHMITT F OF 6	GEORGE		ZUTZENDORF	01/01/1828	A		FILM
SCHMITT F OF 6	MARTIN		WILWISHEIM	01/01/1828	A		PRIV
SCHMITT F OF 7	FRANCOIS JOS		MARLENHEIM	01/01/1828	A		FILM
SCHMITT F OF 7	JEROME		REINHARDSMUENSTER	01/01/1828	A		FILM
SCHMITT F OF 8	JACQUES		HATTMATT	01/01/1828	A		FILM
SCHMITT F OF 8	MICHEL		BRUMATH	01/01/1828	A		FILM
SCHMITT M STOCKER	CHRISTINE		GOERSDORF	01/01/1740	A		SUESS
SCHMITT MN BACHER 2C	SALOME	1826	WEISSENBURG	01/01/1865	NY		NO.2
SCHMITT MN BUFFLER	MARGUERITE	1811	GUEBWILLER	02/18/1840	NY		FILM
SCHMITT W 1 CH	EVE MARIE		KESKASTEL	01/01/1817	A		FILM
SCHMITT W 1CH	CHRISTINE	1822	FELLERINGEN	07/08/1846	PH		FILM
SCHMITT W 3D	MARIE ANNE		ILLHAEUSERN	02/14/1855	NY		FILM
SCHMITT W 5CH	LUISE	1817	ARTZENHEIM	11/08/1855	A		FILM
SCHMITT W W	ALEXANDRE		ROESCHWOOG	03/14/1817	A		FILM
SCHMITT W W	ANTOINE	1822	NEUSPACH LE BAS	06/26/1847	NY		FILM
SCHMITT W W 1CH	ANDRE		KESKASTEL	03/17/1817	A		FILM
SCHMITT W W 1CH	GEORGES		MULHAUSEN	01/01/1828	A		FILM
SCHMITT W W 1CH	JOSEPH	1827	FESSENEHIM	06/04/1852	NY		FILM
SCHMITT W W 2CH	ANTOINE	1820	HIRTZFELDEN	12/01/1847	NY		FILM
SCHMITT W W 2CH	FRANCOIS JOSEPH		MARLENHEIM	01/01/1828	A		FILM
SCHMITT W W 2CH	JEAN	1801	WEITERSWILLER	10/24/1839	A		FILM
SCHMITT W W 3CH	GEORGE		ESCHBOURG	03/31/1817	A		FILM
SCHMITT W W 3CH	JOSEPH	1819	JONCHERRY	02/22/1847	NY		FILM
SCHMITTENKNECHT	MICHEL		THAL	01/01/1828	A		FILM
SCHMITTHEISSLER	FRANZ JOSEF	1841	OBERLAUTERBACH	01/01/1866	NY	FARM	NO.2
SCHMODRY	JOSEPH	1804	KAYSERSBERG	05/10/1856	NY		FILM
SCHMOHL	CLAIRE	1814	DIRMETTINGEN W	10/27/1855	NY		FILM
SCHMOL	IGNACE		DRUSENHEIM	03/24/1838	A		FILM
SCHMOL	MADELAINE		DRUSENHEIM	03/24/1838	A		FILM
SCHMOL	MARIE EVE		DRUSENHEIM	03/24/1838	A		FILM
SCHMOL	MICHEL		DRUSENHEIM	03/24/1838	A		FILM
SCHMOL W W 2CH	JOSEPH		DRUSENHEIM	03/24/1838	A		FILM
SCHMOTTERER W W	SEBASTIEN	1815	KAYSERSBERG	12/14/1855	NY		FILM
SCHMUCK	GERTRUDE		SOUFFLENHEIM	03/02/1838	A		FILM
SCHMUTZ	GEORGES		OBENHEIM	03/10/1838	A		FILM
SCHMUTZ	MARIE	1814	COLMAR	09/16/1850	NO		FILM
SCHNABEL W W 2CH	FRANCOIS	1802	BOUXWILLER	09/03/1846	PA		FILM
SCHNABELE W W 4 CH	JACQUES	1785	BALDENHEIM	03/17/1845	NY		FILM
SCHNAEBELE	LAURENT		BALDENHEIM	03/06/1838	A		FILM

```
                              Birth                                          225
Lastname               Firstname      Year  Birthplace          Emigration De Prof Source
----------------------------------------------------------------------------------------
SCHNAITER              JEAN ERNES      1808 BROGGINGEN           06/20/1846 NY        FILM
SCHNEBELEN             BARTHELEMY      1824 HOMBOURG             11/01/1844 TX BAKE   PASS
SCHNEBELEN             MEINRAD         1817 SENTHEIM             08/27/1847 NY        FILM
SCHNEBELEN CH 1        JOSEPH          1847 GUEWENHEIM           01/01/1869 TX DRIV   PASS
SCHNEBELIN             ANTOINE         1803 BANTZENHEIM          11/13/1844 NO        FILM
----------------------------------------------------------------------------------------
SCHNEBELIN             BARTHOLEMI      1824 BANTZENHEIM          01/14/1848 A         FILM
SCHNEBELIN             FRANCOIS JOSEPH 1795 BANTZENHEIM          01/14/1848 A         FILM
SCHNEBELIN             JUSTINE         1825 CERNAY               06/15/1850 NY        FILM
SCHNECKENBURGER        JOSEPH          1835 ALTKIRCH             04/24/1857 NY        FILM
SCHNEHMACHER W W 3CH   JOSEPH          1826 AMMERSCHWIHR         11/03/1854 A         FILM
----------------------------------------------------------------------------------------
SCHNEIDER              ADAM            1845 TRIEMBACH            01/01/1867 NO        NO.2
SCHNEIDER              ADAM                 WEISLINGEN           01/01/1828 A         FILM
SCHNEIDER              ALEXANDRE       1824 HUSSEREN             09/24/1844 NY        FILM
SCHNEIDER              ALOYSE          1832 PFASTATT             03/07/1854 NY        FILM
SCHNEIDER              ANDRE           1828 MULHOUSE             08/05/1857 SL        FILM
----------------------------------------------------------------------------------------
SCHNEIDER              ANNA BARBARA    1840 LEMBACH              01/01/1866 NY        NO.2
SCHNEIDER              ANTOINE         1814 NIEDERENTZEN         09/01/1851 TX CHAR   PASS
SCHNEIDER              ANTOINE         1823 HETTENSCHLAG         09/10/1851 TX        FILM
SCHNEIDER              ANTON                TRIMBACH             01/01/1850 NO        PRIV
SCHNEIDER              ANTON           1815 MUNCHHOUSE           01/01/1868 NY FARM   NO.2
----------------------------------------------------------------------------------------
SCHNEIDER              BARBE                GERMANY             04/01/1849 NY         FILM
SCHNEIDER              BARTHOLOMEUS    1846 DUERRENBACH          01/01/1866 NY        NO.2
SCHNEIDER              BENOIT          1823 RUMERSHEIM           05/01/1852 TX CULT   PASS
SCHNEIDER              CHARLES              SCHOENBOURG          01/01/1828 A         FILM
SCHNEIDER              CHARLES ANTOINE 1833 MULHOUSE             09/18/1854 NY        FILM
----------------------------------------------------------------------------------------
SCHNEIDER              CHRETIEN             RUNTZENHEIM          01/01/1828 A         FILM
SCHNEIDER              CHRETIEN             DURSTEL              03/18/1838 A         FILM
SCHNEIDER              CONRAD HENRY    1827 BESSONCOURT          03/31/1865 NY        FILM
SCHNEIDER              EDMOND               LEUTENHEIM           03/01/1838 A         FILM
SCHNEIDER              EDUARD          1811 SELTZ  BAS RHIN      10/25/1843 TX        FILM
----------------------------------------------------------------------------------------
SCHNEIDER              ELISABETH       1858 DRACHENBRONN         01/01/1865 NY        NO.2
SCHNEIDER              ELISABETH       1834 ST MARIE AUX MINES   08/29/1854 NY        FILM
SCHNEIDER              ELISABETH       1832 MULHOUSE             08/05/1857 SL        FILM
SCHNEIDER              ELISE                GERMANY              04/01/1849 NY        FILM
SCHNEIDER              EUGENE          1820 BESSONCOURT          03/31/1838 NY        FILM
----------------------------------------------------------------------------------------
SCHNEIDER              EVA             1842 NIEDERROEDERN        01/01/1868 NY        NO.2
SCHNEIDER              FELIX           1835 DOLLENDORF           10/25/1843 TX        FILM
SCHNEIDER              FERDINANT            LICHTENBERG          01/01/1828 A         FILM
SCHNEIDER              FRANCOISE PAULI 1835 NANCY                06/25/1856 NY        FILM
SCHNEIDER              FRANZ           1815 MUNCHHOUSE           01/01/1865 NY FARM   NO.2
----------------------------------------------------------------------------------------
SCHNEIDER              FRANZ           1831 WEISSENBURG          01/01/1865 NY WINE   NO.2
SCHNEIDER              FRANZ ANTON     1814 MUNCHHOUSE           01/01/1867 NY        NO.2
SCHNEIDER              FRANZ ANTON     1849 MUNCHHOUSE           01/01/1868 NY FARM   NO.2
SCHNEIDER              FRANZISKA       1839 DOLLENDORF           10/25/1843 TX        FILM
SCHNEIDER              FREDERIC             RUNTZENHEIM          01/01/1828 A         FILM
----------------------------------------------------------------------------------------
SCHNEIDER              FRIEDRICH       1859 DRACHENBRONN         01/01/1866 NY        NO.2
SCHNEIDER              GEORG           1856 DRACHENBRON          01/01/1865 NY        NO.2
SCHNEIDER              GEORG           1860 DRACHENBRONN         01/01/1866 NY        NO.2.
SCHNEIDER              GEORGES              DETTWILLER           01/01/1831 A         FILM
SCHNEIDER              GEORGES              UHLWILLER            03/03/1838 A         FILM
```

Lastname	Firstname	Birth Year	Birthplace	Emigration	De	Prof	Source
SCHNEIDER	GEORGES	1820	HARBOURG	05/31/1849	NY		FILM
SCHNEIDER	HEINRICH	1858	DRACHENBRONN	01/01/1866	NY		NO.2
SCHNEIDER	HENRY	1855	BESSONCOURG	01/01/1828	A		FILM
SCHNEIDER	JACOB	1830	HOFFEN	01/01/1869	NY		NO.2
SCHNEIDER	JEAN	1817	MASSEVAUX	04/24/1852	NY		FILM
SCHNEIDER	JEAN THIEBAUD	1823	TRAUBACH LE BAS	03/06/1849	NY		FILM
SCHNEIDER	JEAN BAPTISTE	1827	HUSSEREN	08/05/1847	PH		FILM
SCHNEIDER	JOHANN	1847	WEISSENBURG	01/01/1865	NY	WINE	NO.2
SCHNEIDER	JOHANN PETER		WEISSENBURG	01/01/1865	NY		NO.2
SCHNEIDER	JOSEPH	1816	BOLLWILLER	12/14/1846	PH		FILM
SCHNEIDER	JOSEPH	1835	ILLHAEUSERN	03/12/1857	NY		FILM
SCHNEIDER	JOSEPHINE	1825	DOLLENDORF	10/25/1843	TX		FILM
SCHNEIDER	MADELAINE		WEISLINGEN	01/01/1828	A		FILM
SCHNEIDER	MADELEINE		TRIMBACH	01/01/1850	NO		PRIV
SCHNEIDER	MADELEINE		GERMANY	04/01/1849	NY		FILM
SCHNEIDER	MAGDALENA	1863	DRACHEDNBRONN	01/01/1855	NY		NO.2
SCHNEIDER	MAGDALENA	1867	TRIEMBACH	01/01/1867	NO		NO.2
SCHNEIDER	MARGARETHE	1852	DRACHENBRONN	01/01/1866	NY		NO.2
SCHNEIDER	MARIANNE	1807	DOLLENDORF	10/25/1843	TX		FILM
SCHNEIDER	MARIANNE		WEISLINGEN	01/01/1828	A		FILLM
SCHNEIDER	MARIE		SCHAFFHAUSEN	01/01/1828	A		FILM
SCHNEIDER	MARIE	1860	BESSONCOURT	03/31/1865	NY		FILM
SCHNEIDER	MARTIN	1847	KAIDENBURG	01/01/1866	NY	FARM	NO.2
SCHNEIDER	MARTIN	1835	ILLHAEUSERN	11/06/1854	NY		FILM
SCHNEIDER	MARTIN		MARLENHEIM	01/01/1828	A		FILM
SCHNEIDER	MATHIAS	1797	ASCHPACH	01/01/1866	NY		NO.2
SCHNEIDER	MICHEL	1850	NIEDERROEDERN	01/01/1867	NY	FARM	NO.2
SCHNEIDER	NICOLAS		DURSTEL	03/18/1838	A		FILM
SCHNEIDER	PETER	1843	WEISSENBURG	01/01/1865	NY	WINE	NO.2
SCHNEIDER	PHILIPP	1798	BISCHOFFSHEIM	04/09/1844	TX		FILM
SCHNEIDER	PHILIPPE		WEISLINGEN	01/01/1828	A		FILM
SCHNEIDER	ROSALINE	1828	DOLLENDORF	10/25/1843	TX		FILM
SCHNEIDER	ROSINE	1823	SELTZ BAS RHIN	10/25/1843	TX		FILM
SCHNEIDER	THEODORE		ERGERSHEIM	01/01/1846	NO		PRIV
SCHNEIDER	VICTOIRE	1864	BESSONCOURT	03/31/1865	NY		FILM
SCHNEIDER	VICTORIA		GRIESHEIM	10/11/1849	A		FILM
SCHNEIDER F F 5CH	JACQUES HENRY		GOERSDORF	03/22/1817	A		FILM
SCHNEIDER F OF 2	GEORGE		PFALZWEYER	01/01/1828	A		FILM
SCHNEIDER F OF 2	PIERRE		WEISLINGEN	01/01/1828	A		FILM
SCHNEIDER F OF 3	LOUIS		SIEWILLER	03/02/1838	A		FILM
SCHNEIDER F OF 4	ADAM		HAMBACH	03/08/1838	A		FILM
SCHNEIDER F OF 4	CHARLES		BALBRONN	02/28/1838	A		FILM
SCHNEIDER F OF 4	LAURENT		EYWILLER	01/01/1828	A		FILM
SCHNEIDER F OF 5	JACQUES		SCHOENBOURG	01/01/1828	A		FILM
SCHNEIDER F OF 7	GEORGE		BRUMATH	03/22/1838	A		FILM
SCHNEIDER F OF 7	HENRI		VOELLARDINGEN	01/01/1828	A		FILM
SCHNEIDER F OF 8	GEORGE		HERBITZHEIM	01/01/1828	A		FILM
SCHNEIDER MN SCHENK	ELISABETH	1837	DRACHENBRONN	01/01/1865	NY		NO.2
SCHNEIDER MN SCHMOLZ	FRANZISKA	1808	MUNCHHOUSE	01/01/1867	NY		NO.2
SCHNEIDER MN SCHUTZ	ELISABETH		MULHOUSE	08/05/1857	SL		FILM

Lastname	Firstname	Birth Year	Birthplace	Emigration	De	Prof	Source
SCHNEIDER MN TREGER	JULIE	1826	DRACHENBRONN	01/01/1866	NY		NO.2
SCHNEIDER W F	JOSEPH	1788	CARSPACH	03/09/1841	NY		FILM
SCHNEIDER W SI 4CH	FRANZISKA	1807	DOLLENDORF	10/25/1843	TX		FILM
SCHNEIDER W W	NICOLAS		EPPING	10/23/1846	NY		FILM
SCHNEIDER W W 1CH	CHARLES		SCHOENBOURG	01/01/1828	A		
SCHNEIDER W W 3 CH	GEORG	1833	DRACHENBRONN	01/01/1865	NY	DAYL	NO.2
SCHNEIDER W W 3CH	NICOLAS		EYWILLER	03/20/1817	A		FILM
SCHNEIDER W W 4 CH	HEINRICH	1828	DRACHENBRONN	01/01/1866	NY	TAYL	NO.2
SCHNEIDER W W 4CH	JOHANN HEINRICH	1801		09/17/1845	A		FILM
SCHNEIDER W W 5CH	GEORGE		HERBITZHEIM	03/03/1817	A		FILM
SCHNEIDER W W 5CH	JOSEPH		SCHOENBURG	01/01/1828	A		FILM
SCHNEIDER W W 6CH	MICHEL		DRACHENBRONN	03/28/1817	A		FILM
SCHNEIDER W W 8 CH	JACQUES		SCHOENBOURG	01/01/1828	A		FILM
SCHNEIDERHAHN	JULES	1866	COURTAVON	05/17/1866	NY		FILM
SCHNEIDT	WILHELM		BILLINGEN B	11/02/1849	A		FILM
SCHNEL W W 4CH	IN ADAMS		ERNOLSHEIM	03/17/1817	A		FILM
SCHNELL	DANIEL	1814	WEINBOURG	08/17/1854	NY		FILM
SCHNELL	GEORGE		ERNOLSHEIM	01/01/1828	A		FILM
SCHNELL F OF 7	MICHEL		ERNOLSHEIM	01/01/1828	A		FILM
SCHNELL F OF 8	GEORGE		ERNOLSHEIM	01/01/1828	A		FILM
SCHNELL W W 1CH	JACQUES	1805	GUEBWILLER	03/16/1849	NO		FILM
SCHNEPF	MARIA ANNA	1837	NEUHAEUSEL	01/01/1869	NO		NO.2
SCHNEPP F OF 7	JACQUES		INGVILLER	01/01/1828	A		FILM
SCHNIEDERLOCHNER	CATHERINE	1762	ZINSWILLER	02/16/1817	A		FILM
SCHNITTER F OF 6	ALEXANDRE		ROESCHWOOG	01/01/1828	A		FILM
SCHNOERINGER	ROSINE	1832	WEISSENBURG	01/01/1865	NY		NO.2
SCHNUR	ANDRE		DRUSSENHEIM	03/24/1818	A		FILM
SCHNURR	VICTOIRE		RENCHEN	05/31/1849	A		FILM
SCHOCK F OF 3	JACQUES		FURCHHAUSEN	01/01/1828	A		FILM
SCHOEFF	ALOISE	1825	BURNHAUPT LE BAS	04/30/1850	NY		FILM
SCHOEFFEL	MICHEL		MONSWILLER	01/01/1828	A		FILM
SCHOEFFEL W 7CH		1800	STRASSBOURG	07/29/1841	NO		FILM
SCHOEFFER	GEORGES	1831	DAMPIERRE LE BAS	05/10/1865	NY		FILM
SCHOEFFER F OF 3	JEAN GOERGE		BRUMATH	03/22/1838	A		FILM
SCHOEFFERT W W 6CH	PIERRE		BADEN	05/10/1833	A		FILM
SCHOEFFIER W W5CH	PHILIPPE		SOUFFLENHEIM	03/02/1838	A		FILM
SCHOEFFLER W W 6CH	ADAM		SOUFFLENHEIM	03/02/1838	A		FILM
SCHOELLER	ANTOINE	1823	WILDENSTEIN	03/10/1848	NO		FILM
SCHOEN	CAROLINE	1815	WEISSENBURG	01/01/1866	NY		NO.2
SCHOEN	PETER	1846	WEISSENBURG	01/01/1869	NY	COOK	NO.2
SCHOEN	THERESE	1828	HECKEN	03/30/1850	NY		FILM
SCHOEN W W 4CH	FRANCOIS PIERRE	1802	TRAUBACH LE BAS	04/20/1846	NY		FILM
SCHOENBERG	CASPARD	1834	OBERBRUCK	09/07/1853	A		FILM
SCHOENBERG	MADELAINE	1832	OBERBRUCK	09/02/1853	A		FILM
SCHOENENBERGER W W C	JOSEPH ANTOINE	1787	BUTZENWHILE	03/30/1847	A		FILM
SCHOENLAUB	CAROLINE	1844	NEHWILLER	01/01/1866	NO		NO.2
SCHOEPPES W W 5CH	NICOLAS		PETERSBACH	03/17/1817	A		FILM
SCHOEPPS	PIERRE		DURSTEL	03/18/1838	A		FILM
SCHOFFA	IGNACE	1813	KOESTLACH	03/07/1840	NY		FILM
SCHOFFMANN W W 7CH	JOSEPH	1808	TRAUBACH LE HAUT	03/03/1846	NY		FILM

Lastname	Firstname	Birth Year	Birthplace	Emigration	De	Prof	Source
SCHOLL W S	JOSEPH	1811	NIEDERLARG	05/31/1854	NY		FILM
SCHOLLER	JACQUES		ALTECKENDORF	01/01/1828	A		FILM
SCHON F OF 4	JACQUET		SCHIRRHOFF	03/01/1838	A		FILM
SCHORP	JOSEPH	1813	BIERINGEN W	11/22/1843	TX		FILM
SCHORR	DOMINIQUE	1836	GUEBWILLER	10/14/1854	NY		FILM
SCHOTHAMMER	ANDRE		SUNDHAUSEN	02/03/1837	A		FILM
SCHOTT	BRIGITTE		KIECHLINGSBERG	05/24/1849	A		FILM
SCHOTT	JEAN			03/20/1819	A		FILM
SCHOTT	JEAN	1830	BLOTZHEIM	08/17/1850	NY		FILM
SCHOTT	JOSEPH		SCHIRRHEIM	05/03/1838	A		FILM
SCHOTT	SIMONE MARIE	1834	OSTHEIM	07/31/1855	NY		FILM
SCHOTT D ANTOINE	THERESE		WITTELSHEIM	01/01/1845	TX		SHIP
SCHOTT F MARIE-ANNE	ANTOINE		WITTELSHEIM	01/01/1845	TX		SHIP
SCHOTT F OF 2	ANTOINE		SCHIRRHEIM	01/01/1828	A		FILM
SCHOTT F OF 2	MARTIN		SCHIRRHEIM	03/05/1838	A		FILM
SCHOTT S ANTOINE	SEBASTIEN		WITTELSHEIM	01/01/1845	TX		SHIP
SCHOTT W BADER J.	ANNE-MARIE		WITTELSHEIM	01/01/1854	TX		SHIP
SCHOTT W D 2CH	ANTOINE	1776	WITTELSHEIM	11/13/1844	TX		FILM
SCHOTT W W 2CH	JOSEPH ANTOINE	1823	KIRCHLINGSBERGEN	08/09/1853	A		FILM
SCHOTT W W 3CH	JOSEPH		GUMBRECHTSHOFEN	09/04/1819	A		FILM
SCHOTTER F OF 6	MICHEL		MARLENHEIM	01/01/1828	A		FILM
SCHOUBART	CHARLES	1828	ST CROIX AUX MINES	11/18/1852	NO		FILM
SCHOULE W W 1CH	ANTOINE	1815	SCHAIBLINGSHAUSEN	01/12/1852	NY		FILM
SCHRAM	ADELE		SCHWEIGHOUSE	/ /	LA		BULL
SCHRAMM	MAGDALENA	1825	BIRLENBACH	01/01/1869	NY		NO.2
SCHRAMM	MARGARETHA	1845	SCHOENBOURG	01/01/1866	NY		NO.2
SCHRAMM H B.MUELLER	LUDWIG		BUEHL	01/01/1841	A		SUESS
SCHRAMM MN MUELLER	EVA BARBARA		BUEHL	01/01/1841	A		SUESS
SCHRAMM S LU.SCHRAM	FRIEDRICH		BUEHL	01/01/1841	A		SUESS
SCHRAPP	JOSEPH	1825	BITSCHWILLER	04/24/1849	NY		FILM
SCHRAUT F OF 3	MICHEL		WEITERSWILLER	01/01/1828	A		FILM
SCHREIBER	JEAN	1812	WESTHALTEN	10/13/1843	A		FILM
SCHREIBER	JOSEPH		BURCKENWALD	01/01/1828	A		FILM
SCHREIBER W W 3CH	ANTOINE	1826	BOONVILLE	02/09/1851	A		FILM
SCHREIBER W W 3CH	JEAN	1802	NIEDERENTZEN	09/07/1846	TX		FILM
SCHREINER	FREDERIC	1828	RIBEAUVILLE	03/03/1849	NO		FILM
SCHREINER W 4CH A SI	BARBE	1792	TEUBINGEN W	07/13/1848	A		FILM
SCHREINER W W 5CH	GUSTAVE	1800	RIQUEWIHR	06/01/1852	NO		FILM
SCHREPFER	JOSEPH		NEUWILLER	01/01/1828	A		FILM
SCHREPPS	NICOLAS		PETERSBACH	03/17/1817	A		FILM
SCHRIEBER CH 3	JEAN	1802	OBERENTZEN	09/01/1846	TX	DAYL	PASS
SCHRIEBER D JEAN	CATHERINE	1838	OBERNETZEN	09/01/1846	TX		PASS
SCHRIEBER D JEAN	MARIE-ANNE	1836	OBERNETZEN	09/01/1846	TX		PASS
SCHRIEBER MN RICH	CATHERINE			09/01/1846	TX		PASS
SCHRIEBER S JEAN	JEAN	1833	OBERENTZEN	09/01/1846	TX		PASS
SCHROEDER	GEORGE		DORLISHEIM	03/03/1838	A		FILM
SCHRUECKER	MARIE		SCHAFFHAUSEN	01/01/1828	A		FILM
SCHTATTER W H A 3 CH	ANNE MARIE		WITTENHEIM	07/17/1832	NY		FILM
SCHUCH W W 2CH	ADAM		HAMBACH	03/20/1817	A		FILM
SCHUE F OF 3			FORTLOUIS	01/01/1828	A		FILM

Lastname	Firstname	Birth Year	Birthplace	Emigration	De	Prof	Source
SCHUEB	URSULE	1829	HERRLISHEIM	02/28/1848	A		FILM
SCHUEFFENAKER	MADELAINE	1796	MASSEVAUX	10/01/1851	SL		FILM
SCHUEFOLT	JEAN BAPTISTE	1807	RIBEAUVILLE	01/15/1845	NY		FILM
SCHUEHMACHER W W 3CH	JOSEPH	1826	AMMERSCHWIHR	01/10/3184	A		FILM
SCHUELER	FRANCOIS ANTOIE	1833	GRUSSENHEIM	12/08/1857	NY		FILM
SCHUELER	FRANCOIS ANTOIE	1823	GRUSSENHEIM	08/12/1857	NY		FILM
SCHUELER	LEONARD		EPPINGEN B	06/04/1849	A		FILM
SCHUELL F OF 7	MICHEL		ERNOLSHEIM	01/01/1828	A		FILM
SCHUEP F OF 6	MICHEL		MOMMENHEIM	02/28/1838	A		FILM
SCHUFFENUKER W W 5CH	JACQUES	1813	RODEREN	09/03/1852	NY		FILM
SCHUH	GEORG	1809	BISCHHEIM	11/22/1843	TX		FILM
SCHUH	GEORGES	1828	ST HYPOLITE	09/21/1852	PH		FILM
SCHUH	JEAN BAPTISTE	1814	LIEPVRE	10/20/1842	NO		FILM
SCHUH	MARIE ANNE	1810	ERSTEIN	08/17/1849	A		FILM
SCHUH	MARIE-ANNE	1819	COLMAR	08/01/1849	TX	SERV	PASS
SCHULER	JACOB		ESSLINGEN W	06/04/1849	A		FILM
SCHULER F OF 5	JACQUES		IMBSHEIM	01/01/1828	A		FILM
SCHULER W W AND FAM	HENRI	1784	BURNHAUPT	04/21/1847	NY		FILM
SCHULLER F OF 5	JACQUES		SUNDHAUSEN	03/02/1837	A		FILM
SCHULLER F OF 6	MATHIAS		SUNDHAUSEN	03/02/1837	A		FILM
SCHULLER W W 2CH	FRANCOIS JOSEPH	1812	BURNHAUPT LE HAUT	08/02/1847	NY		FILM
SCHULTZ	EUGENE	1832	BRUNSTATT	06/06/1855	A		FILM
SCHULTZ	JOHANN HEINRICH		LANGENSOULTZBACH	01/01/1817	A		NO.2
SCHULTZ	MAURICE	1833	HOUSSEN	08/21/1854	NY		FILM
SCHULTZ F OF 4	JACQUES		OBERMODERN	01/01/1828	A		FILM
SCHULTZ W W 1S	MARTIN		OBERHOFFEN	03/01/1838	A		FILM
SCHULTZ W W 3CH	GO HENRY		LANGENSOULTZBACH	03/17/1817	A		FILM
SCHUMACHER	HENRI		BRETTEN B	06/21/1849	A		FILM
SCHUMACHER	JEAN	1823	RIXHEIM	10/17/1850	NY		FILM
SCHUMACHER	JEAN MICHEL	1819	KUNHEIM	03/11/1841	NY		FILM
SCHUMACHER	JOSEPH	1833	PFEFFERHAUSEN	04/01/1853	NY		FILM
SCHUMACHER W S	ANDRE	1799	ST HYPOLITE	12/07/1853	PH		FILM
SCHUMACHER W W 3CH	JACQUES		BADEN	06/27/1833	A		FILM
SCHUMBERGER	MATHIAS	1836	ASPACH LE BAS	03/21/1854	NY		FILM
SCHUMEBERG	MARIE ANNE	1834	RECOUVRANCE	03/15/1851	NO		FILM
SCHUPP	CONRAD	1829	DORNACH	08/13/1849	NY		FILM
SCHUR	JEAN	1835	WALDIGHOFFEN	12/13/1865	NY		FILM
SCHURB W W	PAUL	1792	MANSPACH	01/10/1846	NY		FILM
SCHURDEVIN	GERMAIN	1825	LEPUIX DELLE	02/19/1852	NY		FILM
SCHURHAMMER	APPOLINE	1816	ODEREN	11/04/1857	TX		FILM
SCHURHAMMER	CATHERINE	1847	ODEREN	11/04/1857	TX		FILM
SCHURHAMMER	JOSEPH	1850	ODEREN	11/04/1857	TX		FILM
SCHURMANN	ELISABETH		ESCHBOURG	01/01/1828	A		FILM
SCHURMANN	MARGERITE		ESCHBOURG	01/01/1828	A		FILM
SCHUSSELE	JEAN GEORGE	1785	GUEBWILLER	01/25/1840	NY		FILM
SCHUSTER	CHRETIEN		OBERHOFFEN	03/01/1838	A		FILM
SCHUSTER	GEORGE	1819	WESTHOFFEN	11/13/1851	A		FILM
SCHUSTER	LOUIS		PFAFFENHOFFEN	01/01/1828	A		FILM
SCHUSTER	MADELEINE		OBERHOFFEN	03/01/1838	A		FILM
SCHUSTER	MARTIN		BUEHL	01/01/1837	A		SUESS

Lastname	Firstname	Birth Year	Birthplace	Emigration	De	Prof	Source
SCHUSTER	MARTIN		PFAFFENHOFFEN	01/01/1828	A		FILM
SCHUSTER F OF 5	MATHIEU		SESSENHEIM	02/23/1838	A		FILM
SCHUSTER W F	CHRISOSTOME		SESSENHEIM	02/23/1838	A		FILM
SCHUTZ	CECILE	1847	MULHOUSE	08/05/1857	SL		FILM
SCHUTZ	ELISABETH	1832	MULHOUSE	05/08/1857	SL		FILM
SCHUTZ	FRIEDRICH		LANGENSOULTZBACH	01/01/1846	A		SUESS
SCHWAB	IGNACE	1824	MELISAY	03/22/1849	NY		FILM
SCHWAB	MARIE	1846	WEISSENBURG	01/01/1865	NY		NO.2
SCHWAB	PAUL		HOFSTETTEN	06/04/1849	A		FILM
SCHWAB F OF 3	LOUIS		EYWILLER	01/01/1828	A		FILM
SCHWACHLER	CATHERINE	1828	MULHOUSE	07/27/1866	NY		FILM
SCHWAECHLER	HORTENSE	1864	MULHOUSE	07/27/1866	NY		FILM
SCHWAECHLER	JOSEPH	1861	MULHOUSE	07/27/1866	NY		FILM
SCHWAECHLER	MELANIE	1858	MULHOUSE	07/27/1866	NY		FILM
SCHWAENDER	JOHANN GEORG		NIEDERBRONN	01/01/1817	A		NO.2
SCHWALB F OF 3	GASPARD		SCHWEIGHAUSEN	01/01/1828	A		FILM
SCHWALEN	FRANZ	1825	ETUFFENT LE HAUT	11/22/1843	TX		FILM
SCHWALEN	LOUISE	1818	ETUFFENT LE HAUT	11/22/1843	TX		FILM
SCHWALEN	MARIE LOUISE	1843	ETUFFENT LE HAUT	11/22/1843	TX		FILM
SCHWALEN	NIKOLAS	1841	ETUFFENT LE HAUT	11/22/1843	TX		FILM
SCHWALEN	NIKOLAS	1826	ETUFFENT LE HAUT	11/22/1843	TX		FILM
SCHWALM	PHILIPPE	1825	COLMAR	04/09/1853	NY		FILM
SCHWALM W W 1CH	ALEXIS	1823	ANJOUTEY	07/09/1850	A		FILM
SCHWANCH W 3 CH	MARIE ANNE		OTTERSTHAL	01/01/1828	A		FILM
SCHWANTZ	DOMINIQUE		HUNSTETTEN B	05/24/1849	A		FILM
SCHWARTZ	ANDRE		APPENWIHR	03/05/1852	NO		FILM
SCHWARTZ	AUGUSTE	1821	HARTMANNSWILLER	03/01/1848	TX	MEDC	PASS
SCHWARTZ	AUGUSTE	1821	CERNAY	03/02/1848	A		FILM
SCHWARTZ	CATHARINA	1809	MUNCHHOUSE	01/01/1865	NY		NO.2
SCHWARTZ	GEORGES	1821	KIFFIS	04/05/1854	NY		FILM
SCHWARTZ	JOSEPH	1831	EBERBACH	01/01/1867	NY	FARM	PRIV
SCHWARTZ	JOSEPH		ROESCHWOOG	01/01/1828	A		FILM
SCHWARTZ	JOSEPH	1813	PFAFFENHEIM	12/24/1842	NY		FILM
SCHWARTZ	JOSEPH FRANCOIS	1822	GROSNE	09/05/1844	NO		FILM
SCHWARTZ	MATHIAS		ROESCHWOOG	01/01/1828	A		FILM
SCHWARTZ	STANISLAS		RUST	05/12/1849	A		FILM
SCHWARTZ	URSANNE JOSEPH	1818	KIFFIS	04/20/1848	NY		FILM
SCHWARTZ F OF 5	ALEXANDRE		MARLENHEIM	01/01/1828	A		FILM
SCHWARTZ F OF 6	JEAN		ROESCHWOOG	01/01/1828	A		FILM
SCHWARTZ F OF 6	MATHIAS		ROESCHWOOG	01/01/1828	A		FILM
SCHWARTZ W 2CH	CATHERINE		FREUDENSTADT W	09/02/1849	NY		FILM
SCHWARTZ W W 2CH	FRANCOIS JOSEPH	1808	KIFFIS	04/20/1848	NY		FILM
SCHWARTZ W W 3CH	ANDRE		HERBITZHEIM	03/17/1817	A		FILM
SCHWARTZ W W 3CH	JACQUES	1827	STRASSBOURG	02/24/1854	NY		FILM
SCHWARTZMANN	ANTOINE	1809	WALHEIM	07/15/1852	MY		FILM
SCHWAUCH W 3CH	MARIE ANNE		OTTERSTHAL	01/01/1828	A		FILM
SCHWEGER	MARIE ANNE		UNTERACHERN B	06/01/1849	A		FILM
SCHWEHRER	ALOYSE	1817	HOLTZWILLER	03/24/1854	NY		FILM
SCHWEIGHOFEN	CHARLES	1815	MULHOUSE	04/23/1849	NY		FILM
SCHWEIN	JEANBAPTISTE	1835	GRUSSENHEIM	11/23/1854	NY		FILM

Lastname	Firstname	Birth Year	Birthplace	Emigration	De	Prof	231 Source
SCHWEIN W W 7CH	FRANCOI XAVIER	1807	GRUSSENHEIM	02/12/1953	A		FILM
SCHWEINSBERGER	SEBASTIAN		GEISWILLER	01/01/1752	A		SUESS
SCHWEISS	ANTOINE		STEINBACH B	05/27/1849	A		FILM
SCHWEITZER	GEORGES		INGENHEIM	01/01/1828	A		FILM
SCHWEITZER	GUILLAUME	1844	HELFRANTZKIRCHEN	10/02/1866	NY		FILM
SCHWEITZER	JACQUES		GEUDERTHEIM	03/01/1838	A		FILM
SCHWEITZER	JEAN		INGENHEIM	01/01/1828	A		FILM
SCHWEITZER	JEAN	1820	HESINGUE	02/18/1843	NY		FILM
SCHWEITZER F OF 2	JEAN GEORGES		INGENHEIM	01/01/1828	A		FILM
SCHWEITZER F OF 3	ANDRE		BISCHWILLER	03/02/1838	A		FILM
SCHWEITZER F OF 4	JEAN GEORGES		INGENHEIM	01/01/1828	A		FILM
SCHWEITZER F OF 5	JEANE JR		INGENHEIM	01/01/1828	A		FILM
SCHWEITZER W W 1CH	JEAN MARTIN		RIBEAUVILLE	09/22/1854	NO		FILM
SCHWEITZER W W 4CH	JOSEPH	1792	LIEPVRE	09/03/1849	NY		FILM
SCHWEITZER W W 4CH	LAURENT		HIRSCHLAND	03/20/1817	A		FILM
SCHWENDENMANN	ANDRE	1800	SENTHEIM	09/17/1844	NO		FILM
SCHWENDER	JEAN GEORGES		NIEDERBRONN	03/21/1817	A		FILM
SCHWENDER W W 1CH	JEAN GEORGES		NIEDERBRONN	03/29/1817	A		FILM
SCHWEYER	ETIENNE		NIEDERMODERN	01/01/1828	A		FILM
SCHWEYER	MARIE ANNE		UNTER ACHERN B	06/11/1849	A		FILM
SCHWEYER	MICHEL		NIEDERMODERN	01/01/1828	A		FILM
SCHWEYER	MICHEL		SCHILLERSDORF	01/01/1828	A		FILM
SCHWEYER	MICHEL	1843	MORSBRONN	01/01/1868	NY	WAMA	NO.2
SCHWEYER F OF 6	GEORGE		INGVILLER	01/01/1828	A		FILM
SCHWEYER S GEORG	PETER		FROESCHWILLER	01/01/1872	A		SUESS
SCHWIMMER	MAXIMILIAN	1829	HOCHSTATT	06/02/1853	NY		FILM
SCHWIND	SEVERIN		AUENHEIM B	05/03/1849	A		FILM
SCHWINDENHAMMER	JEAN	1821	LA CHAPELLE SOUS RE	02/05/1848	NY		FILM
SCHWISER	NIKOLAUS	1799	KIBURG	11/15/1846	TX		FILM
SCHWITZGAEBEL H PREF	G.J.	1788	ROPPENHEIM	/ /		HU	NO.1
SCHWOB	VICTOR	1832	MELISAY	10/16/1855	NO		FILM
SCHWOB W W 3CH	JOSEPH	1806	MANSPACH	03/29/1848	A		FILM
SCHWOEBBLE	JEAN GEORGE		BADEN	06/27/1833	A		FILM
SCHWOERER	EDOUARD		DURBACH B	05/11/1849	A		FILM
SCHWOG	CHARLES	1836	PFASTATT	03/15/1854	NY		FILM
SCHWUIER W 3CH	MICHEL		HERMERSWILLER	03/29/1817	A		FILM
SCKIEUR W W	ANDRE		DRUSENHEIM	03/24/1838	A		FILM
SEE	GUSTAVE	1821	RIBEAUVILLE	08/19/1850	CA		FILM
SEEBURGER	BLAISE	1831	GOENLINGEN W	08/02/1854	NY		FILM
SEEGER	GEORGE		GERMANY	04/01/1849	NY		FILM
SEEGMUELLER W W 3CH	SEBASTIEN	1823	BERGHEIM	10/11/1854	NY		FILM
SEGUIN	DAVID	1826	MULHOUSE	08/24/1847	SL		FILM
SEGWARTH	JACQUES	1829	FELLERINGEN	04/20/1852	PH		FILM
SEIBEL	GUILLAUME		BRUCKHEBEL	04/03/1849	NY		FILM
SEIBOLD F OF 2	FREDERIC		SESSENHEIM	02/23/1838	A		FILM
SEIBOLD F OF 2 SENIO	PHILIPPE		SESSENHEIM	02/23/1838	A		FILM
SEIBOLD JUNIOR F OF2	PHILIPPE		SESSENHEIM	02/23/1838	A		FILM
SEIGNIEU 2CH	MARIE ANNE		THANN	10/10/1845	NY		FILM
SEIHEL	GUILLAUME		BRUCHKEBEL	04/03/1849	NY		FILM
SEILE	FIDELE		HEMMENDORF	05/03/1849	NY		FILM

Lastname	Firstname	Birth Year	Birthplace	Emigration	De	Prof	Source
SEILER	BERNHARD		LEUTENHEIM	03/01/1838	A		FILM
SEILER	EDUARD	1824	ILLZACH	12/05/1849	NY		FILM
SEILER	JEAN GUILLAUME	1781	SARREBOURG	07/01/1859	SL		FILM
SEILER	MARIE ANNE		LEUTENHEIM	03/01/1838	A		FILM
SEILER	MICHEL		LEUTENHEIM	01/01/1838	A		FILM
SEILER F OF 7	MICHEL		WALDOWISHEIM	01/01/1828	A		FILM
SEILER W W 6 CH	JACQUES		PETITE PIERRE	03/11/1817	A		FILM
SEILLER	ANDRE	1813	ISSENHEIM	06/15/1849	NY		FILM
SEILLER	JEAN	1803	MASSEVAUX	04/01/1847	NY		FILM
SEILLER	JEAN BAPTISTE	1824	MASSEVAUX	04/01/1847	NY		FILM
SEILLER	JOSEPH	1830	WEGSCHEID	04/29/1852	A		FILM
SEILLER	SIMON NICOLAS	1830	KIRCHBERG	12/27/1853	NY		FILM
SEILLER W 3 CH	JEAN	1806	MASSEVAUX	03/31/1847	NY		FILM
SEITENZAHL	MADELAINE		BILLINGEN B	11/02/1849	A		FILM
SEITER	CATHERINA	1857	MOTHERN	01/01/1866	CI		NO.2
SEITER	ELISABETH	1866	MOTHERN	01/01/1866	CI		NO.2
SEITER	FREDERIC	1828	KANDEL BA	04/23/1849	NY		FILM
SEITER	JOHANN	1862	MOTHERN	01/01/1866	CI		NO.2
SEITER	MARGARARETHE	1859	MOTHERN	01/01/1869	CI		NO.2
SEITER MN ZIMMERMANN	MARGARETHE	1833	MOTHERN	01/01/1866	CI		NO.2
SEITER W W 4 CH	JOHANN	1826	MOTHERN	01/01/1866	CI		NO.2
SEITHER	JEAN BAPTISTE		FORT LOUIS	01/01/1828	A		FILM
SEITHER	JOSEPH		FORT LOUIS	01/01/1828	A		FILM
SEITZ	AMBROSIUS	1826	TRIEMBACH	01/01/1865	NY		NO.2
SEITZ	ANNA MARIA		REICHSHOFFEN	01/01/1865	NY		NO.2
SEITZ	GEORG	1799	RITTERSHOFEN	01/01/1865	NY	WOCA	NO.2
SEITZ	JOSEF		REICHSHOFFEN	01/01/1865	NY		NO.2
SEITZ	JOSEF	1858	RITTERSHOFEN	01/01/1865	NY	MILL	NO.2
SEITZ	MARIA ANNA	1847	LOBSANN	01/01/1867	NY		NO.2
SELIG MN RITZENTHALR	CATHERINE		JEBSHEIM	09/14/1857	NY		FILM
SELIG W FAMILY	JEAN	1821	JEBSHEIM	08/21/1854	NY		FILM
SELIG W W 2 S	MARTIN	1825	JEBSHEIM	09/14/1857	NY		FILM
SELINGER	AUGUSTE		STADELHOFEN B	07/29/1849	A		FILM
SELIS W W 2 CH	NICOLAS		VOLSBURG	03/06/1817	A		FILM
SELL	ELEANORE		ROTHENBURG	05/09/1849	NY		FILM
SELL	ELEANORE		ROTHENBURG	05/09/1849	NY		FILM
SELLET W 2CH	ANNE MARIE		REMINGUE	09/26/1854	NY		FILM
SELLET W W 5CH	MONRAD	1812	REININGUE	09/21/1854	NY		FILM
SELTER	JEAN		ETZINGEN W	05/30/1849	NY		FILM
SEMBACH	JEAN	1843	JEBSHEIM	07/04/1857	NY		FILM
SENDER	JOSEPH	1827	BURNHAUPT LE BAS	07/04/1855	NY		FILM
SENDER	SEBASTIEN	1832	BURNHAUPT LE BAS	03/06/1856	NY		FILM
SENDER	THIEBAUT	1835	BURNHAUPT LE BAS	06/03/1856	NY		FILM
SENDER MN BISANTZ	MARIE AGATHE	1806	BURNHAUPT LE BAS	02/18/1857	NY		FILM
SENDER W W 5 CH	JEAN JACQUES	1806	BURRHAUPT LE BAS	02/18/1857	NY		FILM
SENF F OF 5	JOSEPH		RASTADT B	04/27/1849	A		FILM
SENGEL	JEAN	1799	ST.MARIE AUX MINES	11/11/1841	NY		FILM
SENGELIN	JEAN	1825	GRENTZINGEN	10/22/1846	NY		FILM
SENGER	LISETTE	1827	ALTENSTADT	01/01/1869	NY		NO.2
SENGER	MARIA	1841	ALTENSTADT	01/01/1869	NY		NO.2

Lastname	Firstname	Birth Year	Birthplace	Emigration	De	Prof	Source
SENGER	MARTIN		ALTENSTADT	01/01/1869	NY		NO.2
SENN MN ADAM W 7CH	ANNE MARIE	1806	GRENTZINGEN	10/22/1846	NY		FILM
SENTER	GUILLAUME	1816	BURNHAUPT LE BAS	05/13/1839	NY		FILM
SEPTER W W 4CH	FORTUNE	1812	NIEDERMORSCHWILLER	06/21/1847	NY		FILM
SERBER	WIDOW	1798	KAYSERSBERG	08/20/1852	NO		FILM
SERENBETZ	LEOPOLD		ZELL B	09/23/1849	A		FILM
SERRE	MARGUERITE	1831	CHAUX	10/12/1852	SL		FILM
SERRE W W 2CH	JACQUES	1797	CHAUX	09/03/1852	NY		FILM
SERRE W W 2CH	VINCENT	1818	CHAUX	02/01/1854	NO		FILM
SESTER W W 3CH	IGNACE	1800	SCHWEIGHAUSEN	05/08/1846	OH		FILM
SETTET W W 5CH	MORAND	1813	REININGUE	09/21/1854	A		FILM
SETZ	JEAN	1825	PFASTATT	04/11/1853	NY		FILM
SEXAUER W W	GEORGES	1798	IRVINGEN	09/11/1851	NY		FILM
SEYREL	LOUISE	1825	BISCHWILLER	04/11/1857	NY		FILM
SIBRE	PROSPORE	1818	BESSONCOURT	10/22/1846	NY		FILM
SICH	JEAN GEORGE		DANNINGEN B	04/23/1849	A		FILM
SICHEL W W 2CH	FRANCOIS JOSEPH	1800	MEMMELSHOFFEN	04/22/1840	NY		FILM
SIEBENHOR	ROSE	1831	NIEDERENTZEN	09/01/1855	TX		PASS
SIEBENPFEIFFER F OF4	PHILIPPE		SIEWILLER	03/02/1838	A		FILM
SIEBER	ANNE MARIE	1839	MEMPRECHTSHOFEN	09/17/1845	TX		FILM
SIEBER	HEINRICH	1841	MEMPRECHTSHOFEN	09/17/1845	TX		FILM
SIEBER	JOHANN	1841	MEMPRECHTSHOFEN	09/17/1845	TX		FILM
SIEBER	JOHANNA MARIA	1845	MEMPRECHTSHOFEN	09/17/1845	TX		FILM
SIEBER	MARIANNE	1809	MEMPRECHTSHOFEN	09/17/1845	TX		FILM
SIEBER W W 4CH	JOHANN	1814	MEMPRECHTSHOFEN	09/17/1845	TX		FILM
SIEBERT	JOSEPH	1808	COLMAR	01/28/1852	NO		FILM
SIEBOLD	JEAN	1816	MAYHAUSEN W	08/07/1856	NY		FILM
SIEBOLD MN BRUN	MADELAINE	1817	MAYHAUSEN W	08/07/1856	NY		FILM
SIEFER F OF 9	MICHEL		IMBSHEIM	01/01/1828	A		FILM
SIEFERT F OF 6	GEORGE MICHEL		LEUTENHEIM	03/01/1838	A		FILM
SIEFERT F OF 8	JEAN		SCHALKENDORF	01/01/1828	A		FILM
SIEFFERMANN W W 1CH	LAURENT	1820	WILLER	04/14/1847	NY		FILM
SIEFFERT F OF 6	JOSEF		MARLENHEIM	01/01/1828	A		FILM
SIEFFERT W 2CH	ROSINE		SCHWABWILLER	03/22/1817	A		FILM
SIEGEL	CAROLINE		GERMANY	04/12/1849	NY		FILM
SIEGEL F OF 5	PIERRE		HIRSCHLAND	03/03/1838	A		FILM
SIEGENTHALER	CHRETIEN	1810	MITTELWIHR	05/09/1849	NY		FILM
SIEGFRIED W 4CH	ELISABETH		SCHIRRHOFFEN	07/27/1853	A		FILM
SIEGLE	CHRETIEN		LEONBERG W	08/17/1849	A		FILM
SIEGRIST F OF 2	PHILIPPE		SUNDHAUSEN	03/02/1837	A		FILM
SIEGRIST F OF 5	HENRI		SUNDHAUSEN	03/02/1837	A		FILM
SIEGRIST F OF 5	PHILIPPE		SUNDHAUSEN	03/02/1837	A		FILM
SIEGRIST F OF 6	GEORGE		SUNDHAUSEN	03/02/1837	A		FILM
SIEGRIST F OF 7	MATHIAS		SUNDHAUSEN	03/02/1837	A		FILM
SIEGRIST F OF 7	MICHEL		TIEFFENBACH	01/01/1828	A		FILM
SIELENHOR	ROSE	1831	NIEDERENTZEN	09/07/1855	TX		FILM
SIFFERLEN	EMERENCE	1840	KRUTH	09/01/1860	TX	SERV	PASS
SIFFERLEN	VENDELIN	1816	KRUTH	08/01/1860	TX	TISS	PASS
SIFFERLEN W JAKOB	AGATHE	1813	KRUTH	11/01/1855	TX	DAYL	PASS
SIGFREID	JOSEPH	1805	RIBEAUVILLE	07/14/1852	NY		FILM

Lastname	Firstname	Birth Year	Birthplace	Emigration	De	Prof	Source
SIGRIST	JEAN MICHEL	1814	BEBLENHEIM	03/17/1845	NY		FILM
SIGRIST	LEONARD		BURCKENWALD	01/01/1828	A		FILM
SIGRIST F OF 3	JOSEPH		BURCKENWALD	01/01/1828	A		FILM
SIGWALD	JULES		GERNSBACH B	08/09/1848	A		FILM
SIGWALD	LOUIS		GERNSBACH B	08/09/1849	A		FILM
SIGWALD	PHILIPPE		GERNSBACH B	08/09/1849	A		FILM
SIGWARTH	JACQUES	1829	FELLERINGEN	04/20/1852	PH		FILM
SIGWARTH	JEAN-JOSEPH	1800	FELLERING	10/01/1854	TX	BRLA	PASS
SIGWARTH W W D 2CH	JOSEPH	1800	WILDENSTEIN	10/20/1854	TX		FILM
SILBEIN W W 4CH	MICHEL		BISSERT	03/06/1817	A		FILM
SILBER	ANDRE		MULLENBACH	08/31/1849	A		FILM
SILBORIESEN	FREDERIC		BOUXWILLER	01/01/1828	A		FILM
SILET W W 1CH	JEAN FRANCOIS	1820	LABROQUE	08/02/1854	NY		FILM
SILNE W W 3CH	ALEXANDRE	1822	RUPPE	03/04/1847	NY		FILM
SIMAON	ANDRE	1826	BERGHOLTZ	02/01/1852	TX	FACT	PASS
SIMCKER W W 2CH	JEAN JACQUES	1805	RIQUEWIHR	11/29/1843	TX		FILM
SIMENDINGER	JOSEPH	1825	PFEFFERHAUSEN	03/10/1847	NY		FILM
SIMLER F OF 7	JOSEPH		SCHIRRHOF	01/13/1838	A		FILM
SIMMONDINGER W S	DOMINIQUE	1807	PFEFFERHAUSEN	11/03/1853	NY		FILM
SIMON	ALEXANDRE	1837	HUSSEREN	06/19/1854	A		FILM
SIMON	ANDRE	1826	BERGHOLTZ	02/19/1852	TX		FILM
SIMON	ANNA MARIA	1838	MOLLAU	11/22/1843	TX		FILM
SIMON	BAPTISTE	1832	MOLLAU	07/20/1854	A		FILM
SIMON	BENJAMIN	1826	RANSPACH	11/22/1843	TX		FILM
SIMON	FRANCOIS ANTOIN	1804	MOLLAU	08/28/1844	NY		FILM
SIMON	FRANCOIS-ANTOIN	1804	RANSPACH	08/01/1844	TX	BAKE	PASS
SIMON	GEORGES	1829	BERGHOLTZ	02/01/1854	TX	SERV	PASS
SIMON	GREGOR	1819	HUSSEREN	11/22/1843	TX		FILM
SIMON	JEAN	1823	RANSPACH	07/27/1853	NY		FILM
SIMON	JEAN BAPTISTE	1821	BERGHOLTZ	02/13/1854	NY		FILM
SIMON	JEAN BATPISTE	1812	BONHOMME	07/06/1852	TX		FILM
SIMON	JEAN-BAPTISTE	1822	ORSCHWIHR	02/01/1854	TX	FILE	PASS
SIMON	JOSEPH		UHLWILLER	03/03/1838	A		FILM
SIMON	JOSEPH	1835	GUEMAR	09/21/1855	NY		FILM
SIMON	MARIE	1837	ERETTE	10/02/1865	NY		FILM
SIMON	MARIE	1844	ERETTE	10/06/1865	NY		FILM
SIMON	MARIE ANNE	1830	EVETTE	10/06/1865	NY		FILM
SIMON	MARIE ANNE	1848	RANSPACH	07/27/1853	NY		FILM
SIMON	MARTIN	1831	HUSSEREN	08/09/1854	PH		FILM
SIMON	MICHAEL	1814	MOLLAU	11/22/1843	TX		FILM
SIMON	ROSALI	1842	MOLLAU	11/22/1843	TX		FILM
SIMON	ROSINE	1797	WEISSENBURG	01/01/1865	NY		NO.2
SIMON	ROSINE	1815	MOLLAU	11/22/1843	TX		FILM
SIMON	SILVESTER	1815	MOLLAU	11/22/1843	TX		FILM
SIMON F OF 8	GEORGES		BISCHWILLER	03/02/1838	A		FILM
SIMON MN KETTERLIN	MARIE LOUISE	1810	MICHELBACH LE BAS	12/13/1856	A		FILM
SIMON W BR AND D	EDUARD	1820	RANSPACH	07/27/1853	NY		FILM
SIMON W CH	MARIE ANNE	1820	ST AMARIN	08/11/1854	CA		FILM
SIMON W W 3CH	ANDRE		DIEBOLSHEIM	06/04/1817	A		FILM
SIMON W W 4CH	FRANCOIS	1793	PUIX	09/03/1852	NY		FILM

Lastname	Firstname	Birth Year	Birthplace	Emigration	De	Prof	Source
SIMONIN	FRANCOIS	1820	EGUENINGUE	05/20/1854	NY		FILM
SIMONIN	GEORGES	1823	RETZWILLER	10/30/1846	NY		FILM
SIMONIN	HILAIRE AMEDEE	1822	MOUTTIER	01/17/1852	NY		FILM
SIMONIN	MARIE	1845	CHENEBIER	01/14/1866	NY		FILM
SIMONIN	VICTOR	1839	CHAMPAGNEY	01/01/1839	NY		FILM
SIMONIS W W 1CH	IGNAZ		REICHSHOFFEN	03/28/1817			FILM
SINELE W M A SI	JEAN PIERRE	1833	COURTELEVANT	09/15/1855	NO		FILM
SINGER	JEAN BAPTISTE		SCHOENBURG	01/01/1828	A		FILM
SINGER W W	JEAN PIERRE	1820	BOURBACH LE BAS	03/02/1851	PH		FILM
SINGER W W 1 S	JEAN PIERRE	1777	SOULTZBACH	08/31/1844	A		FILM
SINGLE	JAQUES		NORTINGEN	05/12/1849	A		FILM
SINGRUN	JOSEPH	1801	RIXHEIM	09/01/1846	TX	DAYL	PASS
SININGER F OF 5	JOSEPH		STEINBOURG	01/01/1828	A		FILM
SINK	MARC	1828	BUTTENHEIM	10/19/1854	NY		FILM
SINN	FREDERIC		GEISINGEN W	05/12/1844	A		FILM
SINS F OF 5	ANTOINE		SIEWILLER	03/02/1838	A		FILM
SINSS W W	NICOLAS		WINGEN	01/01/1828	A		FILM
SINT W W 1CH	MICHEL		WEYER	03/23/1817	A		FILM
SIRFASS	CHARLES		MACKWILLER	03/03/1817	A		FILM
SITTER	ETIENNE		FORT LOUIS	01/01/1828	A		FILM
SITTER	JEAN	1813	WILLER	08/17/1843	NY		FILM
SITTER	JEAN VICTOIRE		FORT LOUIS	01/01/1828	A		FILM
SITTER	NICOLAS		BISSERT	01/01/1828	A		FILM
SITTERLE	ETIENNE	1824	BLODELSHEIM	10/01/1851	TX	SADD	PASS
SITTERLE	ETIENNE	1824	BLODELSHEIM	10/17/1851	TX		FILM
SITTERLEN W 4D 9S	AGATHE	1813	KRUTH	11/10/1855	TX		FILM
SITTERLEN W W 5CH	THIEBAUD	1800	GUEWENHEIM	02/16/1846	NY		FILM
SITTLER F OF 5	JACQUES		MUTTERSHOLTZ	04/05/1838	A		FILM
SITTRE W W 3 CH	JOSEPH	1806	BRETTEN	10/10/1844	NO		FILM
SLENTZEL W W	FRANCOIS		SAVERNE	03/31/1817	A		FILM
SLOEBER	MICHEL	1817	PFAFTENHEIM	08/19/1848	NY		FILM
SOEHNLEN	ADELE	1818	SENTHEIM	11/22/1843	TX		FILM
SOEHNLEN	LUDWIG	1825	SENTHEIM	11/22/1843	TX		FILM
SOEHNLEN	SEBASTIEN	1806	BOURBACH LE BAS	09/24/1845	NY		FILM
SOEHNLEN	THEOBALD	1824	SENTHEIM	11/22/1843	TX		FILM
SOENNLEN	THIEBAUD	1805	BOURBACH LE BAS	09/24/1845	NY		FILM
SOHM	THERESE		BERNOLSHEIM	03/03/1838	A		FILM
SOHN	BARBE	1821	MIETERSHEIM	03/02/1851	NO		FILM
SOHN	BARBE	1821	MIETERSHEIM	03/31/1848	NY		FILM
SOHN	JOHANN JACOB		MATTSTALL	01/01/1817	NY		NO.2
SOHN W W 3CH	JEAN JACQUES		MATTSTALL	03/11/1817	A		FILM
SOHN W W	IGNACE	1787	ROUFFACH	12/15/1845	A		FILM
SOHN W W 1CH	NICOLAS		WEISLINGEN	03/18/1817	A		FILM
SOHN W W 5 CH	JEAN JACQUES		MATTSTALL	03/11/1817	A		FILM
SOHNLE W W 2 CH	JOSEPH	1819	BRUEBACH LE BAS	09/03/1847	OH		FILM
SOLLINGER W W 2 CH	PIERRE		WINGEN	03/17/1817	A		FILM
SOMME	IGNACE	1819	SCHLESTADT	05/08/1841	NY		FILM
SOMMER	CHRETIEN		SELESTAT	02/22/1819	A		FILM
SOMMER	CHRETIEN	1827	ST.MARIE AUX MINES	10/20/1846	NY		FILM
SOMMER	JOSEPH	1817	SELESTAT	05/31/1841	NY		FILM

Lastname	Firstname	Birth Year	Birthplace	Emigration	De	Prof	Source
SOMMER F OF 10	JOSEPH		DOSSENHEIM	01/01/1828	A		FILM
SOMMER W W 1 CH	JEAN		NEHWILLER	03/11/1817	A		FILM
SOMMER W W 6CH	CHRETIEN		ERBOLSHEIM	03/01/1819	A		FILM
SOMMEREISEN W W 2 CH	JEAN BAPTISTE	1810	ROUFFACH	12/29/1842	A		FILM
SOMMEREISEN W W 2 CH	JOSEPH	1803	ROUFFACH	11/15/1843	A		FILM
SONET	ALEXIS EUGENE	1835	BEFALY	10/06/1854	NY		FILM
SONNET	JOSEPH THOMAS	1801	CERNAY	09/01/1854	NY		FILM
SONNSTAETT F OF 5	LOUIS		RYWILLER	01/01/1828	A		FILM
SONNTAG	JACOB	1845	LAUTERBURG	01/01/1867	A		NO.2
SONNTAG W W	ALEXIS	1809	BERRWILLER	03/30/1854	NY		FILM
SONTAG	ANDRE	1814	RAEDERSDORF	02/28/1852	NY		FILM
SONTAG W W 6CH	PIERRE		DEHLINGEN	03/03/1817	A		FILM
SORGINO	FREDERICH		INGWILLER	01/01/1828	A		FILM
SORGINO	HENRI		INGVILLER	01/01/1828	A		FILM
SORGINO	SOPHIE		INGVILLER	01/01/1828	A		FILM
SORGIUS F OF 8	GEORGE		SCHILLERSDORF	01/01/1828	A		FILM
SORVELET	CHARLES	1840	COURCHATON ? FRANCE	11/05/1866	NY		FILM
SORWENDEL	JOSEPH	1816	DURRENBACH	10/09/1846	NY		FILM
SOSENHEIMER	EVE	1820	BOMERSHEIM	03/03/1855	NY		FILM
SOTTER F OF 3	JOSEPH		HOCHFELDEN	01/01/1828	A		FILM
SOUDAIN	HENRI	1802	COURTELEVANT	09/11/1855	NO		FILM
SOUDRICKER W 3 CH	HENRY		DRACHENBRONN	03/28/1817	A		FILM
SOUGOFSQUI W W 2CH	JOSEPH		HIRSCHLAND	03/20/1817	A		FILM
SOULIER	NICOLAS		KESKASTEL	01/01/1817	A		FILM
SOULT	FRANCOIS XAVIER	1824	SENTHEIM	10/16/1855	NY		FILM
SOUX	MARIE	1853	SELTZ	01/01/1867	WA		NO.2
SPAALST F OF 6	JEAN		DETTWILLER	01/01/1828	A		FILM
SPAEDY CH 4	FRANCOIS JOSEPH	1810	NIEDERENTZEN	03/01/1849	TX	CULT	PASS
SPAN F OF 6	MARTIN		SIEWILLER	03/02/1838	A		FILM
SPANN W W 4 CH	MARTIN		PETERSBACH	03/17/1817	A		FILM
SPANY	URA		MERWILLIERS	04/09/1844	TX		FILM
SPECHER	GOTHARD	1850	KAPPELEN HAUT RHIN	08/03/1865	NY		FILM
SPECHT	ALEXANDRE		MARTENHEIM	01/01/1828	A		FILM
SPECHT	JAQUES		MARLENHEIM	01/01/1828	A		FILM
SPECHT	MARIE	1836	OSTHEIM	02/08/1856	NY		FILM
SPECHT	VALENTIN	1820	HEISSEREN	05/11/1844	NO		FILM
SPECHT F OF 7	FRANCOIS JOSEPH		MARLENHEIM	01/01/1828	A		FILM
SPECHT F OF 7	LAURENT		UHLWILLER	01/01/1828	A		FILM
SPECHT S GEORG	FRIEDRICH		HATTEN	01/01/1846	A		SUESS
SPECHT W W 2CH	MICHEL	1789	URBES	05/16/1845	NY		FILM
SPECHT W W 5 CH	DAVID	1808	OFTHEIM	03/19/1853	NY		FILM
SPECK	NICOLAS	1805	BITSCHWILLER	10/22/1845	NY		FILM
SPECKER	ROSINE	1841	KOPPELEN HAUT RHIN	08/03/1865	NY		FILM
SPEITEL	DOROTHEE		ROTHENBURG W	03/06/1838	A		FILM
SPENGLER	ELISABETH		ENGENTHAL	03/06/1838	A		FILM
SPENGLER	HUBERT		ENGENTHAL	03/06/1838	A		FILM
SPENGLER	JOSEF		ENGENTHAL	03/06/1838	A		FILM
SPENGLER	THERESE		ENGENTHAL	01/01/1828	A		FILM
SPENGLER W W 6 CH	PIERRE		ENGENTHAL	03/06/1838	A		FILM
SPENLE	MARIELOUISE	1806	RIQUEWIHR	03/25/1856	NY		FILM

Lastname	Firstname	Birth Year	Birthplace	Emigration	De	Prof	Source
SPENLE'	LOUISE	1838	RIQUEWIHR	03/25/1856	NY		FILM
SPENLINHAUER	ANDRE	1815	VIEUX FERRETTE	12/23/1845	NY		FILM
SPEOTET W W 2CH	MICHEL	1789	URBES	05/16/1848	NY		FILM
SPERR F OF 4	JACQUES		BRUMATH	01/01/1828	A		FILM
SPETTEL	JEAN BAPTISTE	1824	HEITEREN	09/14/1846	TX		FILM
SPETTEL	JOHANN BAPTISTE	1826	HEITEREN	11/15/1846	TX		FILM
SPETTEL	JOSEPH	1826	AMMERSCHWIHR	03/14/1853	NY		FILM
SPETTNAGEL	THERESE		KIGLINGSBERGEN	03/07/1849	NY		FILM
SPIELMANN	BARTHELEMY	1825	GROSSWALSTATT	05/10/1853	NY		FILM
SPIELMANN	WENDELIN		HOFSTETTEN	06/04/1849	A		FILM
SPIESS	FRANCOIS JOSEPH		ST.MARIE AUX MINES	04/13/1847	NO		FILM
SPINNER	FRANCOIS JOSEPH	1827	SOULTZMATT	11/15/1852	NY		FILM
SPOETTER W W	GUILLAUME	1813	ZERHAT	04/19/1853	NY		FILM
SPONY	AUGUSTE	1833	PFASTATT	01/23/1854	NY		FILM
SPONY	JACQUES	1827	GUNDOLSHEIM	09/19/1848	TX		FILM
SPONY	JAQUES	1827	GUNDOLSHEIM	09/01/1848	TX	GARD	PASS
SPONY	JEANNE	1827	LUTTERBACH	09/09/1854	NO		FILM
SPONY	THIEBAUD	1830	LUTTERBACH	04/07/1854	NY		FILM
SPONY MN BURGARD 2CH	ANASTASE	1797	LUTTERBACH	03/11/1854	NY		FILM
SPORTZ	CATHERINE		GERMANY	04/01/1849	NY		FILM
SPRATTLER	FRANCOIS JOSEPH	1816	GUEMAR	04/05/1843	NY		FILM
SPRATTLER W W 2 CH	ANTOINE	1806	GUEMAR	01/22/1839	NY		FILM
SPRATTLER W W 4 CH	ANTOINE	1776	GUEMAR	04/10/1839	NY		FILM
SPRENG	FREDERIC		SCHWEIGHAUSEN	01/01/1828	A		FILM
SPRENG	GEORGE FREDERIC		SCHWEIGHAUSEN	01/01/1828	A		FILM
SPRENG	MADELAINE		SCHWEIGHAUSEN	01/01/1828	A		FILM
SPRENG F OF 2	DOROTHEE		SCHWEIGHAUSEN	01/01/1828	A		FILM
SPRENG F OF 2	JACQUES		SCHWEIGHAUSEN	01/01/1828	A		FILM
SPRENG F OF 3	CHRETIEN		SCHWEIGHAUSEN	01/01/1828	A		FILM
SPRENG F OF 6	PHILIPPE GEORGE		SCHWEIGHAUSEN	01/01/1828	A		FILM
SPRENG F OF 8	CHRETIEN		SCHWEIGHAUSEN	01/01/1828	A		FILM
SPRENG W S	FREDERIC		SCHWEIGHAUSEN	01/01/1828	A		FILM
SPRING	GEORGE FREDERIC		SCHWEIGHAUSEN	01/01/1828	A		FILM
SPRINGER	PIERRE		RUNTZENHEIM	01/01/1828	A		FILM
SPRINGER W W	JEROME		ROESCHWOOG	03/14/1817	A		FILM
SPRINGINSFELD	ANTOINE	1828	FISLIS	08/14/1851	PH		FILM
SPUMER	FRANCOIS JOSEPH	1827	SOULTZ MATT	11/15/1852	NY		FILM
STAAT	JACQUES		DETTWILLER	01/01/1828	A		FILM
STAAT F OF 7	GEORGES		SCHWEIGHAUSEN	01/01/1828	A		FILM
STACKER	ANTOINE	1803	BERRWILLER	06/01/1852	TX		FILM
STACKLIN	JOSEPH	1826	GUEBWILLER	07/07/1849	NY		FILM
STADELMANN	JOSEPH	1834	ODEREN	11/01/1857	TX	FACT	PASS
STADLER	MARGUERITE	1816	ERNISHEIM	03/18/1850	NY		FILM
STADLER W W 1 CH	FREDERIC	1821	HUNAWIHR	11/11/1854	NY		FILM
STADTLER W W	JEAN	1825	LUTTERBACH	09/09/1854	NO		FILM
STAEBLER	JEAN BAPTISTE	1831	BOLLWILLER	07/11/1856	A		FILM
STAEBLER F OF 3	HENRY		GRIESHEIM	03/04/1838	A		FILM
STAEBLER W W 1 S 1D	BLAISE	1800	HARTMANNSWILLER	07/11/1856	A		FILM
STAEDEL	VENDELIN		HAGUENAU	03/01/1838	A		FILM
STAEMPFLE W 5 CH	JOSEPH	1803	BUREN	05/24/1845	A		FILM

Lastname	Firstname	Birth Year	Birthplace	Emigration	De	Prof	Source
STAEPZ W W CH	FREDERICK	1820	CAMBOURG	03/17/1853	NY		FILM
STAFFELBACH W W 1CH	IGNACE		BURNHAUPT LE BAS	05/23/1846	NY		FILM
STAHL	FRANCOI ANTOINE	1823	OTTROTT LE BAS	09/03/1857	NY		FILM
STAHL	FRANCOIS XAVIER	1810	ORSCHWIHR	12/01/1847	TX	VINT	PASS
STAHL	MAGDALENA	1847	STEINSELTZ	01/01/1869	NY		NO.2
STAHL	MARGUERITE	1794	STRASSBOURG	03/25/1846	NO		FILM
STAHL F OF 3	BARBE		GERSTHEIM	03/03/1838	A		FILM
STAHL F OF 3	JEAN		GERSTHEIM	03/03/1838	A		FILM
STAHL W W 1 CH	CHARLES		STRASSBOURG	02/23/1819	A		FILM
STAINACHRE	GEORGE	1827	EVETTE	10/06/1865	NY		FILM
STAINACHRE	GEORGE	1857	EVETTE	10/06/1865	NY		FILM
STAINACHRE	MARIE	1858	EVETTE	10/06/1865	NY		FILM
STALDER W F	JEAN	1826	ESCHOLZMATT SWISS	04/15/1853	NY		FILM
STAMBACH W W 2CH	GEORGES		MULHAUSEN	01/01/1828	A		FILM
STAMLER	GEORGE		EHENGEN ?	04/21/1849	NY		FILM
STAMMLER F OF 2	GEORGE		ECKARTSWILLER	01/01/1828	A		FILM
STAMMLER F OF 5	MARGUERITE		ECKARTSWILLER	01/01/1828	A		FILM
STANIMLER W W 1 CH	GEORGE		MACKWILLER	03/03/1817	A		FILM
STANISIERE	JEAN BAPTISTE	1826	LIEPRE	05/11/1846	NO		FILM
STANISIERE	MARGUERITE	1813	VALLEMAND ROMBACH	08/24/1838	NY		FILM
STANISIERES	JEAN JOSEPH	1822	LIEPRE	08/17/1847	NY		FILM
STARCK	GEORGES		HEMMENDORF W	05/03/1849	NY		FILM
STARCK	SALOME		HEMMENDORF	05/03/1849	NY		FILM
STARCK W W 7 CH	ADAM		LAHR	03/06/1817	A		FILM
STAUB	CATHERINE SALOM	1790	LANGENSOULTZBACH	03/14/1838	A		FILM
STAUB F OF 3	JACQUES		STRUTH	01/01/1828	A		FILM
STAUB F OF 5	JEAN		ZUTZENDORF	01/01/1828			FILM
STAUB W W 4 CH	NICOLAS		STRUTH	03/20/1817	A		FILM
STAUDESCHER	HENRI		KENTZINGEN	04/21/1849	A		FILM
STAUDESCHER	ROBERT		KENTZINGEN	04/21/1849	A		FILM
STAUFER	JACQUES	1825	ALTKIRCH	05/01/1860	NY		FILM
STAUFFEN	BENOIT	1859	LEYMEN	03/14/1866	A		FILM
STAUFFER	BABETTE	1848	LEYMEN	02/28/1866	NY		FILM
STAUFFER	BARBE	1819	ALTKIRCH	03/14/1866	NY		FILM
STAUFFER	BENJAMIN	1847	LEYMEN	02/28/1866	NY		FILM
STAUFFER	CHARLES JACQUES	1766	MORVILLERS	03/27/1844	NY		FILM
STAUFFER	CHRETIEN	1860	ALTKIRCH	03/14/1866	NY		FILM
STAUFFER	JACOBINE	1850	ALTKIRCH	03/14/1866	NY		FILM
STAUFFER	JACQUES	1852	LEYMEN	02/28/1866	NY		FILM
STAUFFER	JACQUES	1853	ALTKIRCH	03/14/1866	NY		FILM
STAUFFER	JEAN	1862	ALTKIRCH	03/14/1866	NY		FILM
STAUFFER	JOSEPH	1819	ALTKIRCH	04/05/1855	NY		FILM
STAUFFER	JOSEPH	1819	ALTKIRCH	10/11/1839	OH		FILM
STAUFFER	JOSEPH	1850	LEYMEN	02/28/1866	A		FILM
STAUFFER	JOSEPH	1856	ALTKIRCH	03/14/1866	NY		FILM
STAUFFER	VERONIQUE	1832	ALTKIRCH	03/14/1866	NY		FILM
STAUFFER W W 11 CH	JOSEPH	1819	ALTKIRCH	04/05/1855	NY		FILM
STAUFFER W W 7 CH	JOSEPH	1825	ALTKIRCH	03/14/1866	NY		FILM
STAUGERT	CHRISTOPH		SUNDHAUSEN	03/02/1837	A		FILM
STAUGERT	DANIEL		SUNDHAUSEN	03/02/1837	A		FILM

Lastname	Firstname	Birth Year	Birthplace	Emigration	De	Prof	Source
STEBER	MARIE ANNE	1825	PFAFFENHEIM	07/28/1854	A		FILM
STEBLEN	CATHERINE	1828	GUEWENHEIM	02/06/1852	NY		FILM
STECK	DAVID		GERMANY	04/12/1849	NY		FILM
STECK	JACOB		GERMANY	04/12/1849	NY		FILM
STECK	KARL	1837	NIEDERROEDERN	01/01/1867	NY	SHMA	NO.2
STEFFAN	ANTOINE	1834	MULHOUSE	01/30/1851	A		FILM
STEFFAN W W 3 CH	MATHIAS	1810	BENNWIHR	11/06/1850	NY		FILM
STEFFAN W W 3CH	BARBE	1806	BENNWIHR	11/06/1850	NY		FILM
STEFFANI	ANTOINE	1810	SCHAFFHAUSEN	11/07/1854	NY		FILM
STEFFANY W 1CH	FRANCOIS	1805	THANN	10/20/1846	A		FILM
STEGERT	ELISE	1829	DANNEMARIE	03/17/1866	NO		FILM
STEGHERK	JEAN	1823	ST CROIX AUX MINES	05/22/1855	NY		FILM
STEHLEN CH 1	ANTOINE		OLTINGUE	10/01/1844	TX	TAYL	PASS
STEHLIN	ALOYSE	1809	OELINGEN	09/24/1844	A		FILM
STEHLIN	ANTOINE	1798	OLTINGUE	10/08/1844	A		FILM
STEHLIN	MARIE URSULA	1829	LUTHER	05/04/1865	NY		FILM
STEHLIN W W	LUDGER	1833	LUTHER	05/04/1865	NY		FILM
STEHLIN W W 3 CH	MARTIN	1795	OLTINGUE	03/08/1844	NY		FILM
STEHLY	SEBASTIEN	1816	RIQUEWIHR	03/06/1855	NO		FILM
STEIBINGER	JEREMIAS		FREUDENSTADT W	10/15/1849	NY		FILM
STEIDEL	LOUISE		OBENHEIM	03/10/1838	A		FILM
STEIDEL MN BURGER	CATHERINA		OBENHEIM	03/10/1838	A		FILM
STEIL	WALBURGA	1841	RANSPACH	11/22/1843	TX		FILM
STEIMELIN	JOSEPH WENDELIN	1816	BALSCHWILLER	05/14/1847	NY		FILM
STEIN	HENRIETTE	1845	OBERLAUTERBACH	01/01/1866	NY		PRIV
STEIN	JAQUES	1847	OBERLAUTERBACH	01/01/1866	NY		PRIV
STEIN	MEINRAD	1821	FRIESSEN	03/25/1852	NO		FILM
STEIN F OF 5	MICHEL		HOCHFELDEN	01/01/1828	A		FILM
STEIN W W 2 CH	CHARLES		SOUFFLENHEIM	03/02/1838	A		FILM
STEINACKRE	GEORGE		ERETTE	10/06/1865	NY		FILM
STEINBACH	ADAM		ECKARTSWILLER	01/01/1828	A		FILM
STEINBACH	PHILLIPPE		WIMMENAU	01/01/1828	A		FILM
STEINBACH F OF 6	MARGUERITE		ECKARTSWILLER	01/01/1828	A		FILM
STEINER	ADAM	1829	KANDEL	04/23/1849	NY		FILM
STEINER	JOSEPH		PHILLIPSBURG	05/15/1849	A		FILM
STEINER	NANETTE		NIEDRHAUSEN B	04/05/1849	A		FILM
STEINLE	ERN		GERMANY	04/05/1849	NY		FILM
STEINMANN	FREDERIC	1803	MULHOUSE	11/24/1849	NO		FILM
STEINMELIN	JOSEPH WENDELIN	1816	BALSCHWILLER	05/14/1847	NY		FILM
STEINMETZ	JEAN		ETTENDORF	10/30/1854	A		FILM
STEINMETZ	MADELAINE		KILLSTEDT	05/28/1817	A		FILM
STEINMETZ	SALOME		WILWISHEIM	01/01/1828	A		FILM
STEINMETZ F OF 7	MARTIN		SCHIRRHEIN	03/05/1838	A		FILM
STEINMETZ F OF 8	ANTOINE		MINVERS	01/01/1828	A		FILM
STEINMETZ W W 6 CH	MATHIEU		ZINSWILLER	03/28/1817	A		FILM
STELL	GEORG	1844	HERMERSWEILER	01/01/1867		CARP	NO.2
STEMB	MARIE	1827	HOMBOURG	02/03/1852	NY		NO.2
STEMELEN	FRANCOIS JOSEPH	1816	UEBERKUMMEN	01/25/1847	NY		FILM
STEMLEN	IGNACE	1827	BELFORT	04/06/1863	NY		FILM
STEMMELEN	MATHIAS	1811	BALSCHWILLER	04/30/1850	NY		FILM

Lastname	Firstname	Birth Year	Birthplace	Emigration	De	Prof	Source
STEMMER	ODILE		WINVERSHEIM	01/01/1828	A		FILM
STEMMLER	ALBERTINE		ALBIRSBACH W	05/12/1849	A		FILM
STENG MN TREJEAN W S		1801	ETEIMBES	04/03/1847	NY		FILM
STENGEL	JEAN		REINHARDSMUNSTER	01/01/1828	A		FILM
STENGEL	MARTIN		REINHARDSMUNSTER	01/01/1828	A		FILM
STENGEL	MARX		REINHARSMUNSTER	01/01/1828	A		FILM
STENGEL F OF 4	ANTOINE		ST . JEAN DE CHOUX	01/01/1828	A		FILM
STENGER	MARTIN	1820	COLMAR	07/09/1851	NY		FILM
STENGER F OF 8	JEAN JACQUES		BOUXWILLER	01/01/1828	A		FILM
STEPHAN	CHARLES		LA PETIT PIERRE	01/01/1828	A		FILM
STEPHAN	JOHANN	1813	FELLERINGEN	11/22/1843	TX		FILM
STEPHAN	PHILIPPINE	1813	BERGHAUPTEN	07/25/1856	NY		FILM
STEPHAN F OF 2	JACQUES		SCHWEIGHAUSEN	01/01/1828	A		FILM
STEPHONIE	EMILE	1839	MULHOUSE	04/29/1853	NY		FILM
STERN	JACOB	1845	LAUTERBURG	01/01/1867	A		NO.2
STERN F OF 5	JACQUES		BOUXWILLER	01/01/1828	A		FILM
STICH	GEORGE		SESSENHEIM	02/23/1838	A		FILM
STICKER	LEONARD	1823	MATHAY	08/20/1853	NY		FILM
STIEFFEL	GEORGES	1828	MULHOUSE	06/18/1849	PH		FILM
STIER	MARIE ANNE	1829	UNGERSHEIM	11/10/1854	A		FILM
STIER W W AND F	DONAL	1819	UNGERSHEIM	11/10/1854	A		FILM
STILTZ	MARGUERITE		NEUHOFF PR	01/01/1851	A		FILM
STINTZY	CASPARD MATHIAS	1819	COLMAR	05/08/1847	NY		FILM
STINTZY MN HELDERE	CATHERINE	1832	COLMAR	10/05/1854	NY		FILM
STINTZY W W 5CH	MATHIAS	1793	COLMAR	09/20/1851	NY		FILM
STIQUEL	CONSTAN	1844	FRAHIER	09/29/1865	NY		FILM
STOBER	WILHELM		SPECK	04/13/1849	NY		FILM
STOBLEN W W 6CH	ALOYSE	1820	GUEWENHEIM	09/11/1851	NY		FILM
STOCK W W 6CH	PIERRE		KESKASTEL	01/01/1817	A		FILM
STOCKBURGER	CATHERINE		VORDEREN ROETHBERG	08/21/1849	A		FILM
STOCKER	ANTOINE	1803	BERRWILLER	06/01/1852	TX		FILM
STOCKER	ANTOINE	1821	BERRWILLER	06/01/1852	TX	CULT	PASS
STOCKER	EDOUARD	1844	MULHOUSE	08/31/1865	NY		FILM
STOCKI	JEAN BAPTISTE		BURCKENWALD	01/01/1828	A		FILM
STOEBER	ANTOINE	1819	PFAFFENHEIM	08/19/1848	NY		FILM
STOECHLIN	MORAND	1831	HAUSGAUEN	12/18/1850	NY		FILM
STOECKEL	ADAM		SCHOENBOURG	01/01/1828	A		FILM
STOECKEL	HENRI		SCHOENBOURG	01/01/1828	A		FILM
STOECKELEN	PIERRE	1812	SOPPE LE BAS	12/30/1839	NY		FILM
STOECKELI	LOUIS	1834	GUEBWILLER	06/27/1854	NY		FILM
STOECKLE	JACQUES	1816	SOPPE LE BAS	04/23/1838	NY		FILM
STOECKLEN W W 6CH	ANTOINE	1809	UBERKUEMMEN	02/22/1854	NY		FILM
STOECKLIN	JEAN	1829	HAUSGAUEN	09/28/1850	NY		FILM
STOECKLIN	JOSEPH	1826	GUEBWILLER	07/07/1849	NY		FILM
STOELTZEL	GEORG		HATTEN III	01/01/1835	A	CARP	SUESS
STOELTZEL S GEORG	HEINRICH		HATTEN III	01/01/1835	A		SUESS
STOESSEL	PIERRE	1833	ASPACH	03/22/1855	NY		FILM
STOFFEL	MARIE MADELAINE	1825	GUIMAR	04/25/1849	A		FILM
STOFFEL W W 2CH	ANDRE	1810	WIEDENSCHLEN	10/13/1838	NO		FILM
STOFFLER	JOHANN	1843	OBERLAUTERBACH	01/01/1865	NY		NO.2

Lastname	Firstname	Birth Year	Birthplace	Emigration	De	Prof	Source
STOLL	GEORGE		ROESCHWOOR OR WOOG	01/01/1828	A		FILM
STOLL W W	FRANCOIS THOMAS		ROESCHWOOG	03/14/1817	A		FILM
STOLL F OF 6	JACQUES		HOERDT	01/01/1828	A		FILM
STOLL F OF 7	MICHEL		HATTMATT	01/01/1828	A		FILM
STOLLE F OF 6	JOSEPH		LICHTENBERG	01/01/1828	A		FILM
STOLSER	MARTIN		GRIESHEIM B	10/11/1849	A		FILM
STOLSER	VICTORIA		GRIESHEIM B	10/11/1849	A		FILM
STOLTZ	ADAM		PETERSBACH	01/01/1828	A		FILM
STOLTZ	ANTON	1844	EBERBACH	01/01/1865	NY	FARM	PRIV
STOLTZ	JACQUES		KIRRVILLER	01/01/1828	A		FILM
STOLTZ	JEAN	1833	SIEGEN	12/24/1852	NY		FILM
STOLTZ	JOSEPH		NIEDERLAUTERBACH	01/01/1850	NO		PRIV
STOLTZ	MICHEL	1831	SIEGEN	12/24/1852	NY		FILM
STOLTZ	ROSINE		NEEWILLER	01/01/1850	NO		PRIV
STOLTZ F OF 7	JACQUES		DETTWILLER	01/01/1828	A		NO.2
STOLTZ MN BURGER 2CH	ELISABETH	1824	CERNAY	04/18/1855	NO		FILM
STOLTZ W 4CH	REGINA		GERMANY	04/12/1849	NY		FILM
STOLTZ W W	JEAN		GERMANY	04/12/1849	NY		FILM
STOLTZ W W 6 CH	IGNACE	1787	MASSEVAUX	04/24/1838	NY		FILM
STOLZ	JOSEF	1847	NIEDERLAUTERBACH	01/01/1865	NO		NO.2
STOLZ	MARIA ANNA	1843	NIEDERROEDERN	01/01/1866	NY		NO.2
STOLZ	ROSINA	1844	NEHWILLER	01/01/1866	NO		NO.2
STORCK	FLORENT		SALENTHAL	04/09/1853	A		FILM
STORCK	JEAN		DETTWILLER	01/01/1828	A		FILM
STOSKOPF	MICHEL		INGENHEIM	01/01/1828	A		FILM
STOSKOPF	VALENTIN		INGENHEIM	01/01/1828	A		FILM
STOUCKLEN	FRANCOIS		CERNAY	08/26/1854	NY		FILM
STOUCKLIN	MARTIN		HAISGAUEN	10/30/1851	NY		FILM
STOUFF	GEROME	1830	FLORIMONT	10/06/1865	NY		FILM
STOUFF	MARIE	1827	FLORIMONT	04/10/1855	NY		FILM
STOUFF W W 4CH	JEAN PIERRE	1786	FLORIMOT	06/25/1846	NY		FILM
STRACK	CHRISTOPHE		SOUFFLENHEIM	03/02/1838	A		FILM
STRACK	PIERRE		SOUFFLENHEIM	03/02/1838	A		FILM
STRACK W W 2 CH	PIERRE		SOUFFLENHEIM	01/01/1838	A		FILM
STRACK W W 2CH	IGNACE		SOUFFLENHEIM	03/02/1838	A		FILM
STRAMP	JACQUES		NIEDERHEIM B	04/23/1849	A		FILM
STRAMP	MICHEL		NIEDERHEIM B	04/23/1849	A		FILM
STRASSEL W 4CH	ANNE MARIE	1800	DORNACH	08/31/1838	A		FILM
STRASSER	KATHERINA	1816	HIRTZFELDEN	11/15/1846	TX		FILM
STRASSER	KATHERINA	1842	HIRTZFELDEN	11/15/1846	TX		FILM
STRASSER W W 1 CH	PAUL	1814	HIRTZFELDEN	11/15/1846	TX		FILM
STRATZ	LOUIS		SIMONSWALD B	08/21/1849	A		FILM
STRAUB	ANNE		ECKWESHEIM	03/01/1838	A		FILM
STRAUB	C		IMMENDINGEN	04/21/1849	NY		FILM
STRAUB	CATHERINE		DEGGINGEN W	06/04/1849	A		FILM
STRAUB	JOSEPH		DEGGINGEN W	06/04/1849	A		FILM
STRAUEL	SEBASTIEN ANTOI	1810	GRUSSENHEIM	10/25/1853	NY		FILM
STRAUEL	VIDALE	1825	GRUSSENHEIM	10/31/1853	NY		FILM
STRAUEL W WCH	FRANCOIS JOSEPH	1788	GRUSSENHEIM	06/09/1853	CH		FILM
STRAUS W 2 D	CATHERINE		SCHWENNINGEN W	05/24/1849	A		FILM

Lastname	Firstname	Birth Year	Birthplace	Emigration	De	Prof	Source
STRAUS W W 1CH	GEORGES	1828	NEUWILLER	08/30/1853	NY		FILM
STRAUSS	GUILLAUME		STUTTGARDT W	05/08/1849	A		FILM
STRAUSS	JACQUES		STUTTGARDT W	05/08/1849	A		FILM
STRAUSS	JEAN		NIEDERROEDERN	01/01/1866	NO		PRIV
STRAUSS	JOHANN	1845	NIEDERROEDERN	01/01/1867	NO	MERC	NO.2
STRAUSS	MOSES	1845	NIEDERROEDERN	01/01/1865	NY	MERC	NO.2
STRAUSS W W 2 CH A M	FRANCOIS	1817	NEUWILLER	10/23/1846	NY		FILM
STREHL	GEORGES	1811	BORGHEIM	03/09/1852	NO		FILM
STRICHER W W 5CH	PIERRE		STRASSBOURG	05/27/1817	A		FILM
STRIEBEL	GEORGE		REICHSHOFFEN	03/22/1817	A		FILM
STRIFF	FLORENT		MARMOUTIER	01/01/1828	A		FILM
STRIFFLER F OF 9	JACQUES		KIRRBERG	03/12/1838	A		FILM
STRINTZ	GEORGE		WEITERSWILLER	01/01/1828	A		FILM
STROBEL	FRANCOIS VICTOR	1830	ISSENHEIM	03/28/1854	NY		FILM
STROBEL	FREDERIC		GERMANY	04/12/1849	NY		FILM
STROBEL	GEORGES	1806	MULHAUSEN	08/10/1846	NO		FILM
STROBEL W F	FRANCOIS JOSEPH	1830	ISSENHEIM	06/08/1854	NY		FILM
STROBEL W W 6CH	IGNACE	1811	RIBEAUVILLE	08/06/1855	NO		FILM
STROEBEL	EDOUARD		KILPERTSAU B	09/28/1849	NY		FILM
STROEBEL	JOHANNA		HILPERTSAU	09/28/1849	NY		FILM
STROEBEL	MARTIN		HILPERTSAU	09/28/1849	NY		FILM
STROHHAECKER W W 5CH	FREDERIC		OBERHOFFEN	03/01/1838	A		FILM
STROHL	CHRETIEN		STRASSBOURG	06/11/1817	A		FILM
STROHMEYER	ELISABETH	1860	LEMBACH	01/01/1866	NY		NO.2
STROHMEYER	FREDERIC	1833	MULHOUSE	07/15/1857	NY		FILM
STROHMEYER	GEORG	1858	LEMBACH	01/01/1866	NY		NO.2
STROHMEYER	JACOB	1862	LEMBACH	01/01/1866	NY		NO.2
STROHMEYER	JOSEF	1864	LEMBACH	01/01/1866	NY		NO.2
STROHMEYER	MAGDALENA	1856	LEMBACH	01/01/1866	NY		NO.W
STROHMEYER H ANNE	F.J.		BURNHAUPT	09/15/1857	NY		FILM
STROHMEYER MN APRIL	MAGDALENA	1827	LEMBACH	01/01/1866	NY		NO.2
STROHMEYER MN WEISS	ANNE	1810	BURNHAUPT-LE-BAS	04/15/1857	NY		FILM
STROHMEYER W W 4CH	FRANCOIS JOSEPH	1813	BURNHAUPT-LE-BAS	04/15/1857	NY		FILM
STROHMEYER W W 5CH	FRANZ JOSEF	1810	LEMBACH	01/01/1866	NY		NO.2
STROHSCHNEIDER F OF2	CATHERINE		GEUDERHEIM	03/01/1838	A		FILM
STROSSER	ANTOINE	1826	HIRTZFELDEN	09/21/1846	TX		FILM
STROSSER	ANTON	1846	HIRTZFELDEN	11/15/1846	TX		FILM
STROSSER W 3 CH	THERESE	1800	HIRTZFELDEN	02/06/1850	A		FILM
STROSSER W W 1CH	PAUL	1813	HIRTZFELDEN	09/21/1846	TX		FILM
STROTTMEYER W W 7 CH	FRANCOIS JOSEPH	1792	BURNHAUPT-LE-BAS	11/12/1844	NY		FILM
STRUB	ANDRE		KERHOFFEN B	05/26/1844	NY		FILM
STRUB	ANNA		NERDINGEN B	10/12/1843	A		FILM
STRUB	FRANCOIS JOSEPH		GERSTHEIM	03/03/1838	A		FILM
STRUB F OF 4	MICHEL		ERNOLSHEIM	01/01/1828	A		FILM
STRUB W 1CH	CATHERINE	1826	HUSSEREN-LES-CHATEAX	09/18/1854	NO		FILM
STRUB W W 5CH	MICHEL		RIEDHEIM	01/01/1828	A		FILM
STRUBINGEN	CHRISOSTOMIUS		GERMANY	04/01/1849	NY		FILM
STRUBLER	FREDERIC		GERSTHEIM	03/03/1838	A		FILM
STRUBLER F OF 4	GEORGE		GERSTHEIM	03/03/1838	A		FILM
STRUBLER F OF 5	ANDRE		GERSTHEIM	03/03/1838	A		FILM

Lastname	Firstname	Birth Year	Birthplace	Emigration	De	Prof	Source
STRUDEL	CHARLES	1815	ILLHAEUSERN	04/03/1844	NY		FILM
STRUSSEL W W 2 CH	GEORGES	1832	WILDHOUSEN	10/06/1851	A		FILM
STUB F OF 5	ETIENNE		ECKARTSWILLER	01/01/1828	A		FILM
STUBEL	JOHANN	1839	ALTENSTADT	01/01/1869	NY	FARM	NO.2
STUBEL	MAGDALENA	1869	ALTENSTADT	01/01/1869	NY		NO.2
STUBEL	REGINA	1843	ALTENSTADT	01/01/1869	NY		NO.2
STUBER	ADAM		ASSWILLER	03/06/1838	A		FILM
STUBER	ADAM		WIMMENAU	01/01/1828	A		FILM
STUBER	JOSEPH		MUNICH	06/01/1849	A		FILM
STUBY F OF 7	JEAN		SCHIRRHEIM	03/05/1838	A		FILM
STUCKER	GEORGES	1824	RAMERSMATT	10/04/1844	NY		FILM
STUCKER	GEORGES	1832	OBERHERGHEIM	10/01/1848	TX		PASS
STUCKER W W 3 CH	THIEBAUD	1786	RAMMERSMATT	10/27/1845	NY		FILM
STUCKER W W 3CH	GEORGES	1824	RAMERSMATT	07/02/1846	NY		FILM
STUCKER W W 7CH	AMBROISE	1795	RAMERSMATT	07/02/1846	NY		FILM
STUCKI W W3 CH	CHRETIEN		STRASSBOURG	03/01/1819	A		FILM
STUCKY	JACQUES	1822	ALTKIRCH	01/22/1847	NY		FILM
STUCKY W 2CH	BARBE	1801	PFASTATT	06/24/1846	NY		FILM
STUCKY WW 5CH	NICOLAS	1789	STAFFELFELDEN	06/24/1846	NY		FILM
STUDER	GEORGES	1832	OBERHERGHEIM	10/20/1848	TX		FILM
STUDER	JOSEPH	1826	LINTHAL	03/11/1854	NY		FILM
STUDER	JOSEPH	1840	OBERHERGHEIM	11/15/1846	TX		FILM
STUDER	MICHEL	1836	OBERHERGHEIM	11/15/1846	TX		FILM
STUDER	THERESE	1807	OBERHERGHEIM	11/15/1846	TX		FILM
STUDER	XAVIER	1824	BOLLWILLER	03/18/1853	TX		FILM
STUDER W S A AUNT	CATHERINE	1813	BURNHAUPT	09/19/1839	NY		FILM
STUDER W W 2CH	GEORG	1804	OBERHERGHEIM	11/15/1846	TX		FILM
STUDER W W 2CH	GEORGES	1804	OBERHERGHEIM	09/14/1846	NY		FILM
STUDER W W A S	AIME	1816	OBERBRUECK	04/09/1847	NO		FILM
STUEPFLER	EMILE	1835	MULHOUSE	01/02/1854	NY		FILM
STUFFEL	GEORGES	1828	MULHOUSE	06/18/1849	PH		FILM
STUHL W W 1CH	CHARLES		STRASSBOURG	02/23/1819	A		FILM
STUHLINGER	JACQUES	1790	ALZEY	11/27/1845	NY		FILM
STUMELEN F OF 6	JEAN	1794	UBERKUMEN	03/21/1854	NY		FILM
STUMPF	AGATHE	1841	INGERSHEIM	08/25/1857	A		FILM
STUMPF	ANNE MARIE	1830	INGERSHEIM	08/25/1857	A		FILM
STUMPF	JOSEF	1827	INGERSHEIM	08/25/1857	A		FILM
STUMPF	JOSEPH	1837	INGERSHEIM	08/25/1857	A		FILM
STUPFEL	ADOLF	1860	MOTHERN	01/01/1867	NY		NO.2
STUPFEL	BENEDICT	1854	MOTHERN	01/01/1867	NY		NO.2
STUPFEL	CATHERINA	1852	MOTHERN	01/01/1867	NY		NO.2
STUPFEL	EVA	1858	MOTHERN	01/01/1867	NY		NO.2
STUPFEL	FRANZ ANTON	1866	MOTHERN	01/01/1867	NY		NO.2
STUPFEL	MAGDALENA	1862	MOTHERN	01/01/1867	NY		NO.2
STUPFEL 6 CH	MICHEL	1822	MOTHERN	01/01/1867	NY	FARM	NO.2
STUPFLER W W 4 CH	SIMON		DIEBOLSHEIM	06/04/1817	A		FILM
STURM	ANDRE	1834	OSTHEIM	01/17/1856	NY		FILM
STURM	ANNE MARIE		OSTHEIM	01/17/1856	NY		FILM
STURM	BENJAMIN		OSTEHIM	01/17/1856	NY		FILM
STURM	CAROLINE		OSTHEIM	01/17/1856	NY		FILM

Lastname	Firstname	Birth Year	Birthplace	Emigration	De	Prof	Source
STURM	CATHERINE		OSTHEIM	01/17/1856	NY		FILM
STURM	DAVID	1828	OSTHEIM	01/17/1856	NY		FILM
STURM	JEAN	1804	OSTEHIM	08/01/1854	NY		FILM
STURM	MARIE SALOME	1831	OSTHEIM	12/11/1855	NY		FILM
STURM W W 1 CH	JEAN	1825	OSTHEIM	03/03/1854	NY		FILM
STUTZ	JACQUEZ	1803	BEBLENHEIM	07/13/1847	A		FILM
STUTZ W W	DANIEL	1818	USTER	08/26/1854	NO		FILM
STUTZER	THERESE		BERNOLSHEIM	03/03/1838	A		FILM
STUTZMANN	CHRETIEN		STRUTH	01/01/1828	A		FILM
STUTZMANN	LOUIS		HERBITZHEIM	01/01/1828	A		FILM
STUTZMANN	MICHEL		TREFFENBACH	01/01/1828	A		FILM
STUTZER W PAULUS GEO	THERESE		BERNOLSHEIM	03/03/1838	A		FILM
SUCHER	FRANZISKA	1845	SURBOURG	01/01/1867	NY		NO.2
SUESS	GEORG		LANGENSOULTZBACH	01/01/0101	A		SUESS
SUESS	KARL		LANGENSOULTZBACH	01/01/1850	A		SUESS
SUESS D KARL	DOROTHEA		FROESCHWILLER	01/01/1857	A		SUESS
SUESS MNAME WEIMER	DOROTHEA		LANGENSOUTZBACH	01/01/0101	A		SUESS
SUESS S KARL	HEINRICH		FROESCHWILLER	01/01/1857	A		SUESS
SUHR W W 2CH	JEAN	1807	GUEMAR	03/17/1853	NY		FILM
SUISER	MICHEL	1826	OSTHEIM	12/14/1848	NY		FILM
SUISSE	JEAN	1826	ST.MARIE AUX MINES	10/23/1846	NY		FILM
SULTER	ARSIDA	1849	SWISS	06/30/1866	NY		FILM
SULTER	DESIRE	1866	SWISS	06/30/1866	NY		FILM
SULTER	JOSEPH	1808	SWISS	06/30/1866	NY		FILM
SULTER	JULES	1841	SWISS	07/01/1865	A		FILM
SULTER	JULES	1843	SWISS	05/04/1865	NY		FILM
SULTER	LOUIS	1837	SWISS	07/01/1865	A		FILM
SULTER	LOUIS	1849	SWISS	05/04/1865	NY		FILM
SULTER	MARIE	1808	SWISS	06/30/1866	NY		FILM
SULTER	MARIE	1845	SWISS	07/01/1865	A		FILM
SULTER	MARIE	1847	SWISS	05/04/1865	NY		FILM
SULZEN W W	LUCAS		KIGLINGSBERGEN	04/07/1849	NY	SL	FILM
SUMMELY W W 2CH	FRANCOIN	1800	LIEPVRE	11/08/1845	SL		FILM
SUMMER	JACQUES	1824	BALLERSDORF	11/21/1853	NY		FILM
SUTELL	BERNHARD	1852	OBERROEDERN	01/01/1868	NY		NO.2
SUTELL	ELISABETH		OBERROEDERN	01/01/1868	NY		NO.2
SUTELL	GEORG	1839	OBERROEDERN	01/01/1868	NY		NO.2
SUTELL	MARIANNE	1847	OBERROEDERN	01/01/1868	NY		NO.2
SUTHER	MARTIN	1828	ENSISHEIM	11/11/1851	NO		FILM
SUTTEL	JAKOB	1850	ALTENSTADT	01/01/1868	NY	BLSM	NO.2
SUTTER	ALOYSE	1819	BIEDERTHAL	05/10/1845	NY		FILM
SUTTER	ANDRE		ROESCHWOOG	01/01/1828	A		FILM
SUTTER	ANNE MARIE	1835	WINTZENHEIM	10/20/1853	A		FILM
SUTTER	BENOIT		RUNTZENHEIM	01/01/1828	A		FILM
SUTTER	FRANCOIS ANTOIN	1813	SENTHEIM	10/01/1851	TX	DAYL	PASS
SUTTER	HENRI	1836	BOERSCH	10/14/1854	NO		FILM
SUTTER	JACQUES		LEHR B	09/28/1849	NY		FILM
SUTTER	JACQUES		RUNTZENHEIM	01/01/1828	A		FILM
SUTTER	LEOPOLD	1829	WINTZENHEIM	03/16/1850	SL		FILM
SUTTER	LOUIS	1828	RIBAUVILLE	06/28/1855	NY		FILM

Lastname	Firstname	Birth Year	Birthplace	Emigration	De Prof	Source
SUTTER JUNIOR	JEAN		BRUMATH	01/01/1828	A	FILM
SUTTER MN WITT	ELISABETH	1810	SEPPOIS LE BAS	02/08/1854	PH	FILM
SUTTER SENIOR	JEAN		BRUMATH	01/01/1828	A	FILM
SYLVESTER	NICOLAS		LA PETIT PIERRE	03/03/1817	A	FILM
SYREM	NIKOLAS	1798	LAUTENBACHZELL	11/22/1843	TX	FILM
SZERLECKI	ARTHUR BOLESLAS	1838	MULHOUSE	10/01/1857	SF	FILM

Lastname	Firstname	Birth Year	Birthplace	Emigration	De	Prof	Source
TACQUARD W W 3CH	JAQUES	1804	VAUTHIERMONT	11/22/1844	NY	DAYL	FILM
TAHL	JOSEF		MORSCHWILLER	01/01/1828	A	FARM	PRIV
TALLEBACH	JAQUES	1828	SAINTE CROIX AUX MIN	10/19/1854	NO		FILM
TALLON	JOSEPHINE		SWISS	10/20/1864	NY		FILM
TALON D OF JOSEPHINE	JOSEPHINE	1857	SWISS	10/20/1864	NY		FILM
TANGER F OF 5	JACQUES		DOSSENHEIM	01/01/1828	A		FILM
TAUFLER	FRANCOIS		WINGEN	01/01/1817	A		FILM
TAUFLER	LAURENT		WINGEN	01/01/1817	A		FILM
TAUGER ? FAMILY OF 5	JAQUES		DOSSENEHIM	01/01/1828	A		FILM
TAUTSCH	FRANCOIS EUGENE	1830	ROUGEMONT	10/15/1844	NO	FARM	FILM
TAVERNIER	PIERRE FRANCOIS	1816	ST.GERMEIN	02/08/1843	NY	FARM	FILM
TAVERNIER W 2 CH	MARIE	1814	COEUVRE SWISS	03/28/1848	NY		FILM
TECK	ANTOINE	1819	VIEUX BRISACH	03/30/1847	NY		PRIV
TECKLER	XAVIER	1809	OFFEMAUT	11/15/1847	TX		PRIV
TECKRE W W 3 CH	NICOLAS	1801	CHAVANNES LES GRANDS	02/25/1845	NY	FARM	FILM
TELTER	JEAN		ETZINGEN? ESSINGEN W	05/30/1849	NY		FILM
TENDRE	CONRAD	1826	ETEIMBES	05/07/1846	NY		FILM
TENKEN	HENRY	1826	CHAVANNE SUR LéTANG	09/03/1850	NO		FARM
TENKEUL	HENRY	1826	CHEVANNE SUR LéTANG	09/03/1850	NO	FARM	FILM
TENN W 7CH	MARIE ANNE	1806	SIGOLSHEIM	09/23/1850	A		FILM
TENNETTE	LEOPOLD	1798	LIEPRE	04/23/1838	NO		FARM
TEUFEL F OF 6	GEORGE		HERLITZHEIM	01/01/1828	A	DAYL	FILM
TEUTAIN MN KRUG	ROSALIE		COLMAR	/ /	A		FILM
TEUTCH W W	PIERRE		MIETESHEIM	01/16/1838	A		FILM
TEUTSCH	BARBE		MIETESHEIM	01/16/1838	NY		FILM
TEUTSCH	MARGARETHE		MIETESHEIM	01/16/1838	NY		FILM
TEUTSCH	MICHEL		MIETESHEIM	01/16/1838	NY		FILM
TEUTSCH	PIERRE		MIETESHEIM	01/16/1838	NY		FILM
TEUTSCH	SALOME		MIETESHEIM	01/16/1838	NY		FILM
TEUTSCH MN STAUB	MARIE		MIETESHEIM	01/16/1838	NY		FILM
TEUTSCH MN STAUB	MARIE		MIETESHEIM	06/01/1838	A		FILM
TEUTSCH W W 6 CH	PIERRE		MIETESHEIM	01/16/1838	NY		FILM
TEXTOR	CHRETIEN		BURBACH	03/02/1838	A		FILM
TEXTOR	HENRI		BURBACH	03/02/1838	A		FILM
TEXTOR	MARGERITE		BURBACH	03/02/1838	A		FILM
TEXTOR	NICOLAS		BURBACH	03/02/1838	A		FILM
TEXTOR	PIERRE		BURBACH	03/02/1838	A		FILM
THAL	JOSEPH		MORSCHWILLER	01/01/1828	A	FARM	FILM
THALL 1CH	CHRISTINE		FROHMUHL	03/06/1817	A		FILM
THALLINGER	JEAN	1825	MUTTERHOLTZ BAS RHIN	06/15/1857	NY		FILM
THALMANN H CATHERIN	FRIEDRICH		NEHWEILER	/ /			SUESS
THALMANN MN DUERRENB	CATHERINA		HATTEN	/ /	A		SUESS
THANANN	JOSEPH	1837	OSTHEIM	05/20/1854	NY		FILM
THANNBERGER	LOUIS OCTAVE	1839	COLMAR	06/01/1857	SL		FILM
THANNBERGER W W 3CH	LOUIS	1805	ALTKIRCH	10/10/1850	SL		FILM
THAUMANN	JOSEPH	1837	OSTHEIM	05/20/1854	NY		FILM
THEOBALT FAMILY OF 6	PHILLIPPE		NEUWILLER	01/01/1828	A		FILM
THIEBAUT	BARBE M	1813	VALDOIS	02/21/1857	NY		FILM
THIENAUN	MARIE ANNA	1834	BERGHEIM	03/21/1854	NY		FILM
THIERING W W 4CH	PIERRE	1816	BELFORT	04/19/1847	NY		FILM

Lastname	Firstname	Birth Year	Birthplace	Emigration	De	Prof	Source
THIERRY	FRAN.XAVIER	1841	BELFORT	12/18/1865	NY		FILM
THIERRY	JAQUES	1828	MULHOUSE	03/24/1848	NY	MECH	FILM
THINAU	MARIE ANNE	1834	BERGHEIM	03/21/1854	NY		FILM
THIRIAN	THERES	1832	BERGHEIM	03/09/1853	A		FILM
THIRIET	JEAN JOSEPH	1822	ST MARIE AUX MINES	03/10/1848	NO		FILM
THOENY W W	GREGOIRE	1817	BARTHOLOMEBERG AUTRC	02/12/1852	NY		FILM
THOMAN	JEAN	1822	INGERSHEIM	02/14/1857	NY		FILM
THOMANN	ANTOINE		DAUENDORF	01/01/1828	A		FILM
THOMANN	CLEMENT	1837	OSTHEIM	02/27/1846	NY	DAYL	FILM
THOMANN	FRANCOIS	1800	WIEDENSOHLEN	08/09/1837	NO	SHMA	FILM
THOMANN	FRANCOIS XAVIER		WIEDENSOHLEN	08/09/1837	NO		FILM
THOMANN	JAQUES FRANCOIS	1800	GUEVENATTEN HAUT RHN	06/09/1856	A		FILM
THOMANN	JEAN BAPTISE	1817	HERRLISHEIM	03/09/1852	NY	FARM	FILM
THOMANN	LAURENT	1825	INGERSHEIM	11/26/1851	NO		FILM
THOMANN	MATHIEU	1826	INGERSHEIM	01/10/1853	NO	WINE	FILM
THOMANN	SAMUEL	1834	MULHOUSE	04/18/1855	A	BUTC	FILM
THOMANN W W 5CH	JEAN	1815	AMMERSCHWIHR	10/27/1854	A	WINE	FILM
THOMANN W W 2 CH	JAQUES FRANCOIS	1800	GUEVENATTEN HAUT RHN	06/25/1856	NY	GEOM	FILM
THOMANN W W 2 CH	XAVIER	1815	OFTEIM	04/01/1855	NY	DAYL	FILM
THOMANN W W 4 CH	GEORGES	1820	INGERSHEIM	04/18/1855	NO	WINE	FILM
THOMANN W W 5 CH	JEAN	1815	AMMERSCHWIR	10/27/1854	BL	WINE	FILM
THOMAS	CAROLINE	1865	SIEGEN	01/01/1869	NY		NO.2
THOMAS	JACOB	1853	ALTENSTEIG	01/01/1868	NY		NO.2
THOMAS	JEAN BAPTISTE	1813	ST.CROIX AUX MINES	03/09/1849	NO		FILM
THOMAS	JOSEPH	1838	KAIDENBURG	01/01/1866	NY	FARM	NO.2
THOMAS	KARL		LANGENSOULTZBACH	01/01/1865	A		SUESS
THOMAS	KATHERINA	1849	ALTENSTADT	01/01/1868	NY		NO.2
THOMAS	MARGARETHE	1832	SIEGEN	01/01/1869	NY		NO.2
THOMAS	MICHEL		BALBRONN	01/01/1828	A		FILM
THOMAS FAMILY OF 5	MICHEL		BATHRONN	01/01/1828	A		FILM
THOMAS MN ZUBER	MARIE	1820	MULHOUSE	03/03/1856	NY		FILM
THOMAS W W	JEAN	1827	LUTTERBACH	05/01/1849	NY		FILM
THOMAS W W 1CH	MICHEL	1811	SCHIRMICH? VOSGES	10/16/1839	NY		FILM
THOMAS W W 4 CH	JEAN PIERRE	1810	PFASTATT	04/29/1847	SL	LAYB	FILM
THOMEN	ANTOINE		SOUFFLENHEIM	01/01/1828	A	FARM	FILM
THOMEN	IGNACE		SOUFFLENHEIM	01/01/1828	A	WEAV	FILM
THOMEN	ROSINE		SOUFFLENHEIM	01/01/1828	A		FILM
THORN	GEORGES	1830	BARTENSTEIN W	03/11/1854	NY		FILM
THORNY W W	GREGOIRE	1817	BARTHOLOMSBERG AUTRI	02/12/1852	NY		FILM
THORU	GEORGES	1830	BARTENSTEIN W	03/11/1854	NY		FILM
THRO	EMILE	1833	MOLLAU	01/09/1849	A		FILM
THRO	FRANCOISE	1830	URBAS	12/18/1852	NO		FILM
THRO	GASPARD	1835	MOLLAU	01/19/1850	A		FILM
THRO	JEAN BAPTISTE	1836	MOLLAU	08/25/1854	A	LAYB	FILM
THRO MN RIETMILLER	MARIANNE W 2CH	1809	LAUTENBACH ZELL	10/19/1854	A		FILM
THRO W CH	FRANCOISE	1812	URBAS	03/10/1842	NO		FILM
THUET	FRANCOIS LOUIS	1839	MEYENHEIM	10/01/1851	TX	BAKE	PASS
THUET	FRANCOIS LOUIS	1831	MAYEN HEIM	10/21/1851	TX	BAKE	FILM
THUET	GEORGES	1820	GUNDOLSHEIM	03/13/1849	NO	SERR	FILM
THUET	JOSEPH	1818	GUNDOLSHEIM	11/01/1843	TX	SERR	PASS

Lastname	Firstname	Birth Year	Birthplace	Emigration	De	Prof	Source
THUET	JOSEPH	1818	GUNDOLSHEIM	11/24/1843	TX	SERR	FILM
THUET W W 1 CH F M	GEORGES	1821	GUNDOLSHEIM	01/09/1851	NO		FILM
THURIN	ALEXANDRE JULE		ST.GERMAIN	11/29/1853	NY		FILM
TIEFENWIRTH	CATHERINE MADE	1813	ZINSWILLER	02/16/1817	A		FILM
TIEFENWIRTH	PHILIPPE	1776	ZINSWEILLER	02/16/1817	A		FILM
TIEFENWIRTH	PHILLIPE HENRY	1811	ZINSWILLER	02/16/1817	A		FILM
TIEFENWIRTH	SALOME	1816	ZINSWILLER	02/16/1817	A		FILM
TIEFENWIRTH W W 3CH	PHILLIPPE		ZINSWILLER	01/01/1817	A	TAIL	FILM
TILGER	PAUL JULES	1821	ULM W	12/08/1853	SL	PHAM	PRIV
TINCKER	JEAN JAQUES	1805	RIQUEWIHR	11/29/1843	A		FILM
TISCHER	ANDRE		KESKASTEL ?	01/01/1828	A	FARM	FILM
TISCHER	CATHARINE		KESKASTEL?	01/01/1828	A		FILM
TISSERAND	HENRI	1820	CRAVANCHE TERR. BELF	12/23/1850	NY	LAYB	FILM
TITUS	SIMON	1826	MOLLAU	09/21/1849	A		FILM
TOCHANN	FRANCOIS JOSEPH	1832	SOULTZ	03/16/1852	NY	FARM	FILM
TOCK	ANTOINE	1819	VIEUX BRISACH	03/30/1847	NY		FILM
TOCKLER	XAVIER	1811	CERNAY	11/01/1846	TX	JOIN	PASS
TOEGEL	FERDINAND		EDLINGEN B	09/01/1849	A		FILM
TOERGEL	VALENTIN	1835	MUNCHHOUSE	01/01/1867	NY		NO.2
TOLTZ	JOSEPH		BOUXWILLER	04/22/1847	NY	FARM	FILM
TOLY	THERESE	1844	FRAHIER ?	04/06/1866	NY	FARM	FILM
TONDRE	CONRAD	1826	ETEIMBES	05/07/1846	NY		FILM
TONDRE	GEORGES	1802	ETEIMBES	03/19/1847	NY		FILM
TONDRE	GEORGES	1827	ETEIMBES	05/02/1846	NY		FILM
TONDRE	GEORGES	1827	ETEIMBES	05/02/1846	NY		FILM
TONHEUL	HENRY	1826	CHAVANNE-SUR-L`ETANG	09/03/1850	NO		FILM
TONNENWIRTH	JEAN		BRUMATH	01/01/1828	A		FILM
TORETAN	THERESE W BATOT			06/01/1846	TX		PASS
TOSNER	WILHELM		HEIDELBERG	06/01/1849	A		FILM
TOTANS	FRAMCOIS	1810	LONGEVILLE	02/14/1855	NY		FILM
TOTANS	PIERRE	1833	GRANDVILLERS	02/03/1851	CH		FILM
TOUPOURE	JUSTIN	1845	FRAHIER	02/08/1866	NY		FILM
TOURET	FRANCOIS	1828	FERETTE	01/27/1847	NY		FILM
TOURNEUR AND CH	CATHERINE	1805	LALLEMAND RAMBACH	01/13/1857	NO		FILM
TOURNIER	CHARLES BENOIT	1830	MULHOUSE	03/12/1852	NY		FILM
TOURNIER	CLAUDE FRANCOIS	1822	AUXELLES HAUT	10/09/1850	NO		FILM
TOURNIER	EUGENE	1836	EGUENIGUE	05/15/1854	NO		FILM
TOURNIER	MARIE THERESE	1819	AUXELLES HAUT	10/01/1851	NO		FILM
TOURNIER	PIERRE FRANCOIS	1829	EGUENIGUE	03/08/1851	NO		FILM
TOUSSAINT	ADELE	1841	MULHOUSE	07/15/1857	NY		FILM
TOUSSAINT	BARBARA	1845	MULHOUSE	07/15/1857	NY		FILM
TOUSSAINT	EMILE	1843	MULHOUSE	07/15/1857	NY		FILM
TOUSSAINT	JEAN BAPTISTE	1812	BADONVILLER	04/13/1849	NO		FILM
TOUSSAINT	JEAN BAPTISTE	1830	ST CROIX AUX MINES	10/14/1854	NY		FILM
TOUSSAINT	JULES	1840	MULHOUSE	07/15/1857	NY		FILM
TOUSSAINT	MARGUERITE		BURBACH	03/02/1838	A		FILM
TOUSSAINT WW AND CH5	JAQUES		WEYER	03/03/1817	A		FILM
TOUZOUNE	JUSTIN	1845	FRAHIER	02/08/1866	NY		FILM
TRABER D JOSEPH	WILHELMINE	1839	HOMBURG	10/25/1843	TX		FILM
TRABER S JOSEPH	DAGOBERT	1840	HOMBURG	10/25/1843	TX		FILM

Lastname	Firstname	Birth Year	Birthplace	Emigration	De	Prof	Source
TRABER S JOSEPH	JOSEPH	1834	HOMBURG	10/25/1843	TX		FILM
TRABER W JOSEPH	MARIE ELISABETH	1809	HOMBURG	10/25/1843	TX		FILM
TRABER WW AND CH 3	JOSEPH	1803	HOMBURG	10/25/1843	TX		FILM
TRAIN	THERESE	1788	PEROUSE	07/24/1852	NY		FILM
TRAISTE	MARIE ANNE	1773	ZINSWEILLER	02/16/1817	A		FILM
TRANDLE	EDOUARD	1827	MULHOUSE	07/01/1847	NY		FILM
TRARALTER	JOSEPH	1796	OBERENTZEN	09/10/1851	TX		FILM
TRARALTER	JOSEPH	1828	OBERENTZEN	09/14/1846	TX		FILM
TRARALTER	NICOLAS	1830	OBERENTZEN	11/04/1848	TX		FILM
TRARALTER CH 7	MARIE AGATHE	1805	OBERENTZEN	03/12/1851	TX		FILM
TRAUT	JOSEPH		ZINSWEILLER	10/15/1826	OH		FILM
TRAUTE D JOSEPH	CATHERINE		ZINSWEILLER	02/16/1817	A		FILM
TRAUTE D JOSEPH	CHARLOTTE	1810	ZINSWEILLER	02/16/1817	A		FILM
TRAUTE D JOSEPH	MARIE ANNE	1816	ZINSWEILLER	02/16/1817	A		FILM
TRAUTE H MARIE	JOSEPH	1787	ZINSWEILLER	02/16/1817	A		FILM
TRAUTH W MULLER LAUR	FRANCOISE	1784	ZINSWEILLER	02/16/1817	A		FILM
TRAUTMANN	CAROLINE	1841	STEINSELTZ	01/01/1869	NY		NO.2
TRAUTMANN	DANIEL	1841	MATTSTALL	01/01/1864	NY		NO.2
TRAUTMANN	JACOB	1848	KUTZENHAUSEN	01/01/1865	NY	FARM	NO.2
TRAUTMANN	ROSALIE	1844	KUTZENHAUSEN	01/01/1865	NY		NO.2
TRAUTTMANN	GASPARD		AUTRICHE	03/23/1817	A		FILM
TRAWALTER	JOSEPH	1796	OBERENTZEN	03/01/1851	TX	CULT	PASS
TRAWALTER	JOSEPH	1828	OBERENTZEN	09/01/1846	TX	DAYL	PASS
TRAWALTER	NICOLAS	1830	OBERENTZEN	11/01/1848	TX	SALK	PASS
TRAWALTER CH 7	MARIE AGATHE	1805	OBERENTZEN	11/01/1851	TX	DAYL	PASS
TRAX	LOUIS		SCHILTIGHEIM	03/03/1817	A		FILM
TREIBER	BONIFACE	1802	BURNHAUPT-HAUT	05/04/1840	NY		FILM
TREIER	JOSEPH		BACKNANG	07/30/1849	A		FILM
TREJAN CH 1		1801	ETEIMBES	04/03/1847	NY		FILM
TRESCH	VINCENT	1819	SOPPE-LE-BAS	08/18/1848	NY		FILM
TRESCH CH 3	MADELEINE	1812	HERICOURT	03/19/1845	NY		FILM
TRIBIS	CHARLES	1803	WASSELONNE	04/23/1840	NY		FILM
TRIEZ	JAQUES	1829	CERNAY	07/22/1852	NY		FILM
TRIGLER	BARTHELEMI	1825	RUSTENHART	09/21/1846	TX		FILM
TRIMBAR	ANDRE			03/18/1817	A		FILM
TRIMBUR	ANDRE		BURBACH	03/18/1817	A		FILM
TRINCANO	MARIE ELISE AUR	1833	PORRENTRUY	03/19/1856	NY		FILM
TRIPONE	FRANCOIS JOSEPH	1803	BELFORT	10/27/1854	A		FILM
TRIPONEZ	AUGUSTE	1829	DENNEY	11/02/1863	NY		FILM
TRISEL	NICOLAS POLUNAI		ESCHBOURG	03/03/1817	A		FILM
TRITZ	ADAM		ADAMSWILLER	02/27/1838	A		FILM
TRITZ	LOUIS		ADAMSWILLER	02/27/1838	A		FILM
TROCKENMILLER	ALLENDE		OBERNDORF	06/21/1849	A		FILM
TROELLER	GEORGES	1825	MITTELWIHR	04/21/1854	NY		FILM
TROELLER	HENRI	1821	MITTLACH	05/24/1850	NY		FILM
TROG	MADELEINE		WEINBOURG	01/01/1828	A		FILM
TROG H RECH M.B.	DIEBOLD		PREUSCHDORF	01/01/1721	A		SUESS
TROG MN RECH	MARIA BARBARA		PREUSCHDORF	01/01/1721	A		SUESS
TROMANN	ANTOINE		DAUENDORF	01/01/1828	A	TURN	FILM
TROMPETTER	JOSEPH		DETTWILLER	01/01/1828	A		FILM

Lastname	Firstname	Birth Year	Birthplace	Emigration	De	Prof	Source
TROMTER	ANDREAS	1848	WINTZENBACH	01/01/1864	NY		NO.2
TROMTER	CAROLINE	1843	WINTZENBACH	01/01/1864	NY		NO.2
TROMTER	CATHARINA	1845	WINTZENBACH	01/01/1864	NY		NO.2
TROMTER	VALENTIN	1851	WINTZENBACH	01/01/1865	NY		NO.2
TROMTER MN SIPP	CATHARINA	1813	WINTZENBACH	01/01/1864	NY		NO.2
TROMTER W W 4CH	ANDREAS	1813	WINTZENBACH	01/01/1864	NY	FARM	NO.2
TROSCHLER	ALBERT	1830	MULHOUSE	08/02/1854	NY		FILM
TROY CH 1	CATHERINE	1827	MORVILLARS	10/11/1855	NY		FILM
TRSTELA CH 2	MARIE ANNE	1824	SERMAMAGNY	06/28/1850	NY		FILM
TRTHAST	JEAN JAQUES	1824	MULHOUSE	08/30/1180	NY		FILM
TRUETH	FRANCOIS ANTOIN		ROESCHWOOG	01/01/1828	A		FILM
TRUTSCH	BARBE		MIETESHEIM	01/16/1838	NY		FILM
TRUTSCH D OF PIERRE	MARGERITE		MIETESHEIM	06/16/1838	NY		FILM
TRUTSCH D OF PIERRE	SALOME		MIETESHEIM	01/16/1838	NY		FILM
TRUTSCH S OF PIERRE	MICHEL		MIETESHEIM	01/16/1838	NY		FILM
TRUTSCH S OF PIERRE	PIERRE		MIETESHEIM	01/16/1838	NY		FILM
TRUTSCH W OF PIERRE	MARIE		MIETESHEIM	01/16/1838	NY		FILM
TRUTSCH W W 4 CH	PIERRE	1795	MIETESHEIM	01/16/1838	NY	FARM	FILM
TSCHAGLE	JOSEPH	1832	ST. AMARIN	08/22/1854	NO		FILM
TSCHAINE	JOSEPH DAMIEN	1810	ST. COSME	03/19/1838	NY		FILM
TSCHAN	ANTOINE	1828	HIRSINGEN	04/23/1857	NY		FILM
TSCHANN	FRANCOISE	1825	FELDKIRCH	01/29/1849	NY		FILM
TSCHANTZ	PIERRE	1828	BOLLWILLER	01/13/1851	NY		FILM
TSCHANTZ WW	PIERRE	1809	ALTKIRCH	04/15/1854	A		FILM
TSCHAUN WW AND CH 4	JEAN	1788	SOPPE-LE-BAS	10/15/1844	A		FILM
TSCHEILLER	LOUIS CHARLES	1810	THANN	08/05/1185	NY		FILM
TSCHIMBER	JOSEPH	1818	WITTERSDORF	11/07/1849	NY		FILM
TSCHIRHART	AUGUSTIN	1812	RODEREN	02/15/1834	A		FILM
TSCHIRHART	LANDELIN	1833	MORTZWILLER	09/02/1853	NY		FILM
TSCHIRHART	NICOLAS	1814	SOPPE-LE-BAS	09/05/1844	NY		FILM
TSCHIRHART	PIERRE		SOPPE-LE-HAUT	/ /	NY		FILM
TSCHIRHART	THEOPHILE	1836	RAEDERSHEIM	12/13/1854	NY		FILM
TSCHIRHART WW CH 4	NICOLAS	1802	SOPPE-LE-HAUT	04/09/1847	NO		FILM
TSCHIRHART WW CH 7	JAQUES	1798	MORTZWILLER	07/22/1851	NO		FILM
TSCHIRRET	THERESE	1821	SOPPE-LE-HAUT	02/20/1840	NY		FILM
TSCHUP	FERDINAND	1841	SIERENTZ	03/14/1863	NY		FILM
TSCHUPP	JEAN	1835	SIERENTZ	09/17/1857	NY		FILM
TUENN WW AND CH 4	CHRISTIAN	1786	SCHRUNTZ	03/10/1838	NY		FILM
TUGLER	BARTHELEMIA	1825	RUSTENHART	09/21/1846	TX		FILM
TUGLER	BARTHELEY	1825	HIRTZFELDEN	09/01/1846	TX	TAYL	PASS
TUHER	FRANCOIS LOUIS	1824	BLODELSHEIM	06/03/1852	NY		FILM
TURC WW AND CH 2	GEORGES		GOERSDORF	03/22/1817	A		FILM
TURCH	MARTIN	1805	HIEHLINSPERGUE	05/15/1845	NY		FILM
TURCHEL CH 1	TSCHIAC	1822	MASSEVAUX	09/15/1851	A		FILM
TURILLOT	LOUIS	1824	FONTENELLE	10/08/1849	NY		FILM
TURIN	ALOYSE	1817	MASSEVAUX	09/01/1847	SL		FILM

Lastname	Firstname	Birth Year	Birthplace	Emigration De	Prof	Source
UBEL	JEAN		NIEDERSOULTZBACH	01/01/1828 A		FILM
UBICINI	OSCAR		BOURGES	06/23/1847 A		FILM
UEBERSCHLAG	MARIE ANNE	1838	MOOS	09/23/1857 NO		.FILM
UHL	CH.		ZUSOLSHOFEN	07/30/1849 A		FILM
UHL	CHRETIEN		MULLENBACH	08/31/1849 A		FILM
UHL	JOSEPH		ZUSOLSHOFEN	07/30/1849 A		FILM
UHL	MICHEL		MULLENBACH	08/23/1849 A		FILM
UHLMANN	FANNY	1838	SOULTZMATT	11/12/1865 NY		FILM
UHLRICH	JEAN		KILLSTETT	05/28/1817 A		FILM
UHLRICH	PHILIPE		KILLSTETT	05/28/1817 A		FILM
UHRBERGER	LOUIS	1812	GRENDELBRUCH	03/15/1838 A		FILM
UHRIG	HELENE		SOUFFLENHEIM	03/02/1838 A		FILM
UHRIN	ALEXANDRE		SARRE UNION	01/01/1828 A		FILM
UHRIN	GEORGES		MARLENHEIM	01/01/1828 A		FILM
UHRIN	JOSEPH		MARLENHEIM	01/01/1828 A		FILM
UHRWILLER	FRANCOIS JOSEPH		HAGEUNAU	03/01/1838 A		FILM
ULIMANN	HIENCHE		DRUSENHEIM	03/24/1838 A		FILM
ULIMANN	JAQUES		DRUSENHEIM	03/24/1838 A		FILM
ULLMANN	LEHMAN	1842	SIERENTZ	02/02/1861 NY		FILM
ULLMANN	MATHIAS	1826	DURMENBACH	04/09/1847 NO		FILM
ULLMANN	SALOMON	1832	DURMENACH	04/19/1851 NO		FILM
ULMANN	ABRAHAM	1836	SIERENTZ	09/17/1857 NY		FILM
ULMANN	JUDAS	1837	SIERENTZ	05/18/1857 NY		FILM
ULMANN	NATHAN	1833	DURMENACH	06/12/1857 NO		FILM
ULMER	ABRAHAM		HECHINGEN	05/16/1849 A		FILM
ULMER	JEANETTE		HECHINGEN	05/16/1849 A		FILM
ULSEMER	MARIE		NIEDERLAUTERBACH	01/01/1850 NO		PRIV
ULSEMER	MARIE ANNA	1796	NIEDERLAUTERBACH	01/01/1865 NO		NO.2
UMBDENSTOCH	DAVID	1835	COLMAR	02/13/1856 NY		FILM
UMDENSTOCH	CHRETIEN	1829	MITTELWIHR	04/07/1847 NY		FILM
UMDENSTOCH	MATHIEU	1817	OSTHEIM	04/13/1847 NY		FILM
UMDENSTOCH D CATHERI	CATHERINE	1834	OSTHEIM	02/13/1856 NY		FILM
UMDENSTOCH D CATHERI	MADELAINE	1836	OSTHEIM	02/13/1856 NY		FILM
UMDENSTOCH D CATHERI	MARIE	1842	OSTHEIM	02/13/1856 NY		FILM
UMDENSTOCH W HENNY	CATHERINE	1809	OSTHEIM	02/13/1856 NY		FILM
UMDENSTOCH WW CH 1	JOSEPH	1819	GUEMAR	04/19/1854 NY		FILM
UMDENSTOCH WW CH 3	MATHIAS	1796	OSTHEIM	02/21/1846 NY		FILM
UMDENSTOCH WW CH	MICHEL	1803	OSTHEIM	04/09/1853 NY		FILM
UMDENSTOCH WW CH 2	JEAN BAPTISTE	1821	GUEMAR	04/19/1854 NY		FILM
UMDENSTOCH WW CH 3	MATHIAS	1796	MITTELWIHR	03/20/1848 NY		FILM
UMEL MN ROTH	ANNE	1803	LACROIX	02/14/1857 NY		FILM
UMPFELBACH	GEORGE		DALHUNDEN	03/02/1838 A		FILM
UNGEREN CH 1	FRANCOISE	1786	DRACHENBRONN	09/03/1849 A		FILM
UNGERER	BARBARA	1835	INGOLSHEIM	01/01/1868 NY		NO.2
UNGERER	BERNHARD	1860	INGOLSHEIM	01/01/1868 NY		NO.2
UNGERER	GEORG	1864	INGOLSHEIM	01/01/1868 NY		NO.2
UNGERER	JOHANN	1843	STEINSELTZ	01/01/1869 NY	FARM	NO.2
UNGERER	MICHEL	1849	KEFFENBACH	01/01/1868 NY	FARM	NO.2
UNGERER	PIERRE	1820	DRACHENBRONN	04/07/1844 A		FILM
UNGERER W W 2 CH	GEORG	1837	INGOLSHEIM	01/01/1868 NY		NO.2

Lastname	Firstname	Birth Year	Birthplace	Emigration	De	Prof	Source
UNTEREINER	JEAN GEORGE	1819	SIEWILLER	01/28/1852	NY		FILM
UNTEREINER	JEANNE		SIEWILLER	03/02/1838	A		FILM
UNTEREINER	MARIE		SIEWILLER	03/02/1838	A		FILM
UNTERNßHER WW CH 3	JEAN NEPON	1802	BUHL	09/19/1845	A		FILM
UPHUS	JOHANN BERNARD	1819	WESTFALEN	09/17/1845	TX		FILM
URBAIN	JEAN NICOLAS	1818	ST CROIX AUX MINES	11/24/1845	SL		FILM
URBAIN	JOSEPH	1813	LIEPRE	08/14/1838	NO		FILM
URBAN	HENRY		SCHWEIGHAUSEN	01/01/1828	A		FILM
URBAN	JEAN		INGENHEIM	01/01/1828	A		FILM
URBAN	JEAN GEORGES	1799	GUEBWILLER	05/27/1844	NY		FILM
URBAN	JOSEPH	1786	RAEDERSHEIM	11/10/1854	A		FILM
URBAN	M. ANNE	1829	RAEDERSHEIM	11/10/1854	A		FILM
URBAN	PHILIPPE		SESSENHEIM	02/23/1838	A		FILM
URNER	JEAN	1812	ST MARIE AUX MINES	07/18/1848	NY		FILM
URSPRUNG	MARIE ANNE	1793	HEITEREN	08/28/1855	NY		FILM
UTARD	FRANCOIS	1826	RIEDWIHR	10/23/1852	NY		FILM
UTERICH	JOSEPH		ROESCHWOOG	01/01/1828	A		FILM

Lastname	Firstname	Birth Year	Birthplace	Emigration	De	Prof	Source
VAELCHER	MICHEL	1812	ORSCHWIHR	10/11/1847	NY		FILM
VAGELWEIDT	SERAPHIN	1801	BISEL	04/29/1847	NY		FILM
VAGNER	BARBE	1814	CHEVENEZ	03/05/1864	NY		FILM
VAGNER	CATHERINE	1857	MULHOUSE	02/20/1864	NY		FILM
VAGNER	CHRISTE	1850	MULHOUSE	02/20/1864	NY		FILM
VAGNER	JEAN	1847	MULHOUSE	02/20/1864	NY		FILM
VAGNER	JOSEPH	1845	MULHOUSE	02/20/1864	NY		FILM
VAGNER WW AND CH	FRANCOIS		ESCHBOURG	03/31/1817	A		FILM
VAGUELEN	MARTIN	1825	ROUGEMONT	12/01/1860	TX	DAYL	PASS
VALBERT	JOSEPHINE	1827	BOUROGNE	02/20/1952	CH		FILM
VALBERT MN TRAIN	THERESE	1788	PEROUSE	07/24/1852	NY		FILM
VALDEJO	SEBASTIEN	1827	LIEPVRE	05/12/1846	NO		FILM
VALETTE	FR. ANT. JEAN		HAGENAU	01/01/1828	A		FILM
VALKRE	PIERRE ANTOINE	1827	LEPUIX	03/17/1854	NY		FILM
VALLAT	CELESTIN	1822	BREBOTTE	08/27/1851	NO		FILM
VALLAT	FRANCOIS	1818	RECAUVRANCE	02/05/1844	NY		FILM
VALLAT	PACIFIQUE	1821	GRANDVILLARS	08/23/1854	NO		FILM
VALLAT	PIERRE	1825	BREBOTTE	03/08/1851	NO		FILM
VALLAT	SOPHIE	1835	GRANDVILLARS	08/21/1855	NO		FILM
VALLAT WW AND CH 6	FRANCOIS	1795	BREBOTTE	02/14/1844	NY		FILM
VALLET WW AND CH 6	SEBASTIEN		SIEWILLER	03/17/1817	A		FILM
VALLEY	MARIE PHILOMENE	1834		04/01/1866	NY		FILM
VALOT	FRANCOIS	1812	FLANCHER-LEBAS	01/13/1847	NY		FILM
VALOT	GEORGE		EVETTE	03/05/1852	OH		FILM
VALOT WW AND CH 2	THEOPHILE	1823	FLANCHER-LE-BAS	06/27/1853	NY		FILM
VALTER MN STOUFF	MARIE	1827	FLORIMOUT	04/10/1855	NY		FILM
VANE	GEORGES	1820	COLMAR	09/06/1849	NO		FILM
VANNIER	PIERRE LOUIS	1834	MONTBELIARD	03/12/1863	NY		FILM
VARIE WW	GEORGES	1820		09/06/1849	NO		FILM
VAUGIER	LOUIS	1847	CHALONVILLARD	02/23/1865	NY		FILM
VAUTHIER	JEAN PIERRE	1811	CHATENOIS HAUT-RHIN	02/09/1839	NY		FILM
VAUTRINOL WW AND CH4	ANTOINE	1817	LIEPRE	10/14/1854	NO		FILM
VAUTRINOLTI	JOSEPH	1807	ST. MARIE AUX MINES	04/13/1849	NO		FILM
VECHTER S VENDELIN	THIEBAUT	1804	ZINSWEILLER	02/16/1817	A		FILM
VEILLER	ANDRE	1813	ISSENHEIM	06/15/1849	NY		FILM
VEIT	CHARLES	1814	COLMAR	06/14/1852	NO		FILM
VEITH	MR.		GERMANY	03/31/1849	A		FILM
VELDEN WW AND CH 3	VALENTIN		NEUHOFF	03/03/1817	A		FILM
VELTEN H HIRDT	PHILIPPE GEORGS		ROPPENHEIM	06/03/1852	AL		NO.1
VELTEN MN HIRDT	MARIE EVE		ROPPENHEIM	06/03/1852	AL		NO.1
VELTER W ROPPI JEAN	ADELE	1845	BIRKENWALD	05/09/1862	A		FILM
VENDELING D JAQUES	ELISABETHE	1791	NEHWILLER	02/20/1817	A		FILM
VENDELING D JAQUES	SALOMEE	1811	NEHWILLER	02/20/1817	A		FILM
VENDELING H SALOMEE	JAQUES	1761	NEHWILLER	02/20/1817	A		FILM
VENDELING MN VERCHMA	SALOMEE		NEHWILLER	02/20/1817	A		FILM
VENDELING S JAQUES	JEAN	1816	NEHWILLER	02/20/1817	A		FILM
VENDELING S JAQUES	JEAN JAQUES	1813	NEHWILLER	02/20/1817	A		FILM
VENDELING S JAQUES	PIERRE	1809	NEHWILLER	02/20/1817	A		FILM
VENDELING WW AND CH3	JAQUES		MERKWILLER	01/01/1817	A		FILM
VENDLING WW AND CH4	FRANCOIS		WEITERSWILLER	03/29/1817	A		FILM

Lastname	Firstname	Birth Year	Birthplace	Emigration	De	Prof	Source
VENDRE WW AND CH 4	PHILIPPE		TIEFFENBACH	01/01/1817	A		FILM
VENDRELY WW AND CH 3	GEORGES	1807	STRASBOURG	04/23/1853	A		FILM
VERAIN	HENRY	1815	VILLESCOT	01/30/1844	NY		FILM
VERASIN	HENRY	1815	VILLESCOT	01/30/1844	NY		FILM
VERCHOT	XAVIER	1845	FRAHIER	02/08/1866	NY		FILM
VERDIN	FLORENT		MARLENHEIM	01/01/1828	A		FILM
VERDIN	NICOLAS		MARLENHEIM	01/01/1828	A		FILM
VERDIN	SALERN		MARLENHEIM	01/01/1828	A		FILM
VERDUN B FRANCOIS	JULIEN	1840	VETRIGNE	09/22/1857	NY		FILM
VERDUN W FRANCOIS	M.A.LOUISE	1833	VETRIGNE	09/22/1857	NY		FILM
VERDUN WW	FRANCOIS	1827	VETRIGNE	09/22/1857	NY		FILM
VERDUN WW AND CH 2	JEAN BAPTISTE	1823	VETRIGNE	09/17/1855	NY		FILM
VERNE	DOMINIQUE	1821	GUEBWILLER	02/17/1844	NY		FILM
VERNETTE WW	LOUIS	1816	BRETTEN	10/10/1844	NO		FILM
VERNIER	HENRIETTE	1832	BELFORT	09/03/1852	A		FILM
VERRIER	CELESTIN	1835	LAMADELEINE	12/13/1853	NY		FILM
VERRIER	FRANCOIS JOSEPH	1832	ST. GERMAIN	01/21/1851	NY		FILM
VETTER	JOACHIM	1814	SONDERSDORF	02/23/1846	A		FILM
VETTER	JOSEPH		HAGUENAU	01/01/1828	A		FILM
VETTER	JOSEPH	1857	LUTHER	05/04/1865	NY		FILM
VETTER	MADELEINE	1860	LUTHER	05/04/1865	NY		FILM
VETTER	MARIE ANNE	1858	LUTHER	05/04/1865	NY		FILM
VETTER	MARTIN	1828	SONDERSDORF	03/02/1847	NY		FILM
VETTER	XAVIER	1823	LUTHER	05/04/1865	NY		FILM
VETTER	XAVIER	1865	LUTHER	05/04/1865	NY		FILM
VETTER W XAVIER	GERTRUDE	1825	LUTHER	05/04/1865	NY		FILM
VETTLER	ROSINE		FREUDENSTADT	09/12/1849	A		FILM
VEUNDEÖING	JACQUES		MERCKWILLER	03/31/1817	A		FILM
VEY WW AND CH 3	JOSEPH	1816	SOPPE-LE-HAUT	05/08/1844	NY		FILM
VEYDMANN WW AND CH 5	DANIEL		PETERSBACH	03/17/1817	A		FILM
VEYH	JEAN MICHEL	1821	SOPPE-LE-HAUT	02/26/1840	NY		FILM
VIELWEBER	DAVID	1780	HUNAWIHR	04/13/1847	NY		FILM
VIENE WW AND CH 5	FRANCOIS	1803	MEZIRE	07/29/1857	NY		FILM
VIENNOT MN LAUTENSCH	ELISABETH	1819	MULHOUSE	09/07/1848	NY		FILM
VIENOT	JEAN	1805	ROCHES	09/20/1847	NY		FILM
VIENOT	PIERRE	1815	ROCHES	09/20/1847	NY		FILM
VIENOT WW AND CH 2	JAQUES	1807	ROCHE LES BLAMONT	03/17/1845	SL		FILM
VIES MN KOCH AND CH	CATHERINE		CERNAY	/ /	A		FILM
VIGNES WW AND CH1	FRANCOIS	1821	CHAVANNES LES GRAND	03/13/1849	NY		FIM
VIGNOS	DENIS	1818	CHAVANNES LES GRAND	11/14/1846	NY		FILM
VIGNOS	JEAN CALUDE	1816	CHAVANNES LES GRAND	11/02/1846	NY		FILM
VIGNOS WW	JEAN CLAUDE	1815	CHAVANNES LES GRAND	02/08/1854	NY		FILM
VILD	JOSEPH		THAL	01/01/1828	A		FILM
VILLAMIE CH 2	FRANCOISE		ST DIZIER	07/18/1855	NY		FILM
VILLAUME WW	JEAN BAPTISTE	1829	VEZELOIS	08/10/1854	NY		FILM
VILLAUMIE	JOSEPH	1830	ST, DIZIER	11/07/1854	NY		FILM
VILLAUMIE CH 2	FRANCOISE	1804	ST. DIZIER	07/18/1855	NY		FILM
VILLEMEZ	PIERRE	1835	BELFORT	10/14/1865	NY		FILM
VILLEMEZ WW	EUGENE	1810	ESSERT	08/02/1852	SL		FILM
VILLEMEZ MN CHATELOT	SOPHIE CH 2	1826	ESSERT	09/01/1854	A		FILM

Lastname	Firstname	Birth Year	Birthplace	Emigration	De	Prof	Source
VILLEMIN	GEORGES	1819	LIEVPRE	09/10/1838	NO		FILM
VILLIER	AIME	1832	ARCEY	10/20/1865	NY		FILM
VILLIER	ANANI	1864	ARCEY	10/07/1865	NY		FILM
VILLIER	ANGELIQUE	1847	ARCEY	10/07/1865	NY		FILM
VILLIER	EUGENIE	1841	ARCEY	10/07/1865	NY		FILM
VILLIER	JEANNE	1826	ARCEY	10/07/1865	NY		FILM
VILLIER	LAURENCE	1861	ARCEY	10/07/1865	NY		FILM
VILLIER	LAURENT		ARCEY	10/07/1865	NY		FILM
VILLINGER	DOMINIQUE		LENZKIRCHE B	09/30/1849	A		FILM
VINCENT	MARTIN	1834	SOPPE-LE-BAS	11/07/1854	NY		FILM
VINCENT MN KNOL	CATHERINE	1800	LIEVPRE	09/30/1854	NO		FILM
VINDELIN	JOSEPH	1799	ZINSWEILLER	02/16/1817	A		FILM
VINDELIN	MICHEL	1802	ZINSWEILLER	02/16/1817	A		FILM
VINDELIN	THIEBAUT	1796	ZINSWEILLER	02/16/1817	A		FILM
VINDELING	VEDELIN		ZINSWILLER	02/16/1817	A		FILM
VINDELING	VENDELIN	1764	ZINSWEILLER	02/16/1817	A		FILM
VINDELING D VENDELIN	CATHERINE	1813	ZINSWEILLER	02/16/1817	A		FILM
VINDELING MN HIHN	MAGDALAINE	1783	ZINSWILLER	02/16/1817	A		FILM
VINDELING S VENDELIN	XAVIER	1811	ZINSWEILLER	02/16/1817	A		FILM
VINEY	JAQUES	1807	ISSENHEIM	06/08/1854	NY		FILM
VINEY	MARIE	1842	HEZIRE	09/15/1866	NY		FILM
VIOLARD	THERESE	1828	BELFORT	07/04/1848	NY		FILM
VIRLOT	FRANCOISE	1812	PLANCHEZ-LE-BAS	01/13/1847	NY		FILM
VIRTH	JULES	1835	BETHONVILLIERS	01/30/1851	NY		FILM
VITEMER	FREDERIC	1839	NOMAIS-DOUBS	11/20/1865	NY		FILM
VITEMER	HENRY	1845	NOMAIS-DOUBS	11/20/1865	NY		FILM
VITEMER	MARIE	1846	NOMAIS-DOUBS	11/20/1865	NY		FILM
VITTMANN	JEAN BAPTISTE	1833	LIEVPRE	12/15/1854	NO		FILM
VIX	BERNARD		ROESCHWOOG	01/01/1828	A		FILM
VIX CH 3	IGNACE	1797	WANZENAU OR WANZENEN	09/13/1848	NY		FILM
VIX H MARIE CH 7	PHILIPPE GEORGE			01/01/1843	A		PRIV
VIX MN CLAESS	MARIE SALOME		ROPPENHEIM	01/01/1843	A		NO.1
VIX S WOLFF MADELEIN	GEORGES MICHAEL	1820	ROPPENHEIM	/ /	A		NO.1
VOEGELE	JOSEPH JUN		SCHWEIGHAUSEN	01/01/1828	A		FILM
VOEGELE	JOSEPH SEN		SCHWEIGHAUSEN	01/01/1828	A		FILM
VOEGELE	PHILIPPE HENRI	1800	OBERBRONN	07/18/1853	A		FILM
VOEGELY D FEDILE	MARIE	1824	CERNAY	10/25/1843	TX		FILM
VOEGELY F MARIE	FREDILE	1791	CERNAY	10/25/1843	TX		FILM
VOEGELY WW AND CH	FIDELE	1822	CERNAY	10/23/1847	NO		FILM
VOEGTLING	HENRI		UTTWILLER	01/01/1828	A		FILM
VOEGTLING	PH. JAQUES		WEITERSWILLER	01/01/1828	A		FILM
VOELCHER	MICHEL	1811	ORSCHWIHR	10/22/1853	NY		FILM
VOGEL	AGATHE		NIEDERLAUTERBACH	01/01/1850	NO		PRIV
VOGEL	AGATHE	1841	NIEDERLAUTERBACH	01/01/1866	NO		PRIV
VOGEL	ANDRE		SOUFFLENHEIM	01/01/1828	A		FILM
VOGEL	ANTOINE	1822	OSTHEIM	02/02/1856	NY		FILM
VOGEL	CHRETIEN		GERMANY	04/12/1849	NY		FILM
VOGEL	CHRETIEN		INGWILLER	01/01/1828	A		FILM
VOGEL	ELISABETH	1842	NEHWILLER	01/01/1866	A		NO.2
VOGEL	FRANCOIS	1834	RIEDSELTZ	10/14/1854	NY		FILM

Lastname	Firstname	Birth Year	Birthplace	Emigration	De	Prof	Source
VOGEL	GEORGES		TIEFFENBACH	01/01/1828	A		FILM
VOGEL	GEORGES	1813	WYDENTOHLEN	10/04/1838	A		FILM
VOGEL	GERTRUDE		NIEDERLAUTERBACH	01/01/1850	NO		PRIV
VOGEL	GERTRUDE	1846	NIEDERLAUTERBACH	01/01/1866	NO		PRIV
VOGEL	GUILLAUME	1824	ST. MARIE AUX MINES	08/29/1848	NY		FILM
VOGEL	HENRY		VOLSBOURG	03/06/1817	A		FILM
VOGEL	IGNACE	1831	BERGHEIM	03/25/1853	NY		FILM
VOGEL	JAQUES		SCHWEIGHAUSEN	01/01/1828	A		FILM
VOGEL	JAQUES	1836	HOLTZWIHR	02/13/1854	NY		FILM
VOGEL	JEAN	1834	HOUSSEN	06/09/1857	NY		FILM
VOGEL	JEAN BAPTISTE	1817	GUEMAR	10/09/1838	NY		FILM
VOGEL	JEAN JAQUES	1814	ST MARIE AUX MINES	07/22/1848	NY		FILM
VOGEL	JOSEPH		STATTMATTEN	01/01/1828	A		FILM
VOGEL	JOSEPH	1825	BERGHEIM	03/17/1853	NY		FILM
VOGEL	JOSEPHINE	1835	PFASTATT	03/18/1857	A		FILM
VOGEL	LOUIS	1842	MARNACH	04/11/1866	NY		FILM
VOGEL	MADELEINE	1835	BEBLENHEIM	07/28/1854	NY		FILM
VOGEL	MARTIN	1816	WYDENTOHLEN	10/04/1838	NO		FILM
VOGEL	MATHIEU	1815	COLMAR	01/15/1850	NO		FILM
VOGEL	PAUL	1808	ILLZACH	04/05/1854	NO		FILM
VOGEL	THIEBAUT		SCHALKENDORF	01/01/1828	A		FILM
VOGEL CH 3	CATHERINE	1800	RIBEAUVILLE	10/07/1854	NY		FILM
VOGEL WW	PAUL		BEBLENHEIM	11/28/1852	NY		FILM
VOGEL WW AND CH 3	JEAN ALOYSE	1819	HOLTZWIHR	12/04/1852	NY		FILM
VOGELBACHER WW	HYPOLITE	1802	ST. HYPOLITE	06/18/1852	NY		FILM
VOGELE	JEROME		SOUFFLENHEIM	01/01/1828	A		FILM
VOGELWEIDT	SERAPHIN	1801	BISEL	04/29/1847	NY		FILM
VOGLER	JACOB		RITTERSHOFEN	01/01/1865	A		NO.2
VOGLER WW AND CH 5	JAQUES		RITTERSHOFFEN	03/28/1817	A		FILM
VOGT	BENEDICT		NIEDERBRONN	05/13/1838	A		FILM
VOGT	CHRETIEN		ERLACH	08/21/1849	A		FILM
VOGT	FIDELE		KRATZINGEN	05/24/1849	A		FILM
VOGT	PIERRE	1811	ROUFFACH	11/15/1843	A		FILM
VOGT CH 5	SALOME	1806	LIESTAL	10/09/1857	NY		FILM
VOGT WW AND CH 6	JEAN GEORGES		HERMERSWILLER	03/29/1817	A		FILM
VOILAND WW AND CH	JAQUES	1814	CRAVANCHE	09/03/1852	NY		FILM
VOILAND WW AND CH 7	THIEBAUD	1809	CRAVANCHE	09/27/1852	NY		FILM
VOILANDS W CHARLES	ADELAINE CH 5	1803	ESSERT	09/03/1857	A		FILM
VOILANDS WW AND CH 5	CHARLES XAVIER	1797	ESSERT	09/03/1857	A		FILM
VOILANT WW AND CH 2	LOUIS	1813	BELFORT	03/19/1847	NY		FILM
VOISARD	JUSTIN	1842	CLERNE	01/26/1862	NY		FILM
VOISIN	MARIE ANNE	1796	REPPE	07/28/1848	A		FILM
VOISINET	CHARLES	1853	EVETTE	03/25/1857	NY		FILM
VOISINET	GEORGES	1803	EVETTE	03/05/1852	A		FILM
VOISINET	GEORGES	1865	EVETTE	10/02/1865	NY		FILM
VOISINET	JOSEPH	1828	EVETTE	03/25/1857	NY		FILM
VOISINET	JOSEPH	1827	EVETTE	10/06/1865	NY		FILM
VOISINET	JOSEPH	1861	EVETTE	10/02/1865	NY		FILM
VOISINET	JULIE	1863	EVETTE	10/02/1865	NY		FILM
VOISINET	LOUISE	1846	ERETTE	03/25/1857	NY		FILM

257

Lastname	Firstname	Birth Year	Birthplace	Emigration	De	Prof	Source
VOISINET D JOSEPH	ROSE	1858	ERETTE	10/02/1865	NY		FILM
VOISINET H SIMON M	JOSEPH	1828	EVETTE	03/25/1857	NY		FILM
VOISINET MN SIMON	M.CATHERINE	1834	EVETTE	03/25/1857	NY		FILM
VOISINET W JOSEPH	M. CATHERINE	1834	EVETTE	03/25/1857	NY		FILM
VOISINET WW AND CH	JOSEPH	1827	EVETTE	10/02/1865	NY		FILM
VOKAL	JEAN		SCHOENBURG	03/17/1817	A		FILM
VOLANT WW AND CH 2	NICOLAS	1801	BELFORT	06/13/1838	NY		FILM
VOLCK	BENEDIQUE		MULLENBACH	08/23/1849	A		FILM
VOLK	ALFRED	1796	FREISTETT	09/17/1845	TX		FILM
VOLK	GEORG	1826	FREISTETT	09/17/1845	TX		FILM
VOLLMER	MATHIEU		INGWILLER	01/01/1828	A		FILM
VOLLMER WH AND CH 3	CATHERINE		ROTHENBURG	04/06/1849	NY		FILM
VOLMAR	LOUIS		WALDOLWISHEIM	01/01/1828	A		FILM
VOLTER	CRESENZ		GRIESHEIM	10/11/1849	A		FILM
VOLTZ	CATHERINE		MELSHEIM	01/01/1828	A		FILM
VOLTZ	GEORGE		SAVERNE	01/01/1828	A		FILM
VOLTZ	PHILIPPE		INGVILLES	01/01/1828	A		FILM
VON VANDRE WW CH 4	PHILIPPE		TIEFFENBACH	03/31/1817	A		FILM
VONAU	IGNACE	1800	CERNAY	11/01/1847	TX	FARR	PASS
VONAU	IGNACE	1800	SCHWABWEILLER	11/13/1847	TX		FILM
VONFILE CH 1	HENRI LE JEUNE	1816	GUNDOLSHEIM	11/01/1848	TX	CULT	PAQSS
VONFLIE	HENRI	1816	GUNDOLSHEIM	11/14/1848	TX		FILM
VONGLIE	JEAN HENRI	1782	GUNDOLSHEIM	11/14/1848	TX		FILM
VONHATTEN WW	MARTIN		SOUFFLENHEIM	01/01/1828	A		FILM
VORFLIE WW	JEAN HENRI SEN	1782	GUNDOLSHEIM	11/14/1848	TX		FILM
VORFLIE WW AND CH	HENRI LEJEUNE	1816	GUNDOLSHEIM	11/14/1848	TX		FILM
VOSELER D JEAN	MADELEINE		PHUNINGEN	09/04/1849	NY		FILM
VOSELER D JEAN	URSULE		PHUNINGEN	09/04/1849	NY		FILM
VOSELER H CHRISTINE	JEAN		PHUNINGEN	09/04/1849	NY		FILM
VOSELER S JEAN	JEAN		PHUNINGEN	09/04/1849	NY		FILM
VOSELER W JEAN CH 3	CHRISTINE		PHUNINGEN	09/04/1849	NY		FILM
VOUILLOT CH	CHARLES LOUIS	1810	BADEREL	04/10/1849	NY		FILM
VOYER	PIERRE CHARLES	1842	CHALONVILLARD	02/29/1864	NY		FILM
VUILLAUME	LOUIS	1809	ST. DIZIER	09/25/1850	NY		FILM
VUILLAUMIE	CHARLES JOSEPH	1826	ST. DIZIER	09/21/1852	NY		FILM
VUILLEQUEZ	PIERRE	1844	BAR	09/07/1865	NY		FILM

Lastname	Firstname	Birth Year	Birthplace	Emigration	De	Prof	Source
WAAG W W 3CH	LOUIS	1810	ANDLAU BAS RHIN	03/29/1847	NY		FILM
WAAG WW AND CH 3	LOUIS	1810	ANDLAU	03/29/1847	NY		FILM
WAANDER	EVE		RUNTZENHEIM	01/01/1828	A		FILM
WACHERMANN	JOSEPH		REICHSHOFFEN	03/22/1817	A		FILM
WACHTER	ANTOINE	1795	BOUXWILLER	04/22/1847	NY		FILM
WACHTER	MARIE CATHERINE	1819	BITSCHWILLER	10/17/1857	IA		FILM
WACHTER	SOPHIE		LANGENENSLINGEN	06/04/1849	A		FILM
WACHTER	THERESE	1815	ST. HYPOLITE	11/07/1845	NO		FILM
WACHTER	THERESE	1815	ST. HYPOLITE	11/07/1854	NO		FILM
WACHTER CH	SOPHIE		LANGENENSLINGEN	06/04/1849	A		FILM
WACHTER W RUILLARD J	M. CATHERINE	1819	BITSCHWILLER	10/17/1857	A		FILM
WACKER	ANTOINE	1795	BOUWILLER	04/22/1847	NY		FILM
WACKERMANN	JOSEPH		REICHSHOFFEN	03/22/1817	A		FILM
WADEL	JEAN	1820	GILDWILLER	11/27/1854	NY		FILM
WADEL	JEAN	1820	GILDWILLER	11/27/1854	A		FILM
WADEL	JOSEP			/ /			
WADEL W W 4CH	JOSEPH	1806	AMMERZWILLER	03/07/1846	OH		FILM
WADEL W W 6CH	JOSEPH	1805	AMMERZWILLER	11/27/1854	NY		FILM
WADEL WW AND CH 4	JOSEPH	1806	AMMERWILLER	03/07/1846	OH		FILM
WADEL WW AND CH 6	JOSEPH	1805	AMMERWILLER	11/27/1854	NY		FILM
WADENPHUL	NICOLAS	1825	MULHAUSEN	09/15/1845	NY		FILM
WADENPHUL	NICOLAS	1825	MULHAUSEN	09/15/1845	NY		FILM
WAEHRLE	VIDAL		HINTERGATTEN	09/30/1849	A		FILM
WAELDE	CATHERINE		NIEDERLAUTERBACH	01/01/1850	NO		PRIV
WAGENHEIM W W 4CH	JOAHNN ADAM		REIPERTSWILLER	01/01/1817	A		FILM
WAGENHEIM WW AND CH4	J. ADAM		REIPERTSWILLER	01/01/1817	A		FILM
WAGLER	JEAN	1821	RIBEAUVILLE	04/17/1848	NY		FILM
WAGLER	JEAN	1821	RIBEAUVILLE	04/17/1848	NY		FILM
WAGLER D CHRETIEN		1842	SENONNES	03/07/1857	NY		FILM
WAGLER D CHRETIEN		1849	SENONNES	03/07/1857	NY		FILM
WAGLER S CHRETIEN		1841	SENONNES	03/07/1857	NY		FILM
WAGLER S CHRETIEN		1846	SENONNES	03/07/1857	NY		FILM
WAGLER S CHRETIEN		1855	SENONNES	03/07/1857	NY		FILM
WAGLER W CHRETIEN		1821	SENONNES	03/07/1857	NY		FILM
WAGLER W W 1CH	JEAN	1811	RIBAUVILLE	02/02/1842	MY		FILM
WAGLER W W 6CH	CHRETIEN	1817	SENONNES	03/07/1857	NY		FILM
WAGLER W W 6CH	JEAN	1804	RIBEAUVILLE	10/11/1854	NY		FILM
WAGLER WW AND CH	CHRETIEN	1776	RIBEAUVILLE	09/13/1848	NY		FILM
WAGLER WW AND CH	JEAN	1811	RIBEAUVILLE	02/02/1842	NY		FILM
WAGLER WW AND CH 6	CHRETIEN	1817	SENONNES	03/07/1857	NY		FILM
WAGLER WW AND CH 6	JEAN	1804	RIBEAUVILLE	10/11/1854	NY		FILM
WAGNER	ALBERT		NIEDERLAUTERBACH	01/01/1850	NO		PRIV
WAGNER	ALBERT	1844	NIEDERLAUTERBACH	01/01/1861	NO		PRIV
WAGNER	ALOISE		NIEDERLAUTERBACH	01/01/1850	NO		PRIV
WAGNER	ALOYSE	1843	NIEDERLAUTERBACH	01/01/1861	NO		PRIV
WAGNER	ANNE CATHERINE		MULHOUSE	05/17/1842	A		FILM
WAGNER	ANNE CATHERINE		MULHOUSE	05/17/1842	SL		FILM
WAGNER	ANSLON		SOUFFELHEIM	03/02/1838	A		FILM
WAGNER	ANSLON		SOUFFLENHEIM	03/02/1838	A		FILM
WAGNER	ANTOINE		BAERENDORF	03/01/1838	A		FILM

Lastname	Firstname	Birth Year	Birthplace	Emigration	De	Prof	Source
WAGNER	ANTOINE		BAERENDORF	01/01/1828	A		FILM
WAGNER	BALTHASAR		DAUENDORF	01/01/1828	A		FILM
WAGNER	BARBE	1806	RIBEAUVILLE	06/29/1854	NY		FILM
WAGNER	BARBE		BAERENDORF	01/01/1828	A		FILM
WAGNER	BARBE	1806	BENNWIHR	06/29/1854	NY		FILM
WAGNER	BARBE	1806	BENNWIHR	06/29/1854	NY		FILM
WAGNER	BLAISE	1815	WITTERSDORF	04/03/1852	NO		FILM
WAGNER	BLAISE	1815	WITTERSDORF	03/04/1852	NO		FILM
WAGNER	CATHERINA	1850	WEISSENBURG	01/01/1868	NY		NO.2
WAGNER	CATHERINE		BAERENDORF	01/01/1828	A		FILM
WAGNER	CECILE	1824	KIENTZHEIMIM	08/18/1853	NO		FILM
WAGNER	CECILE	1824	KIENTZHEIM	08/18/1853	NO		FILM
WAGNER	CHARLES		STRUTH	01/01/1828	A		FILM
WAGNER	CHARLES		STRUTH	01/01/1828	A		FILM
WAGNER	CHRISTOPHE	1799	GEMUNDER PRUSSIA	08/23/1851	A		FILM
WAGNER	ELISABETH			08/23/1851	A		FILM
WAGNER	ELISABETH		NEUHOFF	08/23/1851	A		FILM
WAGNER	ELISABETH	1845	LEMBACH	01/01/1866	NY		NO.2
WAGNER	ELISABETH		GEMUNDER PRUSSIA	08/23/1851	A		FILM
WAGNER	ETIENNE		MARMONTIER	01/01/1828	A		FILM
WAGNER	IGNACE		NIEDERLAUTERBACH	01/01/1850	NO		PRIV
WAGNER	IGNACE	1811	NIEDERLAUTERBACH	01/01/1861	NO	HADR	PRIV
WAGNER	IGNACE		ROHRWILLER	03/12/1838	A		FILM
WAGNER	JACQUES		DETTENWILLER	01/01/1828	A		FILM
WAGNER	JACQUES		BAERENDORF	01/01/1828	A		FILM
WAGNER	JAQUES		DETTWILLER	01/01/1828	A		FILM
WAGNER	JEAN		NIEDERLAUTERBACH	01/01/1850	NO		PRIV
WAGNER	JEAN		REICHENBACH	04/27/1849	A		FILM
WAGNER	JEAN	1840	NIEDERLAUTERBACH	01/01/1861	NO		PRIV
WAGNER	JEAN		REICHENBACH B	04/27/1849	A		FILM
WAGNER	JOSEPH		NIEDERLAUTERBACH	01/01/1850	NO		PRIV
WAGNER	JOSEPH	1824	WITTERSDORF	03/04/1852	NO		FILM
WAGNER	MAGDALENA	1848	LEMBACH	01/01/1866	NY		NO.2
WAGNER	MARGUERITE		BAERENDORF	01/01/1828	A		FILM
WAGNER	MICHEL		BAERENDORF	01/01/1828	A		FILM
WAGNER	PIERRE		BAERENDORF	01/01/1828	A		FILM
WAGNER	ROSINE		NIEDERLAUTERBACH	01/01/1850	NO		PRIV
WAGNER	ROSINE		ROHRWILLER	03/12/1838	A		FILM
WAGNER	THERESE		ROHRWILLER	03/12/1838	A		FILM
WAGNER	ULRICH	1797	WALHISWIL	11/15/1846	TX		FILM
WAGNER	VENDELIN		ROHRWILLER	01/01/1828	A		FILM
WAGNER	XAVER	1805	ROUFFACH	11/15/1846	TX		FILM
WAGNER	XAVIER	1805	ROUFFACH	11/15/1846	TX		FILM
WAGNER CH 1	SERAPHIN	1824	RIXHEIM	10/01/1847	TX	CULT	PASS
WAGNER S ANTOINE	MICHEL		BAERENDORF	03/01/1838	A		FILM
WAGNER D ANTOINE	CATHRINE		BAERENDORF	03/01/1838	A		FILM
WAGNER D ANTOINE	CHRISTINE		BAERENDORF	03/01/1838	A		FILM
WAGNER D ANTOINE	MARGUERITTE		BAERENDORF	03/01/1838	A		FILM
WAGNER D LOUDAIN	MADELEINE		ROHRWILLER	03/12/1838	A		FILM
WAGNER D LOUDAIN	ROSINE		ROHRWILLER	03/12/1838	A		FILM

Lastname	Firstname	Birth Year	Birthplace	Emigration	De	Prof	Source
WAGNER D LOUDIN	THERESE		ROHRWILLER	03/12/1838	A		FILM
WAGNER F OF 10	ANTOINE		BAERENDORF	01/01/1828	A		FILM
WAGNER F OF 4	BALTHASAR		DAUENDORF	01/01/1828	A		FILM
WAGNER F OF 6	ETIENNE		MARMOUTIES	01/01/1828	A		FILM
WAGNER MN STILTZ	MARGUERITE	1802	NEUHOFF PR	08/23/1851	A		FILM
WAGNER MN STILTZ	MARGUERITTE	1803	NEUHOFF	01/01/1852	A		FILM
WAGNER MN VOELGER	ROSE	1791	ROUFFACH	10/04/1851	A		FILM
WAGNER S ANTOINE	ANTOINE		BAERENDORF	03/01/1838	A		FILM
WAGNER S ANTOINE	BARBE		BAERENDORF	03/01/1838	A		FILM
WAGNER S ANTOINE	JAQUES		BAERENDORF	03/01/1838	A		FILM
WAGNER S ANTOINE	PIERRE		BAERENDORF	03/01/1838	A		FILM
WAGNER S LOUDAIN	IGNACE		ROHRWILLER	03/12/1838	A		FILM
WAGNER S LOUDAIN	WENDELIN		ROHRWILLER	03/12/1838	A		FILM
WAGNER S PETIT	CATHERINE		MULHOUSE	05/17/1842	SL		FILM
WAGNER W D	LOUDAIN		ROHRWILLER	03/12/1838	A		FILM
WAGNER W W	XAVIER	1805	ROUFFACH	09/17/1846	TX		FILM
WAGNER W W 1 S A BR	JOSEPH	1814	VOGELGRUN	04/29/1851	NY		FILM
WAGNER W W 4CH	SERAPHIN	1824	RIXHEIM	10/28/1847	TX		FILM
WAGNER W W 5CH	ADAM		ESCHBOURG	03/17/1817	A		FILM
WAGNER W W 5CH	LOUDAIN		ROHRWILLER	01/01/1828	A		FILM
WAGNER W W AND D	CHRISTOPHE		NEUHOFF PR	08/23/1851	A		FILM
WAGNER W.S.B.	GEORG		NIEDERKUTZENHAUSEN	01/01/1836	A		SUESS
WAGNER WW	XAVIER	1805	ROUFFACH	09/17/1846	TX		FILM
WAGNER WW AND CH	JOSEPH	1814	BIESHEIM	04/29/1851	NY		FILM
WAGNER WW AND CH 4	SERAPHIN	1824	RIXHEIM	10/28/1847	TX		FILM
WAGNER WW AND CH 5	ADAM		ESCHBOURG	03/17/1817	A		FILM
WAGNER WW AND CH 6	LOUDAIN		ROHRWILLER	03/12/1838	A		FILM
WAHL	ALOIS	1842	BETTLACH	03/01/1860	NO		FILM
WAHL	ANDRE	1815	FESSENHEIM	02/17/1852	NO		FILM
WAHL	ANTON	1839	SCHAFFHAUSEN	01/01/1865	NY		NO.2
WAHL	BERNARDINE		WEILER W	05/09/1849	NY		FILM
WAHL	CHRETIEN		BACKNANG W	07/30/1849	A		FILM
WAHL	CHRETIEN		RUNTZENHEIM	01/01/1828	A		FILM
WAHL	CHRETIEN		SCHERTZHEIM	08/13/1849	A		FILM
WAHL	FRANCOIS	1826	BETTLACH	10/25/1856	NO		FILM
WAHL	HENRIETTE	1825	BLOTZHEIM	10/20/1865	A		FILM
WAHL	JACQUES		RUNTZENHEIM	01/01/1828	A		FILM
WAHL	JAQUES		RUNTZENHEIM	01/01/1828	A		FILM
WAHL	MICHEL		PFALZWEILER	01/01/1828	A		FILM
WAHL	SALOME		HAUFFENHEIM	05/17/1865	A		FILM
WAHL	SALOME		KAUFFENHEIM	05/17/1856	A		FILM
WAHL	THERES		RIEGEL B	05/24/1849	A		FILM
WAHL	THERESE		RIEGEL	05/24/1844	A		FILM
WAHL BR SALOME	GEORGES	1831	ROPPENHEIM	08/13/1852	A		NO.1
WAHL F OF 4	MICHEL		PFALZWEYER	01/01/1828	A		FILM
WAHL H ANNA MARIA	MICHAEL	1803		01/01/1858	A		PRIV
WAHL H ANNA MARIA	MICHAEL	1803	ROPPENHEIM	01/01/1858	A		NO.1
WAHL H SPITTLER	GEORG		ROPPENHEIM	/ /	AL		NO.1
WAHL MN MAREY	ANNA MARIA	1799		01/01/1858	A		PRIV
WAHL MN MAREY	ANNA MARIA	1799	ROPPENHEIM	01/01/1858	A		NO.1

Lastname	Firstname	Birth Year	Birthplace	Emigration	De	Prof	Source
WAHL SI GEORGES	LOUISE	1831	ROPPENHEIM	07/12/1847	A		NO.1
WAHL SI LUOISE	SALOME	1821	ROPPENHEIM	06/26/1845	A		NO.1
WAHL W W 4CH	MICHEL		ESCHBOURG	03/17/1847	A		FILM
WAHRUNG	ADAM		DIEMINGEN	03/03/1838	A		FILM
WALBRETTE	LAZARUS	1857	SCHWENHEIM	/ /	LA		BULL
WALCH	JEAN	1828	FORTSCHWIHR	02/18/1854	NO		FILM
WALCH	THERESE	1823	NIEDERENTZEN	04/14/1849	NY		FILM
WALCH	XAVIER	1827	MERTZEN	05/17/1850	A		FILM
WALCH WW AND CH	LOUIS	1815	ST. AMARIN	12/21/1846	NY		FILM
WALCHER	JOSEPH	1821	ROUGEGOUTTE	05/20/1865	NY		FILM
WALCHER	JOST	1838	CERNAY	01/20/1857	NO		FILM
WALCKER	JEAN JUN.		SESSENHEIM	01/01/1828	A		FILM
WALCKER	JOSEPH	1821	ROUGEGOUTTE	05/20/1865	NY		FILM
WALCKER F OF 5	JEAN		SESSENHEIM	02/23/1838	A		FILM
WALDI W BAUMANN	CATHERINE		NIEDERLAUTERBACH	01/01/1861	NO		PRIV
WALDSHUST	JEAN	1800	CARSPACH	10/25/1853	A		FILM
WALDVOGEL WW CH 5	FRANCOIS	1809	HOUSSEN	03/30/1853	NY		FILM
WALEDIECH	BERNARD	1816	FERRETTE	05/05/1840	NO		FILM
WALHRE	JOSEPH	1816	LEPUIX	03/30/1847	NY		FILM
WALIKER	JEAN JUN.		SESSENHEIM	02/23/1838	A		FILM
WALIKER F OF 5	JEAN		SESSENHEIM	02/23/1838	A		FILM
WALKER	JOSEPH	1804	SEPPOIS-LE-BAS	04/24/1846	NY		FILM
WALKER	JOSEPH	1833	SEPPOIS-LE-BAS	05/25/1852	NY		FILM
WALKRE	JOSEPH	1816	LEPUIX	03/30/1847	NY		FILM
WALLACH	BARBARA	1829	LAUTERBURG	01/01/1865	NY		NO.2
WALLACH	HENRIETTE	1865	LAUTERBURG	01/01/1865	NY		NO.2
WALLACH W W 1 CH	MOSES ARON	1829	LAUTERBURG	01/01/1865	NY	MERC	NO.2
WALLER	JOSEPH	1833	SEPPOIS-LE-BAS	05/25/1852	NY		FILM
WALLES	JULES	1831	PARIS	04/27/1846	NY		FILM
WALLIS	JOSEPH	1831	PARIS	04/27/1846	NY		FILM
WALLIS	JULES	1824	PARIS	11/09/1842	NY		FILM
WALLIS	JULES	1830	PARIS	11/09/1843	NY		FILM
WALLIS	JULES	1831	PARIS	04/27/1846	NY		FILM
WALLSCHMIT W W	JEAN NEPOMUCENE	1813	GUEBWILLER	06/09/1838	NY		FILM
WALLSCHMIT WW	JEAN NEPOMUK	1813	GUEBWILLER	06/09/1838	NY		FILM
WALPLER	FREDERIC GUILAU	1790	STRASBOURG	09/21/1841	NO		FILM
WALPLER	OSKAR	1824	STRASSBOURG	09/21/1841	NO		FILM
WALTER	ANTOINE		ECKARTSWILLER	01/01/1828	A		FILM
WALTER	ANTOINE		SULZBACH	05/12/1849	A		FILM
WALTER	ANTON	1831	SURBOURG	01/01/1866	NY		NO.2
WALTER	CATHERINE		INGENHEIM	01/01/1828	A		FILM
WALTER	CHARLES		BALBRONN	02/28/1838	A		FILM
WALTER	EVE		INGENHEIM	01/01/1828	A		FILM
WALTER	FREDERIQUE	1823	MUNTZENHEIM	09/17/1857	NY		FILM
WALTER	GEORG	1839	OBERROEDERN	01/01/1867	NY		NO.2
WALTER	GEORG	1839	OBERSEEBACH	01/01/1867	NY	WEAV	NO.2
WALTER	GEORGE		GEUTERTHEIM	03/01/1838	A		FILM
WALTER	GEORGE	1839	ILLKIRCH	03/16/1866	NY		FILM
WALTER	GEORGES	1821	MUNTZENHEIM	02/06/1852	NY		FILM
WALTER	ISIDOR		ZINSHEIM	04/14/1849	NY		FILM

Lastname	Firstname	Birth Year	Birthplace	Emigration	De	Prof	Source
WALTER	ISIDOR		ZINSHEIM B	04/14/1844	NY		FILM
WALTER	JEAN		BALDENHEIM	03/06/1838	A		FILM
WALTER	JEAN	1819	JEBSHEIM	03/14/1849	NY		FILM
WALTER	LAURENT		REIPERTSWILLER	01/01/1817	A		FILM
WALTER	LORENTZ		STEINBACH B	10/04/1849	A		FILM
WALTER	LOUISE		DURLACH B	05/12/1849	NY		FILM
WALTER	MARIE	1830	MUNTZENHEIM	02/25/1853	CH		FILM
WALTER	MARTIN	1798	FELLERING	09/28/1841	NO		FILM
WALTER	MATHIAS		HAGENAU	03/01/1838	A		FILM
WALTER	MICHEL		GEUDERTHEIM	03/01/1838	A		FILM
WALTER	MICHEL		PRINTZHEIM	01/01/1834	A		FILM
WALTER	PHILIPPE JAQUES		BOUXWILLER	01/01/1828	A		FILM
WALTER	XAVIER	1831	WILLER	10/23/1857	A		FILM
WALTER WW AND CH 3	LAURENT		REIPERTSWILLER	01/01/1817	A		FILM
WALTER F OF 4	GEORGE		GEUDERTHEIM	03/01/1838	A		FILM
WALTER F OF 6	ANTOINE		ECKARTSWILLER	01/01/1828	A		FILM
WALTER F OF 6	MARTIN	1788	FELLERING	09/28/1841	NO		FILM
WALTER H MARIE LOUIS	FRANCOIS JOSEPH	1829	WILLER	07/27/1853	NY		FILM
WALTER MN DIETRICH	MARIE LOUISE		WILLER BAS RHIN	07/27/1853	NY		FILM
WALTER S MICHAEL	FRITZ		FROESCHWILLER	01/01/1857	A		SUES*
WALTER W BR A S	MARIE THERESE	1793	DIRLINGSDORF	02/16/1854	NY		FILM
WALTER W FRANCOIS	MARIE LOUISE		WILLER	07/27/1853	NY		FILM
WALTER W W	FRANCOISJOSEPH	1829	WILLER BAS RHIN	07/27/1853	NY		FILM
WALTER W W 1 S	FREDERIC	1813	MULHOUSEN	11/02/1847	NO		FILM
WALTER W W 1CH	JEAN	1820	VIEUX FERRETTE	05/26/1845	NY		FILM
WALTER WW AND CH 1	FREDERIC	1813	MULHOUSE	11/02/1847	NO		FILM
WALTER WW AND CH 1	JEAN	1820	VIEUX FERRETTE	05/26/1845	NY		FILM
WALTHER	ADELE	1832	ANDLAU BAS RHIN	10/20/1854	NO		FILM
WALTHER	ANTOINE		SULZBACH W	05/12/1849	A		FILM
WALTHER	JACOB	1836	LEMBACH	01/01/1864	NY	BAKE	NO.2
WALTHER	MARIE THERESE	1793	DIRLINSDORF	02/16/1854	NY		FILM
WALTHER	PHILLIP		BUCHSWEILER	01/01/1840	LA		BULL
WALTHER F OF 8	PHILIPPE JACQUS		BOUXWILLER	01/01/1828	A		FILM
WALTHER F OF5	MATHIAS		HAGUENAU	03/01/1838	A		FILM
WALTZ	EVE		RENCHEN B	05/31/1849	A		FILM
WALTZ	FRANCOIS		KUPPENHEIM B	09/20/1849	A		FILM
WALTZER	LOUIS	1820	SENTHEIM	09/09/1847	NY		FILM
WAMIER	GEORGE		FORT LOUIS	01/01/1828	A		FILM
WAMPFLER	J. NICOLAS		HERBITZHEIM	01/01/1828	A		FILM
WANDER	EVE		RUNTZENHEIM	01/01/1828	A		FILM
WANDER WW AND CH 2	JAQUES		MEMMELSHOFFEN	03/28/1817	A		FILM
WANNER	JAQUES	1834	WENTZWILLER	05/26/1866	NY		FILM
WANTZ	JOSEPH		SOUFFELNHEIM	03/02/1838	A		FILM
WANTZ W W	JOSEPH		SOUFFLENHEIM	03/02/1838	A		FILM
WANTZ WW	JOSEPH		SOUFFLENHEIM	01/01/1838	A		FILM
WAPLER	EMILE	1790	STRASSBOURG	07/07/1840	NO		FILM
WAPLER	EMILE	1820	STRASBOURG	09/05/1843	NO		FILM
WAPLER	EMILE	1820	STRASBOURG	09/09/1845	NO		FILM
WAPLER	EMILE	1820	STRASBOURG	09/05/1843	NO		FILM
WAPLER	FREDERIC GUILLA	1789	STRASBOURG	11/21/1843	NO		FILM

Lastname	Firstname	Birth Year	Birthplace	Emigration	De	Prof	Source
WAPLER	FREDERIC GUILLA	1790	STRASBOURG	07/07/1840	NO		FILM
WAPLER MN STAHL	MARGUERITE	1794	STRASBOURG	03/25/1846	NO		FILM
WASMER	CHRETIEN		REICHENBACH	04/27/1844	A		FILM
WASMER	JACOB		REICHENBACH	04/27/1849	A		FILM
WASMER	JEAN		REICHENBACH	04/27/1849	A		FILM
WASMER	SABINE		REICHENBACH	04/27/1849	A		FILM
WASS S H.M.WAAS	MATHIAS W CHIDR		MITSCHDORF	01/01/1730	A		SUESS
WASSEN WW AND CH 3	ANTOINE	1805	BOURBACH-LE-BAS	10/31/1844	NO		FILM
WATTEN	ANDRE	1827	JEBSHEIM	05/15/1847	NY		FILM
WATTER	GEORGES	1821	MUNTZENHEIM	02/06/1852	NY		FILM
WATTSTEIN			DEUTSCHLAND	04/12/1849	A		FILM
WATTSTEIN			GERMANY	04/12/1849	A		FILM
WEBER	ANA MARIA		ETZINGEN	05/30/1849	NY		FILM
WEBER	CATHERINE		FREUDENSTADT	04/20/1849	NY		FILM
WEBER	CHARLES		SUNDHAUSEN	03/02/1837	A		FILM
WEBER	FLORENT		SINGRIST	01/01/1828	A		FILM
WEBER	FREDERIC	1825	MUNSTER	10/09/1846	NY		FILM
WEBER	GEORGE		SINGRIST	01/01/1828	A		FILM
WEBER	GEORGES	1819	NEUVILLER	07/07/1854	NY		FILM
WEBER	HENRI	1833	KANDEL	04/23/1849	NY		FILM
WEBER	JEAN	1828	SUHR	05/01/1857	A		FILM
WEBER	JOSEPH	1804	MUTZACH	04/09/1844	TX		FILM
WEBER	JOSEPH	1811	ALTKIRCH	09/12/1849	NY		FILM
WEBER	JOSEPH	1831	APPENWIHR	08/10/1849	NY		FILM
WEBER	KARL	1841	CLIMBACH	01/01/1841	NY		NO.2
WEBER	LAURENT		WASSELONNE	01/01/1828	A		FILM
WEBER	LAURENT	1834	SIEGEN	01/26/1857	NY		FILM
WEBER	MADELEINE	1831	RIQUEWIHR	07/16/1851	NY		FILM
WEBER	MARIANNE	1842	EBERBACH	01/01/1865	NY		NO.2
WEBER	MARIE ANNE	1810	OBERDORFF	03/19/1840	NY		FILM
WEBER	MARTIN	1850	MERCKWILLER	01/01/1869	NY		NO.2
WEBER	MATHIAS	1829	WECHOLSHEIM	02/25/1852	A		FILM
WEBER	MATHIAS	1829	WECKOLSHEIM	02/01/1852	TX	DAYL	PASS
WEBER	MAX		GOSSHEIM	04/21/1849	A		FILM
WEBER	MICHEL	1840	ROUFFACH	05/09/1843	A		FILM
WEBER	PETER	1807	MUTRACH	04/09/1844	TX		FILM
WEBER	PHILIPPE		ESCHBOURG	01/01/1828	A		FILM
WEBER	PHILLIP	1820	EBERBACH	01/01/1865	NY		NO.2
WEBER	PIERRE	1816	SOURGFELDEN	08/21/1847	A		FILM
WEBER	PIGMENIUS	1832	HUSSEREN-WASSELING	08/04/1854	NO		FILM
WEBER	SYLVESTRE	1822	HUSSEREN	10/31/1845	NO		FILM
WEBER	THIEBAUD	1822	OFFHEIM	09/18/1849	NY		FILM
WEBER	VALENTIN DE BAM	1837	HUSSEREN	02/07/1848	NO		FILM
WEBER WW	JOSEPH	1817	HEITEREN	02/06/1852	NY		FILM
WEBER S ANTOINE		1837	COLMAR	06/24/1856	A		FILM
WEBER S ANTOINE		1847	COLMAR	06/24/1856	A		FILM
WEBER W ANTOINE		1802	COLMAR	06/24/1856	A		FILM
WEBER WW AND CH 2	ANTOINE	1806	COLMAR	06/24/1856	A		FILM
WEBER WW AND CH 7	NICOLAS	1789	OSTHEIM	03/07/1845	NY		FILM
WECHERLEN WW CH 5	FRANCOIS THIEBA		CLEEBOURG	03/28/1817	A		FILM

Lastname	Firstname	Birth Year	Birthplace	Emigration	De	Prof	Source
WECKER	GEORGES	1827	MITTELWIHR	06/01/1846	TX	DAYL	PASS
WECKER	SEBASTIEN		OERMINGEN	03/23/1817	A		FILM
WECKER CH 3	NICOLAS	1814	RIQUEWIHR	06/01/1846	TX	DAYL	PASS
WECKER WW AND CH 1	JEAN GEORGES	1811	MITTELWIHR	06/27/1846	TX		FILM
WECKER WW AND CH 2	MATHIAS	1817	BIERSHEIM	05/23/1849	NY		FILM
WECKERLE	JEAN		CLEEBOURG	01/01/1817	A		PRIV
WECKERLE	JOHANN	1850	BREMMELBACH	01/01/1867	NY		NO.2
WECKERLE	MAGDALENA	1848	BREMMELBACH	01/01/1867	NY		NO.2
WECKERLIN	DOMINIQUE	1819	GUEBWILLER	06/30/1849	NY		FILM
WEGER	FREDERICH		SCHERTZHEIM	08/13/1849	A		FILM
WEHNING	THEODOR	1816	WESTFALEN	09/17/1845	TX		FILM
WEHRING WW AND CH 2	PIERRE		SOUWEILER	03/29/1817	A		FILM
WEHRUNG	PIERRE		BERG	03/01/1838	A		FILM
WEHRUNG	PIERRE		SIEWILLER	03/02/1838	A		FILM
WEHRUNG WW AND CH 2	PIERRE		SOUWEILLER	03/29/1817	A		FILM
WEIBEL	CATHERINE	1829	MOOSCH	10/24/1854	NY		FILM
WEIBEL	LOUIS		WIMMENAU	01/01/1828	A		FILM
WEIBEL	MARIE ANNE	1833	MOOSCH	10/27/1854	NY		FILM
WEIDAMNN	NICOLAS		THAL	01/01/1828	A		FILM
WEIDENACKER	DOROTHE		GERMANY	04/12/1849	NY		FILM
WEIDMANN	ANDRE		BETTWILLER	02/28/1838	A		FILM
WEIDMANN	AUGUSTE	1835	WEGSCHEID	03/17/1854	NY		FILM
WEIDRECHT WW			FREISTEDT	04/08/1849	A		FILM
WEIGEL	JOSEPH		OBERLAUTERBACH	01/01/1850	NO		PRIV
WEIGEL	JOSEPH	1837	OBERLAUTERBACH	01/01/1869	NO	DAYL	PRIV
WEIGEL F KLEIN	MADELEINE		NIEDERLAUTERBACH	01/01/1866	NO		PRIV
WEIL	ALBERT		WISSEMBOURG	01/01/1869	NO		PRIV
WEIL	BENJAMIN	1847	SOULTZ-SOUS-FORET	01/01/1865	NY		NO.2
WEIL	GEORGE		NIEDERMODERN	01/01/1828	A		FILM
WEIL	GEORGES		SIEWILLER	03/02/1838	A		FILM
WEIL	HELENE		WISSEMBOURG	01/01/1869	NO		PRIV
WEIL	JACOB		RENINGEN	04/18/1849	NY		FILM
WEIL	KARL	1847	SURBOURG	01/01/1865	NY	MERC	NO.2
WEIL	LOUIS		SCHWEIGHAUSEN	01/01/1828	A		FILM
WEIL	MARGTE		NIEDERMODERN	01/01/1828	A		FILM
WEIL	MICHEL		STRUTH	01/01/1828	A		FILM
WEIL	MICHEL		MARMOUTIER	01/01/1828	A		FILM
WEIL	MOSES	1849	SURBOURG	01/01/1865	NY		NO.2
WEIL	REGINE	1821	WATTWILLER	11/02/1843	NO		FILM
WEIL	SALOMON	1835	BIESHEIM	07/14/1852	NO		FILM
WEIL	SCHILI		TIEFFENBACH	01/01/1828	A		FILM
WEIL WW AND CH 7	GEORGES		MULHOUSE	01/01/1828	A		FILM
WEILER	ANNA MARIA	1829	ROPPENHEIM	03/09/1848	A		NO.1
WEILER	GEORGE		GERSTHEIM	03/03/1838	A		FILM
WEILER	JOHANN		STUPFRICH	09/30/1849	A		FILM
WEILING H MADELEINE	MARTIN	1798		/ /	A		PRIV
WEILING MN MEISTERKN MADELEINE CH 4		1805		/ /	A		PRIV
WEILL	BENJAMIN	1827	SOULTZMATT	08/09/1848	NY		FILM
WEILL	DAVID	1831	WATTWILLER	11/30/1854	NY		FILM
WEILL	GERTRUDE	1825	REICHSHOFFEN	/ /	LA		BULL

Lastname	Firstname	Birth Year	Birthplace	Emigration	De	Prof	Source
WEILL	JAQUES	1831	BOLLWILLER	04/24/1857	SF		FILM
WEILL	KARL		SCHIRRHOFEN	/ /	LA		BULL
WEILL	LEOPOLD	1836	CERNAY	10/31/1854	NO		FILM
WEILL	SUZANNE	1833	WATTWILLER	11/07/1854	NY		FILM
WEILLER	ANDRE	1813	ISSENHEIM	06/15/1849	NY		PRIV
WEIMANN	JEAN	1821	GOMMERSDORF	04/17/1844	NY		FILM
WEIMER	JACOB FRIEDRICH		LANGENSOULTZBACH	01/01/1848	A		SUESS
WEIMER	NICHEL		MEHWILLER	04/11/1818	A		FILM
WEIMZAEPF	MICHEL	1820	UNGERSHEIM	07/21/1847	A		FILM
WEINAMNN	CAROLINE	1839	MULHOUSE	07/14/1857	NY		FILM
WEINBERGER	REINE		BRUMATH	01/01/1828	A		FILM
WEINGARTHNER WW	MARTIN	1809	OBERHERGHEIM	10/14/1847	NY		FILM
WEINIG	LEON	1837	OSTHEIM	07/12/1856	NY		FILM
WEINLING	ANTOINE		SCHERLENHEIM	01/09/1838	A		FILM
WEINMANN WW AND CH 2	FRANCOIS JOSEPH	1808	THANN	03/29/1847	NY		FILM
WEINSTEIN	CHARLES		HERBITZHEIM	01/01/1828	A		FILM
WEINZAEPFLEN WW CH2	ANTOINE	1813	UNGERSHEIM	07/10/1849	A		FILM
WEINZORN				/ /			
WEINZORN WW AND CH	JOSEPH	1826	COLMAR	02/03/1852	NY		FILM
WEIRS WW AND CH 4	ANDRE		REICHSHOFFEN	03/28/1817	A		FILM
WEIS CH 2	JEAN		ETTENDORF	01/01/1828	A		FILM
WEIS CH 5	FRANCOIS MICHEL		ETTENDORF	01/01/1828	A		FILM
WEIS WW	FRANCOIS JOSEPH	1803	BURNHAUPT	05/05/1840	NY		FILM
WEISCHMANN			FRANCE	/ /	NY		FILM
WEISS	ADOLPHE	1826	MULHOUSE	11/18/1854	NY		FILM
WEISS	ANTOINE		FORT LOUIS	01/01/1828	A		FILM
WEISS	BERNARD	1789	MOTHERN	01/01/1867	NY		NO.2
WEISS	CATHERINE	1826	BRECHAUMOMT	03/12/1847	NY		FILM
WEISS	CHARLES	1816	MULHOUSE	08/05/1845	NO		FILM
WEISS	CHRETIEN		BETTWILLER	02/28/1838	A		FILM
WEISS	DANIEL		SARRE UNION	01/01/1828	A		FILM
WEISS	GEORGE		ESCHENTZWILLER	01/01/1828	A		FILM
WEISS	HENRY		KESKASTEL	01/01/1828	A		FILM
WEISS	HENRY JUN		KESKASTEL	01/01/1828	A		FILM
WEISS	JAQUES		PFAFFENHOFFEN	01/01/1828	A		FILM
WEISS	JAQUES	1816	LIEPRE	05/13/1846	NO		FILM
WEISS	JEAN		MOMMENHEIM	02/28/1838	A		FILM
WEISS	JEAN		WASSELONNE	01/01/1828	A		FILM
WEISS	JEAN	1826	GRANDVILLARS	04/17/1855	NY		FILM
WEISS	JOSEPH		MARLENHEIM	01/01/1828	A		FILM
WEISS	JOSEPH		SCHWEIGHAUSEN	01/01/1828	A		FILM
WEISS	MARIE ANNE		WASSELONNE	01/01/1828	A		FILM
WEISS	MARIE ANNE	1786	HOCHSTATT	06/20/1856	TX		FILM
WEISS	MARTIN		SCHIRRHEIM	01/01/1828	A		FILM
WEISS	MICHAEL		NEEWILLER	01/01/1850	NO		PRIV
WEISS	MICHEL		KORK	04/21/1849	NY		FILM
WEISS	MICHEL		MERCKWILLER	01/01/1868	NY		NO.2
WEISS	MICHEL	1849	NEHWILLER	01/01/1866	NO	FARM	NO.2
WEISS	SEBASTIEN	1803	ST. CROIX EN PLAINE	08/21/1845	NY		FILM
WEISS	THERESE		MARLENHEIM	01/01/1828	A		FILM

Lastname	Firstname	Birth Year	Birthplace	Emigration	De	Prof	Source
WEISS	THERESE	1797	BERGHEIM	03/25/1856	NY		FILM
WEISS WW	EMILE EUGENE	1828	ESCHENTZWILLER	03/26/1851	NY		FILM
WEISS H DIEBOLD MARI	GEORGE		KORK	04/21/1844	NY		FILM
WEISS W ALEXIS	VICTOIRE		WANTZENAU	03/07/1838	A		FILM
WEISS W STROHMEYER F	ANNE	1810	BURNHAUPT	09/15/1857	NY		FILM
WEISS WW	FRANCOIS JOSEPH	1803	BURNHAUPT-BAS	05/05/1840	NY		FILM
WEISS WW AND CH 3	PIERRE		RATZWILLER	03/03/1817	A		FILM
WEISS WW AND CH 4	ALEXIS		WANTZENAU	03/07/1838	A		FILM
WEISS WW AND CH 6	NICOLAS		ALTWILLER	03/18/1817	A		FILM
WEISSBACK	FRANCOISE	1833	BOLLWILLER	03/16/1857	NY		FILM
WEISSE	HENRY		KESKASTEL	01/01/1828	A		FILM
WEISSENBORN	GUSTAVE		LUDINGEN	09/30/1849	A		FILM
WEISSENBURGER	BENEDICT	1849	MOTHERN	01/01/1867	NY		NO.2
WEISSENBURGER	JOHANN	1861	MOTHERN	01/01/1869	NY		NO.2
WEISSHAAR	JOSEF	1845	KUTZENHAUSEN	01/01/1866	NY	DAYL	NO.2
WEITH	ALBERT	1845	WEISSENBURG	01/01/1869	NO	MERC	NO.2
WEITH	HELENE	1843	WEISSENBURG	01/01/1869	NO		NO.2
WEITHAS WW AND CH 3	JEAN	1805	WUSENHEIM	04/26/1852	NY		FILM
WEITZ	ERNST JOSEPH		BLODELSHEIM	10/15/1851	TX		FILM
WEITZ	ETIENNE		BLODELSHEIM	10/15/1851	TX		FILM
WEITZ	GEORGES GUILLAU	1825	MULHOUSE	12/09/1953	NY		FILM
WEITZ MN NICOLAI	AMELIE	1817	MULHOUSE	08/12/1854	NY		FILM
WEIXLER CH	URSULA	1824	LEUTKIRCHEN	10/25/1844	NO		FILM
WEIZER	GEORGE		DETTWILLER	01/01/1828	A		FILM
WELCHER	THIEBAULT	1814	MALMERSPACH	10/24/1854	TX		FILM
WELCHER W JOSEPH	MARIANNE	1816	MALMERSPACH	11/15/1846	TX		FILM
WELCHER WW	JOSEPH	1812	MALMERSPACH	11/15/1846	TX		FILM
WELCKER	HUBERT	1826	RANSPACH	08/08/1844	NY		FILM
WELCKER	MARTIN	1835	MOOSCH	06/19/1854	NY		FILM
WELCKER	SARAPHIN	1830	MOOSCH	06/08/1854	NY		FILM
WELDE	TINA		LANDAU	10/31/1849	NY		FILM
WELDY CH 2	ANDRE	1777	OBERBERGHEIM	10/14/1847	NY		FIM
WELDY WW AND CH 2	JEAN	1811	OBERBERGHEIM	10/14/1847	NY		FILM
WELKER	THIEBAUD	1814	MALMERSPACH	10/01/1854	TX	CULT	PASS
WELSCHINGER	JOSEPH	1798	URSCHENHEIM	08/27/1850	NY		FILM
WELTERLE WW	JEAN	1825	BOURBACH LE BAS	04/19/1852	NY		FILM
WENCK	GEORGE		ZUTZENDORF	01/01/1828	A		FILM
WENDE	PIERRE	1814	ROPPWILLER	04/11/1855	A		FILM
WENDEL	JOSEPH	1806	BADEN	09/17/1845	TX		FILM
WENDLING	ANNE AMRIE		BRUMATH	01/01/1828	A		FILM
WENDLING	FRANCOIS ANTION			/ /			
WENDLING	GEORGE		HOCHFRANKENHEIM	01/01/1828	A		FILM
WENDLING	GEORGE		OBERMODERN	01/01/1828	A		FILM
WENDLING	GEORGE		ZUTZENDORF	01/01/1828	A		FILM
WENDLING	JACOB		NEHWILLER	01/01/1817	A		NO.2
WENDLING	JAQUES		BRUMATH	01/01/1828	A		FILM
WENDLING	JEAN		BRUMATH	03/22/1838	A		FILM
WENDLING	JEAN		MORSCHWILLER	03/04/1838	A		FILM
WENDLING	JOSEPH		MORSCHWILLER	03/04/1838	A		FILM
WENDLING	JOSEPH	1816	WILLGOTTHEIM	02/12/1846	NY		FILM

Lastname	Firstname	Birth Year	Birthplace	Emigration	De	Prof	Source
WENDLING	MADELEINE		MORSCHWILLER	03/04/1838	A		FILM
WENDLING	MARGUERITTE		BUESWILLER	01/01/1828	A		FILM
WENDLING	MICHEL		BOUXWILLER	/ /			
WENDLING	NICHOLAS	1815	UHLWILLER	06/20/1837	A		PRIV
WENDLING	NICOLAS		UHLWILLER	03/03/1838	A		FILM
WENDLING	PHILIPPE		BALDENHEIM	03/06/1838	A		FILM
WENDLING MN MARY	ELISABETH	1813	ROESCHWOOG	06/20/1837	A		PRIV
WENDLING WW	JAQUES		MULHOUSE	01/01/1828	A		FILM
WENDLING WW	JEAN THIEBAUD	1813	MICHELBACH	07/03/1846	NY		
WENDLING WW AND CH 2	ANDRE	1806	GUEWENHEIM	06/03/1846	NY		FILM
WENDLING WW AND CH 2	FRANCOIS SERAPH	1824	GRUSSENHEIM	10/20/1854	NY		FILM
WENDLING WW AND CH 3	JAQUES		MULHOUSE	01/01/1828	A		FILM
WENGER	GEORGE		PETERSBACH	01/01/1828	A		FILM
WENGER	MICHEL		ALTECKENDORF	01/01/1828	A		FILM
WENGER WW AND CH 2	BARBE	1824	ST. LOUIS	04/19/1853	NY		FILM
WENGER WW AND CH 5	PH. JAQUES		GUMBRECHTSHOFFEN	04/09/1819	A		FILM
WENGLER	GEORGE		RUNTZENHEIM	01/01/1828	A		FILM
WENIGER	JEAN	1827	MUNSTER	05/12/1849	NY		FILM
WENINO	HENRI	1828	GRIESBACH	05/25/1852	NY		FILM
WENINO	MARTIN	1832	GRIESBACH	06/08/1854	NY		FILM
WENINO	PAUL	1835	GRIESBACH	08/25/1853	NY		FILM
WENIZAEPFLEN	ROMAIN	1813	UNGERSHEIM	07/15/1839	PH		FILM
WENNER	MAGDALENA		ALTENSTADT	01/01/1869	NY		NO.2
WENSO WW	NICOLAS	1817	KAYSERSBERG	02/16/1849	NY		FILM
WENTZER	ANNE MERIE	1826	KAYSERSBERG	02/15/1849	NY		FILM
WEPF WW AND CH 2	JEAN BAPTISTE	1817	NIEDERENTZEN	11/14/1848	TX		FILM
WEPFER	JOSEPH	1824	THANN	04/01/1847	NY		FILM
WEPFER	JUSTINE	1831	THANN	03/31/1857	NY		FILM
WERCK	MICHEL		MARLENHEIM	01/01/1828	A		FILM
WERCKLE F OF 3	PIERRE		HAMBACH	03/08/1838	A		FILM
WERCKLE F OF 6	ANDRE		HAMBACH	03/08/1838	A		FILM
WERCKLE W W 3CH	MICHEL	1823	LUTTERBACH	03/15/1854	NY		FILM
WERLE F OF 4	LOUIS		ESCHBOURG	01/01/1828	A		FILM
WERLE W W	LAURENT	1820	GUEBWILLER	08/02/1854	NY		FILM
WERLE W W 1CH	MICHEL		ESCHBOURG	01/01/1828	A		FILM
WERLIN	ANNA MARIA	1844	LAUTERBURG	01/01/1865	NY		NO.2
WERLIN	FRANCOIS	1815	DELLE	05/05/1840	NY		FILM
WERLING F OF 4	ETTIENNE		WANTZENAU	03/01/1838	A		FILM
WERMEL	BARBE	1827	KANDEL	04/23/1849	NY		FILM
WERMEL	MICHEL	1830	KANDEL	04/23/1849	NY		FILM
WERNER	CAROLINA		GRABEN B	06/21/1849	A		FILM
WERNER	IGANCE		DRUSENHEIM	03/24/1838	A		FILM
WERNER	ULLE		GRABEN B	06/21/1849	A		FILM
WERNER S FRIEDR.WERN	CARL		HATTEN	01/01/1846	A		SUESS
WERNER W W 1CH	GEORGES	1812	BERGHEIM	09/03/1849	A		FILM
WERNER W W 3CH	IGNACE	1816	BERGHEIM	12/21/1854	NY		FILM
WERNERD	JOSEPHINE	1866	DUERRENBACH	01/01/1866	NY		NO.2
WERNERS F OF 8	PHILIPPE		BOUXWILLER	01/01/1828	A		FILM
WERNERT	CHRISOSTE		SOUFFLENHEIM	01/01/1828	A		FILM
WERNERT	XAVIER		DURRENBACH	06/24/1854	A		FILM

Lastname	Firstname	Birth Year	Birthplace	Emigration	De	Prof	Source
WERNERT F OF 4	MICHEL		IMBSHEIM	01/01/1828	A		FILM
WERNERT W W 2 CH	ANTOINE	1822	BERGHEIM	12/21/1854	NY		FILM
WERNET	JACOB	1851	ALTENSTADT	01/01/1866	NY		NO.2
WERNETTE	JEAN BAPTISTE	1813	WITTELSHEIM	11/13/1844	TX		FILM
WERNHER	FRIEDRICH	1840	HOFFEN	01/01/1869	NY		NO.2
WERRIER	ISIDORE	1855	LA CHAPELLE SOUS CHX	03/09/1866	NY		FILM
WERRIER	MARIE	1819	LA CHAPELLE SOUS CHU	03/09/1866	NY		FILM
WERRIER	VINCENT	1815	LA CHAPELLE SOUS CHX	03/09/1866	NY		FILM
WERSCHINE W W 6CH	JOSEPH	1807	RODEREN	06/24/1856	NY		FILM
WERTH	BLAISE	1808	HISRINGUE	04/01/1841	NY		FILM
WERTZ W 4CH	BARBE	1811	COLMAR	11/26/1853	SL		FILM
WESCHLE	ANDRE		HAMBACH	03/08/1838	A		FILM
WEST F OF 7	CHRISTMANN		IMBSHEIM	01/01/1828	A		FILM
WESTE	MICHAEL	1816		04/09/1844	TX		FILM
WESTRICH	PIERRE	1828	TURCHHEIM	10/01/1849	A		FILM
WETTERHOLD W W 7CH	JACQUES		EYWILLER	03/20/1817	A		FILM
WETTLING F OF 6	MARTIN		ROPPENHEIM	03/06/1838	A		FILM
WETTLING H MEISTERKN	MARTIN 4CHILDRE	1798	ROPPENHEIM	/ /	A		NO.1
WETTLING MN MEISTERK	MADELAINE	1805	ROPPENHEIM	/ /	A		NO.1
WETTSTEIN	MARIE		KEHL	04/07/1849	NY		FILM
WETZEL	ANTON	1840	MUNCHHOUSE	01/01/1867	NY		NO.2
WETZEL	CHARLES	1825	ALTKIRCH	09/18/1854	NY		FILM
WETZEL	FRANCOIS JOSEPH	1817	ANGEOT	03/04/1846	NY		FILM
WETZEL	JEAN	1821	MUNSTER	10/09/1846	NY		FILM
WETZEL	JEAN	1824	BUETHWILLER	10/07/1847	NY		FILM
WETZEL	JEAN	1830	LAUW	03/08/1852	NY		FILM
WETZEL H GEIST B.	HANS MARTIN		PREUSCHDORF	01/01/1721	A	MILL	SUESS
WETZEL MN GEIST	BARBARA		PREUSCHDORF	01/01/1721	A		SUESS
WETZSTEIN	CRESZENTIA		HENGENLAU	05/02/1849	NY		FILM
WEXLER	URSULA	1816	BLODELSHEIM	12/01/1844	TX		SHIP
WEY	JEAN	1823	BOURBACH LE BASD	05/23/1846	NY		FILM
WEY W W 2CH	LAURENT	1822	BOURBACH LE BAS	01/13/1854	NY		FILM
WEYD F OF 9	MICHEL		NEUWILLER	01/01/1828	A		FILM
WEYDELICH	EHRARD		WEISACH W	06/01/1849	A		FILM
WEYDMANN F OF 11	JEAN		MORSCHWILLER	03/04/1838	A		FILM
WEYER W W 3CH	JOSEPH		ENGENTHAL	03/06/1838	A		FILM
WEYGANT W W 1 CH	MATERNE		DIEBOLSHEIM	06/04/1817	A		FILM
WEYH F OF 4	MARTIN		KINTZHEIM	02/28/1838	A		FILM
WEYHNACHTER	JEAN		ESCHBOURG	03/03/1817	A		FILM
WEYL	ELIE		HAGUENAU	03/01/1838	A		FILM
WEYL	NATHAN		WESTHAUSEN	02/26/1838	A		FILM
WEYL F OF 2	JOSEPH		FESSENHEIM	02/27/1838	A		FILM
WEYMANN	FRANCOIS	1826	VIEUX THANN	10/24/1846	NY		FILM
WEYMANN	JOSEPHINE	1836	THANN	04/11/1857	A		FILM
WEYMANN W SI	JOSEPH	1833	THANN	05/08/1855	A		FILM
WEYMANN W W	JEAN ANDRE	1826	RIBAUVILLE	03/07/1855	NY		FILM
WGNER	MADELAINE		ROHRWILLER	01/01/1828	A		FILM
WICK W W BRAUN	MICHEL	1820	ALTKIRCH	07/07/1854	NY		FILM
WICKERSHEIM	MATHIAS	1799	OSTHEIM	10/06/1846	NY		FILM
WICKERSHEIM W W 4CH	JEAN	1796	OSTHEIM	10/12/1846	CH		FILM

Lastname	Firstname	Birth Year	Birthplace	Emigration	De	Prof	Source
WICKERSHEIM W W 5CH	FREDERIC	1790	OSTHEIM	03/17/1845	NY		FILM
WICKY W W 3CH	JOSEPH	1809	KIRCHBERG	10/29/1845	NY		FILM
WIDEMEYER W W	JACQUES		NOLSHEIM	03/03/1817	A		FILM
WIDMER	PIERRE	1815	VOUFREY	10/24/1839	A		FILM
WIDOLF	MORAND	1834	WITTERSDORF	11/27/1852	NO		FILM
WIDOLF W W 5CH	MORAND	1803	EMLINGEN	03/25/1856	A		FILM
WIDREKHER	JEAN BAPTISTE	1818	LIEPVRE	07/12/1848	NO		FILM
WIE W W 4CH	ANTOINE	1807	ALTKIRCH	03/11/1854	A		FILM
WIEDEMANN	HENRIETTE		WITTENDORF	05/12/1849	A		FILM
WIEDERSTEIN W W 2CH	JEAN		FROHMUHL	01/01/1817	A		FILM
WIEDLING	JACQUES		KURTZENHAUSEN	03/03/1838	A		FILM
WIEGET W W A D	JEAN	1795	MUSSLEBACH	04/16/1853	NY		FILM
WIEHL	MARTIN		GEISINGEN W	05/12/1849	A		FILM
WIEKERSHEIM W W 5CH	MICHEL	1805	OSTHEIM	03/25/1846	NY		FILM
WIEMAND	URSULA	1823	MUELHAUSEN	10/25/1843	TX		FILM
WIESER	JEAN	1806	NIEDERBRUCH	05/25/1846	NY		FILM
WIESER F OF7	PIERRE		PFALZWEYER	01/01/1828	A		FILM
WIESSENBORN	HERMANN		LUDINGEN B	09/30/1849	A		FILM
WIESSER	IGANCE		MOEHRINGEN	04/21/1849	NY		FILM
WILD	MICHEL		WEITERSWILLER	01/01/1828	A		FILM
WILD W 4 CH	GEORGES	1797	BARTENHEIM	07/20/1847	NY		FILM
WILD F OF 5	JOSEPH		SINGRIST	01/01/1828	A		FILM
WILD F OF 6	CHRETIEN		WEITERSWILLER	01/01/1828	A		FILM
WILD F OF 7	JACQUES		HATTMATT	01/01/1828	A		FILM
WILDT	MADELAINE		PETERSBACH	01/01/1828	A		FILM
WILFERSHEIM	CATHERINE BARBE	1829	RIGUEWIHR	03/31/1852	NY		FILM
WILGAINSS	CHRETIEN		ROPPENHEIM	03/06/1838	A		FILM
WILHELM	AGATHE	1817	FELLERINGEN	11/04/1857	TX		FILM
WILHELM	AGNES	1817	ODEREN	11/04/1857	TX		FILM
WILHELM	ANDRE		RUNTZENHEIM	01/01/1828	A		FILM
WILHELM	JACQUES		RUNTZENHEIM	01/01/1828	A		FILM
WILHELM	JACUQES		BERG	03/01/1838	A		FILM
WILHELM	JEAN ADAM		LEUTENHEIM	03/01/1838	A		FILM
WILHELM	JOSEPH	1820	ODEREM	10/21/1844	NO		FILM
WILHELM	MARIE ANNE		LEUTENHEIM	03/07/1838	A		FILM
WILHELM	MICHEL	1823	POSTROFF	05/22/1848	NY		FILM
WILHELM	NICOLAS		BERG	03/01/1838	A		FILM
WILHELM	PIERRE		ALTWILLER	01/01/1828	A		FILM
WILHELM F OF 8	MATHIAS		ROESCHWOOG	01/01/1828	A		FILM
WILHELM W W 3CH	MAURICE	1822	GUEBWILLER	12/13/1853	NY		FILM
WILHELM W W 4CH	CHARLES GOTTLIB	1804	ROSENFELD	02/14/1855	NY		FILM
WILHELM W W 4CH	JEAN	1808	OBERANSPACH	04/07/1857	A		FILM
WILL	JACQUES		BURBACH	03/02/1838	A		FILM
WILLARD	MOZIRE		MARMOUTIER	01/01/1828	A		FILM
WILLIA	MARIE	1833	ROPPENTZWILLER	08/16/1865	NY		FILM
WILLIEN W 2CH	MARIE ANNE	1811	THANN	10/10/1845	NY		FILM
WILLIG	ANNE MARIE	1827	DURMENACH	07/23/1851	NY		FILM
WILLIG	MARIE ANNE	1801	NIEDERBERGHEIM	09/16/1850	NO		FILM
WILLIG F OF 2	NICOLAS		DOMFESSEL	01/01/1828	A		FILM
WILLMANN	XAVIER ANTOINE	1803	MARCKENHEIM	03/01/1838	A		FILM

270

Lastname	Firstname	Birth Year	Birthplace	Emigration	De	Prof	Source
WILLMENG	IGNACE STANSISL	1822	GRUSSENHEIM	10/10/1852	NY		FILM
WILLY	JOSEPH	1820	MORTZWILLER	04/29/1839	NY		FILM
WILLY	PIERRE		MORTZWILLER	04/29/1839	NY		FILM
WILPERS	HEINRICH	1812	WESTFALEN	09/17/1845	TX		FILM
WILTENMUTH	CAROLINE		TIEFFENBACH	01/01/1828	A		FILM
WIMMER	ELISABETH		FORT LOUIS	01/01/1828	A		FILM
WIMMER	FRANCOIS JOSEPH	1826	KIRCHBERG	07/28/1854	A		FILM
WIMMER F OF 2	ANTOINE		FORT-LOUIS	01/01/1828	A		FILM
WIMMER F OF 5	LAURENT		FORT LOUIS	01/01/1828	A		FILM
WINCKEL	JACQUES	1837	OSTHEIM	12/05/1856	NY		FILM
WINCKELMANN	FREDERIC		MONTBELIARD	03/11/1841	A		FILM
WINCKELSASS	FREDERIC		SESSENHEIM	01/23/1838	A		FILM
WINCKELSASS F OF 5	LOUIS		SESSENHEIM	02/23/1838	A		FILM
WINCKLER	JOSEF		BINZGEN	05/23/1833	A		FILM
WINCKLER	PERRE	1820	MOLLAU	01/12/1848	NO		FILM
WINCKLER	XAVIER	1835	ODEREN	08/01/1860	TX	CARP	PASS
WINCKLER W 2CH	MARIE ANNE	1823	NEUF BRISACH	08/30/1850	NY		FILM
WINDISDAERFFER	FRANCOIS		STEINBOURG	01/01/1828	A		FILM
WINDSTEIN	GEORGE		WEISLINGEN	01/01/1828	A		FILM
WINDSTEIN	HENRI		SCHOENBURG	01/01/1828	A		FILM
WINDSTEIN F OF 6	GEORGES		WEISLINGEN	01/01/1828	A		FILM
WINDSTEIN W W 2 CH	JEAN		FROHMUHL	01/01/1817	A		FILM
WINDSTEIN W W 5CH	ANDRE	1805	KUENHEIM	02/22/1856	CH		FILM
WINIGER MN MUNSINGER	MADALEINE	1808	KUENHEIM	02/22/1856	CH		FILM
WINKLER	DAVID	1814	RANSPACH	11/22/1843	TX		FILM
WINKLER	FRANZISKA	1818	RANSPACH	11/22/1843	TX		FILM
WINKLER	FRANZISKA	1835	RANSPACH	11/22/1843	TX		FILM
WINKLER	GENOVEVA	1816	RANSPACH	11/15/1846	TX		FILM
WINKLER	JAKOB	1779	RANSPACH	11/15/1846	TX		FILM
WINKLER	JOSEF	1816	RANSPACH	11/15/1846	TX		FILM
WINKLER	JOSEPHINE	1844	RANSPACH	11/15/1846	TX		FILM
WINKLER	MARIE ANNE	1841	RANSPACH	11/22/1843	TX		FILM
WINKLER W W 2D	JAKOB	1811	RANSPACH	11/22/1843	TX		FILM
WINTER	GODEFROY ERNST	1821	BACKNANG W	11/19/1847	NY		FILM
WINTER	GREGOR		WITTENDORF W	05/12/1849	A		FILM
WINTERBERGER	ADOLPHE	1827	HUTTENHEIM	04/23/1853	NO		FILM
WINTERHALTER W W 5CH	GREGOIRE	1814	BALGAU	03/10/1851	NO		FILM
WINTZ F OF 2	MICHEL		WEYERSHEIM	03/01/1838	A		FILM
WINTZ F OF 5	FLORENT		WANTZENAU	03/01/1838	A		FILM
WINTZ MN DIEBOLD	ANNE		INGENHEIM	02/08/1828	A		FILM
WINTZ W W 2S	ETIENNE	1777	INGENHEIM	02/08/1828	A		FILM
WIPF	SEBASTIEN	1828	NIEDERENTZEN	09/07/1846	TX		FILM
WIPFF	FRANCOIS JOSEPH	1820	NIEDERENTZEN	09/01/1846	TX	MILL	PASS
WIPFF	FRANCOIS JOSEPH	1820	NIEDERENTZEN	09/07/1846	TX		FILM
WIPFF BR FRANCOIS J.	JEAN-BAPTISTE		NIEDERENTZEN	09/01/1846	TX		PASS
WIPFF CH 2	JEAN-BAPTISTE	1817	NIEDERENTZEN	11/01/1848	TX	CULT	PASS
WIPFF MN KEMPF W 3CH	CECILE	1795	NIEDERENTZEN	02/13/1850	TX		FILM
WIPFF SI FRANCOIS J.	AGATHA		NIEDERENTZEN	09/01/1846	TX		PASS
WIPPS	SEBASTIEN	1828	NIEDERENTZEN	11/15/1846	TX		FILM
WIRA	FRANCOIS	1832	BISEL	04/05/1855	NY		FILM

Lastname	Firstname	Birth Year	Birthplace	Emigration	De	Prof	Source
WIRA W 4CH	ANNE MARIA	1799	PFEFFERHOUSE	09/06/1854	NY		FILM
WIRTH	ANTOINE	1814	MASSEVAUX	04/02/1847	NY		FILM
WIRTH W W 1CH	JOSEPH	1830	HINNSPRUNG	09/06/1854	NY		FILM
WIRTH W W 5CH	NICOLAS	1815	GALTINGUE	03/07/1846	NY		FILM
WISSANG	ANETTE	1854	RANSPACH	09/05/1857	A		FILM
WISSANG	JEAN	1816	FELLERINGEN	11/05/1844	NY		FILM
WISSANG W D ANNETTE	WALBURGA	1823	RANSPACH	09/05/1857	A		FILM
WISSANT	APPOLINE	1825	FELLERINGEN	06/28/1850	NY		FILM
WISSANT	MARIE	1824	FELLERINGEN	07/08/1852	PH		FILM
WISSANT	REINE	1826	FELLERINGEN	07/08/1852	PH		FILM
WISSERT	JACOB		ENDINGEN B	07/31/1849	A		FILM
WISSERTZ	JOSEPH		ENDINGEN B	07/31/1849	A		FILM
WISSLER	DOMINIQUE	1833	MERXHEIM	12/02/1851	A		FILM
WISSLER W W 3CH	ANDRE	1799	MERXHEIM	10/24/1854	A		FILM
WITMER W W 3CH	DANIEL	1817	WUNFREY	07/10/1855	NY		FILM
WITT	ANTOINE	1812	BISEL	04/28/1847	NY		FILM
WITT	CHARLES	1810	SEPPOIS-LE-BAS	03/23/1840	PH		FILM
WITT F OF 4	CHRETIEN		SCHIRRHEIM	03/05/1838	A		FILM
WITT W 4CH	ELISABETH	1810	SEPPOIS-LE-BAS	02/08/1854	PH		FILM
WITT W W 6 CH	GREGOIRE	1809	SEPPOIS LE BAS	05/28/1847	NY		FILM
WITTER	GEORGE		IMBSHEIM	01/01/1828	A		FILM
WITTER W W 5CH	JACQUES		HATTMATT	03/31/1817	A		FILM
WITTIG W W 4CH	CONRAD	1815	OLTINGUE	03/15/1854	NY		FILM
WITTMANN	JOSEPH		FESSENHEIM	02/27/1838	A		FILM
WITTMANN	PHILIPPE		RATZWILLER	01/01/1828	A		FILM
WITTMANN W W 3CH	NICOLAS	1810	THANN	02/10/1846	NY		FILM
WITTMAR W W 4 CH	JACQUES		EYWILLER	03/20/1817	A		FILM
WITTMER	MADELAINE	1825	JEBSHEIM	08/23/1854	NY		FILM
WITZ	REMI LEGER	1825	GUEMAR	01/26/0182	NY		FILM
WITZ W W 3CH	RENWALD	1813	GUEBERSWIHR	11/29/1851	TX		FILM
WITZ CH 3	ROMUALD	1813	AMMERSCHWIHR	11/01/1851	TX	CARP	PASS
WITZ MN FICHTER W 4H	ANNE MARIE		SELESTATT	05/27/1817	A		FILM
WODLI S PETER	PETER		FROESCHWILLER	01/01/1863	A		SUESS
WOEHL	MARTIN	1866	OBERSEEBACH	01/01/1866	NY		NO.2
WOEHL	MICHEL	1863	OBERSEEBACH	01/01/1866	NY		NO.2
WOEHL MN WAGNER	CATHERINA	1840	OBERSEEBACH	01/01/1866	NY		NO.2
WOEHL W W 2 CH	MICHEL	1840	OBERSEEBACH	01/01/1866	NY	FARM	NO.2
WOELFERSHEIM	MADELAINE		OSTHEIM	01/17/1856	NY		FILM
WOELFERSHEIM	SALOME		OSTHEIM	01/17/1856	NY		FILM
WOELFERSHEIM MN HAFF	MADELAINE		OSTHEIM	01/17/1856	NY		FILM
WOELFERSHEIM W W 2CH	JEAN	1823	OSTHEIM	01/17/1856	NY		FILM
WOELFLE	ADELE	1831	MULHOUSE	02/28/1855	PH		FILM
WOELFLIN	JEAN MICHEL	1823	SUNDHOFFEN	10/20/1856	NO		FILM
WOHL	ANTOINE		MOLSHEIM	03/03/1838	A		FILM
WOHLFAHRT	CAROLINE	1828	CLEEBOURG	01/01/1868	NY		PRIV
WOHLFAHRT	JOHANN	1825	WUERTTEMBERG	11/15/1846	TX		FILM
WOHLHUTER	KATHARINA	1849	ROPPENHEIM	04/21/1852	AL		NO.1
WOHLHUTER	LORENZ	1844	ROPPENHEIM	04/21/1852	AL		NO.1
WOHLHUTER	MICHAEL	1842	ROPPENHEIM	04/21/1852	AL		NO.1
WOHLHUTER H BOHL 3CH	MICHEL	1807	ROPPENHEIM	04/21/1852	AL		NO.1

Lastname	Firstname	Birth Year	Birthplace	Emigration	De	Prof	Source
WOHLHUTER H MEEDER 9			ROPPENHEIM	/ /	AL		NO.1
WOHLHUTER MN BOHL	CATHARINA		ROPPENHEIM	04/21/1852	AL		NO.1
WOHLHUTER MN MEEDER	CATHERIN 9CH.		ROPPENHEIM	/ /	AL		NO.1
WOHLSCHLAG W W 1CH	ANDRE	1814	GUEBERSCHWIHR	03/25/1847	NY		FILM
WOHLZUMUTH	JOSEPH	1798	WOLFGANTZEN	04/21/1857	NY		FILM
WOHNENBURGER	JOHANN	1825	RIEDISHEIM	10/25/1843	TX		FILM
WOLCH	THERESE	1823	NIEDERENTZEN	04/14/1849	NY		FILM
WOLF	BARBE	1819	SELTZ BAS RHIN	10/15/1846	NY		FILM
WOLF	CHRITINE		GEUDERTHEIM	03/01/1838	A		FILM
WOLF	JACQUES		COSSWILLER	03/01/1838	A		FILM
WOLF	JACQUES	1821	WALTENHEIM	10/02/1855	SF		FILM
WOLF	JEAN		GEUDERTHEIM	03/01/1838	A		FILM
WOLF	JEAN ADAM		GUNDENBACH	04/26/1858	A		FILM
WOLF	JOSEPH	1810	ILLFURTH	05/07/1851	NY		FILM
WOLF	MADELAINE		LICHTENBERG	01/01/1828	A		FILM
WOLF W W 2 CH	BENJAMIN	1800	ESSLINGEN	09/13/1844	SL		FILM
WOLFARTH W 2CH	ANNE MARIE	1800	SOPPE LE BAS	05/06/1840	NY		FILM
WOLFF	CHRETIEN		RUNTZENHEIM	01/01/1828	A		FILM
WOLFF	GEORGE MICHEL		ROPPENHEIM	03/06/1838	A		FILM
WOLFF	JACQUES		SESSENHEIM	02/23/1838	A		FILM
WOLFF	JEAN		GERMANY	04/12/1849	NY		FILM
WOLFF	JOSEF		KUTZENHAUSEN	01/01/1817	A		NO.2
WOLFF	LOUIS		STEINBOURG	01/01/1828	A		FILM
WOLFF	MICHEL		GERMANY	04/12/1849	NY		FILM
WOLFF	MICHEL		LUPSTEIN	01/01/1828	A		FILM
WOLFF	MICHEL	1851	ALTENSTADT	01/01/1869	NY		NO.2
WOLFF	VALENTIN	1825	GUEBWILLER	08/22/1189	NY		FILM
WOLFF W W 6CH	MATHIEU		UHRWILLER	03/14/1817	A		FILM
WOLFF CH 2	JEAN	1814	MEYENHEIM	11/01/1851	TX	CARP	PASS
WOLFF CH 4	XAVIER		MEYENHEIM	12/01/1851	TX	CULT	PASS
WOLFF D XAVIER	REGINE	1851	MEYENHEIM	12/01/1851	TX		PASS
WOLFF F OF 2	JACQUES		SESSENHEIM	01/01/1828	A		FILM
WOLFF F OF 4	JEAN		STRASBOURG	09/01/1835	A		FILM
WOLFF F OF 6	HENRY		BOUXWILLER	01/01/1828	A		FILM
WOLFF F OF 6	JACQUES		BOUXWILLER	01/01/1828	A		FILM
WOLFF F OF 7	FRANCOIS JOSEPH		AUENHEIM	03/01/1838	A		FILM
WOLFF F OF 9	ADAM		SESSENHEIM	02/23/1838	A		FILM
WOLFF F OF3	LUC		ROESCHWOOG	01/01/1828	A		FILM
WOLFF F OF4	LAURENT		SESSENHEIM	02/23/1838	A		FILM
WOLFF H M. GERLING	JOHANN		BUEHL	01/01/1834	A		SUESS
WOLFF MN GERLING	MARGARETHA		BUEHL	01/01/1834	A		SUESS
WOLFF S XAVIER	JAQUES		MEYENHEIM	12/01/1851	TX		PASS
WOLFF S XAVIER	JOSEPH		MEYENHEIM	12/01/1851	TX		PASS
WOLFF S XAVIER	SEBASTIEN		MEYENHEIM	12/01/1851	TX		PASS
WOLFF W W	JEAN		MEYENHEIM	11/27/1851	TX		FILM
WOLFF W W 4CH	XAVIER	1822	MEYENHEIM	01/01/1828	A		FILM
WOLFHUEGEL F OF 6	JACQUES		BRUMATH	01/01/1828	A		FILM
WOLFSTIRN	EVE	1830	CLEEBOURG	01/01/1855	NY	SERV	PRIV
WOLFSTIRN	FREDERIC	1838	NY	01/01/1867	NY	TAYL	PRIV
WOLHUTTER F OF 5	PHILIPPE		RUNTZENHEIM	01/01/1828	A		FILM

Lastname	Firstname	Birth Year	Birthplace	Emigration	De	Prof	Source
WOLJING W W 6 CH	ANDRE		SOUFFLENHEIM	03/14/1817	A		FILM
WOLL F OF 4	WALTHER		HERBITZHEIM	01/01/1828	A		FILM
WOLLENSACK	JOSEPH		ROTHENBURG W	05/03/1849	NY		FILM
WOLLENSCHLAEGER	FRANCISKA	1839	SELTZ	01/01/1868	NY		NO.2
WOLLENSCHLAEGER	JOSEF	1846	SELTZ	01/01/1868	NY	FARM	NO.2
WOLLJUNG	CATHERINE		GEISWILLER	01/01/1828	A		FILM
WOLLJUNG F OF4	JEAN		HATTMATT	01/01/1828	A		FILM
WOLLJUNG W W	NICOLAS		GEISWILLER	01/01/1828	A		FILM
WOLTISPERGER	BERNARD	1827	MUNCHHAUSEN	09/20/1851	NY		FILM
WOLTLY W W 1CH	CHRETIEN		WEISLINGEN	03/23/1817	A		FILM
WORD	CHARLES		NIEDERLAUTERBACH	01/01/1850	NO		PRIV
WORD	CHARLES	1854	NIEDERLAUTERBACH	01/01/1861	NO		PRIV
WORHEN	EUPHROSINE		ETTENHEIM B	04/01/1849	NY		FILM
WOTTLING	MAXIMIN	1834	GUEMAR	03/04/1857	NY		FILM
WUEHRLIN	MARIE ANNE	1814	SOULTZMATT	09/22/1848	NO		FILM
WUERTENSCHLAG W BR	JACQUES	1821	CERNAY	10/29/1847	NY		FILM
WUERTZ	ANNA MARIA	1840	LEMBACH	01/01/1866	NY		NO.2
WUERTZ F OF 5	NICOLAS		REIPERTSWILLER	01/01/1828	A		FILM
WUHRLIN	JEAN BAPTISTE	1823	HARTMANNSWILLER	09/23/1848	NO		FILM
WUKER W W 3CH	NICOLAS	1814	MITTELWIHR	08/17/1852	TX		FILM
WULER	DUCARTHE		UNZHURST B	08/14/1849	A		FILM
WUNMANN	CAROLINE	1839	MULHOUSE	07/14/1187	NY		FILM
WURBACH	JEAN	1802	KUNHEIM	03/25/1841	NY		FILM
WURGEL	PETER	1845	MUNCHHOUSE	01/01/1868	NY	FARM	NO.2
WURGEL	PHILIPPINE	1863	MUNCHHOUSE	01/01/1867	NY		NO.2
WURGEL	SUSANNA	1861	MUNCHHOUSE	01/01/1867	NY		NO.2
WURGEL	VALENTIN	1865	MUNCHHOUSE	01/01/1867	NY		NO.2
WURGEL MN HORNUNG	CATHERINA	1839	MUNCHHOUSE	01/01/1867	NY		NO.2
WURGEL W W 3 CH	JOHANN MICHEL	1835	MUNCHHOUSE	01/01/1867	NY	FARM	NO.2
WURMSCHMITT F OF2	JEAN		HATTMATT	01/01/1828	A		FILM
WURSTEISEN	CATHERINE		DEHLINGEN	01/01/1828	A		FILM
WURSTEISSEN W 3CH	MARIE ANNE	1790	MULHAUSEN	07/26/1845	NY		FILM
WURSTLER	ADAM		FRIEDENSTADT	10/15/1849	NY		FILM
WURTZ	JEAN DAVID	1822	MITTELWIHR	05/14/1855	NY		FILM
WURTZ	JOHANN	1852	DUERRENBACH	01/01/1866	NY		NO.2
WURTZ	LOUIS		WESTHOFFEN	01/01/1828	A		FILM
WURTZ F OF 2	PHILIPPE		SAVENNE	01/01/1828	A		FILM
WUST	HENRIETTE	1844	CLEEBOURG	01/01/1868	NY		PRIV
WUST	REINE	1816	SCHLEITHAL BAS RHIN	10/23/1846	NY		FILM
WYBRECHT	CHARLES	1831	RIXHEIM	09/14/1857	A	PRIN	FILM
WUSTNER S JACOB	JACOB		FROESCHWILLER	01/01/1874	A		SUESS

Lastname	Firstname	Birth Year	Birthplace	Emigration	De	Prof	Source
ZAEDER	BENJAMIN	1835	GUEBWILLER	08/10/1854	A	DRAW	FILM
ZAEDER	JOSEPH	1819	GUEBWILLER	04/14/1854	A	MERC	FILM
ZAEPFEL	ALEXANDRE	1815	HIRTZFELDEN	02/01/1850	TX		PASS
ZAEPFEL	ALEXANDRE	1815	MONTPELLIER	02/14/1850	A	POET	FILM
ZAEPFEL	HILAIRE	1821	HIRTZFELDEN	02/01/1850	TX		PASS
ZAEPFEL	HILARIE	1830	HIRTZFELDEN	02/18/1859	A	GWON	FILM
ZAHN	FRANCOIS JOSEPH		WANTZENAU	01/01/1828	A	MILL	FILM
ZAHN	FRANCOISE		GEININGEN (W)	05/12/1849	A		FILM
ZAHN	JOSEPH		GEININGEN (W)	05/12/1849	A		FILM
ZAHN	MARTIN		GEININGEN (W)	05/12/1849	A		FILM
ZAHN	ORTRUDE		WANTZENAU	01/01/1828	A		FILM
ZAHN W HEYGEL JOSEPH	SOPHIE		WANTZENAU	01/01/1828	A		FILM
ZARLINDEN	CHARLES	1817	MASSEVAUX	03/22/1847	TX		FILM
ZEER	JEAN BAPTISTE	1803	MITTELWIHR	10/14/1846	TX	TISS	FILM
ZEHLER	MAXIME	1826	BERGHEIM	10/08/1849	A	TEAC	FILM
ZEHR	FREDERIC		STRUTH	01/01/1828	A	DAYL	FILM
ZEHR	THIEBAUD		STRUTH	01/01/1828	A	CULT	FILM
ZEIL	L.		DURACH(B)	03/31/1849	NY		FILM
ZEILER	THIEBAUD		UHRWILLER	01/01/1828	NY	DAYL	FILM
ZEITER	GEORGE		UHRWILLER	04/09/1819	A	TISS	FILM
ZEITER	JACOB		UHRWILLER	01/01/1817	A		NO.2
ZEITVOGEL	FRANCOIS		SINSHEIM(B)	04/14/1849	A		FILM
ZEITVOGEL	MATERN		SINSHEIM (B)	04/14/1849	A		FILM
ZEITVOGEL	ROSALIE		SINSHEIM (B)	04/14/1849	A		FILM
ZELLE	EUGENE	1826	BELFORT	08/14/1849	NO	BAKE	FILM
ZELLE	PHILIBERT	1823	BELFORT	08/14/1849	NO	JOIN	FILM
ZELLER	GEORG		DURBACH (B)	04/08/1849	A		FILM
ZELLER	MARIE ANNE	1827	LIEPVRE	09/30/1854	A	TISS	FILM
ZELLER	PHILIPP		DURBACH (B)	04/08/1849	A		FILM
ZELLER	THEOPHILE	1813	PLANCHERBAS	08/03/1846	A	TAYL	FILM
ZELTMANN	ERNST		DOBEL	04/10/1849	A		FILM
ZENGERLE	BENOIT	1802	SCHNAPSEEN	06/15/1846	NY		FILM
ZENGERLEN D FRANCOIS	ANNE-MARIE	1852	FELLERING	08/01/1860	TX		PASS
ZENGERLEN D FRANCOIS	CATHERINE	1850	FELLERING	08/01/1860	TX		PASS
ZENGERLEN D FRANCOIS	JUSTINE	1855	FELLERING	08/01/1860	TX		PASS
ZENGERLEN H CATHERIN	FRANCOIS JOSEPH	1831	FELLERING	08/01/1860	TX	BRLA	PASS
ZENGERLEN MN HALLER	CATHERINE	1826	FELLERING	08/01/1860	TX		PASS
ZENGERLEN S FRANCOIS	EDOUARD	1859	FELLERING	08/01/1860	TX		PASS
ZENO	FRANCOIS		GUTHENBERG	07/31/1849	A		FILM
ZENTNER	FRANCOIS ANTOIN		RHINAU	02/27/1838	A	DAYL	FILM
ZEPPENFELD	FRANCOIS	1800	OLPE(P)	08/20/1841	NY	TANN	FILM
ZERR	AUGUSTIN	1828	MITTELWIHR	09/23/1850	TX	SERV	FILM
ZERR	CATHARINA	1837	NIEDERLAUTERBACH	01/01/1865	NO		NO.2
ZERR	CATHERINE	1833	NIEDERLAUTERBACH	01/01/1861			PRIV
ZERR	FRANCOIS	1829	BOURGFELDEN	05/20/1856	NY	FACT	FILM
ZERR	JOHANN	1845	NEHWILLER	01/01/1866	A		NO.2
ZERR H KATHARINA	JOHANN	1801	MITTELWIHR	11/15/1846	TX		FILM
ZERR CH 2	JEAN-BAPTISTE	1825	MITTELWIHR	11/01/1854	TX	DAYL	PASS
ZERR D JOHANN	ANNA MARIA	1838	MITTELWIHR	11/15/1846	TX		FILM
ZERR D JOHANN	BARBARA	1836	MITTELWIHR	11/15/1846	TX		FILM

Lastname	Firstname	Birth Year	Birthplace	Emigration	De	Prof	Source
ZERR D JOHANN	KATHARINA	1830	MITTELWIHR	11/15/1846	TX		FILM
ZERR W JOHANN BAPTIS	KATHARINA	1802	MITTELWIHR	11/15/1846	TX		FILM
ZETWOCH	IGNACE		SOUFFLENHEIM	01/01/1828	A	CARP	FILM
ZEUSER	FREDERIC SON		WICKERSHEIM	01/01/1828	A	HOST	FILM
ZEUSER	PHILIPPE		WICKERSHEIM	01/01/1828	A		FILM
ZEYER	JOSEPH	1817	FRANKEN	11/22/1843	TX	CULT	FILM
ZIEBEL CH 4	LOUIS		UHRWILLER	03/14/1817	A		FILM
ZIEBLER	JOHANN	1796	MAINVILLER	11/15/1846	TX	CULT	FILM
ZIEGER	HENRI	1824	NIEDERMORSCHWIHR	06/26/1847	A		FILM
ZIEGLER	FREDERIC		WICKERSHEIM	01/01/1828	A	MERC	FILM
ZIEGLER	JEAN		KUTTOLSHEIM	01/01/1828	AM		FILM
ZIEGLER	JOSEPH	1813	ENDINGEN(B)	04/16/1840	NY	MECH	FIOLM
ZIEGLER	JULES	1827	GUEBWILLER	02/26/1849	CA	MERC	FILM
ZIEGLER	MATHAEUS		WITTENDORF(W)	05/12/1849	A		FILM
ZIEGLER	MAURICE	1823	GUEBWILLER	05/03/1852	NO	FOND	FILM
ZIEGLER	SEBASTIEN	1816	GUEBWILLER	08/18/1849	NO	TOUR	FILM
ZIEGLER	WENDELIN		STADELHOFEN (B)	07/29/1849	A		FILM
ZIEGLER CH 2	FREDERIC	1809	RIQUEWIHR	11/01/1854	TX		PASS
ZIEGLER WW AND CH 2	ANDRE	1816	ORSCHWIHR	11/26/1851	A	VINT	FILM
ZIEGLER WW ANS CH 2	FREDERIC	1829	RIQUEWIHR	11/09/1854	TX	BAKE	FILM
ZIMBER	BARNABAS		IFFEZHEIM(B)	03/31/1849	NY		FILOM
ZIMBER	SALOME	1822	STRASBOURG	08/01/1855	NY	TAYL	FILM
ZIMBERLIN	FERDINAND	1823	PFETTERHAUSEN	04/01/1853	NY	DAYL	FILM
ZIMMER	CATHERINE	1810	INGENHEIM	02/18/1828	A		FILM
ZIMMER	CLEMENT		KILSTETT	05/12/1817	A	TISS	FILM
ZIMMER	GEORGE		REIPERTSWILLER	01/01/1828	A	FILM	ZIMBER
ZIMMER	JEAN MICHEL	1790	LEIDERHEIM(B)	02/18/1828	A	BRLA	FILM
ZIMMER	MICHEL		INGENHEIM	01/01/1828	A	BRLA	FILM
ZIMMER	NICOLAS		WASSELONNE	01/01/1828	A	MEDC	FILM
ZIMMER D JEAN MICHEL	ROSINE	1837	INGENHEIM	02/18/1828	A		FILM
ZIMMER F ROSINE	JEAN MICHEL		INGENHEIM	02/18/1828	A		FILM
ZIMMERLE	JEAN		MUTTERSHOLTZ	04/15/1838	A	TISS	FILM
ZIMMERLE	JOSEPH	1792	OBERHERGHEIM	02/25/1848	A	SHMA	FILM
ZIMMERMANN	ADAM		BRUMATH	01/01/1828	A	BAKE	FILM
ZIMMERMANN	ANTOINE	1823	RINDLINGEN	02/07/1854	A	BAKE	FILM
ZIMMERMANN	CATHERINE		DONAUESCHINGEN(B)	08/21/1849	A		FILM
ZIMMERMANN	ETIENNE	1800	RIXHEIM	11/01/1851	TX	DAYL	PASS
ZIMMERMANN	ETIENNE	1810	RIXHEIM	11/18/1851	TX	DAYL	FILM
ZIMMERMANN	FELIX		OBERKIRCH(B)	04/06/1849	NY		FILM
ZIMMERMANN	GEORGE		DETTWILLER	01/01/1828	A	TISS	FILM
ZIMMERMANN	GEORGES		INGENHEIM	01/01/1828	A	CULT	FILM
ZIMMERMANN	JEAN		DORNACH	03/22/1849	NY	CULT	FILM
ZIMMERMANN	JEAN	1792	HEGENHEIM	04/05/1841	A	TENA	FILM
ZIMMERMANN	LAURENT		FORT LOUIS	01/01/1828	A	SOLD	FILM
ZIMMERMANN	MICHEL	1816	HERICOURT	07/27/1847	A	SERR	FILM
ZIMMERMANN	MICHEL	1851	WINTZENBACH	01/01/1865	NY		NO.2
ZIMMERMANN	SALOME	1818	ST.CROIX EN PLAINES	09/16/1839	A		FILM
ZIMMERMANN CH 2	APPOLINE	1818	ODEREN	11/01/1857	TX	FACT	PASS
ZIMMERMANN D JOSEPH	AGATHE	1832	FELLERING	04/09/1844	TX		FILM
ZIMMERMANN D JOSEPH	KAROLINE	1829	FELLERING	04/09/1844	TX		FILM

Lastname	Firstname	Birth Year	Birthplace	Emigration	De	Prof	Source
ZIMMERMANN D JOSEPH	MARIA ANNA	1825	FELLERING	04/09/1844	TX		FILM
ZIMMERMANN H MARIA	JOSEPH	1797	FELLERING	04/09/1844	TX		FILM
ZIMMERMANN M M.DIETS	FRIEDRICH		HATTEN	01/01/1841	A		SUESS
ZIMMERMANN MN DIETSC	MAGDALENA		HATTEN	01/01/1841	A		SUESS
ZIMMERMANN S JOSEPH	ALEXANDER	1832	FELLERING	04/09/1844	TX		FILM
ZIMMERMANN S JOSEPH	GUSTAV	1843	FELLERING	04/09/1844	TX		FILM
ZIMMERMANN S JOSEPH	HEINRICH	1827	FELLERING	04/09/1844	TX		FILM
ZIMMERMANN S JOSEPH	JOHANN BAPTISTE	1839	FELLERING	04/09/1844	TX		FILM
ZIMMERMANN S JOSEPH	JOSEPH	1822	FELLERING	04/09/1844	TX		FILM
ZIMMERMANN S JOSEPH	TIBOT	1825	FELLERING	04/09/1844	TX		FILM
ZIMMERMANN W JOSEPH	MARIA ANNA	1799	FELLERING	04/09/1844	TX		FILM
ZIMMETH	JOSEPH		ROESCHWOOG	01/01/1828	A	CULT	FILM
ZIMPELMANN	JOHANN	1848	OBERSEEBACH	01/01/1866	NY		NO.2
ZIMPELMANN	N	1845	OBERSEEBACH	01/01/1866	NY		NO.2
ZIMPELMANN	SALOME	1848	OBERSEEBACH	01/01/1866	NY		NO.2
ZINCK	CHRISTIAN	1829	GUEBWILLER	09/10/1857	NY	MECH	FILM
ZINCK	FRANCOIS JOSEPH	1787	WITTENHEIM	10/08/1844	A	SHMA	FILM
ZINCK	JACOB	1827	SARSBACH VALDEN (B)	06/16/1853	A	SHMA	FILM
ZINCK CH 1	JOSEPH	1787		10/01/1844	TX	SHMA	PASS
ZINK	ALOISE		BUEHLERTAL (B)	04/19/1849	NY		FILM
ZINNBIEHL	GEORGES	1820	RIXHEIM	08/18/1847	A	WOCA	FILM
ZINNSTEIN	LOUIS		OBERHAUSBERGEN	01/01/1828	A		FILM
ZINSMEISTER	HUBERT	1815	BLOTZHEIM	09/01/1846	TX	JOIN	PASS
ZIPPER	VIKTOIRE	1844	VIEUX FERRETTE	02/22/1866	NY	TAYL	FILM
ZIPSE	JAKOB		STEIN (B)	04/11/1849	A		FILM
ZIRCHER	NICOLAS		SCHIRRHEIN	01/01/1828	A	DAYL	FILM
ZOEBST	JEAN GEORGES	1808	UHRWILLER	02/17/1828	A		FILM
ZOLLER	CATHERINE		ERNOLSHEIM	01/01/1828	A	DAYL	FILM
ZOLLER	DANIEL		ERNOLSHEIM	01/01/1828	A	DAYL	FILM
ZOLLER	FREDERIC		ERNOLSHEIM	01/01/1828	A	TAYL	FILM
ZOLLER	MAGDALENA	1836	SELTZ	01/01/1865	NY		NO.2
ZOLLER	MICHEL		ERNOLSHEIM	01/01/1828	A	TISS	FILM
ZOLLER	PHILIPPE		DALHUNDEN	03/02/1838	A	DAYL	FILM
ZOLLER	ROSINE		ERNOLSHEIM	01/01/1828	A		FILM
ZOLLINER	ETIENNE	1802	DURMANACH	06/04/1857	NY	BRLA	FILM
ZOLLINER S ETIENNE	JULES	1842	DURMANACH	06/04/1857	NY		FILM
ZONNER	JEAN THIEBAUD	1820	FALKWILLER	02/19/1850	A	CULT	FILM
ZORN	CHRISTOPH		EIDINGEN (B)	04/21/1849	A		FILM
ZORN	FLORENZ		SCHOENBORG	01/01/1828	A	TEAC	FILM
ZORN	JAQUES		ZITTERSHEIM	01/01/1828	A	TISS	FILM
ZORN	JOSEPH		SCHOENBOURG	01/01/1828	A	TAYL	FILM
ZORN	JOSEPHINE		WATZENAU	01/01/1828	US		FILM
ZORN	PIERRE		SCHOENBURG	01/01/1828	US		FILM
ZUBER	MICHEL		OTTERSTHAL	01/01/1828	A	VINT	FILM
ZUBER W THOMAS EDUAR	MARIE	1820	MITTELSCHAEFFELSHEIM	05/03/1856	A		FILM
ZUCK	SEBASTIEN	1829	MUNCHHAUSEN	09/20/1851	A	DAYL	FILM
ZUERCHER D JOHANN	HORTENSE	1841	MULHOUSE	04/08/1844	A		FILM
ZUERCHER D JOHANN	MARIA	1823	MULHOUSE	04/08/1844	A		FILM
ZUERCHER H DOROTHEA	JOHANN ULRICH	1797	MULHOUSE	04/08/1844	A	BAKE	FILM
ZUERCHER H MAGDALENA	NIKOLAUS	1806	MULHOUSE	04/08/1844	A	CULT	FILM

Lastname	Firstname	Birth Year	Birthplace	Emigration	De	Prof	Source
ZUERCHER W JOHANN	DOROTHEA	1797	MULHOUSE	04/08/1844	A		FILM
ZUERCHER W NIKOLAUS	MAGDALENA	1808	MULHOUSE	04/08/1844	A		FILM
ZUFALL	FRANCOIS		DETTWILLER	01/01/1828	A	CARP	FILM
ZUFF	CHRISTIAN		NEUWILLER	01/01/1828	A	JOIN	FILM
ZUICK	MR		GERMANY	04/16/1849	A		FILM
ZUMBIEHL	ANTOINE	1838	NIEDERENTZEN	11/04/1857	A	CULT	FILM
ZUMBIEHL	ANTOINE	1838	OBERENTZEN	11/01/1857	TX	CULT	PASS
ZUPPE	PIERRE		DURSTEL	03/18/1838	A	SHMA	FILM
ZURBRICK	NIKOLAUS		PFALZWEYER	01/01/1828	A		FILM
ZURCHER	CHRISTIAN		TIEFENBACH	01/01/1828	A		FILM
ZURCHER	JAKOB	1816	OBERENTZEN	09/10/1851	A	CULT	FILM
ZURCHER	LEOPOLD	1821	OBERENTZEN	09/14/1846	A	CULT	FILM
ZURCHER	NICOLAS	1818	MULHOUSE	02/19/1842	A	DYER	FILM
ZURCHER BR REGINE	LEOPOLD	1821	OBERENTZEN	09/01/1846	TX	CULT	PASS
ZURCHER CH 1	JOSEPH	1816	OBERENTZEN	09/01/1851	TX	CULT	PASS
ZURCHER SI LEOPOLD	REGINE		OBERENTZEN	09/01/1846	TX		PASS
ZURLER	JEAN	1796	MUNWILLER	09/19/1846	TX		FILM
ZUSSY	MARTIN	1820	ST. AMARIN	01/01/1860	TX	WOCA	PASSS
ZWELLER				/ /			
ZWIEBEL	ARMAND		STRUTH	01/01/1828	A	DAYL	FILM
ZWIEBEL	DOROTHEE		STRUTH	01/01/1828	A		FILM
ZWIEBEL	MADELEINE		PETERSBACH	01/01/1828	A		FILM
ZWILLING	CAROLINE		WALTENHEIM	01/01/1832	A		FILM